PENGUIN EDUCATION

PENGUIN ENGLISH POETS
GENERAL EDITOR: CHRISTOPHER RICKS

Robert Browning
The Ring and the Book

EDITED BY RICHARD D. ALTICK

Robert Browning

The Ring and the Book

EDITED BY RICHARD D. ALTICK

PENGUIN BOOKS

Penguin Books Ltd, Harmondsworth,
Middlesex, England
Penguin Books Inc., 7110 Ambassador Road,
Baltimore, Md 21207, U.S.A.
Penguin Books Australia Ltd,
Ringwood, Victoria, Australia

First published 1971
Introduction and notes copyright © Richard D. Altick, 1971

Made and printed in Great Britain by
Hazell Watson & Viney Ltd,
Aylesbury, Bucks
Set in Monotype Ehrhardt

Contents

Table of Dates

1845   *10 January* First letter to Elizabeth Barrett.
20 May First visit to Wimpole Street.
November *Bells and Pomegranates* VII:
Dramatic Romances and Lyrics.

1846   *April* *Bells and Pomegranates* VIII: *Luria* and
A Soul's Tragedy.
12 September Marriage to Elizabeth Barrett.
19 September They leave England for Pisa.

1847   *Summer* Settle at Casa Guidi, Florence.

1849   First collected edition of poems.
9 March Son, Robert Wiedemann Barrett, born.

1850   *April* *Christmas-Eve and Easter-Day.*

1855   *November* *Men and Women.*

1855–6   *Autumn–Winter* Visit to London.

1860   *June* Discovers the Old Yellow Book in a
Florentine market.

1861   *29 June* Elizabeth Barrett Browning dies.

1862   Settles at 19 Warwick Crescent, London, his home
for most of his remaining years.

1863   Collected edition (the so-called 'third').

1864   *May* *Dramatis Personae.*
Autumn Begins writing *The Ring and the Book.*

1866   Death of his father.

1868–9   *21 November–27 February* *The Ring and the Book.*

1871   *August* *Balaustion's Adventure.*
December *Prince Hohenstiel-Schwangau.*

1872   *June* *Fifine at the Fair.*

1873   *May* *Red Cotton Night-Cap Country.*

1875   *April* *Aristophanes' Apology.*
November *The Inn Album.*

1876   *July* *Pacchiarotto and How He Worked in
Distemper.*

1877   *October* *The Agamemnon of Aeschylus.*

1878   *May* *La Saisiaz* and *The Two Poets of Croisic.*

1879   *April   Dramatic Idyls*

1880   *June   Dramatic Idyls: Second Series.*

1881   F. J. Furnivall founds the Browning Society.

1883   *March   Jocoseria.*

1884   *November   Ferishtah's Fancies.*

1887   *January   Parleyings with Certain People of Importance in Their Day.*

1888–9   'Fourth and complete edition' of *Poetical Works* (the last supervised by Browning).

1889   *12 December   Asolando* published; Browning dies in Venice the same evening.
        31 December   Buried in Westminster Abbey.

Introduction

As Browning vivaciously describes the event in the poem's first 119 lines, *The Ring and the Book* had its genesis in Florence on a June day in 1860. Browsing in the second-hand market in the Piazza di San Lorenzo, he paused at a stall laden with odds and ends in various stages of damage and decrepitude, and there picked up an old book in which was bound a collection of documents produced during and after a sensational Roman murder trial in 1698. At the age of forty-eight, Browning was a seasoned connoisseur equally of crime, of the mysterious ways of human psychology, and of historical events which, whatever their initial fame, had long since vanished from memory. The material in this battered square volume, he saw at a glance, was almost providentially designed to engage a man of his intellectual curiosity and tastes. He bought it for some small change and began to read it as he made his way back across the Arno to the Casa Guidi, where he was living with his wife and their eleven-year-old son Pen.

The pamphlets and letters contained in the Old Yellow Book, as he came to call it, proved on closer inspection to be a baffling, intriguing mixture of controversy, contradiction, pedantic legal arguments, even more pedantic law Latin – and obscure questions of human character and motivation. Within a year or two, if not immediately, Browning began to think of basing a large poem on it. But the death of his wife, his subsequent re-settling in England after fifteen years' residence in Italy, and the distractions associated with preparing his son for Oxford and his newest poems for publication (in the volume entitled *Dramatis Personae*, 1864) prevented him from going on with the project. Meanwhile, with his characteristic impetuous generosity, he offered the subject of the Franceschini murders to several of his acquaintances, including Tennyson and Anthony Trollope. Fortunately, no doubt, he found no takers.

Modern scholars conclude from such scanty evidence as is available that Browning brought his hitherto nebulous plans for *The Ring and the Book* to fruitful focus in the summer of 1864. While on holiday in a village in the Pyrenees, he visited a nearby mountain gorge called the *pas de Roland* (because traditionally it was reputed to have been kicked open by Roland) and there conceived the epic length and the twelve-book structure of what he came to call 'my great venture, the murder-poem'. In the same autumn he began the actual writing at his home in Warwick Crescent, Paddington, and soon progressed to the point where, in the periodic bulletins he issued to his friends, he was able to reckon his output by the thousands of lines. By 1 November 1865, the count was 15,000 lines. The remaining 6000 lines took longer – he was on several occasions forced to suspend work for considerable lengths of time – so that the poem was completed only in the spring of 1868.

As a working title Browning had used the name of 'the collection of law-papers' (presumably, therefore, *The Old Yellow Book*), but when the poem was in type he suggested to his publishers, Smith, Elder and Company, that it be called *The Franceschini*, perhaps by analogy with Shelley's *The Cenci*. An alternative possibility, *The Book and the Ring*, he rejected as 'too pretty-fairy-story-like'; Thackeray, one recalls, had published a fairy story entitled *The Rose and the Ring* in 1855. But poet and publisher ultimately agreed upon a transposition of the two nouns, and it was as *The Ring and the Book* that the poem was published in four volumes between 21 November 1868 and 27 February 1869.

The text of that first edition is reproduced in the present volume. For the second edition of 1872, and again for the edition included in his collected *Poetical Works* (1889), Browning made many hundreds of revisions in the interest of smoother versification (perhaps the most frequent motive), greater clarity, improved idiom, simplified syntactical order, consistency of grammatical mood or tense, and – very occasionally – strengthened dramatic emphasis and the elimination of especially infelicitous sound patterns. The great majority of these amendments involved mere adjustment of punctuation or the transposition of words within a single line or two. Many unquestionably served their purpose.

Browning's revising eye and ear were by no means sure, however. Although the reasons for most of his alterations can be understood, the results make a considerable number seem hardly worth the trouble. His concentration on minutiae frequently drifted into a profitless concern with trivia, and more than a few of his emendations actually left the text worse off:

1868–9 Nor lifted courteous cap to – how bend him
1889   Nor lifted courteous cap to – him how bend (IV 938)

1868–9 Had clearly cut the tangle in a trice.
1889   Had clearly cut the embroilment in a trice. (VIII 780)

1868–9 *Ob*, for, because of, *keep her claws off!* Ah,
1889   *Ob*, for, because of, *keep her claws off!* Tush! (VIII 969)

1868–9 Hath so the Molinism-canker, lords, | Eaten to the bone?
1872   Hath so the Molinism, the canker, lords, | Eaten to our bone? (VIII 1072–3)

1868–9 Save by the magnet moves the manly mind?
1872   Yet spare love, loadstone moving manly mind? (IX 485)

1868–9 Guido must needs trip on a stumbling-block
1872   Needs must trip Guido on a stumbling-block (X 811)

1868–9 Omniscience sees, Omnipotence could stop, | All-mercifulness pardons
1872   Omniscience sees, Omnipotence could stop, | Omnibenevolence pardons (XI 1999–2000)

1868–9 Unmanned, remade: I hold it probable –
1872   Unmanned, remanned: I hold it probable (XI 2391)
          (an ill-advised variation on the notorious 'Go get you manned by Manning and new-manned | By Newman' of I 444–5)

1868–9 Guido was last to mount the scaffold-steps
1872 To mount the scaffold-steps, Guido was last (XII 167)

Too often Browning merely substituted one inversion for another, or paid for a slightly smoother metre by inserting a gratuitous monosyllable to eke out the line.

'Revision' in the case of this poem therefore was by no means necessarily synonymous with 'improvement'. One has the impression that the diligence with which Browning reviewed and touched up the text in 1872 and 1889 was not matched by enthusiasm for the task or by a consistently sure craftsman's sense. Might it be said that he was, in effect, the captive of his peculiar idiom, which by its very nature was not freely amenable (or 'malleolable') to successful revision? In any event, it is fair to say that the original version is in no way artistically inferior to the revised ones.

In the absence of any clear-cut qualitative differences, the choice of the one to reprint can legitimately be made on historical rather than critical grounds. And here the text of 1868–9 has a superior claim, because it represents the poem – his avowed *magnum opus* – in the precise form in which Browning chose to submit it to the 'British Public, who may like me yet'. It was upon this text, and not any later one, that the fate of his poetic reputation hinged. With all its small blemishes (as, judging from the number of his revisions, he must subsequently have regarded them), this was the text on which Browning was content to rest his case for the long-withheld approval of his contemporaries and which inspired such immediate critical plaudits as the *Athenaeum*'s 'the supremest poetical achievement of our time ... the most precious and profound spiritual treasure that England has produced since the days of Shakespeare'.

In the present edition, no attempt has been made to provide a systematic record of Browning's revisions. A partial account is available in Cook's *Commentary*, Appendix XI, and an exhaustive apparatus of variant readings will be included in the edition of the poem which Roma A. King Jr has prepared for the *Complete Works of Robert Browning* now in course of publication by the Ohio University Press, Athens, Ohio. The only alterations to which the reader's attention is called in the notes are those in which patent obscurities in the original version are clarified, meanings changed, errors corrected (in two or three instances) or lines added. The additions are fully listed in order to account for the discrepant line numbering, in Books VIII, IX, XI and XII, between the first edition and that of 1889. (Additional discrepancies were introduced in some later editions by the practice of counting two half-lines as a single one.)

Several typographical errors in 1868–9 have been silently corrected: a period substituted for a comma (II 982); 'craves' for 'cravse' (III 1406); 'Court' for 'Count' (V 45, last word); '*Contaminatam*' for '*Comtaminatam*' (VIII 923); and 'pact' for 'past' (VIII 1587). The inverted commas which introduced each line of quoted matter in the first edition have been eliminated. In conformity with Penguin style single quotation marks have been substituted for double ones and, accordingly, double ones used for quotations-within-quotations. Otherwise the spelling and punctuation are reproduced in the form in which Browning passed them for the press.

The annotation has been carried out on a scale which is necessarily extensive but which seeks at the same time to be as economical as possible in face of the twin challenges of Browning's wide range of curious information and his immense and flexible vocabulary. Without the prior labours of A. K. Cook to draw upon, preparation of the body of notes would have been an even more formidable task than it in fact was. Despite all that has been transported to the present site from Cook's *Commentary*, a great deal of ore remains in that capacious mine. Everything that has been transferred has been freshly verified, although one hastens to add that Cook's references prove to be remarkably accurate. A number of allusions which he left unglossed have been explained.

Further Reading

EDITIONS

The three editions with textual significance are the first (4 volumes, 1868–9), the second (4 volumes, 1872), and that included in volumes 8–10 of the *Poetical Works of Robert Browning* (1888–94; the volumes in question are dated 1889). Most of the subsequent editions of Browning's poetry, such as the 'Florentine' edition by C. Porter and H. A. Clarke (New York, 1898) and the 'Centenary' edition by F. G. Kenyon (10 volumes, 1912) print the finally revised text of 1889, as will the definitive *Complete Works of Robert Browning* now in progress. Two readily available editions – the Everyman (1911, etc.) and the Oxford (1912, etc.) – print the 1868–9 text, while the Norton Library edition (1961) reproduces that of 1889.

BIBLIOGRAPHIES AND REFERENCE WORKS

L. N. Broughton and B. F. Stelter, *A Concordance to the Poems of Robert Browning*, 2 vols., Stechert, 1924–5.

L. N. Broughton, C. S. Northup, and R. Pearsall, *Robert Browning: A Bibliography, 1830–1950*, Cornell University Press, 1953. (Later material is listed in B. Litzinger and K. L. Knickerbocker, *The Browning Critics*, University of Kentucky Press, 1965, and in the annual bibliographies of studies in Victorian literature in the *MLA International Bibliography* and *Victorian Studies*.)

A. K. Cook, *A Commentary upon Browning's 'The Ring and the Book'*, Oxford University Press, 1920.

W. C. DeVane, *A Browning Handbook*, 2nd edn, Appleton-Century-Crofts, 1955.

BIOGRAPHY AND CRITICISM

R. D. Altick and J. F. Loucks II, *Browning's Roman Murder Story: A Reading of 'The Ring and the Book'*, University of Chicago Press, 1968.

I. Armstrong, '*The Ring and the Book:* The Uses of Prolixity', *The Major Victorian Poets: Reconsiderations*, Routledge & Kegan Paul, 1969, ch. 8.

B. Brugière, 'Guido dans *The Ring and the Book* de Robert Browning', *Études Anglaises* XXI, 1968, 19–34.

B. Corrigan, *Curious Annals: New Documents Relating to Browning's Roman Murder Story*, University of Toronto Press, 1956. (The Italian text of the documents is reproduced in the same author's 'Browning's Roman Murder Story', *English Miscellany* (Rome) XI, 1960, 333–400.)

W. Coyle, 'Molinos: "The Subject of the Day" in *The Ring and the Book*', *Publications of the Modern Language Association of America* LXVII, 1952, 308–14.

P. A. Cundiff, 'The Clarity of Browning's Ring Metaphor', *Publications of the Modern Language Association of America* LXIII, 1948, 1276–82.

P. A. Cundiff *et al.* (Three articles on the gold-alloy metaphor and the distinction between 'truth' and 'fancy' in Book I), *Victorian Newsletter* 15–17, Spring 1959–Spring 1960.

R. Curle (ed.), *Robert Browning and Julia Wedgwood: A Broken Friendship as Revealed by Their Letters*, Stokes, 1937.

W. C. DeVane, 'The Virgin and the Dragon', *Yale Review*, new series XXXVII, 1947, 33–46.

F. E. Faverty, 'The Absconded Abbot in *The Ring and the Book*', *Studies in Philology* XXXVI, 1939, 88–104.

B. R. Friedman, 'To Tell the Sun from the Druid Fire: Imagery of Good and Evil in *The Ring and the Book*', *Studies in English Literature* VI, 1966, 693–708.

J. M. Gest, *The Old Yellow Book . . . : A New Translation*, 2nd edn, University of Pennsylvania Press, 1927.

R. Gridley, 'Browning's Pompilia', *Journal of English and Germanic Philology* LXVII, 1968, 64–83.

R. Gridley, 'Browning's Two Guidos', *University of Toronto Quarterly* XXXVII, 1967, 51–68.

W. H. Griffin and H. C. Minchin, *The Life of Robert Browning*, 3rd edn, Methuen, 1938.

C. W. Hodell, *The Old Yellow Book*, Carnegie Institution of Washington, 1908.

P. Honan, *Browning's Characters*, Yale University Press, 1961.

H. James, 'The Novel in *The Ring and the Book*', *Quarterly Review* CCXVII, 1912, 68–87. (Reprinted in his *Notes on Novelists*, 1914.)

E. D. H. Johnson, *The Alien Vision of Victorian Poetry*, Princeton University Press, 1952.

E. D. H. Johnson, 'Browning's Pluralistic Universe: A Reading of *The Ring and the Book*', *University of Toronto Quarterly* XXXI, 1961, 20–41.

J. Killham, 'Browning's "Modernity": *The Ring and the Book* and Relativism', in I. Armstrong (ed.), *The Major Victorian Poets: Reconsiderations*, Routledge & Kegan Paul, 1969, ch. 7.

R. A. King Jr, *The Focusing Artifice: The Poetry of Robert Browning*, Ohio University Press, 1968.

R. Langbaum, *The Poetry of Experience*, Random House, 1957.

B. R. McElderry Jr, 'The Narrative Structure of Browning's *The Ring and the Book*', *Research Studies of the State College of Washington* XI, 1943, 193–233.

B. R. McElderry Jr, 'Victorian Evaluation of *The Ring and the Book*', *Research Studies of the State College of Washington* VII, 1939, 75–89.

C. T. Phipps, 'Adaptation from the Past, Creation for the Present: A Study of Browning's "The Pope"', *Studies in Philology* LXV, 1968, 702–22.

C. T. Phipps, 'Browning's Canon Giuseppe Caponsacchi: Warrior-Priest, Dantean Lover, Critic of Society', *English Literary History* XXXVI, 1969, 696–718.

W. O. Raymond, *The Infinite Moment and Other Essays in Robert Browning*, 2nd edn, University of Toronto Press, 1965.

J. E. Shaw, 'The "Donna Angelicata" in *The Ring and the Book*', *Publications of the Modern Language Association of America* XLI, 1926, 55–81.

W. D. Shaw, *The Dialectical Temper: The Rhetorical Art of Robert Browning*, Cornell University Press, 1968.

L. Snitslaar, *Sidelights on Robert Browning's 'The Ring and the Book'*, Swets and Zeitlinger, Amsterdam, 1934.

M. R. Sullivan, *Browning's Voices in 'The Ring and the Book': A Study of Method and Meaning*, University of Toronto Press, 1969.

Victorian Poetry. Double number commemorating the centennial of *The Ring and the Book*, VI, nos. 3–4 (Autumn–Winter 1968).

G. R. Wasserman, 'The Meaning of Browning's Ring-Figure', *Modern Language Notes* LXXVI, 1961, 420–26.

W. Whitla, *The Central Truth: The Incarnation in Browning's Poetry*, University of Toronto Press, 1963.

D. H. Willey, 'Moral Meaning in *The Ring and the Book*', *Research Studies of the State College of Washington* XX, 1952, 93–111.

E. H. Yarrill, 'Browning's "Roman Murder Story" as Recorded in a Hitherto Unknown Italian Contemporary Manuscript', *Baylor Bulletin* XLII, 1939, no. 4.

BOOK I

The Ring and the Book

Do you see this Ring?
               'T is Rome-work, made to match
(By Castellani's imitative craft)
Etrurian circlets found, some happy morn,
After a dropping April; found alive
Spark-like 'mid unearthed slope-side figtree-roots
That roof old tombs at Chiusi: soft, you see,
Yet crisp as jewel-cutting. There's one trick,
(Craftsmen instruct me) one approved device
10 And but one, fits such slivers of pure gold
As this was, – such mere oozings from the mine,
Virgin as oval tawny pendent tear
At beehive-edge when ripened combs o'erflow, –
To bear the file's tooth and the hammer's tap:
Since hammer needs must widen out the round,
And file emboss it fine with lily-flowers,
Ere the stuff grow a ring-thing right to wear.
That trick is, the artificer melts up wax
With honey, so to speak; he mingles gold
20 With gold's alloy, and, duly tempering both,
Effects a manageable mass, then works.
But his work ended, once the thing a ring,
Oh, there's repristination! Just a spirt
O' the proper fiery acid o'er its face,
And forth the alloy unfastened flies in fume;
While, self-sufficient now, the shape remains,
The rondure brave, the lilied loveliness,
Gold as it was, is, shall be evermore:
Prime nature with an added artistry –
30 No carat lost, and you have gained a ring.

What of it? 'T is a figure, a symbol, say;
A thing's sign: now for the thing signified.

Do you see this square old yellow Book, I toss
I' the air, and catch again, and twirl about
By the crumpled vellum covers, – pure crude fact
Secreted from a man's life when hearts beat hard,
And brains, high-blooded, ticked two centuries since?
Examine it yourselves! I found this book,
Gave a *lira* for it, eightpence English just,
40 (Mark the predestination!) when a Hand,
Always above my shoulder, pushed me once,
One day still fierce 'mid many a day struck calm,
Across a Square in Florence, crammed with booths,
Buzzing and blaze, noontide and market-time;
Toward Baccio's marble, – ay, the basement-ledge
O' the pedestal where sits and menaces
John of the Black Bands with the upright spear,
'Twixt palace and church, – Riccardi where they lived,
His race, and San Lorenzo where they lie.
50 This book, – precisely on that palace-step
Which, meant for lounging knaves o' the Medici,
Now serves re-venders to display their ware, –
'Mongst odds and ends of ravage, picture-frames
White through the worn gilt, mirror-sconces chipped,
Bronze angel-heads once knobs attached to chests,
(Handled when ancient dames chose forth brocade)
Modern chalk drawings, studies from the nude,
Samples of stone, jet, breccia, porphyry
Polished and rough, sundry amazing busts
60 In baked earth, (broken, Providence be praised!)
A wreck of tapestry, proudly-purposed web
When reds and blues were indeed red and blue,
Now offered as a mat to save bare feet
(Since carpets constitute a cruel cost)
Treading the chill scagliola bedward: then
A pile of brown-etched prints, two *crazie* each,
Stopped by a conch a-top from fluttering forth

    – Sowing the Square with works of one and the same
    Master, the imaginative Sienese
70 Great in the scenic backgrounds – (name and fame
    None of you know, nor does he fare the worse:)
    From these . . . Oh, with a Lionard going cheap
    If it should prove, as promised, that Joconde
    Whereof a copy contents the Louvre! – these
    I picked this book from. Five compeers in flank
    Stood left and right of it as tempting more –
    A dogseared Spicilegium, the fond tale
    O' the Frail One of the Flower, by young Dumas,
    Vulgarized Horace for the use of schools,
80 The Life, Death, Miracles of Saint Somebody,
    Saint Somebody Else, his Miracles, Death and Life, –
    With this, one glance at the lettered back of which,
    And 'Stall!' cried I: a *lira* made it mine.

    Here it is, this I toss and take again;
    Small-quarto size, part print part manuscript:
    A book in shape but, really, pure crude fact
    Secreted from man's life when hearts beat hard,
    And brains, high-blooded, ticked two centuries since.
    Give it me back! The thing's restorative
90 I' the touch and sight.

                That memorable day,
    (June was the month, Lorenzo named the Square)
    I leaned a little and overlooked my prize
    By the low railing round the fountain-source
    Close to the statue, where a step descends:
    While clinked the cans of copper, as stooped and rose
    Thick-ankled girls who brimmed them, and made place
    For marketmen glad to pitch basket down,
    Dip a broad melon-leaf that holds the wet,
100 And whisk their faded fresh. And on I read
    Presently, though my path grew perilous
    Between the outspread straw-work, piles of plait
    Soon to be flapping, each o'er two black eyes

And swathe of Tuscan hair, on festas fine:
Through fire-irons, tribes of tongs, shovels in sheaves,
Skeleton bedsteads, wardrobe-drawers agape,
Rows of tall slim brass lamps with dangling gear, –
And worse, cast clothes a-sweetening in the sun:
None of them took my eye from off my prize.
110　Still read I on, from written title-page
To written index, on, through street and street,
At the Strozzi, at the Pillar, at the Bridge;
Till, by the time I stood at home again
In Casa Guidi by Felice Church,
Under the doorway where the black begins
With the first stone-slab of the staircase cold,
I had mastered the contents, knew the whole truth
Gathered together, bound up in this book,
Print three-fifths, written supplement the rest.
120　'*Romana Homicidiorum*' – nay,
Better translate – 'A Roman murder-case:
Position of the entire criminal cause
Of Guido Franceschini, nobleman,
With certain Four the cutthroats in his pay,
Tried, all five, and found guilty and put to death
By heading or hanging as befitted ranks,
At Rome on February Twenty Two,
Since our salvation Sixteen Ninety Eight:
Wherein it is disputed if, and when,
130　Husbands may kill adulterous wives, yet 'scape
The customary forfeit.'

　　　　　　　　Word for word,
So ran the title-page: murder, or else
Legitimate punishment of the other crime,
Accounted murder by mistake, – just that
And no more, in a Latin cramp enough
When the law had her eloquence to launch,
But interfilleted with Italian streaks
When testimony stooped to mother-tongue, –
140　That, was this old square yellow book about.

Now, as the ingot, ere the ring was forged,
Lay gold, (beseech you, hold that figure fast!)
So, in this book lay absolutely truth,
Fanciless fact, the documents indeed,
Primary lawyer-pleadings for, against,
The aforesaid Five; real summed-up circumstance
Adduced in proof of these on either side,
Put forth and printed, as the practice was,
At Rome, in the Apostolic Chamber's type,

150 And so submitted to the eye o' the Court
Presided over by His Reverence
Rome's Governor and Criminal Judge, – the trial
Itself, to all intents, being then as now
Here in the book and nowise out of it;
Seeing, there properly was no judgment-bar,
No bringing of accuser and accused,
And whoso judged both parties, face to face
Before some court, as we conceive of courts.
There was a Hall of Justice; that came last:

160 For justice had a chamber by the hall
Where she took evidence first, summed up the same,
Then sent accuser and accused alike,
In person of the advocate of each,
To weigh that evidence' worth, arrange, array
The battle. 'T was the so-styled Fisc began,
Pleaded (and since he only spoke in print
The printed voice of him lives now as then)
The public Prosecutor – 'Murder's proved;
With five . . . what we call qualities of bad,

170 Worse, worst, and yet worse still, and still worse yet;
Crest over crest crowning the cockatrice,
That beggar hell's regalia to enrich
Count Guido Franceschini: punish him!'
Thus was the paper put before the court
In the next stage, (no noisy work at all,)
To study at ease. In due time like reply
Came from the so-styled Patron of the Poor,
Official mouthpiece of the five accused

Too poor to fee a better, – Guido's luck
180 Or else his fellows', which, I hardly know, –
An outbreak as of wonder at the world,
A fury-fit of outraged innocence,
A passion of betrayed simplicity:
'Punish Count Guido? For what crime, what hint
O' the colour of a crime, inform us first!
Reward him rather! Recognize, we say,
In the deed done, a righteous judgment dealt!
All conscience and all courage, – there's our Count
Charactered in a word; and, what's more strange,
190 He had companionship in privilege,
Found four courageous conscientious friends:
Absolve, applaud all five, as props of law,
Sustainers of society! – perchance
A trifle over-hasty with the hand
To hold her tottering ark, had tumbled else;
But that's a splendid fault whereat we wink,
Wishing your cold correctness sparkled so!'
Thus paper second followed paper first,
Thus did the two join issue – nay, the four,
200 Each pleader having an adjunct. 'True, he killed
– So to speak – in a certain sort – his wife,
But laudably, since thus it happed!' quoth one:
Whereat, more witness and the case postponed.
'Thus it happed not, since thus he did the deed,
And proved himself thereby portentousest
Of cutthroats and a prodigy of crime,
As the woman that he slaughtered was a saint,
Martyr and miracle!' quoth the other to match:
Again, more witness, and the case postponed.
210 'A miracle, ay – of lust and impudence;
Hear my new reasons!' interposed the first:
' – Coupled with more of mine!' pursued his peer.
'Beside, the precedents, the authorities!'
From both at once a cry with an echo, that!
That was a firebrand at each fox's tail
Unleashed in a cornfield: soon spread flare enough,

As hurtled thither and there heaped themselves
From earth's four corners, all authority
And precedent for putting wives to death,
220 Or letting wives live, sinful as they seem.
How legislated, now, in this respect,
Solon and his Athenians? Quote the code
Of Romulus and Rome! Justinian speak!
Nor modern Baldo, Bartolo be dumb!
The Roman voice was potent, plentiful;
Cornelia de Sicariis hurried to help
Pompeia de Parricidiis; Julia de
Something-or-other jostled *Lex* this-and-that;
King Solomon confirmed Apostle Paul:
230 That nice decision of Dolabella, eh?
That pregnant instance of Theodoric, oh!
Down to that choice example Aelian gives
(An instance I find much insisted on)
Of the elephant who, brute-beast though he were,
Yet understood and punished on the spot
His master's naughty spouse and faithless friend;
A true tale which has edified each child,
Much more shall flourish favoured by our court!
Pages of proof this way, and that way proof,
240 And always – once again the case postponed.

Thus wrangled, brangled, jangled they a month,
– Only on paper, pleadings all in print,
Nor ever was, except i' the brains of men,
More noise by word of mouth than you hear now –
Till the court cut all short with 'Judged, your cause.
Receive our sentence! Praise God! We pronounce
Count Guido devilish and damnable:
His wife Pompilia in thought, word and deed,
Was perfect pure, he murdered her for that:
250 As for the Four who helped the One, all Five –
Why, let employer and hirelings share alike
In guilt and guilt's reward, the death their due!'

So was the trial at end, do you suppose?
'Guilty you find him, death you doom him to?
Ay, were not Guido, more than needs, a priest,
Priest and to spare!' – this was a shot reserved;
I learn this from epistles which begin
Here where the print ends, – see the pen and ink
Of the advocate, the ready at a pinch! –
260 'My client boasts the clerkly privilege,
Has taken minor orders many enough,
Shows still sufficient chrism upon his pate
To neutralize a blood-stain: *presbyter,*
Primae tonsurae, subdiaconus,
Sacerdos, so he slips from underneath
Your power, the temporal, slides inside the robe
Of mother Church: to her we make appeal
By the Pope, the Church's head!'

                              A parlous plea,
270 Put in with noticeable effect, it seems;
'Since straight,' – resumes the zealous orator,
Making a friend acquainted with the facts, –
'Once the word "clericality" let fall,
Procedure stopped and freer breath was drawn
By all considerate and responsible Rome.'
Quality took the decent part, of course;
Held by the husband, who was noble too:
Or, for the matter of that, a churl would side
With too-refined susceptibility,
280 And honour which, tender in the extreme,
Stung to the quick, must roughly right itself
At all risks, not sit still and whine for law
As a Jew would, if you squeezed him to the wall,
Brisk-trotting through the Ghetto. Nay, it seems,
Even the Emperor's Envoy had his say
To say on the subject; might not see, unmoved,
Civility menaced throughout Christendom
By too harsh measure dealt her champion here.
Lastly, what made all safe, the Pope was kind,

290 From his youth up, reluctant to take life,
If mercy might be just and yet show grace;
Much more unlikely then, in extreme age,
To take a life the general sense bade spare.
'T was plain that Guido would go scatheless yet.

But human promise, oh, how short of shine!
How topple down the piles of hope we rear!
How history proves . . . nay, read Herodotus!
Suddenly starting from a nap, as it were,
A dog-sleep with one shut, one open orb,
300 Cried the Pope's great self, – Innocent by name
And nature too, and eighty-six years old,
Antonio Pignatelli of Naples, Pope
Who had trod many lands, known many deeds,
Probed many hearts, beginning with his own,
And now was far in readiness for God, –
'Twas he who first bade leave those souls in peace,
Those Jansenists, re-nicknamed Molinists,
('Gainst whom the cry went, like a frowsy tune,
Tickling men's ears – the sect for a quarter of an hour
310 I' the teeth of the world which, clown-like, loves to chew
Be it but a straw twixt work and whistling-while,
Taste some vituperation, bite away,
Whether at marjoram-sprig or garlic-clove,
Aught it may sport with, spoil, and then spit forth)
'Leave them alone,' bade he, 'those Molinists!
Who may have other light than we perceive,
Or why is it the whole world hates them thus?'
Also he peeled off that last scandal-rag
Of Nepotism; and so observed the poor
320 That men would merrily say, 'Halt, deaf and blind,
Who feed on fat things, leave the master's self
To gather up the fragments of his feast,
These be the nephews of Pope Innocent! –
His own meal costs but five carlines a day,
Poor-priest's allowance, for he claims no more.'
– He cried of a sudden, this great good old Pope,

When they appealed in last resort to him,
'I have mastered the whole matter: I nothing doubt.
Though Guido stood forth priest from head to heel,
330   Instead of, as alleged, a piece of one, –
And further, were he, from the tonsured scalp
To the sandaled sole of him, my son and Christ's,
Instead of touching us by finger-tip
As you assert, and pressing up so close
Only to set a blood-smutch on our robe, –
I and Christ would renounce all right in him.
Am I not Pope, and presently to die,
And busied how to render my account,
And shall I wait a day ere I decide
340   On doing or not doing justice here?
Cut off his head to-morrow by this time,
Hang up his four mates, two on either hand,
And end one business more!'

So said, so done –
Rather so writ, for the old Pope bade this,
I find, with his particular chirograph,
His own no such infirm hand, Friday night;
And next day, February Twenty Two,
Since our salvation Sixteen Ninety Eight,
350   – Not at the proper head-and-hanging-place
On bridge-foot close by Castle Angelo,
Where custom somewhat staled the spectacle,
('Twas not so well i' the way of Rome, beside,
The noble Rome, the Rome of Guido's rank)
But at the city's newer gayer end, –
The cavalcading promenading place
Beside the gate and opposite the church
Under the Pincian gardens green with Spring,
'Neath the obelisk 'twixt the fountains in the Square,
360   Did Guido and his fellows find their fate,
All Rome for witness, and – my writer adds –
Remonstrant in its universal grief,
Since Guido had the suffrage of all Rome.

This is the bookful; thus far take the truth,
The untempered gold, the fact untampered with,
The mere ring-metal ere the ring be made!
And what has hitherto come of it? Who preserves
The memory of this Guido, and his wife
Pompilia, more than Ademollo's name,
370 The etcher of those prints, two *crazie* each,
Saved by a stone from snowing broad the Square
With scenic backgrounds? Was this truth of force?
Able to take its own part as truth should,
Sufficient, self-sustaining? Why, if so –
Yonder's a fire, into it goes my book,
As who shall say me nay, and what the loss?
You know the tale already: I may ask,
Rather than think to tell you, more thereof, –
Ask you not merely who were he and she,
380 Husband and wife, what manner of mankind,
But how you hold concerning this and that
Other yet-unnamed actor in the piece.
The young frank handsome courtly Canon, now,
The priest, declared the lover of the wife,
He who, no question, did elope with her,
For certain bring the tragedy about,
Giuseppe Caponsacchi; – his strange course
I' the matter, was it right or wrong or both?
Then the old couple, slaughtered with the wife
390 By the husband as accomplices in crime,
Those Comparini, Pietro and his spouse, –
What say you to the right or wrong of that,
When, at a known name whispered through the door
Of a lone villa on a Christmas night,
It opened that the joyous hearts inside
Might welcome as it were an angel-guest
Come in Christ's name to knock and enter, sup
And satisfy the loving ones he saved;
And so did welcome devils and their death?
400 I have been silent on that circumstance
Although the couple passed for close of kin

To wife and husband, were by some accounts
Pompilia's very parents: you know best.
Also that infant the great joy was for,
That Gaetano, the wife's two-weeks' babe,
The husband's first-born child, his son and heir,
Whose birth and being turned his night to day –
Why must the father kill the mother thus
Because she bore his son and saved himself?

410 Well, British Public, ye who like me not,
(God love you!) and will have your proper laugh
At the dark question, laugh it! I laugh first.
Truth must prevail, the proverb vows; and truth
– Here is it all i' the book at last, as first
There it was all i' the heads and hearts of Rome
Gentle and simple, never to fall nor fade
Nor be forgotten. Yet, a little while,
The passage of a century or so,
Decads thrice five, and here's time paid his tax,
420 Oblivion gone home with her harvesting,
And all left smooth again as scythe could shave.
Far from beginning with you London folk,
I took my book to Rome first, tried truth's power
On likely people. 'Have you met such names?
Is a tradition extant of such facts?
Your law-courts stand, your records frown a-row:
What if I rove and rummage?' ' – Why, you'll waste
Your pains and end as wise as you began!'
Everyone snickered: 'names and facts thus old
430 Are newer much than Europe news we find
Down in to-day's *Diario*. Records, quotha?
Why, the French burned them, what else do the French?
The rap-and-rending nation! And it tells
Against the Church, no doubt, – another gird
At the Temporality, your Trial, of course?'
' – Quite otherwise this time,' submitted I;
Clean for the Church and dead against the world,
The flesh and the devil, does it tell for once.'

'– The rarer and the happier! All the same,
440 Content you with your treasure of a book,
And waive what's wanting! Take a friend's advice!
It's not the custom of the country. Mend
Your ways indeed and we may stretch a point:
Go get you manned by Manning and new-manned
By Newman and, mayhap, wise-manned to boot
By Wiseman, and we'll see or else we won't!
Thanks meantime for the story, long and strong,
A pretty piece of narrative enough,
Which scarce ought so to drop out, one would think,
450 From the more curious annals of our kind.
Do you tell the story, now, in off-hand style,
Straight from the book? Or simply here and there,
(The while you vault it through the loose and large)
Hang to a hint? Or is there book at all,
And don't you deal in poetry, make-believe,
And the white lies it sounds like?'

                     Yes and no!
From the book, yes; thence bit by bit I dug
The lingot truth, that memorable day,
460 Assayed and knew my piecemeal gain was gold, –
Yes; but from something else surpassing that,
Something of mine which, mixed up with the mass,
Made it bear hammer and be firm to file.
Fancy with fact is just one fact the more;
To-wit, that fancy has informed, transpierced,
Thridded and so thrown fast the facts else free,
As right through ring and ring runs the djereed
And binds the loose, one bar without a break.
I fused my live soul and that inert stuff,
470 Before attempting smithcraft, on the night
After the day when, – truth thus grasped and gained, –
The book was shut and done with and laid by
On the cream-coloured massive agate, broad
'Neath the twin cherubs in the tarnished frame
O' the mirror, tall thence to the ceiling-top.

And from the reading, and that slab I leant
My elbow on, the while I read and read,
I turned, to free myself and find the world,
And stepped out on the narrow terrace, built
480   Over the street and opposite the church,
And paced its lozenge-brickwork sprinkled cool;
Because Felice-church-side stretched, a-glow
Through each square window fringed for festival,
Whence came the clear voice of the cloistered ones
Chanting a chant made for midsummer nights –
I know not what particular praise of God,
It always came and went with June. Beneath
I' the street, quick shown by openings of the sky
When flame fell silently from cloud to cloud,
490   Richer than that gold snow Jove rained on Rhodes,
The townsmen walked by twos and threes, and talked,
Drinking the blackness in default of air –
A busy human sense beneath my feet:
While in and out the terrace-plants, and round
One branch of tall datura, waxed and waned
The lamp-fly lured there, wanting the white flower.
Over the roof o' the lighted church I looked
A bowshot to the street's end, north away
Out of the Roman gate to the Roman road
500   By the river, till I felt the Apennine.
And there would lie Arezzo, the man's town,
The woman's trap and cage and torture-place,
Also the stage where the priest played his part,
A spectacle for angels, – ay, indeed,
There lay Arezzo! Farther then I fared,
Feeling my way on through the hot and dense,
Romeward, until I found the wayside inn
By Castelnuovo's few mean hut-like homes
Huddled together on the hill-foot bleak,
510   Bare, broken only by that tree or two
Against the sudden bloody splendour poured
Cursewise in his departure by the day
On the low house-roof of that squalid inn

Where they three, for the first time and the last,
Husband and wife and priest, met face to face.
Whence I went on again, the end was near,
Step by step, missing none and marking all,
Till Rome itself, the ghastly goal, I reached.
Why, all the while, – how could it otherwise? –
520 The life in me abolished the death of things,
Deep calling unto deep: as then and there
Acted itself over again once more
The tragic piece. I saw with my own eyes
In Florence as I trod the terrace, breathed
The beauty and the fearfulness of night,
How it had run, this round from Rome to Rome –
Because, you are to know, they lived at Rome,
Pompilia's parents, as they thought themselves,
Two poor ignoble hearts who did their best
530 Part God's way, part the other way than God's,
To somehow make a shift and scramble through
The world's mud, careless if it splashed and spoiled,
Provided they might so hold high, keep clean
Their child's soul, one soul white enough for three,
And lift it to whatever star should stoop,
What possible sphere of purer life than theirs
Should come in aid of whiteness hard to save.
I saw the star stoop, that they strained to touch,
And did touch and depose their treasure on,
540 As Guido Franceschini took away
Pompilia to be his for evermore,
While they sang 'Now let us depart in peace,
Having beheld thy glory, Guido's wife!'
I saw the star supposed, but fog o' the fen,
Gilded star-fashion by a glint from hell;
Having been heaved up, haled on its gross way,
By hands unguessed before, invisible help
From a dark brotherhood, and specially
Two obscure goblin creatures, fox-faced this,
550 Cat-clawed the other, called his next of kin
By Guido the main monster, – cloaked and caped,

Making as they were priests, to mock God more, –
Abate Paul, Canon Girolamo.
These who had rolled the starlike pest to Rome
And stationed it to suck up and absorb
The sweetness of Pompilia, rolled again
That bloated bubble, with her soul inside,
Back to Arezzo and a palace there –
Or say, a fissure in the honest earth
560 Whence long ago had curled the vapour first,
Blown big by nether fires to appal day:
It touched home, broke, and blasted far and wide.
I saw the cheated couple find the cheat
And guess what foul rite they were captured for, –
Too fain to follow over hill and dale
That child of theirs caught up thus in the cloud
And carried by the Prince o' the Power of the Air
Whither he would, to wilderness or sea.
I saw them, in the potency of fear,
570 Break somehow through the satyr-family
(For a grey mother with a monkey-mien,
Mopping and mowing, was apparent too,
As, confident of capture, all took hands
And danced about the captives in a ring)
– Saw them break through, breathe safe, at Rome again,
Saved by the selfish instinct, losing so
Their loved one left with haters. These I saw,
In recrudescency of baffled hate,
Prepare to wring the uttermost revenge
580 From body and soul thus left them: all was sure,
Fire laid and cauldron set, the obscene ring traced,
The victim stripped and prostrate: what of God?
The cleaving of a cloud, a cry, a crash,
Quenched lay their cauldron, cowered i' the dust the crew,
As, in a glory of armour like Saint George,
Out again sprang the young good beauteous priest
Bearing away the lady in his arms,
Saved for a splendid minute and no more.
For, whom i' the path did that priest come upon,

590 He and the poor lost lady borne so brave,
     – Checking the song of praise in me, had else
     Swelled to the full for God's will done on earth –
     Whom but a dusk misfeatured messenger,
     No other than the angel of this life,
     Whose care is lest men see too much at once.
     He made the sign, such God-glimpse must suffice,
     Nor prejudice the Prince o' the Power of the Air,
     Whose ministration piles us overhead
     What we call, first, earth's roof and, last, heaven's floor,
600 Now grate o' the trap, then outlet of the cage:
     So took the lady, left the priest alone,
     And once more canopied the world with black.
     But through the blackness I saw Rome again,
     And where a solitary villa stood
     In a lone garden-quarter: it was eve,
     The second of the year, and oh so cold!
     Ever and anon there flittered through the air
     A snow-flake, and a scanty couch of snow
     Crusted the grass-walk and the garden-mould.
610 All was grave, silent, sinister, – when, ha?
     Glimmeringly did a pack of were-wolves pad
     The snow, those flames were Guido's eyes in front,
     And all five found and footed it, the track,
     To where a threshold-streak of warmth and light
     Betrayed the villa-door with life inside,
     While an inch outside were those blood-bright eyes,
     And black lips wrinkling o'er the flash of teeth,
     And tongues that lolled – Oh God that madest man!
     They parleyed in their language. Then one whined –
620 That was the policy and master-stroke –
     Deep in his throat whispered what seemed a name –
     'Open to Caponsacchi!' Guido cried:
     'Gabriel!' cried Lucifer at Eden-gate.
     Wide as a heart, opened the door at once,
     Showing the joyous couple, and their child
     The two-weeks' mother, to the wolves, the wolves
     To them. Close eyes! And when the corpses lay

Stark-stretched, and those the wolves, their wolf-work done,
Were safe-embosomed by the night again,
630 I knew a necessary change in things;
As when the worst watch of the night gives way,
And there comes duly, to take cognisance,
The scrutinizing eye-point of some star –
And who despairs of a new daybreak now?
Lo, the first ray protruded on those five!
It reached them, and each felon writhed transfixed.
Awhile they palpitated on the spear
Motionless over Tophet: stand or fall?
'I say, the spear should fall – should stand, I say!'
640 Cried the world come to judgment, granting grace
Or dealing doom according to world's wont,
Those world's-bystanders grouped on Rome's cross-road
At prick and summons of the primal curse
Which bids man love as well as make a lie.
There prattled they, discoursed the right and wrong,
Turned wrong to right, proved wolves sheep and sheep
     wolves,
So that you scarce distinguished fell from fleece;
Till out spoke a great guardian of the fold,
Stood up, put forth his hand that held the crook,
650 And motioned that the arrested point decline:
Horribly off, the wriggling dead-weight reeled,
Rushed to the bottom and lay ruined there.
Though still at the pit's mouth, despite the smoke
O' the burning, tarriers turned again to talk
And trim the balance, and detect at least
A touch of wolf in what showed whitest sheep,
A cross of sheep redeeming the whole wolf, –
Vex truth a little longer: – less and less,
Because years came and went, and more and more
660 Brought new lies with them to be loved in turn.
Till all at once the memory of the thing, –
The fact that, wolves or sheep, such creatures were, –
Which hitherto, however men supposed,
Had somehow plain and pillar-like prevailed

I' the midst of them, indisputably fact,
Granite, time's tooth should grate against, not graze, –
Why, this proved sandstone, friable, fast to fly
And give its grain away at wish o' the wind.
Ever and ever more diminutive,
670 Base gone, shaft lost, only entablature,
Dwindled into no bigger than a book,
Lay of the column; and that little, left
By the roadside 'mid the ordure, shards and weeds.
Until I haply, wandering that way,
Kicked it up, turned it over, and recognized,
For all the crumblement, this abacus,
This square old yellow book, – could calculate
By this the lost proportions of the style.

This was it from, my fancy with those facts,
680 I used to tell the tale, turned gay to grave,
But lacked a listener seldom; such alloy,
Such substance of me interfused the gold
Which, wrought into a shapely ring therewith,
Hammered and filed, fingered and favoured, last
Lay ready for the renovating wash
O' the water. 'How much of the tale was true?'
I disappeared; the book grew all in all;
The lawyer's pleadings swelled back to their size, –
Doubled in two, the crease upon them yet,
690 For more commodity of carriage, see! –
And these are letters, veritable sheets
That brought posthaste the news to Florence, writ
At Rome the day Count Guido died, we find,
To stay the craving of a client there,
Who bound the same and so produced my book.
Lovers of dead truth, did ye fare the worse?
Lovers of live truth, found ye false my tale?

Well, now; there's nothing in nor out o' the world
Good except truth: yet this, the something else,
700 What's this then, which proves good yet seems untrue?

This that I mixed with truth, motions of mine
That quickened, made the inertness malleolable
O' the gold was not mine, – what's your name for this?
Are means to the end, themselves in part the end?
Is fiction which makes fact alive, fact too?
The somehow may be thishow.
                              I find first
Writ down for very A.B.C. of fact,
'In the beginning God made heaven and earth;'
710 From which, no matter with what lisp, I spell
And speak you out a consequence – that man,
Man, – as befits the made, the inferior thing, –
Purposed, since made, to grow, not make in turn,
Yet forced to try and make, else fail to grow, –
Formed to rise, reach at, if not grasp and gain
The good beyond him, – which attempt is growth, –
Repeats God's process in man's due degree,
Attaining man's proportionate result, –
Creates, no, but resuscitates, perhaps.
720 Inalienable, the arch-prerogative
Which turns thought, act – conceives, expresses too!
No less, man, bounded, yearning to be free,
May so project his surplusage of soul
In search of body, so add self to self
By owning what lay ownerless before, –
So find, so fill full, so appropriate forms –
That, although nothing which had never life
Shall get life from him, be, not having been,
Yet, something dead may get to live again,
730 Something with too much life or not enough,
Which, either way imperfect, ended once:
An end whereat man's impulse intervenes,
Makes new beginning, starts the dead alive,
Completes the incomplete and saves the thing.
Man's breath were vain to light a virgin wick, –
Half-burned-out, all but quite-quenched wicks o' the lamp
Stationed for temple-service on this earth,
These indeed let him breathe on and relume!

For such man's feat is, in the due degree,
740   – Mimic creation, galvanism for life,
But still a glory portioned in the scale.
Why did the mage say, – feeling as we are wont
For truth, and stopping midway short of truth,
And resting on a lie, – 'I raise a ghost?'
'Because', he taught adepts, 'man makes not man.
Yet by a special gift, an art of arts,
More insight and more outsight and much more
Will to use both of these than boast my mates,
I can detach from me, commission forth
750   Half of my soul; which in its pilgrimage
O'er old unwandered waste ways of the world,
May chance upon some fragment of a whole,
Rag of flesh, scrap of bone in dim disuse,
Smoking flax that fed fire once: prompt therein
I enter, spark-like, put old powers to play,
Push lines out to the limit, lead forth last
(By a moonrise through a ruin of a crypt)
What shall be mistily seen, murmuringly heard,
Mistakenly felt: then write my name with Faust's!'
760   Oh, Faust, why Faust? Was not Elisha once? –
Who bade them lay his staff on a corpse-face.
There was no voice, no hearing: he went in
Therefore, and shut the door upon them twain,
And prayed unto the Lord: and he went up
And lay upon the corpse, dead on the couch,
And put his mouth upon its mouth, his eyes
Upon its eyes, his hands upon its hands,
And stretched him on the flesh; the flesh waxed warm:
And he returned, walked to and fro the house,
770   And went up, stretched him on the flesh again,
And the eyes opened. 'Tis a credible feat
With the right man and way.

                    Enough of me!
The Book! I turn its medicinable leaves
In London now till, as in Florence erst,

A spirit laughs and leaps through every limb,
And lights my eye, and lifts me by the hair,
Letting me have my will again with these
– How title I the dead alive once more?

780 Count Guido Franceschini the Aretine,
Descended of an ancient house, though poor,
A beak-nosed bushy-bearded black-haired lord,
Lean, pallid, low of stature yet robust,
Fifty years old, – having four years ago
Married Pompilia Comparini, young,
Good, beautiful, at Rome, where she was born,
And brought her to Arezzo, where they lived
Unhappy lives, whatever curse the cause, –
This husband, taking four accomplices,
790 Followed this wife to Rome, where she was fled
From their Arezzo to find peace again,
In convoy, eight months earlier, of a priest,
Aretine also, of still nobler birth,
Giuseppe Caponsacchi, – and caught her there
Quiet in a villa on a Christmas night,
With only Pietro and Violante by,
Both her putative parents; killed the three,
Aged, they, seventy each, and she, seventeen,
And, two weeks since, the mother of his babe
800 First-born and heir to what the style was worth
O' the Guido who determined, dared and did
This deed just as he purposed point by point.
Then, bent upon escape, but hotly pressed,
And captured with his co-mates that same night,
He, brought to trial, stood on this defence –
Injury to his honour caused the act;
That since his wife was false, (as manifest
By flight from home in such companionship,)
Death, punishment deserved of the false wife
810 And faithless parents who abetted her
I' the flight aforesaid, wronged nor God nor man,
'Nor false she, nor yet faithless they,' replied

The accuser; 'cloaked and masked this murder glooms;
True was Pompilia, loyal too the pair;
Out of the man's own heart this monster curled,
This crime coiled with connivancy at crime,
His victim's breast, he tells you, hatched and reared;
Uncoil we and stretch stark the worm of hell!'
A month the trial swayed this way and that
820 Ere judgment settled down on Guido's guilt;
Then was the Pope, that good Twelfth Innocent,
Appealed to: who well weighed what went before,
Affirmed the guilt and gave the guilty doom.

Let this old woe step on the stage again!
Act itself o'er anew for men to judge,
Not by the very sense and sight indeed –
(Which take at best imperfect cognizance,
Since, how heart moves brain, and how both move hand,
What mortal ever in entirety saw?)
830 – No dose of purer truth than man digests,
But truth with falsehood, milk that feeds him now,
Not strong meat he may get to bear some day –
To-wit, by voices we call evidence,
Uproar in the echo, live fact deadened down,
Talked over, bruited abroad, whispered away,
Yet helping us to all we seem to hear:
For how else know we save by worth of word?

Here are the voices presently shall sound
In due succession. First, the world's outcry
840 Around the rush and ripple of any fact
Fallen stonewise, plumb on the smooth face of things;
The world's guess, as it crowds the bank o' the pool,
At what were figure and substance, by their splash:
Then, by vibrations in the general mind,
At depth of deed already out of reach.
This threefold murder of the day before, –
Say, Half-Rome's feel after the vanished truth;
Honest enough, as the way is: all the same,

Harbouring in the centre of its sense
850 A hidden germ of failure, shy but sure,
Should neutralize that honesty and leave
That feel for truth at fault, as the way is too.
Some prepossession such as starts amiss,
By but a hair's breadth at the shoulder-blade,
The arm o' the feeler, dip he ne'er so brave;
And so leads waveringly, lets fall wide
O' the mark his finger meant to find, and fix
Truth at the bottom, that deceptive speck.
With this Half-Rome, – the source of swerving, call
860 Over-belief in Guido's right and wrong
Rather than in Pompilia's wrong and right:
Who shall say how, who shall say why? 'T is there –
The instinctive theorizing whence a fact
Looks to the eye as the eye likes the look.
Gossip in a public place, a sample-speech.
Some worthy, with his previous hint to find
A husband's side the safer, and no whit
Aware he is not Aeacus the while, –
How such an one supposes and states fact
870 To whosoever of a multitude
Will listen, and perhaps prolong thereby
The not-unpleasant flutter at the breast,
Born of a certain spectacle shut in
By the church Lorenzo opposite. So, they lounge
Midway the mouth o' the street, on Corso side,
'Twixt palace Fiano and palace Ruspoli,
Linger and listen; keeping clear o' the crowd,
Yet wishful one could lend that crowd one's eyes,
(So universal is its plague of squint)
880 And make hearts beat our time that flutter false:
– All for the truth's sake, mere truth, nothing else!
How Half-Rome found for Guido much excuse.

Next, from Rome's other half, the opposite feel
For truth with a like swerve, like unsuccess, –
Or if success, by no more skill but luck:

This time, through rather siding with the wife,
However the fancy-fit inclined that way,
Than with the husband. One wears drab, one, pink;
Who wears pink, ask him 'Which shall win the race,
890 Of coupled runners like as egg and egg?'
' – Why, if I must choose, he with the pink scarf.'
Doubtless for some such reason choice fell here.
A piece of public talk to correspond
At the next stage of the story; just a day
Let pass and new day bring the proper change.
Another sample-speech i' the market-place
O' the Barberini by the Capucins;
Where the old Triton, at his fountain-sport,
Bernini's creature plated to the paps,
900 Puffs up steel sleet which breaks to diamond dust,
A spray of sparkles snorted from his conch,
High over the caritellas, out o' the way
O' the motley merchandizing multitude.
Our murder has been done three days ago,
The frost is over and gone, the south wind laughs,
And, to the very tiles of each red roof
A-smoke i' the sunshine, Rome lies gold and glad:
So, listen how, to the other half of Rome,
Pompilia seemed a saint and martyr both!

910 Then, yet another day let come and go,
With pause prelusive still of novelty,
Hear a fresh speaker! – neither this nor that
Half-Rome aforesaid; something bred of both:
One and one breed the inevitable three,
Such is the personage harangues you next;
The elaborated product, *tertium quid*:
Rome's first commotion in subsidence gives
The curd o' the cream, flower o' the wheat, as it were,
And finer sense o' the city. Is this plain?
920 You get a reasoned statement of the case,
Eventual verdict of the curious few
Who care to sift a business to the bran

Nor coarsely bolt it like the simpler sort.
Here, after ignorance, instruction speaks;
Here, clarity of candour, history's soul,
The critical mind, in short: no gossip-guess.
What the superior social section thinks,
In person of some man of quality
Who, – breathing musk from lace-work and brocade,
930 His solitaire amid the flow of frill,
Powdered peruke on nose, and bag at back,
And cane dependent from the ruffled wrist, –
Harangues in silvery and selectest phrase
'Neath waxlight in a glorified saloon
Where mirrors multiply the girandole:
Courting the approbation of no mob,
But Eminence This and All-Illustrious That
Who take snuff softly, range in well-bred ring,
Card-table-quitters for observance' sake,
940 Around the argument, the rational word –
Still, spite its weight and worth, a sample-speech.
How quality dissertated on the case.

So much for Rome and rumour; smoke comes first:
Once the smoke risen untroubled, we descry
Clearlier what tongues of flame may spire and spit
To eye and ear, each with appropriate tinge
According to its food, pure or impure.
The actors, no mere rumours of the act,
Intervene. First you hear Count Guido's voice,
950 In a small chamber that adjoins the court,
Where Governor and Judges, summoned thence,
Tommati, Venturini and the rest,
Find the accused ripe for declaring truth.
Soft-cushioned sits he; yet shifts seat, shirks touch,
As, with a twitchy brow and wincing lip
And cheek that changes to all kinds of white,
He proffers his defence, in tones subdued
Near to mock-mildness now, so mournful seems
The obtuser sense truth fails to satisfy;

960 Now, moved, from pathos at the wrong endured,
To passion; for the natural man is roused
At fools who first do wrong, then pour the blame
Of their wrong-doing, Satan-like, on Job.
Also his tongue at times is hard to curb;
Incisive, nigh satiric bites the phrase,
Rough-raw, yet somehow claiming privilege
– It is so hard for shrewdness to admit
Folly means no harm when she calls black white!
– Eruption momentary at the most,
970 Modified forthwith by a fall o' the fire,
Sage acquiescence; for the world's the world,
And, what it errs in, Judges rectify:
He feels he has a fist, then folds his arms
Crosswise and makes his mind up to be meek.
And never once does he detach his eye
From those ranged there to slay him or to save,
But does his best man's-service for himself,
Despite, – what twitches brow and makes lip wince, –
His limbs' late taste of what was called the Cord,
980 Or Vigil-torture more facetiously.
Even so; they were wont to tease the truth
Out of loath witness (toying, trifling time)
By torture: 'twas a trick, a vice of the age,
Here, there and everywhere, what would you have?
Religion used to tell Humanity
She gave him warrant or denied him course.
And since the course was much to his own mind,
Of pinching flesh and pulling bone from bone
To unhusk truth a-hiding in its hulls,
990 Nor whisper of a warning stopped the way,
He, in their joint behalf, the burly slave,
Bestirred him, mauled and maimed all recusants,
While, prim in place, Religion overlooked;
And so had done till doomsday, never a sign
Nor sound of interference from her mouth,
But that at last the burly slave wiped brow,
Let eye give notice as if soul were there,

Muttered ''Tis a vile trick, foolish more than vile,
Should have been counted sin; I make it so:
1000 At any rate no more of it for me –
Nay, for I break the torture-engine thus!'
Then did Religion start up, stare amain,
Look round for help and see none, smile and say
'What, broken is the rack? Well done of thee!
Did I forget to abrogate its use?
Be the mistake in common with us both!
– One more fault our blind age shall answer for,
Down in my book denounced though it must be
Somewhere. Henceforth find truth by milder means!'
1010 Ah but, Religion, did we wait for thee
To ope the book, that serves to sit upon,
And pick such place out, we should wait indeed!
That is all history: and what is not now,
Was then, defendants found it to their cost.
How Guido, after being tortured, spoke.

Also hear Caponsacchi who comes next,
Man and priest – could you comprehend the coil! –
In days when that was rife which now is rare.
How, mingling each its multifarious wires,
1020 Now heaven, now earth, now heaven and earth at once,
Had plucked at and perplexed their puppet here,
Played off the young frank personable priest;
Sworn fast and tonsured plain heaven's celibate,
And yet earth's clear-accepted servitor,
A courtly spiritual Cupid, squire of dames
By law of love and mandate of the mode.
The Church's own, or why parade her seal,
Wherefore that chrism and consecrative work?
Yet verily the world's, or why go badged
1030 A prince of sonneteers and lutanists,
Show colour of each vanity in vogue
Borne with decorum due on blameless breast?
All that is changed now, as he tells the court
How he had played the part excepted at;

Tells it, moreover, now the second time:
Since, for his cause of scandal, his own share
I' the flight from home and husband of the wife,
He has been censured, punished in a sort
By relegation, – exile, we should say,
1040 To a short distance for a little time, –
Whence he is summoned on a sudden now,
Informed that she, he thought to save, is lost,
And, in a breath, bidden re-tell his tale,
Since the first telling somehow missed effect,
And then advise in the matter. There stands he,
While the same grim black-panelled chamber blinks
As though rubbed shiny with the sins of Rome
Told the same oak for ages – wave-washed wall
Whereto has set a sea of wickedness.
1050 There, where you yesterday heard Guido speak,
Speaks Caponsacchi; and there face him too
Tommati, Venturini and the rest
Who, eight months earlier, scarce repressed the smile,
Forewent the wink; waived recognition so
Of peccadillos incident to youth,
Especially youth high-born; for youth means love,
Vows can't change nature, priests are only men,
And love needs stratagem and subterfuge:
Which age, that once was youth, should recognize,
1060 May blame, but needs not press too hard against.
Here sit the old Judges then, but with no grace
Of reverend carriage, magisterial port.
For why? The accused of eight months since, – the same
Who cut the conscious figure of a fool,
Changed countenance, dropped bashful gaze to ground,
While hesitating for an answer then, –
Now is grown judge himself, terrifies now
This, now the other culprit called a judge,
Whose turn it is to stammer and look strange,
1070 As he speaks rapidly, angrily, speech that smites:
And they keep silence, bear blow after blow,
Because the seeming solitary man,

Speaking for God, may have an audience too,
Invisible, no discreet judge provokes.
How the priest Caponsacchi said his say.

Then a soul sighs its lowest and its last
After the loud ones, – so much breath remains
Unused by the four-days'-dying; for she lived
Thus long, miraculously long, 't was thought,
1080 Just that Pompilia might defend herself.
How, while the hireling and the alien stoop,
Comfort, yet question, – since the time is brief,
And folk, allowably inquisitive,
Encircle the low pallet where she lies
In the good house that helps the poor to die, –
Pompilia tells the story of her life.
For friend and lover, – leech and man of law
Do service; busy helpful ministrants
As varied in their calling as their mind,
1090 Temper and age: and yet from all of these,
About the white bed under the arched roof,
Is somehow, as it were, evolved a one, –
Small separate sympathies combined and large,
Nothings that were, grown something very much:
As if the bystanders gave each his straw,
All he had, though a trifle in itself,
Which, plaited all together, made a Cross
Fit to die looking on and praying with,
Just as well as if ivory or gold.
1100 So, to the common kindliness she speaks,
There being scarce more privacy at the last
For mind than body: but she is used to bear,
And only unused to the brotherly look.
How she endeavoured to explain her life.

Then, since a Trial ensued, a touch o' the same
To sober us, flustered with frothy talk,
And teach our common sense its helplessness.
For why deal simply with divining-rod,

Scrape where we fancy secret sources flow,
1110 And ignore law, the recognized machine,
Elaborate display of pipe and wheel
Framed to unchoak, pump up and pour apace
Truth in a flowery foam shall wash the world?
The patent truth-extracting process, – ha?
Let us make all that mystery turn one wheel,
Give you a single grind of law at least!
One orator, of two on either side,
Shall teach us the puissance of the tongue
– That is, o' the pen which simulated tongue
1120 On paper and saved all except the sound
Which never was. Law's speech beside law's thought?
That were too stunning, too immense an odds:
That point of vantage, law let nobly pass.
One lawyer shall admit us to behold
The manner of the making out a case,
First fashion of a speech; the chick in egg,
And masterpiece law's bosom incubates.
How Don Giacinto of the Arcangeli,
Called Procurator of the Poor at Rome,
1130 Now advocate for Guido and his mates, –
The jolly learned man of middle age,
Cheek and jowl all in laps with fat and law,
Mirthful as mighty, yet, as great hearts use,
Despite the name and fame that tempt our flesh,
Constant to that devotion of the hearth,
Still captive in those dear domestic ties! –
How he, – having a cause to triumph with,
All kind of interests to keep intact,
More than one efficacious personage
1140 To tranquillize, conciliate and secure,
And above all, public anxiety
To quiet, show its Guido in good hands, –
Also, as if such burdens were too light,
A certain family-feast to claim his care,
The birthday-banquet for the only son –
Paternity at smiling strife with law –

How he brings both to buckle in one bond;
And, thick at throat, with waterish under-eye,
Turns to his task and settles in his seat
1150 And puts his utmost means to practice now:
Wheezes out law and whiffles Latin forth,
And, just as though roast lamb would never be,
Makes logic levigate the big crime small:
Rubs palm on palm, rakes foot with itchy foot,
Conceives and inchoates the argument,
Sprinkling each flower appropriate to the time,
– Ovidian quip or Ciceronian crank,
A-bubble in the larynx while he laughs,
As he had fritters deep down frying there.
1160 How he turns, twists, and tries the oily thing
Shall be – first speech for Guido 'gainst the Fisc.

Then with a skip as it were from heel to head,
Leaving yourselves fill up the middle bulk
O' the Trial, reconstruct its shape august,
From such exordium clap we to the close;
Give you, if we dare wing to such a height,
The absolute glory in some full-grown speech
On the other side, some finished butterfly,
Some breathing diamond-flake with leaf-gold fans,
1170 That takes the air, no trace of worm it was,
Or cabbage-bed it had production from.
Giovambattista o' the Bottini, Fisc,
Pompilia's patron by the chance of the hour,
To-morrow her persecutor, – composite, he,
As becomes who must meet such various calls –
Odds of age joined in him with ends of youth.
A man of ready smile and facile tear,
Improvised hopes, despairs at nod and beck,
And language – ah, the gift of eloquence!
1180 Language that goes as easy as a glove
O'er good and evil, smoothens both to one.
Rashness helps caution with him, fires the straw,
In free enthusiastic careless fit,
On the first proper pinnacle of rock

Which happens, as reward for all that zeal,
To lure some bark to founder and bring gain:
While calm sits Caution, rapt with heavenward eye,
A true confessor's gaze amid the glare,
Beaconing to the breaker, death and hell.
1190 'Well done, thou good and faithful!' she approves:
'Hadst thou let slip a faggot to the beach,
The crew had surely spied thy precipice
And saved their boat; the simple and the slow,
Who should have prompt forestalled the wrecker's fee:
Let the next crew be wise and hail in time!'
Just so compounded is the outside man,
Blue juvenile pure eye and pippin cheek,
And brow all prematurely soiled and seamed
With sudden age, bright devastated hair.
1200 Ah, but you miss the very tones o' the voice,
The scrannel pipe that screams in heights of head,
As, in his modest studio, all alone,
The tall wight stands a-tiptoe, strives and strains,
Both eyes shut, like the cockerel that would crow,
Tries to his own self amorously o'er
What never will be uttered else than so –
To the four walls, for Forum and Mars' Hill,
Speaks out the poesy which, penned, turns prose.
Clavecinist debarred his instrument,
1210 He yet thrums – shirking neither turn nor trill,
With desperate finger on dumb table-edge –
The sovereign rondo, shall conclude his *Suite*,
Charm an imaginary audience there,
From old Corelli to young Handel, both
I' the flesh at Rome, ere he perforce go print
The cold black score, mere music for the mind –
The last speech against Guido and his gang,
With special end to prove Pompilia pure.
How the Fisc vindicates Pompilia's fame.

1220 Then comes the all but end, the ultimate
Judgment save yours. Pope Innocent the Twelfth,
Simple, sagacious, mild yet resolute,

Till in its silkiness the trap-teeth join;
Then you know how the bristling fury foams.
1300 They listen, this wrapped in his folds of red,
While his feet fumble for the filth below;
The other, as beseems a stouter heart,
Working his best with beads and cross to ban
The enemy that comes in like a flood
Spite of the standard set up, verily
And in no trope at all, against him there:
For at the prison-gate, just a few steps
Outside, already, in the doubtful dawn,
Thither, from this side and from that, slow sweep
1310 And settle down in silence solidly,
Crow-wise, the frightful Brotherhood of Death.
Black-hatted and black-hooded huddle they,
Black rosaries a-dangling from each waist;
So take they their grim station at the door,
Torches alight and cross-bones-banner spread,
And that gigantic Christ with open arms,
Grounded. Nor lacks there aught but that the group
Break forth, intone the lamentable psalm,
'Out of the deeps, Lord, have I cried to thee!' –
1320 When inside, from the true profound, a sign
Shall bear intelligence that the foe is foiled,
Count Guido Franceschini has confessed,
And is absolved and reconciled with God.
Then they, intoning, may begin their march,
Make by the longest way for the People's Square,
Carry the criminal to his crime's award:
A mob to cleave, a scaffolding to reach,
Two gallows and Mannaia crowning all.
How Guido made defence a second time.

1330 Finally, even as thus by step and step
I led you from the level of to-day
Up to the summit of so long ago,
Here, whence I point you the wide prospect round –
Let me, by like steps, slope you back to smooth,

Land you on mother-earth, no whit the worse,
To feed o' the fat o' the furrow: free to dwell,
Taste our time's better things profusely spread
For all who love the level, corn and wine,
Much cattle and the many-folded fleece.
1340 Shall not my friends go feast again on sward,
Though cognizant of country in the clouds
Higher than wistful eagle's horny eye
Ever unclosed for, 'mid ancestral crags,
When morning broke and Spring was back once more,
And he died, heaven, save by his heart, unreached?
Yet heaven my fancy lifts to, ladder-like, –
As Jack reached, holpen of his beanstalk-rungs!

A novel country: I might make it mine
By choosing which one aspect of the year
1350 Suited mood best, and putting solely that
On panel somewhere in the House of Fame,
Landscaping what I saved, not what I saw:
– Might fix you, whether frost in goblin-time
Startled the moon with his abrupt bright laugh,
Or, August's hair afloat in filmy fire,
She fell, arms wide, face foremost on the world,
Swooned there and so singed out the strength of things.
Thus were abolished Spring and Autumn both,
The land dwarfed to one likeness of the land,
1360 Life cramped corpse-fashion. Rather learn and love
Each facet-flash of the revolving year! –
Red, green and blue that whirl into a white,
The variance now, the eventual unity,
Which make the miracle. See it for yourselves,
This man's act, changeable because alive!
Action now shrouds, now shows the informing thought;
Man, like a glass ball with a spark a-top,
Out of the magic fire that lurks inside,
Shows one tint at a time to take the eye:
1370 Which, let a finger touch the silent sleep,
Shifted a hair's-breadth shoots you dark for bright,

Suffuses bright with dark, and baffles so
Your sentence absolute for shine or shade.
Once set such orbs, – white styled, black stigmatized, –
A-rolling, see them once on the other side
Your good men and your bad men every one,
From Guido Franceschini to Guy Faux,
Oft would you rub your eyes and change your names.

Such, British Public, ye who like me not,
1380 (God love you!) – whom I yet have laboured for,
Perchance more careful whoso runs may read
Than erst when all, it seemed, could read who ran, –
Perchance more careless whoso reads may praise
Than late when he who praised and read and wrote
Was apt to find himself the self-same me, –
Such labour had such issue, so I wrought
This arc, by furtherance of such alloy,
And so, by one spirt, take away its trace
Till, justifiably golden, rounds my ring.

1390 A ring without a posy, and that ring mine?

O lyric Love, half-angel and half-bird
And all a wonder and a wild desire, –
Boldest of hearts that ever braved the sun,
Took sanctuary within the holier blue,
And sang a kindred soul out to his face, –
Yet human at the red-ripe of the heart –
When the first summons from the darkling earth
Reached thee amid thy chambers, blanched their blue,
And bared them of the glory – to drop down,
1400 To toil for man, to suffer or to die, –
This is the same voice: can thy soul know change?
Hail then, and hearken from the realms of help!
Never may I commence my song, my due
To God who best taught song by gift of thee,
Except with bent head and beseeching hand –
That still, despite the distance and the dark,

What was, again may be; some interchange
Of grace, some splendour once thy very thought,
Some benediction anciently thy smile:
1410 – Never conclude, but raising hand and head
Thither where eyes, that cannot reach, yet yearn
For all hope, all sustainment, all reward,
Their utmost up and on, – so blessing back
In those thy realms of help, that heaven thy home,
Some whiteness which, I judge, thy face makes proud,
Some wanness where, I think, thy foot may fall!

BOOK II

Half-Rome

What, you, Sir, come too? (Just the man I'd meet.)
Be ruled by me and have a care o' the crowd:
This way, while fresh folk go and get their gaze:
I'll tell you like a book and save your shins.
Fie, what a roaring day we've had! Whose fault?
Lorenzo in Lucina, – here's a church
To hold a crowd at need, accommodate
All comers from the Corso! If this crush
Make not its priests ashamed of what they show
10 For temple-room, don't prick them to draw purse
And down with bricks and mortar, eke us out
The beggarly transept with its bit of apse
Into a decent space for Christian ease,
Why, to-day's lucky pearl is cast to swine.
Listen and estimate the luck they've had!
(The right man, and I hold him.)
                                        Sir, do you see,
They laid both bodies in the church, this morn
The first thing, on the chancel two steps up,
20 Behind the little marble balustrade;
Disposed them, Pietro the old murdered fool
To the right of the altar, and his wretched wife
On the other side. In trying to count stabs,
People supposed Violante showed the most,
Till somebody explained us that mistake;
His wounds had been dealt out indifferent where,
But she took all her stabbings in the face,
Since punished thus solely for honour's sake,
Honoris causâ, that's the proper term.
30 A delicacy there is, our gallants hold,

When you avenge your honour and only then,
That you disfigure the subject, fray the face,
Not just take life and end, in clownish guise.
It was Violante gave the first offence,
Got therefore the conspicuous punishment:
While Pietro, who helped merely, his mere death
Answered the purpose, so his face went free.
We fancied even, free as you please, that face
Showed itself still intolerably wronged;
40 Was wrinkled over with resentment yet,
Nor calm at all, as murdered faces use,
Once the worst ended: an indignant air
O' the head there was – 'tis said the body turned
Round and away, rolled from Violante's side
Where they had laid it loving-husband-like.
If so, if corpses can be sensitive,
Why did not he roll right down altar-step,
Roll on through nave, roll fairly out of church,
Deprive Lorenzo of the spectacle,
50 Pay back thus the succession of affronts
Whereto this church had served as theatre?
For see: at that same altar where he lies,
To that same inch of step, was brought the babe
For blessing after baptism, and there styled
Pompilia, and a string of names beside,
By his bad wife, some seventeen years ago,
Who purchased her simply to palm on him,
Flatter his dotage and defraud the heirs.
Wait awhile! Also to this very step
60 Did this Violante, twelve years afterward,
Bring, the mock-mother, that child-cheat full-grown,
Pompilia, in pursuance of her plot,
And there brave God and man a second time
By linking a new victim to the lie.
There, having made a match unknown to him,
She, still unknown to Pietro, tied the knot
Which nothing cuts except this kind of knife;
Yes, made her daughter, as the girl was held,

Marry a man, and honest man beside,
70   And man of birth to boot, – clandestinely
Because of this, because of that, because
O' the devil's will to work his worst for once, –
Confident she could top her part at need
And, when her husband must be told in turn,
Ply the wife's trade, play off the sex's trick
And, alternating worry with quiet qualms,
Bravado with submissiveness, quick fool
Her Pietro into patience: so it proved.
Ay, 'tis four years since man and wife they grew,
80   This Guido Franceschini and this same
Pompilia, foolishly thought, falsely declared
A Comparini and the couple's child:
Just at this altar where, beneath the piece
Of Master Guido Reni, Christ on cross,
Second to nought observable in Rome,
That couple lie now, murdered yestereve.
Even the blind can see a providence here.

From dawn till now that it is growing dusk,
A multitude has flocked and filled the church,
90   Coming and going, coming back again,
Till to count crazed one. Rome was at the show.
People climbed up the columns, fought for spikes
O' the chapel-rail to perch themselves upon,
Jumped over and so broke the wooden work
Painted like porphyry to deceive the eye;
Serve the priests right! The organ-loft was crammed,
Women were fainting, no few fights ensued,
In short, it was a show repaid your pains:
For, though their room was scant undoubtedly,
100   Yet they did manage matters, to be just,
A little at this Lorenzo. Body o' me!
I saw a body exposed once . . . never mind!
Enough that here the bodies had their due.
No stinginess in wax, a row all round,
And one big taper at each head and foot.

So, people pushed their way, and took their turn,
Saw, threw their eyes up, crossed themselves, gave place
To pressure from behind, since all the world
Knew the old pair, could talk the tragedy
110 Over from first to last: Pompilia too,
Those who had known her – what 't was worth to them!
Guido's acquaintance was in less request;
The Count had lounged somewhat too long in Rome,
Made himself cheap; with him were hand and glove
Barbers and blear-eyed, as the ancient sings.
Also he is alive and like to be:
Had he considerately died, – aha!
I jostled Luca Cini on his staff,
Mute in the midst, the whole man one amaze,
120 Staring amain and crossing brow and breast.
'How now?' asked I. ''Tis seventy years,' quoth he,
'Since I first saw, holding my father's hand,
Bodies set forth: a many have I seen,
Yet all was poor to this I live and see.
Here the world's wickedness seals up the sum:
What with Molinos' doctrine and this deed,
Antichrist's surely come and doomsday near.
May I depart in peace, I have seen my see.'
'Depart then,' I advised, 'nor block the road
130 For youngsters still behindhand with such sights!'
'Why no,' rejoins the venerable sire,
'I know it's horrid, hideous past belief,
Burdensome far beyond what eye can bear;
But they do promise, when Pompilia dies
I' the course o' the day, – and she can't outlive night, –
They'll bring her body also to expose
Beside the parents, one, two, three a-breast;
That were indeed a sight which, might I see,
I trust I should not last to see the like!'
140 Whereat I bade the senior spare his shanks,
Since doctors give her till to-night to live
And tell us how the butchery happened. 'Ah,
But you can't know!' sighs he, 'I'll not despair:

Beside I'm useful at explaining things –
As, how the dagger laid there at the feet,
Caused the peculiar cuts; I mind its make,
Triangular i' the blade, a Genoese,
Armed with those little hook-teeth on the edge
To open in the flesh nor shut again:
150 I like to teach a novice: I shall stay!'
And stay he did, and stay be sure he will.

A personage came by the private door
At noon to have his look: I name no names:
Well then, His Eminence the Cardinal,
Whose servitor in honourable sort
Guido was once, the same who made the match,
(Will you have the truth?) whereof we see effect.
No sooner whisper ran he was arrived
Than up pops Curate Carlo, a brisk lad,
160 Who never lets a good occasion slip,
And volunteers improving the event.
We looked he'd give the history's self some help,
Treat us to how the wife's confession went
(This morning she confessed her crime, we know)
And, may-be, throw in something of the Priest –
If he's not ordered back, punished anew,
The gallant, Caponsacchi, Lucifer
I' the garden where Pompilia, Eve-like, lured
Her Adam Guido to his fault and fall.
170 Think you we got a sprig of speech akin
To this from Carlo, with the Cardinal there?
Too wary, he was, too widely awake, I trow.
He did the murder in a dozen words;
Then said that all such outrages crop forth
I' the course of nature, when Molinos' tares
Are sown for wheat, flourish and choke the Church:
So slid on to the abominable sect
And the philosophic sin – we've heard all that,
And the Cardinal too, (who book-made on the same)
180 But, for the murder, left it where he found.

Oh but he's quick, the Curate, minds his game!
And, after all, we have the main o' the fact:
Case could not well be simpler, – mapped, as it were,
We follow the murder's maze from source to sea,
By the red line, past mistake: one sees indeed
Not only how all was and must have been,
But cannot other than be to the end of time.
Turn out here by the Ruspoli! Do you hold
Guido was so prodigiously to blame?
190   A certain cousin of yours has told you so?
Exactly! Here's a friend shall set you right,
Let him but have the handsel of your ear.

These wretched Comparini were once gay
And galiard, of the modest middle class:
Born in this quarter seventy years ago,
And married young, they lived the accustomed life,
Citizens as they were of good repute:
And, childless, naturally took their ease
With only their two selves to care about
200   And use the wealth for: wealthy is the word,
Since Pietro was possessed of house and land –
And specially one house, when good days were,
In Via Vittoria, the aspectable street
Where he lived mainly; but another house
Of less pretension did he buy betimes,
The villa, meant for jaunts and jollity,
I' the Pauline district, to be private there –
Just what puts murder in an enemy's head.
Moreover, – and here's the worm i' the core, the germ
210   O' the rottenness and ruin which arrived, –
He owned some usufruct, had moneys' use
Lifelong, but to determine with his life
In heirs' default: so, Pietro craved an heir,
(The story always old and always new)
Shut his fool's-eyes fast on the visible good
And wealth for certain, opened them owl-wide
On fortune's sole piece of forgetfulness,

The child that should have been and would not be.

Hence, seventeen years ago, conceive his glee
220 When first Violante, 'twixt a smile and a blush,
With touch of agitation proper too,
Announced that, spite of her unpromising age,
The miracle would in time be manifest,
An heir's birth was to happen: and it did.
Somehow or other, – how, all in good time!
By a trick, a sleight of hand you are to hear, –
A child was born, Pompilia, for his joy,
Plaything at once and prop, a fairy-gift,
A saints' grace or, say, grant of the good God, –
230 A fiddle-pin's end! What imbeciles are we!
Look now: if some one could have prophesied,
'For love of you, for liking to your wife,
I undertake to crush a snake I spy
Settling itself i' the soft of both your breasts.
Give me yon babe to strangle painlessly!
She'll soar to the safe: you'll have your crying out,
Then sleep, then wake, then sleep, then end your days
In peace and plenty, mixed with mild regret,
Thirty years hence when Christmas takes old folk' –
240 How had old Pietro sprung up, crossed himself,
And kicked the conjuror! Whereas you and I,
Being wise with after-wit, had clapped our hands;
Nay, added, in the old fool's interest,
'Strangle the black-eyed babe, so far so good,
But on condition you relieve the man
O' the wife and throttle him Violante too –
She is the mischief!'

We had hit the mark.
She, whose trick brought the babe into the world,
250 She it was, when the babe was grown a girl,
Judged a new trick should reinforce the old,
Send vigour to the lie now somewhat spent
By twelve years' service; lest Eve's rule decline

Over this Adam of hers, whose cabbage-plot
Throve dubiously since turned fools'-paradise,
Spite of a nightingale on every stump.
Pietro's estate was dwindling day by day,
While he, rapt far above such mundane care,
Crawled all-fours with his baby pick-a-back,
260   Sat at serene cats'-cradle with his child,
Or took the measured tallness, top to toe,
Of what was grown a great girl twelve years old:
Till sudden at the door a tap discreet,
A visitor's premonitory cough,
And poverty had reached him in her rounds.

This came when he was past the working-time,
Had learned to dandle and forgot to dig,
And who must but Violante cast about,
Contrive and task that head of hers again?
270   She who had caught one fish, could make that catch
A bigger still, in angler's policy:
So, with an angler's mercy for the bait,
Her minnow was set wriggling on its barb
And tossed to the mid-stream; that is, this grown girl
With the great eyes and bounty of black hair
And first crisp youth that tempts a jaded taste,
Was whisked i' the way of a certain man, who snapped.

Count Guido Franceschini the Aretine
Was head of an old noble house enough,
280   Not over-rich, you can't have everything,
But such a man as riches rub against,
Readily stick to, – one with a right to them
Born in the blood: 'twas in his very brow
Always to knit itself against the world,
So be beforehand when that stinted due
Service and suit: the world ducks and defers.
As such folks do, he had come up to Rome
To better his fortune, and, since many years,
Was friend and follower of a cardinal;

290 Waiting the rather thus on providence,
That a shrewd younger poorer brother yet,
The Abate Paolo, a regular priest,
Had long since tried his powers and found he swam
With the deftest on the Galilean pool:
But then he was a web-foot, free o' the wave,
And no ambiguous dab-chick hatched to strut,
Humbled by any fond attempt to swim
When fiercer fowl usurped his dunghill-top –
A whole priest, Paolo, no mere piece of one
300 Like Guido tacked thus to the Church's tail!
Guido moreover, as the head o' the house,
Claiming the main prize, not the lesser luck,
The centre lily, no mere chickweed fringe.

He waited and learned waiting, thirty years;
Got promise, missed performance – what would you have?
No petty post rewards a nobleman
For spending youth in splendid lackey-work,
And there's concurrence for each rarer prize;
When that falls, rougher hand and readier foot
310 Push aside Guido spite of his black looks.
The end was, Guido, when the warning showed,
The first white hair i' the glass, gave up the game,
Determined on returning to his town,
Making the best of bad incurable,
Patching the old palace up and lingering there
The customary life out with his kin,
Where honour helps to spice the scanty bread.

Just as he trimmed his lamp and girt his loins
To go his journey and be wise at home,
320 In the right mood of disappointed worth,
Who but Violante sudden spied her prey
(Where was I with that angler-simile?)
And threw her bait, Pompilia, where he sulked –
A gleam i' the gloom!

What if he gained thus much,
Wrung out this sweet drop from the bitter Past,
Bore off this rose-bud from the prickly brake
To justify such torn clothes and scratched hands,
And, after all, brought something back from Rome?
330 Would not a wife serve at Arezzo well
To light the dark house, lend a look of youth
To the mother's face grown meagre, left alone
And famished with the emptiness of hope,
Old Donna Beatrice? Wife you want
Would you play family-representative,
Carry you elder-brotherly, high and right
O'er what may prove the natural petulance
Of the third brother, younger, greedier still,
Girolamo, also a fledgeling priest,
340 Beginning life in turn with callow beak
Agape for luck, no luck had stopped and stilled.
Such were the pinks and greys about the bait
Persuaded Guido gulp down hook and all.

What constituted him so choice a catch,
You question? Past his prime and poor beside?
Ask that of any she who knows the trade.
Why first, here was a nobleman with friends,
A palace one might run to and be safe
When presently the threatened fate should fall,
350 A big-browed master to block door-way up,
Parley with people bent on pushing by
And praying the mild Pietro quick clear scores:
Is birth a privilege and power or no?
Also, – but judge of the result desired,
By the price paid and manner of the sale.
The Count was made woo, win and wed at once:
Asked, and was haled for answer, lest the heat
Should cool, to San Lorenzo, one blind eve,
And had Pompilia put into his arms
360 O' the sly there, by a hasty candle-blink,
With sanction of some priest-confederate

Properly paid to make short work and sure.

So did old Pietro's daughter change her style
For Guido Franceschini's lady-wife
Ere Guido knew it well; and why this haste
And scramble and indecent secrecy?
'Lest Pietro, all the while in ignorance,
Should get to learn, gainsay and break the match:
His peevishness had promptly put aside
370   Such honour and refused the proffered boon,
Pleased to become authoritative once.
She remedied the wilful man's mistake – '
Did our discreet Violante. Rather say,
Thus did she, lest the object of her game,
Guido the gulled one, give him but a chance,
A moment's respite, time for thinking twice,
Might count the cost before he sold himself,
And try the clink of coin they paid him with.

But passed, the bargain struck, the business done,
380   Once the clandestine marriage over thus,
All parties made perforce the best o' the fact;
Pietro could play vast indignation off,
Be ignorant and astounded, dupe alike
At need, of wife, daughter and son-in-law,
While Guido found himself in flagrant fault,
Must e'en do suit and service, soothe, subdue
A father not unreasonably chafed,
Bring him to terms by paying son's devoir.
Pleasant initiation!

390   The end, this:
Guido's broad back was saddled to bear all –
Pietro, Violante, and Pompilia too, –
Three lots cast confidently in one lap,
Three dead-weights with one arm to lift the three
Out of their limbo up to life again:
The Roman household was to strike fresh root

In a new soil, graced with a novel name,
Gilt with an alien glory, Aretine
Henceforth and never Roman any more,
400 By treaty and engagement: thus it ran:
Pompilia's dowry for Pompilia's self
As a thing of course, – she paid her own expense;
No loss nor gain there: but the couple, you see,
They, for their part, turned over first of all
Their fortune in its rags and rottenness
To Guido, fusion and confusion, he
And his with them and theirs, – whatever rag
With a coin residuary fell on floor
When Brother Paolo's energetic shake
410 Should do the relics justice: since 'twas thought,
Once vulnerable Pietro out of reach,
That, left at Rome as representative,
The Abate, backed by a potent patron here,
And otherwise with purple flushing him,
Might play a good game with the creditor,
Make up a moiety which, great or small,
Should go to the common stock – if anything,
Guido's, so far repayment of the cost
About to be, – and if, as looked more like,
420 Nothing, – why, all the nobler cost were his
Who guaranteed, for better or for worse,
To Pietro and Violante, house and home,
Kith and kin, with the pick of company
And life o' the fat o' the land while life should last.
How say you to the bargain at first blush?
Why did a middle-aged not-silly man
Show himself thus besotted all at once?
Quoth Solomon, one black eye does it all.

They went to Arezzo, – Pietro and his spouse,
430 With just the dusk o' the day of life to spend,
Eager to use the twilight, taste a treat,
Enjoy for once with neither stay nor stint
The luxury of lord-and-lady-ship,

And realise the stuff and nonsense long
A-simmer in their noddles; vent the fume
Born there and bred, the citizen's conceit
How fares nobility while crossing earth,
What rampart or invisible body-guard
Keeps off the taint of common life from such.
440 They had not fed for nothing on the tales
Of grandees who give banquets worthy Jove,
Spending gold as if Plutus paid a whim,
Served with obeisances as when . . . what God?
I'm at the end of my tether; 'tis enough
You understand what they came primed to see:
While Guido who should minister the sight,
Stay all this qualmish greediness of soul
With apples and with flagons – for his part,
Was set on life diverse as pole from pole:
450 Lust of the flesh, lust of the eye, – what else
Was he just now awake from, sick and sage,
After the very debauch they would begin? –
Suppose such stuff and nonsense really were.
That bubble, they were bent on blowing big,
He had blown already till he burst his cheeks,
And hence found soapsuds bitter to the tongue.
He hoped now to walk softly all his days
In soberness of spirit, if haply so,
Pinching and paring he might furnish forth
460 A frugal board, bare sustenance, no more,
Till times, that could not well grow worse, should mend.

Thus minded then, two parties mean to meet
And make each other happy. The first week,
And fancy strikes fact and explodes in full.
'This,' shrieked the Comparini, 'this the Count,
The palace, the signorial privilege,
The pomp and pageantry were promised us?
For this have we exchanged our liberty,
Our competence, our darling of a child?
470 To house as spectres in a sepulchre

Under this black stone heap, the street's disgrace,
Grimmest as that is of the gruesome town,
And here pick garbage on a pewter plate
Or cough at verjuice dripped from earthenware?
Oh Via Vittoria, oh the other place
I' the Pauline, did we give you up for this?
Where's the foregone housekeeping good and gay,
The neighbourliness, the companionship,
The treat and feast when holidays came round,
480 The daily feast that seemed no treat at all,
Called common by the uncommon fools we were!
Even the sun that used to shine at Rome,
Where is it? Robbed and starved and frozen too,
We will have justice, justice if there be!'
Did not they shout, did not the town resound!
Guido's old lady-mother Beatrice,
Who since her husband, Count Tommaso's death,
Had held sole sway i' the house, – the doited crone
Slow to acknowledge, curtsey and abdicate, –
490 Was recognized of true novercal type,
Dragon and devil. His brother Girolamo
Came next in order: priest was he? The worse!
No way of winning him to leave his mumps
And help the laugh against old ancestry
And formal habits long since out of date,
Letting his youth be patterned on the mode
Approved of where Violante laid down law.
Or did he brighten up by way of change?
Dispose himself for affability?
500 The malapert, too complaisant by half
To the alarmed young novice of a bride!
Let him go buzz, betake himself elsewhere
Nor singe his fly-wings in the candle-flame!

Four months' probation of this purgatory,
Dog-snap and cat-claw, curse and counterblast,
The devil's self had been sick of his own din;
And Pietro, after trumpeting huge wrongs

At church and market-place, pillar and post,
Square's corner, street's end, now the palace-step
510 And now the wine-house bench – while, on her side,
Violante up and down was voluble
In whatsoever pair of ears would perk
From goody, gossip, cater-cousin and sib,
Curious to peep at the inside of things
And catch in the act pretentious poverty
At its wits' end to keep appearance up,
Make both ends meet, – nothing the vulgar loves
Like what this couple pitched them right and left, –
Then, their worst done that way, they struck tent, marched:
520 – Renounced their share o' the bargain, flung what dues
Guido was bound to pay, in Guido's face,
Left their hearts'-darling, treasure of the twain
And so forth, the poor inexperienced bride,
To her own devices, bade Arezzo rot
And the life signorial, and sought Rome once more.

I see the comment ready on your lip,
'The better fortune, Guido's – free at least
By this defection of the foolish pair,
He could begin make profit in some sort
530 Of the young bride and the new quietness,
Lead his own life now, henceforth breathe unplagued.'
Could he? You know the sex like Guido's self.
Learn the Violante-nature!

                    Once in Rome,
By way of helping Guido lead such life,
Her first act to inaugurate return
Was, she got pricked in conscience: Jubilee
Gave her the hint. Our Pope, as kind as just,
Attained his eighty years, announced a boon
540 Should make us bless the fact, held Jubilee –
Short shrift, prompt pardon for the light offence,
And no rough dealing with the regular crime
So this occasion were not suffered slip –

Otherwise, sins commuted as before,
Without the least abatement in the price.
Now, who had thought it? All this while, it seems,
Our sage Violante had a sin of a sort
She must compound for now or not at all:
Now be the ready riddance! She confessed
550 Pompilia was a fable not a fact:
She never bore a child in her whole life.
Had this child been a changeling, that were grace
In some degree, exchange is hardly theft;
You take your stand on truth ere leap your lie:
Here was all lie, no touch of truth at all,
All the lie hers – not even Pietro guessed
He was as childless still as twelve years since.
The babe had been a find i' the filth-heap, Sir,
Catch from the kennel! There was found at Rome,
560 Down in the deepest of our social dregs,
A woman who professed the wanton's trade
Under the requisite thin coverture,
Communis meretrix and washer-wife:
The creature thus conditioned found by chance
Motherhood like a jewel in the muck,
And straightway either trafficked with her prize
Or listened to the tempter and let be, –
Made pact abolishing her place and part
In womankind, beast-fellowship indeed –
570 She sold this babe eight months before its birth
To our Violante, Pietro's honest spouse,
Well-famed and widely-instanced as that crown
To the husband, virtue in a woman's shape.
She it was, bought and paid for, passed the thing
Off as the flesh and blood and child of her
Despite the flagrant fifty years, – and why?
Partly to please old Pietro, fill his cup
With wine at the late hour when lees are left,
And send him from life's feast rejoicingly, –
580 Partly to cheat the rightful heirs, agape,
Each uncle's cousin's brother's son of him,

For that same principal of the usufruct
It vext him he must die and leave behind.

Such was the sin had come to be confessed.
Which of the tales, the first or last, was true?
Did she so sin once, or, confessing now,
Sin for the first time? Either way you will.
One sees a reason for the cheat: one sees
A reason for a cheat in owning cheat
590   Where no cheat had been. What of the revenge?
What prompted the contrition all at once,
Made the avowal easy, the shame slight?
Why, prove they but Pompilia not their child,
No child, no dowry; this, supposed their child,
Had claimed what this, shown alien to their blood,
Claimed nowise: Guido's claim was through his wife,
Null then and void with hers. The biter bit,
Do you see! For such repayment of the past,
One might conceive the penitential pair
600   Ready to bring their case before the courts,
Publish their infamy to all the world
And, arm in arm, go chuckling thence content.

Is this your view? 'Twas Guido's anyhow
And colourable: he came forward then,
Protested in his very bride's behalf
Against this lie and all it led to, least
Of all the loss o' the dowry; no! From her
And him alike he would expunge the blot,
Erase the brand of such a bestial birth,
610   Participate in no hideous heritage
Gathered from the gutter to be garnered up
And glorified in a palace. Peter and Paul!
But that who likes may look upon the pair
Exposed in yonder church, and show his skill
By saying which is eye and which is mouth
Thro' those stabs thick and threefold, – but for that –
A strong word on the liars and their lie

Might crave expression and obtain it, Sir!
– Though prematurely, since there's more to come,
620 More that will shake your confidence in things
Your cousin tells you, – may I be so bold?

This makes the first act of the farce, – anon
The stealing sombre element comes in
Till all is black or blood-red in the piece.
Guido, thus made a laughing-stock abroad,
A proverb for the market-place at home,
Left alone with Pompilia now, this graft
So reputable on his ancient stock,
This plague-seed set to fester his sound flesh,
630 What did the Count? Revenge him on his wife?
Unfasten at all risks to rid himself
The noisome lazar-badge, fall foul of fate,
And, careless whether the poor rag was ware
O' the part it played, or helped unwittingly,
Bid it go burn and leave his frayed flesh free?
Plainly, did Guido open both doors wide,
Spurn thence the cur-cast creature and clear scores
As man might, tempted in extreme like this?
No, birth and breeding, and compassion too
640 Saved her such scandal. She was young, he thought,
Not privy to the treason, punished most
I' the proclamation of it; why make her
A party to the crime she suffered by?
Then the black eyes were now her very own,
Not any more Violante's: let her live,
Lose in a new air, under a new sun,
The taint of the imputed parentage
Truely or falsely, take no more the touch
Of Pietro and his partner anyhow!
650 All might go well yet.

So she thought, herself,
It seems, since what was her first act and deed
When news came how these kindly ones at Rome

Had stripped her naked to amuse the world
With spots here, spots there and spots everywhere?
– For I should tell you that they noised abroad
Not merely the main scandal of her birth,
But slanders written, printed, published wide,
Pamphlets which set forth all the pleasantry
660 Of how the promised glory was a dream,
The power a bubble and the wealth – why, dust.
There was a picture, painted to the life,
Of those rare doings, that superlative
Initiation in magnificence
Conferred on a poor Roman family
By favour of Arezzo and her first
And famousest, the Franceschini there.
You had the Countship holding head aloft
Bravely although bespattered, shifts and straits
670 In keeping out o' the way o' the wheels o' the world,
The comic of those home-contrivances
When the old lady-mother's wit was taxed
To find six clamorous mouths in food more real
Than fruit plucked off the cobwebbed family-tree,
Or acorns shed from its gilt mouldered frame –
Cold glories served up with three-pauls' worth' sauce.
What, I ask, – when the drunkenness of hate
Hiccuped return for hospitality,
Befouled the table they had feasted on,
680 Or say, – God knows I'll not prejudge the case, –
Grievances thus distorted, magnified,
Coloured by quarrel into calumny, –
What side did our Pompilia first espouse?
Her first deliberate measure was, she wrote,
Pricked by some loyal impulse, straight to Rome
And her husband's brother the Abate there,
Who, having managed to effect the match,
Might take men's censure for its ill success.
She made a clean breast also in her turn;
690 She qualified the couple handsomely!
Since whose departure, hell, she said, was heaven,

And the house, late distracted by their peals,
Quiet as Carmel where the lilies live.
Herself had oftentimes complained: but why?
All her complaints had been their prompting, tales
Trumped up, devices to this very end.
Their game had been to thwart her husband's love
And cross his will, malign his words and ways,
So reach this issue, furnish this pretence
700 For impudent withdrawal from their bond, –
Theft, indeed murder, since they meant no less
Whose last injunction to her simple self
Had been – what parents'-precept do you think?
That she should follow after with all speed,
Fly from her husband's house clandestinely,
Join them at Rome again, but first of all
Pick up a fresh companion in her flight,
Putting so youth and beauty to fit use,
Some gay, dare-devil, cloak-and-rapier spark
710 Capable of adventure, – helped by whom
She, some fine eve when lutes were in the air,
Having put poison in the posset-cup,
Laid hands on money, jewels and the like,
And, to conceal the thing with more effect,
By way of parting benediction too,
Fired the house, – one would finish famously
I' the tumult, slip out, scurry off and away
And turn up merrily at home once more.
Fact this, and not a dream o' the devil, Sir!
720 And more than this, a fact none dare dispute,
Word for word, such a letter did she write,
And such the Abate read, nor simply read
But gave all Rome to ruminate upon,
In answer to such charges as, I say,
The couple sought to be beforehand with.

The cause thus carried to the courts at Rome,
Guido away, the Abate had no choice
But stand forth, take his absent brother's part,

Defend the honour of himself beside.
730 He made what head he might against the pair,
Maintained Pompilia's birth legitimate
And all her rights intact – hers, Guido's now –
And so far by his tactics turned their flank,
The enemy being beforehand in the place,
That, though the courts allowed the cheat for fact,
Suffered Violante to parade her shame,
Publish her infamy to heart's content,
And let the tale o' the feigned birth pass for proved, –
Yet they stopped there, refused to intervene
740 And dispossess the innocents, befooled
By gifts o' the guilty, at guilt's new caprice:
They would not take away the dowry now
Wrongfully given at first, nor bar at all
Succession to the aforesaid usufruct,
Established on a fraud, nor play the game
Of Pietro's child and now not Pietro's child
As it might suit the gamester's purpose. Thus
Was justice ever ridiculed in Rome:
Such be the double verdicts favoured here
750 Which send away both parties to a suit
Nor puffed up nor cast down, – for each a crumb
Of right, for neither of them the whole loaf.
Whence, on the Comparini's part, appeal –
Counter-appeal on Guido's, – that's the game:
And so the matter stands, even to this hour,
Bandied as balls are in a tennis-court,
And so might stand, unless some heart broke first,
Till doomsday.

                    Leave it thus, and now revert
760 To the old Arezzo whence we moved to Rome.
We've had enough o' the parents, false or true,
Now for a touch o' the daughter's quality.
The start's fair henceforth – every obstacle
Out of the young wife's footpath – she's alone –
Left to walk warily now: how does she walk?

Why, once a dwelling's doorpost marked and crossed
In rubric by the enemy on his rounds
As eligible, as fit place of prey,
Baffle him henceforth, keep him out who can!
770 Stop up the door at the first hint of hoof,
Presently at the window taps a horn,
And Satan's by your fireside, never fear!
Pompilia, left alone now, found herself;
Found herself young too, sprightly, fair enough,
Matched with a husband old beyond his age
(Though that was something like four times her own)
Because of cares past, present and to come:
Found too the house dull and its inmates dead,
So, looked outside for light and life.

780   And lo
There in a trice did turn up life and light,
The man with the aureole, sympathy made flesh,
The all-consoling Caponsacchi, Sir!
A priest – what else should the consoler be?
With goodly shoulderblade and proper leg,
A portly make and a symmetric shape,
And curls that clustered to the tonsure quite.
This was a bishop in the bud, and now
A canon full-blown so far: priest, and priest
790 Nowise exorbitantly overworked,
The courtly Christian, not so much Saint Paul
As a saint of Caesar's household: there posed he
Sending his god-glance after his shot shaft,
Apollos turned Apollo, while the snake
Pompilia writhed transfixed through all her spires.
He, not a visitor at Guido's house,
Scarce an acquaintance, but in prime request
With the magnates of Arezzo, was seen here,
Heard there, felt everywhere in Guido's path
800 If Guido's wife's path be her husband's too.
Now he threw comfits at the theatre
Into her lap, – what harm in Carnival?

Now he pressed close till his foot touched her gown,
His hand brushed hers, – how help on promenade?
And, ever on weighty business, found his steps
Incline to a certain haunt of doubtful fame
Which fronted Guido's palace by mere chance;
While – how do accidents sometimes combine!
Pompilia chose to cloister up her charms
810 Just in a chamber that o'erlooked the street,
Sat there to pray, or peep thence at mankind.

This passage of arms and wits amused the town.
At last the husband lifted eyebrow, – bent
On day-book and the study how to wring
Half the due vintage from the worn-out vines
At the villa, teaze a quarter the old rent
From the farmstead, tenants swore would tumble soon, –
Pricked up his ear a-singing day and night
With 'ruin, ruin;' – and so surprised at last –
820 Why, what else but a titter? Up he jumps.
Back to mind come those scratchings at the grange,
Prints of the paw about the outhouse; rife
In his head at once again are word and wink,
Mum here and *budget* there, the smell o' the fox,
The musk o' the gallant. 'Friends, there's falseness here!'

The proper help of friends in such a strait
Is waggery, the world over. Laugh him free
O' the regular jealous-fit that's incident
To all old husbands that wed brisk young wives,
830 And he'll go duly docile all his days.
'Somebody courts your wife, Count? Where and when?
How and why? Mere horn-madness: have a care!
Your lady loves her own room, sticks to it,
Locks herself in for hours, you say yourself.
And – what, it's Caponsacchi means you harm?
The Canon? We caress him, he's the world's,
A man of such acceptance, – never dream,
Though he were fifty times the fox you fear,

He'd risk his brush for your particular chick,
840   When the wide town's his hen-roost! Fie o' the fool!'
So they dispensed their comfort of a kind.
Guido at last cried 'Something is in the air,
Under the earth, some plot against my peace:
The trouble of eclipse hangs overhead,
How it should come of that officious orb
Your Canon in my system, you must say:
I say – that from the pressure of this spring
Began the chime and interchange of bells,
Ever one whisper, and one whisper more,
850   And just one whisper for the silvery last,
Till all at once a-row the bronze-throats burst
Into a larum both significant
And sinister: stop it I must and will.
Let Caponsacchi take his hand away
From the wire! – disport himself in other paths
Than lead precisely to my palace-gate, –
Look where he likes except one window's way
Where, cheek on hand, and elbow set on sill,
Happens to lean and say her litanies
860   Every day and all day long, just my wife –
Or wife and Caponsacchi may fare the worse!'

Admire the man's simplicity, 'I'll do this,
I'll not have that, I'll punish and prevent!' –
'Tis easy saying. But to a fray, you see,
Two parties go. The badger shows his teeth:
The fox nor lies down sheep-like nor dares fight.
Oh, the wife knew the appropriate warfare well,
The way to put suspicion to the blush!
At first hint of remonstrance, up and out
870   I' the face of the world, you found her: she could speak,
State her case, – Franceschini was a name,
Guido had his full share of foes and friends –
Why should not she call these to arbitrate?
She bade the Governor do governance,
Cried out on the Archbishop, – why, there now,

Take him for sample! Three successive times,
Had he to reconduct her by main-force
From where she took her station opposite
His shut door, – on the public steps thereto,
880   Wringing her hands, when he came out to see,
And shrieking all her wrongs forth at his foot, –
Back to the husband and the house she fled:
Judge if that husband warmed him in the face
Of friends or frowned on foes as heretofore!
Judge if he missed the natural grin of folk,
Or lacked the customary compliment
Of cap and bells, the luckless husband's fit!

So it went on and on till – who was right?
One merry April morning, Guido woke
890   After the cuckoo, so late, near noonday,
With an inordinate yawning of the jaws,
Ears plugged, eyes gummed together, palate, tongue
And teeth one mud-paste made of poppy-milk;
And found his wife flown, his scrutoire the worse
For a rummage, – jewelry that was, was not,
Some money there had made itself wings too, –
The door lay wide and yet the servants slept
Sound as the dead, or dosed which does as well.
In short, Pompilia, she who, candid soul,
900   Had not so much as spoken all her life
To the Canon, nay, so much as peeped at him
Between her fingers while she prayed in church, –
This lamb-like innocent of fifteen years
(Such she was grown to by this time of day)
Had simply put an opiate in the drink
Of the whole household overnight, and then
Got up and gone about her work secure,
Laid hand on this waif and the other stray,
Spoiled the Philistine and marched out of doors
910   In company of the Canon who, Lord's love,
What with his daily duty at the church,
Nightly devoir where ladies congregate,

Had something else to mind, assure yourself,
Beside Pompilia, paragon though she be,
Or notice if her nose were sharp or blunt!
Well, anyhow, albeit impossible,
Both of them were together jollily
Jaunting it Rome-ward, half-way there by this,
While Guido was left go and get undrugged,
920   Gather his wits up, groaningly give thanks
When neighbours crowded round him to condole.
'Ah,' quoth a gossip, 'well I mind me now,
The Count did always say he thought he felt
He feared as if this very chance might fall!
And when a man of fifty finds his corns
Ache and his joints throb, and foresees a storm,
Though neighbours laugh and say the sky is clear,
Let us henceforth believe him weatherwise!'
Then was the story told, I'll cut you short:
930   All neighbours knew: no mystery in the world.
The lovers left at nightfall – over night
Had Caponsacchi come to carry off
Pompilia, – not alone, a friend of his,
One Guillichini, the more conversant
With Guido's housekeeping that he was just
A cousin of Guido's and might play a prank –
(Have not you too a cousin that 's a wag?)
– Lord and a Canon also, – what would you have?
Such are the red-clothed milk-swollen poppy-heads
940   That stand and stiffen 'mid the wheat o' the Church! –
This worthy came to aid, abet his best.
And so the house was ransacked, booty bagged,
The lady led downstairs and out of doors
Guided and guarded till, the city passed,
A carriage lay convenient at the gate.
Good-bye to the friendly Canon; the loving one
Could peradventure do the rest himself.
In jumps Pompilia, after her the priest,
'Whip, driver! Money makes the mare to go,
950   And we've a bagful. Take the Roman road!'

So said the neighbours. This was eight hours since.

Guido heard all, swore the befitting oaths,
Shook off the relics of his poison-drench,
Got horse, was fairly started in pursuit
With never a friend to follow, found the track
Fast enough, 't was the straight Perugia way,
Trod soon upon their very heels, too late
By a minute only at Camoscia, at
Chiusi, Foligno, ever the fugitives
960   Just ahead, just out as he galloped in,
Getting the good news ever fresh and fresh,
Till, lo, at the last stage of all, last post
Before Rome, – as we say, in sight of Rome
And safety (there's impunity at Rome
For priests, you know) at – what's the little place?
What some call Castelnuovo, some just call
The Osteria, because o' the post-house inn,
There, at the journey's all but end, it seems,
Triumph deceived them and undid them both,
970   Secure they might foretaste felicity
Nor fear surprisal: so, they were surprised.
There did they halt at early evening, there
Did Guido overtake them: 't was day-break;
He came in time enough, not time too much,
Since in the courtyard stood the Canon's self
Urging the drowsy stable-grooms to haste
Harness the horses, have the journey end,
The trifling four-hours'-running, so reach Rome.
And the other runaway, the wife? Upstairs,
980   Still on the couch where she had spent the night,
One couch in one room, and one room for both.
So gained they six hours, so were lost thereby.

Sir, what's the sequel? Lover and beloved
Fall on their knees? No impudence serves here?
They beat their breasts and beg for easy death,
Confess this, that and the other? – anyhow

Confess there wanted not some likelihood
To the supposition so preposterous,
That, O Pompilia, thy sequestered eyes
990 Had noticed, straying o'er the prayerbook's edge,
More of the Canon than that black his coat,
Buckled his shoes were, broad his hat of brim:
And that, O Canon, thy religious care
Had breathed too soft a *benedicite*
To banish trouble from a lady's breast
So lonely and so lovely, nor so lean!
This you expect? Indeed, then, much you err.
Not to such ordinary end as this
Had Caponsacchi flung the cassock far,
1000 Doffed the priest, donned the perfect cavalier;
The die was cast: over shoes over boots:
And just as she, I presently shall show,
Pompilia, soon looked Helen to the life,
Recumbent upstairs in her pink and white,
So, in the inn-yard, bold as 't were Troy-town,
There strutted Paris in correct costume,
Cloak, cap and feather, no appointment missed,
Even to a wicked-looking sword at side,
He seemed to find and feel familiar at.
1010 Nor wanted words as ready and as big
As the part he played, the bold abashless one.
'I interposed to save your wife from death,
Yourself from shame, the true and only shame:
Ask your own conscience else! – or, failing that,
What I have done I answer, anywhere,
Here, if you will; you see I have a sword:
Or, since I have a tonsure as you taunt,
At Rome, by all means, – priests to try a priest.
Only, speak where your wife's voice can reply!'
1020 And then he fingered at the sword again.
So, Guido called, in aid and witness both,
The Public Force. The Commissary came,
Officers also; they secured the priest;
Then, for his more confusion, mounted up

With him, a guard on either side, the stair
To the bed-room where still slept or feigned a sleep
His paramour and Guido's wife: in burst
The company and bade her wake and rise.

Her defence? This. She woke, saw, sprang upright
1030 I' the midst and stood as terrible as truth,
Sprang to her husband's side, caught at the sword
That hung there useless, since they held each hand
O' the lover, had disarmed him properly,
And in a moment out flew the bright thing
Full in the face of Guido, – but for help
O' the guards who held her back and pinioned her
With pains enough, she had finished you my tale
With a flourish of red all round it, pinked her man
Prettily; but she fought them one to six.
1040 They stopped that, – but her tongue continued free:
She spat forth such invective at her spouse,
O'erfrothed him with such foam of murderer,
Thief, pandar – that the popular tide soon turned,
The favour of the very *shirri*, straight
Ebbed from the husband, set toward his wife,
People cried 'Hands off, pay a priest respect!'
And 'persecuting fiend' and 'martyred saint'
Began to lead a measure from lip to lip.

But facts are facts and flinch not; stubborn things,
1050 And the question 'Prithee, friend, how comes my purse
I' the poke of you?' – admits of no reply.
Here was a priest found out in masquerade,
A wife caught playing truant if no more;
While the Count, mortified in mien enough,
And, nose to face, an added palm in length,
Was plain writ 'husband' every piece of him:
Capture once made, release could hardly be.
Beside, the prisoners both made appeal,
'Take us to Rome!'
1060   Taken to Rome they were;

The husband trooping after, piteously,
Tail between legs, no talk of triumph now –
No honour set firm on its feet once more
On two dead bodies of the guilty, – nay,
No dubious salve to honour's broken pate
From chance that, after all, the hurt might seem
A skin-deep matter, scratch that leaves no scar:
For Guido's first search, – ferreting, poor soul,
Here, there and everywhere in the vile place
1070 Abandoned to him when their backs were turned,
Found, – furnishing a last and best regale, –
All the love-letters bandied twixt the pair
Since the first timid trembling into life
O' the love-star till its stand at fiery full.
Mad prose, mad verse, fears, hopes, triumph, despair,
Avowal, disclaimer, plans, dates, names, – was nought
Wanting to prove, if proof consoles at all,
That this had been but the fifth act o' the piece
Whereof the due proemium, months ago
1080 These playwrights had put forth, and ever since
Matured the middle, added 'neath his nose.
He might go cross himself: the case was clear.

Therefore to Rome with the clear case; there plead
Each party its best, and leave the law do right,
Let her shine forth and show, as God in heaven,
Vice prostrate, virtue pedestalled at last,
The triumph of truth! What else shall glad our gaze
When once authority has knit the brow
And set the brain behind it to decide
1090 Between the wolf and sheep turned litigants?
'This is indeed a business' law shook head:
'A husband charges hard things on a wife,
The wife as hard o' the husband: whose fault here?
A wife that flies her husband's house, does wrong:
The male friend's interference looks amiss,
Lends a suspicion: but suppose the wife,
On the other hand, be jeopardized at home –

Nay, that she simply hold, ill-groundedly,
An apprehension she is jeopardized, –
1100 And further, if the friend partake the fear,
And, in a commendable charity
Which trusteth all, trust her that she mistrusts, –
What do they but obey the natural law?
Pretence may this be and a cloak for sin,
And circumstances that concur i' the close
Hint as much, loudly – yet scarce loud enough
To drown the answer "strange may yet be true:"
Innocence often looks like guiltiness.
The accused declare that in thought, word and deed,
1110 Innocent were they both from first to last
As male-babe haply laid by female-babe
At church on edge of the baptismal font
Together for a minute, perfect-pure.
Difficult to believe, yet possible,
As witness Joseph, the friend's patron-saint.
The night at the inn – there charity nigh chokes
Ere swallow what they both asseverate;
Though down the gullet faith may feel it go,
When mindful of what flight fatigued the flesh
1120 Out of its faculty and fleshliness,
Subdued it to the soul, as saints assure:
So long a flight necessitates a fall
On the first bed, though in a lion's den,
And the first pillow, though the lion's back:
Difficult to believe, yet possible.
Last come the letters' bundled beastliness –
Authority repugns give glance to twice,
Turns head, and almost lets her whip-lash fall;
Yet here a voice cries "Respite!" from the clouds –
1130 The accused, both in a tale, protest, disclaim,
Abominate the horror: "Not my hand"
Asserts the friend – "Nor mine" chimes in the wife,
"Seeing I have no hand, nor write at all."
Illiterate – for she goes on to ask,
What if the friend did pen now verse now prose,

Commend it to her notice now and then?
'Twas pearls to swine: she read no more than wrote,
And kept no more than read, for as they fell
She ever brushed the burr-like things away,
1140 Or, better, burned them, quenched the fire in smoke.
As for this fardel, filth and foolishness,
She sees it now the first time: burn it too!
While for his part the friend vows ignorance
Alike of what bears his name and bears hers:
'Tis forgery, a felon's masterpiece,
And, as 'tis said the fox still finds the stench,
Home-manufacture and the husband's work.
Though he confesses, the ingenuous friend,
That certain missives, letters of a sort,
1150 Flighty and feeble, which assigned themselves
To the wife, no less have fallen, far too oft,
In his path: wherefrom he understood just this –
That were they verily the lady's own,
Why, she who penned them, since he never saw
Save for one minute the mere face of her,
Since never had there been the interchange
Of word with word between them all their life,
Why, she must be the fondest of the frail,
And fit, she for the "*apage*" he flung,
1160 Her letters for the flame they went to feed.
But, now he sees her face and hears her speech,
Much he repents him if, in fancy-freak
For a moment the minutest measurable,
He coupled her with the first flimsy word
O' the self-spun fabric some mean spider-soul
Furnished forth: stop his films and stamp on him!
Never was such a tangled knottiness,
But thus authority cuts the Gordian through,
And mark how her decision suits the need!
1170 Here's troublesomeness, scandal on both sides,
Plenty of fault to find, no absolute crime:
Let each side own its fault and make amends!
What does a priest in cavalier's attire

Consorting publicly with vagrant wives
In quarters close as the confessional,
Though innocent of harm? 'Tis harm enough:
Let him pay it, and be relegate a good
Three years, to spend in some place not too far
Nor yet too near, midway twixt near and far,
1180 Rome and Arezzo, – Civita we choose,
Where he may lounge away time, live at large,
Find out the proper function of a priest,
Nowise an exile, – that were punishment,
But one our love thus keeps out of harm's way
Not more from the husband's anger than, mayhap
His own . . . say, indiscretion, waywardness,
And wanderings when Easter eves grow warm.
For the wife, – well, our best step to take with her,
On her own showing, were to shift her root
1190 From the old cold shade and unhappy soil
Into a generous ground that fronts the south:
Where, since her callow soul, a-shiver late,
Craved simply warmth and called mere passers-by
To the rescue, she should have her fill of shine.
Do house and husband hinder and not help?
Why then, forget both and stay here at peace,
Come into our community, enroll
Herself along with those good Convertites,
Those sinners saved, those Magdalens re-made,
1200 Accept their ministration, well bestow
Her body and patiently possess her soul,
Until we see what better can be done.
Last for the husband: if his tale prove true,
Well is he rid of two domestic plagues –
The wife that ailed, do whatsoever he would,
And friend of hers that undertook the cure.
See, what a double load we lift from breast!
Off he may go, return, resume old life,
Laugh at the priest here and Pompilia there
1210 In limbo each and punished for their pains,
And grateful tell the inquiring neighbourhood –

In Rome, no wrong but has its remedy.'
The case was closed. Now, am I fair or no
In what I utter? Do I state the facts,
Having forechosen a side? I promised you!

The Canon Caponsacchi, then, was sent
To change his garb, re-trim his tonsure, tie
The clerkly silk round, every plait correct,
Make the impressive entry on his place
1220 Of relegation, thrill his Civita,
As Ovid, a like sufferer in the cause,
Planted a primrose-patch by Pontus: where,
What with much culture of the sonnet-stave
And converse with the aborigines,
Soft savagery of eyes unused to roll,
And hearts that all awry went pit-a-pat
And wanted setting right in charity,
What were a couple of years to while away?
Pompilia, as enjoined, betook herself
1230 To the aforesaid Convertites, the sisterhood
In Via Lungara, where the light ones live,
Spin, pray, then sing like linnets o'er the flax.
'Anywhere, anyhow, out of my husband's house,
Is heaven,' cried she, – was therefore suited so.
But for Count Guido Franceschini, he –
The injured man thus righted – found no heaven
I' the house when he returned there, I engage,
Was welcomed by the city turned upside down
In a chorus of inquiry. 'What, back – you?
1240 And no wife? Left her with the Penitents?
Ah, being young and pretty, 'twere a shame
To have her whipped in public: leave the job
To the priests who understand! Such priests as yours –
(Pontifex Maximus whipped Vestals once)
Our madcap Caponsacchi: think of him!
So, he fired up, showed fight and skill of fence?
Ay, you drew also, but you did not fight!
The wiser, 'tis a word and a blow with him,

'True Caponsacchi, of old Head-i'-the-Sack
1250 That fought at Fiesole ere Florence was:
He had done enough, to firk you were too much.
And did the little lady menace you,
Make at your breast with your own harmless sword?
The spitfire! Well, thank God you're safe and sound,
Have kept the sixth commandment whether or no
The lady broke the seventh: I only wish
I were as saint-like, could contain me so.
I am a sinner, I fear I should have left
Sir Priest no nose-tip to turn up at me!'
1260 You, Sir, who listen but interpose no word,
Ask yourself, had you borne a baiting thus?
Was it enough to make a wise man mad?
Oh, but I'll have your verdict at the end!

Well, not enough, it seems: such mere hurt falls,
Frets awhile, and aches long, then less and less,
And so is done with. Such was not the scheme
O' the pleasant Comparini: on Guido's wound
Ever in due succession, drop by drop,
Came slow distilment from the alembic here
1270 Set on to simmer by Canidian hate,
Corrosives keeping the man's misery raw.
First fire-drop, – when he thought to make the best
O' the bad, to wring from out the sentence passed,
Poor, pitiful, absurd although it were,
Yet what might eke him out result enough
And make it worth his while he had the right
And not the wrong i' the matter judged at Rome. ·
Inadequate her punishment, no less
Punished in some slight sort his wife had been;
1280 Then, punished for adultery, what else?
On such admitted crime he thought to seize,
And institute procedure in the courts
Which cut corruption of this kind from man,
Cast loose a wife proved loose and castaway:
He claimed in due form a divorce at least.

This claim was met now by a counterclaim:
Pompilia sought divorce from bed and board
Of Guido, whose outrageous cruelty,
Whose mother's malice and whose brother's hate
1290 Were just the white o' the charge, such dreadful depths
Blackened its centre, – hints of worse than hate,
Love from that brother, by that Guido's guile,
That mother's prompting. Such reply was made,
So was the engine loaded, wound up, sprung
On Guido, who received the bolt in breast;
But no less bore up, giddily perhaps.
He had the Abate Paolo still in Rome,
Brother and friend and fighter on his side:
They rallied in a measure, met the foe
1300 Manlike, joined battle in the public courts,
As if to shame supine law from her sloth:
And waiting her award, let beat the while
Arezzo's banter, Rome's buffoonery,
On this ear and on that ear, deaf alike,
Safe from worse outrage. Let a scorpion nip,
And never mind till he contorts his tail!
But there was sting i' the creature; thus it struck.
Guido had thought in his simplicity –
That lying declaration of remorse,
1310 That story of the child which was no child
And motherhood no motherhood at all,
– That even this sin might have its sort of good
Inasmuch as no question could be more,
Call it false, call the story true, no claim
Of further parentage pretended now:
The parents had abjured all right, at least,
I' the woman still his wife: to plead right now
Were to declare the abjuration false:
He was relieved from any fear henceforth
1320 Their hands might touch, their breath defile again
Pompilia with his name upon her yet.
Well, no: the next news was, Pompilia's health
Demanded change after full three long weeks

Spent in devotion with the Sisterhood, –
Rendering sojourn, – so the court opined, –
Too irksome, since the convent's walls were high
And windows narrow, nor was air enough
Nor light enough, but all looked prison-like,
The last thing which had come in the court's head.
1330 Propose a new expedient therefore, – this!
She had demanded – had obtained indeed,
By intervention of whatever friends
Or perhaps lovers – (beauty in distress,
In one whose tale is the town-talk beside,
Never lacks friendship's arm about her neck) –
Not freedom, scarce remitted penalty,
Solely the transfer to some private place
Where better air, more light, new food might be –
Incarcerated (call it, all the same)
1340 At some sure friend's house she must keep inside,
Be found in at requirement fast enough, –
Domus pro carcere, in Roman style.
You keep the house i' the main, as most men do
And all good women: but free otherwise,
Should friends arrive, to lodge and entertain.
And such a *domum*, such a dwelling-place,
Having all Rome to choose from, where chose she?
What house obtained Pompilia's preference?
Why, just the Comparini's – just, do you mark,
1350 Theirs who renounced all part and lot in her
So long as Guido could be robbed thereby,
And only fell back on relationship
And found their daughter safe and sound again
So soon as that might stab him: yes, the pair
Who, as I told you, first had baited hook
With this poor gilded fly Pompilia-thing,
Then caught the fish, pulled Guido to the shore
And gutted him, – now found a further use
For the bait, would trail the gauze wings yet again
1360 I' the way of what new swimmer passed their stand.
They took Pompilia to their hiding-place –

Not in the heart of Rome as formerly,
Under observance, subject to control –
But out o' the way, – or in the way, who knows?
That blind mute villa lurking by the gate
At Via Paulina, not so hard to miss
By the honest eye, easy enough to find
In twilight by marauders: where perchance
Some muffled Caponsacchi might repair,
1370 Employ odd moments when he too tried change,
Found that a friend's abode was pleasanter
Than relegation, penance and the rest.

Come, here's the last drop does its worst to wound,
Here's Guido poisoned to the bone, you say,
Your boasted still's full strain and strength: not so!
One master-squeeze from screw shall bring to birth
The hoard i' the heart o' the toad, hell's quintessence.
He learned the true convenience of the change,
And why a convent wants the cheerful hearts
1380 And helpful hands which female straits require,
When, in the blind mute villa by the gate,
Pompilia – what? sang, danced, saw company?
– Gave birth, Sir, to a child, his son and heir,
Or Guido's heir and Caponsacchi's son.
I want your word now: what do you say to this?
What would say little Arezzo and great Rome,
And what did God say and the devil say
One at each ear o' the man, the husband, now
The father? Why, the overburdened mind
1390 Broke down, what was a brain became a blaze.
In fury of the moment – (that first news
Fell on the Count among his vines, it seems,
Doing his farm-work,) – why, he summoned steward,
Called in the first four hard hands and stout hearts
From field and furrow, poured forth his appeal,
Not to Rome's law and gospel any more,
But this clown with a mother or a wife,
That clodpole with a sister or a son:

And, whereas law and gospel held their peace,
1400 What wonder if the sticks and stones cried out?

All five soon somehow found themselves at Rome,
At the villa door: there was the warmth and light –
The sense of life so just an inch inside –
Some angel must have whispered 'One more chance!'

He gave it: bade the others stand aside:
Knocked at the door, – 'Who is it knocks?' cried one.
'I will make,' surely Guido's angel said,
'One final essay, last experiment,
Speak the word, name the name from out all names
1410 Which, if, – as doubtless strong illusions are,
And strange disguisings whence even truth seems false,
And, for I am a man, I dare not do
God's work until assured I see with God, –
If I should bring my lips to breathe that name
And they be innocent, – nay, by one touch
Of innocence redeemed from utter guilt, –
That name will bar the door and bid fate pass.
I will not say "It is a messenger,
A neighbour, even a belated man,
1420 Much less your husband's friend, your husband's self:"
At such appeal the door is bound to ope.
But I will say' – here's rhetoric and to spare!
Why, Sir, the stumbling-block is cursed and kicked,
Block though it be; the name that brought offence
Will bring offence: the burnt child dreads the fire
Although that fire feed on a taper-wick
Which never left the altar nor singed fly:
And had a harmless man tripped you by chance,
How would you wait him, stand or step aside,
1430 When next you heard he rolled your way? Enough.

'Giuseppe Caponsacchi!' Guido cried;
And open flew the door: enough again.

Vengeance, you know, burst, like a mountain-wave
That holds a monster in it, over the house,
And wiped its filthy four walls free again
With a wash of hell-fire, – father, mother, wife,
Killed them all, bathed his name clean in their blood,
And, reeking so, was caught, his friends and he,
Haled hither and imprisoned yesternight
1440 O' the day all this was.
                              Now the whole is known,
And how the old couple come to lie in state
Though hacked to pieces, – never, the expert say,
So thorough a study of stabbing – while the wife
Viper-like, very difficult to slay,
Writhes still through every ring of her, poor wretch,
At the Hospital hard by – survives, we'll hope,
To somewhat purify her putrid soul
By full confession, make so much amends
1450 While time lasts; since at day's end die she must.

For Caponsacchi, – why, they'll have him here,
The hero of the adventure, who so fit
To tell it in the coming Carnival?
'Twill make the fortune of whate'er saloon
Hears him recount, with helpful cheek, and eye
Hotly indignant now, now dewy-dimmed,
The incidents of flight, pursuit, surprise,
Capture, with hints of kisses all between –
While Guido, the most unromantic spouse,
1460 No longer fit to laugh at since the blood
Gave the broad farce an all too brutal air,
Why, he and those [f]our luckless friends of his
May tumble in the straw this bitter day –
Laid by the heels i' the New Prison, I hear,
To bide their trial, since trial, and for the life,
Follows if but for form's sake: yes, indeed!

But with a certain issue: no dispute,

'Try him,' bids law: formalities oblige:
But as to the issue, – look me in the face! –
1470 If the law thinks to find them guilty, Sir,
Master or men – touch one hair of the five,
Then I say in the name of all that's left
Of honour in Rome, civility i' the world
Whereof Rome boasts herself the central source, –
There's an end to all hope of justice more.
Astraea's gone indeed, let hope go too!
Who is it dares impugn the natural law?
Deny God's word 'the faithless wife shall die?'
What, are we blind? How can we fail to see,
1480 This crowd of miseries make the man a mark,
Accumulate on one devoted head
For our example, yours and mine who read
Its lesson thus – 'Henceforward let none dare
Stand, like a natural in the public way,
Letting the very urchins twitch his beard
And tweak his nose, to earn a nickname so,
Of the male-Grissel or the modern Job!'
Had Guido, in the twinkling of an eye,
Summed up the reckoning, promptly paid himself,
1490 That morning when he came up with the pair
At the wayside inn, – exacted his just debt
By aid of what first mattock, pitchfork, axe
Came to hand in the helpful stable-yard,
And with that axe, if providence so pleased,
Cloven each head, by some Rolando-stroke,
In one clean cut from crown to clavicle,
– Slain the priest-gallant, the wife-paramour,
Sticking, for all defence, in each skull's cleft
The rhyme and reason of the stroke thus dealt,
1500 To-wit, those letters and last evidence
Of shame, each package in its proper place, –
Bidding, who pitied, undistend the skulls, –
I say, the world had praised the man. But no!
That were too plain, too straight, too simply just!
He hesitates, calls law forsooth to help.

And law, distasteful to who calls in law
When honour is beforehand and would serve,
What wonder if law hesitate in turn,
Plead her disuse to calls o' the kind, reply
1510 Smiling a little ''Tis yourself assess
The worth of what's lost, sum of damage done:
What you touched with so light a finger-tip,
You whose concern it was to grasp the thing,
Why must law gird herself and grapple with?
Law, alien to the actor whose warm blood
Asks heat from law whose veins run lukewarm milk, –
What you dealt lightly with, shall law make out
Heinous forsooth?'
                        Sir, what's the good of law
1520 In a case o' the kind? None, as she all but says.
Call in law when a neighbour breaks your fence,
Cribs from your field, tampers with rent or lease,
Touches the purse or pocket, – but wooes your wife?
No: take the old way trod when men were men!
Guido preferred the new path, – for his pains,
Stuck in a quagmire, floundered worse and worse
Until he managed somehow scramble back
Into the safe sure rutted road once more,
Revenged his own wrong like a gentleman.
1530 Once back 'mid the familiar prints, no doubt
He made too rash amends for his first fault,
Vaulted too loftily over what barred him late,
And lit i' the mire again, – the common chance,
The natural over-energy: the deed
Maladroit yields three deaths instead of one,
And one life left: for where's the Canon's corpse?
All which is the worse for Guido, but, be frank –
The better for you and me and all the world,
Husbands of wives, especially in Rome.
1540 The thing is put right, in the old place, – ay,
The rod hangs on its nail behind the door,
Fresh from the brine: a matter I commend
To the notice, during Carnival that's near,

Of a certain what's-his-name and jackanapes
Somewhat too civil of eves with lute and song
About a house here, where I keep a wife.
(You, being his cousin, may go tell him so.)

BOOK III

The Other Half-Rome

Another day that finds her living yet,
Little Pompilia, with the patient brow
And lamentable smile on those poor lips,
And, under the white hospital-array,
A flower-like body, to frighten at a bruise
You'd think, yet now, stabbed through and through again,
Alive i' the ruins. 'T is a miracle.
It seems that, when her husband struck her first,
She prayed Madonna just that she might live
10   So long as to confess and be absolved;
And whether it was that, all her sad life long,
Never before successful in a prayer,
This prayer rose with authority too dread, –
Or whether, because earth was hell to her,
By compensation, when the blackness broke
She got one glimpse of quiet and the cool blue,
To show her for a moment such things were, –
Or else, – as the Augustinian Brother thinks,
The friar who took confession from her lip, –
20   When a probationary soul that moves
From nobleness to nobleness, as she,
Over the rough way of the world, succumbs,
Bloodies its last thorn with unflinching foot,
The angels love to do their work betimes,
Staunch some wounds here nor leave so much for God.
Who knows? However it be, confessed, absolved,
She lies, with overplus of life beside
To speak and right herself from first to last,
Right the friend also, lamb-pure, lion-brave,
30   Care for the boy's concerns, to save the son

From the sire, her two-weeks' infant orphaned thus,
And – with best smile of all reserved for him –
Pardon that sire and husband from the heart.
A miracle, so tell your Molinists!

There she lies in the long white lazar-house.
Rome has besieged, these two days, never doubt,
Saint Anna's where she waits her death, to hear
Though but the chink o' the bell, turn o' the hinge
When the reluctant wicket opes at last,
40   Lets in, on now this and now that pretence,
Too many by half, – complain the men of art, –
For a patient in such plight. The lawyers first
Paid the due visit – justice must be done;
They took her witness, why the murder was;
Then the priests followed properly, – a soul
To shrive; 't was Brother Celestine's own right,
The same who noises thus her gifts abroad:
But many more, who found they were old friends,
Pushed in to have their stare and take their talk
50   And go forth boasting of it and to boast.
Old Monna Baldi chatters like a jay,
Swears – but that, prematurely trundled out
Just as she felt the benefit begin,
The miracle was snapped up by somebody, –
Her palsied limb 'gan prick and promise life
At touch o' the bedclothes merely, – how much more
Had she but brushed the body as she tried!
Cavalier Carlo – well, there's some excuse
For him – Maratta who paints Virgins so –
60   He too must fee the porter and slip by
With pencil cut and paper squared, and straight
There was he figuring away at face –
'A lovelier face is not in Rome,' cried he,
'Shaped like a peacock's egg, the pure as pearl,
That hatches you anon a snow-white chick.'
Then, oh that pair of eyes, that pendent hair,
Black this, and black the other! Mighty fine –

But nobody cared ask to paint the same,
Nor grew a poet over hair and eyes
70 Four little years ago when, ask and have,
The woman who wakes all this rapture leaned
Flower-like from out her window long enough,
As much uncomplimented as uncropped
By comers and goers in Via Vittoria: eh?
'T is just a flower's fate: past parterre we trip,
Till peradventure someone plucks our sleeve –
'Yon blossom at the briar's end, that's the rose
Two jealous people fought for yesterday
And killed each other: see, there's undisturbed
80 A pretty pool at the root, of rival red!'
Then cry we, 'Ah, the perfect paragon!'
Then crave we, 'Just one keepsake-leaf for us!'

Truth lies between: there's anyhow a child
Of seventeen years, whether a flower or weed,
Ruined: who did it shall account to Christ –
Having no pity on the harmless life
And gentle face and girlish form he found,
And thus flings back: go practise if you please
With men and women: leave a child alone
90 For Christ's particular love's sake! – so I say.

Somebody, at the bedside, said much more,
Took on him to explain the secret cause
O' the crime: quoth he, 'Such crimes are very rife,
Explode nor make us wonder now-a-days,
Seeing that Antichrist disseminates
That doctrine of the Philosophic Sin:
Molinos' sect will soon make earth too hot!'
'Nay,' groaned the Augustinian, 'what's there new?
Crime will not fail to flare up from men's hearts
100 While hearts are men's and so born criminal;
Which one fact, always old yet ever new,
Accounts for so much crime that, for my part,
Molinos may go whistle to the wind

That waits outside a certain church, you know!'

Though really it does seem as if she here,
Pompilia, living so and dying thus,
Has had undue experience how much crime
A heart can hatch. Why was she made to learn
– Not you, not I, not even Molinos' self –
110   What Guido Franceschini's heart could hold?
Thus saintship is effected probably;
No sparing saints the process! – which the more
Tends to the reconciling us, no saints,
To sinnership, immunity and all.

For see now: Pietro and Violante's life
Till seventeen years ago, all Rome might note
And quote for happy – see the signs distinct
Of happiness as we yon Triton's trump.
What could they be but happy? – balanced so,
120   Nor low i' the social scale nor yet too high,
Nor poor nor richer than comports with ease,
Nor bright and envied, nor obscure and scorned,
Nor so young that their pleasures fell too thick,
Nor old past catching pleasure when it fell,
Nothing above, below the just degree,
All at the mean where joy's components mix.
So again, in the couple's very souls
You saw the adequate half with half to match,
Each having and each lacking somewhat, both
130   Making a whole that had all and lacked nought;
The round and sound, in whose composure just
The acquiescent and recipient side
Was Pietro's, and the stirring striving one
Violante's: both in union gave the due
Quietude, enterprise, craving and content,
Which go to bodily health and peace of mind.
But, as 't is said a body, rightly mixed,
Each element in equipoise, would last
Too long and live for ever, – accordingly

140   Holds a germ – sand-grain weight too much i' the scale –
     Ordained to get predominance one day
     And so bring all to ruin and release, –
     Not otherwise a fatal germ lurked here:
     'With mortals much must go, but something stays;
     Nothing will stay of our so happy selves.'
     Out of the very ripeness of life's core
     A worm was bred – 'Our life shall leave no fruit.'
     Enough of bliss, they thought, could bliss bear seed,
     Yield its like, propagate a bliss in turn
150   And keep the kind up; not supplant themselves
     But put in evidence, record they were,
     Show them, when done with, i' the shape of a child.
     ''T is in a child, man and wife grow complete,
     One flesh: God says so: let him do his work!'

     Now, one reminder of this gnawing want,
     One special prick o' the maggot at the core,
     Always befell when, as the day came round,
     A certain yearly sum, – our Pietro being,
     As the long name runs, an usufructuary, –
160   Dropped in the common bag as interest
     Of money, his till death, not afterward,
     Failing an heir: an heir would take and take,
     A child of theirs be wealthy in their place
     To nobody's hurt – the stranger else seized all.
     Prosperity rolled river-like and stopped,
     Making their mill go; but when wheel wore out,
     The wave would find a space and sweep on free
     And, half-a-mile off, grind some neighbour's corn.

     Adam-like, Pietro sighed and said no more:
170   Eve saw the apple was fair and good to taste,
     So, plucked it, having asked the snake advice.
     She told her husband God was merciful,
     And his and her prayer granted at the last:
     Let the old mill-stone moulder, – wheel unworn,
     Quartz from the quarry, shot into the stream

Adroitly, should go bring grist as before –
Their house continued to them by an heir,
Their vacant heart replenished with a child.
We have her own confession at full length
180 Made in the first remorse: 't was Jubilee
Pealed in the ear o' the conscience and it woke.
She found she had offended God no doubt,
So much was plain from what had happened since,
Misfortune on misfortune; but she harmed
No one i' the world, so far as she could see.
The act had gladdened Pietro to the height,
Her husband – God himself must gladden so
Or not at all – (thus much seems probable
From the implicit faith, or rather say
190 Stupid credulity of the foolish man
Who swallowed such a tale nor strained a whit
Even at his wife's far-over-fifty years
Matching his sixty-and-under.) Him she blessed,
And as for doing any detriment
To the veritable heir, – why, tell her first
Who was he? Which of all the hands held up
I' the crowd, would one day gather round their gate,
Did she so wrong by intercepting thus
The ducat, spendthrift fortune thought to fling
200 For a scramble just to make the mob break shins?
She kept it, saved them kicks and cuffs thereby.
While at the least one good work had she wrought,
Good, clearly and incontestably! Her cheat –
What was it to its subject, the child's self,
But charity and religion? See the girl!
A body most like – a soul too probably –
Doomed to death, such a double death as waits
The illicit offspring of a common trull,
Sure to resent and forthwith rid herself
210 Of a mere interruption to sin's trade,
In the efficacious way old Tiber knows.
Was not so much proved by the ready sale
O' the child, glad transfer of this irksome chance?

Well then, she had caught up this castaway:
This fragile egg, some careless wild bird dropped,
She had picked from where it waited the foot-fall,
And put in her own breast till forth broke finch
Able to sing God praise on mornings now.
What so excessive harm was done? – she asked.

220 To which demand the dreadful answer comes –
For that same deed, now at Lorenzo's church,
Both agents, conscious and inconscious, lie;
While she, the deed was done to benefit,
Lies also, the most lamentable of things,
Yonder where curious people count her breaths,
Calculate how long yet the little life
Unspilt may serve their turn nor spoil the show,
Give them their story, then the church its group.

Well, having gained Pompilia, the girl grew
230 I' the midst of Pietro here, Violante there,
Each, like a semicircle with stretched arms,
Joining the other round her preciousness –
Two walls that go about a garden-plot
Where a chance sliver, branchlet slipt from bole
Of some tongue-leaved eye-figured Eden tree,
Filched by two exiles and borne far away,
Patiently glorifies their solitude, –
Year by year mounting, grade by grade surmounts
The builded brick-work, yet is compassed still,
240 Still hidden happily and shielded safe, –
Else why should miracle have graced the ground?
But on the twelfth sun that brought April there
What meant that laugh? The coping-stone was reached;
Nay, a light tuft of bloom towered above
To be toyed with by butterfly or bee,
Done good to or else harm to from outside:
Pompilia's root, stem and a branch or two
Home enclosed still, the rest would be the world's.
All which was taught our couple though obtuse,

250 Since walls have ears, when one day brought a priest,
Smooth-mannered soft-speeched sleek-cheeked visitor,
The notable Abate Paolo – known
As younger brother of a Tuscan house
Whereof the actual representative,
Count Guido, had employed his youth and age
In culture of Rome's most productive plant –
A cardinal: but years pass and change comes,
In token of which, here was our Paolo brought
To broach a weighty business. Might he speak?
260 Yes – to Violante somehow caught alone
While Pietro took his after-dinner doze,
And the young maiden, busily as befits,
Minded her broider-frame three chambers off.

So – giving now his great flap-hat a gloss
With flat o' the hand between-whiles, soothing now
The silk from out its creases o'er the calf,
Setting the stocking clerical again,
But never disengaging, once engaged,
The thin clear grey hold of his eyes on her –
270 He dissertated on that Tuscan house,
Those Franceschini, – very old they were –
Not rich however – oh, not rich, at least,
As people look to be who, low i' the scale
One way, have reason, rising all they can
By favour of the money-bag: 't is fair –
Do all gifts go together? But do n't suppose
That being not so rich means all so poor!
Say rather, well enough – i' the way, indeed,
Ha, ha, to better fortune than the best,
280 Since if his brother's patron-friend kept faith,
Put into promised play the Cardinalate,
Their house might wear the red cloth that keeps warm,
Would but the Count have patience – there's the point!
For he was slipping into years apace,
And years make men restless – they needs must see
Some certainty, some sort of end assured,

Sparkle, tho' from the topmost beacon-tip
That warrants life a harbour through the haze.
In short, call him fantastic as you choose,
290 Guido was home-sick, yearned for the old sights
And usual faces, – fain would settle himself
And have the patron's bounty when it fell
Irrigate far rather than deluge near,
Go fertilize Arezzo, not flood Rome.
Sooth to say, 't was the wiser wish: the Count
Proved wanting in ambition, – let us avouch,
Since truth is best, – in callousness of heart,
Winced at those pin-pricks whereby honours hang
A ribbon o'er each puncture: his – no soul
300 Ecclesiastic (here the hat was brushed)
Humble but self-sustaining, calm and cold,
Having, as one who puts his hand to the plough,
Renounced the over-vivid family-feel –
Poor brother Guido! All too plain, he pined
Amid Rome's pomp and glare for dinginess
And that dilapidated palace-shell
Vast as a quarry and, very like, as bare –
Since to this comes old grandeur now-a-days –
Or that absurd wild villa in the waste
310 O' the hill side, breezy though, for who likes air,
Vittiano, nor unpleasant with its vines,
Outside the city and the summer heats.
And now his harping on this one tense chord
The villa and the palace, palace this
And villa the other, all day and all night
Creaked like the implacable cicala's cry
And made one's ear-drum ache: nought else would serve
But that, to light his mother's visage up
With second youth, hope, gaiety again,
320 He must find straightway, woo and haply win
And bear away triumphant back, some wife.
Well now, the man was rational in his way –
He, the Abate, – ought he to interpose?
Unless by straining still his tutelage

(Priesthood leaps over elder-brothership)
Across this difficulty: then let go,
Leave the poor fellow in peace! Would that be wrong?
There was no making Guido great, it seems,
Spite of himself: then happy be his dole!
330 Indeed, the Abate's little interest
Was somewhat nearly touched i' the case, they saw:
Since if his simple kinsman so were bent,
Began his rounds in Rome to catch a wife,
Full soon would such unworldliness surprise
The rare bird, sprinkle salt on phoenix' tail,
And so secure the nest a sparrow-hawk.
No lack of mothers here in Rome, – no dread
Of daughters lured as larks by looking-glass!
The first name-pecking credit-scratching fowl
340 Would drop her unfledged cuckoo in our nest
To gather greyness there, give voice at length
And shame the brood . . . but it was long ago
When crusades were, and we sent eagles forth!
No, that at least the Abate could forestall.
He read the thought within his brother's word,
Knew what he purposed better than himself.
We want no name and fame – having our own:
No worldly aggrandizement – such we fly:
But if some wonder of a woman's-heart
350 Were yet untainted on this grimy earth,
Tender and true – tradition tells of such –
Prepared to pant in time and tune with ours –
If some good girl (a girl, since she must take
The new bent, live new life, adopt new modes)
Not wealthy – Guido for his rank was poor –
But with whatever dowry came to hand,
There were the lady-love predestinate!
And somehow the Abate's guardian eye —
Scintillant, rutilant, fraternal fire, –
360 Roving round every way had seized the prize
– The instinct of us, we, the spiritualty!
Come, cards on table; was it true or false

That here – here in this very tenement –
Yea, Via Vittoria did a marvel hide,
Lily of a maiden, white with intact leaf
Guessed thro' the sheath that saved it from the sun?
A daughter with the mother's hands still clasped
Over her head for fillet virginal,
A wife worth Guido's house and hand and heart?
370 He came to see; had spoken, he could no less –
(A final cherish of the stockinged calf)
If harm were, – well, the matter was off his mind.

Then with the great air did he kiss, devout,
Violante's hand, and rise up his whole height
(A certain purple gleam about the black)
And go forth grandly, – as if the Pope came next.
And so Violante rubbed her eyes awhile,
Got up too, walked to wake her Pietro soon
And pour into his ear the mighty news
380 How somebody had-somehow somewhere seen
Their tree-top-tuft of bloom above the wall,
And came now to apprise them the tree's self
Was no such crab-sort as should feed the swine,
But veritable gold, the Hesperian ball
Ordained for Hercules to haste and pluck,
And bear and give the Gods to banquet with –
Hercules standing ready at the door.
Whereon did Pietro rub his eyes in turn,
Look very wise, a little woeful too,
390 Then, periwig on head, and cane in hand,
Sally forth dignifiedly into the Square
Of Spain across Babbuino the six steps,
Toward the Boat-fountain where our idlers lounge, –
Ask, for form's sake, who Hercules might be,
And have congratulation from the world.

Heartily laughed the world in his fool's-face
And told him Hercules was just the heir
To the stubble once a corn-field, and brick-heap

Where used to be a dwelling-place now burned.
400 Guido and Franceschini; a Count, – ay:
But a cross i' the poke to bless the Countship? No!
All gone except sloth, pride, rapacity,
Humours of the imposthume incident
To rich blood that runs thin, – nursed to a head
By the rankly-salted soil – a cardinal's court
Where, parasite and picker-up of crumbs,
He had hung on long, and now, let go, said some,
But shaken off, said others, – in any case
Tired of the trade and something worse for wear,
410 Was wanting to change town for country quick,
Go home again: let Pietro help him home!
The brother, Abate Paolo, shrewder mouse,
Had pricked for comfortable quarters, inched
Into the core of Rome, and fattened so;
But Guido, over-burly for rat's hole
Suited to clerical slimness, starved outside,
Must shift for himself: and so the shift was this!
What, was the snug retreat of Pietro tracked,
The little provision for his old age snuffed?
420 'Oh, make your girl a lady, an you list,
But have more mercy on our wit than vaunt
Your bargain as we burgesses who brag!
Why, Goodman Dullard, if a friend must speak,
Would the Count, think you, stoop to you and yours
Were there the value of one penny-piece
To rattle 'twixt his palms – or likelier laugh,
Bid your Pompilia help you black his shoe?'

Home again, shaking oft the puzzled pate,
Went Pietro to announce a change indeed,
430 Yet point Violante where some solace lay
Of a rueful sort, – the taper, quenched so soon,
Had ended merely in a snuff, not stink –
Congratulate there was one hope the less
Not misery the more: and so an end.

The marriage thus impossible, the rest
Followed: our spokesman, Paolo, heard his fate,
Resignedly Count Guido bore the blow:
Violante wiped away the transient tear,
Renounced the playing Danae to gold dreams,
440 Praised much her Pietro's prompt sagaciousness,
Found neighbours' envy natural, lightly laughed
At gossips' malice, fairly wrapped herself
In her integrity three folds about,
And, letting pass a little day or two,
Threw, even over that integrity,
Another wrappage, namely one thick veil
That hid her, matron-wise, from head to foot,
And, by the hand holding a girl veiled too,
Stood, one dim end of a December day,
450 In Saint Lorenzo on the altar-step –
Just where she lies now and that girl will lie –
Only with fifty candles' company
Now – in the place of the poor winking one
Which saw, – doors shut and sacristan made sure, –
A priest – perhaps Abate Paolo – wed
Guido clandestinely, irrevocably
To his Pompilia aged thirteen years
And five months, – witness the church register, –
Pompilia, (thus become Count Guido's wife
460 Clandestinely, irrevocably his,)
Who all the while had borne, from first to last,
As brisk a part i' the bargain, as yon lamb,
Brought forth from basket and set out for sale,
Bears while they chaffer, wary market-man
And voluble housewife, o'er it, – each in turn
Patting the curly calm inconscious head,
With the shambles ready round the corner there,
When the talk's talked out and a bargain struck.

Transfer complete, why, Pietro was apprised.
470 Violante sobbed the sobs and prayed the prayers
And said the serpent tempted so she fell,

Till Pietro had to clear his brow apace
And make the best of matters: wrath at first, –
How else? pacification presently,
Why not? – could flesh withstand the impurpled one,
The very Cardinal, Paolo's patron-friend?
Who, justifiably surnamed 'a hinge,'
Knew where the mollifying oil should drop
To cure the creak o' the valve, – considerate
480 For frailty, patient in a naughty world,
He even volunteered to supervise
The rough draught of those marriage-articles
Signed in a hurry by Pietro, since revoked:
Trust's politic, suspicion does the harm,
There is but one way to brow-beat this world,
Dumb-founder doubt, and repay scorn in kind, –
To go on trusting, namely, till faith move
Mountains.

            And faith here made the mountains move.
490 Why, friends whose zeal cried 'Caution ere too late!' –
Bade 'Pause ere jump, with both feet joined, on slough!' –
Counselled 'If rashness then, now temperance!'–
Heard for their pains that Pietro had closed eyes,
Jumped and was in the middle of the mire,
Money and all, just what should sink a man.
By the mere marriage, Guido gained forthwith
Dowry, his wife's right; no rescinding there:
But Pietro, why must he needs ratify
One gift Violante gave, pay down one doit
500 Promised in first fool's-flurry? Grasp the bag
Lest the son's service flag, – is reason and rhyme,
Above all when the son's a son-in-law.
Words to the wind! The parents cast their lot
Into the lap o' the daughter: and the son
Now with a right to lie there, took what fell,
Pietro's whole having and holding, house and field,
Goods, chattels and effects, his worldly worth
Present and in perspective, all renounced

In favour of Guido. As for the usufruct –
510   The interest now, the principal anon,
Would Guido please to wait, at Pietro's death:
Till when, he must support the couple's charge,
Bear with them, housemates, pensionaries, pawned
To an alien for fulfilment of their pact.
Guido should at discretion deal them orts,
Bread-bounty in Arezzo the strange place, –
They who had lived deliciously and rolled
Rome's choicest comfit 'neath the tongue before.
Into this quag, 'jump' bade the Cardinal!
520   And neck-deep in a minute there flounced they.

But they touched bottom at Arezzo: there –
Four months' experience of how craft and greed
Quickened by penury and pretentious hate
Of plain truth, brutify and bestialize, –
Four months' taste of apportioned insolence,
Cruelty graduated, dose by dose
Of ruffianism dealt out at bed and board,
And lo, the work was done, success clapped hands.
The starved, stripped, beaten brace of stupid dupes
530   Broke at last in their desperation loose,
Fled away for their lives, and lucky so;
Found their account in casting coat afar
And bearing off a shred of skin at least:
Left Guido lord o' the prey, as the lion is,
And, careless what came after, carried their wrongs
To Rome, – I nothing doubt, with such remorse
As folly feels, since pain can make it wise,
But crime, past wisdom, which is innocence,
Needs not be plagued with till a later day.

540   Pietro went back to beg from door to door,
In hope that memory not quite extinct
Of cheery days and festive nights would move
Friends and acquaintance – after the natural laugh,
And tributary 'Just as we foretold –'

To show some bowels, give the dregs o' the cup,
Scraps of the trencher, to their host that was,
Or let him share the mat with the mastiff, he
Who lived large and kept open house so long.
Not so Violante: ever a-head i' the march,
550 Quick at the bye-road and the cut-across,
She went first to the best adviser, God –
Whose finger unmistakably was felt
In all this retribution of the past.
Here was the prize of sin, luck of a lie!
But here too was the Holy Year would help,
Bound to rid sinners of sin vulgar, sin
Abnormal, sin prodigious, up to sin
Impossible and supposed for Jubilee' sake:
To lift the leadenest of lies, let soar
560 The soul unhampered by a feather-weight.
'I will' said she 'go burn out this bad hole
That breeds the scorpion, baulk the plague at least
Its hope of further creeping progeny:
I will confess my fault, be punished, yes,
But pardoned too: Saint Peter pays for all.'

So, with the crowd she mixed, made for the dome,
Through the great door new-broken for the nonce
Marched, muffled more than ever matron-wise,
Up the left nave to the formidable throne,
570 Fell into file with this the poisoner
And that the parricide, and reached in turn
The poor repugnant Penitentiary
Set at this gully-hole o' the world's discharge
To help the frightfullest of filth have vent,
And then knelt down and whispered in his ear
How she had bought Pompilia, palmed the babe
On Pietro, passed the girl off as their child
To Guido, and defrauded of his due
This one and that one, – more than she could name,
580 Until her solid piece of wickedness
Happened to split and spread woe far and wide:

Contritely now she brought the case for cure.

Replied the throne – 'Ere God forgive the guilt,
Make man some restitution! Do your part!
The owners of your husband's heritage,
Barred thence by this pretended birth and heir, –
Tell them, the bar came so, is broken so,
Theirs be the due reversion as before!
Your husband who, no partner in the guilt,
590 Suffers the penalty, led blindfold thus
By love of what he thought his flesh and blood
To alienate his all in her behalf, –
Tell him too such contract is null and void!
Last, he who personates your son-in-law,
Who with sealed eyes and stopped ears, tame and mute,
Took at your hand that bastard of a whore
You called your daughter and he calls his wife, –
Tell him, and bear the anger which is just!
Then, penance so performed, may pardon be!'

600 Who could gainsay this just and right award?
Nobody in the world: but, out o' the world,
Who knows? – might timid intervention be
From any makeshift of an angel-guide,
Substitute for celestial guardianship,
Pretending to take care of the girl's self:
'Woman, confessing crime is healthy work,
And telling truth relieves a liar like you,
But what of her my unconsidered charge?
No thought of, while this good befalls yourself,
610 What in the way of harm may find out her?'
No least thought, I assure you: truth being truth,
Tell it and shame the devil!
                              Said and done:
Home went Violante and disbosomed all:
And Pietro who, six months before, had borne
Word after word of such a piece of news
Like so much cold steel inched through his breast-blade,

Now at its entry gave a leap for joy,
As who – what did I say of one in a quag? –
620 Should catch a hand from heaven and spring thereby
Out of the mud, on ten toes stand once more.
'What? All that used to be, may be again?
My money mine again, my house, my land,
My chairs and tables, all mine evermore?
What, the girl's dowry never was the girl's,
And, unpaid yet, is never now to pay?
Then the girl's self, my pale Pompilia child
That used to be my own with her great eyes –
He who drove us forth, why should he keep her
630 When proved as very a pauper as himself?
Will she come back, with nothing changed at all,
And laugh "But how you dreamed uneasily!
I saw the great drops stand here on your brow –
Did I do wrong to wake you with a kiss?"
No, indeed, darling! No, for wide awake
I see another outburst of surprise:
The lout-lord, bully-beggar, braggart-sneak,
Who not content with cutting purse, crops ear –
Assuredly it shall be salve to mine
640 When this great news red-letters him, the rogue!
Ay, let him taste the teeth o' the trap, this fox,
Give us our lamb back, golden fleece and all,
Let her creep in and warm our breasts again!
What care for the past? – we three are our old selves,
Who know now what the outside world is worth.'
And so, he carried case before the courts;
And there Violante, blushing to the bone,
Made public declaration of her fault,
Renounced her motherhood, and prayed the law
650 To interpose, frustrate of its effect
Her folly, and redress the injury done.

Whereof was the disastrous consequence,
That though indisputably clear the case
(For thirteen years are not so large a lapse,

And still six witnesses survived in Rome
To prove the truth o' the tale) – yet, patent wrong
Seemed Guido's; the first cheat had chanced on him:
Here was the pity that, deciding right,
Those who began the wrong would gain the good.
660 Guido pronounced the story one long lie
Lied to do robbery and take revenge:
Or say it were no lie at all but truth,
Then, it both robbed the right heirs and shamed him
Without revenge to humanize the deed:
What had he done when first they shamed him thus?
But that were too fantastic: losels they,
And leasing this world's-wonder of a lie,
They lied to blot him though it brand themselves.

So answered Guido through the Abate's mouth.
670 Wherefore the court, its customary way,
Inclined to the middle course the sage affect –
They held the child to be a changeling, – good:
But, lest the husband got no good thereby,
They willed the dowry, though not hers at all,
Should yet be his, if not by right then grace –
Part-payment for the plain injustice done.
But then, that other contract, Pietro's work,
Renunciation of his own estate,
That must be cancelled – give him back his goods,
680 He was no party to the cheat at least!
So ran the judgment: – whence a prompt appeal
On both sides, seeing right is absolute.
Cried Pietro 'Is Pompilia not my child?
Why give her my child's dowry?' – 'Have I right
To the dowry, why not to the rest as well?'
Cried Guido, or cried Paolo in his name:
Till law said 'Reinvestigate the case!'
And so the matter pends, unto this day.

Hence new disaster – that no outlet seemed;
690 Whatever the fortune of the battle-field,

No path whereby the fatal man might march
Victorious, wreath on head and spoils in hand,
And back turned full upon the baffled foe, –
Nor cranny whence, desperate and disgraced,
Stripped to the skin, he might be fain to crawl
Worm-like, and so away with his defeat
To other fortune and the novel prey.
No, he was pinned to the place there, left alone
With his immense hate and, the solitary
700 Subject to satisfy that hate, his wife.
'Cast her off? Turn her naked out of doors?
Easily said! But still the action pends,
Still dowry, principal and interest.
Pietro's possessions, all I bargained for, –
Any good day, be but my friends alert,
May give them me if she continue mine.
Yet, keep her? Keep the puppet of my foes –
Her voice that lisps me back their curse – her eye
They lend their leer of triumph to – her lip
710 I touch and taste their very filth upon?'

In short, he also took the middle course
Rome taught him – did at last excogitate
How he might keep the good and leave the bad
Twined in revenge, yet extricable, – nay
Make the very hate's eruption, very rush
Of the unpent sluice of cruelty relieve
His heart first, then go fertilize his field.
What if the girl-wife, tortured with due care,
Should take, as though spontaneously, the road
720 It were impolitic to thrust her on?
If, goaded, she broke out in full revolt,
Followed her parents i' the face o' the world,
Branded as runaway not castaway,
Self-sentenced and self-punished in the act?
So should the loathed form and detested face
Launch themselves into hell and there be lost
While he looked o'er the brink with folded arms;

So should the heaped-up shames go shuddering back
O' the head o' the heapers, Pietro and his wife,
730   And bury in the breakage three at once:
While Guido, left free, no one right renounced,
Gain present, gain prospective, all the gain,
None of the wife except her rights absorbed,
Should ask law what it was law paused about –
If law were dubious still whose word to take,
The husband's – dignified and derelict,
Or the wife's – the . . . what I tell you. It should be.

Guido's first step was to take pen, indite
A letter to the Abate, – not his own,
740   His wife's, – she should re-write, sign, seal and send.
She liberally told the household-news,
Rejoiced her vile progenitors were fled,
Revealed their malice – how they even laid
A last injunction on her, when they fled,
That she should forthwith find a paramour,
Complot with him to gather spoil enough
Then burn the house down, – taking previous care
To poison all its inmates overnight, –
And so companioned, so provisioned too,
750   Follow to Rome and all join fortunes gay.
This letter, traced in pencil-characters,
Guido as easily got retraced in ink
By his wife's pen, guided from end to end,
As it had been just so much Hebrew, Sir:
For why? That wife could broider, sing perhaps,
Pray certainly, but no more read than write
This letter 'which yet write she must,' he said
'Being half courtesy and compliment,
Half sisterliness: take the thing on trust!'
760   She had as readily re-traced the words
Of her own death-warrant, – in some sort 't was so.
This letter the Abate in due course
Communicated to such curious souls
In Rome as needs must pry into the cause

Of quarrel, why the Comparini fled
The Franceschini, whence the grievance grew,
What the hubbub meant: 'Nay, – see the wife's own word,
Authentic answer! Tell detractors too
There's a plan formed, a programme figured here
770 – Pray God no after-practice put to proof,
This letter cast no light upon, one day!'

So much for what should work in Rome, – back now
To Arezzo, go on with the project there,
Forward the next step with as bold a foot,
And plague Pompilia to the height, you see!
Accordingly did Guido set himself
To worry up and down, across, around,
The woman, hemmed in by her household-bars, –
Chased her about the coop of daily life,
780 Having first stopped each outlet thence save one
Which, like bird with a ferret in her haunt,
She needs must seize as sole way of escape
Though there was tied and twittering a decoy
To seem as if it tempted, – just the plume
O' the popinjay, and not a respite there
From tooth and claw of something in the dark, –
Giuseppe Caponsacchi.
                              Now begins
The tenebrific passage of the tale:
790 How hold a light, display the cavern's gorge?
How, in this phase of the affair, show truth?
Here is the dying wife who smiles and says
'So it was, – so it was not, – how it was,
I never knew nor ever care to know –'
Till they all weep, physician, man of law,
Even that poor old bit of battered brass
Beaten out of all shape by the world's sins,
Common utensil of the lazar-house –
Confessor Celestino groans ''T is truth,
800 All truth and only truth: there's something else,
Some presence in the room beside us all,

Something that every lie expires before:
No question she was pure from first to last.'
So far is well and helps us to believe:
But beyond, she the helpless, simple-sweet
Or silly-sooth, unskilled to break one blow
At her good fame by putting finger forth, –
How can she render service to the truth?
The bird says 'So I fluttered where a springe
810   Caught me: the springe did not contrive itself,
That I know: who contrived it, God forgive!'
But we, who hear no voice and have dry eyes,
Must ask, – we cannot else, absolving her, –
How of the part played by that same decoy
I' the catching, caging? Was himself caught first?
We deal here with no innocent at least,
No witless victim, – he's a man of the age
And a priest beside, – persuade the mocking world
Mere charity boiled over in this sort!
820   He whose own safety too, – (the Pope's apprised –
Good-natured with the secular offence,
The Pope looks grave on priesthood in a scrape)
Our priest's own safety therefore, may-be life,
Hangs on the issue! You will find it hard.
Guido is here to meet you with fixed foot,
Stiff like a statue – 'Leave what went before!
My wife fled i' the company of a priest,
Spent two days and two nights alone with him:
Leave what came after!' He is hard to throw.
830   Moreover priests are merely flesh and blood;
When we get weakness, and no guilt beside,
We have no such great ill-fortune: finding grey,
We gladly call that white which might be black,
Too used to the double-dye. So, if the priest
Moved by Pompilia's youth and beauty, gave
Way to the natural weakness. . . . Anyhow
Here be facts, charactery; what they spell
Determine, and thence pick what sense you may!
There was a certain young bold handsome priest

840 Popular in the city, far and wide
Famed, for Arezzo's but a little place,
As the best of good companions, gay and grave
At the decent minute; settled in his stall,
Or sideling, lute on lap, by lady's couch,
Ever the courtly Canon: see in such
A star shall climb apace and culminate,
Have its due handbreadth of the heaven at Rome,
Though meanwhile pausing on Arezzo's edge,
As modest candle 'mid the mountain fog,
850 To rub off redness and rusticity
Ere it sweep chastened, gain the silver-sphere.
Whether through Guido's absence or what else,
This Caponsacchi, favourite of the town,
Was yet no friend of his nor free o' the house,
Though both moved in the regular magnates' march –
Each must observe the other's tread and halt
At church, saloon, theatre, house of play.
Who could help noticing the husband's slouch,
The black of his brow – or miss the news that buzzed
860 Of how the little solitary wife
Wept and looked out of window all day long?
What need of minute search into such springs
As start men, set o' the move? – machinery
Old as earth, obvious as the noonday sun.
Why, take men as they come, – an instance now, –
Of all those who have simply gone to see
Pompilia on her deathbed since four days,
Half at the least are, call it how you please,
In love with her – I don't except the priests
870 Nor even the old confessor whose eyes run
Over at what he styles his sister's voice
Who died so early and weaned him from the world.
Well, had they viewed her ere the paleness pushed
The last o' the red o' the rose away, while yet
Some hand, adventurous 'twixt the wind and her,
Might let the life run back and raise the flower
Rich with reward up to the guardian's face, –

Would they have kept that hand employed the same
At fumbling on with prayer-book pages? No!
880 Men are men: why then need I say one word
More than this, that our man the Canon here
Saw, pitied, loved Pompilia?

              This is why;
This startling why: that Caponsacchi's self –
Whom foes and friends alike avouch, for good
Or ill, a man of truth whate'er betide,
Intrepid altogether, reckless too
How his own fame and fortune, tossed to the winds,
Suffer by any turn the adventure take,
890 Nay, more – not thrusting, like a badge to hide,
'Twixt shirt and skin a joy which shown is shame –
But flirting flag-like i' the face o' the world
This tell-tale kerchief, this conspicuous love
For the lady, – oh, called innocent love, I know!
Only, such scarlet fiery innocence
As most men would try muffle up in shade, –
– 'Tis strange then that this else abashless mouth
Should yet maintain, for truth's sake which is God's,
That it was not he made the first advance,
900 That, even ere word had passed between the two,
Pompilia penned him letters, passionate prayers,
If not love, then so simulating love
That he, no novice to the taste of thyme,
Turned from such over-luscious honey-clot
At end o' the flower, and would not lend his lip
Till . . . but the tale here frankly outsoars faith:
There must be falsehood somewhere. For her part,
Pompilia quietly constantly avers
She never penned a letter in her life
910 Nor to the Canon nor any other man,
Being incompetent to write and read:
Nor had she ever uttered word to him, nor he
To her till that same evening when they met,
She on her window-terrace, he beneath

I' the public street, as was their fateful chance,
And she adjured him in the name of God
Find out and bring to pass where, when and how
Escape with him to Rome might be contrived.
Means found, plan laid and time fixed, she avers,
920 And heart assured to heart in loyalty,
All at an impulse! All extemporized
As in romance-books! Is that credible?
Well, yes: as she avers this with calm mouth
Dying, I do think 'Credible!' you'd cry –
Did not the priest's voice come to break the spell:
They questioned him apart, as the custom is,
When first the matter made a noise at Rome,
And he, calm, constant then as she is now,
For truth's sake did assert and reassert
930 Those letters called him to her and he came,
– Which damns the story credible otherwise.
Why should this man, – mad to devote himself,
Careless what comes of his own fame, the first, –
Be studious thus to publish and declare
Just what the lightest nature loves to hide,
Nor screen a lady from the byword's laugh
'First spoke the lady, last the cavalier!'
– I say, – why should the man tell truth just here
When graceful lying meets such ready shrift?
940 Or is there a first moment for a priest
As for a woman, when invaded shame
Must have its first and last excuse to show?
Do both contrive love's entry in the mind
Shall look, i' the manner of it, a surprise,
That after, once the flag o' the fort hauled down,
Effrontery may sink drawbridge, open gate,
Welcome and entertain the conqueror?
Or what do you say to a touch of the devil's worst?
Can it be that the husband, he who wrote
950 The letter to his brother I told you of,
I' the name of her it meant to criminate, –
What if he wrote those letters to the priest?

Further the priest says, when it first befell,
This folly o' the letters, that he checked the flow,
Put them back lightly each with its reply.
Here again vexes new discrepancy:
There never reached her eye a word from him;
He did write but she could not read – she could
Burn what offended wifehood, womanhood,
960 So did burn: never bade him come to her,
Yet when it proved he must come, let him come,
And when he did come though uncalled, she spoke·
Prompt by an inspiration: thus it was.
Will you go somewhat back to understand?

When first, pursuant to his plan, there sprung,
Like an uncaged beast, Guido's cruelty
On the weak shoulders of his wife, she cried
To those whom law appoints resource for such,
The secular guardian – that's the Governor,
970 And the Archbishop, – that's the spiritual guide,
And prayed them take the claws from out her flesh.
Now, this is ever the ill consequence
Of being noble, poor and difficult,
Ungainly, yet too great to disregard, –
That the born peers and friends hereditary
Though disinclined to help from their own store
The opprobrious wight, put penny in his poke
From purse of theirs or leave the door ajar
When he goes wistful by at dinner-time, –
980 Yet, if his needs conduct him where they sit
Smugly in office, judge this, bishop that,
Dispensers of the shine and shade o' the place –
And if, the friend's door shut and purse undrawn,
The potentate may find the office-hall
Do as good service at no cost – give help
By-the-bye, pay up traditional dues at once
Just through a feather-weight too much i' the scale,
A finger-tip forgot at the balance-tongue, –
Why, only churls refuse, or Molinists.

990 Thus when, in the first roughness of surprise
At Guido's wolf-face whence the sheepskin fell,
The frightened couple, all bewilderment,
Rushed to the Governor, – who else rights wrong?
Told him their tale of wrong and craved redress –
Why, then the Governor woke up to the fact
That Guido was a friend of old, poor Count! –
So, promptly paid his tribute, promised the pair,
Wholesome chastisement should soon cure their qualms
Next time they came and prated and told lies:
1000 Which stopped all prating, sent them dumb to Rome.
Well, now it was Pompilia's turn to try:
The troubles pressing on her, as I said,
Three times she rushed, maddened by misery,
To the other mighty man, sobbed out her prayer
At footstool of the Archbishop – fast the friend
Of her husband also! Oh, good friends of yore!
So, the Archbishop, not to be outdone
By the Governor, break custom more than he,
Thrice bade the foolish woman stop her tongue,
1010 Unloosed her hands from harassing his gout,
Coached her and carried her to the Count again,
– His old friend should be master in his house,
Rule his wife and correct her faults at need!
Well, driven from post to pillar in this wise,
She, as a last resource, betook herself
To one, should be no family-friend at least,
A simple friar o' the city; confessed to him,
Then told how fierce temptation of release
By self-dealt death was busy with her soul,
1020 And urged that he put this in words, write plain
For one who could not write, set down her prayer
That Pietro and Violante, parent-like
If somehow not her parents, should for love
Come save her, pluck from out the flame the brand
Themselves had thoughtlessly thrust in so deep
To send gay-coloured sparkles up and cheer
Their seat at the chimney-corner. The good friar

Promised as much at the moment; but, alack,
Night brings discretion: he was no one's friend,
Yet presently found he could not turn about
Nor take a step i' the case and fail to tread
On someone's toe who either was a friend,
Or a friend's friend, or friend's friend thrice-removed,
And woe to friar by whom offences come!
So, the course being plain, – with a general sigh
At matrimony the profound mistake, –
He threw reluctantly the business up,
Having his other penitents to mind.

If then, all outlets thus secured save one,
At last she took to the open, stood and stared
With her wan face to see where God might wait –
And there found Caponsacchi wait as well
For the precious something at perdition's edge,
He only was predestinate to save, –
And if they recognised in a critical flash
From the zenith, each the other, her need of him,
His need of . . . say, a woman to perish for,
The regular way o' the world, yet break no vow,
Do no harm save to himself, – if this were thus?
How do you say? It were improbable;
So is the legend of my patron-saint.

Anyhow, whether, as Guido states the case,
Pompilia, – like a starving wretch i' the street
Who stops and rifles the first passenger
In the great right of an excessive wrong, –
Did somehow call this stranger and he came, –
Or whether the strange sudden interview
Blazed as when star and star must needs go close
Till each hurts each and there is loss in heaven –
Whatever way in this strange world it was, –
Pompilia and Caponsacchi met, in fine,
She at her window, he i' the street beneath,
And understood each other at first look.

All was determined and performed at once.
And on a certain April evening, late
I' the month, this girl of sixteen, bride and wife
Three years and over, – she who hitherto
Had never taken twenty steps in Rome
Beyond the church, pinned to her mother's gown,
1070 Nor, in Arezzo, knew her way through street
Except what led to the Archbishop's door, –
Such an one rose up in the dark, laid hand
On what came first, clothes and a trinket or two,
Belongings of her own in the old day, –
Stole from the side o' the sleeping spouse – who knows?
Sleeping perhaps, silent for certain, – slid
Ghost-like from great dark room to great dark room,
In through the tapestries and out again
And onward, unembarrassed as a fate,
1080 Descended staircase, gained last door of all,
Sent it wide open at first push of palm,
And there stood, first time, last and only time,
At liberty, alone in the open street, –
Unquestioned, unmolested found herself
At the city gate, by Caponsacchi's side,
Hope there, joy there, life and all good again,
The carriage there, the convoy there, light there
Broadening into a full blaze at Rome
And breaking small what long miles lay between;
1090 Up she sprang, in he followed, they were safe.

The husband quotes this for incredible,
All of the story from first word to last:
Sees the priest's hand throughout upholding hers,
Traces his foot to the alcove, that night,
Whither and whence blindfold he knew the way,
Proficient in all craft and stealthiness;
And cites for proof a servant, eye that watched
And ear that opened to purse secrets up,
A woman-spy, – suborned to give and take
1100 Letters and tokens, do the work of shame

The more adroitly that herself, who helped
Communion thus between a tainted pair,
Had long since been a leper thick in spot,
A common trull o' the town: she witnessed all,
Helped many meetings, partings, took her wage
And then told Guido the whole matter. Lies!
The woman's life confutes her word, – her word
Confutes itself: 'Thus, thus and thus I lied.'
'And thus, no question, still you lie,' we say.

1110 'Ay, but at last, e'en have it how you will,
Whatever the means, whatever the way, explodes
The consummation' – the accusers shriek:
'Here is the wife avowedly found in flight,
And the companion of her flight, a priest;
She flies her husband, he the church his spouse:
What is this?'

       Wife and priest alike reply
'This is the simple thing it claims to be,
A course we took for life and honour's sake,
1120 Very strange, very justifiable.'
She says, 'God put it in my head to fly,
As when the martin migrates: autumn claps
Her hands, cries "Winter's coming, will be here,
Off with you ere the white teeth overtake!
Flee!" So I fled: this friend was the warm day,
The south wind and whatever favours flight;
I took the favour, had the help, how else?
And so we did fly rapidly all night,
All day, all night – a longer night – again,
1130 And then another day, longest of days,
And all the while, whether we fled or stopped,
I scarce know how or why, one thought filled both,
" Fly and arrive!" So long as I found strength
I talked with my companion, told him much,
Knowing that he knew more, knew me, knew God
And God's disposal of me, – but the sense

O' the blessed flight absorbed me in the main,
And speech became mere talking through a sleep,
Till at the end of that last longest night
1140 In a red daybreak, when we reached an inn
And my companion whispered "Next stage – Rome!"
Sudden the weak flesh fell like piled-up cards,
All the frail fabric at a finger's touch,
And prostrate the poor soul too, and I said
"But though Count Guido were a furlong off,
Just on me, I must stop and rest awhile!"
Then something like a white wave o' the sea
Broke o'er my brain and buried me in sleep
Blessedly, till it ebbed and left me loose,
1150 And where was I found but on a strange bed
In a strange room like hell, roaring with noise,
Ruddy with flame, and filled with men, in front
Whom but the man you call my husband, ay –
Count Guido once more between heaven and me,
For there my heaven stood, my salvation, yes –
That Caponsacchi all my heaven of help,
Helpless himself, held prisoner in the hands
Of men who looked up in my husband's face
To take the fate thence he should signify,
1160 Just as the way was at Arezzo: then,
Not for my sake but his who had helped me –
I sprang up, reached him with one bound, and seized
The sword o' the felon, trembling at his side,
Fit creature of a coward, unsheathed the thing
And would have pinned him through the poison-bag
To the wall and left him there to palpitate,
As you serve scorpions, but men interposed –
Disarmed me, gave his life to him again
That he might take mine and the other lives,
1170 And he has done so. I submit myself!'
The priest says – oh, and in the main result
The facts asseverate, he truly says,
As to the very act and deed of him,

However you mistrust the mind o' the man –
The flight was just for flight's sake, no pretext
For aught except to set Pompilia free:
He says 'I cite the husband's self's worst charge
In proof of my best word for both of us.
Be it conceded that so many times
1180 We took our pleasure in his palace: then,
What need to fly at all? – or flying no less,
What need to outrage the lips sick and white
Of a woman, and bring ruin down beside,
By halting when Rome lay one stage beyond?'
So does he vindicate Pompilia's fame,
Confirm her story in all points but one –
This; that, so fleeing and so breathing forth
Her last strength in the prayer to halt awhile,
She makes confusion of the reddening white
1190 Which was the sunset when her strength gave way,
And the next sunrise and its whitening red
Which she revived in when her husband came:
She mixes both times, morn and eve, in one,
Having lived through a blank of night 'twixt each
Though dead-asleep, unaware as a corpse,
She on the bed above; her friend below
Watched in the doorway of the inn the while,
Stood i' the red o' the morn, that she mistakes,
In act to rouse and quicken the tardy crew
1200 And hurry out the horses, have the stage
Over, the last league, reach Rome and be safe:
When up came Guido.
                    Guido's tale begins –
How he and his whole household, drunk to death
By some enchanted potion, poppied drugs
Plied by the wife, lay powerless in gross sleep
And left the spoilers unimpeded way,
Could not shake off their poison and pursue,
Till noontide, then made shift to get on horse
1210 And did pursue: which means, he took his time,
Pressed on no more than lingered after, step

By step, just making sure o' the fugitives,
Till at the nick of time, he saw his chance,
Seized it, came up with and surprised the pair.
How he must needs have gnawn lip and gnashed teeth,
Taking successively at tower and town,
Village and roadside, still the same report
'Yes, such a pair arrived an hour ago,
Sat in the carriage just where your horse stands,
1220 While we got horses ready, – turned deaf ear
To all entreaty they would even alight;
Counted the minutes and resumed their course.'
Would they indeed escape, arrive at Rome,
Leave no least loop to let damnation through,
And foil him of his captured infamy,
Prize of guilt provèd and perfect? So it seemed:
Till, oh the happy chance, at last stage, Rome
But two short hours off, Castelnuovo reached,
The guardian angel gave reluctant place,
1230 Satan stepped forward with alacrity,
Pompilia's flesh and blood succumbed, perforce
A halt was, and her husband had his will.
Perdue he couched, counted out hour by hour
Till he should spy in the east a signal-streak –
Night had been, morrow was, triumph would be.
Do you see the plan deliciously complete?
The rush upon the unsuspecting sleep,
The easy execution, the outcry
Over the deed 'Take notice all the world!
1240 These two dead bodies, locked still in embrace, –
The man is Caponsacchi and a priest,
The woman is my wife: they fled me late,
Thus have I found and you behold them thus,
And may judge me: do you approve or no?'

Success did seem not so improbable,
But that already Satan's laugh was heard,
His black back turned on Guido – left i' the lurch
Or rather, baulked of suit and service now,

That he improve on both by one deed more,
1250 Burn up the better at no distant day,
Body and soul one holocaust to hell.
Anyhow, of this natural consequence
Did just the last link of the long chain snap:
For his eruption was o' the priest, alive
And alert, calm, resolute and formidable,
Not the least look of fear in that broad brow –
One not to be disposed of by surprise,
And armed moreover – who had guessed as much?
Yes, there stood he in secular costume
1260 Complete from head to heel, with sword at side,
He seemed to know the trick of perfectly.
There was no prompt suppression of the man
As he said calmly 'I have saved your wife
From death; there was no other way but this;
Of what do I defraud you except death?
Charge any wrong beyond, I answer it.'
Guido, the valorous, had met his match,
Was forced to demand help instead of fight,
Bid the authorities o' the place lend aid
1270 And make the best of a broken matter so.
They soon obeyed the summons – I suppose,
Apprized and ready, or not far to seek –
Laid hands on Caponsacchi, found in fault,
A priest yet flagrantly accoutred thus, –
Then, to make good Count Guido's further charge,
Proceeded, prisoner made lead the way,
In a crowd, upstairs to the chamber-door
Where wax-white, dead asleep, deep beyond dream,
As the priest laid her, lay Pompilia yet.

1280 And as he mounted step and step with the crowd
How I see Guido taking heart again!
He knew his wife so well and the way of her –
How at the outbreak she would shroud her shame
In hell's heart, would it mercifully yawn –
How, failing that, her forehead to his foot,

She would crouch silent till the great doom fell,
Leave him triumphant with the crowd to see!
Guilt motionless or writhing like a worm?
No! Second misadventure, this worm turned,
1290 I told you: would have slain him on the spot
With his own weapon, but they seized her hands:
Leaving her tongue free, as it tolled the knell
Of Guido's hope so lively late. The past
Took quite another shape now. She who shrieked
'At least and for ever I am mine and God's,
Thanks to his liberating angel Death –
Never again degraded to be yours
The ignoble noble, the unmanly man,
The beast below the beast in brutishness!' –
1300 This was the froward child, 'the restif lamb
Used to be cherished in his breast,' he groaned –
'Eat from his hand and drink from out his cup,
The while his fingers pushed their loving way
Through curl on curl of that soft coat – alas,
And she all silverly baaed gratitude
While meditating mischief!' – and so forth.
He must invent another story now!
The ins and outs o' the rooms were searched: he found
Or showed for found the abominable prize –
1310 Love-letters from his wife who cannot write,
Love-letters in reply o' the priest – thank God! –
Who can write and confront his character
With this, and prove the false thing forged throughout:
Spitting whereat, he needs must spatter who
But Guido's self? – that forged and falsified
One letter called Pompilia's, past dispute:
Then why not these to make sure still more sure?

So was the case concluded then and there:
Guido preferred his charges in due form,
1320 Called on the law to adjudicate, consigned
The accused ones to the Prefect of the place.
(Oh mouse-birth of that mountain-like revenge!)

And so to his own place betook himself
After the spring that failed, – the wildcat's way.
The captured parties were conveyed to Rome;
Investigation followed here i' the court –
Soon to review the fruit of its own work,
From then to now being eight months and no more.
Guido kept out of sight and safe at home:
1330 The Abate, brother Paolo, helped most
At words when deeds were out of question, pushed
Nearest the purple, best played deputy,
So, pleaded, Guido's representative
At the court shall soon try Guido's self, – what's more,
The court that also took – I told you, Sir –
That statement of the couple, how a cheat
Had been i' the birth of the babe, no child of theirs.
That was the prelude; this, the play's first act:
Whereof we wait what comes, crown, close of all.

1340 Well, the result was something of a shade
On the parties thus accused, – how otherwise?
Shade, but with shine as unmistakable.
Each had a prompt defence: Pompilia first –
'Earth was made hell to me who did no harm:
I only could emerge one way from hell
By catching at the one hand held me, so
I caught at it and thereby stepped to heaven:
If that be wrong, do with me what you will!'
Then Caponsacchi with a grave grand sweep
1350 O' the arm as though his soul warned baseness off –
'If as a man, then much more as a priest
I hold me bound to help weak innocence:
If so my worldly reputation burst,
Being the bubble it is, why, burst it may:
Blame I can bear though not blameworthiness.
But use your sense first, see if the miscreant here
The man who tortured thus the woman, thus
Have not both laid the trap and fixed the lure
Over the pit should bury body and soul!

1360 His facts are lies: his letters are the fact –
An infiltration flavoured with himself!
As for the fancies – whether . . . what is it you say?
The lady loves me, whether I love her
In the forbidden sense of your surmise, –
If, with the midday blaze of truth above,
The unlidded eye of God awake, aware,
You needs must pry about and track the course
Of each stray beam of light may traverse earth,
To the night's sun and Lucifer himself,
1370 Do so, at other time, in other place,
Not now nor here! Enough that first to last
I never touched her lip nor she my hand
Nor either of us thought a thought, much less
Spoke a word which the Virgin might not hear.
Be that your question, thus I answer it.'

Then the court had to make its mind up, spoke.
'It is a thorny question, and a tale
Hard to believe, but not impossible:
Who can be absolute for either side?
1380 A middle course is happily open yet.
Here has a blot surprised the social blank, –
Whether through favour, feebleness or fault,
No matter, leprosy has touched our robe
And we're unclean and must be purified.
Here is a wife makes holiday from home,
A priest caught playing truant to his church,
In masquerade moreover: both allege
Enough excuse to stop our lifted scourge
Which else would heavily fall. On the other hand,
1390 Here is a husband, ay and man of mark,
Who comes complaining here, demands redress
As if he were the pattern of desert –
The while those plaguy allegations frown,
Forbid we grant him the redress he seeks.
To all men be our moderation known!
Rewarding none while compensating each,

Hurting all round though harming nobody,
Husband, wife, priest, scot-free not one shall 'scape,
Yet priest, wife, husband, boast the unbroken head
1400 From application of our excellent oil:
So that, whatever be the fact, in fine,
It makes no miss of justice in a sort.
First, let the husband stomach as he may,
His wife shall neither be returned him, no –
Nor branded, whipped and caged, but just consigned
To a convent and the quietude she craves;
So is he rid of his domestic plague:
What better thing can happen to a man?
Next, let the priest retire – unshent, unshamed,
1410 Unpunished as for perpetrating crime,
But relegated (not imprisoned, Sirs!)
Sent for three years to clarify his youth
At Civita, a rest by the way to Rome:
There let his life skim off its last of lees
Nor keep this dubious colour. Judged the cause:
All parties may retire, content, we hope.'
That's Rome's way, the traditional road of law;
Whither it leads is what remains to tell.

The priest went to his relegation-place,
1420 The wife to her convent, brother Paolo
To the arms of brother Guido with the news
And this beside – his charge was countercharged;
The Comparini, his old brace of hates,
Were breathed and vigilant and venomous now –
Has shot a second bolt where the first stuck,
And followed up the pending dowry-suit
By a procedure should release the wife
From so much of the marriage-bond as barred
Escape when Guido turned the screw too much
1430 On his wife's flesh and blood, as husband may.
No more defence, she turned and made attack,
Claimed now divorce from bed and board, in short:
Pleaded such subtle strokes of cruelty,

Such slow sure siege laid to her body and soul,
As, proved, – and proofs seemed coming thick and fast, –
Would gain both freedom and the dowry back
Even should the first suit leave them in his grasp:
So urged the Comparini for the wife.
Guido had gained not one of the good things
1440 He grasped at by his creditable plan
O' the flight and following and the rest: the suit
That smouldered late was fanned to fury new,
This adjunct came to help with fiercer fire,
While he had got himself a quite new plague –
Found the world's face an universal grin
At this last best of the Hundred Merry Tales
Of how a young and spritely clerk devised
To carry off a spouse that moped too much,
And cured her of the vapours in a trice:
1450 And how the husband, playing Vulcan's part,
Told by the Sun, started in hot pursuit
To catch the lovers, and came halting up,
Cast his net and then called the Gods to see
The convicts in their rosy impudence –
Whereat said Mercury 'Would that I were Mars!'
Oh it was rare, and naughty all the same!
Brief, the wife's courage and cunning, – the priest's show
Of chivalry and adroitness, – last not least,
The husband – how he ne'er showed teeth at all,
1460 Whose bark had promised biting; but just sneaked
Back to his kennel, tail 'twixt legs, as 't were, –
All this was hard to gulp down and digest.
So pays the devil his liegeman, brass for gold.
But this was at Arezzo: here in Rome
Brave Paolo bore up against it all –
Battled it out, nor wanting to himself
Nor Guido nor the House whose weight he bore
Pillar-like, not by force of arm but brain.
He knew his Rome, what wheels we set to work;
1470 Plied influential folk, pressed to the ear
Of the efficacious purple, pushed his way

To the old Pope's self, – past decency indeed, –
Praying him take the matter in his hands
Out of the regular court's incompetence;
But times are changed and nephews out of date
And favouritism unfashionable: the Pope
Said 'Render Caesar what is Caesar's due!'
As for the Comparini's counter-plea,
He met that by a counter-plea again,
1480 Made Guido claim divorce – with help so far
By the trial's issue: for, why punishment
However slight unless for guiltiness
However slender? – and a molehill serves
Much as a mountain of offence this way.
So was he gathering strength on every side
And growing more and more to menace – when
All of a terrible moment came the blow
That beat down Paolo's fence, ended the play
O' the foil and brought Mannaia on the stage.

1490 Five months had passed now since Pompilia's flight,
Months spent in peace among the Convert nuns:
This, – being, as it seemed, for Guido's sake
Solely, what pride might call imprisonment
And quote as something gained, to friends at home, –
This naturally was at Guido's charge:
Grudge it he might, but penitential fare,
Prayers, preachings, who but he defrayed the cost?
So, Paolo dropped, as proxy, doit by doit
Like heart's blood, till – what's here? What notice comes?
1500 The Convent's self makes application bland
That, since Pompilia's health is fast o' the wane,
She may have leave to go combine her cure
Of soul with cure of body, mend her mind
Together with her thin arms and sunk eyes
That want fresh air outside the convent-wall,
Say in a friendly house, – and which so fit
As a certain villa in the Pauline way,
That happens to hold Pietro and his wife,

The natural guardians? 'Oh, and shift the care
1510 You shift the cost, too; Pietro pays in turn,
And lightens Guido of a load! And then,
Villa or convent, two names for one thing,
Always the sojourn means imprisonment,
Domum pro carcere – nowise we relax,
Nothing abate: how answers Paolo?'

You,
What would you answer? All so smooth and fair,
Even Paul's astuteness sniffed no harm i' the world.
He authorised the transfer, saw it made
1520 And, two months after, reaped the fruit of the same,
Having to sit down, rack his brain and find
What phrase should serve him best to notify
Our Guido that by happy providence
A son and heir, a babe was born to him
I' the villa, – go tell sympathising friends!
Yes, such had been Pompilia's privilege:
She, when she fled, was one month gone with child,
Known to herself or unknown, either way
Availing to explain (say men of art)
1530 The strange and passionate precipitance
Of maiden startled into motherhood
Which changes body and soul by nature's law.
So when the she-dove breeds, strange yearnings come
For the unknown shelter by undreamed-of shores,
And there is born a blood-pulse in her heart
To fight if needs be, though with flap of wing,
For the wool-flock or the fur-tuft, though a hawk
Contest the prize, – wherefore, she knows not yet.
Anyhow, thus to Guido came the news.
1540 'I shall have quitted Rome ere you arrive
To take the one step left,' – wrote Paolo.
Then did the winch o' the winepress of all hate,
Vanity, disappointment, grudge and greed,
Take the last turn that screws out pure revenge
With a bright bubble at the brim beside –
By an heir's birth he was assured at once

O' the main prize, all the money in dispute:
Pompilia's dowry might revert to her
Or stay with him as law's caprice should point, –
1550 But now – now – what was Pietro's shall be hers,
What was hers shall remain her own, – if hers,
Why then,   oh, not her husband's but – her heir's!
That heir being his too, all grew his at last
By this road or by that road, since they join.
Before, why, push he Pietro out o' the world, –
The current of the money stopped, you see,
Pompilia being proved no Pietro's child:
Or let it be Pompilia's life he quenched,
Again the current of the money stopped, –
1560 Guido debarred his rights as husband soon,
So the new process threatened; – now, the chance,
Now, the resplendent minute! Clear the earth,
Cleanse the house, let the three but disappear
A child remains, depositary of all,
That Guido may enjoy his own again!
Repair all losses by a master-stroke,
Wipe out the past, all done and left undone,
Swell the good present to best evermore,
Die into new life, which let blood baptize!

1570 So, i' the blue of a sudden sulphur-blaze,
And why there was one step to take at Rome,
And why he should not meet with Paolo there,
He saw – the ins and outs to the heart of hell –
And took the straight line thither swift and sure.
He rushed to Vittiano, found four sons o' the soil,
Brutes of his breeding, with one spark i' the clod
That served for a soul, the looking up to him
Or aught called Franceschini as life, death,
Heaven, hell, – lord paramount, assembled these,
1580 Harangued, equipped, instructed, pressed each clod
With his will's imprint; then took horse, plied spur,
And so arrived, all five of them, at Rome
On Christmas-Eve, and forthwith found themselves

Installed i' the vacancy and solitude
Left them by Paolo, the considerate man
Who, good as his word, disappeared at once
As if to leave the stage free. A whole week
Did Guido spend in study of his part,
Then played it fearless of a failure. One,
1590 Struck the year's clock whereof the hours are days,
And off was rung o' the little wheels the chime
'Good will on earth and peace to man:' but, two,
Proceeded the same bell and, evening come,
The dreadful five felt finger-wise their way
Across the town by blind cuts and black turns
To the little lone suburban villa; knocked –
'Who may be outside?' called a well-known voice.
'A friend of Caponsacchi's bringing friends
A letter.'
       That's a test, the excusers say:
1600 Ay, and a test conclusive, I return.
What? Had that name brought touch of guilt or taste
Of fear with it, aught to dash the present joy
With memory of the sorrow just at end, –
She, happy in her parents' arms at length
With the new blessing of the two weeks' babe, –
How had that name's announcement moved the wife?
Or, as the other slanders circulate,
Were Caponsacchi no rare visitant
On nights and days whither safe harbour lured,
1610 What bait had been i' the name to ope the door?
The promise of a letter? Stealthy guests
Have secret watchwords, private entrances:
The man's own self might have been found inside
And all the scheme made frustrate by a word.
No: but since Guido knew, none knew so well,
The man had never since returned to Rome
Nor seen the wife's face more than villa's front,
So, could not be at hand to warn or save, –
For that, he took this sure way to the end.
1620 'Come in,' bade poor Violante cheerfully,

Drawing the door-bolt: that death was the first,
Stabbed through and through. Pietro, close on her heels,
Set up a cry – 'Let me confess myself!
Grant but confession!' Cold steel was the grant.
Then came Pompilia's turn.

       Then they escaped.
The noise o' the slaughter roused the neighbourhood.
They had forgotten just the one thing more
Which saves i' the circumstance, the ticket to-wit
1630 Which puts post-horses at a traveller's use:
So, all on foot, desperate through the dark
Reeled they like drunkards along open road,
Accomplished a prodigious twenty miles
Homeward, and gained Baccano very near,
Stumbled at last, deaf, dumb, blind through the feat,
Into a grange and, one dead heap, slept there
Till the pursuers hard upon their trace
Reached them and took them, red from head to heel,
And brought them to the prison where they lie.
1640 The couple were laid i' the church two days ago,
And the wife lives yet by miracle.

       All is told.
You hardly need ask what Count Guido says,
Since something he must say. 'I own the deed – '
(He cannot choose, – but) 'I declare the same
Just and inevitable, – since no way else
Was left me, but by this of taking life,
To save my honour which is more than life.
I exercised a husband's rights.' To which
1650 The answer is as prompt – 'There was no fault
In any one o' the three to punish thus:
Neither i' the wife, who kept all faith to you,
Nor in the parents, whom yourself first duped,
Robbed and maltreated, then turned out of doors.
You wronged and they endured wrong; yours the fault.
Next, had endurance overpassed the mark
And turned resentment needing remedy, –

Nay, put the absurd impossible case, for once –
You were all blameless of the blame alleged
1660 And they blameworthy where you fix all blame,
Still, why this violation of the law?
Yourself elected law should take its course,
Avenge wrong, or show vengeance not your right;
Why, only when the balance in law's hand
Trembles against you and inclines the way
O' the other party, do you make protest,
Renounce arbitrament, flying out of court,
And crying "Honour's hurt the sword must cure?"
Aha, and so i' the middle of each suit
1670 Trying i' the courts, – and you had three in play
With an appeal to the Pope's self beside, –
What, you may chop and change and right your wrongs
Leaving the law to lag as she thinks fit?'

That were too temptingly commodious, Count!
One would have still a remedy in reserve
Should reach the safest oldest sinner, you see!
One's honour forsooth? Does that take hurt alone
From the extreme outrage? I who have no wife,
Being yet sensitive in my degree
1680 As Guido, – must discover hurt elsewhere
Which, half compounded-for in days gone by,
May profitably break out now afresh,
Need cure from my own expeditious hands.
The lie that was, as it were, imputed me
When you objected to my contract's clause, –
The theft as good as, one may say, alleged,
When you, co-heir in a will, excepted, Sir,
To my administration of effects,
– Aha, do you think law disposed of these?
1690 My honour's touched and shall deal death around!
Count, that were too commodious, I repeat!
If any law be imperative on us all,
Of all are you the enemy: out with you
From the common light and air and life of man!

BOOK IV

Tertium Quid

True, Excellency – as his Highness says,
Though she's not dead yet, she's as good as stretched
Symmetrical beside the other two;
Though he's not judged yet, he's the same as judged,
So do the facts abound and superabound:
And nothing hinders, now, we lift the case
Out of the shade into the shine, allow
Qualified persons to pronounce at last,
Nay, edge in an authoritative word
10 Between this rabble's-brabble of dolts and fools
Who make up reasonless unreasoning Rome.
'Now for the Trial!' they roar: 'the Trial to test
The truth, weigh husband and weigh wife alike
I' the scales of law, make one scale kick the beam!'
Law's a machine from which, to please the mob,
Truth the divinity must needs descend
And clear things at the play's fifth act – aha!
Hammer into their noddles who was who
And what was what. I tell the simpletons
20 'Could law be competent to such a feat
'T were done already: what begins next week
Is end o' the Trial, last link of a chain
Whereof the first was forged three years ago
When law addressed herself to set wrong right,
And proved so slow in taking the first step
That ever some new grievance, – tort, retort,
On one or the other side, – o'ertook i' the game,
Retarded sentence, till this deed of death
Is thrown in, as it were, last bale to boat
30 Crammed to the edge with cargo – or passengers?

"*Trecentos inseris: ohe, jam satis est!*
Huc appelle!" – passengers, the word must be.'
Long since, the boat was loaded to my eyes.
To hear the rabble and brabble, you'd call the case
Fused and confused past human finding out.
One calls the square round, t' other the round square –
And pardonably in that first surprise
O' the blood that fell and splashed the diagram:
But now we've used our eyes to the violent hue
40 Can't we look through the crimson and trace lines?
It makes a man despair of history,
Eusebius and the established fact – fig's end!
Oh, give the fools their Trial, rattle away
With the leash of lawyers, two on either side –
One barks, one bites, – Masters Arcangeli
And Spreti, – that's the husband's ultimate hope
Against the Fisc and the other kind of Fisc,
Bound to do barking for the wife: bow – wow!
Why, Excellency, we and his Highness here
50 Would settle the matter as sufficiently
As ever will Advocate This and Fiscal That
And Judge the Other, with even – a word and a wink –
We well know who for ultimate arbiter.
Let us beware o' the basset-table – lest
We jog the elbow of Her Eminence,
Jostle his cards, – he'll rap you out a . . . st !
By the window-seat! And here's the Marquis too!
Indulge me but a moment: if I fail
– Favoured with such an audience, understand! –
60 To set things right, why, class me with the mob
As understander of the mind of man!

The mob, – now, that's just how the error comes!
Bethink you that you have to deal with *plebs*,
The commonalty; this is an episode
In burgess-life, – why seek to aggrandize,
Idealize, denaturalize the class?
People talk just as if they had to do

With a noble pair that . . . Excellency, your ear!
Stoop to me, Highness, – listen and look yourselves!

70 This Pietro, this Violante, live their life
At Rome in the easy way that's far from worst
Even for their betters, – themselves love themselves,
Spend their own oil in feeding their own lamp
That their own faces may grow bright thereby.
They get to fifty and over: how's the lamp?
Full to the depth o' the wick, – moneys so much;
And also with a remnant, – so much more
Of moneys, – which there's no consuming now,
But, when the wick shall moulder out some day,
80 Failing fresh twist of tow to use up dregs,
Will lie a prize for the passer-by, – to-wit
Anyone that can prove himself the heir,
Seeing, the couple are wanting in a child:
Meantime their wick swims in the safe broad bowl
O' the middle rank, – not raised a beacon's height
For wind to ravage, nor swung till lamp graze ground
As watchman's cresset, he pokes here and there,
Going his rounds to probe the ruts i' the road
Or fish the luck o' the puddle. Pietro's soul
90 Was satisfied when crony smirked, 'No wine
Like Pietro's, and he drinks it every day!'
His wife's heart swelled her boddice, joyed its fill
When neighbours turned heads wistfully at church,
Sighed at the load of lace that came to pray.
Well, having got through fifty years of flare,
They burn out so, indulge so their dear selves,
That Pietro finds himself in debt at last,
As he were any lordling of us all:
And, for the dark begins to creep on day,
00 Creditors grow uneasy, talk aside,
Take counsel, then importune all at once.
For if the good fat rosy careless man,
Who has not laid a ducat by, decease –
Let the lamp fall, no heir at hand to catch –

Why, being childless, there's a spilth i' the street
O' the remnant, there's a scramble for the dregs
By the stranger: so, they grant him no long day
But come in a body, clamour to be paid.

What's his resource? He asks and straight obtains
110 The customary largess, dole dealt out
To, what we call our 'poor dear shame-faced ones,'
In secret once a month to spare the shame
O' the slothful and the spendthrift, – pauper-saints
The Pope puts meat i' the mouth of, ravens they,
And providence he – just what the mob admires!
That is, instead of putting a prompt foot
On selfish worthless human slugs whose slime
Has failed to lubricate their path in life,
Why, the Pope picks the first ripe fruit that falls
120 And gracious puts it in the vermin's way.
Pietro could never save a dollar? Straight
He must be subsidized at our expense:
And for his wife – the harmless household sheep
One ought not to see harassed in her age –
Judge, by the way she bore adversity,
O' the patient nature you ask pity for!
How long, now, would the roughest marketman,
Handling the creatures huddled to the knife,
Harass a mutton ere she made a mouth
130 Or menaced biting? Yet the poor sheep here,
Violante, the old innocent burgess-wife,
In her first difficulty showed great teeth
Fit to crunch up and swallow a good round crime.
She meditates the tenure of the Trust,
Fidei commissum is the lawyer-phrase,
These funds that only want an heir to take –
Goes o'er the gamut o' the creditor's cry
By semitones from whine to snarl high up
And growl down low, one scale in sundry keys, –
140 Pauses with a little compunction for the face
Of Pietro frustrate of its ancient cheer, —

Never a bottle now for friend at need, –
Comes to a stop on her own frittered lace
And neighbourly condolences thereat,
Then makes her mind up, sees the thing to do:
And so, deliberately snaps house-book clasp,
Posts off to vespers, missal beneath arm,
Passes the proper San Lorenzo by,
Dives down a little lane to the left, is lost
50 In a labyrinth of dwellings best unnamed,
Selects a certain blind one, black at base,
Blinking at top, – the sign of we know what, –
One candle in a casement set to wink
Streetward, do service to no shrine inside, –
Mounts thither by the filthy flight of stairs,
Holding the cord by the wall, to the tip-top,
Gropes for the door i' the dark, ajar of course,
Raps, opens, enters in: up starts a thing
Naked as needs be – 'What, you rogue, 't is you?
60 Back, – how can I have taken a farthing yet?
Mercy on me, poor sinner that I am!
Here's . . . why, I took you for Madonna's self
With all that sudden swirl of silk i' the place!
What may your pleasure be, my bonny dame?'
Your Excellency supplies aught left obscure?
One of those women that abound in Rome,
Whose needs oblige them eke out one poor trade
By another vile one: her ostensible work
Was washing clothes, out in the open air
170 At the cistern by Citorio; but true trade –
Whispering to idlers when they stopped and praised
The ancles she let liberally shine
In kneeling at the slab by the fountain-side,
That there was plenty more to criticise
At home, that eve, i' the house where candle blinked
Decorously above, and all was done
I' the holy fear of God and cheap beside.
Violante, now, had seen this woman wash,
Noticed and envied her propitious shape,

180 Tracked her home to her house-top, noted too,
And now was come to tempt her and propose
A bargain far more shameful than the first
Which trafficked her virginity away
For a melon and three pauls at twelve years old.
Five minutes' talk with this poor child of Eve,
Struck was the bargain, business at an end –
'Then, six months hence, that person whom you trust,
Comes, fetches whatsoever babe it be;
I keep the price and secret, you the babe,
190 Paying beside for mass to make all straight:
Meantime, I pouch the earnest-money-piece.'

Down stairs again goes fumbling by the rope
Violante, triumphing in a flourish of fire
From her own brain, self-lit by such success, –
Gains church in time for the '*Magnificat*'
And gives forth 'My reproof is taken away,
And blessed shall mankind proclaim me now,'
So that the officiating priest turns round
To see who proffers the obstreperous praise:
200 Then home to Pietro, the enraptured-much
But puzzled-more when told the wondrous news –
How orisons and works of charity,
(Beside that pair of pinners and a coif,
Birth-day surprise last Wednesday was five weeks)
Had borne fruit in the Autumn of his life, –
They, or the Orvieto in a double dose.
Anyhow, she must keep house next six months,
Lie on the settle, avoid the three-legged stool,
And, chiefly, not be crossed in wish or whim,
210 And the result was like to be an heir.

Accordingly, when time was come about,
He found himself the sire indeed of this
Francesca Vittoria Pompilia and the rest
O' the names whereby he sealed her his next day.
A crime complete in its way is here, I hope?

Lies to God, lies to man, every way lies
To nature and civility and the mode:
Flat robbery of the proper heirs thus foiled
O' the due succession, – and, what followed thence,
20   Robbery of God, through the confessor's ear
Debarred the most note-worthy incident
When all else done and undone twelve month through
Was put in evidence at Easter-time.
All other peccadillos! – but this one
To the priest who comes next day to dine with us?
'T were inexpedient; decency forbade.

Is so far clear? You know Violante now,
Compute her capability of crime
By this authentic instance? Black hard cold
30   Crime like a stone you kick up with your foot
I' the middle of a field?

                    I thought as much.
But now, a question, – how long does it lie,
The bad and barren bit of stuff you kick,
Before encroached on and encompassed round
With minute moss, weed, wild-flower – made alive
By worm, and fly, and foot of the free bird?
Your Highness, – healthy minds let bygones be,
Leave old crimes to grow young and virtuous-like
40   I' the sun and air; so time treats ugly deeds:
They take the natural blessing of all change.
There was the joy o' the husband silly-sooth,
The softening of the wife's old wicked heart,
Virtues to right and left, profusely paid
If so they might compensate the saved sin.
And then the sudden existence, dewy-dear,
O' the rose above the dungheap, the pure child
As good as new created, since withdrawn
From the horror of the pre-appointed lot
50   With the unknown father and the mother known
Too well, – some fourteen years of squalid youth,

And then libertinage, disease, the grave –
Hell in life here, hereafter life in hell:
Look at that horror and this soft repose!
Why, moralist, the sin has saved a soul!
Then, even the palpable grievance to the heirs –
'Faith, this was no frank setting hand to throat
And robbing a man, but . . . Excellency, by your leave,
How did you get that marvel of a gem,
260   The sapphire with the Graces grand and Greek?
The story is, stooping to pick a stone
From the pathway through a vineyard – no-man's-land –
To pelt a sparrow with, you chanced on this:
Why now, do those five clowns o' the family
O' the vinedresser digest their porridge worse
That not one keeps it in his goatskin pouch
To do flints'-service with the tinder-box?
Do n't cheat me, do n't cheat you, do n't cheat a friend!
But are you so hard on who jostles just
270   A stranger with no natural sort of claim
To the havings and the holdings (here's the point)
Unless by misadventure, and defect
Of that which ought to be – nay, which there's none
Would dare so much as wish to profit by –
Since who dares put in just so many words
'May Pietro fail to have a child, please God!
So shall his house and goods belong to me,
The sooner that his heart will pine betimes?'
Well then, God do n't please, nor his heart shall pine!
280   Because he has a child at last, you see,
Or selfsame thing as though a child it were,
He thinks, whose sole concern it is to think:
If he accepts it why should you demur?

Moreover, say that certain sin there seem,
The proper process of unsinning sin
Is to begin well-doing somehow else.
Pietro, – remember, with no sin at all
I' the substitution, – why, this gift of God

Flung in his lap from over Paradise
90 Steadied him in a moment, set him straight
On the good path he had been straying from.
Henceforward no more wilfulness and waste,
Cuppings, carousings, – these a sponge wiped out.
All sort of self-denial was easy now
For the child's sake, the chatelaine to be,
Who must want much and might want who knows what?
And so, the debts were paid, habits reformed,
Expense curtailed, the dowry set to grow.
As for the wife, – I said, hers the whole sin:
00 So, hers the exemplary penance. 'T was a text
Whereon folk preached and praised, the district through:
'Oh, make us happy and you make us good!
It all comes of God giving her a child:
Such graces follow God's best earthly gift!'

Here you put by my guard, pass to my heart
By the home-thrust – 'There's a lie at base of all.'
Why, thou exact Prince, is it a pearl or no,
Yon globe upon the Principessa's neck?
That great round glory of pellucid stuff,
10 A fish secreted round a grain of grit!
Do you call it worthless for the worthless core?
(She do n't, who well knows what she changed for it!)
So, to our brace of burgesses again!
You see so far i' the story, who was right,
Who wrong, who neither, do n't you? What, you do n't?
Eh? Well, admit there's somewhat dark i' the case,
Let's on – the rest shall clear, I promise you.
Leap over a dozen years: you find, these passed,
An old good easy creditable sire,
20 A careful housewife's beaming bustling face,
Both wrapped up in the love of their one child,
The strange tall pale beautiful creature grown
Lily-like out o' the cleft i' the sun-smit rock
To bow its white miraculous birth of buds
I' the way of wandering Joseph and his spouse, –

So painters fancy: here it was a fact.
And this their lily, – could they but transplant
And set in vase to stand by Solomon's porch
'Twixt lion and lion! – this Pompilia of theirs,
330 Could they see worthily married, well bestowed
In house and home! And why despair of this
With Rome to choose from, save the topmost rank?
Themselves would help the choice with heart and soul,
Throw their late savings in a common heap
Should go with the dowry, to be followed in time
By the heritage legitimately hers:
And when such paragon was found and fixed,
Why, they might chant their 'Nunc dimittas' straight.

Indeed the prize was simply full to a fault;
340 Exorbitant for the suitor they should seek,
And social class to choose among, these cits.
Yet there's a latitude: exceptional white
Amid the general brown o' the species, lurks
A burgess nearly an aristocrat,
Legitimately in reach: look out for him!
What banker, merchant, has seen better days,
What second-rate painter a-pushing up,
Poet a-slipping down, shall bid the best
For this young beauty with the thumping purse?
350 Alack, had it been but one of such as these
So like the real thing they may pass for it,
All had gone well! Unluckily fate must needs
It proved to be the impossible thing itself;
The truth and not the sham: hence ruin to them all.

For, Guido Franceschini was the head
Of an old family in Arezzo, old
To that degree they could afford be poor
Better than most: the case is common too.
Out of the vast door 'scutcheoned overhead,
360 Creeps out a serving-man on Saturdays
To cater for the week, – turns up anon

I' the market, chaffering for the lamb's least leg,
Or the quarter-fowl, less entrails, claws and comb:
Then back again with prize, – a liver begged
Into the bargain, gizzard overlooked, –
He's mincing these to give the beans a taste,
When, at your knock, he leaves the simmering soup,
Waits on the curious stranger-visitant,
Napkin in half-wiped hand, to show the rooms,
370 Point pictures out have hung their hundred years,
'Priceless,' he tells you, – puts in his place at once
The man of money: yes, you're banker-king
Or merchant-kaiser, wallow in your wealth
While patron, the house-master, can't afford
To stop our ceiling-hole that rain so rots –
But he's the man of mark, and there's his shield,
And yonder's the famed Rafael, first in kind,
The painter painted for his grandfather –
You have paid a paul to see: 'Good morning, Sir!'
380 Such is the law of compensation. Here
The poverty was getting too acute;
There gaped so many noble mouths to feed,
Beans must suffice unflavoured of the fowl.
The mother, – hers would be a spun-out life
I' the nature of things; the sisters had done well
And married men of reasonable rank:
But that sort of illumination stops,
Throws back no heat upon the parent-hearth.
The family instinct felt out for its fire
390 To the Church, – the Church traditionally helps
A second son: and such was Paolo,
Established here at Rome these thirty years,
Who played the regular game, – priest and Abate,
Made friends, owned house and land, became of use
To a personage: his course lay clear enough.
The youngest caught the sympathetic flame,
And, though unfledged wings kept him still i' the cage,
Yet he shot up to be a Canon, so
Clung to the higher perch and crowed in hope.

400 Even our Guido, eldest brother, went
As far i' the way o' the Church as safety seemed,
He being Head o' the House, ordained to wive, ⌐
So, could but dally with an Order or two
And testify good-will i' the cause: he clipt
His top-hair and thus far affected Christ,
But main promotion must fall otherwise,
Though still from the side o' the Church: and here was he
At Rome, since first youth, worn threadbare of soul
By forty-six years' rubbing on hard life,
410 Getting fast tired o' the game whose word is – 'Wait!'
When one day, – he too having his Cardinal
To serve in some ambiguous sort, as serve
To draw the coach the plumes o' the horses' heads, –
The Cardinal saw fit to dispense with him,
Ride with one plume the less; and off it dropped.

Guido thus left, – with a youth spent in vain
And not a penny in purse to show for it,
Advised with Paolo, bent no doubt in chafe
The black brows somewhat formidably the while.
420 'Where is the good I came to get at Rome?
Where the repayment of the servitude
To a purple popinjay, whose feet I kiss,
Knowing his father wiped the shoes of mine?'

'Patience,' pats Paolo the recalcitrant –
'You have not had, so far, the proper luck,
Nor do my gains suffice to keep us both:
A modest competency is mine, not more.
You are the Count however, yours the style,
Heirdom and state, – you can't expect all good.
430 Had I, now, held your hand of cards ... well, well –
What's yet unplayed, I'll look at, by your leave,
Over your shoulder, – I who made my game,
Let's see, if I can't help to handle yours.
Fie on you, all the Honours in your fist,
Countship, Househeadship, – how have you misdealt!

Why, in the first place, they will marry a man!
Notum tonsoribus! To the Tonsor then!
Come, clear your looks, and choose your freshest suit,
And, after function's done with, down we go
440 To the woman-dealer in perukes, a wench
I and some others settled in the shop
At Place Colonna: she's an oracle. Hmm!
"Dear, 'tis my brother: brother, 'tis my dear.
Dear, give us counsel! Whom do you suggest
As properest party in the quarter round,
For the Count here? – he is minded to take wife,
And further tells me he intends to slip
Twenty zecchines under the bottom-scalp
Of his old wig when he sends it to revive
450 For the wedding: and I add a trifle too.
You know what personage I'm potent with." '
And so plumped out Pompilia's name the first.
She told them of the household and its ways,
The easy husband and the shrewder wife
In Via Vittoria, – how the tall young girl,
With hair black as yon patch and eyes as big
As yon pomander to make freckles fly,
Would have so much for certain, and so much more
In likelihood, – why, it suited, slipt as smooth
460 As the Pope's pantoufle does on the Pope's foot.
'I'll to the husband!' Guido ups and cries.
'Ay, so you'd play your last court-card, no doubt!'
Puts Paolo in with a groan – 'Only, you see,
'Tis I, this time, that supervise your lead.
Priests play with women, maids, wives, mothers, – why?
These play with men and take them off our hands.
Did I come, counsel with some cut-beard gruff
Or rather this sleek young-old barberess?
Go, brother, stand you rapt in the ante-room
470 Of Her Efficacity my Cardinal
For an hour, – he likes to have lord-suitors lounge, –
While I betake myself to the grey mare,
The better horse, – how wise the people's word! –

And wait on Madam Violante.'
                                   Said and done.
He was at Via Vittoria in three skips:
Proposed at once to fill up the one want
O' the burgess-family which, wealthy enough,
And comfortable to heart's desire, yet crouched
480   Outside a gate to heaven, – locked, bolted, barred,
Whereof Count Guido had a key he kept
Under his pillow, but Pompilia's hand
Might slide behind his neck and pilfer thence.
The key was fairy; mention of it, made
Violante feel the thing shoot one sharp ray
That reached the heart o' the woman. 'I assent:
Yours be Pompilia, hers and ours that key
To all the glories of the greater life!
There's Pietro to convince: leave that to me!'

490   Then was the matter broached to Pietro; then
Did Pietro make demand and get response
That in the Countship was a truth, but in
The counting up of the Count's cash, a lie:
He thereupon stroked grave his chin, looked great,
Declined the honour. Then the wife wiped one –
Winked with the other eye turned Paolo-ward,
Whispered Pompilia, stole to church at eve,
Found Guido there and got the marriage done,
And finally begged pardon at the feet
500   Of her dear lord and master. Whereupon
Quoth Pietro – 'Let us make the best of things!'
'I knew your love would licence us,' quoth she:
Quoth Paolo once more, 'Mothers, wives and maids,
These be the tools wherewith priests manage men.'

Now, here take breath and ask, – which bird o' the brace
Decoyed the other into clapnet? Who
Was fool, who knave? Neither and both, perchance.
There was a bargain mentally proposed
On each side, straight and plain and fair enough;

510 Mind knew its own mind: but when mind must speak,
    The bargain have expression in plain terms,
    There was the blunder incident to words,
    And in the clumsy process, fair turned foul.
    The straight backbone-thought of the crooked speech
    Were just – 'I Guido truck my name and rank
    For so much money and youth and female charms.' –
    'We Pietro and Violante give our child
    And wealth to you for a rise i' the world thereby.'
    Such naked truth while chambered in the brain
520 Shocks nowise: walk it forth by way of tongue, –
    Out on the cynical unseemliness!
    Hence was the need, on either side, of a lie
    To serve as decent wrappage: so, Guido gives
    Money for money, – and they, bride for groom,
    Having, he, not a doit, they, not a child
    Honestly theirs, but this poor waif and stray.
    According to the words, each cheated each;
    But in the inexpressive barter of thoughts,
    Each did give and did take the thing designed,
530 The rank on this side and the cash on that –
    Attained the object of the traffic, so.
    The way of the world, the daily bargain struck
    In the first market! Why sells Jack his ware?
    'For the sake of serving an old customer.'
    Why does Jill buy it? 'Simply not to break
    A custom, pass the old stall the first time.'
    Why, you know where the gist is of the exchange:
    Each sees a profit, throws the fine words in.
    Don't be too hard o' the pair! Had each pretence
540 Been simultaneously discovered, stripped
    From off the body o' the transaction, just
    As when a cook ... will Excellency forgive?
    Strips away those long loose superfluous legs
    From either side the crayfish, leaving folk
    A meal all meat henceforth, no garnishry,
    (With your respect, Prince!) – balance had been kept,
    No party blamed the other, – so, starting fair,

All subsequent fence of wrong returned by wrong
I' the matrimonial thrust and parry, at least
550 Had followed on equal terms. But, as it chanced,
One party had the advantage, saw the cheat
Of the other first and kept its own concealed:
And the luck o' the first discovery fell, beside,
To the least adroit and self-possessed o' the pair.
'Twas foolish Pietro and his wife saw first
The nobleman was penniless, and screamed
'We are cheated!'

          Such unprofitable noise
Angers at all times: but when those who plague,
560 Do it from inside your own house and home,
Gnats which yourself have closed the curtain round,
Noise goes too near the brain and makes you mad.
The gnats say, Guido used the candle-flame
Unfairly, – worsened that first bad of his,
By practise of all kind of cruelty
To oust them and suppress the wail and whine, –
That speedily he so scared and bullied them,
Fain were they, long before five months were out,
To beg him grant, from what was once their wealth,
570 Just so much as would help them back to Rome
Where, when they had finished paying the last doit
O' the dowry, they might beg from door to door.
So say the Comparini – as if it were
In pure resentment for this worse than bad,
That then Violante, feeling conscience prick,
Confessed her substitution of the child
Whence all the harm came, – and that Pietro first
Bethought him of advantage to himself
I' the deed, as part revenge, part remedy
580 For all miscalculation in the pact.

On the other hand 'Not so!' Guido retorts –
'I am the wronged, solely, from first to last,
Who gave the dignity I engaged to give,

Which was, is, cannot but continue gain.
My being poor was a bye-circumstance,
Miscalculated piece of untowardness,
Might end to-morrow did heaven's windows ope,
Or uncle die and leave me his estate.
You should have put up with the minor flaw,
590 Getting the main prize of the jewel. If wealth,
Not rank, had been prime object in your thoughts,
Why not have taken the butcher's son, the boy
O' the baker or candlestick-maker? In all the rest,
It was yourselves broke compact and played false,
And made a life in common impossible.
Show me the stipulation of our bond
That you should make your profit of being inside
My house, to hustle and edge me out o' the same,
First make a laughing-stock of mine and me,
600 Then round us in the ears from morn to night
(Because we show wry faces at your mirth)
That you are robbed, starved, beaten and what not!
You fled a hell of your own lighting-up,
Pay for your own miscalculation too:
You thought nobility, gained at any price,
Would suit and satisfy, – find the mistake,
And now retaliate, not on yourselves, but me.
And how? By telling me, i' the face of the world,
I it is have been cheated all this while,
610 Abominably and irreparably, – my name
Given to a cur-cast mongrel, a drab's brat,
A beggar's bye-blow, – thus depriving me
Of what yourselves allege the whole and sole
Aim on my part i' the marriage, – money to-wit.
This thrust I have to parry by a guard
Which leaves me open to a counter-thrust
On the other side, – no way but there's a pass
Clean through me. If I prove, as I hope to do,
There's not one truth in this your odious tale
620 O' the buying, selling, substituting – prove
Your daughter was and is your daughter, – well,

And her dowry hers and therefore mine, – what then?
Why, where's the appropriate punishment for this
Enormous lie hatched for mere malice' sake
To ruin me? Is that a wrong or no?
And if I try revenge for remedy,
Can I well make it strong and bitter enough?'

I anticipate however – only ask,
Which of the two here sinned most? A nice point!
630   Which brownness is least black, – decide who can,
Wager-by-battle-of-cheating! What do you say,
Highness? Suppose, your Excellency, we leave
The question at this stage, proceed to the next,
Both parties step out, fight their prize upon,
In the eye o' the world?

                    They brandish law 'gainst law;
The grinding of such blades, each parry of each,
Throws terrible sparks off, over and above the thrusts,
And makes more sinister the fight, to the eye,
640   Than the very wounds that follow. Beside the tale
Which the Comparini have to re-assert,
They needs must write, print, publish all abroad
The straitnesses of Guido's household life –
The petty nothings we bear privately
But break down under when fools flock around.
What is it all to the facts o' the couple's case,
How helps it prove Pompilia not their child,
If Guido's mother, brother, kith and kin
Fare ill, lie hard, lack clothes, lack fire, lack food?
650   That's one more wrong than needs.

                              On the other hand,
Guido, – whose cue is to dispute the truth
O' the tale, reject the shame it throws on him, –
He may retaliate, fight his foe in turn
And welcome, we allow. Ay, but he can't!
He's at home, only acts by proxy here:

Law may meet law, – but all the gibes and jeers,
The superfluity of naughtiness,
Those libels on his House, – how reach at them?
660 Two hateful faces, grinning all a-glow,
Not only make parade of spoil they filched,
But foul him from the height of a tower, you see.
Unluckily temptation is at hand –
To take revenge on a trifle overlooked,
A pet lamb they have left in reach outside,
Whose first bleat, when he plucks the wool away,
Will strike the grinners grave: his wife remains
Who, four months earlier, some thirteen years old,
Never a mile away from mother's house
670 And petted to the height of her desire,
Was told one morning that her fate was come,
She must be married – just as, a month before,
Her mother told her she must comb her hair
And twist her curls into one knot behind.
These fools forgot their pet lamb, fed with flowers,
Then 'ticed as usual by the bit of cake,
Out of the bower into the butchery.
Plague her, he plagues them threefold: but how plague?
The world may have its word to say to that:
680 You can't do some things with impunity.
What remains . . . well, it is an ugly thought . . .
But that he drive herself to plague herself –
Herself disgrace herself and so disgrace
Who seek to disgrace Guido?

                              There's the clue
To what else seems gratuitously vile,
If, as is said, from this time forth the rack
Was tried upon Pompilia: 't was to wrench
Her limbs into exposure that brings shame.
690 The aim o' the cruelty being so crueller still,
That cruelty almost grows compassion's self
Could one attribute it to mere return
O' the parents' outrage, wrong avenging wrong.

They see in this a deeper deadlier aim,
Not to vex just a body they held dear,
But blacken too a soul they boasted white,
And show the world their saint in a lover's arms,
No matter how driven thither, – so they say.

On the other hand, so much is easily said,
700 And Guido lacks not an apologist.
The pair had nobody but themselves to blame,
Being selfish beasts throughout, no less, no more:
– Cared for themselves, their supposed good, nought else,
And brought about the marriage; good proved bad,
As little they cared for her its victim – nay,
Meant she should stay behind and take the chance,
If haply they might wriggle themselves free.
They baited their own hook to catch a fish
With this poor worm, failed o' the prize, and then
710 Sought how to unbait tackle, let worm float
Or sink, amuse the monster while they 'scaped.
Under the best stars Hymen brings above,
Had all been honesty on either side,
A common sincere effort to good end,
Still, this would prove a difficult problem, Prince!
– Given, a fair wife, aged thirteen years,
A husband poor, care-bitten, sorrow-sunk,
Little, long-nosed, bush-bearded, lantern-jawed,
Forty-six-years full, – place the two grown one,
720 She, cut off sheer from every natural aid,
In a strange town with no familiar face –
He, in his own parade-ground or retreat
As need were, free from challenge, much less check
To an irritated, disappointed will –
How evolve happiness from such a match?
'T were hard to serve up a congenial dish
Out of these ill-agreeing morsels, Duke,
By the best exercise of the cook's craft,
Best interspersion of spice, salt and sweet!
730 But let two ghastly scullions concoct mess

With brimstone, pitch, vitriol and devil's-dung –
Throw in abuse o' the man, his body and soul,
Kith, kin and generation, shake all slab
At Rome, Arezzo, for the world to nose,
Then end by publishing, for fiend's arch-prank,
That, over and above sauce to the meat's self,
Why, even the meat, bedevilled thus in dish,
Was never a pheasant but a carrion-crow –
Prince, what will then the natural loathing be?
740 What wonder if this? – the compound plague o' the pair
Pricked Guido, – not to take the course they hoped,
That is, submit him to their statement's truth,
Accept its obvious promise of relief,
And thrust them out of doors the girl again
Since the girl's dowry would not enter there,
– Quit of the one if baulked of the other: no!
Rather did rage and hate so work in him,
Their product proved the horrible conceit
That he should plot and plan and bring to pass
750 His wife might, of her own free will and deed,
Relieve him of her presence, get her gone,
And yet leave all the dowry safe behind,
Confirmed his own henceforward past dispute,
While blotting out, as by a belch of hell,
Their triumph in her misery and death.

You see, the man was Aretine, had touch
O' the subtle air that breeds the subtle wit;
Was noble too, of old blood thrice-refined
That shrinks from clownish coarseness in disgust:
760 Allow that such an one may take revenge,
You do n't expect he'll catch up stone and fling,
Or try cross-buttock, or whirl quarter-staff?
Instead of the honest drubbing clowns bestow,
When out of temper at the dinner spoilt,
On meddling mother-in-law and tiresome wife, –
Substitute for the clown a nobleman,
And you have Guido, practising, 't is said,

Unmitigably from the very first,
The finer vengeance: this, they say, the fact
770 O' the famous letter shows – the writing traced
At Guido's instance by the timid wife
Over the pencilled words himself writ first –
Wherein she, who could neither write nor read,
Was made unblushingly declare a tale
To the brother, the Abate then in Rome,
How her putative parents had impressed,
On their departure, their enjoinment; bade
'We being safely arrived here, follow, you!
Poison your husband, rob, set fire to all,
780 And then by means o' the gallant you procure
With ease, by helpful eye and ready tongue,
The brave youth ready to dare, do and die,
You shall run off and merrily reach Rome
Where we may live like flies in honey-pot:' –
Such being exact the programme of the course
Imputed her as carried to effect.

They also say, – to keep her straight therein,
All sort of torture was piled, pain on pain,
On either side Pompilia's path of life,
790 Built round about and over against by fear,
Circumvallated month by month, and week
By week, and day by day, and hour by hour,
Close, closer and yet closer still with pain,
No outlet from the encroaching pain save just
Where stood one saviour like a piece of heaven,
Hell's arms would strain round but for this blue gap.
She, they say further, first tried every chink,
Every imaginable break i' the fire,
As way of escape: ran to the Commissary,
800 Who bade her not malign his friend her spouse;
Flung herself thrice at the Archbishop's feet,
Where three times the Archbishop let her lie,
Spend her whole sorrow and sob full heart forth,
And then took up the slight load from the ground

And bore it back for husband to chastise, –
Mildly of course, – but natural right is right.
So went she slipping ever yet catching at help,
Missing the high till come to lowest and last,
No more than a certain friar of mean degree,
Who heard her story in confession, wept,
Crossed himself, showed the man within the monk.
'Then, will you save me, you the one i' the world?
I cannot even write my woes, nor put
My prayer for help in words a friend may read, –
I no more own a coin than have an hour
Free of observance, – I was watched to church,
Am watched now, shall be watched back presently, –
How buy the skill of scribe i' the market-place?
Pray you, write down and send whatever I say
O' the need I have my parents take me hence!'
The good man rubbed his eyes and could not choose –
Let her dictate her letter in such a sense
That parents, to save breaking down a wall,
Might lift her over: she went back, heaven in her heart.
Then the good man took counsel of his couch,
Woke and thought twice, the second thought the best:
'Here am I, foolish body that I be,
Caught all but pushing, teaching, who but I,
My betters their plain duty, – what, I dare
Help a case the Archbishop would not help,
Mend matters, peradventure, God loves mar?
What hath the married life but strifes and plagues
For proper dispensation? So a fool
Once touched the ark, – poor Hophni that I am!
Oh married ones, much rather should I bid,
In patience all of ye possess your souls!
This life is brief and troubles die with it:
Where were the prick to soar up homeward else?'
So saying, he burnt the letter he had writ,
Said *Ave* for her intention, in its place,
Took snuff and comfort, and had done with all.
Then the grim arms stretched yet a little more

And each touched each, all but one streak i' the midst,
Whereat stood Caponsacchi, who cried, 'This way,
Out by me! Hesitate one moment more
And the fire shuts out me and shuts in you!
Here my hand holds you life out!' Whereupon
She clasped the hand, which closed on hers and drew
Pompilia out o' the circle now complete.
850 Whose fault or shame but Guido's? – ask her friends.

But then this is the wife's – Pompilia's tale –
Eve's . . . no, not Eve's, since Eve, to speak the truth,
Was hardly fallen (our candour might pronounce)
So much of paradisal nature, Eve's,
When simply saying in her own defence
'The serpent tempted me and I did eat.'
Her daughters ever since prefer to urge
'Adam so starved me I was fain accept
The apple any serpent pushed my way.'
860 What an elaborate theory have we here,
Ingeniously nursed up, pretentiously
Brought forth, pushed forward amid trumpet-blast,
To account for the thawing of an icicle,
Show us there needed Etna vomit flame
Ere run the chrystal into dew-drops! Else,
How, unless hell broke loose to cause the step,
How could a married lady go astray?
Bless the fools! And 't is just this way they are blessed,
And the world wags still, – because fools are sure
870 – Oh, not of my wife nor your daughter! No!
But of their own: the case is altered quite.
Look now, – last week, the lady we all love, –
Daughter o' the couple we all venerate,
Wife of the husband we all cap before,
Mother o' the babes we all breathe blessings on, –
Was caught in converse with a negro page.
Hell thawed that icicle, else 'Why was it –
Why?' asked and echoed the fools. 'Because, you fools, –'
So did the dame's self answer, she who could,

With that fine candour only forthcoming
When 't is no odds whether withheld or no –
'Because my husband was the saint you say,
And, – with that childish goodness, absurd faith,
Stupid self-satisfaction, you so praise, –
Saint to you, insupportable to me.
Had he, – instead of calling me fine names,
Lucretia and Susanna and so forth,
And curtaining Correggio carefully
Lest I be taught that Leda had two legs, –
– But once never so little tweaked my nose
For peeping through my fan at Carnival,
Confessing thereby "I have no easy task –
I need use all my powers to hold you mine,
And then, – why 't is so doubtful if they serve,
That – take this, as an earnest of despair!"
Why, we were quits – I had wiped the harm away,
Thought "The man fears me!" and foregone revenge.'
We must not want all this elaborate work
To solve the problem why young fancy-and-flesh
Slips from the dull side of a spouse in years,
Betakes it to the breast of brisk-and-bold
Whose love-scrapes furnish talk for all the town!

Accordingly, one word on the other side
Tips over the piled-up fabric of a tale.
Guido says – that is, always, his friends say –
It is unlikely from the wickedness,
That any man treat any woman so.
The letter in question was her very own,
Unprompted and unaided: she could write –
As able to write as ready to sin, or free,
When there was danger, to deny both facts.
He bids you mark, herself from first to last
Attributes all the so-styled torture just
To jealousy, – jealousy of whom but just
This very Caponsacchi! How suits here
This with the other alleged motive, Prince?

Would Guido make a terror of the man
He meant should tempt the woman, as they charge?
Do you fright your hare that you may catch your hare?
920　Consider too, the charge was made and met
At the proper time and place where proofs were plain –
Heard patiently and disposed of thoroughly
By the highest powers, possessors of most light,
The Governor, for the law, and the Archbishop
For the gospel: which acknowledged primacies,
'T is impudently pleaded, he could warp
Into a tacit partnership with crime –
He being the while, believe their own account,
Impotent, penniless and miserable!
930　He further asks – Duke, note the knotty point! –
How he, – concede him skill to play such part
And drive his wife into a gallant's arms, –
Could bring the gallant to play his part too
And stand with arms so opportunely wide?
How bring this Caponsacchi, – with whom, friends
And foes alike agree, throughout his life
He never interchanged a civil word
Nor lifted courteous cap to – how bend him,
To such observancy of beck and call,
940　– To undertake this strange and perilous feat
For the good of Guido, using, as the lure,
Pompilia whom, himself and she avouch,
He had nor spoken with nor seen, indeed,
Beyond sight in a public theatre,
When she wrote letters (she that could not write!)
The importunate shamelessly-protested love
Which brought him, though reluctant, to her feet,
And forced on him the plunge which, howsoe'er
She might swim up i' the whirl, must bury him
950　Under abysmal black: a priest contrive
No mitigable amour to be hushed up,
But open flight and noon-day infamy?
Try and concoct defence for such revolt!
Take the wife's tale as true, say she was wronged, –

Pray, in what rubric of the breviary
Do you find it registered the part of a priest
That to right wrongs he skip from the church-door,
Go journeying with a woman that's a wife,
And be pursued, o'ertaken and captured ... how?
In a lay-dress, playing the sentinel
Where the wife sleeps (says he who best should know)
And sleeping, sleepless, both have spent the night!
Could no one else be found to serve at need –
No woman – or if man, no safer sort
Than this not well-reputed turbulence?

Then, look into his own account o' the case!
He, being the stranger and astonished one,
Yet received protestations of her love
From lady neither known nor cared about:
Love, so protested, bred in him disgust
After the wonder, – or incredulity,
Such impudence seeming impossible.
But, soon assured such impudence might be,
When he had seen with his own eyes at last
Letters thrown down to him i' the very street
From behind lattice where the lady lurked,
And read their passionate summons to her side –
Why then, a thousand thoughts swarmed up and in, –
How he had seen her once, a moment's space,
Observed she was so young and beautiful,
Heard everywhere report she suffered much
From a jealous husband thrice her age, – in short
There flashed the propriety, expediency
Of treating, trying might they come to terms,
– At all events, granting the interview
Prayed for, and so adapted to assist
Decision as to whether he advance,
Stand or retire, in his benevolent mood.
Therefore the interview befell at length;
And at this one and only interview,
He saw the sole and single course to take –

Bade her dispose of him, head, heart and hand,
Did her behest and braved the consequence,
Not for the natural end, the love of man
For woman whether love be virtue or vice,
But, please you, altogether for pity's sake –
Pity of innocence and helplessness!
And how did he assure himself of both?
Had he been the house-inmate, visitor,
1000 Eye-witness of the described martyrdom,
So, competent to pronounce its remedy
Ere rush on such extreme and desperate course,
Involving such enormity of harm,
Moreover, to the husband judged thus, doomed
And damned without a word in his defence?
But no, – the truth was felt by instinct here!
– Process which saves a world of trouble and time,
And there's his story: what do you say to it,
Trying its truth by your own instinct too,
1010 Since that's to be the expeditious mode?
'And now, do hear my version,' Guido cries:
'I accept argument and inference both.
It would indeed have been miraculous
Had such a confidency sprung to birth
With no more fanning from acquaintanceship
Than here avowed by my wife and this priest.
Only, it did not: you must substitute
The old stale unromantic way of fault,
The commonplace adventure, mere intrigue
1020 In the prose form with the unpoetic tricks,
Cheatings and lies: they used the hackney chair
Satan jaunts forth with, shabby and serviceable,
No gilded jimcrack-novelty from below,
To bowl you along thither, swift and sure.
That same officious go-between, the wench
That gave and took the letters of the two,
Now offers self and service back to me:
Bears testimony to visits night by night
When all was safe, the husband far and away, –

1030 To many a timely slipping out at large
By light o' the morning-star, ere he should wake.
And when the fugitives were found at last,
Why, with them were found also, to belie
What protest they might make of innocence,
All documents yet wanting, if need were,
To establish guilt in them, disgrace in me –
The chronicle o' the converse from its rise
To culmination in this outrage: read!
Letters from wife to priest, from priest to wife, –
1040 Here they are, read and say where they chime in
With the other tale, superlative purity
O' the pair of saints! I stand or fall by these.'

But then on the other side again, – how say
The pair of saints? That not one word is theirs –
No syllable o' the batch or writ or sent
Or yet received by either of the two.
'Found,' says the priest, 'because he needed them,
Failing all other proofs, to prove our fault:
So, here they are, just as is natural.
1050 Oh yes – we had our missives, each of us!
Not these, but to the full as vile, no doubt:
Hers as from me, – she could not read, so burnt, –
Mine as from her, – I burnt because I read.
Who forged and found them? *Cui profuerint!*'
(I take the phrase out of your Highness' mouth)
'He who would gain by her fault and my fall,
The trickster, schemer and pretender – he
Whose whole career was lie entailing lie
Sought to be sealed truth by the worst lie last!'

1060 Guido rejoins – 'Did the other end o' the tale
Match this beginning! 'Tis alleged I prove
A murderer at the end, a man of force
Prompt, indiscriminate, effectual: good!
Then what need all this trifling woman's-work,
Letters and embassies and weak intrigue,

When will and power were mine to end at once
Safely and surely? Murder had come first
Not last with such a man, assure yourselves!
The silent *acquetta*, stilling at command –
1070 A drop a day i' the wine or soup, the dose, –
The shattering beam that breaks above the bed
And beats out brains, with nobody to blame
Except the wormy age which eats even oak, –
Nay, the staunch steel or trusty cord, – who cares
I' the blind old palace, a pitfall at each step,
With none to see, much more to interpose
O' the two, three creeping house-dog-servant-things
Born mine and bred mine? – had I willed gross death,
I had found nearer paths to thrust him prey
1080 Than this that goes meandering here and there
Through half the world and calls down in its course
Notice and noise, – hate, vengeance, should it fail,
Derision and contempt though it succeed!
Moreover, what o' the future son and heir?
The unborn babe about to be called mine, –
What end in heaping all this shame on him,
Were I indifferent to my own black share?
Would I have tried these crookednesses, say,
Willing and able to effect the straight?'

1090 'Ay, would you!' – one may hear the priest retort,
'Being as you are, i' the stock, a man of guile,
And ruffianism but an added graft.
You, a born coward, try a coward's arms,
Trick and chicane, – and only when these fail
Does violence follow, and like fox you bite
Caught out in stealing. Also, the disgrace
You hardly shrunk at, wholly shrivelled her:
You plunged her thin white delicate hand i' the flame
Along with your coarse horny brutish fist,
1100 Held them a second there, then drew out both
– Yours roughed a little, hers ruined through and through.
Your hurt would heal forthwith at ointment's touch –

Namely, succession to the inheritance
Which bolder crime had lost you: let things change,
The birth o' the boy warrant the bolder crime,
Why, murder was determined, dared and done.
For me,' the priest proceeds with his reply,
'The look o' the thing, the chances of mistake,
All were against me, – that, I knew the first:
110 But, knowing also what my duty was,
I did it: I must look to men more skilled
I' the reading hearts than ever was the world.'

Highness, decide! Pronounce, Her Excellency!
Or . . . even leave this argument in doubt,
Account it a fit matter, taken up
With all its faces, manifold enough,
To put upon – what fronts us, the next stage,
Next legal process! – Guido, in pursuit,
Coming up with the fugitives at the inn,
120 Caused both to be arrested then and there
And sent to Rome for judgment on the case –
Thither, with all his armoury of proofs
Betook himself, and there we'll meet him now,
Waiting the further issue.

           Here some smile
'And never let him henceforth dare to plead, –
Of all pleas and excuses in the world
For any deed hereafter to be done, –
His irrepressible wrath at honour's wound!
130 Passion and madness irrepressible?
Why, Count and cavalier, the husband comes
And catches foe i' the very act of shame:
There's man to man, – nature must have her way, –
We look he should have cleared things on the spot.
Yes, then, indeed – even tho' it prove he erred –
Though the ambiguous first appearance, mount
Of solid injury, melt soon to mist,
Still, – had he slain the lover and the wife –

Or, since she was a woman and his wife,
1140 Slain him, but stript her naked to the skin
Or at best left no more of an attire
Than patch sufficient to pin paper to,
Some one love-letter, infamy and all,
As passport to the Paphos fit for such,
Safe-conduct to her natural home the stews, –
Good! One had recognised the power o' the pulse.
But when he stands, the stock-fish, – sticks to law –
Offers the hole in his heart, all fresh and warm,
For scrivener's pen to poke and play about –
1150 Can stand, can stare, can tell his beads perhaps,
Oh, let us hear no syllable o' the rage!
Such rage were a convenient afterthought
For one who would have shown his teeth belike,
Exhibited unbridled rage enough,
Had but the priest been found, as was to hope,
In serge, not silk, with crucifix, not sword:
Whereas the grey innocuous grub, of yore,
Had hatched a hornet, tickle to the touch,
The priest was metamorphosed into knight.
1160 And even the timid wife, whose cue was – shriek,
Bury her brow beneath his trampling foot, –
She too sprang at him like a pythoness:
So, gulp down rage, passion must be postponed,
Calm be the word! Well, our word is – we brand
This part o' the business, howsoever the rest
Befall.'
      'Nay,' interpose as prompt his friends –
'This is the world's way! So you adjudge reward
To the forbearance and legality
1170 Yourselves begin by inculcating – ay,
Exacting from us all with knife at throat!
This one wrong more you add to wrong's amount, –
You publish all, with the kind comment here,
"Its victim was too cowardly for revenge." '
Make it your own case, – you who stand apart!
The husband wakes one morn from heavy sleep,

With a taste of poppy in his mouth, – rubs eyes,
Finds his wife flown, his strong box ransacked too,
Follows as he best can, overtakes i' the end.
180 You bid him use his privilege: well, it seems
He's scarce cool-blooded enough for the right move –
Does not shoot when the game were sure, but stands
Bewildered at the critical minute, – since
He has the first flash of the fact alone
To judge from, act with, not the steady lights
Of after-knowledge, – yours who stand at ease
To try conclusions: he's in smother and smoke,
You outside, with explosion at an end:
The sulphur may be lightning or a squib –
190 He'll know in a minute, but till then, he doubts.
Back from what you know to what he knew not!
Hear the priest's lofty 'I am innocent,'
The wife's as resolute 'You are guilty!' Come!
Are you not staggered? – pause, and you lose the move!
Nought left you but a low appeal to law,
'Coward' tied to your tail for compliment!
Another consideration: have it your way!
Admit the worst: his courage failed the Count,
He's cowardly like the best o' the burgesses
200 He's grown incorporate with, – a very cur,
Kick him from out your circle by all means!
Why, trundled down this reputable stair,
Still, the Church-door lies wide to take him in,
And the Court-porch also: in he sneaks to each, –
'Yes, I have lost my honour and my wife,
And, being moreover an ignoble hound,
I dare not jeopardise my life for them!'
Religion and Law lean forward from their chairs,
'Well done, thou good and faithful servant!' Ay,
210 Not only applaud him that he scorned the world,
But punish should he dare do otherwise.
If the case be clear or turbid, – you must say!

Thus, anyhow, it mounted to the stage

In the law-courts, – let's see clearly from this point! –
Where the priest tells his story true or false,
And the wife her story, and the husband his,
All with result as happy as before.
The courts would nor condemn nor yet acquit
This, that or the other, in so distinct a sense
1220 As end the strife to either's absolute loss:
Pronounced, in place of something definite,
'Each of the parties, whether goat or sheep
I' the main, has wool to show and hair to hide.
Each has brought somehow trouble, is somehow cause
Of pains enough, – even though no worse were proved.
Here is a husband, cannot rule his wife
Without provoking her to scream and scratch
And scour the fields, – causelessly, it may be:
Here is that wife, – who makes her sex our plague,
1230 Wedlock, our bugbear, – perhaps with cause enough:
And here is the truant priest o' the trio, worst
Or best – each quality being conceivable.
Let us impose a little mulct on each.
We punish youth in state of pupilage
Who talk at hours when youth is bound to sleep,
Whether the prattle turn upon Saint Rose
Or Donna Olimpia of the Vatican:
'T is talk, talked wisely or unwisely talked,
I' the dormitory where to talk at all,
1240 Transgresses, and is mulct: as here we mean.
For the wife, – let her betake herself, for rest,
After her run, to a House of Convertites –
Keep there, as good as real imprisonment:
Being sick and tired, she will recover so.
For the priest, spritely strayer out of bounds,
Who made Arezzo hot to hold him, – Rome
Profits by his withdrawal from the scene.
Let him be relegate to Civita,
Circumscribed by its bounds till matters mend:
1250 There he at least lies out o' the way of harm
From foes – perhaps from the too friendly fair.

And finally for the husband, whose rash rule
Has but itself to blame for this ado, –
If he be vexed that, in our judgments dealt,
He fails obtain what he accounts his right,
Let him go comforted with the thought, no less,
That, turn each sentence howsoever he may,
There's satisfaction to extract therefrom.
For, does he wish his wife proved innocent?
1260 Well, she's not guilty, he may safely urge,
Has missed the stripes dishonest wives endure –
This being a fatherly pat o' the cheek, no more.
Does he wish her guilty? Were she otherwise
Would she be locked up, set to say her prayers,
Prevented intercourse with the outside world,
And that suspected priest in banishment,
Whose portion is a further help i' the case?
Oh, ay, you all of you want the other thing,
The extreme of law, some verdict neat, complete, –
1270 Either, the whole o' the dowry in your poke
With full release from the false wife, to boot,
And heading, hanging for the priest, beside –
Or, contrary, claim freedom for the wife,
Repayment of each penny paid her spouse,
Amends for the past, release for the future! Such
Is wisdom to the children of this world;
But we've no mind, we children of the light,
To miss the advantage of the golden mean,
And push things to the steel point.' Thus the courts.

1280 Is it settled so far? Settled or disturbed,
Console yourselves: 't is like . . . an instance, now!
You've seen the puppets, of Place Navona, play, –
Punch and his mate, – how threats pass, blows are dealt,
And a crisis comes: the crowd or clap or hiss
Accordingly as disposed for man or wife –
When down the actors duck awhile perdue,
Donning what novel rag-and-feather trim
Best suits the next adventure, new effect:

R.B. – 9

And, – by the time the mob is on the move,
1290 With something like a judgment *pro* and *con*, –
There's a whistle, up again the actors pop
In t' other tatter with fresh-tinseled staves,
To re-engage in one last worst fight more
Shall show, what you thought tragedy was farce.
Note, that the climax and the crown of things
Invariably is, the devil appears himself,
Armed and accoutred, horns and hoofs and tail!
Just so, nor otherwise it proved – you'll see:
Move to the murder, never mind the rest!

1300 Guido, at such a general duck-down,
I' the breathing-space, – of wife to convent here,
Priest to his relegation, and himself
To Arezzo, – had resigned his part perforce
To brother Abate, who bustled, did his best,
Retrieved things somewhat, managed the three suits –
Since, it should seem, there were three suits-at-law
Behoved him look to, still, lest bad grow worse:
First civil suit, – the one the parents brought,
Impugning the legitimacy of his wife,
1310 Affirming thence the nullity of her rights:
This was before the Rota, – Molinès,
That's judge there, made that notable decree
Which partly leaned to Guido, as I said, –
But Pietro had appealed against the same
To the very court will judge what we judge now –
Tommati and his fellows, – Suit the first.
Next civil suit, – demand on the wife's part
Of separation from the husband's bed
On plea of cruelty and risk to life –
1320 Claims restitution of the dowry paid,
Immunity from paying any more:
This second, the Vicegerent has to judge.
Third and last suit, – this time, a criminal one, –
Answer to, and protection from, both these, –
Guido's complaint of guilt against his wife

In the Tribunal of the Governor,
Venturini, also judge of the present cause.
Three suits of all importance plaguing him,
Beside a little private enterprise
1330 Of Guido's, – essay at a shorter cut.
For Paolo, knowing the right way at Rome,
Had, even while supcrintending these three suits
I' the regular way, each at its proper court,
Ingeniously made interest with the Pope
To set such tedious regular forms aside,
And, acting the supreme and ultimate judge,
Declare for the husband and against the wife.
Well, at such crisis and extreme of straits,
The man at bay, buffeted in this wise,
1340 Happened the strangest accident of all.
'Then,' sigh friends, 'the last feather broke his back,
Made him forget all possible remedies
Save one – he rushed to, as the sole relief
From horror and the abominable thing.'
'Or rather,' laugh foes, 'then did there befall
The luckiest of conceivable events,
Most pregnant with impunity for him,
Which henceforth turned the flank of all attack,
And bade him do his wickedest and worst.'
1350 – The wife's withdrawal from the Convertites,
Visit to the villa where her parents lived,
And birth there of his babe. Divergence here!
I simply take the facts, ask what they show.

First comes this thunderclap of a surprise:
Then follow all the signs and silences
Premonitory of earthquake. Paolo first
Vanished, was swept off somewhere, lost to Rome:
(Wells dry up, while the sky is sunny and blue.)
Then Guido girds himself for enterprise,
1360 Hies to Vittiano, counsels with his steward,
Comes to terms with four peasants young and bold,
And starts for Rome the Holy, reaches her

At very holiest, for 't is Christmas Eve,
And makes straight for the Abate's dried-up font,
The lodge where Paolo ceased to work the pipes.
And then, rest taken, observation made
And plan completed, all in a grim week,
The five proceed in a body, reach the place,
– Pietro's, by the Paolina, silent, lone,
1370 And stupefied by the propitious snow, –
At one in the evening: knock: a voice 'Who's there?'
'Friends with a letter from the priest your friend.'
At the door, straight smiles old Violante's self.
She falls, – her son-in-law stabs through and through,
Reaches thro' her at Pietro – 'With your son
This is the way to settle suits, good sire!'
He bellows 'Mercy for heaven, not for earth!
Leave to confess and save my sinful soul,
Then do your pleasure on the body of me!'
1380 – 'Nay, father, soul with body must take its chance!'
He presently got his portion and lay still.
And last, Pompilia rushes here and there
Like a dove among lightnings in her brake,
Falls also: Guido's, this last husband's-act.
He lifts her by the long dishevelled hair,
Holds her away at arms' length with one hand,
While the other tries if life come from the mouth –
Looks out his whole heart's hate on the shut eyes,
Draws a deep satisfied breath, 'So – dead at last!'
1390 Throws down the burthen on dead Pietro's knees,
And ends all with 'Let us away, my boys!'

And, as they left by one door, in at the other
Tumbled the neighbours – for the shrieks had pierced
To the mill and the grange, this cottage and that shed.
Soon followed the Public Force; pursuit began
Though Guido had the start and chose the road:
So, that same night was he, with the other four,
Overtaken near Baccano, – where they sank
By the way-side, in some shelter meant for beasts,

1400 And now lay heaped together, nuzzling swine,
Each wrapped in bloody cloak, each grasping still
His unwiped weapon, sleeping all the same
The sleep o' the just, – a journey of twenty miles
Bringing just and unjust to a level, you see.
The only one i' the world that suffered aught
By the whole night's toil and trouble, flight and chase,
Was just the officer who took them, Head
O' the Public Force, – Patrizj, zealous soul,
Who, having duty to sustain the flesh,
1410 Got heated, caught a fever and so died:
A warning to the over-vigilant,
    – Virtue in a chafe should change her linen quick,
Lest pleurisy get start of providence.
(That's for the Cardinal, and told, I think!)

Well, they bring back the company to Rome.
Says Guido, 'By your leave, I fain would ask
How you found out 't was I who did the deed?
What put you on my trace, a foreigner,
Supposed in Arezzo, – and assuredly safe
1420 Except for an oversight: who told you, pray?'
'Why, naturally your wife!' Down Guido drops
O' the horse he rode, – they have to steady and stay,
At either side the brute that bore him, bound,
So strange it seemed his wife should live and speak!
She had prayed – at least so people tell you now –
For but one thing to the Virgin for herself,
Not simply, as did Pietro 'mid the stabs, –
Time to confess and get her own soul saved –
But time to make the truth apparent, truth
1430 For God's sake, lest men should believe a lie:
Which seems to have been about the single prayer
She ever put up, that was granted her.
With this hope in her head, of telling truth, –
Being familiarized with pain, beside, –
She bore the stabbing to a certain pitch
Without a useless cry, was flung for dead

On Pietro's lap, and so attained her point.
Her friends subjoin this – have I done with them? –
And cite the miracle of continued life
1440 (She was not dead when I arrived just now)
As attestation to her probity.

Does it strike your Excellency? Why, your Highness,
The self-command and even the final prayer,
Our candour must acknowledge explainable
As easily by the consciousness of guilt.
So, when they add that her confession runs
She was of wifehood one white innocence
In thought, word, act, from first of her short life
To last of it; praying, i' the face of death,
1450 That God forgive her other sins – not this,
She is charged with and must die for, that she failed
Anyway to her husband: while thereon
Comments the old Religious – 'So much good,
Patience beneath enormity of ill,
I hear to my confusion, woe is me,
Sinner that I stand, shamed in the walk and gait
I have practised and grown old in, by a child!' –
Guido's friends shrug the shoulder, 'Just this same
Prodigious absolute calm in the last hour
1460 Confirms us, – being the natural result
Of a life which proves consistent to the close.
Having braved heaven and deceived earth throughout,
She braves still and deceives still, gains thereby
Two ends, she prizes beyond earth or heaven:
First sets her lover free, imperilled sore
By the new turn things take: he answers yet
For the part he played: they have summoned him indeed:
The past ripped up, he may be punished still:
What better way of saving him than this?
1470 Then, – thus she dies revenged to the uttermost
On Guido, drags him with her in the dark,
The lower still the better, do you doubt?
Thus, two ways, does she love her love to the end,

And hate her hate, – death, hell is no such price
To pay for these, – lovers and haters hold.'
But there's another parry for the thrust.
'Confession,' cry folks – 'a confession, think!
Confession of the moribund is true!'
Which of them, my wise friends? This public one,
1480 Or the private other we shall never know?
The private may contain, – your casuists teach, –
The acknowledgment of, and the penitence for,
That other public one, so people say.
However it be, – we trench on delicate ground,
Her Eminence is peeping o'er the cards, –
Can one find nothing in behalf of this
Catastrophe? Deaf folks accuse the dumb!
You criticize the drunken reel, fool's-speech,
Maniacal gesture of the man, – we grant!
1490 But who poured poison in his cup, we ask?
Recall the list of his excessive wrongs,
First cheated in his wife, robbed by her kin,
Rendered anon the laughing-stock o' the world
By the story, true or false, of his wife's birth, –
The last seal publicly apposed to shame
By the open flight of wife and priest, – why, Sirs,
Step out of Rome a furlong, would you know
What anotherguess tribunal than ours here,
Mere worldly Court without the help of grace,
1500 Thinks of just that one incident o' the flight?
Guido preferred the same complaint before
The court at Arezzo, bar of the Granduke, –
In virtue of it being Tuscany
Where the offence had rise and flight began, –
Self-same complaint he made in the sequel here
Where the offence grew to the full, the flight
Ended: offence and flight, one fact judged twice
By two distinct tribunals, – what result?
There was a sentence passed at the same time
1510 By Arezzo and confirmed by the Granduke,
Which nothing baulks of swift and sure effect

But absence of the guilty, (flight to Rome
Frees them from Tuscan jurisdiction now)
– Condemns the wife to the opprobrious doom
Of all whom law just lets escape from death.
The Stinche, House of Punishment, for life, –
That's what the wife deserves in Tuscany:
Here, she deserves – remitting with a smile
To her father's house, main object of the flight!
1520 The thief presented with the thing he steals!

At this discrepancy of judgments – mad,
The man took on himself the office, judged;
And the only argument against the use
O' the law he thus took into his own hands
Is . . . what, I ask you? – that, revenging wrong,
He did not revenge sooner, kill at first
Whom he killed last! That is the final charge.
Sooner? What's soon or late i' the case? – ask we.
A wound i' the flesh no doubt wants prompt redress;
1530 It smarts a little to-day, well in a week,
Forgotten in a month; or never, or now, revenge!
But a wound to the soul? That rankles worse and worse.
Shall I comfort you, explaining – 'Not this once
But now it may be some five hundred times
I called you ruffian, pandar, liar and rogue:
The injury must be less by lapse of time?'
The wrong is a wrong, one and immortal too,
And that you bore it those five hundred times,
Let it rankle unrevenged five hundred years,
1540 Is just five hundred wrongs the more and worse!
Men, plagued this fashion, get to explode this way,
If left no other.

   'But we left this man
Many another way, and there's his fault,'
'T is answered – 'He himself preferred our arm
O' the law to fight his battle with. No doubt
We did not open him an armoury

To pick and choose from, use, and then reject.
He tries one weapon and fails, – he tries the next
1550 And next: he flourishes wit and common sense,
They fail him, – he plies logic doughtily,
It fails him too, – thereon, discovers last
He has been blind to the combustibles –
That all the while he is a-glow with ire,
Boiling with irrepressible rage, and so
May try explosives and discard cold steel, –
So hire assassins, plot, plan, execute!
Is this the honest self-forgetting rage
We are called to pardon? Does the furious bull
1560 Pick out four help mates from the grazing herd
And journey with them over hill and dale
Till he find his enemy?

              What rejoinder? save
That friends accept our bull-similitude.
Bull-like, – the indiscriminate slaughter, rude
And reckless aggravation of revenge,
Where all i' the way o' the brute who never once
Ceases, amid all provocation more,
To bear in mind the first tormentor, first
1570 Giver o' the wound that goaded him to fight:
And, though a dozen follow and reinforce
The aggressor, wound in front and wound in flank,
Continues undisturbedly pursuit,
And only after prostrating his prize
Turns on the pettier, makes a general prey.
So Guido rushed against Violante, first
Author of all his wrongs, *fons et origo*
Malorum – increasingly drunk, – which justice done,
He finished with the rest. Do you blame a bull?

1580 In truth you look as puzzled as ere I preached!
How is that? There are difficulties perhaps
On any supposition, and either side.
Each party wants too much, claims sympathy

For its object of compassion, more than just.
Cry the wife's friends, 'O the enormous crime
Caused by no provocation in the world!'
'Was not the wife a little weak?' – inquire –
'Punished extravagantly, if you please,
But meriting a little punishment?
1590 One treated inconsiderately, say,
Rather than one deserving not at all
Treatment and discipline o' the harsher sort?'
No, they must have her purity itself,
Quite angel, – and her parents angels too
Of an aged sort, immaculate, word and deed,
At all events, so seeming, till the fiend,
Even Guido, by his folly, forced from them
The untoward avowal of the trick o' the birth,
Would otherwise be safe and secret now.
1600 Why, here you have the awfulest of crimes
For nothing! Hell broke loose on a butterfly!
A dragon born of rose-dew and the moon!
Yet here is the monster! Why, he's a mere man –
Born, bred and brought up in the usual way.
His mother loves him, still his brothers stick
To the good fellow of the boyish games;
The Governor of his town knows and approves,
The Archbishop of the place knows and assists:
Here he has Cardinal This to vouch for the past,
1610 Cardinal That to trust for the future, – match
And marriage were a Cardinal's making, – in short,
What if a tragedy be acted here
Impossible for malice to improve,
And innocent Guido with his innocent four
Be added, all five, to the guilty three,
That we of these last days be edified
With one full taste o' the justice of the world?

The long and the short is, truth is what I show: –
Undoubtedly no pains ought to be spared
1620 To give the mob an inkling of our lights.

It seems unduly harsh to put the man
To the torture, as I hear the court intends,
Though readiest way of twisting out the truth;
He is noble, and he may be innocent:
On the other hand, if they exempt the man
(As it is also said they hesitate
On the fair ground, presumptive guilt is weak
I' the case of nobility and privilege), –
What crime that ever was, ever will be,
1630 Deserves the torture? Then abolish it!
You see the reduction *ad absurdum*, Sirs?

Her Excellency must pronounce, in fine!
What, she prefers going and joining play?
Her Highness finds it late, intends retire?
I am of their mind: only, all this talk, talked,
'T was not for nothing that we talked, I hope?
Both know as much about it, now, at least,
As all Rome: no particular thanks, I beg!
(You'll see, I have not so advanced myself,
1640 After my teaching the two idiots here!)

BOOK V

Count Guido Franceschini

Thanks, Sir, but, should it please the reverend Court,
I feel I can stand somehow, half sit down
Without help, make shift to even speak, you see,
Fortified by the sip of . . . why, 't is wine,
Velletri, – and not vinegar and gall,
So changed and good the times grow! Thanks, kind Sir!
Oh, but one sip's enough! I want my head
To save my neck, there's work awaits me still.
How cautious and considerate . . . aie, aie, aie,
Not your fault, sweet Sir! Come, you take to heart
An ordinary matter. Law is law.
Noblemen were exempt, the vulgar thought,
From racking, but, since law thinks otherwise,
I have been put to the rack: all's over now,
And neither wrist – what men style, out of joint:
If any harm be, 't is the shoulder-blade,
The left one, that seems wrong i' the socket, – Sirs,
Much could not happen, I was quick to faint,
Being past my prime of life, and out of health.
In short I thank you, – yes, and mean the word.
Needs must the Court be slow to understand
How this quite novel form of taking pain,
This getting tortured merely in the flesh,
Amounts to almost an agreeable change
In my case, me fastidious, plied too much
With opposite treatment, used (forgive the joke)
To the rasp-tooth toying with this brain of mine,
And, in and out my heart, the play o' the probe.
Four years have I been operated on
I' the soul, do you see – its tense or tremulous part –

My self-respect, my care for a good name,
Pride in an old one, love of kindred – just
A mother, brothers, sisters, and the like,
That looked up to my face when days were dim,
And fancied they found light there – no one spot,
Foppishly sensitive, but has paid its pang.
That, and not this you now oblige me with,
That was the Vigil-torment, if you please!
The poor old noble House that drew the rags
40 O' the Franceschini's once superb array
Close round her, hoped to slink unchallenged by, –
Pluck off these! Turn the drapery inside out
And teach the tittering town how scarlet wears!
Show men the lucklessness, the improvidence
Of the easy-natured Count before this Court,
The father I have some slight feeling for,
Who let the world slide, nor foresaw that friends
Then proud to cap and kiss the patron's shoe,
Would, when the purse he left held spider-webs,
50 Properly push his child to wall one day!
Mimic the tetchy humour, furtive glance
And brow where half was furious half fatigued,
O' the same son got to be of middle age,
Sour, saturnine, – your humble servant here, –
When things go cross and the young wife, he finds
Take to the window at a whistle's bid,
And yet demurs thereon, preposterous fool! –
Whereat the worthies judge he wants advice
And beg to civilly ask what's evil here,
60 Perhaps remonstrate on the habit they deem
He's given unduly to, of beating her
... Oh, sure he beats her – why says John so else,
Who is cousin to George who is sib to Tecla's self
Who cooks the meal and combs the lady's hair?
What? 'T is my wrist you merely dislocate
For the future when you mean me martyrdom?
– Let the old mother's economy alone,
How the brocade-strips saved o' the seamy side

O' the wedding-gown buy raiment for a year?
70 – How she can dress and dish up – lordly dish
Fit for a duke, lamb's head and purtenance –
With her proud hands, feast household so a week?
No word o' the wine rejoicing God and man
The less when three-parts water? Then, I say,
A trifle of torture to the flesh, like yours,
While soul is spared such foretaste of hell-fire,
Is naught. But I curtail the catalogue
Through policy, – a rhetorician's trick, –
Because I would reserve some choicer points
80 O' the practice, more exactly parallel –
(Having an eye to climax) with what gift,
Eventual grace the Court may have in store
I' the way of plague – my crown of punishments.
When I am hanged or headed, time enough
To prove the tenderness of only that,
Mere heading, hanging, – not their counterpart,
Not demonstration public and precise
That I, having married the mongrel of a drab,
Am bound to grant that mongrel-brat, my wife,
90 Her mother's birthright-licence as is just, –
Let her sleep undisturbed, i' the family style,
Her sleep out in the embraces of a priest,
Nor disallow their bastard as my heir!
Your sole mistake, – dare I submit so much
To the reverend Court? – has been in all this pains
To make a stone roll down hill, – rack and wrench
And rend a man to pieces, all for what?
Why – make him ope mouth in his own defence,
Show cause for what he has done, the irregular deed,
00 (Since that he did it, scarce dispute can be)
And clear his fame a little, beside the luck
Of stopping even yet, if possible,
Discomfort to his flesh from noose or axe –
For that, out come the implements of law!
May it content my lords the gracious Court
To listen only half so patient-long

As I will in that sense profusely speak,
And – fie, they shall not call in screws to help!
I killed Pompilia Franceschini, Sirs;
110   Killed too the Comparini, husband, wife,
Who called themselves, by a notorious lie,
Her father and her mother to ruin me.
There's the irregular deed: you want no more
Than right interpretation of the same,
And truth so far – am I to understand?
To that then, with convenient speed, – because
Now I consider, – yes, despite my boast,
There is an ailing in this omoplat
May clip my speech all too abruptly close,
120   Whatever the good-will in me. Now for truth!

I' the name of the indivisible Trinity!
Will my lords, in the plentitude of their light,
Weigh well that all this trouble has come on me
Through my persistent treading in the paths
Where I was trained to go, – wearing that yoke
My shoulder was predestined to receive,
Born to the hereditary stoop and crease?
Noble, I recognized my nobler still,
The Church, my suzerain; no mock-mistress, she;
130   The secular owned the spiritual: mates of mine
Have thrown their careless hoofs up at her call
'Forsake the clover and come drag my wain!'
There they go cropping: I protruded nose
To halter, bent my back of docile beast,
And now am whealed, one wide wound all of me,
For being found at the eleventh hour o' the day
Padding the mill-track, not neck-deep in grass:
– My one fault, I am stiffened by my work,
– My one reward, I help the Court to smile!

140   I am representative of a great line,
One of the first of the old families
In Arezzo, ancientest of Tuscan towns.

When my worst foe is fain to challenge this,
His worst exception runs – not first in rank
But second, noble in the next degree
Only; not malice 'self maligns me more.
So, my lord opposite has composed, we know,
A marvel of a book, sustains the point
That Francis boasts the primacy 'mid saints;
150 Yet not inaptly hath his argument
Obtained response from yon my other lord
In thesis published with the world's applause
– Rather 't is Dominic such post befits:
Why, at the worst, Francis stays Francis still,
Second in rank to Dominic it may be,
Still, very saintly, very like our Lord;
And I at least descend from a Guido once
Homager to the Empire, nought below –
Of which account as proof that, none o' the line
160 Having a single gift beyond brave blood,
Or able to do aught but give, give, give
In blood and brain, in house and land and cash,
Not get and garner as the vulgar may,
We became poor as Francis or our Lord.
Be that as it likes you, Sirs, – whenever it chanced
Myself grew capable anyway of remark,
(Which was soon – penury makes wit premature)
This struck me, I was poor who should be rich
Or pay that fault to the world which trifles not
170 When lineage lacks the flag yet lifts the pole:
Therefore I must make move forthwith, transfer
My stranded self, born fish with gill and fin
Fit for the deep sea, now left flap bare-backed
In slush and sand, a show to crawlers vile
Reared of the low-tide and aright therein.
The enviable youth with the old name,
Wide chest, stout arms, sound brow and pricking veins,
A heartful of desire, man's natural load,
A brainful of belief, the noble's lot, –
180 All this life, cramped and gasping, high and dry

I' the wave's retreat, – the misery, good my lords,
Which made you merriment at Rome of late, –
It made me reason, rather – muse, demand
– Why our bare dropping palace, in the street
Where such-an-one whose grandfather sold tripe
Was adding to his purchased pile a fourth
Tall tower, could hardly show a turret sound?
Why Countess Beatrice, whose son I am,
Cowered in the winter-time as she spun flax,
190 Blew on the earthen basket of live ash,
Instead of jaunting forth in coach and six
Like such-another widow who ne'er was wed?
I asked my fellows, how came this about?
'Why, Jack, the suttler's child, perhaps the camp's,
Went to the wars, fought sturdily, took a town
And got rewarded as was natural.
She of the coach and six – excuse me there!
Why, do n't you know the story of her friend?
A clown dressed vines on somebody's estate,
200 His boy recoiled from muck, liked Latin more,
Stuck to his pen and got to be a priest,
Till one day . . . do n't you mind that telling tract
Against Molinos, the old Cardinal wrote?
He penned and dropped it in the patron's desk
Who, deep in thought and absent much of mind,
Licensed the thing, allowed it for his own;
Quick came promotion, – *suum cuique*, Count!
Oh, he can pay for coach and six, be sure!'
' – Well, let me go, do likewise: war 's the word –
210 That way the Franceschini worked at first,
I'll take my turn, try soldiership.' – 'What, you?
The eldest son and heir and prop o' the house,
So do you see your duty? Here's your post,
Hard by the hearth and altar. (Roam from roof,
This youngster, play the gypsy out of doors,
And who keeps kith and kin that fall on us?)
Stand fast, stick tight, conserve your gods at home!'
' – Well then, the quiet course, the contrary trade!

We had a cousin amongst us once was Pope,
220 And minor glories manifold. Try the Church,
The tonsure, and, – since heresy's but half-slain
Even by the Cardinal's tract he thought he wrote, –
Have at Molinos!' – 'Have at a fool's head!
You a priest? How were marriage possible?
There must be Franceschini till time ends –
That's your vocation. Make your brothers priests,
Paul shall be porporate, and Girolamo step
Red-stockinged in the presence when you choose,
But save one Franceschini for the age!
230 Be not the vine but dig and dung its root,
Be not a priest but gird up priesthood's loins,
With one foot in Arezzo stride to Rome,
Spend yourself there and bring the purchase back!
Go hence to Rome, be guided!'

                    So I was.
I turned alike from the hill-side zig-zag thread
Of way to the table-land a soldier takes,
Alike from the low-lying pasture-place
Where churchmen graze, recline and ruminate,
240 – Ventured to mount no platform like my lords
Who judge the world, bear brain I dare not brag –
But stationed me, might thus the expression serve,
As who should fetch and carry, come and go,
Meddle and make i' the cause my lords love most –
The public weal, which hangs to the law, which holds
By the Church, which happens to be through God himself.
Humbly I helped the Church till here I stand, –
Or would stand but for the omoplat, you see!
Bidden qualify for Rome, I, having a field,
250 Went, sold it, laid the sum at Peter's foot:
Which means – I settled home-accounts with speed,
Set apart just a modicum should suffice
To keep the villa's head above the waves
Of weed inundating its oil and wine,
And prop roof, stanchion wall o' the palace so

It should keep breath i' the body, hold its own
Amid the advance of neighbouring loftiness –
(People like building where they used to beg) –
Till succoured one day, – shared the residue
260 Between my mother and brothers and sisters there,
Black-eyed babe Donna This and Donna That,
As near to starving as might decently be,
– Left myself journey-charges, change of suit,
A purse to put i' the pocket of the Groom
O' the Chamber of the patron, and a glove
With a ring to it for the digits of the niece
Sure to be helpful in his household, – then
Started for Rome, and led the life prescribed.
Close to the Church, though clean of it, I assumed
270 Three or four orders of no consequence,
– They cast out evil spirits and exorcise,
For example; bind a man to nothing more,
Give clerical savour to his layman's-salt,
Facilitate his claim to loaf and fish
Should miracle leave, beyond what feeds the flock,
Fragments to brim the basket of a friend –
While, for the world's sake, I rode, danced and gamed,
Quitted me like a courtier, measured mine
With whatsoever blade had fame in fence,
280 – Ready to let the basket go its round
Even though my turn was come to help myself,
Should Dives count on me at dinner-time
As just the understander of a joke
And not immoderate in repartee.
Utrique sic paratus, Sirs, I said
'Here,' (in the fortitude of years fifteen,
So good a pedagogue is penury)
'Here wait, do service, – serving and to serve!
And, in due time, I nowise doubt at all,
290 The recognition of my service comes.
Next year I'm only sixteen. I can wait.'

I waited thirty years, may it please the Court:

Saw meanwhile many a denizen o' the dung
Hop, skip, jump o'er my shoulder, make him wings
And fly aloft, – succeed, in the usual phrase.
Everyone soon or late comes round by Rome:
Stand still here, you'll see all in turn succeed.
Why, look you, so and so, the physician here,
My father's lacquey's son we sent to school,
Doctored and dosed this Eminence and that,
Salved the last Pope his certain obstinate sore,
Soon bought land as became him, names it now:
I grasp bell at his griffin-guarded gate,
Traverse the half-mile avenue, – a term,
A cypress, and a statue, three and three, –
Deliver message from my Monsignor,
With varletry at lounge i' the vestibule
I'm barred from, who bear mud upon my shoe.
My father's chaplain's nephew, Chamberlain, –
Nothing less, please you! – courteous all the same,
– He does not see me though I wait an hour
At his staircase-landing 'twixt the brace of busts,
A noseless Sylla, Marius maimed to match,
My father gave him for a hexastich
Made on my birth-day, – but he sends me down,
To make amends, that relic I prize most –
The unburnt end o' the very candle, Sirs,
Purfled with paint so prettily round and round,
He carried in such state last Peter's-day, –
In token I, his gentleman and squire,
Had held the bridle, walked his managed mule
Without a tittup the procession through.
Nay, the official, – one you know, sweet lords! –
Who drew the warrant for my transfer late
To the New Prisons from Tordinona, – he
Graciously had remembrance – 'Francesc . . . ha?
His sire, now – how a thing shall come about! –
Paid me a dozen florins above the fee,
For drawing deftly up a deed of sale
When troubles fell so thick on him, good heart,

And I was prompt and pushing! By all means!
At the New Prisons be it his son shall lie, –
Anything for an old friend!' and thereat
Signed name with triple flourish underneath.
These were my fellows, such their fortunes now,
While I – kept fasts and feasts innumerable,
Matins and vespers, functions to no end
I' the train of Monsignor and Eminence,
As gentleman-squire, and for my zeal's reward
340 Have rarely missed a place at the table-foot
Except when some Ambassador, or such like,
Brought his own people. Brief, one day I felt
The tick of time inside me, turning-point
And slight sense there was now enough of this:
That I was near my seventh climacteric,
Hard upon, if not over, the middle life,
And, although fed by the east-wind, fulsome-fine
With foretaste of the Land of Promise, still
My gorge gave symptom it might play me false;
350 Better not press it further, – be content
With living and dying only a nobleman,
Who merely had a father great and rich,
Who simply had one greater and richer yet,
And so on back and back till first and best
Began i' the night; I finish in the day.
'The mother must be getting old,' I said;
'The sisters are well wedded away, our name
Can manage to pass a sister off, at need,
And do for dowry: both my brothers thrive –
360 Regular priests they are, nor, bat-like, 'bide
'Twixt flesh and fowl with neither privilege.
My spare revenue must keep me and mine.
I am tired: Arezzo's air is good to breathe;
Vittiano, – one limes flocks of thrushes there;
A leathern coat costs little and lasts long:
Let me bid hope good-bye, content at home!'
Thus, one day, I disbosomed me and bowed.
Whereat began the little buzz and thrill

O' the gazers round me; each face brightened up:
370 As when at your Casino, deep in dawn,
A gamester says at last, 'I play no more,
Forego gain, acquiesce in loss, withdraw
Anyhow:' and the watchers of his ways,
A trifle struck compunctious at the word,
Yet sensible of relief, breathe free once more,
Break up the ring, venture polite advice –
'How, Sir? So scant of heart and hope indeed?
Retire with neither cross nor pile from play?–
So incurious, so short-casting? – give your chance
380 To a younger, stronger, bolder spirit belike,
Just when luck turns and the fine throw sweeps all?'
Such was the chorus: and its goodwill meant –
'See that the loser leave door handsomely!
There's an ill look, – it's sinister, spoils sport,
When an old bruised and battered year-by-year
Fighter with fortune, not a penny in poke,
Reels down the steps of our establishment
And staggers on broad daylight and the world,
In shagrag beard and doleful doublet, drops
390 And breaks his heart on the outside: people prate
"Such is the profit of a trip upstairs!"
Contrive he sidle forth, baulked of the blow
Best dealt by way of moral, bidding down
No curse but blessings rather on our heads
For some poor prize he bears at tattered breast,
Some palpable sort of kind of good to set
Over and against the grievance: give him quick!'
Whereon protested Paul, 'Go hang yourselves!
Leave him to me. Count Guido and brother of mine,
400 A word in your ear! Take courage since faint heart
Ne'er won . . . aha, fair lady, do n't men say?
There's a *sors*, there's a right Virgilian dip!
Do you see the happiness o' the hint? At worst,
If the Church want no more of you, the Court
No more, and the Camp as little, the ingrates, – come,
Count you are counted: still you've coat to back,

Not cloth of gold and tissue, as we hoped,
But cloth with sparks and spangles on its frieze
From Camp, Court, Church, enough to make a shine,
410 Entitle you to carry home a wife
With the proper dowry, let the worst betide!
Why, it was just a wife you meant to take!'

Now, Paul's advice was weighty: priests should know:
And Paul apprised me, ere the week was out,
That Pietro and Violante, the easy pair,
The cits enough, with stomach to be more,
Had just the daughter and exact the sum
To truck for the quality of myself: 'She's young,
Pretty and rich: you're noble, classic, choice.
420 Is it to be a match?' 'A match,' said I.
Done! He proposed all, I accepted all,
And we performed all. So I said and did
Simply. As simply followed, not at first
But with the outbreak of misfortune, still
One comment on the saying and doing – 'What?
No blush at the avowal you dared buy
A girl of age beseems your granddaughter,
Like ox or ass? Are flesh and blood a ware?
Are heart and soul a chattel?'
430   Softly, Sirs!
Will the Court of its charity teach poor me
Anxious to learn, of any way i' the world,
Allowed by custom and convenience, save
This same which, taught from my youth up, I trod?
Take me along with you; where was the wrong step?
If what I gave in barter, style and state
And all that hangs to Franceschinihood,
Were worthless, – why, society goes to ground,
Its rules are idiot's-rambling. Honour of birth, –
440 If that thing has no value, cannot buy
Something with value of another sort,
You've no reward nor punishment to give

I' the giving or the taking honour; straight
Your social fabric, pinnacle to base,
Comes down a-clatter like a house of cards.
Get honour, and keep honour free from flaw,
Aim at still higher honour, – gabble o' the goose!
Go bid a second blockhead like myself
Spend fifty years in guarding bubbles of breath,
450 Soapsuds with air i' the belly, gilded brave,
Guarded and guided, all to break at touch
O' the first young girl's hand and first old fool's purse!
All my privation and endurance, all
Love, loyalty and labour dared and did,
Fiddle-de-dee! – why, doer and darer both, –
Count Guido Franceschini had hit the mark
Far better, spent his life with more effect,
As a dancer or a prizer, trades that pay!
On the other hand, bid this buffoonery cease,
460 Admit that honour is a privilege,
The question follows, privilege worth what?
Why, worth the market-price, – now up, now down,
Just so with this as with all other ware:
Therefore essay the market, sell your name,
Style and condition to who buys them best!
'Does my name purchase,' had I dared inquire,
'Your niece, my lord?' there would have been rebuff
Though courtesy, your Lordship cannot else –
'Not altogether! Rank for rank may stand:
470 But I have wealth beside, you – poverty;
Your scale flies up there: bid a second bid,
Rank too and wealth too!' Reasoned like yourself!
But was it to you I went with goods to sell?
This time 'twas my scale quietly kissed the ground,
Mere rank against mere wealth – some youth beside,
Some beauty too, thrown into the bargain, just
As the buyer likes or lets alone. I thought
To deal o' the square: others find fault, it seems:
The thing is, those my offer most concerned,
480 Pietro, Violante, cried they fair or foul?

What did they make o' the terms? Preposterous terms?
Why then accede so promptly, close with such
Nor take a minute to chaffer? Bargain struck,
They straight grew bilious, wished their money back,
Repented them, no doubt: why, so did I,
So did your Lordship, if town-talk be true,
Of paying a full farm's worth for that piece
By Pietro of Cortona — probably
His scholar Ciro Ferri may have retouched —
490 You caring more for colour than design —
Getting a little tired of cupids too.
That's incident to all the folk who buy!
I am charged, I know, with gilding fact by fraud;
I falsified and fabricated, wrote
Myself down roughly richer than I prove,
Rendered a wrong revenue, — grant it all!
Mere grace, mere coquetry such fraud, I say:
A flourish round the figures of a sum
For fashion's sake, that deceives nobody.
500 The veritable back-bone, understood
Essence of this same bargain, blank and bare,
Being the exchange of quality for wealth, —
What may such fancy-flights be? Flecks of oil
Flirted by chapmen where plain dealing grates.
I may have dripped a drop — 'My name I sell;
Not but that I too boast my wealth' — as they,
' — We bring you riches; still our ancestor
Was hardly the rapscallion, folks saw flogged,
But heir to we know who, were rights of force!'
510 They knew and I knew where the back-bone lurked
I' the writhings of the bargain, lords, believe!
I paid down all engaged for, to a doit,
Delivered them just that which, their life long,
They hungered in the hearts of them to gain —
Incorporation with nobility thus
In word and deed: for that they gave me wealth.
But when they came to try their gain, my gift,
Quit Rome and qualify for Arezzo, take

The tone o' the new sphere that absorbed the old,
520 Put away gossip Jack and goody Joan
And go become familiar with the Great,
Greatness to touch and taste and handle now, –
Why, then, – they found that all was vanity,
Vexation, and what Solomon describes!
The old abundant city-fare was best,
The kindly warmth o' the commons, the glad clap
Of the equal on the shoulder, the frank grin
Of the underling at all so many spoons
Fire-new at neighbourly treat, – best, best and best
530 Beyond compare! – down to the loll itself
O' the pot-house settle, – better such a bench
Than the stiff crucifixion by my dais
Under the piece-meal damask canopy
With the coroneted coat of arms a-top!
Poverty and privation for pride's sake,
All they engaged to easily brave and bear, –
With the fit upon them and their brains a-work, –
Proved unendurable to the sobered sots.
A banished prince, now, will exude a juice
540 And salamander-like support the flame:
He dines on chesnuts, chucks the husks to help
The broil o' the brazier, pays the due baioc,
Goes off light-hearted: his grimace begins
At the funny humours of the christening-feast
Of friend the money-lender, – then he's touched
By the flame and frizzles at the babe to kiss!
Here was the converse trial, opposite mind:
Here did a petty nature split on rock
Of vulgar wants predestinate for such –
550 One dish at supper and weak wine to boot!
The prince had grinned and borne: the citizen shrieked,
Summoned the neighbourhood to attest the wrong,
Made noisy protest he was murdered, – stoned
And burned and drowned and hanged, – then broke away,
He and his wife, to tell their Rome the rest.
And this you admire, you men o' the world, my lords?

This moves compassion, makes you doubt my faith?
Why, I appeal to . . . sun and moon? Not I!
Rather to Plautus, Terence, Boccaccio's Book,
560 My townsman, frank Ser Franco's merry Tales, –
To all who strip a vizard from a face,
A body from its padding, and a soul
From froth and ignorance it styles itself, –
If this be other than the daily hap
Of purblind greed that dog-like still drops bone,
Grasps shadow, and then howls the case is hard!

So much for them so far: now for myself,
My profit or loss i' the matter: married am I:
Text whereon friendly censors burst to preach.
570 Ay, at Rome even, long ere I was left
To regulate her life for my young bride
Alone at Arezzo, friendliness outbroke
(Sifting my future to predict its fault)
'Purchase and sale being thus so plain a point,
How of a certain soul bound up, may-be,
I' the barter with the body and money-bags?
From the bride's soul what is it you expect?'
Why, loyalty and obedience, – wish and will
To settle and suit her fresh and plastic mind
580 To the novel, nor disadvantageous mould!
Father and mother shall the woman leave,
Cleave to the husband, be it for weal or woe:
There is the law: what sets this law aside
In my particular case? My friends submit
'Guide, guardian, benefactor, – fee, faw, fum,
The fact is you are forty-five years old,
Nor very comely even for that age:
Girls must have boys.' Why, let girls say so then,
Nor call the boys and men, who say the same,
590 Brute this and beast the other as they do!
Come, cards on table! When you chaunt us next
Epithalamium full to overflow
With praise and glory of white womanhood,

The chaste and pure – troll no such lies o'er lip!
Put in their stead a crudity or two,
Such short and simple statement of the case
As youth chalks on our walls at spring of year!
No! I shall still think nobler of the sex,
Believe a woman still may take a man
600 For the short period that his soul wears flesh,
And, for the soul's sake, understand the fault
Of armour frayed by fighting. Tush, it tempts
One's tongue too much! I'll say – the law's the law:
With a wife I look to find all wifeliness,
As when I buy, timber and twig, a tree –
I buy the song o' the nightingale inside.

Such was the pact: Pompilia from the first
Broke it, refused from the beginning day
Either in body or soul to cleave to mine,
610 And published it forthwith to all the world.
No rupture, – you must join ere you can break, –
Before we had cohabited a month
She found I was a devil and no man, –
Made common cause with those who found as much,
Her parents, Pietro and Violante, – moved
Heaven and earth to the rescue of all three.
In four months' time, the time o' the parents' stay,
Arezzo was a-ringing, bells in a blaze,
With the unimaginable story rife
620 I' the mouth of man, woman and child – to-wit
My misdemeanour. First the lighter side,
Ludicrous face of things, – how very poor
The Franceschini had become at last,
The meanness and the misery of each shift
To save a soldo, stretch and make ends meet.
Next, the more hateful aspect, – how myself
With cruelty beyond Caligula's
Had stripped and beaten, robbed and murdered them,
The good old couple, I decoyed, abused,
630 Plundered and then cast out, and happily so,

Since, – in due course the abominable comes, –
Woe worth the poor young wife left lonely here!
Repugnant in my person as my mind,
I sought, – was ever heard of such revenge?
– To lure and bind her to so cursed a couch,
Such co-embrace with sulphur, snake and toad,
That she was fain to rush forth, call the stones
O' the common street to save her, not from hate
Of mine merely, but . . . must I burn my lips
640   With the blister of the lie? . . . the satyr-love
Of who but my own brother, the young priest,
Too long enforced to lenten fare belike,
Now tempted by the morsel tossed him full
I' the trencher where lay bread and herbs at best.
Mark, this yourselves say! – this, none disallows,
Was charged to me by the universal voice
At the instigation of my four-months' wife! –
And then you ask 'Such charges so preferred,
(Truly or falsely, here concerns us not)
650   Pricked you to punish now if not before? –
Did not the harshness double itself, the hate
Harden?' I answer 'Have it your way and will!'
Say my resentment grew apace: what then?
Do you cry out on the marvel? When I find
That pure smooth egg which, laid within my nest,
Could not but hatch a comfort to us all,
Issues a cockatrice for me and mine,
Do you stare to see me stamp on it? Swans are soft:
Is it not clear that she you call my wife,
660   That any wife of any husband, caught
Whetting a sting like this against his breast, –
Speckled with fragments of the fresh-broke shell,
Married a month and making outcry thus, –
Proves a plague-prodigy to God and man?
She married: what was it she married for,
Counted upon and meant to meet thereby?
'Love' suggests some one, 'love, a little word
Whereof we have not heard one syllable.'

So, the Pompilia, child, girl, wife, in one,
670   Wanted the beating pulse, the rolling eye,
The frantic gesture, the devotion due
From Thyrsis to Neaera! Guido's love –
Why not provençal roses in his shoe,
Plume to his cap, and trio of guitars
At casement, with a bravo close beside?
Good things all these are, clearly claimable
When the fit price is paid the proper way.
Had it been some friend's wife, now, threw her fan
At my foot, with just this pretty scrap attached,
680   'Shame, death, damnation – fall these as they may,
So I find you, for a minute! Come this eve!'
– Why, at such sweet self-sacrifice, – who knows?
I might have fired up, found me at my post,
Ardent from head to heel, nor feared catch cough.
Nay, had some other friend's . . . say, daughter, tripped
Upstairs and tumbled flat and frank on me,
Bareheaded and barefooted, with loose hair
And garments all at large, – cried 'Take me thus!
Duke So-and-So, the greatest man in Rome –
690   To escape his hand and heart have I broke bounds,
Traversed the town and reached you!' – Then, indeed,
The lady had not reached a man of ice!
I would have rummaged, ransacked at the word
Those old odd corners of an empty heart
For remnants of dim love the long disused,
And dusty crumblings of romance! But here,
We talk of just a marriage, if you please –
The every-day conditions and no more;
Where do these bind me to bestow one drop
700   Of blood shall dye my wife's true-love-knot pink?
Pompilia was no pigeon, Venus' pet,
That shuffled from between her pressing paps
To sit on my rough shoulder, – but a hawk,
I bought at a hawk's price and carried home
To do hawk's service – at the Rotunda, say,
Where, six o' the callow nestlings in a row,

You pick and choose and pay the price for such.
I have paid my pound, await my penny's worth,
So, hoodwink, starve and properly train my bird,
710   And, should she prove a haggard, – twist her neck!
Did I not pay my name and style, my hope
And trust, my all? Through spending these amiss
I am here! 'T is scarce the gravity of the Court
Will blame me that I never piped a tune,
Treated my falcon-gentle like my finch.
The obligation I incurred was just
To practise mastery, prove my mastership: –
Pompilia's duty was – submit herself,
Afford me pleasure; perhaps cure my bile.
720   Am I to teach my lords what marriage means,
What God ordains thereby and man fulfils
Who, docile to the dictate, treads the house?
My lords have chosen the happier part with Paul
And neither marry nor burn, – yet priestliness
Can find a parallel to the marriage-bond
In its own blessed special ordinance
Whereof indeed was marriage made the type:
The Church may show her insubordinate,
As marriage her refractory. How of the Monk
730   Who finds the claustral regimen too sharp
After the first month's essay? What's the mode
With the Deacon who supports indifferently
The rod o' the Bishop when he tastes its smart
Full four weeks? Do you straightway slacken hold
Of the innocents, the all-unwary ones
Who, eager to profess, mistook their mind? –
Remit a fast-day's rigour to the Monk
Who fancied Francis' manna meant roast quails,
Concede the Deacon sweet society,
740   He never thought the Levite-rule renounced, –
Or rather prescribe short chain and sharp scourge
Corrective of such peccant humours? This –
I take to be the Church's mode, and mine.
If I was over-harsh, – the worse i' the wife

Who did not win from harshness as she ought,
Wanted the patience and persuasion, lore
Of love, should cure me and console herself.
Put case that I mishandle, flurry and fright
My hawk through clumsiness in sportsmanship,
750 Twitch out five pens where plucking one would serve –
What, shall she bite and claw to mend the case?
And, if you find I pluck five more for that,
Shall you weep 'How he roughs the turtle there?'

Such was the starting; now of the further step.
In lieu of taking penance in good part,
The Monk, with hue and cry, summons a mob
To make a bonfire of the convent, say, –
And the Deacon's pretty piece of virtue (save
The ears o' the Court! I try to save my head)
760 Instructed by the ingenuous postulant,
Taxes the Bishop with adultery, (mud
Needs must pair off with mud, and filth with filth) –
Such being my next experience: who knows not –
The couple, father and mother of my wife,
Returned to Rome, published before my lords,
Put into print, made circulate far and wide
That they had cheated me who cheated them?
Pompilia, I supposed their daughter, drew
Breath first 'mid Rome's worst rankness, through the deed
770 Of a drab and a rogue, was bye-blow bastard-babe
Of a nameless strumpet, passed off, palmed on me
As the daughter with the dowry. Daughter? Dirt
O' the kennel! Dowry? Dust o' the street! Nought more,
Nought less, nought else but – oh – ah – assuredly
A Franceschini and my very wife!
Now take this charge as you will, for false or true, –
This charge, preferred before your very selves
Who judge me now, – I pray you, adjudge again,
Classing it with the cheats or with the lies,
780 By which category I suffer most!
But of their reckoning, theirs who dealt with me

In either fashion, – I reserve my word,
Justify that in its place; I am now to say,
Whichever point o' the charge might poison most,
Pompilia's duty was no doubtful one.
You put the protestation in her mouth
'Henceforward and forevermore, avaunt
Ye fiends, who drop disguise and glare revealed
In your own shape, no longer father mine
790 Nor mother mine! Too nakedly you hate
Me whom you looked as if you loved once, – me
Whom, whether true or false, your tale now damns,
Divulged thus to my public infamy,
Private perdition, absolute overthrow.
For, hate my husband to your hearts' content,
I, spoil and prey of you from first to last,
I who have done you the blind service, lured
The lion to your pit-fall, – I, thus left
To answer for my ignorant bleating there,
800 I should have been remembered and withdrawn
From the first o' the natural fury, not flung loose
A proverb and a byeword men will mouth
At the cross-way, in the corner, up and down
Rome and Arezzo, – there, full in my face,
If my lord, missing them and finding me,
Content himself with casting his reproach
To drop i' the street where such impostors die.
Ah, but – that husband, what the wonder were! –
If, far from casting thus away the rag
810 Smeared with the plague, his hand had chanced upon,
Sewn to his pillow by Locusta's wile, –
Far from abolishing, root, stem and branch,
The misgrowth of infectious mistletoe
Foisted into his stock for honest graft, –
If he, repudiate not, renounce nowise,
But, guarding, guiding me, maintain my cause
By making it his own, (what other way?)
– To keep my name for me, he call it his,
Claim it of who would take it by their lie, –

820 To save my wealth for me – or babe of mine
Their lie was framed to beggar at the birth –
He bid them loose grasp, give our gold again:
Refuse to become partner with the pair
Even in a game which, played adroitly, gives
Its winner life's great wonderful new chance, –
Of marrying, to-wit, a second time, –
Ah, did he do thus, what a friend were he!
Anger he might show, – who can stamp out flame
Yet spread no black o' the brand? – yet, rough albeit
830 In the act, as whose bare feet feel embers scorch,
What grace were his, what gratitude were mine!'
Such protestation should have been my wife's.
Looking for this, do I exact too much?
Why, here's the, – word for word so much, no more, –
Avowal she made, her pure spontaneous speech
To my brother the Abate at first blush,
Ere the good impulse had begun to fade –
So did she make confession for the pair,
So pour forth praises in her own behalf.
840 'Ay, the false letter,' interpose my lords –
'The simulated writing, – 't was a trick:
You traced the signs, she merely marked the same,
The product was not hers but yours.' Alack,
I want no more impulsion to tell truth
From the other trick, the torture inside there!
I confess all – let it be understood –
And deny nothing! If I baffle you so,
Can so fence, in the plenitude of right,
That my poor lathen dagger puts aside
850 Each pass o' the Bilboa, beats you all the same, –
What matters inefficiency of blade?
Mine and not hers the letter, – conceded, lords!
Impute to me that practice! – take as proved
I taught my wife her duty, made her see
What it behoved her see and say and do,
Feel in her heart and with her tongue declare,
And, whether sluggish or recalcitrant,

Forced her to take the right step, I myself
Marching in mere marital rectitude!
860 And who finds fault here, say the tale be true?
Would not my lords commend the priest whose zeal
Seized on the sick, morose or moribund,
By the palsy-smitten finger, made it cross
His brow correctly at the critical time?
– Or answered for the inarticulate babe
At baptism, in its stead declared the faith,
And saved what else would perish unprofessed?
True, the incapable hand may rally yet,
Renounce the sign with renovated strength, –
870 The babe may grow up man and Molinist, –
And so Pompilia, set in the good path
And left to go alone there, soon might see
That too frank-forward, all too simple-strait
Her step was, and decline to tread the rough,
When here lay, tempting foot, the meadow-side,
And there the coppice called with singing-birds!
Soon she discovered she was young and fair,
That many in Arezzo knew as much, –
Yes, this next cup of bitterness, my lords,
880 Had to begin go filling, drop by drop,
Its measure up of full disgust for me,
Filtered into by every noisome drain –
Society's sink toward which all moisture runs.
Would not you prophesy – 'She on whose brow is stamped
The note of the imputation that we know, –
Rightly or wrongly mothered with a whore, –
Such an one, to disprove the frightful charge,
What will she but exaggerate chastity,
Err in excess of wifehood, as it were,
890 Renounce even levities permitted youth,
Though not youth struck to age by a thunderbolt?
Cry "wolf" i' the sheepfold, where's the sheep dares bleat,
Knowing the shepherd listens for a growl?'
So you expect. How did the devil decree?
Why, my lords, just the contrary of course!

It was in the house from the window, at the church
From the hassock, – where the theatre lent its lodge,
Or staging for the public show left space, –
That still Pompilia needs must find herself
900   Launching her looks forth, letting looks reply
As arrows to a challenge; on all sides
Ever new contribution to her lap,
Till one day, what is it knocks at my clenched teeth
But the cup full, curse-collected all for me?
And I must needs drink, drink this gallant's praise,
That minion's prayer, the other fop's reproach,
And come at the dregs to – Caponsacchi! Sirs,
I, – chin deep in a marsh of misery,
Struggling to extricate my name and fame
910   And fortune from the marsh would drown them all,
My face the sole unstrangled part of me, –
I must have this new gad-fly in that face,
Must free me from the attacking lover too!
Men say I battled ungracefully enough –
Was harsh, uncouth and ludicrous beyond
The proper part o' the husband: have it so!
Your lordships are considerate at least –
You order me to speak in my defence
Plainly, expect no quavering tuneful trills
920   As when you bid a singer solace you, –
Nor look that I shall give it, for a grace,
Stans pede in uno: – you remember well
In the one case, 't is a plainsong too severe,
This story of my wrongs, – and that I ache
And need a chair, in the other. Ask you me
Why, when I felt this trouble flap my face,
Already pricked with every shame could perch, –
When, with her parents, my wife plagued me too, –
Why I enforced not exhortation mild
930   To leave whore's-tricks and let my brows alone,
With mulct of comfits, promise of perfume?

'Far from that! No, you took the opposite course,

Breathed threatenings, rage and slaughter!' What you will!
And the end has come, the doom is verily here,
Unhindered by the threatening. See fate's flare
Full on each face of the dead guilty three!
Look at them well, and now, lords, look at this!
Tell me: if on that day when I found first
That Caponsacchi thought the nearest way
940 To his church was some half-mile round by my door,
And that he so admired, shall I suppose,
The manner of the swallows' come-and-go
Between the props o' the window over-head, –
That window happening to be my wife's –
As to stand gazing by the hour on high,
Of May-eves, while she sat and let him smile, –
If I, – instead of threatening, talking big,
Showing hair-powder, a prodigious pinch,
For poison in a bottle, – making believe
950 At desperate doings with a bauble-sword,
And other bugaboo-and-baby-work, –
Had, with the vulgarest household implement,
Calmly and quietly cut off, clean thro' bone,
But one joint of one finger of my wife,
Saying 'For listening to the serenade,
Here's your ring-finger shorter a full third:
Be certain I will slice away next joint,
Next time that anybody underneath
Seems somehow to be sauntering as he hoped
960 A flower would eddy out of your hand to his
While you please fidget with the branch above
O' the rose-tree in the terrace!' – had I done so,
Why, there had followed a quick sharp scream, some pain,
Much calling for plaister, damage to the dress,
A somewhat sulky countenance next day,
Perhaps reproaches, – but reflections too!
I don't hear much of harm that Malchus did
After the incident of the ear, my lords!
Saint Peter took the efficacious way;
970 Malchus was sore but silenced for his life:

He did not hang himself i' the Potter's Field
Like Judas, who was trusted with the bag
And treated to sops after he proved a thief.
So, by this time, my true and obedient wife
Might have been telling beads with a gloved hand;
Awkward a little at pricking hearts and darts
On sampler possibly, but well otherwise:
Not where Rome shudders now to see her lie.
I give that for the course a wise man takes;
980 I took the other however, tried the fool's,
The lighter remedy, brandished rapier dread
With cork-ball at the tip, boxed Malchus' ear
Instead of severing the cartilage,
Called her a terrible nickname, and the like
And there an end: and what was the end of that?
What was the good effect o' the gentle course?
Why, one night I went drowsily to bed,
Dropped asleep suddenly, not suddenly woke,
But did wake with rough rousing and loud cry,
990 To find noon in my face, a crowd in my room,
Fumes in my brain, fire in my throat, my wife
Gone God knows whither, – rifled vesture-chest,
And ransacked money-coffer. 'What does it mean?'
The servants had been drugged too, stared and yawned,
'It must be that our lady has eloped!'
– 'Whither and with whom?' – 'With whom but the
     Canon's self?
One recognizes Caponsacchi there!' –
(By this time the admiring neighbourhood
Joined chorus round me while I rubbed my eyes)
1000 "T is months since their intelligence began, –
A comedy the town was privy to, –
He wrote and she wrote, she spoke, he replied,
And going in and out your house last night
Was easy work for one . . . to be plain with you . . .
Accustomed to do both, at dusk and dawn
When you were absent, – at the villa, you know,
Where husbandry required the master-mind.

Did not you know? Why, we all knew, you see!'
And presently, bit by bit, the full and true
1010 Particulars of the tale were volunteered
With all the breathless zeal of friendship – 'Thus
Matters were managed: at the seventh hour of night' . . .
– 'Later, at daybreak' . . . 'Caponsacchi came' . . .
– 'While you and all your household slept like death,
Drugged as your supper was with drowsy stuff' . . .
– 'And your own cousin Guillichini too –
Either or both entered your dwelling-place,
Plundered it at their pleasure, made prize of all,
Including your wife . . .' – 'Oh, your wife led the way,
1020 Out of doors, on to the gate . . .' – 'But gates are shut,
In a decent town, to darkness and such deeds:
They climbed the wall – your lady must be lithe –
At the gap, the broken bit . . .' – 'Torrione, true!
To escape the questioning guard at the proper gate,
Clemente, where at the inn, hard by, "the Horse,"
Just outside, a calash in readiness
Took the two principals, all alone at last,
To gate San Spirito, which o'erlooks the road,
Leads to Perugia, Rome and liberty.'
1030 Bit by bit thus made-up mosaic-wise,
Flat lay my fortune, – tesselated floor,
Imperishable tracery devils should foot
And frolic it on, around my broken gods,
Over my desecrated hearth.
                                        So much
For the terrible effect of threatening, Sirs!

Well, this way I was shaken wide awake,
Doctored and drenched, somewhat unpoisoned so;
Then, set on horseback and bid seek the lost,
1040 I started alone, head of me, heart of me
Fire, and each limb as languid . . . ah, sweet lords,
Bethink you! – poison-torture, try persuade
The next refractory Molinist with that! . . .
Floundered thro' day and night, another day

And yet another night, and so at last,
As Lucifer kept falling to find hell,
Tumbled into the court-yard of an inn
At the end, and fell on whom I thought to find,
Even Caponsacchi, – what part once was priest,
1050 Cast to the winds now with the cassock-rags:
In cape and sword a cavalier confessed,
There stood he chiding dilatory grooms,
Chafing that only horseflesh and no team
Of eagles would supply the last relay,
Whirl him along the league, the one post more
Between the couple and Rome and liberty.
'T was dawn, the couple were rested in a sort,
And though the lady, tired, – the tenderer sex, –
Still lingered in her chamber, – to adjust
1060 The limp hair, look for any blush astray, –
She would descend in a twinkling, – 'Have you out
The horses therefore!'
              So did I find my wife.
Is the case complete? Do your eyes here see with mine?
Even the parties dared deny no one
Point out of all these points.
              What follows next?
'Why, that then was the time,' you interpose,
'Or then or never, while the fact was fresh,
1070 To take the natural vengeance: there and thus
They and you, – somebody had stuck a sword
Beside you while he pushed you on your horse, –
'T was requisite to slay the couple, Count!'
Just so my friends say – 'Kill!' they cry in a breath,
Who presently, when matters grow to a head
And I do kill the offending ones indeed, –
When crime of theirs, only surmised before,
Is patent, proved indisputably now, –
When remedy for wrong, untried at the time,
1080 Which law professes shall not fail a friend,
Is thrice tried now, found threefold worse than null, –
When what might turn to transient shade, who knows?

Solidifies into a blot which breaks
Hell's black off in pale flakes for fear of mine, –
Then, when I claim and take revenge – 'So rash?'
They cry – 'so little reverence for the law?'

Listen, my masters, and distinguish here!
At first, I called in law to act and help:
Seeing I did so, 'Why, 't is clear,' they cry,
1090 'You shrank from gallant readiness and risk,
Were coward: the thing's inexplicable else.'
Sweet my lords, let the thing be! I fall flat,
Play the reed, not the oak, to breath of man.
Only, inform my ignorance! Say I stand
Convicted of the having been afraid,
Proved a poltroon, no lion but a lamb, –
Does that deprive me of my right of lamb
And give my fleece and flesh to the first wolf?
Are eunuchs, women, children, shieldless quite
1100 Against attack their own timidity tempts?
Cowardice were misfortune and no crime!
– Take it that way, since I am fallen so low
I scarce dare brush the fly that blows my face,
And thank the man who simply spits not there, –
Unless the Court be generous, comprehend
How one brought up at the very feet of law
As I, awaits the grave Gamaliel's nod
Ere he clench fist at outrage, – much less, stab!
– How, ready enough to rise at the right time,
1110 I still could recognise no time mature
Unsanctioned by a move o' the judgment-seat,
So, mute in misery, eyed my masters here
Motionless till the authoritative word
Pronounced amercement. There's the riddle solved:
This is just why I slew nor her nor him,
But called in law, law's delegate in the place,
And bade arrest the guilty couple, Sirs!
We had some trouble to do so – you have heard
They braved me, – he with arrogance and scorn,

120 She, with a volubility of curse,
     A conversancy in the skill of tooth
     And claw to make suspicion seem absurd,
     Nay, an alacrity to put to proof
     At my own throat my own sword, teach me so
     To try conclusions better the next time, –
     Which did the proper service with the mob.
     They never tried to put on mask at all:
     Two avowed lovers forcibly torn apart,
     Upbraid the tyrant as in a playhouse scene,
130 Ay, and with proper clapping and applause
     From the audience that enjoys the bold and free.
     I kept still, said to myself, 'There's law!' Anon
     We searched the chamber where they passed the night,
     Found what confirmed the worst was feared before,
     However needless confirmation now –
     The witches' circle intact, charms undisturbed
     That raised the spirit and succubus, – letters, to-wit,
     Love-laden, each the bag o' the bee that bore
     Honey from lily and rose to Cupid's hive, –
140 Now, poetry in some rank blossom-burst,
     Now, prose, – 'Come here, go there, wait such a while,
     He's at the villa, now he's back again:
     We are saved, we are lost, we are lovers all the same!'
     All in order, all complete, – even to a clue
     To the drowsiness that happed so opportune –
     No mystery, when I read 'Of all things, find
     What wine Sir Jealousy decides to drink –
     Red wine? Because a sleeping-potion, dust
     Dropped into white, discolours wine and shows.'

150 – 'Oh, but we did not write a single word!
     Somebody forged the letters in our name! – '
     Both in a breath protested presently.
     Aha, Sacchetti again! – 'Dame,' – quoth the Duke,
     'What meaneth this epistle, counsel me,
     I pick from out thy placket and peruse,
     Wherein my page averreth thou art white

And warm and wonderful 'twixt pap and pap?'
'Sir,' laughed the Lady ''t is a counterfeit!
Thy page did never stroke but Dian's breast,
1160 The pretty hound I nurture for thy sake:
To lie were losel, – by my fay, no more!'
And no more say I too, and spare the Court.

Ah, the Court! yes, I come to the Court's self;
Such the case, so complete in fact and proof
I laid at the feet of law, – there sat my lords,
Here sit they now, so may they ever sit
In easier attitude than suits my haunch!
In this same chamber did I bare my sores
O' the soul and not the body, – shun no shame,
1170 Shrink from no probing of the ulcerous part,
Since confident in Nature, – which is God, –
That she who, for wise ends, concocts a plague,
Curbs, at the right time, the plague's virulence too:
Law renovates even Lazarus, – cures me!
Caesar thou seekest? To Caesar thou shalt go!
Caesar's at Rome; to Rome accordingly!

The case was soon decided: both weights, cast
I' the balance, vibrate, neither kicks the beam,
Here away, there away, this now and now that.
1180 To every one o' my grievances law gave
Redress, could purblind eye but see the point.
The wife stood a convicted runagate
From house and husband, – driven to such a course
By what she somehow took for cruelty,
Oppression and imperilment of life –
Not that such things were, but that so they seemed:
Therefore, the end conceded lawful, (since
To save life there's no risk should stay our leap)
It follows that all means to the lawful end
1190 Are lawful likewise, – poison, theft and flight.
As for the priest's part, did he meddle or make,
Enough that he too thought life jeopardised;

Concede him then the colour charity
Cast on a doubtful course, – if blackish white
Or whitish black, will charity hesitate?
What did he else but act the precept out,
Leave, like a provident shepherd, his safe flock
To follow the single lamb and strayaway?
Best hope so and think so, – that the ticklish time
200 I' the carriage, the tempting privacy, the last
Somewhat ambiguous accident at the inn,
– All may bear explanation: may? then, must!
The letters, – do they so incriminate?
But what if the whole prove a prank o' the pen,
Flight of the fancy, none of theirs at all,
Bred of the vapours of my brain belike,
Or at worst mere exercise of scholar's-wit
In the courtly Caponsacchi: verse, convict?
Did not Catullus write less seemly once?
210 Yet *doctus* and unblemished he abides.
Wherefore so ready to infer the worst?
Still, I did righteously in bringing doubts
For the law to solve, – take the solution now!
'Seeing that the said associates, wife and priest,
Bear themselves not without some touch of blame
– Else why the pother, scandal and outcry
Which trouble our peace and require chastisement?
We, for complicity in Pompilia's flight
And deviation, and carnal intercourse
220 With the same, do set aside and relegate
The Canon Caponsacchi for three years
At Civita in the neighbourhood of Rome:
And we consign Pompilia to the care
Of a certain Sisterhood of penitents
I' the city's self, expert to deal with such.'
Word for word, there's your judgment! Read it, lords,
Re-utter your deliberate penalty
For the crime yourselves establish! Your award –
Who chop a man's right-hand off at the wrist
230 For tracing with forefinger words in wine

O' the table of a drinking-booth that bear
Interpretation as they mocked the Church!
– Who brand a woman black between the breasts
For sinning by connection with a Jew:
While for the Jew's self – pudency be dumb!
You mete out punishment such and such, yet so
Punish the adultery of wife and priest!
Take note of that, before the Molinists do,
And read me right the riddle, since right must be!
1240 While I stood rapt away with wonderment,
Voices broke in upon my mood and muse.
'Do you sleep?' began the friends at either ear,
'The case is settled, – you willed it should be so –
None of our counsel, always recollect!
With law's award, budge! Back into your place!
Your betters shall arrange the rest for you.
We'll enter a new action, claim divorce:
Your marriage was a cheat themselves allow:
You erred i' the person, – might have married thus
1250 Your sister or your daughter unaware.
We'll gain you, that way, liberty at least,
Sure of so much by law's own showing. Up
And off with you and your unluckiness –
Leave us to bury the blunder, sweep things smooth!'
I was in humble frame of mind, be sure!
I bowed, betook me to my place again.
Station by station I retraced the road,
Touched at this hostel, passed this post-house by,
Where, fresh-remembered yet, the fugitives
1260 Had risen to the heroic stature: still –
'That was the bench they sat on, – there's the board
They took the meal at, – yonder garden-ground
They leaned across the gate of,' – ever a word
O' the Helen and the Paris, with 'Ha! you're he,
The ... much-commiserated husband?' Step
By step, across the pelting, did I reach
Arezzo, underwent the archway's grin,
Traversed the length of sarcasm in the street,

Found myself in my horrible house once more,
1270 And after a colloquy ... no word assists!
With the mother and the brothers, stiffened me
Strait out from head to foot as dead man does,
And, thus prepared for life as he for hell,
Marched to the public Square and met the world.
Apologise for the pincers, palliate screws?
Ply me with such toy-trifles, I entreat!
Trust who has tried both sulphur and sops-in-wine!

I played the man as I best might, bade friends
Put non-essentials by and face the fact.
1280 'What need to hang myself as you advise?
The paramour is banished, – the ocean's width,
Or the suburb's length, – to Ultima Thule, say,
Or Proxima Civitas, what's the odds of name
And place? He's banished, and the fact's the thing.
Why should law banish innocence an inch?
Here's guilt then, what else do I care to know?
The adulteress lies imprisoned, – whether in a well
With bricks above and a snake for company,
Or tied by a garter to a bed-post, – much
I mind what's little, – least's enough and to spare!
1290 The little fillip on the coward's cheek
Serves as though crab-tree cudgel broke his pate.
Law has pronounced there's punishment, less or more:
And I take note o' the fact and use it thus –
For the first flaw in the original bond,
I claim release. My contract was to wed
The daughter of Pietro and Violante. Both
Protest they never had a child at all.
Then I have never made a contract: good!
1300 Cancel me quick the thing pretended one.
I shall be free. What matter if hurried over
The harbour-boom by a great favouring tide,
Or the last of a spent ripple that lifts and leaves?
The Abate is about it. Laugh who wins!
You shall not laugh me out of faith in law!

I listen, through all your noise, to Rome!'

                                  Rome spoke.

In three months letters thence admonished me,
'Your plan for the divorce is all mistake.

1310 It would hold, now, had you, taking thought to wed
Rachel of the blue eye and golden hair,
Found swarth-skinned Leah cumber couch next day:
But Rachel, blue-eyed golden-haired aright,
Proving to be only Laban's child, not Lot's,
Remains yours all the same for ever more.
No whit to the purpose is your plea: you err
I' the person and the quality – nowise
In the individual, – that's the case in point!
You go to the ground, – are met by a cross-suit

1320 For separation, of the Rachel here,
From bed and board, – she is the injured one,
You did the wrong and have to answer it.
As for the circumstance of imprisonment
And colour it lends to this your new attack,
Never fear, that point is considered too!
The durance is already at an end;
The convent-quiet preyed upon her health,
She is transferred now to her parents' house
– No-parents, when that cheats and plunders you,

1330 But parentage again confessed in full,
When such confession pricks and plagues you more –
As now – for, this their house is not the house
In Via Vittoria wherein neighbours' watch
Might incommode the freedom of your wife,
But a certain villa smothered up in vines
At the town's edge by the gate i' the Pauline way,
Out of eye-reach, out of ear-shot, little and lone,
Whither a friend, – at Civita, we hope,
A good half-dozen-hours' ride off, – might, some eve,

1340 Betake himself, and whence ride back, some morn,
Nobody the wiser: but be that as it may,
Do not afflict your brains with trifles now.
You have still three suits to manage, all and each

Ruinous truly should the event play false.
It is indeed the likelier so to do,
That brother Paul, your single prop and stay,
After a vain attempt to bring the Pope
To set aside procedures, sit himself
And summarily use prerogative,
1350 Afford us the infallible finger's tact
To disentwine your tangle of affairs,
Paul, – finding it moreover past his strength
To stem the irruption, bear Rome's ridicule
Of . . . since friends must speak . . . to be round with you . . .
Of the old outwitted husband, wronged and wroth,
Pitted against a brace of juveniles –
A brisk priest who is versed in Ovid's art
More than his Summa, and a gamesome wife
Able to act Corinna without book,
1360 Beside the waggish parents who played dupes
To dupe the duper – (and truly divers scenes
Of the Arezzo palace, tickle rib
And teaze eye till the tears come, so we laugh;
Nor wants the shock at the inn its comic force,
And then the letters and poetry – *merum sal!*)
– Paul, finally, in such a state of things,
After a brief temptation to go jump
And join the fishes in the Tiber, drowns
Sorrow another and a wiser way:
1370 House and goods, he has sold all off, is gone,
Leaves Rome, – whether for France or Spain, who knows?
Or Britain almost divided from our orb.
You have lost him anyhow.'
                              Now, – I see my lords
Shift in their seat, – would I could do the same!
They probably please expect my bile was moved
To purpose, nor much blame me: now, they judge,
The fiery titillation urged my flesh
Break through the bonds. By your pardon, no, sweet Sirs!
1380 I got such missives in the public place;
When I sought home, – with such news, mounted stair

And sat at last in the sombre gallery,
('T was Autumn, the old mother in bed betimes,
Having to bear that cold, the finer frame
Of her daughter-in-law had found intolerable –
The brother, walking misery away
O' the mountain-side with dog and gun belike)
As I supped, ate the coarse bread, drank the wine
Weak once, now acrid with the toad's-head-squeeze,
1390 My wife's bestowment, – I broke silence thus:
'Let me, a man, manfully meet the fact,
Confront the worst o' the truth, end, and have peace!
I am irremediably beaten here, –
The gross illiterate vulgar couple, – bah!
Why, they have measured forces, mastered mine,
Made me their spoil and prey from first to last.
They have got my name, – 't is nailed now fast to theirs,
The child or changeling is anyway my wife;
Point by point as they plan they execute,
1400 They gain all, and I lose all – even to the lure
That led to loss, – they have the wealth again
They hazarded awhile to hook me with,
Have caught the fish and find the bait entire:
They even have their child or changeling back
To trade with, turn to account a second time.
The brother, presumably might tell a tale
Or give a warning, – he, too, flies the field,
And with him vanish help and hope of help.
They have caught me in the cavern where I fell,
1410 Covered my loudest cry for human aid
With this enormous paving-stone of shame.
Well, are we demigods or merely clay?
Is success still attendant on desert?
Is this, we live on, heaven and the final state,
Or earth which means probation to the end?
Why claim escape from man's predestined lot
Of being beaten and baffled? – God's decree,
In which I, bowing bruised head, acquiesce.
One of us Franceschini fell long since

1420 I' the Holy Land, betrayed, tradition runs,
To Paynims by the feigning of a girl
He rushed to free from ravisher, and found
Lay safe enough with friends in ambuscade
Who flayed him while she clapped her hands and laughed:
Let me end, falling by a like device.
It will not be so hard. I am the last
O' my line which will not suffer any more.
I have attained to my full fifty years,
(About the average of us all, 'tis said,
1430 Though it seems longer to the unlucky man)
– Lived through my share of life; let all end here,
Me and the house and grief and shame at once.
Friends my informants, – I can bear your blow!'
And I believe 't was in no unmeet match
For the stoic's mood, with something like a smile,
That, when morose December roused me next,
I took into my hand, broke seal to read
The new epistle from Rome. 'All to no use!
Whate'er the turn next injury take,' smiled I,
1440 'Here's one has chosen his part and knows his cue.
I am done with, dead now; strike away, good friends!
Are the three suits decided in a trice?
Against me, – there's no question! How does it go?
Is the parentage of my wife demonstrated
Infamous to her wish? Parades she now
Loosed of the cincture that so irked the loin?
Is the last penny extracted from my purse
To mulct me for demanding the first pound
Was promised in return for value paid?
1450 Has the priest, with nobody to court beside,
Courted the Muse in exile, hitched my hap
Into a rattling ballad-rhyme which, bawled
At tavern-doors, wakes rapture everywhere,
And helps cheap wine down throat this Christmas time,
Beating the bagpipes? Any or all of these!
As well, good friends, you cursed my palace here
To its old cold stone face, – stuck your cap for crest

Over the shield that's extant in the Square, –
Or spat on the statue's cheek, the impatient world
1460 Sees cumber tomb-top in our family church:
Let him creep under covert as I shall do,
Half below-ground already indeed. Good-bye!
My brothers are priests, and childless so; that's well –
And, thank God most for this, no child leave I –
None after me to bear till his heart break
The being a Franceschini and my son!'

'Nay,' said the letter, 'but you have just that!
A babe, your veritable son and heir –
Lawful, – 't is only eight months since your wife
1470 Left you, – so, son and heir, your babe was born
Last Wednesday in the villa, – you see the cause
For quitting Convent without beat of drum,
Stealing a hurried march to this retreat
That's not so savage as the Sisterhood
To slips and stumbles: Pietro's heart is soft,
Violante leans to pity's side, – the pair
Ushered you into life a bouncing boy:
And he's already hidden away and safe
From any claim on him you mean to make –
1480 They need him for themselves, – don't fear, they know
The use o' the bantling, – the nerve thus laid bare
To nip at, new and nice, with finger-nail!'

Then I rose up like fire, and fire-like roared.
What, all is only beginning not ending now?
The worm which wormed its way from skin through flesh
To the bone and there lay biting, did its best,
What, it goes on to scrape at the bone's self,
Will wind to inmost marrow and madden me?
There's to be yet my representative,
1490 Another of the name shall keep displayed
The flag with the ordure on it, brandish still
The broken sword has served to stir a jakes?
Who will he be, how will you call the man?

A Franceschini, – when who cut my purse,
Filched my name, hemmed me round, hustled me hard
As rogues at a fair some fool they strip i' the midst,
When these count gains, vaunt pillage presently: –
But a Caponsacchi, oh, be very sure!
When what demands its tribute of applause
1500 Is the cunning and impudence o' the pair of cheats,
The lies and lust o' the mother, and the brave
Bold carriage of the priest, worthily crowned
By a witness to his feat i' the following age, –
And how this three-fold cord could hook and fetch
And land leviathan that king of pride!
Or say, by some mad miracle of chance,
Is he indeed my flesh and blood, this babe?
Was it because fate forged a link at last
Betwixt my wife and me, and both alike
1510 Found we had henceforth some one thing to love,
Was it when she could damn my soul indeed
She unlatched door, let all the devils o' the dark
Dance in on me to cover her escape?
Why then, the surplusage of disgrace, the spilth
Over and above the measure of infamy,
Failing to take effect on my coarse flesh
Seasoned with scorn now, saturate with shame, –
Is saved to instil on and corrode the brow,
The baby-softness of my first-born child –
1520 The child I had died to see though in a dream,
The child I was bid strike out for, beat the wave
And baffle the tide of troubles where I swam,
So I might touch shore, lay down life at last
At the feet so dim and distant and divine
Of the apparition, as 't were Mary's babe
Had held, through night and storm, the torch aloft, –
Born now in very deed to bear this brand
On forehead and curse me who could not save!
Rather be the town-talk true, Square's jest, street's jeer
1530 True, my own inmost heart's confession true,
And he's the priest's bastard and none of mine!

Ay, there was cause for flight, swift flight and sure!
The husband gets unruly, breaks all bounds
When he encounters some familiar face,
Fashion of feature, brow and eyes and lips
Where he least looked to find them, – time to fly!
This bastard then, a nest for him is made,
As the manner is of vermin, in my flesh –
Shall I let the filthy pest buzz, flap and sting,
1540 Busy at my vitals and, nor hand nor foot
Lift, but let be, lie still and rot resigned?
No, I appeal to God, – what says Himself,
How lessons Nature when I look to learn?
Why, that I am alive, am still a man
With brain and heart and tongue and right-hand too –
Nay, even with friends, in such a cause as this,
To right me if I fail to take my right.
No more of law; a voice beyond the law
Enters my heart, *Quis est pro Domino?*

1550 Myself, in my own Vittiano, told the tale
To my own serving-people summoned there:
Told the first half of it, scarce heard to end
By judges who got done with judgment quick
And clamoured to go execute her 'hest –
Who cried 'Not one of us that dig your soil
And dress your vineyard, prune your olive-trees,
But would have brained the man debauched our wife,
And staked the wife whose lust allured the man,
And paunched the Duke, had it been possible,
1560 Who ruled the land, yet barred us such revenge!'
I fixed on the first whose eyes caught mine, some four,
Resolute youngsters with the heart still fresh,
Filled my purse with the residue o' the coin
Uncaught-up by my wife whom haste made blind,
Donned the first rough and rural garb I found,
Took whatsoever weapon came to hand,
And out we flung and on we ran or reeled
Romeward, I have no memory of our way,

Only that, when at intervals the cloud
1570 Of horror about me opened to let in life,
I listened to some song in the ear, some snatch
Of a legend, relic of religion, stray
Fragment of record very strong and old
Of the first conscience, the anterior right,
The God's-gift to mankind, impulse to quench
The antagonistic spark of hell and tread
Satan and all his malice into dust,
Declare to the world the one law, right is right.
Then the cloud re-encompassed me, and so
1580 I found myself, as on the wings of winds,
Arrived: I was at Rome on Christmas Eve.

Festive bells – everywhere the Feast o' the Babe,
Joy upon earth, peace and good will to man!
I am baptized. I started and let drop
The dagger. 'Where is it, His promised peace?'
Nine days o' the Birth-Feast did I pause and pray
To enter into no temptation more.
I bore the hateful house, my brother's once,
Deserted, – let the ghost of social joy
1590 Mock and make mouths at me from empty room
And idle door that missed the master's step, –
Bore the frank wonder of incredulous eyes,
As my own people watched without a word,
Waited, from where they huddled round the hearth
Black like all else, that nod so slow to come –
I stopped my ears even to the inner call
Of the dread duty, heard only the song
'Peace upon earth,' saw nothing but the face
O' the Holy Infant and the halo there
1600 Able to cover yet another face
Behind it, Satan's which I else should see.
But, day by day, joy waned and withered off:
The Babe's face, premature with peak and pine,
Sank into wrinkled ruinous old age,
Suffering and death, then mist-like disappeared,

And showed only the Cross at end of all,
Left nothing more to interpose 'twixt me
And the dread duty, – for the angel's song,
'Peace upon earth,' louder and louder pealed
1610 'O Lord, how long, how long be unavenged?'
On the ninth day, this grew too much for man.
I started up – 'Some end must be!' At once,
Silence: then, scratching like a death-watch-tick,
Slowly within my brain was syllabled,
'One more concession, one decisive way
And but one, to determine thee the truth, –
This way, in fine, I whisper in thy ear:
Now doubt, anon decide, thereupon act!'

'That is a way, thou whisperest in my ear!
1620 I doubt, I will decide, then act,' said I –
Then beckoned my companions: 'Time is come!'

And so, all yet uncertain save the will
To do right, and the daring aught save leave
Right undone, I did find myself at last
I' the dark before the villa with my friends,
And made the experiment, the final test,
Ultimate chance that ever was to be
For the wretchedness inside. I knocked – pronounced
The name, the predetermined touch for truth,
1630 'What welcome for the wanderer? Open straight –'
To the friend, physician, friar upon his rounds,
Traveller belated, beggar lame and blind? –
No, but – 'to Caponsacchi!' And the door
Opened.
      And then, – why, even then, I think,
I' the minute that confirmed my worst of fears,
Surely, – I pray God that I think aright! –
Had but Pompilia's self, the tender thing
Who once was good and pure, was once my lamb
1640 And lay in my bosom, had the well-known shape
Fronted me in the door-way, – stood there faint

With the recent pang, perhaps, of giving birth
To what might, though by miracle, seem my child, –
Nay more, I will say, had even the aged fool
Pietro, the dotard, in whom folly and age
Wrought, more than enmity or malevolence,
To practice and conspire against my peace, –
Had either of these but opened, I had paused.
But it was she the hag, she that brought hell
1650 For a dowry with her to her husband's house,
She the mock-mother, she that made the match
And married me to perdition, spring and source
O' the fire inside me that boiled up from heart
To brain and hailed the Fury gave it birth, –
Violante Comparini, she it was,
With the old grin amid the wrinkles yet,
Opened: as if in turning from the Cross,
With trust to keep the sight and save my soul,
I had stumbled, first thing, on the serpent's head
1660 Coiled with a leer at foot of it.

       There was the end!
Then was I rapt away by the impulse, one
Immeasurable everlasting wave of a need
To abolish that detested life. 'T was done:
You know the rest and how the folds o' the thing,
Twisting for help, involved the other two
More or less serpent-like: how I was mad,
Blind, stamped on all, the earth-worms with the asp,
And ended so.
1670   You came on me that night,
Your officers of justice, – caught the crime
In the first natural frenzy of remorse?
Twenty miles off, sound sleeping as a child
On a cloak i' the straw which promised shelter first,
With the bloody arms beside me, – was it not so?
Wherefore not? Why, how else should I be found?
I was my own self, had my sense again,
My soul safe from the serpents. I could sleep:
Indeed and, dear my lords, I shall sleep now,

1680 Spite of my shoulder, in five minutes' space,
When you dismiss me, having truth enough!
It is but a few days are passed, I find,
Since this adventure. Do you tell me, four?
Then the dead are scarce quiet where they lie,
Old Pietro, old Violante, side by side
At the church Lorenzo, – oh, they know it well!
So do I. But my wife is still alive,
Has breath enough to tell her story yet,
Her way, which is not mine, no doubt at all.

1690 And Caponsacchi, you have summoned him, –
Was he so far to send for? Not at hand?
I thought some few o' the stabs were in his heart,
Or had not been so lavish, – less had served.
Well, he too tells his story, – florid prose
As smooth as mine is rough. You see, my lords,
There will be a lying intoxicating smoke
Born of the blood, – confusion probably, –
For lies breed lies – but all that rests with you!
The trial is no concern of mine; with me

1700 The main of the care is over: I at least
Recognise who took that huge burthen off,
Let me begin to live again. I did
God's bidding and man's duty, so, breathe free;
Look you to the rest! I heard Himself prescribe,
That great Physician, and dared lance the core
Of the bad ulcer; and the rage abates,
I am myself and whole now: I prove cured
By the eyes that see, the ears that hear again,
The limbs that have relearned their youthful play,

1710 The healthy taste of food and feel of clothes
And taking to our common life once more,
All that now urges my defence from death.
The willingness to live, what means it else?
Before, – but let the very action speak!
Judge for yourselves, what life seemed worth to me
Who, not by proxy but in person, pitched
Head-foremost into danger as a fool

That never cares if he can swim or no –
So he but find the bottom, braves the brook.
1720 No man omits precaution, quite neglects
Secrecy, safety, schemes not how retreat,
Having schemed he might advance. Did I so scheme?
Why, with a warrant which 't is ask and have,
With horse thereby made mine without a word,
I had gained the frontier and slept safe that night.
Then, my companions, – call them what you please,
Slave or stipendiary, – what need of one
To me whose right-hand did its owner's work?
Hire an assassin yet expose yourself?
1730 As well buy glove and then thrust naked hand
I' the thorn-bush. No, the wise man stays at home,
Sends only agents out, with pay to earn:
At home, when they come back, – he straight discards
Or else disowns. Why use such tools at all
When a man's foes are of his house, like mine,
Sit at his board, sleep in his bed? Why noise,
When there's the *acquetta* and the silent way?
Clearly my life was valueless.

But now
1740 Health is returned, and sanity of soul
Nowise indifferent to the body's harm.
I find the instinct bids me save my life;
My wits, too, rally round me; I pick up
And use the arms that strewed the ground before,
Unnoticed or spurned aside: I take my stand,
Make my defence. God shall not lose a life
May do Him further service, while I speak
And you hear, you my judges and last hope!
You are the law: 't is to the law I look.
1750 I began life by hanging to the law,
To the law it is I hang till life shall end.
My brother made appeal to the Pope, 't is true,
To stay proceedings, judge my cause himself
Nor trouble law, – some fondness of conceit

That rectitude, sagacity sufficed
The investigator in a case like mine,
Dispensed with the machine of law. The Pope
Knew better, set aside my brother's plea
And put me back to law, – referred the cause
1760 *Ad judices meos*, – doubtlessly did well.
Here, then, I clutch my judges, – I claim law –
Cry, by the higher law whereof your law
O' the land is humbly representative, –
Cry, on what point is it, where either accuse,
I fail to furnish you defence? I stand
Acquitted, actually or virtually,
By every intermediate kind of court
That takes account of right or wrong in man,
Each unit in the series that begins
1770 With God's throne, ends with the tribunal here.
God breathes, not speaks, his verdicts, felt not heard,
Passed on successively to each court I call
Man's conscience, custom, manners, all that make
More and more effort to promulgate, mark
God's verdict in determinable words,
Till last come human jurists – solidify
Fluid result, – what's fixable lies forged,
Statute, – the residue escapes in fume,
Yet hangs aloft, a cloud, as palpable
1780 To the finer sense as word the legist welds.
Justinian's Pandects only make precise
What simply sparkled in men's eyes before,
Twitched in their brow or quivered on their lip,
Waited the speech they called but would not come.
These courts then, whose decree your own confirms, –
Take my whole life, not this last act alone,
Look on it by the light reflected thence!
What has Society to charge me with?
Come, unreservedly, – favour nor fear, –
1790 I am Guido Franceschini, am I not?
You know the courses I was free to take?
I took just that which let me serve the Church,

I gave it all my labour in body and soul
Till these broke down i' the service. 'Specify?'
Well, my last patron was a Cardinal.
I left him unconvicted of a fault –
Was even helped, by way of gratitude,
Into the new life that I left him for,
This very misery of the marriage, – he
1800 Made it, kind soul, so far as in him lay –
Signed the deed where you yet may see his name.
He is gone to his reward, – dead, being my friend
Who could have helped here also, – that, of course!
So far, there's my acquittal, I suppose.
Then comes the marriage itself – no question, lords,
Of the entire validity of that!
In the extremity of distress, 't is true,
For after-reasons, furnished abundantly,
I wished the thing invalid, went to you
1810 Only some months since, set you duly forth
My wrong and prayed your remedy, that a cheat
Should not have force to cheat my whole life long.
'Annul a marriage? 'T is impossible!
Though ring about your neck be brass not gold,
Needs must it clasp, gangrene you all the same!'
Well, let me have the benefit, just so far,
O' the fact announced, – my wife then is my wife,
I have allowance for a husband's right.
I am charged with passing right's due bound, – such acts
1820 As I thought just, my wife called cruelty,
Complained of in due form, – convoked no court
Of common gossipry, but took her wrongs –
And not once, but so long as patience served –
To the town's top, jurisdiction's pride of place,
To the Archbishop and the Governor.
These heard her charge with my reply, and found
That futile, this sufficient: they dismissed
The hysteric querulous rebel, and confirmed
Authority in its wholesome exercise,
1830 They, with directest access to the facts.

    ' – Ay, for it was their friendship favoured you,
Hereditary alliance against a breach
I' the social order: prejudice for the name
Of Franceschini!' – So I hear it said:
But not here. You, lords, never will you say
'Such is the nullity of grace and truth,
Such the corruption of the faith, such lapse
Of law, such warrant have the Molinists
For daring reprehend us as they do, –
1840 That we pronounce it just a common case,
Two dignitaries, each in his degree
First, foremost, this the spiritual head, and that
The secular arm o' the body politic,
Should, for mere wrongs' love and injustice' sake,
Side with, aid and abet in cruelty
This broken beggarly noble, – bribed perhaps
By his watered wine and mouldy crust of bread –
Rather than that sweet tremulous flower-like wife
Who kissed their hands and curled about their feet
1850 Looking the irresistible loveliness
In tears that takes man captive, turns' . . . enough!
Do you blast your predecessors? What forbids
Posterity to trebly blast yourselves
Who set the example and instruct their tongue?
You dreaded the crowd, succumbed to the popular cry,
Or else, would nowise seem defer thereto
And yield to public clamour though i' the right!
You ridded your eye of my unseemliness,
The noble whose misfortune wearied you, –
1860 Or, what's more probable, made common cause
With the cleric section, punished in myself
Maladroit uncomplaisant laity,
Defective in behaviour to a priest
Who claimed the customary partnership
I' the house and the wife. Lords, any lie will serve!
Look to it, – or allow me freed so far!

Then I proceed a step, come with clean hands

Thus far, re-tell the tale told eight months since.
The wife, you allow so far, I have not wronged,
1870 Has fled my roof, plundered me and decamped
In company with the priest her paramour:
And I gave chace, came up with, caught the two
At the wayside inn where both had spent the night,
Found them in flagrant fault, and found as well,
By documents with name and plan and date,
The fault was furtive then that's flagrant now,
Their intercourse a long established crime.
I did not take the license law's self gives
To slay both criminals o' the spot at the time,
1880 But held my hand, – preferred play prodigy
Of patience which the world calls cowardice,
Rather than seem anticipate the law
And cast discredit on its organs, – you –
So, to your bar I brought both criminals,
And made my statement: heard their counter-charge
Nay, – their corroboration of my tale,
Nowise disputing its allegements, not
I' the main, not more than nature's decency
Compels men to keep silence in this kind, –
1890 Only contending that the deeds avowed
Would take another colour and bear excuse.
You were to judge between us; so you did.
You disregard the excuse, you breathe away
The colour of innocence and leave guilt black,
'Guilty' is the decision of the court,
And that I stand in consequence untouched,
One white integrity from head to heel.
Not guilty? Why then did you punish them?
True, punishment has been inadequate –
1900 'T is not I only, not my friends that joke,
My foes that jeer, who echo 'inadequate' –
For, by a chance that comes to help for once,
The same case simultaneously was judged
At Arezzo, in the province of the Court
Where the crime had beginning but not end.

They then, deciding on but half o' the crime,
The effraction, robbery, – features of the fault
I never cared to dwell upon at Rome, –
What was it they adjudged as penalty
1910 To Pompilia, – the one criminal o' the pair
Amenable to their judgment, not the priest
Who is Rome's? Why, just imprisonment for life
I' the Stinche. There was Tuscany's award
To a wife that robs her husband: you at Rome
Having to deal with adultery in a wife
And, in a priest, breach of the priestly vow,
Give gentle sequestration for a month
In a manageable Convent, then release,
You call imprisonment, in the very house
1920 O' the very couple, the sole aim and end
Of the culprits' crime was – there to reach and rest
And there take solace and defy me: well, –
This difference 'twixt their penalty and yours
Is immaterial: make your penalty less –
Merely that she should henceforth wear black gloves
And white fan, she who wore the opposite –
Why, all the same the fact o' the thing subsists.
Reconcile to your conscience as you may,
Be it on your own heads, you pronounced one half
1930 O' the penalty for heinousness like hers
And his, that's for a fault at Carnival
Of comfit-pelting past discretion's law,
Or accident to handkerchief in Lent
Which falls perversely as a lady kneels
Abruptly, and but half conceals her neck!
I acquiesce for my part, – punished, though
By a pin-point scratch, means guilty: guilty means
– What have I been but innocent hitherto?
Anyhow, here the offence, being punished, ends.

1940 Ends? – for you deemed so, did you not, sweet lords?
That was throughout the veritable aim
O' the sentence light or heavy, – to redress

Recognised wrong? You righted me, I think?
Well then, – what if I, at this last of all,
Demonstrate you, as my whole pleading proves,
No particle of wrong received thereby
One atom of right? – that cure grew worse disease?
That in the process you call 'justice done'
All along you have nipped away just inch
1950 By inch the creeping climbing length of plague
Breaking my tree of life from root to branch,
And left me, after all and every act
Of your interference, – lightened of what load?
At liberty wherein? Mere words and wind!
'Now I was saved, now I should feel no more
The hot breath, find a respite from fixed eye
And vibrant tongue!' Why, scarce your back was turned,
There was the reptile, that feigned death at first,
Renewing its detested spire and spire
1960 Around me, rising to such heights of hate
That, so far from mere purpose now to crush
And coil itself on the remains of me,
Body and mind, and there flesh fang content,
Its aim is now to evoke life from death,
Make me anew, satisfy in my son
The hunger I may feed but never sate,
Tormented on to perpetuity, –
My son, whom, dead, I shall know, understand,
Feel, hear, see, never more escape the sight
1970 In heaven that's turned to hell, or hell returned
(So, rather, say) to this same earth again, –
Moulded into the image and made one,
Fashioned of soul as featured like in face,
First taught to laugh and lisp and stand and go
By that thief, poisoner and adulteress
I call Pompilia, he calls . . . sacred name,
Be unpronounced, be unpolluted here!
And last led up to the glory and prize of hate
By his . . . foster-father, Caponsacchi's self,
1980 The perjured priest, pink of conspirators,

Tricksters and knaves, yet polished, superfine,
Manhood to model adolescence by . . .
Lords, look on me, declare, – when, what I show,
Is nothing more nor less than what you deemed
And doled me out for justice, – what did you say?
For reparation, restitution and more, –
Will you not thank, praise, bid me to your breasts
For having done the thing you thought to do,
And thoroughly trampled out sin's life at last?
1990 I have heightened phrase to make your soft speech serve,
Doubled the blow you but essayed to strike,
Carried into effect your mandate here
That else had fallen to ground: mere duty done,
Oversight of the master just supplied
By zeal i' the servant: I, being used to serve,
Have simply . . . what is it they charge me with?
Blackened again, made legible once more
Your own decree, not permanently writ,
Rightly conceived but all too faintly traced, –
2000 It reads efficient, now, comminatory,
A terror to the wicked, answers so
The mood o' the magistrate, the mind of law.
Absolve, then, me, law's mere executant!
Protect your own defender, – save me, Sirs!
Give me my life, give me my liberty,
My good name and my civic rights again!
It would be too fond, too complacent play
Into the hands o' the devil, should we lose
The game here, I for God: a soldier-bee
2010 That yields his life, exenterate with the stroke
O' the sting that saves the hive. I need that life,
Oh, never fear! I'll find life plenty use
Though it should last five years more, aches and all!
For, first thing, there's the mother's age to help –
Let her come break her heart upon my breast,
Not on the blank stone of my nameless tomb!
The fugitive brother has to be bidden back
To the old routine, repugnant to the tread,
Of daily suit and service to the Church, –

2020 Thro' gibe and jest, those stones that Shimei flung!
Ay, and the spirit-broken youth at home,
The awe-struck altar-ministrant, shall make
Amends for faith now palsied at the source,
Shall see truth yet triumphant, justice yet
A victor in the battle of this world!
Give me – for last, best gift, my son again,
Whom law makes mine, – I take him at your word,
Mine be he, by miraculous mercy, lords!
Let me lift up his youth and innocence
2030 To purify my palace, room by room
Purged of the memories, lend from his bright brow
Light to the old proud paladin my sire
Shrunk now for shame into the darkest shade
O' the tapestry, showed him once and shrouds him now!
Then may we, – strong from that rekindled smile, –
Go forward, face new times, the better day.
And when, in times made better through your brave
Decision now, – might but Utopia be! –
Rome rife with honest women and strong men,
2040 Manners reformed, old habits back once more,
Customs that recognize the standard worth, –
The wholesome household rule in force again,
Husbands once more God's representative,
Wives like the typical Spouse once more, and Priests
No longer men of Belial, with no aim
At leading silly women captive, but
Of rising to such duties as yours now, –
Then will I set my son at my right-hand
And tell his father's story to this point,
2050 Adding 'The task seemed superhuman, still
I dared and did it, trusting God and law:
And they approved of me: give praise to both!'
And if, for answer, he shall stoop to kiss
My hand, and peradventure start thereat, –
I engage to smile 'That was an accident
I' the necessary process, – just a trip
O' the torture-irons in their search for truth, –
Hardly misfortune, and no fault at all.'

BOOK VI

Giuseppe Caponsacchi

Answer you, Sirs? Do I understand aright?
Have patience! In this sudden smoke from hell, –
So things disguise themselves, – I cannot see
My own hand held thus broad before my face
And know it again. Answer you? Then that means
Tell over twice what I, the first time, told
Six months ago: 't was here, I do believe,
Fronting you same three in this very room,
I stood and told you: yet now no one laughs,
Who then ... nay, dear my lords, but laugh you did,
As good as laugh, what in a judge we style
Laughter – no levity, nothing indecorous, lords!
Only, – I think I apprehend the mood:
There was the blameless shrug, permissible smirk,
The pen's pretence at play with the pursed mouth,
The titter stifled in the hollow palm
Which rubbed the eyebrow and caressed the nose,
When I first told my tale: they meant, you know,
'The sly one, all this we are bound believe!
Well, he can say no other than what he says.
We have been young, too, – come, there's greater guilt!
Let him but decently disembroil himself,
Scramble from out the scrape nor move the mud, –
We solid ones may risk a finger-stretch!'
And now you sit as grave, stare as aghast
As if I were a phantom: now 't is – 'Friend,
Collect yourself!' – no laughing matter more –
'Counsel the Court in this extremity,
Tell us again!' – tell that, for telling which,
I got the jocular piece of punishment,

Was sent to lounge a little in the place
Whence now of a sudden here you summon me
To take the intelligence from just – your lips
You, Judge Tommati, who then tittered most, –
That she I helped eight months since to escape
Her husband, is retaken by the same,
Three days ago, if I have seized your sense, –
(I being disallowed to interfere,
Meddle or make in a matter none of mine,
40 For you and law were guardians quite enough
O' the innocent, without a pert priest's help) –
And that he has butchered her accordingly,
As she foretold and as myself believed, –
And, so foretelling and believing so,
We were punished, both of us, the merry way:
Therefore, tell once again the tale! For what?
Pompilia is only dying while I speak!
Why does the mirth hang fire and miss the smile?
My masters, there's an old book, you should con
50 For strange adventures, applicable yet,
'T is stuffed with. Do you know that there was once
This thing: a multitude of worthy folk
Took recreation, watched a certain group
Of soldiery intent upon a game, –
How first they wrangled, but soon fell to play,
Threw dice, – the best diversion in the world.
A word in your ear, – they are now casting lots,
Ay, with that gesture quaint and cry uncouth,
For the coat of One murdered an hour ago!
60 I am a priest, – talk of what I have learned.
Pompilia is bleeding out her life belike,
Gasping away the latest breath of all,
This minute, while I talk – not while you laugh?

Yet, being sobered now, what is it you ask
By way of explanation? There's the fact!
It seems to fill the universe with sight
And sound, – from the four corners of this earth

Tells itself over, to my sense at least.
But you may want it lower set i' the scale, –
70 Too vast, too close it clangs in the ear, perhaps;
You 'd stand back just to comprehend it more:
Well then, let me, the hollow rock, condense
The voice o' the sea and wind, interpret you
The mystery of this murder. God above!
It is too paltry, such a transference
O' the storm's roar to the cranny of the stone!

This deed, you saw begin – why does its end
Surprise you? Why should the event enforce
The lesson, we ourselves learned, she and I,
80 From the first o' the fact, and taught you, all in vain?
This Guido from whose throat you took my grasp,
Was this man to be favoured, now, or feared,
Let do his will, or have his will restrained,
In the relation with Pompilia? – say!
Did any other man need interpose
– Oh, though first comer, though as strange at the work
As fribble must be, coxcomb, fool that's near
To knave as, say, a priest who fears the world –
Was he bound brave the peril, save the doomed,
90 Or go on, sing his snatch and pluck his flower,
Keep the straight path and let the victim die?
I held so; you decided otherwise,
Saw no such peril, therefore no such need
To stop song, loosen flower, and leave path: Law,
Law was aware and watching, would suffice,
Wanted no priest's intrusion, palpably
Pretence, too manifest a subterfuge!
Whereupon I, priest, coxcomb, fribble and fool,
Ensconced me in my corner, thus rebuked,
100 A kind of culprit, over-zealous hound
Kicked for his pains to kennel; I gave place,
To you, and let the law reign paramount:
I left Pompilia to your watch and ward,
And now you point me – there and thus she lies!

Men, for the last time, what do you want with me?
Is it, – you acknowledge, as it were, a use,
A profit in employing me? – at length
I may conceivably help the august law?
I am free to break the blow, next hawk that swoops
110 On next dove, nor miss much of good repute?
Or what if this your summons, after all,
Be but the form of mere release, no more,
Which turns the key and lets the captive go?
I have paid enough in person at Civita,
Am free, – what more need I concern me with?
Thank you! I am rehabilitated then,
A very reputable priest. But she –
The glory of life, the beauty of the world,
The splendour of heaven, . . . well, Sirs, does no one
    move?
120 Do I speak ambiguously? The glory, I say,
And the beauty, I say, and splendour, still say I,
Who, a priest, trained to live my whole life long
On beauty and splendour, solely at their source,
God, – have thus recognized my food in one,
You tell me, is fast dying while we talk,
Pompilia, – how does lenity to me,
Remit one death-bed pang to her? Come, smile!
The proper wink at the hot-headed youth
Who lets his soul show, through transparent words,
130 The mundane love that's sin and scandal too!
You are all struck acquiescent now, it seems:
It seems the oldest, gravest signor here,
Even the redoubtable Tommati, sits
Chop-fallen, – understands how law might take
Service like mine, of brain and heart and hand,
In good part. Better late than never, law!
You understand of a sudden, gospel too
Has a claim here, may possibly pronounce
Consistent with my priesthood, worthy Christ,
140 That I endeavoured to save Pompilia?

Then,
You were wrong, you see: that's well to see, though late:
That's all we may expect of man, this side
The grave: his good is – knowing he is bad:
Thus will it be with us when the books ope
And we stand at the bar on judgment-day.
Well then, I have a mind to speak, see cause
To relume the quenched flax by this dreadful light,
Burn my soul out in showing you the truth.
150 I heard, last time I stood here to be judged,
What is priest's-duty, – labour to pluck tares
And weed the corn of Molinism; let me
Make you hear, this time, how, in such a case,
Man, be he in the priesthood or at plough,
Mindful of Christ or marching step by step
With . . . what's his style, the other potentate
Who bids have courage and keep honour safe,
Nor let minuter admonition teaze? –
How he is bound, better or worse, to act.
160 Earth will not end through this misjudgment, no!
For you and the others like you sure to come,
Fresh work is sure to follow, – wickedness
That wants withstanding. Many a man of blood,
Many a man of guile will clamour yet,
Bid you redress his grievance, – as he clutched
The prey, forsooth a stranger stepped between,
And there's the good gripe in pure waste! My part
Is done; i' the doing it, I pass away
Out of the world. I want no more with earth.
170 Let me, in heaven's name, use the very snuff
O' the taper in one last spark shall show truth
For a moment, show Pompilia who was true!
Not for her sake, but yours: if she is dead,
Oh, Sirs, she can be loved by none of you
More or least priestly! Saints, to do us good,
Must be in heaven, I seem to understand:
We never find them saints before, at least.
Be her first prayer then presently for you –

She has done the good to me . . .
180   What is all this?
There, I was born, have lived, shall die, a fool!
This is a foolish outset: – might with cause
Give colour to the very lie o' the man,
The murderer, – make as if I loved his wife,
In the way he called love. He is the fool there!
Why, had there been in me the touch of taint,
I had picked up so much of knaves'-policy
As hide it, keep one hand pressed on the place
Suspected of a spot would damn us both.
190 Or no, not her! – not even if any of you
Dares think that I, i' the face of death, her death
That's in my eyes and ears and brain and heart,
Lie, – if he does, let him! I mean to say,
So he stop there, stay thought from smirching her
The snow-white soul that angels fear to take
Untenderly. But, all the same, I know
I too am taintless, and I bare my breast.
You can't think, men as you are, all of you,
But that, to hear thus suddenly such an end
200 Of such a wonderful white soul, that comes
Of a man and murderer calling the white black,
Must shake me, trouble and disadvantage. Sirs,
Only seventeen!

                          Why, good and wise you are!
You might at the beginning stop my mouth:
So, none would be to speak for her, that knew.
I talk impertinently, and you bear,
All the same. This it is to have to do
With honest hearts: they easily may err,
210 But in the main they wish well to the truth.
You are Christians; somehow, no one ever plucked
A rag, even, from the body of the Lord,
To wear and mock with, but, despite himself,
He looked the greater and was the better. Yes,
I shall go on now. Does she need or not

I keep calm? Calm I'll keep as monk that croons
Transcribing battle, earthquake, famine, plague,
From parchment to his cloister's chronicle.
Not one word more from the point now!

220   I begin.
Yes, I am one of your body and a priest.
Also I am a younger son o' the House
Oldest now, greatest once, in my birth-town
Arezzo, I recognize no equal there –
(I want all arguments, all sorts of arms
That seem to serve, – use this for a reason, wait!)
Not therefore thrust into the Church, because
O' the piece of bread one gets there. We were first
Of Fiesole, that rings still with the fame
230 Of Capo-in-Sacco our progenitor:
When Florence ruined Fiesole, our folk
Migrated to the victor-city, and there
Flourished, – our palace and our tower attest,
In the Old Mercato, – this was years ago,
Four hundred, full, – no, it wants fourteen just.
Our arms are those of Fiesole itself,
The shield quartered with white and red: a branch
Are the Salviati of us, nothing more.
That were good help to the Church? But better still –
240 Not simply for the advantage of my birth
I' the way of the world, was I proposed for priest;
But because there's an illustration, late
I' the day, that's loved and looked to as a saint
Still in Arezzo, he was bishop of,
Sixty years since: he spent to the last doit
His bishop's-revenue among the poor,
And used to tend the needy and the sick,
Barefoot, because of his humility.
He it was, – when the Granduke Ferdinand
250 Swore he would raze our city, plough the place
And sow it with salt, because we Aretines
Had tied a rope about the neck, to hale

The statue of his father from its base
For hate's sake, – he availed by prayers and tears
To pacify the Duke and save the town.
This was my father's father's brother. You see,
For his sake, how it was I had a right
To the self-same office, bishop in the egg,
So, grew i' the garb and prattled in the school,
260 Was made expect, from infancy almost,
The proper mood o' the priest; till time ran by
And brought the day when I must read the vows,
Declare the world renounced and undertake
To become priest and leave probation, – leap
Over the ledge into the other life,
Having gone trippingly hitherto up to the height
O'er the wan water. Just a vow to read!

I stopped short awe-struck. 'How shall holiest flesh
Engage to keep such vow inviolate,
270 How much less mine, – I know myself too weak,
Unworthy! Choose a worthier stronger man!'
And the very Bishop smiled and stopped the mouth
In its mid-protestation. 'Incapable?
Qualmish of conscience? Thou ingenuous boy!
Clear up the clouds and cast thy scruples far!
I satisfy thee there's an easier sense
Wherein to take such vow than suits the first
Rough rigid reading. Mark what makes all smooth,
Nay, has been even a solace to myself!
280 The Jews who needs must, in their synagogue,
Utter sometimes the holy name of God,
A thing their superstition boggles at,
Pronounce aloud the ineffable sacrosanct, –
How does their shrewdness help them? In this wise;
Another set of sounds they substitute,
Jumble so consonants and vowels – how
Should I know? – that there grows from out the old
Quite a new word that means the very same –
And o'er the hard place slide they with a smile.

290   Giuseppe Maria Caponsacchi mine,
      Nobody wants you in these latter days
      To prop the Church by breaking your back-bone, –
      As the necessary way was once, we know,
      When Dioclesian flourished and his like;
      That building of the buttress-work was done
      By martyrs and confessors: let it bide,
      Add not a brick, but, where you see a chink,
      Stick in a sprig of ivy or root a rose
      Shall make amends and beautify the pile!
300   We profit as you were the painfullest
      O' the martyrs, and you prove yourself a match
      For the cruellest confessor ever was,
      If you march boldly up and take your stand
      Where their blood soaks, their bones yet strew the soil,
      And cry "Take notice, I the young and free
      And well-to-do i' the world, thus leave the world,
      Cast in my lot thus with no gay young world
      But the grand old Church: she tempts me of the two!"
      Renounce the world? Nay, keep and give it us!
310   Let us have you, and boast of what you bring.
      We want the pick o' the earth to practise with,
      Not its offscouring, halt and deaf and blind
      In soul and body. There's a rubble-stone
      Unfit for the front o' the building, stuff to stow
      In a gap behind and keep us weather-tight;
      There 's porphyry for the prominent place. Good lack!
      Saint Paul has had enough and to spare, I trow,
      Of ragged run-away Onesimus:
      He wants the right-hand with the signet-ring
320   Of King Agrippa, now, to shake and use.
      I have a heavy scholar cloistered up,
      Close under lock and key, kept at his task
      Of letting Fenelon know the fool he is,
      In a book I promise Christendom next Spring.
      Why, if he covets so much meat, the clown,
      As a lark's wing next Friday, or, any day,
      Diversion beyond catching his own fleas,

He shall be properly swinged, I promise him.
But you, who are so quite another paste
330 Of a man, – do you obey me? Cultivate
Assiduous, that superior gift you have
Of making madrigals – (who told me? Ah!)
Get done a Marinesque Adoniad straight
With a pulse o' the blood a–pricking, here and there,
That I may tell the lady, "And he's ours!" '

So I became a priest: those terms changed all,
I was good enough for that, nor cheated so;
I could live thus and still hold head erect.
Now you see why I may have been before
340 A fribble and coxcomb, yet, as priest, break word
Nowise, to make you disbelieve me now.
I need that you should know my truth. Well, then,
According to prescription did I live,
– Conformed myself, both read the breviary
And wrote the rhymes, was punctual to my place
I' the Pieve, and as diligent at my post
Where beauty and fashion rule. I throve apace,
Sub-deacon, Canon, the authority
For delicate play at tarocs, and arbiter
350 O' the magnitude of fan-mounts: all the while
Wanting no whit the advantage of a hint
Benignant to the promising pupil, – thus:
'Enough attention to the Countess now,
The young one; 't is her mother rules the roast,
We know where, and puts in a word: go pay
Devoir to-morrow morning after mass!
Break that rash promise to preach, Passion-week!
Has it escaped you the Archbishop grunts
And snuffles when one grieves to tell his Grace
360 No soul dares treat the subject of the day
Since his own masterly handling it (ha, ha!)
Five years ago, – when somebody could help
And touch up an odd phrase in time of need,
(He, he!) – and somebody helps you, my son!

Therefore, don't prove so indispensable
At the Pieve, sit more loose i' the seat, nor grow
A fixture by attendance morn and eve!
Arezzo's just a haven midway Rome –
Rome's the eventual harbour, – make for port,
370 Crowd sail, crack cordage! And your cargo be
A polished presence, a genteel manner, wit
At will, and tact at every pore of you!
I sent our lump of learning, Brother Clout,
And Father Slouch, our piece of piety,
To see Rome and try suit the Cardinal.
Thither they clump-clumped, beads and book in hand,
And ever since 't is meat for man and maid
How both flopped down, prayed blessing on bent pate
Bald many an inch beyond the tonsure's need,
380 Never once dreaming, the two moony dolts,
There's nothing moves his Eminence so much
As – far from all this awe at sanctitude –
Heads that wag, eyes that twinkle, modified mirth
At the closet-lectures on the Latin tongue
A lady learns so much by, we know where.
Why, body o' Bacchus, you should crave his rule
For pauses in the elegiac couplet, chasms
Permissible only to Catullus! There!
Now go do duty: brisk, break Priscian's head
390 By reading the day's office – there's no help.
You've Ovid in your poke to plaster that;
Amen's at the end of all: then sup with me!'

Well, after three or four years of this life,
In prosecution of my calling, I
Found myself at the theatre one night
With a brother Canon, in a mood and mind
Proper enough for the place, amused or no:
When I saw enter, stand, and seat herself
A lady, young, tall, beautiful, strange and sad.
400 It was as when, in our cathedral once,
As I got yawningly through matin-song,

I saw *facchini* bear a burden up,
Base it on the high-altar, break away
A board or two, and leave the thing inside
Lofty and lone: and lo, when next I looked,
There was the Rafael! I was still one stare,
When – 'Nay, I'll make her give you back your gaze' –
Said Canon Conti; and at the word he tossed
A paper-twist of comfits to her lap,
410 And dodged and in a trice was at my back
Nodding from over my shoulder. Then she turned,
Looked our way, smiled the beautiful sad strange smile.
'Is not she fair? 'T is my new cousin,' said he:
'The fellow lurking there i' the black o' the box
Is Guido, the old scapegrace: she's his wife,
Married three years since: how his Countship sulks!
He has brought little back from Rome beside,
After the bragging, bullying. A fair face,
And – they do say – a pocket-full of gold
420 When he can worry both her parents dead.
I don't go much there, for the chamber's cold
And the coffee pale. I got a turn at first
Paying my duty, – I observed they crouched
– The two old frightened family spectres, close
In a corner, each on each like mouse on mouse
I' the cat's cage: ever since, I stay at home.
Hallo, there's Guido, the black, mean and small,
Bends his brows on us – please to bend your own
On the shapely nether limbs of Light-skirts there
430 By way of a diversion! I was a fool
To fling the sweetmeats. Prudence, for God's love!
To-morrow I'll make my peace, e'en tell some fib,
Try if I can't find means to take you there.'
That night and next day did the gaze endure,
Burnt to my brain, as sunbeam thro' shut eyes,
And not once changed the beautiful sad strange smile.
At vespers Conti leaned beside my seat
I' the choir, – part said, part sung – '*In ex-cel-sis* –
All's to no purpose: I have louted low,

440 But he saw you staring – *quia sub* – do n't incline
To know you nearer: him we would not hold
For Hercules, – the man would lick your shoe
If you and certain efficacious friends
Managed him warily, – but there's the wife:
Spare her, because he beats her, as it is,
She's breaking her heart quite fast enough – *jam tu* –
So, be you rational and make amends
With little Light-skirts yonder – *in secula*
Secu-lo-o-o-o-rum. Ah, you rogue! Every one knows
450 What great dame she makes jealous: one against one,
Play, and win both!'

              Sirs, ere the week was out,
I saw and said to myself 'Light-skirts hides teeth
Would make a dog sick, – the great dame shows spite
Should drive a cat mad: 't is but poor work this –
Counting one's fingers till the sonnet's crowned.
I doubt much if Marino really be
A better bard than Dante after all.
'T is more amusing to go pace at eve
460 I' the Duomo, – watch the day's last gleam outside
Turn, as into a skirt of God's own robe,
Those lancet-windows' jewelled miracle, –
Than go eat the Archbishop's ortolans,
Digest his jokes. Luckily Lent is near:
Who cares to look will find me in my stall
At the Pieve, constant to this faith at least –
Never to write a canzonet any more.'

So, next week, 't was my patron spoke abrupt,
In altered guise, 'Young man, can it be true
470 That after all your promise of sound fruit,
You have kept away from Countess young or old
And gone play truant in church all day long?
Are you turning Molinist?' I answered quick
'Sir, what if I turned Christian? It might be.
The fact is, I am troubled in my mind,
Beset and pressed hard by some novel thoughts.

This your Arezzo is a limited world;
There's a strange Pope, – 't is said, a priest who thinks.
Rome is the port, you say: to Rome I go.
480 I will live alone, one does so in a crowd,
And look into my heart a little.' 'Lent
Ended,' – I told friends, – 'I shall go to Rome.'

One evening I was sitting in a muse
Over the opened 'Summa,' darkened round
By the mid-March twilight, thinking how my life
Had shaken under me, – broke short indeed
And showed the gap 'twixt what is, what should be, –
And into what abysm the soul may slip,
Leave aspiration here, achievement there,
490 Lacking omnipotence to connect extremes –
Thinking moreover . . . oh, thinking, if you like,
How utterly dissociated was I
A priest and celibate, from the sad strange wife
Of Guido, – just as an instance to the point,
Nought more, – how I had a whole store of strengths
Eating into my heart, which craved employ,
And she, perhaps, need of a finger's help, –
And yet there was no way in the wide world
To stretch out mine and so relieve myself –
500 How when the page o' the Summa preached its best,
Her smile kept glowing out of it, as to mock
The silence we could break by no one word, –
There came a tap without the chamber-door,
And a whisper, when I bade who tapped speak out,
And, in obedience to my summons, last
In glided a masked muffled mystery,
Laid lightly a letter on the opened book,
Then stood with folded arms and foot demure,
Pointing as if to mark the minutes' flight.

510 I took the letter, read to the effect
That she, I lately flung the comfits to,
Had a warm heart to give me in exchange,

And gave it, – loved me and confessed it thus,
And bade me render thanks by word of mouth,
Going that night to such a side o' the house
Where the small terrace overhangs a street
Blind and deserted, not the street in front:
Her husband being away, the surly patch,
At his villa of Vittiano.

520   'And you?' – I asked:
'What may you be?' – 'Count Guido's kind of maid –
Most of us have two functions in his house.
We all hate him, the lady suffers much,
'T is just we show compassion, furnish aid,
Specially since her choice is fixed so well.
What answer may I bring to cheer the sweet
Pompilia?'

       Then I took a pen and wrote.
'No more of this! That you are fair, I know:
530 But other thoughts now occupy my mind.
I should not thus have played the insensible
Once on a time. What made you, – may one ask, –
Marry your hideous husband? 'T was a fault,
And now you taste the fruit of it. Farewell.'

'There!' smiled I as she snatched it and was gone –
'There, let the jealous miscreant, – Guido's self,
Whose mean soul grins through this transparent trick, –
Be baulked so far, defrauded of his aim!
What fund of satisfaction to the knave,
540 Had I kicked this his messenger down stairs,
Trussed to the middle of her impudence,
Setting his heart at ease so! No, indeed!
There's the reply which he shall turn and twist
At pleasure, snuff at till his brain grow drunk,
As the bear does when he finds a scented glove
That puzzles him, – a hand and yet no hand,
Of other perfume than his own foul paw!

  Last month, I had doubtless chosen to play the dupe,
  Accepted the mock-invitation, kept
550 The sham appointment, cudgel beneath cloak,
  Prepared myself to pull the appointer's self
  Out of the window from his hiding-place
  Behind the gown of this part-messenger
  Part-mistress who would personate the wife.
  Such had seemed once a jest permissible:
  Now, I am not i' the mood.'
        Back next morn brought
  The messenger, a second letter in hand.
  'You are cruel, Thyrsis, and Myrtilla moans
560 Neglected but adores you, makes request
  For mercy: why is it you dare not come?
  Such virtue is scarce natural to your age:
  You must love someone else; I hear you do,
  The Baron's daughter or the Advocate's wife,
  Or both, – all's one, would you make me the third –
  I take the crumbs from table gratefully
  Nor grudge who feasts there. 'Faith, I blush and blaze!
  Yet if I break all bounds, there's reason sure,
  Are you determinedly bent on Rome?
570 I am wretched here, a monster tortures me:
  Carry me with you! Come and say you will!
  Concert this very evening! Do not write!
  I am ever at the window of my room
  Over the terrace, at the *Ave*. Come!'

  I questioned – lifting half the woman's mask
  To let her smile loose. 'So, you gave my line
  To the merry lady?' 'She kissed off the wax,
  And put what paper was not kissed away,
  In her bosom to go burn: but merry, no!
580 She wept all night when evening brought no friend,
  Alone, the unkind missive at her breast;
  Thus Philomel, the thorn at her breast too,
  Sings' . . 'Writes this second letter?' 'Even so!

Then she may peep at vespers forth?' – 'What risk
Do we run o' the husband?' – 'Ah, – no risk at all!
He is more stupid even than jealous. Ah –
That was the reason? Why, the man 's away!
Beside, his bugbear is that friend of yours,
Fat little Canon Conti. He fears him –
590 How should he dream of you? I told you truth –
He goes to the villa at Vittiano – 't is
The time when Spring-sap rises in the vine –
Spends the night there. And then his wife's a child,
Does he think a child outwits him? A mere child:
Yet so full grown, a dish for any duke.
Do n't quarrel longer with such cates, but come!'

I wrote 'In vain do you solicit me.
I am a priest: and you are wedded wife,
Whatever kind of brute your husband prove.
600 I have scruples, in short. Yet should you really show
Sign at the window . . . but nay, best be good!
My thoughts are elsewhere.' – 'Take her that!'
                                   – 'Again
Let the incarnate meanness, cheat and spy,
Mean to the marrow of him, make his heart
His food, anticipate hell's worm once more!
Let him watch shivering at the window – ay,
And let this hybrid, this his light-of-love
And lackey-of-lies, – a sage economy, –
610 Paid with embracings for the rank brass coin, –
Let her report and make him chuckle o'er
The break-down of my resolution now,
And lour at disappointment in good time!
– So tantalize and so enrage by turns,
Until the two fall each on the other like
Two famished spiders, as the coveted fly
That toys long, leaves their net and them at last!'
And so the missives followed thick and fast
For a month, say, – I still came at every turn
620 On the soft sly adder, endlong 'neath my tread.

I was met i' the street, made sign to in the church,
A slip was found i' the door-sill, scribbled word
'Twixt page and page o' the prayer-book in my place:
A crumpled thing dropped even before my feet,
Pushed through the blind, above the terrace-rail,
As I passed, by day, the very window once.
And ever from corners would be peering up
The messenger, with the self-same demand
'Obdurate still, no flesh but adamant?
630 Nothing to cure the wound, assuage the throe
O' the sweetest lamb that ever loved a bear?'
And ever my one answer in one tone –
'Go your ways, temptress! Let a priest read, pray,
Unplagued of vain talk, visions not for him!
In the end, you 'll have your will and ruin me!'

One day, a variation: thus I read:
'You have gained little by timidity.
My husband has found out my love at length,
Sees cousin Conti was the stalking-horse,
640 And you the game he covered, poor fat soul!
My husband is a formidable foe,
Will stick at nothing to destroy you. Stand
Prepared, or better, run till you reach Rome!
I bade you visit me, when the last place
My tyrant would have turned suspicious at,
Or cared to seek you in, was . . . why say, where?
But now all's changed: beside, the season's past
At the villa, – wants the master's eye no more.
Anyhow, I beseech you, stay away
650 From the window! He might well be posted there.'

I wrote – 'You raise my courage, or call up
My curiosity, who am but man.
Tell him he owns the palace, not the street
Under – that 's his and yours and mine alike.
If it should please me pad the path this eve,

Guido will have two troubles, first to get
Into a rage and then get out again.
Be cautious, though: at the *Ave*!'

                                You of the court!
660 When I stood question here and reached this point
O' the narrative, – search notes and see and say
If some one did not interpose with smile
And sneer, 'And prithee why so confident
That the husband must, of all needs, not the wife,
Fabricate thus, – what if the lady loved?
What if she wrote the letters?'

                               Learned Sir,
I told you there's a picture in our church.
Well, if a low-browed verger sidled up
670 Bringing me, like a blotch, on his prod's point,
A transfixed scorpion, let the reptile writhe,
And then said, 'See a thing that Rafael made –
This venom issued from Madonna's mouth!' –
I should reply, 'Rather, the soul of you
Has issued from your body, like from like,
By way of the ordure-corner!'

                               But no less,
I tired of the same black teazing lie
Obtruded thus at every turn; the pest
680 Was far too near the picture, anyhow:
One does Madonna service, making clowns
Remove their dung-heap from the sacristy.
'I will to the window, as he tempts,' said I:
'Yes, whom the easy love has failed allure,
This new bait of adventure may, – he thinks.
While the imprisoned lady keeps afar,
There will they lie in ambush, heads alert,
Kith, kin, and Count mustered to bite my heel.
No mother nor brother viper of the brood
690 Shall scuttle off without the instructive bruise!'
So, I went: crossed street and street: 'The next street's turn,

I stand beneath the terrace, see, above,
The black of the ambush-window. Then, in place
Of hand's throw of soft prelude over lute
And cough that clears way for the ditty last,' –
I began to laugh already – 'he will have
Out of the hole you hide in, on to the front,
Count Guido Franceschini, show yourself!
Hear what a man thinks of a thing like you,
700 And after, take this foulness in your face!'

The words lay living on my lip, I made
The one turn more – and there at the window stood,
Framed in its black square length, with lamp in hand,
Pompilia; the same great, grave, griefful air
As stands i' the dusk, on altar that I know,
Left alone with one moonbeam in her cell,
Our Lady of all the Sorrows. Ere I knelt –
Assured myself that she was flesh and blood –
She had looked one look and vanished.

710   I thought – 'Just so:
It was herself, they have set her there to watch –
Stationed to see some wedding-band go by,
On fair pretence that she must bless the bride,
Or wait some funeral with friends wind past,
And crave peace for the corpse that claims its due.
She never dreams they used her for a snare,
And now withdraw the bait has served its turn.
Well done, the husband, who shall fare the worse!'
And on my lip again was – 'Out with thee,
720 Guido!' When all at once she re-appeared;
But, this time, on the terrace overhead,
So close above me, she could almost touch
My head if she bent down; and she did bend,
While I stood still as stone, all eye, all ear.

She began – 'You have sent me letters, Sir:
I have read none, I can neither read nor write;

But she you gave them to, a woman here,
One of the people in whose power I am,
Partly explained their sense, I think, to me
730 Obliged to listen while she inculcates
That you, a priest, can dare love me, a wife,
Desire to live or die as I shall bid,
(She makes me listen if I will or no)
Because you saw my face a single time.
It cannot be she says the thing you mean;
Such wickedness were deadly to us both:
But good true love would help me now so much –
I tell myself, you may mean good and true.
You offer me, I seem to understand,
740 Because I am in poverty and starve,
Much money, where one piece would save my life.
The silver cup upon the altar-cloth
Is neither yours to give nor mine to take;
But I might take one bit of bread therefrom,
Since I am starving, and return the rest,
Yet do no harm: this is my very case.
I am in that strait, I may not abstain
From so much of assistance as would bring
The guilt of theft on neither you nor me;
750 But no superfluous particle of aid.
I think, if you will let me state my case,
Even had you been so fancy-fevered here,
Not your sound self, you must grow healthy now –
Care only to bestow what I can take.
That it is only you in the wide world,
Knowing me nor in thought nor word nor deed,
Who, all unprompted save by your own heart,
Come proffering assistance now, – were strange
But that my whole life is so strange: as strange
760 It is, my husband whom I have not wronged
Should hate and harm me. For his own soul's sake,
Hinder the harm! But there is something more,
And that the strangest: it has got to be

Somehow for my sake too, and yet not mine,
– This is a riddle – for some kind of sake
Not any clearer to myself than you,
And yet as certain as that I draw breath, –
I would fain live, not die – oh no, not die!
My case is, I was dwelling happily
770 At Rome with those dear Comparini, called
Father and mother to me; when at once
I found I had become Count Guido's wife:
Who then, not waiting for a moment, changed
Into a fury of fire, if once he was
Merely a man: his face threw fire at mine,
He laid a hand on me that burned all peace,
All joy, all hope, and last all fear away,
Dipping the bough of life, so pleasant once,
In fire which shrivelled leaf and bud alike,
780 Burning not only present life but past,
Which you might think was safe beyond his reach.
He reached it, though, since that beloved pair,
My father once, my mother all those years,
That loved me so, now say I dreamed a dream
And bid me wake, henceforth no child of theirs,
Never in all the time their child at all.
Do you understand? I cannot: yet so it is.
Just so I say of you that proffer help:
I cannot understand what prompts your soul,
790 I simply needs must see that it is so,
Only one strange and wonderful thing more.
They came here with me, those two dear ones, kept
All the old love up, till my husband, till
His people here so tortured them, they fled.
And now, is it because I grow in flesh
And spirit one with him their torturer,
That they, renouncing him, must cast off me?
If I were graced by God to have a child,
Could I one day deny God graced me so?
800 Then, since my husband hates me, I shall break
No law that reigns in this fell house of hate,

By using – letting have effect so much
Of hate as hides me from that whole of hate
Would take my life which I want and must have –
Just as I take from your excess of love
Enough to save my life with, all I need.
The Archbishop said to murder me were sin:
My leaving Guido were a kind of death
With no sin, – more death, he must answer for.
810   Hear now what death to him and life to you
I wish to pay and owe. Take me to Rome!
You go to Rome, the servant makes me hear.
Take me as you would take a dog, I think,
Masterless left for strangers to maltreat:
Take me home like that – leave me in the house
Where the father and the mother are; and soon
They'll come to know and call me by my name,
Their child once more, since child I am, for all
They now forget me, which is the worst o' the dream –
820   And the way to end dreams is to break them, stand,
Walk, go: then help me to stand, walk and go!
The Governor said the strong should help the weak:
You know how weak the strongest women are.
How could I find my way there by myself?
I cannot even call out, make them hear –
Just as in dreams: I have tried and proved the fact.
I have told this story and more to good great men,
The Archbishop and the Governor: they smiled.
"Stop your mouth, fair one!" – presently they frowned,
830   "Get you gone, disengage you from our feet!"
I went in my despair to an old priest,
Only a friar, no great man like these two,
But good, the Augustinian, people name
Romano, – he confessed me two months since:
He fears God, why then needs he fear the world?
And when he questioned how it came about
That I was found in danger of a sin –
Despair of any help from providence, –
"Since, though your husband outrage you," said he,

840 "That is a case too common, the wives die
Or live, but do not sin so deep as this" –
Then I told – what I never will tell you –
How, worse than husband's hate, I had to bear
The love, – soliciting to shame called love, –
Of his brother, – the young idle priest i' the house
With only the devil to meet there. "This is grave –
Yes, we must interfere: I counsel, – write
To those who used to be your parents once,
Of dangers here, bid them convey you hence!"

850 "But," said I, "when I neither read nor write?"
Then he took pity and promised "I will write."
If he did so, – why, they are dumb or dead:
Either they give no credit to the tale,
Or else, wrapped wholly up in their own joy
Of such escape, they care not who cries, still
I' the clutches. Anyhow, no word arrives.
All such extravagance and dreadfulness
Seems incident to dreaming, cured one way, –
Wake me! The letter I received this morn,

860 Said – if the woman spoke your very sense –
"You would die for me:" I can believe it now:
For now the dream gets to involve yourself.
First of all, you seemed wicked and not good,
In writing me those letters: you came in
Like a thief upon me. I this morning said
In my extremity, entreat the thief!
Try if he have in him no honest touch!
A thief might save me from a murderer.
'T was a thief said the last kind word to Christ:

870 Christ took the kindness and forgave the theft:
And so did I prepare what I now say.
But now, that you stand and I see your face,
Though you have never uttered word yet, – well, I know,
Here too has been dream-work, delusion too,
And that at no time, you with the eyes here,
Ever intended to do wrong by me,

Nor wrote such letters therefore. It is false,
And you are true, have been true, will be true.
To Rome then, – when is it you take me there?
880   Each minute lost is mortal. When? – I ask.'

I answered 'It shall be when it can be.
I will go hence and do your pleasure, find
The sure and speedy means of travel, then
Come back and take you to your friends in Rome.
There wants a carriage, money and the rest, –
A day's work by to-morrow at this time.
How shall I see you and assure escape?'

She replied, 'Pass, to-morrow at this hour.
If I am at the open window, well:
890   If I am absent, drop a handkerchief
And walk by! I shall see from where I watch,
And know that all is done. Return next eve,
And next, and so till we can meet and speak!'
'To-morrow at this hour I pass,' said I.
She was withdrawn.
                        Here is another point
I bid you pause at. When I told thus far,
Someone said, subtly, 'Here at least was found
Your confidence in error, – you perceived
900   The spirit of the letters, in a sort,
Had been the lady's, if the body should be
Supplied by Guido: say, he forged them all!
Here was the unforged fact – she sent for you,
Spontaneously elected you to help,
– What men call, loved you: Guido read her mind,
Gave it expression to assure the world
The case was just as he foresaw: he wrote,
She spoke.'
                        Sirs, that first simile serves still, –
910   That falsehood of a scorpion hatched, I say,
Nowhere i' the world but in Madonna's mouth.

Go on! Suppose, that falsehood foiled, next eve
Pictured Madonna raised her painted hand,
Fixed the face Rafael bent above the Babe,
On my face as I flung me at her feet:
Such miracle vouchsafed and manifest,
Would that prove the first lying tale was true?
Pompilia spoke, and I at once received,
Accepted my own fact, my miracle
920　Self-authorised and self-explained, – she chose
To summon me and signify her choice.
Afterward, – oh! I gave a passing glance
To a certain ugly cloud-shape, goblin-shred
Of hell-smoke hurrying past the splendid moon
Out now to tolerate no darkness more,
And saw right through the thing that tried to pass
For truth and solid, not an empty lie:
'So, he not only forged the words for her
But words for me, made letters he called mine:
930　What I sent, he retained, gave these in place,
All by the mistress-messenger! As I
Recognized her, at potency of truth,
So she, by the crystalline soul, knew me,
Never mistook the signs. Enough of this –
Let the wraith go to nothingness again,
Here is the orb, have only thought for her!'

'Thought?' nay, Sirs, what shall follow was not thought:
I have thought sometimes, and thought long and hard.
I have stood before, gone round a serious thing,
940　Tasked my whole mind to touch and clasp it close,
As I stretch forth my arm to touch this bar.
God and man, and what duty I owe both, –
I dare to say I have confronted these
In thought: but no such faculty helped here.
I put forth no thought, – powerless, all that night
I paced the city: it was the first Spring.
By the invasion I lay passive to,
In rushed new things, the old were rapt away;

Alike abolished – the imprisonment
950 Of the outside air, the inside weight o' the world
That pulled me down. Death meant, to spurn the ground,
Soar to the sky, – die well and you do that.
The very immolation made the bliss;
Death was the heart of life, and all the harm
My folly had crouched to avoid, now proved a veil
Hiding all gain my wisdom strove to grasp:
As if the intense centre of the flame
Should turn a heaven to that devoted fly
Which hitherto, sophist alike and sage,
960 Saint Thomas with his sober grey goose-quill,
And sinner Plato by Cephisian reed,
Would fain, pretending just the insect's good,
Whisk off, drive back, consign to shade again.
Into another state, under new rule
I knew myself was passing swift and sure;
Whereof the initiatory pang approached,
Felicitous annoy, as bitter-sweet
As when the virgin-band, the victors chaste,
Feel at the end the earthly garments drop,
970 And rise with something of a rosy shame
Into immortal nakedness: so I
Lay, and let come the proper throe would thrill
Into the ecstacy and outthrob pain.

I' the grey of dawn it was I found myself
Facing the pillared front o' the Pieve – mine,
My church: it seemed to say for the first time
'But am not I the Bride, the mystic love
O' the Lamb, who took thy plighted troth, my priest,
To fold thy warm heart on my heart of stone
980 And freeze thee nor unfasten any more?
This is a fleshly woman, – let the free
Bestow their life-blood, thou art pulseless now!'
See! Day by day I had risen and left this church
At the signal waved me by some foolish fan,
With half a curse and half a pitying smile

For the monk I stumbled over in my haste,
Prostrate and corpse-like at the altar-foot
Intent on his *corona;* then the church
Was ready with her quip, if word conduced,
990   To quicken my pace nor stop for prating – 'There!
Be thankful you are no such ninny, go
Rather to teach a black-eyed novice cards
Than gabble Latin and protrude that nose
Smoothed to a sheep's through no brains and much faith!'
That sort of incentive! Now the church changed tone –
Now, when I found out first that life and death
Are means to an end, that passion uses both,
Indisputably mistress of the man
Whose form of worship is self-sacrifice –
1000   Now, from the stone lungs sighed the scrannel voice
'Leave that live passion, come be dead with me!'
As if, i' the fabled garden, I had gone
On great adventure, plucked in ignorance
Hedge-fruit, and feasted to satiety,
Laughing at such high fame for hips and haws,
And scorned the achievement: then come all at once
O' the prize o' the place, the thing of perfect gold,
The apple's self: and, scarce my eye on that,
Was 'ware as well o' the seven-fold dragon's watch.

1010   Sirs, I obeyed. Obedience was too strange, –
This new thing that had been struck into me
By the look o' the lady, – to dare disobey
The first authoritative word. 'T was God's.
I had been lifted to the level of her,
Could take such sounds into my sense. I said
'We two are cognizant o' the Master now;
It is she bids me bow the head: how true,
I am a priest! I see the function here;
I thought the other way self-sacrifice:
1020   This is the true, seals up the perfect sum.
I pay it, sit down, silently obey.'

So, I went home. Dawn broke, noon broadened, I –
I sat stone-still, let time run over me.
The sun slanted into my room, had reached
The west. I opened book, – Aquinas blazed
With one black name only on the white page.
I looked up, saw the sunset: vespers rang:
'She counts the minutes till I keep my word
And come say all is ready. I am a priest.
1030 Duty to God is duty to her: I think
God, who created her, will save her too
Some new way, by one miracle the more,
Without me. Then, prayer may avail perhaps.'
I went to my own place i' the Pieve, read
The office: I was back at home again
Sitting i' the dark. 'Could she but know – but know
That, were there good in this distinct from God's,
Really good as it reached her, though procured
By a sin of mine, – I should sin: God forgives.
1040 She knows it is no fear withholds me: fear?
Of what? Suspense here is the terrible thing.
If she should, as she counts the minutes, come
On the fantastic notion that I fear
The world now, fear the Archbishop, fear perhaps
Count Guido, he who, having forged the lies,
May wait the work, attend the effect, – I fear
The sword of Guido! Let God see to that –
Hating lies, let not her believe a lie!'

Again the morning found me. 'I will work,
1050 Tie down my foolish thoughts. Thank God so far!
I have saved her from a scandal, stopped the tongues
Had broken else into a cackle and hiss
Around the noble name. Duty is still
Wisdom: I have been wise.' So the day wore.

At evening – 'But, achieving victory,
I must not blink the priest's peculiar part,
Nor shrink to counsel, comfort: priest and friend –

How do we discontinue to be friends?
I will go minister, advise her seek
1060 Help at the source; – above all, not despair:
There may be other happier help at hand.
I hope it, – wherefore then neglect to say?'

There she stood – leaned there, for the second time,
Over the terrace, looked at me, then spoke:
'Why is it you have suffered me to stay
Breaking my heart two days more than was need?
Why delay help, your own heart yearns to give?
You are again here, in the self-same mind,
I see here, steadfast in the face of you, –
1070 You grudge to do no one thing that I ask.
Why then is nothing done? You know my need.
Still, through God's pity on me, there is time
And one day more: shall I be saved or no?'
I answered – 'Lady, waste no thought, no word
Even to forgive me! Care for what I care –
Only! Now follow me as I were fate!
Leave this house in the dark to-morrow night,
Just before daybreak: – there's new moon this eve –
It sets, and then begins the solid black.
1080 Descend, proceed to the Torrione, step
Over the low dilapidated wall,
Take San Clemente, there's no other gate
Unguarded at the hour: some paces thence
An inn stands; cross to it; I shall be there.'

She answered, 'If I can but find the way.
But I shall find it. Go now!'

                              I did go,
Took rapidly the route myself prescribed,
Stopped at Torrione, climbed the ruined place,
1090 Proved that the gate was practicable, reached
The inn, no eye, despite the dark, could miss,
Knocked there and entered, made the host secure:

'With Caponsacchi it is ask and have;
I know my betters. Are you bound for Rome?
I get swift horse and trusty man,' said he.

Then I retraced my steps, was found once more
In my own house for the last time: there lay
The broad pale opened Summa. 'Shut his book,
There's other showing! 'T was a Thomas too
1100 Obtained, – more favoured than his namesake here, –
A gift, tied faith fast, foiled the tug of doubt, –
Our Lady's girdle; down he saw it drop
As she ascended into heaven, they say:
He kept that safe and bade all doubt adieu.
I too have seen a lady and hold a grace.'

I know not how the night passed: morning broke:
Presently came my servant. 'Sir, this eve –
Do you forget?' I started. – 'How forget?
What is it you know?' – 'With due submission, Sir,
1110 This being last Monday in the month but one
And a vigil, since to-morrow is Saint George,
And feast day, and moreover day for copes,
And Canon Conti now away a month,
And Canon Crispi sour because, forsooth,
You let him sulk in stall and bear the brunt
Of the octave ... Well, Sir, 'tis important!'
                                              'True!'
'Hearken, I have to start for Rome this night.
No word, lest Crispi overboil and burst!
1120 Provide me with a laic dress! Throw dust
I' the Canon's eye, stop his tongue's scandal so!
See there's a sword in case of accident.'
I knew the knave, the knave knew me.

                                   And thus
Through each familiar hindrance of the day
Did I make steadily for its hour and end, –
Felt time's old barrier-growth of right and fit

Give way through all its twines, and let me go;
Use and wont recognized the excepted man,
1130 Let speed the special service, – and I sped
Till, at the dead between midnight and morn,
There was I at the goal, before the gate,
With a tune in the ears, low leading up to loud,
A light in the eyes, faint that would soon be flare,
Ever some spiritual witness new and new
In faster frequence, crowding solitude
To watch the way o' the warfare, – till, at last,
When the ecstatic minute must bring birth,
Began a whiteness in the distance, waxed
1140 Whiter and whiter, near grew and more near,
Till it was she: there did Pompilia come:
The white I saw shine through her was her soul's,
Certainly, for the body was one black,
Black from head down to foot. She did not speak,
Glided into the carriage, – so a cloud
Gathers the moon up. 'By San Spirito,
To Rome, as if the road burned underneath!
Reach Rome, then hold my head in pledge, I pay
The run and the risk to heart's content!' Just that,
1150 I said, – then, in another tick of time,
Sprang, was beside her, she and I alone.

So it began, our flight thro' dusk to clear,
Through day and night and day again to night
Once more, and to last dreadful dawn of all.
Sirs, how should I lie quiet in my grave
Unless you suffer me wring, drop by drop,
My brain dry, make a riddance of the drench
Of minutes with a memory in each,
Recorded motion, breath or look of hers,
1160 Which poured forth would present you one pure glass,
Mirror you plain, – as God's sea, glassed in gold,
His saints, – the perfect soul Pompilia? Men,
You must know that a man gets drunk with truth
Stagnant inside him! Oh, they've killed her, Sirs!

Can I be calm?
     Calmly! Each incident
Proves, I maintain, that action of the flight
For the true thing it was. The first faint scratch
O' the stone will test its nature, teach its worth
1170 To idiots who name Parian, coprolite.
After all, I shall give no glare – at best
Only display you certain scattered lights
Lamping the rush and roll of the abyss –
Nothing but here and there a fire-point pricks
Wavelet from wavelet: well!
      For the first hour
We both were silent in the night, I know:
Sometimes I did not see nor understand.
Blackness engulphed me, – partial stupor, say –
1180 Then I would break way, breathe through the surprise,
And be aware again, and see who sat
In the dark vest with the white face and hands.
I said to myself – 'I have caught it, I conceive
The mind o' the mystery: 't is the way they wake
And wait, two martyrs somewhere in a tomb
Each by each as their blessing was to die;
Some signal they are promised and expect,
When to arise before the trumpet scares:
So, through the whole course of the world they wait
1190 The last day, but so fearless and so safe!
No otherwise, in safety and not fear,
I lie, because she lies too by my side.'
You know this is not love, Sirs, – it is faith,
The feeling that there's God, he reigns and rules
Out of this low world: that is all; no harm!
At times she drew a soft sigh – music seemed
Always to hover just above her lips
Not settle, – break a silence music too.

In the determined morning, I first found
1200 Her head erect, her face turned full to me,
Her soul intent on mine through two wide eyes.

I answered them. 'You are saved hitherto.
We have passed Perugia, – gone round by the wood,
Not through, I seem to think, – and opposite
I know Assisi; this is holy ground.'
Then she resumed. 'How long since we both left
Arezzo?' – 'Years – and certain hours beside.'

It was at . . . ah, but I forget the names!
'T is a mere post-house and a hovel or two, –
1210 I left the carriage and got bread and wine
And brought it her. – 'Does it detain to eat?'
' – They stay perforce, change horses, – therefore eat!
We lose no minute: we arrive, be sure!'
She said – I know not where – there's a great hill
Close over, and the stream has lost its bridge,
One fords it. She began – 'I have heard say
Of some sick body that my mother knew,
'T was no good sign when in a limb diseased
All the pain suddenly departs, – as if
1220 The guardian angel discontinued pain
Because the hope of cure was gone at last:
The limb will not again exert itself,
It needs be pained no longer: so with me,
– My soul whence all the pain is past at once:
All pain must be to work some good in the end.
True, this I feel now, this may be that good,
Pain was because of, – otherwise, I fear!'

She said, – a long while later in the day,
When I had let the silence be, – abrupt –
1230 'Have you a mother?' – 'She died, I was born.'
'A sister then?' – 'No sister.' – 'Who was it –
What woman were you used to serve this way,
Be kind to, till I called you and you came?'
I did not like that word. Soon afterward –
'Tell me, are men unhappy, in some kind
Of mere unhappiness at being men,
As women suffer, being womanish?

Have you, now, some unhappiness, I mean,
Born of what may be man's strength overmuch,
1240 To match the undue susceptibility,
The sense at every pore when hate is close?
It hurts us if a baby hides its face
Or child strikes at us punily, calls names
Or makes a mouth, – much more if stranger men
Laugh or frown, – just as that were much to bear!
Yet rocks split, – and the blow-ball does no more,
Quivers to feathery nothing at a touch;
And strength may have its drawback, weakness scapes.'

Once she asked 'What is it that made you smile,
1250 At the great gate with the eagles and the snakes,
Where the company entered, 't is a long time since?'
' – Forgive – I think you would not understand:
Ah, but you ask me, – therefore, it was this.
That was a certain bishop's villa-gate,
I knew it by the eagles, – and at once
Remembered this same bishop was just he
People of old were wont to bid me please
If I would catch preferment: so, I smiled
Because an impulse came to me, a whim –
1260 What if I prayed the prelate leave to speak,
Began upon him in his presence-hall
– "What, still at work so grey and obsolete?
Still rocheted and mitred more or less?
Do n't you feel all that out of fashion now?
I find out when the day of things is done!"'

At eve we heard the *angelus*: she turned –
'I told you I can neither read nor write.
My life stopped with the play-time; I will learn,
If I begin to live again: but you –
1270 Who are a priest – wherefore do you not read
The service at this hour? Read Gabriel's song,
The lesson, and then read the little prayer
To Raphael, proper for us travellers!'

I did not like that, neither, but I read.

When we stopped at Foligno it was dark.
The people of the post came out with lights:
The driver said, 'This time to-morrow, may
Saints only help, relays continue good,
Nor robbers hinder, we arrive at Rome.'
1280 I urged, – 'Why tax your strength a second night?
Trust me, alight here and take brief repose!
We are out of harm's reach, past pursuit: go sleep
If but an hour! I keep watch, guard the while
Here in the doorway.' But her whole face changed,
The misery grew again about her mouth,
The eyes burned up from faintness, like the fawn's
Tired to death in the thicket, when she feels
The probing spear o' the huntsman. 'Oh, no stay!'
She cried, in the fawn's cry, 'On to Rome, on, on –
1290 Unless 't is you who fear, – which cannot be!'

We did go on all night; but at its close
She was troubled, restless, moaned low, talked at whiles
To herself, her brow on quiver with the dream:
Once, wide awake, she menaced, at arms' length
Waved away something – 'Never again with you!
My soul is mine, my body is my soul's:
You and I are divided ever more
In soul and body: get you gone!' Then I –
'Why, in my whole life I have never prayed!
1300 Oh, if the God, that only can, would help!
Am I his priest with power to cast out fiends?
Let God arise and all his enemies
Be scattered!' By morn, there was peace, no sigh
Out of the deep sleep.

                            When she woke at last,
I answered the first look – 'Scarce twelve hours more,
Then, Rome! There probably was no pursuit,
There cannot now be peril: bear up brave!

Just some twelve hours to press through to the prize –
1310 Then, no more of the terrible journey!' 'Then,
No more o' the journey: if it might but last!
Always, my life-long, thus to journey still!
It is the interruption that I dread, –
With no dread, ever to be here and thus!
Never to see a face nor hear a voice!
Yours is no voice; you speak when you are dumb;
Nor face, I see it in the dark. I want
No face nor voice that change and grow unkind.'
That I liked, that was the best thing she said.

1320 In the broad day, I dared entreat, 'Descend!'
I told a woman, at the garden-gate
By the post-house, white and pleasant in the sun,
'It is my sister, – talk with her apart!
She is married and unhappy, you perceive;
I take her home because her head is hurt;
Comfort her as you women understand!'
So, there I left them by the garden-wall,
Paced the road, then bade put the horses to,
Came back, and there she sat: close to her knee,
1330 A black-eyed child still held the bowl of milk,
Wondered to see how little she could drink,
And in her arms the woman's infant lay.
She smiled at me 'How much good this has done!
This is a whole night's rest and how much more!
I can proceed now, though I wish to stay.
How do you call that tree with the thick top
That holds in all its leafy green and gold
The sun now like an immense egg of fire?'
(It was a million-leaved mimosa.) 'Take
1340 The babe away from me and let me go!'
And in the carriage 'Still a day, my friend!
And perhaps half a night, the woman fears.
I pray it finish since it cannot last.
There may be more misfortune at the close,
And where will you be? God suffice me then!'

And presently – for there was a roadside-shrine –
'When I was taken first to my own church
Lorenzo in Lucina, being a girl,
And bid confess my faults, I interposed
1350 "But teach me what fault to confess and know!"
So, the priest said – "You should bethink yourself:
Each human being needs must have done wrong!"
Now, be you candid and no priest but friend –
Were I surprised and killed here on the spot,
A runaway from husband and his home,
Do you account it were in sin I died?
My husband used to seem to harm me, not . . .
Not on pretence he punished sin of mine,
Nor for sin's sake and lust of cruelty,
1360 But as I heard him bid a farming-man
At the villa take a lamb once to the wood
And there ill-treat it, meaning that the wolf
Should hear its cries, and so come, quick be caught,
Enticed to the trap: he practised thus with me
That so, whatever were his gain thereby,
Others than I might become prey and spoil.
Had it been only between our two selves, –
His pleasure and my pain, – why, pleasure him
By dying, nor such need to make a coil!
1370 But this was worth an effort, that my pain
Should not become a snare, prove pain threefold
To other people – strangers – or unborn –
How should I know? I sought release from that –
I think, or else from, – dare I say, some cause
Such as is put into a tree, which turns
Away from the northwind with what nest it holds, –
The woman said that trees so turn: now, friend,
Tell me, because I cannot trust myself!
You are a man: what have I done amiss?'
1380 You must conceive my answer, – I forget –
Taken up wholly with the thought, perhaps,
This time she might have said, – might, did not say –
'You are a priest.' She said, 'my friend.'

                                        Day wore,
We passed the places, somehow the calm went,
Again the restless eyes began to rove
In new fear of the foe mine could not see:
She wandered in her mind, – addressed me once
'Gaetano!' – that is not my name: whose name?
1390 I grew alarmed, my head seemed turning too:
I quickened pace with promise now, now threat:
Bade drive and drive, nor any stopping more.
'Too deep i' the thick of the struggle, struggle through!
Then drench her in repose though death's self pour
The plenitude of quiet, – help us, God,
Whom the winds carry!'

                            Suddenly I saw
The old tower, and the little white-walled clump
Of buildings and the cypress-tree or two, –
1400 'Already Castelnuovo – Rome!' I cried,
'As good as Rome, – Rome is the next stage, think!
This is where travellers' hearts are wont to beat.
Say you are saved, sweet lady!' Up she woke.
The sky was fierce with colour from the sun
Setting. She screamed out 'No, I must not die!
Take me no farther, I should die: stay here!
I have more life to save than mine!'
                                        She swooned.
We seemed safe: what was it foreboded so?
1410 Out of the coach into the inn I bore
The motionless and breathless pure and pale
Pompilia, – bore her through a pitying group
And laid her on a couch, still calm and cured
By deep sleep of all woes at once. The host
Was urgent 'Let her stay an hour or two!
Leave her to us, all will be right by morn!'
Oh, my foreboding! But I could not choose.

I paced the passage, kept watch all night long.
I listened, – not one movement, not one sigh.

1420 'Fear not: she sleeps so sound!' they said – but I
Feared, all the same, kept fearing more and more,
Found myself throb with fear from head to foot,
Filled with a sense of such impending woe,
That, at first pause of night, pretence of gray,
I made my mind up it was morn. – 'Reach Rome,
Lest hell reach her! A dozen miles to make,
Another long breath, and we emerge!' I stood
I' the court-yard, roused the sleepy grooms. 'Have out
Carriage and horse, give haste, take gold!' – said I.

1430 While they made ready in the doubtful morn, –
'T was the last minute, – needs must I ascend
And break her sleep; I turned to go.

                              And there
Faced me Count Guido, there posed the mean man
As master, – took the field, encamped his rights,
Challenged the world: there leered new triumph, there
Scowled the old malice in the visage bad
And black o' the scamp. Soon triumph suppled the tongue
A little, malice glued to his dry throat,

1440 And he part howled, part hissed . . . oh, how he kept
Well out o' the way, at arm's length and to spare! –
'My salutation to your priestship! What?
Matutinal, busy with book so soon
Of an April day that's damp as tears that now
Deluge Arezzo at its darling's flight? –
'T is unfair, wrongs feminity at large,
To let a single dame monopolize
A heart the whole sex claims, should share alike:
Therefore I overtake you, Canon! Come!

1450 The lady, – could you leave her side so soon?
You have not yet experienced at her hands
My treatment, you lay down undrugged, I see!
Hence this alertness – hence no death-in-life
Like what held arms fast when she stole from mine.
To be sure, you took the solace and repose
That first night at Foligno! – news abound
O' the road by this time, – men regaled me much,

As past them I came halting after you,
Vulcan pursuing Mars, as poets sing, –
1460 Still at the last here pant I, but arrive,
Vulcan – and not without my Cyclops too,
The Commissary and the unpoisoned arm
O' the Civil Force, should Mars turn mutineer.
Enough of fooling: capture the culprits, friend!
Here is the lover in the smart disguise
With the sword, – he is a priest, so mine lies still:
There upstairs hides my wife the runaway,
His leman: the two plotted, poisoned first,
Plundered me after, and eloped thus far
1470 Where now you find them. Do your duty quick!
Arrest and hold him! That's done: now catch her!'
During this speech of that man, – well, I stood
Away, as he managed, – still, I stood as near
The throat of him, – with these two hands, my own, –
As now I stand near yours, Sir, – one quick spring,
One great good satisfying gripe, and lo!
There had he lain abolished with his lie,
Creation purged o' the miscreate, man redeemed,
A spittle wiped off from the face of God!
1480 I, in some measure, seek a poor excuse
For what I left undone, in just this fact
That my first feeling at the speech I quote
Was – not of what a blasphemy was dared,
Not what a bag of venomed purulence
Was split and noisome, – but how splendidly
Mirthful, what ludicrous a lie was launched!
Would Molière's self wish more than hear such man
Call, claim such woman for his own, his wife,
Even though, in due amazement at the boast,
1490 He had stammered, she moreover was divine?
She to be his, – were hardly less absurd
Than that he took her name into his mouth,
Licked, and then let it go again, the beast,
Signed with his slaver. Oh, she poisoned him,
Plundered him, and the rest! Well, what I wished

Was, that he would but go on, say once more
So to the world, and get his meed of men,
The fist's reply to the filth. And while I mused,
The minute, oh the misery, was gone!
1500 On either idle hand of me there stood
Really an officer, nor laughed i' the least.
They rendered justice to his reason, laid
Logic to heart, as 't were submitted them
'Twice two makes four.'
               'And now, catch her!' – he cried.
That sobered me. 'Let myself lead the way –
Ere you arrest me, who am somebody,
And, as you hear, a priest and privileged, –
To the lady's chamber! I presume you – men
1510 Expert, instructed how to find out truth,
Familiar with the guise of guilt. Detect
Guilt on her face when it meets mine, then judge
Between us and the mad dog howling there!'
Up we all went together, in they broke
O' the chamber late my chapel. There she lay,
Composed as when I laid her, that last eve,
O' the couch, still breathless, motionless, sleep's self,
Wax-white, seraphic, saturate with the sun
O' the morning that now flooded from the front
1520 And filled the window with a light like blood.
'Behold the poisoner, the adulteress,
– And feigning sleep too! Seize, bind!' – Guido hissed.

She started up, stood erect, face to face
With the husband: back he fell, was buttressed there
By the window all a-flame with morning-red,
He the black figure, the opprobrious blur
Against all peace and joy and light and life.
'Away from between me and hell!' – she cried:
'Hell for me, no embracing any more!
1530 I am God's, I love God, God – whose knees I clasp,
Whose utterly most just award I take,
But bear no more love-making devils: hence!'

I may have made an effort to reach her side
From where I stood i' the door-way, – anyhow
I found the arms, I wanted, pinioned fast,
Was powerless in the clutch to left and right
O' the rabble pouring in, rascality
Enlisted, rampant on the side of hearth
Home and the husband, – pay in prospect too!
1540 They heaped themselves upon me. – 'Ha! – and him
Also you outrage? Him too, my sole friend,
Guardian and saviour? That I baulk you of,
Since – see how God can help at last and worst!'
She sprung at the sword that hung beside him, seized,
Drew, brandished it, the sunrise burned for joy
O' the blade, 'Die,' cried she, 'devil, in God's name!'
Ah, but they all closed round her, twelve to one,
– The unmanly men, no woman-mother made,
Spawned somehow! Dead-white and disarmed she lay.
1550 No matter for the sword, her word sufficed
To spike the coward through and through: he shook,
Could only spit between the teeth – 'You see?
You hear? Bear witness, then! Write down ... but, no –
Carry these criminals to the prison-house,
For first thing! I begin my search meanwhile
After the stolen effects, gold, jewels, plate,
Money and clothes, they robbed me of and fled:
With no few amorous pieces, verse and prose,
I have much reason to expect to find.'

1560 When I saw, that, – no more than the first mad speech,
Made out the speaker mad and a laughing-stock,
So neither did this next device explode
One listener's indignation, – that a scribe
Did sit down, set himself to write indeed,
And sundry knaves began to peer and pry
In corner and hole, – that Guido, wiping brow
And getting him a countenance, was fast
Losing his fear, beginning to strut free
O' the stage of his exploit, snuff here, sniff there, –

1570 I took the truth in, guessed sufficiently
The service for the moment – 'What I say,
Slight at your peril! We are aliens here,
My adversary and I, called noble both;
I am the nobler, and a name men know.
I could refer our cause to our own court
In our own country, but prefer appeal
To the nearer jurisdiction. Being a priest,
Though in a secular garb, – for reasons good
I shall adduce in due time to my peers, –
1580 I demand that the Church I serve, decide
Between us, right the slandered lady there.
A Tuscan noble, I might claim the Duke:
A priest, I rather choose the Church, – bid Rome
Cover the wronged with her inviolate shield.'

There was no refusing this: they bore me off,
They bore her off, to separate cells o' the same
Ignoble prison, and, separate, thence to Rome.
Pompilia's face, then and thus, looked on me
The last time in this life: not one sight since,
1590 Never another sight to be! And yet
I thought I had saved her. I appealed to Rome:
It seems I simply sent her to her death.
You tell me she is dying now, or dead;
I cannot bring myself to quite believe
This is a place you torture people in:
What if this your intelligence were just
A subtlety, an honest wile to work
On a man at unawares? 'T were worthy you.
No, Sirs, I cannot have the lady dead!
1600 That erect form, flashing brow, fulgurant eye,
That voice immortal (oh, that voice of hers!)
That vision in the blood-red day-break – that
Leap to life of the pale electric sword
Angels go armed with, – that was not the last
O' the lady! Come, I see through it, you find –
Know the manoeuvre! Also herself said

I had saved her: do you dare say she spoke false?
Let me see for myself if it be so!
Though she were dying, a priest might be of use,
1610 The more when he's a friend too, – she called me
Far beyond 'friend.' Come, let me see her – indeed
It is my duty, being a priest: I hope
I stand confessed, established, proved a priest?
My punishment had motive that, a priest
I, in a laic garb, a mundane mode,
Did what were harmlessly done otherwise.
I never touched her·with my finger-tip
Except to carry her to the couch, that eve,
Against my heart, beneath my head, bowed low,
1620 As we priests carry the paten: that is why
– To get leave and go see her of your grace –
I have told you this whole story over again.
Do I deserve grace? For I might lock lips,
Laugh at your jurisdiction: what have you
To do with me in the matter? I suppose
You hardly think I donned a bravo's dress
To have a hand in the new crime; on the old,
Judgment's delivered, penalty imposed,
I was chained fast at Civita hand and foot –
1630 She had only you to trust to, you and Rome,
Rome and the Church, and no pert meddling priest
Two days ago, when Guido, with the right,
Hacked her to pieces. One might well be wroth;
I have been patient, done my best to help:
I come from Civita and punishment
As friend of the court – and for pure friendship's sake
Have told my tale to the end, – nay, not the end –
For, wait – I'll end – not leave you that excuse!

When we were parted, – shall I go on there?
640 I was presently brought to Rome – yes, here I stood
Opposite yonder very crucifix –
And there sat you and you, Sirs, quite the same.
I heard charge, and bore question, and told tale

Noted down in the book there, – turn and see
If, by one jot or tittle, I vary now!
I' the colour the tale takes, there's change perhaps;
'T is natural, since the sky is different,
Eclipse in the air now; still, the outline stays.
I showed you how it came to be my part
1650 To save the lady. Then your clerk produced
Papers, a pack of stupid and impure
Banalities called letters about love –
Love, indeed, – I could teach who styled them so,
Better, I think, though priest and loveless both!
'– How was it that a wife, young, innocent,
And stranger to your person, wrote this page?' –
'– She wrote it when the Holy Father wrote
The bestiality that posts thro' Rome,
Put in his mouth by Pasquin.' – 'Nor perhaps
1660 Did you return these answers, verse and prose,
Signed, sealed and sent the lady? There's your hand!'
' – This precious piece of verse, I really judge
Is meant to copy my own character,
A clumsy mimic; and this other prose,
Not so much even; both rank forgery:
Verse, quotha? Bembo's verse! When Saint John wrote
The tract "*De Tribus*," I wrote this to match.'
' – How came it, then, the documents were found
At the inn on your departure?' – 'I opine,
1670 Because there were no documents to find
In my presence, – you must hide before you find.
Who forged them, hardly practised in my view;
Who found them, waited till I turned my back.'
' – And what of the clandestine visits paid,
Nocturnal passage in and out the house
With its lord absent? 'T is alleged you climbed . . .'
'– Flew on a broomstick to the man i' the moon!
Who witnessed or will testify this trash?'
' – The trusty servant, Margherita's self,
1680 Even she who brought you letters, you confess,
And, you confess, took letters in reply:

Forget not we have knowledge of the facts!'
' – Sirs, who have knowledge of the facts, defray
The expenditure of wit I waste in vain,
Trying to find out just one fact of all!
She who brought letters from who could not write,
And took back letters to who could not read, –
Who was that messenger, of your charity?'
' – Well, so far favours you the circumstance
690 That this same messenger ... how shall we say? ...
Sub imputatione meretricis
Laborat, – which makes accusation null:
We waive this woman's: – nought makes void the next.
Borsi, called Venerino, he who drove,
O' the first night when you fled away, at length
Deposes to your kissings in the coach,
– Frequent, frenetic ...' 'When deposed he so?'
'After some weeks of sharp imprisonment ...'
' – Granted by friend the Governor, I engage – '
700 ' – For his participation in your flight!
At length his obduracy melting made
The avowal mentioned ...' 'Was dismissed forthwith
To liberty, poor knave, for recompense.
Sirs, give what credit to the lie you can!
For me, no word in my defence I speak,
And God shall argue for the lady!'
                                        So
Did I stand question, and make answer, still
With the same result of smiling disbelief,
710 Polite impossibility of faith
In such affected virtue in a priest;
But a showing fair play, an indulgence, even,
To one no worse than others after all –
Who had not brought disgrace to the order, played
Discreetly, ruffled gown nor ripped the cloth
In a bungling game at romps: I have told you, Sirs –
If I pretended simply to be pure
Honest and Christian in the case, – absurd!
As well go boast myself above the needs

1720 O' the human nature, careless how meat smells,
Wine tastes, – a saint above the smack! But once
Abate my crest, own flaws i' the flesh, agree
To go with the herd, be hog no more nor less,
Why, hogs in common herd have common rights –
I must not be unduly borne upon,
Who had just romanced a little, sown wild oats,
But 'scaped without a scandal, flagrant fault.
My name helped to a mirthful circumstance:
'Joseph' would do well to amend his plea:
1730 Undoubtedly – some toying with the wife,
But as for ruffian violence and rape,
Potiphar pressed too much on the other side!
The intrigue, the elopement, the disguise, – well charged!
The letters and verse looked hardly like the truth.
Your apprehension was – of guilt enough
To be compatible with innocence,
So, punished best a little and not too much.
Had I struck Guido Franceschini's face,
You had counselled me withdraw for my own sake,
1740 Baulk him of bravo-hiring. Friends came round,
Congratulated, 'Nobody mistakes!
The pettiness o' the forfeiture defines
The peccadillo: Guido gets his share:
His wife is free of husband and hook-nose,
The mouldy viands and the mother-in-law.
To Civita with you and amuse the time,
Travesty us '*De Raptu Helenae!*'
A funny figure must the husband cut
When the wife makes him skip, – too ticklish, eh?
1750 Do it in Latin, not the Vulgar, then!
Scazons – we'll copy and send his Eminence!
Mind – one iambus in the final foot!
He'll rectify it, be your friend for life!'
Oh, Sirs, depend on me for much new light
Thrown on the justice and religion here
By this proceeding, much fresh food for thought!

And I was just set down to study these
In relegation, two short days ago,
Admiring how you read the rules, when, clap,
1760 A thunder comes into my solitude –
I am caught up in a whirlwind and cast here,
Told of a sudden, in this room where so late
You dealt out law adroitly, that those scales,
I meekly bowed to, took my allotment from,
Guido has snatched at, broken in your hands,
Metes to himself the murder of his wife,
Full measure, pressed down, running over now!
Can I assist to an explanation? – Yes,
I rise in your esteem, sagacious Sirs,
1770 Stand up a renderer of reasons, not
The officious priest would personate Saint George
For a mock Princess in undragoned days.
What, the blood startles you? What, after all
The priest who needs must carry sword on thigh
May find imperative use for it? Then, there was
A Princess, was a dragon belching flame,
And should have been a Saint George also? Then,
There might be worse schemes than to break the bonds
At Arezzo, lead her by the little hand,
1780 Till she reached Rome, and let her try to live?
But you were the law and the gospel, – would one please
Stand back, allow your faculty elbow-room?
You blind guides who must needs lead eyes that see!
Fools, alike ignorant of man and God!
What was there here should have perplexed your wit
For a wink of the owl-eyes of you? How miss, then,
What's now forced on you by this flare of fact –
As if Saint Peter failed to recognise
Nero as no apostle, John or James,
1790 Till someone burned a martyr, made a torch
O' the blood and fat to show his features by!
Could you fail read this cartulary aright
On head and front of Franceschini there,
Large-lettered like hell's masterpiece of print, –

That he, from the beginning pricked at heart
By some lust, letch of hate against his wife,
Plotted to plague her into overt sin
And shame, would slay Pompilia body and soul,
And save his mean self – miserably caught
1800 I' the quagmire of his own tricks, cheats and lies?
– That himself wrote those papers, – from himself
To himself, – which, i' the name of me and her,
His mistress-messenger gave her and me,
Touching us with such pustules of the soul
That she and I might take the taint, be shown
To the world and shuddered over, speckled so?
– That the agent put her sense into my words,
Made substitution of the thing she hoped,
For the thing she had and held, its opposite,
1810 While the husband in the background bit his lips
At each fresh failure of his precious plot?
– That when at the last we did rush each on each,
By no chance but because God willed it so –
The spark of truth was struck from out our souls –
Made all of me, descried in the first glance,
Seem fair and honest and permissible love
O' the good and true – as the first glance told me
There was no duty patent in the world
Like daring try be good and true myself,
1820 Leaving the shows of things to the Lord of Show
And Prince o' the Power of the Air. Our very flight,
Even to its most ambiguous circumstance,
Irrefragably proved how futile, false . . .
Why, men – men and not boys – boys and not babes –
Babes and not beasts – beasts and not stocks and stones! –
Had the liar's lie been true one pin-point speck,
Were I the accepted suitor, free o' the place,
Disposer of the time, to come at a call
And go at a wink as who should say me nay, –
1830 What need of flight, what were the gain therefrom
But just damnation, failure or success?
Damnation pure and simple to her the wife

And me the priest – who bartered private bliss
For public reprobation, the safe shade
For the sunshine which men see to pelt me by:
What other advantage, – we who led the days
And nights alone i' the house, – was flight to find?
In our whole journey did we stop an hour,
Diverge a foot from strait road till we reached
1840 Or would have reached – but for that fate of ours –
The father and mother, in the eye of Rome,
The eye of yourselves we made aware of us
At the first fall of misfortune? And indeed
You did so far give sanction to our flight,
Confirm its purpose, as lend helping hand,
Deliver up Pompilia not to him
She fled, but those the flight was ventured for.
Why then could you, who stopped short, not go on
One poor step more, and justify the means,
1850 Having allowed the end? – not see and say
'Here's the exceptional conduct that should claim
To be exceptionally judged on rules
Which, understood, make no exception here' –
Why play instead into the devil's hands
By dealing so ambiguously as gave
Guido the power to intervene like me,
Prove one exception more? I saved his wife
Against law: against law he slays her now:
Deal with him!

1860   I have done with being judged.
I stand here guiltless in thought, word and deed,
To the point that I apprise you, – in contempt
For all misapprehending ignorance
O' the human heart, much more the mind of Christ, –
That I assuredly did bow, was blessed
By the revelation of Pompilia. There!
Such is the final fact I fling you, Sirs,
To mouth and mumble and misinterpret: there!
'The priest's in love,' have it the vulgar way!

1870 Unpriest me, rend the rags o' the vestment, do –
Degrade deep, disenfranchise all you dare –
Remove me from the midst, no longer priest
And fit companion for the like of you –
Your gay Abati with the well-turned leg
And rose i' the hat-rim, Canons, cross at neck
And silk mask in the pocket of the gown,
Brisk bishops with the world's musk still unbrushed
From the rochet; I'll no more of these good things:
There's a crack somewhere, something that's unsound
1880 I' the rattle!

      For Pompilia – be advised,
Build churches, go pray! You will find me there,
I know, if you come, – and you will come, I know.
Why, there's a Judge weeping! Did not I say
You were good and true at bottom? You see the truth –
I am glad I helped you: she helped me just so.

      But for Count Guido, – you must counsel there!
I bow my head, bend to the very dust,
Break myself up in shame of faultiness.
1890 I had him one whole moment, as I said –
As I remember, as will never out
O' the thoughts of me, – I had him in arm's reach
There, – as you stand, Sir, now you cease to sit, –
I could have killed him ere he killed his wife,
And did not: he went off alive and well
And then effected this last feat – through me!
Me – not through you – dismiss that fear! 'T was you
Hindered me staying here to save her, – not
From leaving you and going back to him
1900 And doing service in Arezzo. Come,
Instruct me in procedure! I conceive –
In all due self-abasement might I speak –
How you will deal with Guido: oh, not death!
Death, if it let her life be: otherwise
Not death, – your lights will teach you clearer! I

Certainly have an instinct of my own
I' the matter: bear with me and weigh its worth!
Let us go away – leave Guido all alone
Back on the world again that knows him now!
1910 I think he will be found (indulge so far!)
Not to die so much as slide out of life,
Pushed by the general horror and common hate
Low, lower, – left o' the very ledge of things,
I seem to see him catch convulsively
One by one at all honest forms of life,
At reason, order, decency and use –
To cramp him and get foothold by at least;
And still they disengage them from his clutch.
'What, you are he, then, had Pompilia once
1920 And so forwent her? Take not up with us!'
And thus I see him slowly and surely edged
Off all the table-land whence life upsprings
Aspiring to be immortality,
As the snake, hatched on hill-top by mischance,
Despite his wriggling, slips, slides, slidders down
Hill-side, lies low and prostrate on the smooth
Level of the outer place, lapsed in the vale:
So I lose Guido in the loneliness,
Silence and dusk, till at the doleful end,
1930 At the horizontal line, creation's verge,
From what just is to absolute nothingness –
Lo, what is this he meets, strains onward still?
What other man deep further in the fate,
Who, turning at the prize of a footfall
To flatter him and promise fellowship,
Discovers in the act a frightful face –
Judas, made monstrous by much solitude!
The two are at one now! Let them love their love
That bites and claws like hate, or hate their hate
940 That mops and mows and makes as it were love!
There, let them each tear each in devil's-fun,
Or fondle this the other while malice aches –
Both teach, both learn detestability!

Kiss him the kiss, Iscariot! Pay that back,
That smatch o' the slaver blistering on your lip –
By the better trick, the insult he spared Christ –
Lure him the lure o' the letters, Aretine!
Lick him o'er slimy-smooth with jelly-filth
O' the verse-and-prose pollution in love's guise!
1950 The cockatrice is with the basilisk!
There let them grapple, denizens o' the dark,
Foes or friends, but indissolubly bound,
In their one spot out of the ken of God
Or care of man, for ever and ever more!

Why, Sirs, what's this? Why, this is sorry and strange! –
Futility, divagation: this from me
Bound to be rational, justify an act
Of sober man! – whereas, being moved so much,
I give you cause to doubt the lady's mind;
1960 A pretty sarcasm for the world! I fear
You do her wit injustice, – all through me!
Like my fate all through, – ineffective help!
A poor rash advocate I prove myself.
You might be angry with good cause: but sure
At the advocate, – only at the undue zeal
That spoils the force of his own plea, I think?
My part was just to tell you how things stand,
State facts and not be flustered at their fume.
But then 't is a priest speaks: as for love, – no!
1970 If you let buzz a vulgar fly like that
About your brains, as if I loved, forsooth,
Indeed, Sirs, you do wrong! We had no thought
Of such infatuation, she and I:
There are many points that prove it: do be just!
I told you, – at one little roadside-place
I spent a good half-hour, paced to and fro
The garden; just to leave her free awhile,
I plucked a handful of Spring herb and bloom:
I might have sat beside her on the bench
1980 Where the children were: I wish the thing had been,

Indeed: the event could not be worse, you know:
One more half-hour of her saved! She's dead now, Sirs!
While I was running on at such a rate,
Friends should have plucked me by the sleeve: I went
Too much o' the trivial outside of her face
And the purity that shone there – plain to mė,
Not to you, what more natural? Nor am I
Infatuated, – oh, I saw, be sure!
Her brow had not the right line, leaned too much,
1990 Painters would say; they like the straight-up Greek:
This seemed bent somewhat with an invisible crown
Of martyr and saint, not such as art approves.
And how the dark orbs dwelt deep underneath,
Looked out of such a sad sweet heaven on me –
The lips, compressed a little, came forward too,
Careful for a whole world of sin and pain.
That was the face, her husband makes his plea,
He sought just to disfigure, – no offence
Beyond that! Sirs, let us be rational!
2000 He needs must vindicate his honour, – ay,
Yet shirks, the coward, in a clown's disguise,
Away from the scene, endeavours to escape.
Now, had he done so, slain and left no trace
O' the slayer, – what were vindicated, pray?
You had found his wife disfigured or a corpse,
For what and by whom? It is too palpable!
Then, here's another point involving law:
I use this argument to show you meant
No calumny against us by that title
2010 O' the sentence, – liars try to twist it so:
What penalty it bore, I had to pay
Till further proof should follow of innocence –
Probationis ob defectum, – proof?
How could you get proof without trying us?
You went through the preliminary form,
Stopped there, contrived this sentence to amuse
The adversary. If the title ran
For more than fault imputed and not proved,

That was a simple penman's error, else
2020 A slip i' the phrase, – as when we say of you
'Charged with injustice' – which may either be
Or not be, – 't is a name that sticks meanwhile.
Another relevant matter: fool that I am!
Not what I wish true, yet a point friends urge:
It is not true, – yet, since friends think it helps, –
She only tried me when some others failed –
Began with Conti, whom I told you of,
And Guillichini, Guido's kinsfolk both,
And when abandoned by them, not before,
2030 Turned to me. That's conclusive why she turned.
Much good they got by the happy cowardice!
Conti is dead, poisoned a month ago:
Does that much strike you as a sin? Not much,
After the present murder, – one mark more
On the Moor's skin, – what is black by blacker still?
Conti had come here and told truth. And so
With Guillichini; he's condemned of course
To the galleys, as a friend in this affair,
Tried and condemned for no one thing i' the world,
2040 A fortnight since by who but the Governor? –
The just judge, who refused Pompilia help
At first blush, being her husband's friend, you know.
There are two tales to suit the separate courts,
Arezzo and Rome: he tells you here, we fled
Alone, unhelped, – lays stress on the main fault,
The spiritual sin, Rome looks to: but elsewhere
He likes best we should break in, steal, bear off,
Be fit to brand and pillory and flog –
That's the charge goes to the heart of the Governor:
2050 If these unpriest me, you and I may yet
Converse, Vincenzo Marzi-Medici!
Oh, Sirs, there are worse men than you, I say!
More easily duped, I mean; this stupid lie,
Its liar never dared propound in Rome,
He gets Arezzo to receive, – nay more,
Gets Florence and the Duke to authorise!

This is their Rota's sentence, their Granduke
Signs and seals! Rome for me henceforward – Rome,
Where better men are, – most of all, that man
2060 The Augustinian of the Hospital,
Who writes the letter, – he confessed, he says,
Many a dying person, never one
So sweet and true and pure and beautiful.
A good man! Will you make him Pope one day?
Not that he is not good too, this we have –
But old, – else he would have his word to speak,
His truth to teach the world: I thirst for truth,
But shall not drink it till I reach the source.

Sirs, I am quiet again. You see, we are
2070 So very pitiable, she and I,
Who had conceivably been otherwise.
Forget distemperature and idle heat!
Apart from truth's sake, what's to move so much?
Pompilia will be presently with God;
I am, on earth, as good as out of it,
A relegated priest; when exile ends,
I mean to do my duty and live long.
She and I are mere strangers now: but priests
Should study passion; how else cure mankind,
2080 Who come for help in passionate extremes?
I do but play with an imagined life
Of who, unfettered by a vow, unblessed
By the higher call, – since you will have it so, –
Leads it companioned by the woman there.
To live, and see her learn, and learn by her,
Out of the low obscure and petty world –
Or only see one purpose and one will
Evolve themselves i' the world, change wrong to right:
To have to do with nothing but the true,
2090 The good, the eternal – and these, not alone
In the main current of the general life,
But small experiences of every day,
Concerns of the particular hearth and home:

To learn not only by a comet's rush
But a rose's birth, – not by the grandeur, God –
But the comfort, Christ. All this, how far away!
Mere delectation, meet for a minute's dream! –
Just as a drudging student trims his lamp,
Opens his Plutarch, puts him in the place
2100 Of Roman, Grecian; draws the patched gown close,
Dreams, 'Thus should I fight, save or rule the world!' –
Then smilingly, contentedly, awakes
To the old solitary nothingness.
So I, from such communion, pass content . . .

O great, just, good God! Miserable me!

BOOK VII
Pompilia

I am just seventeen years and five months old,
And, if I lived one day more, three full weeks;
'T is writ so in the church's register,
Lorenzo in Lucina, all my names
At length, so many names for one poor child,
– Francesca Camilla Vittoria Angela
Pompilia Comparini, – laughable!
Also 't is writ that I was married there
Four years ago: and they will add, I hope,
10 When they insert my death, a word or two, –
Omitting all about the mode of death, –
This, in its place, this which one cares to know,
That I had been a mother of a son
Exactly two weeks. It will be through grace
O' the Curate, not through any claim I have;
Because the boy was born at, so baptized
Close to, the Villa, in the proper church:
A pretty church, I say no word against,
Yet stranger-like, – while this Lorenzo seems
20 My own particular place, I always say.
I used to wonder, when I stood scarce high
As the bed here, what the marble lion meant,
With half his body rushing from the wall,
Eating the figure of a prostrate man –
(To the right, it is, of entry by the door)
An ominous sign to one baptized like me,
Married, and to be buried there, I hope.
And they should add, to have my life complete,
He is a boy and Gaetan by name –
30 Gaetano, for a reason, – if the friar

Don Celestine will ask this grace for me
Of Curate Ottoboni: he it was
Baptized me: he remembers my whole life
As I do his grey hair.

             All these few things
I know are true, – will you remember them?
Because time flies. The surgeon cared for me,
To count my wounds, – twenty-two dagger-wounds,
Five deadly, but I do not suffer much –
40 Or too much pain, – and am to die to-night.

Oh how good God is that my babe was born,
– Better than born, baptized and hid away
Before this happened, safe from being hurt!
That had been sin God could not well forgive:
He was too young to smile and save himself.
When they took, two days after he was born,
My babe away from me to be baptized
And hidden awhile, for fear his foe should find, –
The country-woman, used to nursing babes,
50 Said 'Why take on so? where is the great loss?
These next three weeks he will but sleep and feed,
Only begin to smile at the month's end;
He would not know you, if you kept him here,
Sooner than that; so, spend three merry weeks
Snug in the Villa, getting strong and stout,
And then I bring him back to be your own,
And both of you may steal to – we know where!'
The month – there wants of it two weeks this day!
Still, I half fancied when I heard the knock
60 At the Villa in the dusk, it might prove she –
Come to say 'Since he smiles before the time,
Why should I cheat you out of one good hour?
Back I have brought him; speak to him and judge!'
Now I shall never see him; what is worse,
When he grows up and gets to be my age,
He will seem hardly more than a great boy;

And if he asks 'What was my mother like?'
People may answer 'Like girls of seventeen' –
And how can he but think of this and that,
70 Lucias, Marias, Sofias, who titter or blush
When he regards them as such boys may do?
Therefore I wish some one will please to say
I looked already old though I was young;
Do I not . . . say, if you are by to speak . . .
Look nearer twenty? No more like, at least,
Girls who look arch or redden when boys laugh,
Than the poor Virgin that I used to know
At our street-corner in a lonely niche, –
The babe, that sat upon her knees, broke off, –
80 Thin white glazed clay, you pitied her the more:
She, not the gay ones, always got my rose.

How happy those are who know how to write!
Such could write what their son should read in time,
Had they a whole day to live out like me.
Also my name is not a common name,
'Pompilia,' and may help to keep apart
A little the thing I am from what girls are.
But then how far away, how hard to find
Will anything about me have become,
90 Even if the boy bethink himself and ask!
No father that he ever knew at all,
Nor ever had – no, never had, I say!
That is the truth, – nor any mother left,
Out of the little two weeks that she lived,
Fit for such memory as might assist:
As good too as no family, no name,
Not even poor old Pietro's name, nor hers,
Poor kind unwise Violante, since it seems
They must not be my parents any more.
100 That is why something put it in my head
To call the boy 'Gaetano' – no old name
For sorrow's sake; I looked up to the sky
And took a new saint to begin anew.

One who has only been made saint – how long?
Twenty-five years: so, carefuller, perhaps,
To guard a namesake than those old saints grow,
Tired out by this time, – see my own five saints!

On second thoughts, I hope he will regard
The history of me as what someone dreamed,
110 And get to disbelieve it at the last:
Since to myself it dwindles fast to that,
Sheer dreaming and impossibility, –
Just in four days too! All the seventeen years,
Not once did a suspicion visit me
How very different a lot is mine
From any other woman's in the world.
The reason must be, 't was by step and step
It got to grow so terrible and strange:
These strange woes stole on tiptoe, as it were,
120 Into my neighbourhood and privacy,
Sat down where I sat, laid them where I lay;
And I was found familiarised with fear,
When friends broke in, held up a torch and cried
'Why, you Pompilia in the cavern thus,
How comes that arm of yours about a wolf?
And the soft length, – lies in and out your feet
And laps you round the knee, – a snake it is!'
And so on.

                    Well, and they are right enough,
130 By the torch they hold up now: for first, observe,
I never had a father, – no, nor yet
A mother: my own boy can say at least
'I had a mother whom I kept two weeks!'
Not I, who little used to doubt . . . I doubt
Good Pietro, kind Violante, gave me birth?
They loved me always as I love my babe
(– Nearly so, that is – quite so could not be –)
Did for me all I meant to do for him,
Till one surprising day, three years ago,

140 They both declared, at Rome, before some judge
In some court where the people flocked to hear,
That really I had never been their child,
Was a mere castaway, the careless crime
Of an unknown man, the crime and care too much
Of a woman known too well, – little to these,
Therefore, of whom I was the flesh and blood:
What then to Pietro and Violante, both
No more my relatives than you or you?
Nothing to them! You know what they declared.

150 So with my husband, – just such a surprise,
Such a mistake, in that relationship!
Everyone says that husbands love their wives,
Guard them and guide them, give them happiness;
'Tis duty, law, pleasure, religion: well,
You see how much of this comes true in mine!
People indeed would fain have somehow proved
He was no husband: but he did not hear,
Or would not wait, and so has killed us all.
Then there is . . . only let me name one more!
160 There is the friend, – men will not ask about,
But tell untruths of, and give nicknames to,
And think my lover, most surprise of all!
Do only hear, it is the priest they mean,
Giuseppe Caponsacchi: a priest – love,
And love me! Well, yet people think he did.
I am married, he has taken priestly vows,
They know that, and yet go on, say, the same,
'Yes, how he loves you!' 'That was love' – they say,
When anything is answered that they ask:
170 Or else 'No wonder you love him' – they say.
Then they shake heads, pity much, scarcely blame –
As if we neither of us lacked excuse,
And anyhow are punished to the full,
And downright love atones for everything!
Nay, I heard read-out in the public court
Before the judge, in presence of my friends,

Letters 't was said the priest had sent to me,
And other letters sent him by myself,
We being lovers!

180   Listen what this is like!
When I was a mere child, my mother . . . that's
Violante, you must let me call her so
Nor waste time, trying to unlearn the word, . . .
She brought a neighbour's child of my own age
To play with me of rainy afternoons;
And, since there hung a tapestry on the wall,
We two agreed to find each other out
Among the figures. 'Tisbe, that is you,
With half-moon on your hair-knot, spear in hand,
190 Flying, but no wings, only the great scarf
Blown to a bluish rainbow at your back:
Call off your hound and leave the stag alone!'
' – And there are you, Pompilia, such green leaves
Flourishing out of your five finger-ends,
And all the rest of you so brown and rough:
Why is it you are turned a sort of tree?'
You know the figures never were ourselves
Though we nicknamed them so. Thus, all my life, –
As well what was, as what, like this, was not, –
200 Looks old, fantastic and impossible:
I touch a fairy thing that fades and fades.
– Even to my babe! I thought, when he was born,
Something began for once that would not end,
Nor change into a laugh at me, but stay
For evermore, eternally quite mine.
Well, so he is, – but yet they bore him off,
The third day, lest my husband should lay traps
And catch him, and by means of him catch me.
Since they have saved him so, it was well done:
210 Yet thence comes such confusion of what was
With what will be, – that late seems long ago,
And, what years should bring round, already come,
Till even he withdraws into a dream

As the rest do: I fancy him grown great,
Strong, stern, a tall young man who tutors me,
Frowns with the others 'Poor imprudent child!
Why did you venture out of the safe street?
Why go so far from help to that lone house?
Why open at the whisper and the knock?'

220 Six days ago when it was New Year's-day,
We bent above the fire and talked of him,
What he should do when he was grown and great.
Violante, Pietro, each had given the arm
I leant on, to walk by, from couch to chair
And fireside, – laughed, as I lay safe at last,
'Pompilia's march from bed to board is made,
Pompilia back again and with a babe,
Shall one day lend his arm and help her walk!'
Then we all wished each other more New Years.

230 Pietro began to scheme – 'Our cause is gained;
The law is stronger than a wicked man:
Let him henceforth go his way, leave us ours!
We will avoid the city, tempt no more
The greedy ones by feasting and parade, –
Live at the other villa, we know where,
Still farther off, and we can watch the babe
Grow fast in the good air; and wood is cheap
And wine sincere outside the city gate.
I still have two or three old friends will grope

240 Their way along the mere half-mile of road,
With staff and lantern on a moonless night
When one needs talk: they'll find me, never fear,
And I'll find them a flask of the old sort yet!'
Violante said 'You chatter like a crow:
Pompilia tires o' the tattle, and shall to-bed:
Do not too much the first day, – somewhat more
To-morrow, and, the next, begin the cape
And hood and coat! I have spun wool enough.'
Oh what a happy friendly eve was that!

250   And, next day, about noon, out Pietro went –
      He was so happy and would talk so much,
      Until Violante pushed and laughed him forth
      Sight-seeing in the cold, – 'So much to see
      I' the churches! Swathe your throat three times!' she cried,
      'And, above all, beware the slippery ways,
      And bring us all the news by supper-time!'
      He came back late, laid by cloak, staff and hat,
      Powdered so thick with snow it made us laugh,
      Rolled a great log upon the ash o' the hearth,
260   And bade Violante treat us to a flask,
      Because he had obeyed her faithfully,
      Gone sight-see through the seven, and found no church
      To his mind like San Giovanni – 'There's the fold,
      And all the sheep together, big as cats!
      And such a shepherd, half the size of life,
      Starts up and hears the angel' – when, at the door,
      A tap: we started up: you know the rest.

      Pietro at least had done no harm, I know;
      Nor even Violante, so much harm as makes
270   Such revenge lawful. Certainly she erred –
      Did wrong, how shall I dare say otherwise? –
      In telling that first falsehood, buying me
      From my poor faulty mother at a price,
      To pass off upon Pietro as his child:
      If one should take my babe, give him a name,
      Say he was not Gaetano and my own,
      But that some other woman made his mouth
      And hands and feet, – how very false were that!
      No good could come of that; and all harm did.
280   Yet if a stranger were to represent
      'Needs must you either give your babe to me
      And let me call him mine for ever more,
      Or let your husband get him' – ah, my God,
      That were a trial I refuse to face!
      Well, just so here: it proved wrong but seemed right
      To poor Violante – for there lay, she said,

My poor real dying mother in her rags,
Who put me from her with the life and all,
Poverty, pain, shame and disease at once,
290 To die the easier by what price I fetched –
Also (I hope) because I should be spared
Sorrow and sin, – why may not that have helped?
My father, – he was no one, any one, –
The worse, the likelier, – call him, – he who came,
Was wicked for his pleasure, went his way,
And left no trace to track by; there remained
Nothing but me, the unnecessary life,
To catch up or let fall, – and yet a thing
She could make happy, be made happy with,
300 This poor Violante, – who would frown thereat?

Well, God, you see! God plants us where we grow.
It is not that, because a bud is born
At a wild briar's end, full i' the wild beast's way,
We ought to pluck and put it out of reach
On the oak-tree top, – say, 'There the bud belongs!'
She thought, moreover, real lies were – lies told
For harm's sake; whereas this had good at heart,
Good for my mother, good for me, and good
For Pietro who was meant to love a babe,
310 And needed one to make his life of use,
Receive his house and land when he should die.
Wrong, wrong and always wrong! how plainly wrong!
For see, this fault kept pricking, as faults do,
All the same at her heart, – this falsehood hatched,
She could not let it go nor keep it fast.
She told me so, – the first time I was found
Locked in her arms once more after the pain,
When the nuns let me leave them and go home,
And both of us cried all the cares away, –
320 This it was set her on to make amends,
This brought about the marriage – simply this!
Do let me speak for her you blame so much!
When Paul, my husband's brother, found me out,

Heard there was wealth for who should marry me,
So, came and made a speech to ask my hand
For Guido, – she, instead of piercing straight
Through the pretence to the ignoble truth,
Fancied she saw God's very finger point,
Designate just the time for planting me,
330 (The wild briar-slip she plucked to love and wear)
In soil where I could strike real root, and grow,
And get to be the thing I called myself:
For, wife and husband are one flesh, God says,
And I, whose parents seemed such and were none,
Should in a husband have a husband now,
Find nothing, this time, but was what it seemed,
– All truth and no confusion any more.
I know she meant all good to me, all pain
To herself, – since how could it be aught but pain,
340 To give me up, so, from her very breast,
The wilding flower-tree-branch that, all those years,
She had got used to feel for and find fixed?
She meant well: has it been so ill i' the main?
That is but fair to ask: one cannot judge
Of what has been the ill or well of life,
The day that one is dying, – sorrows change
Into not altogether sorrow-like;
I do see strangeness but scarce misery,
Now it is over, and no danger more.
350 My child is safe; there seems not so much pain.
It comes, most like, that I am just absolved,
Purged of the past, the foul in me, washed fair, –
One cannot both have and not have, you know, –
Being right now, I am happy and colour things.
Yes, every body that leaves life sees all
Softened and bettered: so with other sights:
To me at least was never evening yet
But seemed far beautifuller than its day,
For past is past.

360   There was a fancy came,

When somewhere, in the journey with my friend,
We stepped into a hovel to get food;
And there began a yelp here, a bark there, –
Misunderstanding creatures that were wroth
And vexed themselves and us till we retired.
The hovel is life: no matter what dogs bit
Or cats scratched in the hovel I break from,
All outside is lone field, moon and such peace –
Flowing in, filling up as with a sea
370 Whereon comes Someone, walks fast on the white,
Jesus Christ's self, Don Celestine declares,
To meet me and calm all things back again.

Beside, up to my marriage, thirteen years
Were, each day, happy as the day was long:
This may have made the change too terrible.
I know that when Violante told me first
The cavalier, – she meant to bring next morn,
Whom I must also let take, kiss my hand, –
Would be at San Lorenzo the same eve
380 And marry me, – which over, we should go
Home both of us without him as before,
And, till she bade speak, I must hold my tongue,
Such being the correct way with girl-brides,
From whom one word would make a father blush, –
I know, I say, that when she told me this,
– Well, I no more saw sense in what she said
Than a lamb does in people clipping wool;
Only lay down and let myself be clipped.
And when next day the cavalier who came
390 (Tisbe had told me that the slim young man
With wings at head, and wings at feet, and sword
Threatening a monster, in our tapestry,
Would eat a girl else, – was a cavalier)
When he proved Guido Franceschini, – old
And nothing like so tall as I myself,
Hook-nosed and yellow in a bush of beard,
Much like a thing I saw on a boy's wrist,

He called an owl and used for catching birds, –
And when he took my hand and made a smile –
400 Why, the uncomfortableness of it all
Seemed hardly more important in the case
Than, – when one gives you, say, a coin to spend, –
Its newness or its oldness; if the piece
Weigh properly and buy you what you wish,
No matter whether you get grime or glare!
Men take the coin, return you grapes and figs.
Here, marriage was the coin, a dirty piece
Would purchase me the praise of those I loved:
About what else should I concern myself?

410 So, hardly knowing what a husband meant,
I supposed this or any man would serve,
No whit the worse for being so uncouth:
For I was ill once and a doctor came
With a great ugly hat, no plume thereto,
Black jerkin and black buckles and black sword,
And white sharp beard over the ruff in front,
And oh so lean, so sour-faced and austere! –
Who felt my pulse, made me put out my tongue,
Then oped a phial, dripped a drop or two
420 Of a black bitter something, – I was cured!
What mattered the fierce beard or the grim face?
It was the physic beautified the man,
Master Malpichi, – never met his match
In Rome, they said, – so ugly all the same!

However, I was hurried through a storm,
Next dark eve of December's deadest day –
How it rained! – through our street and the Lion's-mouth
And the bit of Corso, – cloaked round, covered close,
I was like something strange or contraband, –
430 Into blank San Lorenzo, up the aisle,
My mother keeping hold of me so tight,
I fancied we were come to see a corpse
Before the altar which she pulled me toward.

There we found waiting an unpleasant priest
Who proved the brother, not our parish friend,
But one with mischief-making mouth and eye,
Paul, whom I know since to my cost. And then
I heard the heavy church-door lock out help
Behind us: for the customary warmth,
440 Two tapers shivered on the altar. 'Quick –
Lose no time!' – cried the priest. And straightway down
From . . . what's behind the altar where he hid –
Hawk-nose and yellowness and bush and all,
Stepped Guido, caught my hand, and there was I
O' the chancel, and the priest had opened book,
Read here and there, made me say that and this,
And after, told me I was now a wife,
Honoured indeed, since Christ thus weds the Church,
And therefore turned he water into wine,
450 To show I should obey my spouse like Christ.
Then the two slipped aside and talked apart,
And I, silent and scared, got down again
And joined my mother who was weeping now.
Nobody seemed to mind us any more,
And both of us on tiptoe found our way
To the door which was unlocked by this, and wide.
When we were in the street, the rain had stopped,
All things looked better. At our own house-door,
Violante whispered 'No one syllable
460 To Pietro! Girl-brides never breathe a word!'
' – Well treated to a wetting, draggle-tails!'
Laughed Pietro as he opened – 'Very near
You made me brave the gutter's roaring sea
To carry off from roost old dove and young,
Trussed up in church, the cote, by me, the kite!
What do these priests mean, praying folk to death
On stormy afternoons, with Christmas close
To wash our sins off nor require the rain?'
Violante gave my hand a timely squeeze,
470 Madonna saved me from immodest speech,
I kissed him and was quiet, being a bride.

When I saw nothing more, the next three weeks,
Of Guido – 'Nor the Church sees Christ' thought I:
'Nothing is changed however, wine is wine
And water only water in our house.
Nor did I see that ugly doctor since
The cure of the illness: just as I was cured,
I am married, – neither scarecrow will return.'

Three weeks, I chuckled – 'How would Giulia stare,
480 And Tecla smile and Tisbe laugh outright,
Were it not impudent for brides to talk!' –
Until one morning, as I sat and sang
At the broidery-frame alone i' the chamber, – loud
Voices, two, three together, sobbings too,
And my name, 'Guido,' 'Paolo,' flung like stones
From each to the other! In I ran to see.
There stood the very Guido and the priest
With sly face, – formal but nowise afraid, –
While Pietro seemed all red and angry, scarce
490 Able to stutter out his wrath in words;
And this it was that made my mother sob,
As he reproached her – 'You have murdered us,
Me and yourself and this our child beside!'
Then Guido interposed 'Murdered or not,
Be it enough your child is now my wife!
I claim and come to take her.' Paul put in,
'Consider – kinsman, dare I term you so? –
What is the good of your sagacity
Except to counsel in a strait like this?
500 I guarantee the parties man and wife
Whether you like or loathe it, bless or ban.
May spilt milk be put back within the bowl –
The done thing, undone? You, it is, we look
For counsel to, you fitliest will advise!
Since milk, though spilt and spoilt, does marble good,
Better we down on knees and scrub the floor,
Than sigh, "the waste would make a syllabub!"
Help us so turn disaster to account,

So predispose the groom, he needs shall grace
510 The bride with favour from the very first,
Not begin marriage an embittered man!'
He smiled, – the game so wholly in his hands!
While fast and faster sobbed Violante – 'Ay,
All of us murdered, past averting now!
O my sin, O my secret!' and such like.

Then I began to half surmise the truth;
Something had happened, low, mean, underhand,
False, and my mother was to blame, and I
To pity, whom all spoke of, none addressed:
520 I was the chattel that had caused a crime.
I stood mute, – those who tangled must untie
The embroilment. Pietro cried 'Withdraw, my child!
She is not helpful to the sacrifice
At this stage, – do you want the victim by
While you discuss the value of her blood?
For her sake, I consent to hear you talk:
Go, child, and pray God help the innocent!'

I did go and was praying God, when came
Violante, with eyes swollen and red enough,
530 But movement on her mouth for make-believe
Matters were somehow getting right again.
She bade me sit down by her side and hear.
'You are too young and cannot understand,
Nor did your father understand at first.
I wished to benefit all three of us,
And when he failed to take my meaning, – why,
I tried to have my way at unaware –
Obtained him the advantage he refused.
As if I put before him wholesome food
540 Instead of broken victual, – he finds change
I' the viands, never cares to reason why,
But falls to blaming me, would fling the plate
From window, scandalize the neighbourhood,
Even while he smacks his lips, – men's way, my child!

But either you have prayed him unperverse
Or I have talked him back into his wits:
And Paolo was a help in time of need, –
Guido, not much – my child, the way of men!
A priest is more a woman than a man,
550 And Paul did wonders to persuade. In short,
Yes, he was wrong, your father sees and says;
My scheme was worth attempting: and bears fruit,
Gives you a husband and a noble name,
A palace and no end of pleasant things.
What do you care about a handsome youth?
They are so volatile, and teaze their wives!
This is the kind of man to keep the house.
We lose no daughter, – gain a son, that's all:
For 'tis arranged we never separate,
560 Nor miss, in our grey time of life, the tints
Of you that colour eve to match with morn.
In good or ill, we share and share alike,
And cast our lots into a common lap,
And all three die together as we lived!
Only, at Arezzo, – that's a Tuscan town,
Not so large as this noisy Rome, no doubt,
But older far and finer much, say folks, –
In a great palace where you will be queen,
Know the Archbishop and the Governor,
570 And we see homage done you ere we die.
Therefore, be good and pardon!' – 'Pardon what?
You know things, I am very ignorant:
All is right if you only will not cry!'

And so an end! Because a blank begins
From when, at the word, she kissed me hard and hot,
And took me back to where my father leaned
Opposite Guido – who stood eyeing him,
As eyes the butcher the cast panting ox
That feels his fate is come, nor struggles more, –
580 While Paul looked archly on, pricked brow at whiles
With the pen-point as to punish triumph there, –

And said 'Count Guido, take your lawful wife
Until death part you!'

      All since is one blank,
Over and ended; a terrific dream.
It is the good of dreams – so soon they go!
Wake in a horror of heart-beats, you may –
Cry, 'The dread thing will never from my thoughts!'
Still, a few daylight doses of plain life,
590 Cock-crow and sparrow-chirp, or bleat and bell
Of goats that trot by, tinkling, to be milked;
And when you rub your eyes awake and wide,
Where is the harm o' the horror? Gone! So here.
I know I wake, – but from what? Blank, I say!
This is the note of evil: for good lasts.
Even when Don Celestine bade 'Search and find!
For your soul's sake, remember what is past,
The better to forgive it,' – all in vain!
What was fast getting indistinct before,
600 Vanished outright. By special grace perhaps,
Between that first calm and this last, four years
Vanish, – one quarter of my life, you know.
I am held up, amid the nothingness,
By one or two truths only – thence I hang,
And there I live, – the rest is death or dream,
All but those points of my support. I think
Of what I saw at Rome once in the Square
O' the Spaniards, opposite the Spanish House:
There was a foreigner had trained a goat,
610 A shuddering white woman of a beast,
To climb up, stand straight on a pile of sticks
Put close, which gave the creature room enough:
When she was settled there he, one by one,
Took away all the sticks, left just the four
Whereon the little hoofs did really rest,
There she kept firm, all underneath was air.
So, what I hold by, are my prayer to God,
My hope, that came in answer to the prayer,

Some hand would interpose and save me – hand
620 Which proved to be my friend's hand: and, – best bliss, –
That fancy which began so faint at first,
That thrill of dawn's suffusion through my dark,
Which I perceive was promise of my child,
The light his unborn face sent long before, –
God's way of breaking the good news to flesh.
That is all left now of those four bad years.
Don Celestine urged 'But remember more!
Other men's faults may help me find your own.
I need the cruelty exposed, explained,
630 Or how can I advise you to forgive?'
He thought I could not properly forgive
Unless I ceased forgetting, – which is true:
For, bringing back reluctantly to mind
My husband's treatment of me, – by a light
That's later than my life-time, I review
And comprehend much and imagine more,
And have but little to forgive at last.
For now, – be fair and say, – is it not true
He was ill-used and cheated of his hope
640 To get enriched by marriage? Marriage gave
Me and no money, broke the compact so:
He had a right to ask me on those terms,
As Pietro and Violante to declare
They would not give me: so the bargain stood:
They broke it, and he felt himself aggrieved,
Became unkind with me to punish them.
They said 't was he began deception first,
Nor, in one point whereto he pledged himself,
Kept promise: what of that, suppose it were?
650 Echoes die off, scarcely reverberate
For ever, – why should ill keep echoing ill,
And never let our ears have done with noise?
Then my poor parents took the violent way
To thwart him, – he must needs retaliate, – wrong,
Wrong, and all wrong, – better say, all blind!
As I myself was, that is sure, who else

Had understood the mystery: for his wife
Was bound in some sort to help somehow there.
It seems as if I might have interposed,
660   Blunted the edge of their resentment so,
Since he vexed me because they first vexed him;
'I will entreat them to desist, submit,
Give him the money and be poor in peace, –
Certainly not go tell the world: perhaps
He will grow quiet with his gains.'

                      Yes, say
Something to this effect and you do well!
But then you have to see first: I was blind.
That is the fruit of all such wormy ways,
670   The indirect, the unapproved of God:
You cannot find their author's end and aim,
Not even to substitute your good for bad,
Your open for the irregular; you stand
Stupefied, profitless, as cow or sheep
That miss a man's mind; anger him just twice
By trial at repairing the first fault.
Thus, when he blamed me, 'You are a coquette,
A lure-owl posturing to attract birds,
You look love-lures at theatre and church,
680   In walk, at window!' – that, I knew, was false:
But why he charged me falsely, whither sought
To drive me by such charge, – how could I know?
So, unaware, I only made things worse.
I tried to soothe him by abjuring walk,
Window, church, theatre, for good and all,
As if he had been in earnest: that, you know,
Was nothing like the object of his charge.
Yes, when I got my maid to supplicate
The priest, whose name she read when she would read
690   Those feigned false letters I was forced to hear
Though I could read no word of, – he should cease
Writing, – nay, if he minded prayer of mine,
Cease from so much as even pass the street

Whereon our house looked, – in my ignorance
I was just thwarting Guido's true intent;
Which was, to bring about a wicked change
Of sport to earnest, tempt a thoughtless man
To write indeed, and pass the house, and more,
Till both of us were taken in a crime.
700 He ought not to have wished me thus act lies,
Simulate folly, – but, – wrong or right, the wish, –
I failed to apprehend its drift. How plain
It follows, – if I fell into such fault,
He also may have overreached the mark,
Made mistake, by perversity of brain,
In the whole sad strange plot, this same intrigue
To make me and my friend unself ourselves,
Be other man and woman than we were!
Think it out, you who have the time! for me, –
710 I cannot say less; more I will not say.
Leave it to God to cover and undo!
Only, my dulness should not prove too much!
– Not prove that in a certain other point
Wherein my husband blamed me, – and you blame,
If I interpret smiles and shakes of head, –
I was dull too. Oh, if I dared but speak!
Must I speak? I am blamed that I forwent
A way to make my husband's favour come.
That is true: I was firm, withstood, refused . . .
720 – Women as you are, how can I find the words?

I felt there was just one thing Guido claimed
I had no right to give nor he to take;
We being in estrangement, soul from soul:
Till, when I sought help, the Archbishop smiled,
Inquiring into privacies of life,
– Said I was blameable – (he stands for God)
Nowise entitled to exemption there.
Then I obeyed, – as surely had obeyed
Were the injunction 'Since your husband bids,
730 Swallow the burning coal he proffers you!'

But I did wrong, and he gave wrong advice
Though he were thrice Archbishop, – that, I know! –
Now I have got to die and see things clear.
Remember I was barely twelve years old –
A child at marriage: I was let alone
For weeks, I told you, lived my child-life still
Even at Arezzo, when I woke and found
First . . . but I need not think of that again –
Over and ended! Try and take the sense
740   Of what I signify, if it must be so.
After the first, my husband, for hate's sake,
Said one eve, when the simpler cruelty
Seemed somewhat dull at edge and fit to bear,
'We have been man and wife six months almost:
How long is this your comedy to last?
Go this night to my chamber, not your own!'
At which word, I did rush – most true the charge –
And gain the Archbishop's house – he stands for God –
And fall upon my knees and clasp his feet,
750   Praying him hinder what my estranged soul
Refused to bear, though patient of the rest:
'Place me within a convent,' I implored –
'Let me henceforward lead the virgin life
You praise in Her you bid me imitate!'
What did he answer? 'Folly of ignorance!
Know, daughter, circumstances make or mar
Virginity, – 't is virtue or 't is vice.
That which was glory in the Mother of God
Had been, for instance, damnable in Eve
760   Created to be mother of mankind.
Had Eve, in answer to her Maker's speech
"Be fruitful, multiply, replenish earth" –
Pouted "But I choose rather to remain
Single" – why, she had spared herself forthwith
Further probation by the apple and snake,
Been pushed straight out of Paradise! For see –
If motherhood be qualified impure,
I catch you making God command Eve sin!

– A blasphemy so like these Molinists',
770 I must suspect you dip into their books.'
Then he pursued ''T was in your covenant!'

No! There my husband never used deceit.
He never did by speech nor act imply
'Because of our souls' yearning that we meet
And mix in soul through flesh, which yours and mine
Wear and impress, and make their visible selves,
– All which means, for the love of you and me,
Let us become one flesh, being one soul!'
He only stipulated for the wealth;
780 Honest so far. But when he spoke as plain –
Dreadfully honest also – 'Since our souls
Stand each from each, a whole world's width between,
Give me the fleshy vesture I can reach
And rend and leave just fit for hell to burn!' –
Why, in God's name, for Guido's soul's own sake
Imperilled by polluting mine, – I say,
I did resist; would I had overcome!

My heart died out at the Archbishop's smile;
– It seemed so stale and worn a way o' the world,
790 As though 't were nature frowning – 'Here is Spring,
The sun shines as he shone at Adam's fall,
The earth requires that warmth reach everywhere:
What, must your patch of snow be saved forsooth
Because you rather fancy snow than flowers?'
Something in this style he began with me.
Last he said, savagely for a good man,
'This explains why you call your husband harsh,
Harsh to you, harsh to whom you love. God's Bread!
The poor Count has to manage a mere child
800 Whose parents leave untaught the simplest things
Their duty was and privilege to teach, –
Goodwives' instruction, gossips' lore: they laugh
And leave the Count the task, – or leave it me!'
Then I resolved to tell a frightful thing.

'I am not ignorant, – know what I say,
Declaring this is sought for hate, not love.
Sir, you may hear things like almighty God.
I tell you that my housemate, yes – the priest
My husband's brother, Canon Girolamo –
810 Has taught me what depraved and misnamed love
Means, and what outward signs denote the sin,
For he solicits me and says he loves,
The idle young priest with nought else to do.
My husband sees this, knows this, and lets be.
Is it your counsel I bear this beside?'
' – More scandal, and against a priest this time!
What, 't is the Canon now?' – less snappishly –
'Rise up, my child, for such a child you are,
The rod were too advanced a punishment!
820 Let's try the honeyed cake. A parable!
"Without a parable spake He not to them."
There was a ripe round long black toothsome fruit,
Even a flower-fig, the prime boast of May:
And, to the tree, said . . . either the spirit o' the fig,
Or, if we bring in men, the gardener,
Archbishop of the orchard – had I time
To try o' the two which fits in best: indeed
It might be the Creator's self, but then
The tree should bear an apple, I suppose, –
830 Well, anyhow, one with authority said
"Ripe fig, burst skin, regale the fig-pecker –
The bird whereof thou art a perquisite!"
"Nay," with a flounce, replied the restif fig,
"I much prefer to keep my pulp myself:
He may go breakfastless and dinnerless,
Supperless of one crimson seed, for me!"
So, back she flopped into her bunch of leaves.
He flew off, left her, – did the natural lord, –
And lo, three hundred thousand bees and wasps
840 Found her out, feasted on her to the shuck:
Such gain the fig's that gave its bird no bite!
The moral, – fools elude their proper lot,

Tempt other fools, get ruined all alike.
Therefore go home, embrace your husband quick!
Which if his Canon brother chance to see,
He will the sooner back to book again.'

So, home I did go; so, the worst befell:
So, I had proof the Archbishop was just man,
And hardly that, and certainly no more.
850 For, miserable consequence to me,
My husband's hatred waxed nor waned at all,
His brother's boldness grew effrontery soon,
And my last stay and comfort in myself
Was forced from me: henceforth I looked to God
Only, nor cared my desecrated soul
Should have fair walls, gay windows for the world.
God's glimmer, that came through the ruin-top,
Was witness why all lights were quenched inside:
Henceforth I asked God counsel, not mankind.

860 So, when I made the effort, saved myself,
They said – 'No care to save appearance here!
How cynic, – when, how wanton, were enough!'
– Adding, it all came of my mother's life –
My own real mother, whom I never knew,
Who did wrong (if she needs must have done wrong)
Through being all her life, not my four years,
At mercy of the hateful, – every beast
O' the field was wont to break that fountain-fence,
Trample the silver into mud so murk
870 Heaven could not find itself reflected there, –
Now they cry 'Out on her, who, plashy pool,
Bequeathed turbidity and bitterness
To the daughter-stream where Guido dipt and drank!'

Well, since she had to bear this brand – let me!
The rather do I understand her now, –
From my experience of what hate calls love, –
Much love might be in what their love called hate.

If she sold . . . what they call, sold . . . me her child –
I shall believe she hoped in her poor heart
880 That I at least might try be good and pure,
Begin to live untempted, not go doomed
And done with ere once found in fault, as she.
Oh and, my mother, it all came to this?
Why should I trust those that speak ill of you,
When I mistrust who speaks even well of them?
Why, since all bound to do me good, did harm,
May not you, seeming as you harmed me most,
Have meant to do most good – and feed your child
From bramble-bush, whom not one orchard-tree
890 But drew-back bough from, nor let one fruit fall?
This it was for you sacrificed your babe?
Gained just this, giving your heart's hope away
As I might give mine, loving it as you,
If . . . but that never could be asked of me!

There, enough! I have my support again,
Again the knowledge that my babe was, is,
Will be mine only. Him, by death, I give
Outright to God, without a further care, –
But not to any parent in the world, –
900 So to be safe: why is it we repine?
What guardianship were safer could we choose?
All human plans and projects come to nought,
My life, and what I know of other lives,
Prove that: no plan nor project! God shall care!

And now you are not tired? How patient then
All of you, – Oh yes, patient this long while
Listening, and understanding, I am sure!
Four days ago, when I was sound and well
And like to live, no one would understand.
910 People were kind, but smiled 'And what of him,
Your friend, whose tonsure, the rich dark-brown hides?
There, there! – your lover, do we dream he was?
A priest too – never were such naughtiness!

Still, he thinks many a long think, never fear,
After the shy pale lady, – lay so light
For a moment in his arms, the lucky one!'
And so on: wherefore should I blame you much?
So we are made, such difference in minds,
Such difference too in eyes that see the minds!
920 That man, you misinterpret and misprise –
The glory of his nature, I had thought,
Shot itself out in white light, blazed the truth
Through every atom of his act with me:
Yet where I point you, through the chrystal shrine,
Purity in quintessence, one dew-drop,
You all descry a spider in the midst.
One says, 'The head of it is plain to see,'
And one, 'They are the feet by which I judge,'
All say, 'Those films were spun by nothing else.'

930 Then, I must lay my babe away with God,
Nor think of him again, for gratitude.
Yes, my last breath shall wholly spend itself
In one attempt more to disperse the stain,
The mist from other breath fond mouths have made,
About a lustrous and pellucid soul:
So that, when I am gone but sorrow stays,
And people need assurance in their doubt
If God yet have a servant, man a friend,
The weak a saviour and the vile a foe, –
940 Let him be present, by the name invoked,
Giuseppe-Maria Caponsacchi!

There,
Strength comes already with the utterance!
I will remember once more for his sake
The sorrow: for he lives and is belied.
Could he be here, how he would speak for me!

I had been miserable three drear years
In that dread palace and lay passive now,

When I first learned there could be such a man.
950 Thus it fell: I was at a public play,
In the last days of Carnival last March,
Brought there I knew not why, but now know well.
My husband put me where I sat, in front;
Then crouched down, breathed cold through me from
     behind,
Stationed i' the shadow, – none in front could see, –
I, it was, faced the stranger-throng beneath,
The crowd with upturned faces, eyes one stare,
Voices one buzz. I looked but to the stage,
Whereupon two lovers sang and interchanged
960 'True life is only love, love only bliss:
I love thee – thee I love!' then they embraced.
I looked thence to the ceiling and the walls, –
Over the crowd, those voices and those eyes, –
My thoughts went through the roof and out, to Rome
On wings of music, waft of measured words, –
Set me down there, a happy child again,
Sure that to-morrow would be festa-day,
Hearing my parents praise past festas more,
And seeing they were old if I was young,
970 Yet wondering why they still would end discourse
With 'We must soon go, you abide your time,
And, – might we haply see the proper friend
Throw his arm over you and make you safe!'

Sudden I saw him; into my lap there fell
A foolish twist of comfits, broke my dream
And brought me from the air and laid me low,
As ruined as the soaring bee that's reached
(So Pietro told me at the Villa once)
By the dust-handful. There the comfits lay:
980 I looked to see who flung them, and I faced
This Caponsacchi, looking up in turn.
Ere I could reason out why, I felt sure,
Whoever flung them, his was not the hand, –
Up rose the round face and good-natured grin

Of him who, in effect, had played the prank,
From covert close beside the earnest face, –
Fat waggish Conti, friend of all the world.
He was my husband's cousin, privileged
To throw the thing: the other, silent, grave,
990 Solemn almost, saw me, as I saw him.

There is a psalm Don Celestine recites,
'Had I a dove's wings, how I fain would flee!'
The psalm runs not 'I hope, I pray for wings,' –
Not 'If wings fall from heaven, I fix them fast,' –
Simply 'How good it were to fly and rest,
Have hope now, and one day expect content!
How well to do what I shall never do!'
So I said 'Had there been a man like that,
To lift me with his strength out of all strife
1000 Into the calm, how I could fly and rest!
I have a keeper in the garden here
Whose sole employment is to strike me low
If ever I, for solace, seek the sun.
Life means with me successful feigning death,
Lying stone-like, eluding notice so,
Forgoing here the turf and there the sky.
Suppose that man had been instead of this!'

Presently Conti laughed into my ear,
– Had tripped up to the raised place where I sat –
1010 'Cousin, I flung them brutishly and hard!
Because you must be hurt, to look austere
As Caponsacchi yonder, my tall friend
A-gazing now. Ah, Guido, you so close?
Keep on your knees, do! Beg her to forgive!
My cornet battered like a cannon-ball.
Good bye, I'm gone!' – nor waited the reply.

That night at supper, out my husband broke,
'Why was that throwing, that buffoonery?
Do you think I am your dupe? What man would dare

1020 Throw comfits in a stranger lady's lap?
'Twas knowledge of you bred such insolence
In Caponsacchi; he dared shoot the bolt,
Using that Conti for his stalking-horse.
How could you see him this once and no more,
When he is always haunting hereabout
At the street-corner or the palace-side,
Publishing my shame and your impudence?
You are a wanton, – I a dupe, you think?
O Christ, what hinders that I kill her quick?'
1030 Whereat he drew his sword and feigned a thrust.

All this, now, – being not so strange to me,
Used to such misconception day by day
And broken-in to bear, – I bore, this time,
More quietly than woman should perhaps;
Repeated the mere truth and held my tongue.

Then he said, 'Since you play the ignorant,
I shall instruct you. This amour, – commenced
Or finished or midway in act, all's one, –
'Tis the town-talk; so my revenge shall be.
1040 Does he presume because he is a priest?
I warn him that the sword I wear shall pink
His lily-scented cassock through and through,
Next time I catch him underneath your eaves!'

But he had threatened with the sword so oft
And, after all, not kept his promise. All
I said was, 'Let God save the innocent!
Moreover, death is far from a bad fate.
I shall go pray for you and me, not him;
And then I look to sleep, come death or, worse,
1050 Life.' So, I slept.

There may have elapsed a week,
When Margherita, – called my waiting-maid,
Whom it is said my husband found too fair –

Who stood and heard the charge and the reply,
Who never once would let the matter rest
From that night forward, but rang changes still
On this the thrust and that the shame, and how
Good cause for jealousy cures jealous fools,
And what a paragon was this same priest
1060 She talked about until I stopped my ears, –
She said, 'A week is gone; you comb your hair,
Then go mope in a corner, cheek on palm,
Till night comes round again, – so, waste a week
As if your husband menaced you in sport.
Have not I some acquaintance with his tricks?
Oh no, he did not stab the serving-man
Who made and sang the rhymes about me once!
For why? They sent him to the wars next day.
Nor poisoned he the foreigner, my friend,
1070 Who wagered on the whiteness of my breast, –
The swarth skins of our city in dispute:
For, though he paid me proper compliment,
The Count well knew he was besotted with
Somebody else, a skin as black as ink,
(As all the town knew save my foreigner)
He found and wedded presently, – "Why need
Better revenge?" – the Count asked. But what's here?
A priest, that does not fight, and cannot wed,
Yet must be dealt with! If the Count took fire
1080 For the poor pastime of a minute, – me –
What were the conflagration for yourself,
Countess and lady-wife and all the rest?
The priest will perish; you will grieve too late:
So shall the city-ladies' handsomest
Frankest and liberalest gentleman
Die for you, to appease a scurvy dog
Hanging's too good for. Is there no escape?
Were it not simple Christian charity
To warn the priest be on his guard, – save him
1090 Assured death, save yourself from causing it?
I meet him in the street. Give me a glove,

A ring to show for token! Mum's the word!'

I answered, 'If you were, as styled, my maid,
I would command you: as you are, you say,
My husband's intimate, – assist his wife
Who can do nothing but entreat "Be still!"
Even if you speak truth and a crime is planned,
Leave help to God as I am forced to do!
There is no other course, or we should craze,
1100 Seeing such evil with no human cure.
Reflect that God, who makes the storm desist,
Can make an angry violent heart subside.
Why should we venture teach Him governance?
Never address me on this subject more!'

Next night she said, 'But I went, all the same,
– Ay, saw your Caponsacchi in his house,
And come back stuffed with news I must outpour.
I told him, "Sir, my mistress is a stone:
Why should you harm her for no good you get?
1110 For you do harm her – prowl about our place
With the Count never distant half the street,
Lurking at every corner, would you look!
'Tis certain she has witched you with a spell.
Are there not other beauties at your beck?
We all know, Donna This and Monna That
Die for a glance of yours, yet here you gaze!
Go make them grateful, leave the stone its cold!"
And he – oh, he turned first white and then red,
And then – "To her behest I bow myself,
1120 Whom I love with my body and my soul:
Only, a word i' the bowing! See, I write
One little word, no harm to see or hear!
Then, fear no further!" This is what he wrote.
I know you cannot read, – therefore, let me!
"*My idol!*" ' ...

But I took it from her hand

And tore it into shreds. 'Why join the rest
Who harm me? Have I ever done you wrong?
People have told me 't is you wrong myself:
1130 Let it suffice I either feel no wrong
Or else forgive it, – yet you turn my foe!
The others hunt me and you throw a noose!'

She muttered, 'Have your wilful way!' I slept.

Whereupon ... no, I leave my husband out!
It is not to do him more hurt, I speak.
Let it suffice, when misery was most,
One day, I swooned and got a respite so.
She stooped as I was slowly coming to,
This Margherita, ever on my trace,
1140 And whispered – 'Caponsacchi!'

                If I drowned,
But woke afloat i' the wave with upturned eyes,
And found their first sight was a star! I turned –
For the first time, I let her have her will,
Heard passively, – 'The imposthume at such head,
One touch, one lancet-puncture would relieve, –
And still no glance the good physician's way
Who rids you of the torment in a trice!
Still he writes letters you refuse to hear.
1150 He may prevent your husband, kill himself,
So desperate and all fordone is he!
Just hear the pretty verse he made to-day!
A sonnet from Mirtillo. "*Peerless fair* ..."
All poetry is difficult to read,
– The sense of it is, anyhow, he seeks
Leave to contrive you an escape from hell,
And for that purpose asks an interview.
I can write, I can grant it in your name,
Or, what is better, lead you to his house.
1160 Your husband dashes you against the stones;
This man would place each fragment in a shrine:

You hate him, love your husband!'

                         I returned,
'It is not true I love my husband, – no,
Nor hate this man. I listen while you speak,
– Assured that what you say is false, the same:
Much as when once, to me a little child,
A rough gaunt man in rags, with eyes on fire,
A crowd of boys and idlers at his heels,
Rushed as I crossed the Square, and held my head
In his two hands, "Here's she will let me speak!
You little girl, whose eyes do good to mine,
I am the Pope, am Sextus, now the Sixth;
And that Twelfth Innocent, proclaimed to-day,
Is Lucifer disguised in human flesh!
The angels, met in conclave, crowned me!" – thus
He gibbered and I listened; but I knew
All was delusion, ere folks interposed
"Unfasten him, the maniac!" Thus I know
All your report of Caponsacchi false,
Folly or dreaming; I have seen so much
By that adventure at the spectacle,
The face I fronted that one first, last time:
He would belie it by such words and thoughts.
Therefore while you profess to show him me,
I ever see his own face. Get you gone!'

' – That will I, nor once open mouth again, –
No, by Saint Joseph and the Holy Ghost!
On your head be the damage, so adieu!'
And so more days, more deeds I must forget,
Till ... what a strange thing now is to declare!
Since I say anything, say all if true!
And how my life seems lengthened as to serve!
It may be idle or inopportune,
But, true? – why, what was all I said but truth,
Even when I found that such as are untrue
Could only take the truth in through a lie?

Now – I am speaking truth to the Truth's self:
God will lend credit to my words this time.

1200 It had got half through April. I arose
One vivid daybreak, – who had gone to bed
In the old way my wont those last three years,
Careless until, the cup drained, I should die.
The last sound in my ear, the over-night,
Had been a something let drop on the sly
In prattle by Margherita, 'Soon enough
Gaieties end, now Easter's past: a week,
And the Archbishop gets him back to Rome, –
Everyone leaves the town for Rome, this Spring, –
1210 Even Caponsacchi, out of heart and hope,
Resigns himself and follows with the flock.'
I heard this drop and drop like rain outside
Fast-falling through the darkness while she spoke:
So had I heard with like indifference,
'And Michael's pair of wings will arrive first
At Rome to introduce the company,
Will bear him from our picture where he fights
Satan, – expect to have that dragon loose
And never a defender!' – my sole thought
1220 Being still, as night came, 'Done, another day!
How good to sleep and so get nearer death!' –
When, what, first thing at daybreak, pierced the sleep
With a summons to me? Up I sprang alive,
Light in me, light without me, everywhere
Change! A broad yellow sun-beam was let fall
From heaven to earth, – a sudden drawbridge lay,
Along which marched a myriad merry motes,
Mocking the flies that crossed them and recrossed
In rival dance, companions new-born too.
1230 On the house-eaves, a dripping shag of weed
Shook diamonds on each dull grey lattice-square,
As first one, then another bird leapt by,
And light was off, and lo was back again,
Always with one voice, – where are two such joys? –

The blessed building-sparrow! I stepped forth,
Stood on the terrace, – o'er the roofs, such sky!
My heart sang, 'I too am to go away,
I too have something I must care about,
Carry away with me to Rome, to Rome!

1240 The bird brings hither sticks and hairs and wool,
And nowhere else i' the world; what fly breaks rank,
Falls out of the procession that befits,
From window here to window there, with all
The world to choose, – so well he knows his course?
I have my purpose and my motive too,
My march to Rome, like any bird or fly!
Had I been dead! How right to be alive!
Last night I almost prayed for leave to die,
Wished Guido all his pleasure with the sword

1250 Or the poison, – poison, sword, was but a trick,
Harmless, may God forgive him the poor jest!
My life is charmed, will last till I reach Rome!
Yesterday, but for the sin, – ah, nameless be
The deed I could have dared against myself!
Now – see if I will touch an unripe fruit,
And risk the health I want to have and use!
Not to live, now, would be the wickedness, –
For life means to make haste and go to Rome
And leave Arezzo, leave all woes at once!'

1260 Now, understand here, by no means mistake!
Long ago had I tried to leave that house
When it seemed such procedure would stop sin;
And still failed more the more I tried – at first
The Archbishop, as I told you, – next, our lord
The Governor, – indeed I found my way,
I went to the great palace where he rules,
Though I knew well 't was he who, – when I gave
A jewel or two, themselves had given me,
Back to my parents, – since they wanted bread,
1270 They who had never let me want a nosegay, – he
Spoke of the jail for felons, if they kept

What was first theirs, then mine, so doubly theirs,
Though all the while my husband's most of all!
I knew well who had spoke the word wrought this:
Yet, being in extremity, I fled
To the Governor, as I say, – scarce opened lip
When – the cold cruel snicker close behind –
Guido was on my trace, already there,
Exchanging nod and wink for shrug and smile,
1280 And I – pushed back to him and, for my pains,
Paid with . . . but why remember what is past?
I sought out a poor friar the people call
The Roman, and confessed my sin which came
Of their sin, – that fact could not be repressed, –
The frightfulness of my despair in God:
And, feeling, through the grate, his horror shake,
Implored him, 'Write for me who cannot write,
Apprise my parents, make them rescue me!
You bid me be courageous and trust God:
1290 Do you in turn dare somewhat, trust and write
"Dear friends, who used to be my parents once,
And now declare you have no part in me,
This is some riddle I want wit to solve,
Since you must love me with no difference.
Even suppose you altered, – there's your hate,
To ask for: hate of you two dearest ones
I shall find liker love than love found here,
If husbands love their wives. Take me away
And hate me as you do the gnats and fleas,
1300 Even the scorpions! How I shall rejoice!"
Write that and save me!' And he promised – wrote
Or did not write; things never changed at all:
He was not like the Augustinian here!
Last, in a desperation I appealed
To friends, whoever wished me better days,
To Guillichini, that's of kin, – 'What, I –
Travel to Rome with you? A flying gout
Bids me deny my heart and mind my leg!'
Then I tried Conti, used to brave – laugh back

1310 The louring thunder when his cousin scowled
At me protected by his presence: 'You –
Who well know what you cannot save me from, –
Carry me off! What frightens you, a priest?'
He shook his head, looked grave – 'Above my strength!
Guido has claws that scratch, shows feline teeth;
A formidabler foe than I dare fret:
Give me a dog to deal with, twice the size!
Of course I am a priest and Canon too,
But . . . by the bye . . . though both, not quite so bold,
1320 As he, my fellow-Canon, brother-priest,
The personage in such ill odour here
Because of the reports – pure birth o' the brain –
Our Caponsacchi, he's your true Saint George
To slay the monster, set the Princess free,
And have the whole High-Altar to himself:
I always think so when I see that piece
I' the Pieve, that's his church and mine, you know:
Though you drop eyes at mention of his name!'

That name had got to take a half-grotesque
1330 Half-ominous, wholly enigmatic sense,
Like any bye-word, broken bit of song
Born with a meaning, changed by mouth and mouth
That mix it in a sneer or smile, as chance
Bids, till it now means nought but ugliness
And perhaps shame.

            – All this intends to say,
That, over-night, the notion of escape
Had seemed distemper, dreaming; and the name, –
Not the man, but the name of him, thus made
1340 Into a mockery and disgrace, – why, she
Who uttered it persistently, had laughed,
'I name his name, and there you start and wince
As criminal from the red tongs' touch!' – yet now,
Now, as I stood letting morn bathe me bright,
Choosing which butterfly should bear my news, –

The white, the brown one, or that tinier blue, –
The Margherita, I detested so,
In she came – 'The fine day, the good Spring time!
What, up and out at window? That is best.
1350 No thought of Caponsacchi? – who stood there
All night on one leg, like the sentry crane,
Under the pelting of your water-spout –
Looked last look at your lattice ere he leave
Our city, bury his dead hope at Rome?
Ay, go to looking-glass and make you fine,
While he may die ere touch one least loose hair
You drag at with the comb in such a rage!'

I turned – 'Tell Caponsacchi he may come!'

'Tell him to come? Ah, but, for charity,
1360 A truce to fooling! Come? What, – come this eve?
Peter and Paul! But I see through the trick –
Yes, come, and take a flower-pot on his head
Flung from your terrace! No joke, sincere truth?'

How plainly I perceived hell flash and fade
O' the face of her, – the doubt that first paled joy,
Then, final reassurance I indeed
Was caught now, never to be free again!
What did I care? – who felt myself of force
To play with the silk, and spurn the horsehair-springe.

1370 'But – do you know that I have bade him come,
And in your own name? I presumed so much,
Knowing the thing you needed in your heart.
But somehow – what had I to show in proof?
He would not come: half-promised, that was all,
And wrote the letters you refused to read.
What is the message that shall move him now?'

'After the Ave Maria, at first dark,
I will be standing on the terrace, say!

I would I had a good long lock of hair
1380 Should prove I was not lying! Never mind!'

Off she went – 'May he not refuse, that's all –
Fearing a trick!'

I answered, 'He will come.'
And, all day, I sent prayer like incense up
To God the strong, God the beneficent,
God ever mindful in all strife and strait,
Who, for our own good, makes the need extreme,
Till at the last He puts forth might and saves.
An old rhyme came into my head and rang
1390 Of how a virgin, for the faith of God,
Hid herself, from the Paynims that pursued,
In a cave's heart; until a thunderstone,
Wrapped in a flame, revealed the couch and prey:
And they laughed – 'Thanks to lightning, ours at last!'
And she cried 'Wrath of God, assert His love!
Servant of God, thou fire, befriend His child!'
And lo, the fire she grasped at, fixed its flash,
Lay in her hand a calm cold dreadful sword
She brandished till pursuers strewed the ground,
1400 So did the souls within them die away,
As o'er the prostrate bodies, sworded, safe,
She walked forth to the solitudes and Christ:
So should I grasp the lightning and be saved!

And still, as the day wore, the trouble grew
Whereby I guessed there would be born a star,
Until at an intense throe of the dusk,
I started up, was pushed, I dare to say,
Out on the terrace, leaned and looked at last
Where the deliverer waited me: the same
1410 Silent and solemn face, I first descried
At the spectacle, confronted mine once more.

So was that minute twice vouchsafed me, so

The manhood, wasted then, was still at watch
To save me yet a second time: no change
Here, though all else changed in the changing world!

I spoke on the instant, as my duty bade,
In some such sense as this, whatever the phrase.
'Friend, foolish words were borne from you to me;
Your soul behind them is the pure strong wind,
1420 Not dust and feathers which its breath may bear:
These to the witless seem the wind itself,
Since proving thus the first of it they feel.
If by mischance you blew offence my way,
The straws are dropt, the wind desists no whit,
And how such strays were caught up in the street
And took a motion from you, why inquire?
I speak to the strong soul, no weak disguise.
If it be truth, – why should I doubt it truth? –
You serve God specially, as priests are bound,
1430 And care about me, stranger as I am,
So far as wish my good, – that miracle
I take to intimate He wills you serve
By saving me, – what else can He direct?
Here is the service. Since a long while now,
I am in course of being put to death:
While death concerned nothing but me, I bowed
The head and bade, in heart, my husband strike.
Now I imperil something more, it seems,
Something that's trulier me than this myself,
1440 Something I trust in God and you to save.
You go to Rome, they tell me: take me there,
Put me back with my people!'

                         He replied –
The first word I heard ever from his lips,
All himself in it, – an eternity
Of speech, to match the immeasurable depths
O' the soul that then broke silence – 'I am yours.'

So did the star rise, soon to lead my step,
Lead on, nor pause before it should stand still
1450 Above the House o' the Babe, – my babe to be,
That knew me first and thus made me know him,
That had his right of life and claim on mine,
And would not let me die till he was born,
But pricked me at the heart to save us both,
Saying 'Have you the will? Leave God the way!'
And the way was Caponsacchi – 'mine,' thank God!
He was mine, he is mine, he will be mine.

No pause i' the leading and the light! I know,
Next night there was a cloud came, and not he:
1460 But I prayed through the darkness till it broke
And let him shine. The second night, he came.

'The plan is rash; the project desperate:
In such a flight needs must I risk your life,
Give food for falsehood, folly or mistake,
Ground for your husband's rancour and revenge' –
So he began again, with the same face.
I felt that, the same loyalty – one star
Turning now red that was so white before –
One service apprehended newly: just
1470 A word of mine and there the white was back!

'No, friend, for you will take me! 'Tis yourself
Risk all, not I, – who let you, for I trust
In the compensating great God: enough!
I know you: when is it that you will come?'

'To-morrow at the day's dawn.' Then I heard
What I should do: how to prepare for flight
And where to fly.

That night my husband bade
' – You, whom I loathe, beware you break my sleep
1480 This whole night! Couch beside me like the corpse

I would you were!' The rest you know, I think –
How I found Caponsacchi and escaped.

And this man, men call sinner? Jesus Christ!
Of whom men said, with mouths Thyself mad'st once,
'He hath a devil' – say he was Thy saint,
My Caponsacchi! Shield and show – unshroud
In Thine own time the glory of the soul
If aught obscure, – if ink-spot, from vile pens
Scribbling a charge against him – (I was glad
1490 Then, for the first time, that I could not write) –
Flirted his way, have flecked the blaze!

For me,
'Tis otherwise: let men take, sift my thoughts
– Thoughts I throw like the flax for sun to bleach!
I did think, do think, in the thought shall die,
That to have Caponsacchi for my guide,
Ever the face upturned to mine, the hand
Holding my hand across the world, – a sense
That reads, as only such can read, the mark
1500 God sets on woman, signifying so
She should – shall peradventure – be divine;
Yet 'ware, the while, how weakness mars the print
And makes confusion, leaves the thing men see,
– Not this man, – who from his own soul, re-writes
The obliterated charter, – love and strength
Mending what's marred: 'So kneels a votarist,
Weeds some poor waste traditionary plot
Where shrine once was, where temple yet may be,
Purging the place but worshipping the while,
1510 By faith and not by sight, sight clearest so, –
Such way the saints work,' – says Don Celestine.
But I, not privileged to see a saint
Of old when such walked earth with crown and palm,
If I call 'saint' what saints call something else –
The saints must bear with me, impute the fault
To a soul i' the bud, so starved by ignorance,

Stinted of warmth, it will not blow this year
Nor recognize the orb which Spring-flowers know.
But if meanwhile some insect with a heart
1520 Worth floods of lazy music, spendthrift joy –
Some fire-fly renounced Spring for my dwarfed cup,
Crept close to me with lustre for the dark,
Comfort against the cold, – what though excess
Of comfort should miscall the creature – sun?
What did the sun to hinder while harsh hands
Petal by petal, crude and colourless,
Tore me? This one heart brought me all the Spring!

Is all told? There's the journey: and where's time
To tell you how that heart burst out in shine?
1530 Yet certain points do press on me too hard.
Each place must have a name, though I forget:
How strange it was – there where the plain begins
And the small river mitigates its flow –
When eve was fading fast, and my soul sank,
And he divined what surge of bitterness,
In overtaking me, would float me back
Whence I was carried by the striding day –
So, – 'This grey place was famous once,' said he –
And he began that legend of the place
1540 As if in answer to the unspoken fear,
And told me all about a brave man dead,
Which lifted me and let my soul go on!
How did he know too, – at that town's approach
By the rock-side, – that in coming near the signs,
Of life, the house-roofs and the church and tower,
I saw the old boundary and wall o' the world
Rise plain as ever round me, hard and cold,
As if the broken circlet joined again,
Tightened itself about me with no break, –
1550 As if the town would turn Arezzo's self, –
The husband there, – the friends my enemies,
All ranged against me, not an avenue
I try, but would be blocked and drive me back

On him, – this other, . . . oh the heart in that!
Did not he find, bring, put into my arms,
A new-born babe? – and I saw faces beam
Of the young mother proud to teach me joy,
And gossips round expecting my surprise
At the sudden hole through earth that lets in heaven.
1560 I could believe himself by his strong will
Had woven around me what I thought the world
We went along in, every circumstance,
Towns, flowers and faces, all things helped so well!
For, through the journey, was it natural
Such comfort should arise from first to last?
As I look back, all is one milky way;
Still bettered more, the more remembered, so
Do new stars bud while I but search for old,
And fill all gaps i' the glory, and grow him –
1570 Him I now see make the shine everywhere.
Even at the last when the bewildered flesh,
The cloud of weariness about my soul
Clogging too heavily, sucked down all sense, –
Still its last voice was, 'He will watch and care;
Let the strength go, I am content: he stays!'
I doubt not he did stay and care for all –
From that sick minute when the head swam round,
And the eyes looked their last and died on him,
As in his arms he caught me and, you say,
1580 Carried me in, that tragical red eve,
And laid me where I next returned to life
In the other red of morning, two red plates
That crushed together, crushed the time between,
And are since then a solid fire to me, –
When in, my dreadful husband and the world
Broke, – and I saw him, master, by hell's right,
And saw my angel helplessly held back
By guards that helped the malice – the lamb prone,
The serpent towering and triumphant – then
1590 Came all the strength back in a sudden swell,
I did for once see right, do right, give tongue

The adequate protest: for a worm must turn
If it would have its wrong observed by God.
I did spring up, attempt to thrust aside
That ice-block 'twixt the sun and me, lay low
The neutralizer of all good and truth.
If I sinned so, – never obey voice more
O' the Just and Terrible, who bids us – 'Bear!'
Not – 'Stand by, bear to see my angels bear!'
1600 I am clear it was on impulse to serve God
Not save myself, – no – nor my child unborn!
Had I else waited patiently till now? –
Who saw my old kind parents, silly-sooth
And too much trustful, for their worst of faults,
Cheated, brow-beaten, stripped and starved, cast out
Into the kennel: I remonstrated,
Then sank to silence, for, – their woes at end,
Themselves gone, – only I was left to plague.
If only I was threatened and belied,
1610 What matter? I could bear it and did bear;
It was a comfort, still one lot for all:
They were not persecuted for my sake
And I, estranged, the single happy one.
But when at last, all by myself I stood
Obeying the clear voice which bade me rise,
Not for my own sake but my babe unborn,
And take the angel's hand was sent to help –
And found the old adversary athwart the path –
Not my hand simply struck from the angel's, but
1620 The very angel's self made foul i' the face
By the fiend who struck there, – that I would not bear,
That only I resisted! So, my first
And last resistance was invincible.
Prayers move God; threats, and nothing else, move men!
I must have prayed a man as he were God
When I implored the Governor to right
My parents' wrongs: the answer was a smile.
The Archbishop, – did I clasp his feet enough,
Hide my face hotly on them, while I told

1630 More than I dared make my own mother know?
The profit was – compassion and a jest.
This time, the foolish prayers were done with, right
Used might, and solemnized the sport at once.
All was against the combat: vantage, mine?
The runaway avowed, the accomplice-wife,
In company with the plan-contriving priest?
Yet, shame thus rank and patent, I struck, bare,
At foe from head to foot in magic mail,
And off it withered, cobweb-armoury
1640 Against the lightning! 'T was truth singed the lies
And saved me, not the vain sword nor weak speech!

You see, I will not have the service fail!
I say, the angel saved me: I am safe!
Others may want and wish, I wish nor want
One point o' the circle plainer, where I stand
Traced round about with white to front the world.
What of the calumny I came across,
What o' the way to the end? – the end crowns all.
The judges judged aright i' the main, gave me
1650 The uttermost of my heart's desire, a truce
From torture and Arezzo, balm for hurt
With the quiet nuns, – God recompense the good!
Who said and sang away the ugly past.
And, when my final fortune was revealed,
What safety while, amid my parents' arms,
My babe was given me! Yes, he saved my babe:
It would not have peeped forth, the bird-like thing,
Through that Arezzo noise and trouble: back
Had it returned nor ever let me see!
1660 But the sweet peace cured all, and let me live
And give my bird the life among the leaves
God meant him! Weeks and months of quietude,
I could lie in such peace and learn so much –
Begin the task, I see how needful now,
Of understanding somewhat of my past, –
Know life a little, I should leave so soon.

Therefore, because this man restored my soul,
All has been right; I have gained my gain, enjoyed
As well as suffered, – nay, got foretaste too
1670 Of better life beginning where this ends –
All through the breathing-while allowed me thus,
Which let good premonitions reach my soul
Unthwarted, and benignant influence flow
And interpenetrate and change my heart,
Uncrossed by what was wicked, – nay, unkind.
For, as the weakness of my time drew nigh,
Nobody did me one disservice more,
Spoke coldly or looked strangely, broke the love
I lay in the arms of, till my boy was born,
1680 Born all in love, with nought to spoil the bliss
A whole long fortnight: in a life like mine
A fortnight filled with bliss is long and much.
All women are not mothers of a boy,
Though they live twice the length of my whole life,
And, as they fancy, happily all the same.
There I lay, then, all my great fortnight long,
As if it would continue, broaden out
Happily more and more, and lead to heaven:
Christmas before me, – was not that a chance?
1690 I never realized God's birth before –
How he grew likest God in being born.
This time I felt like Mary, had my babe
Lying a little on my breast like hers.
So all went on till, just four days ago –
The night and the tap.

　　　　　　　O it shall be success
To the whole of our poor family! My friends
... Nay, father and mother, – give me back my word!
They have been rudely stripped of life, disgraced
1700 Like children who must needs go clothed too fine,
Carry the garb of Carnival in Lent:
If they too much affected frippery,
They have been punished and submit themselves,

Say no word: all is over, they see God
Who will not be extreme to mark their fault
Or He had granted respite: they are safe.

For that most woeful man my husband once,
Who, needing respite, still draws vital breath,
I – pardon him? So far as lies in me,
1710 I give him for his good the life he takes,
Praying the world will therefore acquiesce.
Let him make God amends, – none, none to me
Who thank him rather that, whereas strange fate
Mockingly styled him husband and me wife,
Himself this way at least pronounced divorce,
Blotted the marriage-bond: this blood of mine
Flies forth exultingly at any door,
Washes the parchment white, and thanks the blow.
We shall not meet in this world nor the next,
1720 But where will God be absent? In His face
Is light, but in His shadow healing too:
Let Guido touch the shadow and be healed!
And as my presence was importunate, –
My earthly good, temptation and a snare, –
Nothing about me but drew somehow down
His hate upon me, – somewhat so excused
Therefore, since hate was thus the truth of him, –
May my evanishment for evermore
Help further to relieve the heart that cast
1730 Such object of its natural loathing forth!
So he was made; he nowise made himself:
I could not love him, but his mother did.
His soul has never lain beside my soul;
But for the unresisting body, – thanks!
He burned that garment spotted by the flesh!
Whatever he touched is rightly ruined: plague
It caught, and disinfection it had craved
Still but for Guido; I am saved through him
So as by fire; to him – thanks and farewell!

1740 Even for my babe, my boy, there's safety thence —
From the sudden death of me, I mean: we poor
Weak souls, how we endeavour to be strong!
I was already using up my life, —
This portion, now, should do him such a good,
This other go to keep off such an ill!
The great life; see, a breath and it is gone!
So is detached, so left all by itself
The little life, the fact which means so much.
Shall not God stoop the kindlier to His work,
1750 His marvel of creation, foot would crush,
Now that the hand He trusted to receive
And hold it, lets the treasure fall perforce?
The better; He shall have in orphanage
His own way all the clearlier: if my babe
Outlive the hour — and he has lived two weeks —
It is through God who knows I am not by.
Who is it makes the soft gold hair turn black,
And sets the tongue, might lie so long at rest,
Trying to talk? Let us leave God alone!
1760 Why should I doubt He will explain in time
What I feel now, but fail to find the words?
My babe nor was, nor is, nor yet shall be
Count Guido Franceschini's child at all —
Only his mother's, born of love not hate!
So shall I have my rights in after-time.
It seems absurd, impossible to-day;
So seems so much else not explained but known.

Ah! Friends, I thank and bless you every one!
No more now: I withdraw from earth and man
1770 To my own soul, compose myself for God.

Well, and there is more! Yes, my end of breath
Shall bear away my soul in being true!
He is still here, not outside with the world,
Here, here, I have him in his rightful place!
'T is now, when I am most upon the move,

I feel for what I verily find – again
The face, again the eyes, again, through all,
The heart and its immeasurable love
Of my one friend, my only, all my own,
1780 Who put his breast between the spears and me.
Ever with Caponsacchi! Otherwise
Here alone would be failure, loss to me –
How much more loss to him, with life debarred
From giving life, love locked from love's display,
The day-star stopped its task that makes night morn!
O lover of my life, O soldier-saint,
No work begun shall ever pause for death!
Love will be helpful to me more and more
I' the coming course, the new path I must tread,
1790 My weak hand in thy strong hand, strong for that!
Tell him that if I seem without him now,
That's the world's insight! Oh, he understands!
He is at Civita – do I once doubt
The world again is holding us apart?
He had been here, displayed in my behalf
The broad brow that reverberates the truth,
And flashed the word God gave him, back to man!
I know where the free soul is flown! My fate
Will have been hard for even him to bear:
1800 Let it confirm him in the trust of God,
Showing how holily he dared the deed!
And, for the rest, – say, from the deed, no touch
Of harm came, but all good, all happiness,
Not one faint fleck of failure! Why explain?
What I see, oh, he sees and how much more!
Tell him, – I know not wherefore the true word
Should fade and fall unuttered at the last –
It was the name of him I sprang to meet
When came the knock, the summons and the end.
1810 'My great heart, my strong hand are back again!'
I would have sprung to these, beckoning across
Murder and hell gigantic and distinct
O' the threshold, posted to exclude me heaven:

He is ordained to call and I to come!
Do not the dead wear flowers when dressed for God?
Say, – I am all in flowers from head to foot!
Say, – not one flower of all he said and did,
Might seem to flit unnoticed, fade unknown,
But dropped a seed has grown a balsam-tree
1820 Whereof the blossoming perfumes the place
At this supreme of moments! He is a priest;
He cannot marry therefore, which is right:
I think he would not marry if he could.
Marriage on earth seems such a counterfeit,
Mere imitation of the inimitable:
In heaven we have the real and true and sure.
'T is there they neither marry nor are given
In marriage but are as the angels: right,
Oh how right that is, how like Jesus Christ
1830 To say that! Marriage-making for the earth,
With gold so much, – birth, power, repute so much,
Or beauty, youth so much, in lack of these!
Be as the angels rather, who, apart,
Know themselves into one, are found at length
Married, but marry never, no, nor give
In marriage; they are man and wife at once
When the true time is: here we have to wait
Not so long neither! Could we by a wish
Have what we will and get the future now,
1840 Would we wish aught done undone in the past?
So, let him wait God's instant men call years;
Meantime hold hard by truth and his great soul,
Do out the duty! Through such souls alone
God stooping shows sufficient of His light
For us i' the dark to rise by. And I rise.

BOOK VIII

Dominus Hyacinthus de Archangelis

Ah, my Giacinto, he's no ruddy rogue,
Is not Cinone? What, to-day we're eight?
Seven and one 's eight, I hope, old curly-pate!
– Branches me out his verb-tree on the slate,
Amo –as –avi –atum –are –ans,
Up to *–aturus,* person, tense, and mood,
Quies me cum subjunctivo (I could cry)
And chews Corderius with his morning crust!
Look eight years onward, and he's perched, he's perched,
10 Dapper and deft on stool beside this chair,
Cinozzo, Cinoncello, who but he?
– Trying his milk-teeth on some crusty case
Like this, papa shall triturate full soon
To smooth Papinianian pulp!
                              It trots
Already through my head, though noon be now,
Does supper-time and what belongs to eve.
Dispose, O Don, o' the day, first work then play!
– The proverb bids. And 'then' means, won't we hold
20 Our little yearly lovesome frolic feast,
Cinuolo's birth-night, Cinicello's own,
That makes gruff January grin perforce!
For too contagious grows the mirth, the warmth
Escaping from so many hearts at once –
When the good wife, buxom and bonny yet,
Jokes the hale grandsire, – such are just the sort
To go off suddenly, – he who hides the key
O' the box beneath his pillow every night, –
Which box may hold a parchment (some one thinks)

30 Will show a scribbled something like a name
'Cinino, Ciniccino,' near the end,
'To whom I give and I bequeath my lands,
Estates, tenements, hereditaments,
When I decease as honest grandsire ought':
Wherefore – yet this one time again perhaps –
Sha'n't my Orvieto fuddle his old nose!
Then, uncles, one or the other, well i' the world,
May – drop in, merely? – trudge through rain and wind,
Rather! The smell-feasts rouse them at the hint
40 There's cookery in a certain dwelling-place!
Gossips, too, each with keepsake in his poke,
Will pick the way, thrid lane by lantern-light,
And so find door, put galligaskin off
At entry of a decent domicile
Cornered in snug Condotti, – all for love,
All to crush cup with Cinucciatolo!

                                      Well,
Let others climb the heights o' the court, the camp!
How vain are chambering and wantonness,
50 Revel and rout and pleasures that make mad!
Commend me to home-joy, the family board,
Altar and hearth! These, with a brisk career,
A source of honest profit and good fame,
Just so much work as keeps the brain from rust,
Just so much play as lets the heart expand,
Honouring God and serving man, – I say,
These are reality, and all else, – fluff,
Nutshell and naught, – thank Flaccus for the phrase!
Suppose I had been Fisc, yet bachelor!

60 Why, work with a will, then! Wherefore lazy now?
Turn up the hour-glass, whence no sand-grain slips
But should have done its duty to the saint
O' the day, the son and heir that 's eight years old!
Let law come dimple Cinoncino's cheek,
And Latin dumple Cinarello's chin,
The while we spread him fine and toss him flat

This pulp that makes the pancake, trim our mass
Of matter into Argument the First,
Prime Pleading in defence of our accused,
70 Which, once a-waft on paper wing, shall soar,
Shall signalize before applausive Rome
What study, and mayhap some mother-wit,
Can do toward making Master fop and Fisc
Old bachelor Bottinius bite his thumb.
Now, how good God is! How falls plumb to point
This murder, gives me Guido to defend
Now, of all days i' the year, just when the boy
Verges on Virgil, reaches the right age
For some such illustration from his sire,
80 Stimulus to himself! One might wait years
And never find the chance which now finds me!
The fact is, there's a blessing on the hearth,
A special providence for fatherhood!
Here's a man, and what's more, a noble, kills
– Not sneakingly but almost with parade –
Wife's father and wife's mother and wife's self
That's mother's self of son and heir (like mine!)
– And here stand I, the favoured advocate,
Who pluck this flower o' the field, no Solomon
90 Was ever clothed in glorious gold to match,
And set the same in Cinoncino's cap!
I defend Guido and his comrades – I!
Pray God, I keep me humble: not to me –
Non nobis, Domine, sed tibi laus!
How the fop chuckled when they made him Fisc!
We'll beat you, my Bottinius, all for love,
All for our tribute to Cinotto's day!
Why, 'sbuddikins, old Innocent himself
May rub his eyes at the bustle, – ask 'What's this
100 Rolling from out the rostrum, as a gust
O' the *Pro Milone* had been prisoned there,
And rattled Rome awake?' Awaken Rome,
How can the Pope doze on in decency?
He needs must wake up also, speak his word,

Have his opinion like the rest of Rome,
About this huge, this hurly-burly case:
He wants who can excogitate the truth,
Give the result in speech, plain black and white,
To mumble in the mouth and make his own
110   – A little changed, good man, a little changed!
No matter, so his gratitude be moved,
By when my Giacintino gets of age,
Mindful of who thus helped him at a pinch,
Archangelus *Procurator Pauperum* –
And proved Hortensius *Redivivus!*
                           Whew!
To earn the *Est-est*, merit the minced herb
That mollifies the liver's leathery slice,
With here a goose-foot, there a cock's-comb stuck,
120   Cemented in an element of cheese!
I doubt if dainties do the grandsire good:
Last June he had a sort of strangling . . . bah!
He's his own master, and his will is made.
So, liver fizz, law flit and Latin fly
As we rub hands o'er dish by way of grace!
May I lose cause if I vent one word more
Except, – with fresh-cut quill we ink the white, –
P-r-o-pro Guidone et Sociis. There!

Count Guido married – or, in Latin due,
130   What? *Duxit in uxorem?* – commonplace!
Taedas jugales iniit, subiit, – ha!
He underwent the matrimonial torch?
Connubio stabili sibi junxit, – hum!
In stable bond of marriage bound his own?
That's clear of any modern taint: and yet . . .

Virgil is little help to who writes prose.
He shall attack me Terence with the dawn,
Shall Cinuccino! Mum, mind business, Sir!
Thus circumstantially evolve we facts,
140   *Ita se habet ideo series facti:*

He wedded, – ah, with owls for augury!
Nupserat, heu sinistris avibus,
One of the blood Arezzo boasts her best,
Dominus Guido, nobili genere ortus,
Pompiliae . . .

But the version afterward!
Curb we this ardour! Notes alone, to-day,
The speech to-morrow and the Latin last:
Such was the rule in Farinacci's time.
Indeed I hitched it into verse and good.

150 Unluckily, law quite absorbs a man,
Or else I think I too had poetized.
'Law is the pork substratum of the fry,
Goose-foot and cocks-comb are Latinity,' –
And in this case, if circumstance assist,
We'll garnish law with idiom, never fear!
Out-of-the-way events extend our scope:
For instance, when Bottini brings his charge,
'That letter which you say Pompilia wrote,
To criminate her parents and herself

160 And disengage her husband from the coil, –
That, Guido Franceschini wrote, say we:
Because Pompilia could nor read nor write,
Therefore he pencilled her such letter first,
Then made her trace in ink the same again.'
– Ha, my Bottini, have I thee on hip?
How will he turn this nor break Tully's pate?
'*Existimandum*' (do n't I hear the dog!)
'*Quod Guido designaverit elementa*
Dictae epistolae, quae fuerint

170 (*Superinducto ab ea calamo*)
Notata atramento' – there's a style! –
'*Quia ipsa scribere nesciebat.*' Boh!
Now, my turn! Either, *Insulse!* – I outburst,
Stupidly put! Inane is the response,
Inanis est responsio, or the like –
To-wit, that each of all those characters,

Quod singula elementa epistolae,
Had first of all been traced for her by him,
Fuerant per eum prius designata,
180 And then, the ink applied a-top of that,
Et deinde, superinducto calamo,
The piece, she says, became her handiwork,
Per eam, efformata, ut ipsa asserit.
Inane were such response! (a second time:)
Her husband outlined her the whole, forsooth?
Vir ejus lineabat epistolam?
What, she confesses that she wrote the thing,
Fatetur eam scripsisse, (scorn that scathes!)
That she might pay obedience to her lord?
190 *Ut viro obtemperaret, apices*
(Here repeat charge with proper varied phrase)
Eo designante, ipsaque calamum
Super inducente? By such argument,
Ita pariter, she seeks to show the same,
(Ay, by Saint Joseph and what saints you please)
Epistolam ostendit, medius fidius,
No voluntary deed but fruit of force!
Non voluntarie sed coacte scriptam!
That's the way to write Latin, friend my Fisc!
200 Bottini is a beast, one barbarous:
Look out for him when he attempts to say
'Armed with a pistol, Guido followed her!'
Will not I be beforehand with my Fisc,
Cut away phrase by phrase from underfoot!
Guido Pompiliam – Guido thus his wife
Following with igneous engine, shall I have?
Armis munitus igneis persequens –
Arma sulphurea gestans, sulphury arms,
Or, might one style a pistol – popping-piece?
210 *Armatus breviori sclopulo?*
We'll let him have been armed so, though it make
Somewhat against us: I had thought to own –
Provided with a simple travelling-sword,
Ense solummodo viatorio

Instructus: but we'll grant the pistol here:
Better we lost the cause than lacked the gird
At the Fisc's Latin, lost the Judge's laugh!
It's Venturini that decides for style.
Tommati rather goes upon the law.
220 So, as to law, –

                 Ah, but with law ne'er hope
To level the fellow, – don't I know his trick!
How he draws up, ducks under, twists aside!
He's a lean-gutted hectic rascal, fine
As pale-haired red-eyed ferret which pretends
'T is ermine, pure soft snow from tail to snout.
He eludes law by piteous looks aloft,
Lets Latin glance off as he makes appeal
To the saint that's somewhere in the ceiling-top, –
230 Do you suppose that I do n't see the beast?
Plague of the ermine-vermin! For it takes,
It takes, and here 's the fellow Fisc, you see,
And Judge, you'll not be long in seeing next!
Confound the fop – he's now at work like me:
Enter his study, as I seem to do,
Hear him read out his writing to himself!
I know he writes as if he spoke: I hear
The hoarse shrill throat, see shut eyes, neck shot-forth,
– I see him strain on tiptoe, soar and pour
240 Eloquence out, nor stay nor stint at all –
Perorate in the air, and so, to press
With the product! What abuse of type is here!
He'll keep clear of my cast, my logic-throw,
Let argument slide, and then deliver swift
Some bowl from quite an unguessed point of stand –
Having the luck o' the last word, the reply!
A plaguy cast, a mortifying stroke:
You face a fellow – cries 'So, there you stand?
But I discourteous jump clean o'er your head!
250 You play ship-carpenter, not pilot so, –
Stop rat-holes, while a sea sweeps through the breach, –

Hammer and fortify at puny points!
Do, clamp and tenon, make all tight and safe!
'Tis here and here and here you ship a sea,
No good of your stopped leaks and littleness!'

Yet what do I name 'little and a leak'?
The main defence o' the murder's used to death,
By this time, dry bare bones, no scrap to pick:
Safer I worked at the new, the unforeseen,
260   The nice bye-stroke, the fine and improvised,
Point that can titillate the brain o' the Bench
Torpid with over-teaching, by this time!
As if Tommati, that has heard, reheard
And heard again, first this side and then that, –
Guido and Pietro, Pietro and Guido din
And deafen, full three years, at each long ear, –
Do n't want amusement for instruction now,
Won't rather feel a flea run o'er his ribs,
Than a daw settle heavily on his head!
270   Oh, I was young and had the trick of fence,
Knew subtle pass and push with careless right –
The left arm ever quietly behind back
With the dagger in 't: not both hands to blade!
Puff and blow, put the strength out, Blunderbore!
That's my subordinate, young Spreti, now,
Pedant and prig, – he'll pant away at proof,
That's his way!

          Now for mine – to rub some life
Into one's choppy fingers this cold day!
280   I trust Cinuzzo ties on tippet, guards
The precious throat on which so much depends!
Guido must be all goose-flesh in his hole,
Despite the prison-straw: bad Carnival
For captives! no sliced fry for him, poor Count!

Carnival-time, – another providence!
The town a-swarm with strangers to amuse,

To edify, to give one's name and fame
In charge of, till they find, some future day,
Cintino come and claim it, his name too,
290 Pledge of the pleasantness they owe papa –
Who else was it, cured Rome of her great qualms,
When she must needs have her own judgment? – ay
Since all her topping wits had set to work,
Pronounced already on the case: mere boys,
Twice Cineruggiolo's age and half his sense,
As good as tell me, when I cross the court,
'Master Arcangeli!' (plucking at my gown)
'We can predict, we comprehend your play,
We'll help you save your client.' Tra-la-la!
300 I've travelled ground, from childhood till this hour,
To have the town anticipate my track!
The old fox takes the plain and velvet path,
The young hound's predilection, – prints the dew,
Do n't he, to suit their pulpy pads of paw?
No! Burying nose deep down i' the briery bush,
Thus I defend Count Guido.
                                        Where are we weak?
First, which is foremost in advantage too,
Our murder, – we call, killing, – is a fact
310 Confessed, defended, made a boast of: good!
To think the Fisc claimed use of torture here,
And got thereby avowal plump and plain
That gives me just the chance I wanted, – scope
Not for brute-force but ingenuity,
Explaining matters, not denying them!
One may dispute, – as I am bound to do,
And shall, – validity of process here:
Inasmuch as a noble is exempt
From torture which plebeians undergo
320 In such a case: for law is lenient, lax,
Remits the torture to a nobleman
Unless suspicion be of twice the strength
Attaches to a man born vulgarly:
We do n't card silk with comb that dresses wool.

Moreover, 'twas severity undue
In this case, even had the lord been lout.
What utters, on this head, our oracle,
Our Farinacci, my Gamaliel erst,
In those immortal 'Questions?' What I quote:
330 'Of all the tools at Law's disposal, sure
That named *Vigiliarum* is the best –
That is, the worst – to whoso has to bear:
Lasting, as it may do, from some seven hours
To ten, (beyond ten, we've no precedent;
Certain have touched their ten but, bah, they died!)
It does so efficaciously convince
That, – speaking by much observation here, –
Out of each hundred cases, by my count,
Never I knew of patients beyond four
340 Withstand its taste, or less than ninety-six
End by succumbing: only martyrs four,
Of obstinate silence, guilty or no, – against
Ninety-six full confessors, innocent
Or otherwise, – so shrewd a tool have we!'
No marvel either: in unwary hands,
Death on the spot is no rare consequence:
As indeed all but happened in this case
To one of ourselves, our young tough peasant-friend
The accomplice called Baldeschi: they were rough,
350 Dosed him with torture as you drench a horse,
Not modify your treatment to a man:
So, two successive days he fainted dead,
And only on the third essay, gave up,
Confessed like flesh and blood. We could reclaim, –
Blockhead Bottini giving cause enough!
But no, – we'll take it as spontaneously
Confessed: we'll have the murder beyond doubt.
Ah, fortunate (the poet's word reversed)
Inasmuch as we know our happiness!
360 Had the antagonist left dubiety,
Here were we proving murder a mere myth,
And Guido innocent, ignorant, absent, – ay,

Absent! He was – why, where should Christian be? –
Engaged in visiting his proper church,
The duty of us all at Christmas-time;
When Caponsacchi, the seducer, stung
To madness by his relegation, cast
About him and contrived a remedy:
To stave off what opprobrium broke afresh,
370 By the birth o' the babe, on him the imputed sire,
He came and quietly sought to smother up
His shame and theirs together, – killed the three,
And fled – (go seek him where you please to search) –
Just at the moment, Guido, touched by grace,
Devotions ended, hastened to the spot,
Meaning to pardon his convicted wife,
'Neither do I condemn thee, go in peace!' –
Who thus arrived i' the nick of time to catch
The charge o' the killing, though great-heartedly
380 He came but to forgive and bring to life.
Doubt ye the force of Christmas on the soul?
'Is thine eye evil because mine is good?'

So, doubtless, had I needed argue here
But for the full confession round and sound!
Thus would you have some kingly alchemist, –
Whose concern should not be with proving brass
Transmutable to gold, but triumphing,
Rather, above his gold changed out of brass,
Not vulgarly to the mere sight and touch,
390 But in the idea, the spiritual display,
Proud apparition buoyed by winged words
Hovering above its birth-place in the brain, –
Here would you have this excellent personage
Forced, by the gross need, to gird apron round,
Plant forge, light fire, ply bellows, – in a word,
Demonstrate – when a faulty pipkin's crack
May disconcert you his presumptive truth!
Here were I hanging to the testimony
Of one of these poor rustics – four, ye Gods!

400 Whom the first taste of friend the Fiscal's cord
Might drive into undoing my whole speech,
Shaming truth so!
                     I wonder, all the same,
Not so much at those peasants' lack of heart;
But – Guido Franceschini, nobleman,
Bear pain no better! Everybody knows
It used once, when my father was a boy,
To form a proper, nay, important point
I' the education of our well-born youth,
410 To take the torture handsomely at need,
Without confessing in this clownish guise.
Each noble had his rack for private use,
And would, for the diversion of a guest,
Bid it be set up in the yard of arms,
To take thereon his hour of exercise, –
Command the varletry stretch, strain their best,
While friends looked on, admired my lord could smile
'Mid tugging which had caused an ox to roar.
Men are no longer men!

420   – And advocates
No longer Farinacci, let men add,
If I one more time fly from point proposed!
So, *Vindicatio*, – here begins the same! –
Honoris causa; so we make our stand:
Honour in us had injury, we shall prove.
Or if we fail to prove such injury
More than misprision of the fact, – what then?
It is enough, authorities declare,
If the result, the deed in question now,
430 Be caused by confidence that injury
Is veritable and no figment: since,
What, though proved fancy afterward, seemed fact
At the time, they argue shall excuse result.
That which we do, persuaded of good cause
For what we do, hold justifiable! –
The casuists bid: man, bound to do his best,

They would not have him leave that best undone
And mean to do the worst, – though fuller light
Show best was worst and worst would have been best.

440 Act by the present light, they ask of man.
Ultra quod hic non agitur, besides
It is not anyway our business here,
De probatione adulterii,
To prove what we thought crime was crime indeed,
Ad irrogandam poenam, and require
Its punishment: such nowise do we seek:
Sed ad effectum, but 't is our concern,
Excusandi, here to simply find excuse,
Occisorem, for who did the killing-work,

450 *Et ad illius defensionem*, (mark
The difference!) and defend the man, just that.
Quo casu levior probatio
Exuberaret, to which end far lighter proof
Suffices than the prior case would claim:
It should be always harder to convict,
In short, than to establish innocence.
Therefore we shall demonstrate first of all
That Honour is a gift of God to man
Precious beyond compare, – which natural sense

460 Of human rectitude and purity, –
Which white, man's soul is born with, brooks no touch:
Therefore, the sensitivest spot of all,
Woundable by a wafture breathed from black,
Is, – honour within honour, like the eye
Centred i' the ball, – the honour of our wife.
Touch us o' the pupil of our honour, then,
Not actually, – since so you slay outright, –
But by a gesture simulating touch,
Presumable mere menace of such taint, –

470 This were our warrant for eruptive ire
'To whose dominion I impose no end.'

(Virgil, now, should not be too difficult
To Cinoncino, – say the early books . . .

Pen, truce to further gambols! *Poscimur!*)

Nor can revenge of injury done here
To the honour proved the life and soul of us,
Be too excessive, too extravagant:
Such wrong seeks and must have complete revenge.
Show we this, first, on the mere natural ground:
480 Begin at the beginning, and proceed
Incontrovertibly. Theodoric,
In an apt sentence Cassiodorus cites,
Propounds for basis of all household law –
I hardly recollect it, but it ends,
'Bird mates with bird, beast genders with his like,
And brooks no interference:' bird and beast?
The very insects . . . if they wive or no,
How dare I say when Aristotle doubts?
But the presumption is they likewise wive,
490 At least the nobler sorts; for take the bee
As instance, – copying King Solomon, –
Why that displeasure of the bee to aught
That savours of incontinency, makes
The unchaste a very horror to the hive?
Whence comes it bees obtain the epithet
Of *castae apes*? notably 'the chaste?'
Because, ingeniously saith Scaliger,
(The young one – see his book of Table-talk)
'Such is their hatred of immodest act,
500 They fall upon the offender, sting to death.'
I mind a passage much confirmative
I' the Idyllist (though I read him Latinized)
'Why' asks a shepherd, 'is this bank unfit
For celebration of our vernal loves?'
'Oh swain,' returns the wiser shepherdess,
'Bees swarm here, and would quick resent our warmth!'
Only cold-blooded fish lack instinct here,
Nor gain nor guard connubiality:
But beasts, quadrupedal, mammiferous,
510 Do credit to their beasthood: witness him,

That Aelian cites, the noble elephant,
(Or if not Aelian, somebody as sage)
Who seeing much offence beneath his nose,
His master's friend exceed in courtesy
The due allowance to that master's wife,
Taught them good manners and killed both at once,
Making his master and all men admire.
Indubitably, then, that master's self
Favoured by circumstance, had done the same
520 Or else stood clear rebuked by his own beast.
Adeo, ut qui honorem spernit, thus,
Who values his own honour not a straw, –
Et non recuperare curat, nor
Labours by might and main to salve its wound,
Se ulciscendo, by revenging him,
Nil differat a belluis, is a brute,
Quinimo irrationabilior
Ipsismet belluis, nay, contrariwise,
Much more irrational than brutes themselves,
530 Should be considered, *reputetur*! How?
If a poor animal feel honour smart,
Taught by blind instinct nature plants in him,
Shall man, – confessed creation's master-stroke,
Nay, intellectual glory, nay, a god,
Nay, of the nature of my Judges here, –
Shall man prove the insensible, the block,
The blot o' the earth he crawls on to disgrace?
(Come, that's both solid and poetic) – man
Derogate, live for the low tastes alone,
540 Mean creeping cares about the animal life?

May Gigia have remembered, nothing stings
Fried liver out of its monotony
Of richness like a root of fennel, chopped
Fine with the parsley: parsley-sprigs, I said –
Was there need I should say 'and fennel too?'
But no, she cannot have been so obtuse!
To our argument! The fennel will be chopped.

From beast to man next mount we – ay, but, mind,
Still mere man, not yet Christian, – that, in time!
550 Not too fast, mark you! 'Tis on Heathen grounds
We next defend our act: then, fairly urge –
If this were done of old, in a green tree,
Allowed in the Spring rawness of our kind,
What may be licenced in the Autumn dry,
And ripe, the latter harvest-tide of man?
If, with his poor and primitive half-lights,
The Pagan, whom our devils served for gods,
Could stigmatise the breach of marriage-vow
As that which blood, blood only might efface, –
560 Absolve the husband, outraged, whose revenge
Anticipated law, plied sword himself, –
How with the Christian in full blaze of day?
Shall not he rather double penalty,
Multiply vengeance, than, degenerate,
Let privilege be minished, droop, decay?
Therefore set forth at large the ancient law!
Superabundant the examples be
To pick and choose from. The Athenian Code,
Solon's, the name is serviceable, – then,
570 The Laws of the Twelve Tables, that fifteenth, –
'Romulus' likewise rolls out round and large.
The Julian; the Cornelian; Gracchus' Law:
So old a chime, the bells ring of themselves!
Spreti can set that going if he please,
I point you, for my part, the belfry out,
Intent to rise from dusk, *diluculum*,
Into the Christian day shall broaden next.

First, the fit compliment to His Holiness
Happily reigning: then sustain the point –
580 All that was long ago declared as law
By the early Revelation, stands confirmed
By Apostle and Evangelist and Saint, –
To-wit – that Honour is the supreme good.
Why should I baulk Saint Jerome of his phrase?

Ubi honor non est, where no honour is,
Ibi contemptus est; and where contempt,
Ibi injuria frequens; and where that,
The frequent injury, *ibi et indignatio*;
And where the indignation, *ibi quies*
590 *Nulla;* and where there is no quietude,
Why, *ibi*, there, the mind is often cast
Down from the heights where it proposed to dwell,
Mens a proposito saepe dejicitur.
And naturally the mind is so cast down,
Since harder 't is, *quum difficilius sit,*
Iram cohibere, to coerce one's wrath,
Quam miracula facere, than work miracles, –
Saint Gregory smiles in his First Dialogue:
Whence we infer, the ingenuous soul, the man
600 Who makes esteem of honour and repute,
Whenever honour and repute are touched,
Arrives at term of fury and despair,
Loses all guidance from the reason-check:
As in delirium, or a frenzy-fit,
Nor fury nor despair he satiates, – no,
Not even if he attain the impossible,
O'erturn the hinges of the universe
To annihilate – not whoso caused the smart
Solely, the author simply of his pain,
610 But the place, the memory, *vituperii,*
O' the shame and scorn: *quia*, – says Solomon,
(The Holy Spirit speaking by his mouth
In Proverbs, the sixth chapter near the end)
– Because, the zeal and fury of a man,
Zelus et furor viri, will not spare,
Non parcet, in the day of his revenge,
In die vindictae, nor will acquiesce,
Nec acquiescet, through a person's prayers,
Cujusdam precibus, – nec suscipiet,
620 Nor yet take, *pro redemptione,* for
Redemption, *dona plurium,* gifts of friends,
Nor money-payment to compound for ache.

Who recognises not my client's case?
Whereto, as strangely consentaneous here,
Adduce Saint Bernard in the Epistle writ
To Robertulus, his nephew: Too much grief,
Dolor quippe nimius non deliberat,
Does not excogitate propriety,
Non verecundatur, nor knows shame at all,
630 *Non consulit rationem*, nor consults
Reason, *non dignitatis metuit*
Damnum, nor dreads the loss of dignity;
Modum et ordinem, order and the mode,
Ignorat, it ignores: why, trait for trait,
Was ever portrait limned so like the life?
(By Cavalier Maratta, shall I say?
I hear he's first in reputation now.)
Yes, that of Samson in the Sacred Text:
That's not so much the portrait as the man!
640 Samson in Gaza was the antetype
Of Guido at Rome: for note the Nazarite!
Blinded he was, – an easy thing to bear,
Intrepidly he took imprisonment,
Gyves, stripes and daily labour at the mill:
But when he found himself, i' the public place,
Destined to make the common people sport,
Disdain burned up with such an impetus
I' the breast of him that, all of him on fire,
Moriatur, roared he, let my soul's self die,
650 *Anima mea*, with the Philistines!
So, pulled down pillar, roof, and death and all,
Multosque plures interfecit, ay,
And many more he killed thus, *moriens*,
Dying, *quam vivus*, than in his whole life,
Occiderat, he ever killed before.
Are these things writ for no example, Sirs?
One instance more, and let me see who doubts!
Our Lord Himself, made up of mansuetude,
Sealing the sum of sufferance up, received
660 Opprobrium, contumely and buffeting

Without complaint: but when He found Himself
Touched in His honour never so little for once,
Then outbroke indignation pent before –
'*Honorem meum nemini dabo!*' 'No,
My honour I to nobody will give!'
And certainly the example so hath wrought,
That whosoever, at the proper worth,
Apprises worldly honour and repute,
Esteems it nobler to die honoured man
670   Beneath Mannaia, than live centuries
Disgraced in the eye o' the world. We find Saint Paul
No recreant to this faith delivered once:
'Far worthier were it that I died,' cries he,
Expedit mihi magis mori, 'than
That anyone should make my glory void,'
Quam ut gloriam meam quis evacuet!
See, *ad Corinthienses:* whereupon
Saint Ambrose makes a comment with much fruit,
Doubtless my Judges long since laid to heart,
680   So I desist from bringing forward here –
(I can't quite recollect it.)

                 Have I proved
Satis superque, both enough and to spare,
That Revelation old and new admits
The natural man may effervesce in ire,
O'erflood earth, o'erfroth heaven with foamy rage,
At the first puncture to his self-respect?
Then, Sirs, this Christian dogma, this law-bud
Full-blown now, soon to bask the absolute flower
690   Of Papal doctrine in our blaze of day, –
Bethink you, shall we miss one promise-streak,
One doubtful birth of dawn crepuscular,
One dew-drop comfort to humanity,
Now that the chalice teems with noonday wine?
Yea, argue Molinists who bar revenge –
Referring just to what makes out our case!
Under old dispensation, argue they,

The doom of the adulterous wife was death,
Stoning by Moses' law. 'Nay, stone her not,
700 Put her away!' next legislates our Lord;
And last of all, 'Nor yet divorce a wife!'
Ordains the Church, 'she typifies ourself,
The Bride no fault shall cause to fall from Christ.'
Then, as no jot nor tittle of the Law
Has passed away – which who presumes to doubt?
As not one word of Christ is rendered vain –
Which, could it be though heaven and earth should pass?
– Where do I find my proper punishment
For my adulterous wife, I humbly ask
710 Of my infallible Pope, – who now remits
Even the divorce allowed by Christ in lieu
Of lapidation Moses licensed me?
The Gospel checks the Law which throws the stone,
The Church tears the divorce-bill Gospel grants,
The wife sins and enjoys impunity!
What profits me the fulness of the days,
The final dispensation, I demand,
Unless Law, Gospel and the Church subjoin
'But who hath barred thee primitive revenge,
720 Which, like fire damped and dammed up, burns more
        fierce?
Use thou thy natural privilege of man,
Else wert thou found like those old ingrate Jews,
Despite the manna-banquet on the board,
A-longing after melons, cucumbers
And such like trash of Egypt left behind!'
(There was one melon, had improved our soup,
But did not Cinoncino need the rind
To make a boat with? So I seem to think.)

Law, Gospel and the Church – from these we leap
730 To the very last revealment, easy rule
Befitting the well-born and thorough-bred
O' the happy day we live in, – not the dark
O' the early rude and acorn-eating race.

'Behold,' quoth James, 'we bridle in a horse
And turn his body as we would thereby!'
Yea, but we change the bit to suit the growth,
And rasp our colt's jaw with a rugged spike
We hasten to remit our managed steed
Who wheels round at persuasion of a touch.
740 Civilization bows to decency,
The acknowledged use and wont, the manners, – mild
But yet imperative law, – which make the man.
Thus do we pay the proper compliment
To rank, and that society of Rome,
Hath so obliged us by its interest,
Taken our client's part instinctively,
As unaware defending its own cause.
What *dictum* doth Society lay down
I' the case of one who hath a faithless wife?
750 Wherewithal should the husband cleanse his way?
Be patient and forgive? Oh, language fails –
Shrinks from depicturing his punishment!
For if wronged husband raise not hue and cry,
Quod si maritus de adulterio non
Conquereretur, he's presumed a – foh!
Presumitur leno: so, complain he must.
But how complain? At your tribunal, lords?
Far weightier challenge suits your sense, I wot!
You sit not to have gentlemen propose
760 Questions gentility can itself discuss.
Did not you prove that to our brother Paul?
The Abate, *quum judicialiter*
Prosequeretur, when he tried the law,
Guidonis causam, in Count Guido's case,
Accidit ipsi, this befell himself,
Quod risum moverit et cachinnos, that
He moved to mirth and cachinnation, all
Or nearly all, *fere in omnibus*
Etiam sensatis et cordatis, men
770 Strong-sensed, sound-hearted, nay, the very Court,
Ipsismet in judicibus, I might add,

Non tamen dicam. In a cause like this,
So multiplied were reasons *pro* and *con*,
Delicate, intertwisted and obscure,
That law were shamed to lend a finger-tip
To unravel, readjust the hopeless twine,
While, half-a-dozen steps outside the court,
There stood a foolish trifler with a tool
A-dangle to no purpose by his side,
780 Had clearly cut the tangle in a trice.
Asserunt enim unanimiter
Doctores, for the Doctors all assert,
That husbands, *quod mariti*, must be held
Viles, cornuti reputantur, vile
And branching forth a florid infamy,
Si propriis manibus, if with their own hands,
Non sumunt, they take not straightway revenge,
Vindictam, but expect the deed be done
By the Court – *expectant illam fieri*
790 *Per judices, qui summopere rident*, which
Gives an enormous guffaw for reply,
Et cachinnantur. For he ran away,
Deliquit enim, just that he might 'scape
The censure of both counsellors and crowd,
Ut vulgi et Doctorum evitaret
Censuram, and lest so he superadd
To loss of honour ignominy too,
Et sic ne istam quoque ignominiam
Amisso honori superadderet.
800 My lords, my lords, the inconsiderate step
Was – we referred ourselves to law at all!
Twit me not with, 'Law else had punished you!'
Each punishment of the extra-legal step,
To which the high-born preferably revert,
Is ever for some oversight, some slip
I' the taking vengeance, not for vengeance' self.
A good thing done unhandsomely turns ill;
And never yet lacked ill the law's rebuke.
For pregnant instance, let us contemplate

810 The luck of Leonardus, – see at large
    Of Sicily's Decisions sixty-first.
    This Leonard finds his wife is false: what then?
    He makes her own son snare her, and entice
    Out of the town-walls to a private walk,
    Wherein he slays her with commodity.
    They find her body half devoured by dogs:
    Leonard is tried, convicted, punished, sent
    To labour in the galleys seven years long:
    Why? For the murder? Nay, but for the mode!
820 *Malus modus occidendi*, ruled the Court,
    An ugly mode of killing, nothing more!
    Another fructuous sample, – see '*De Re
    Criminali*,' in Matthaeus' divine piece.
    Another husband, in no better plight,
    Simulates absence, thereby tempts the wife;
    On whom he falls, out of sly ambuscade,
    Backed by a brother of his, and both of them
    Armed to the teeth with arms that law had blamed.
    Nimis dolose, overwilily,
830 *Fuisse operatum*, was it worked,
    Pronounced the law: had all been fairly done
    Law had not found him worthy, as she did,
    Of four years' exile. Why cite more? Enough
    Is good as a feast – (unless a birthday-feast
    For one's Cinuccio: so, we'll finish here)
    My lords, we rather need defend ourselves
    Inasmuch as for a twinkling of an eye
    We hesitatingly appealed to law, –
    Rather than deny that, on mature advice,
840 We blushingly bethought us, bade revenge
    Back to the simple proper private way
    Of decent self-dealt gentlemanly death.
    Judges, there is the law, and this beside,
    The testimony! Look to it!
                          Pause and breathe!
    So far is only too plain; we must watch,
    Bottini will scarce hazard an attack

Here: let's anticipate the fellow's play,
And guard the weaker places – warily ask,
850 What if considerations of a sort,
Reasons of a kind, arise from out the strange
Peculiar unforeseen new circumstance
Of this our (candour owns) abnormal act,
To bar the right of us revenging so?
'Impunity were otherwise your meed:
Go slay your wife and welcome,' – may be urged, –
'But why the innocent old couple slay,
Pietro, Violante? You may do enough,
Not too much, not exceed the golden mean:
860 Neither brute-beast nor Pagan, Gentile, Jew,
Nor Christian, no nor votarist of the mode,
Were free at all to push revenge so far!'

No, indeed? Why, thou very sciolist!
The actual wrong, Pompilia seemed to do,
Was virtual wrong done by the parents here –
Imposing her upon us as their child –
Themselves allow: then, her fault was their fault,
Her punishment be theirs accordingly!
But wait a little, sneak not off so soon!
870 Was this cheat solely harm to Guido, pray?
The precious couple you call innocent, –
Why, they were felons that law failed to clutch,
Qui ut fraudarent, who that they might rob,
Legitime vocatos, folks law called,
Ad fidei commissum, true heirs to the Trust,
Partum supposuerunt, feigned this birth,
Immemores reos factos esse, blind
To the fact that, guilty, they incurred thereby,
Ultimi supplicii, hanging or aught worse.
880 Do you blame us that we turn law's instruments
Not mere self-seekers, – mind the public weal,
Nor make the private good our sole concern?
That having – shall I say – secured a thief,
Not simply we recover from his pouch

The stolen article our property,
But also pounce upon our neighbour's purse
We opportunely find reposing there,
And do him justice while we right ourselves?
He owes us, for our part, a drubbing say,
890 But owes our neighbour just a dance i' the air
Under the gallows: so we throttle him.
The neighbour's Law, the couple are the Thief,
We are the over-ready to help Law –
Zeal of her house hath eaten us up: for which,
Can it be, Law intends to eat up us,
Crudum Priamum, devour poor Priam raw,
('T was Jupiter's own joke) with babes to boot,
Priamique pisinnos, in Homeric phrase?
Shame! – and so ends the period prettily.

900 But even, – prove the pair not culpable,
Free as unborn babe from connivance at,
Participation in, their daughter's fault:
Ours the mistake. Is that a rare event?
Non semel, it is anything but rare,
In contingentia facti, that by chance,
Impunes evaserunt, go scot-free,
Qui, such well-meaning people as ourselves,
Justo dolore moti, who aggrieved
With cause, *apposuerunt manus*, lay
910 Rough hands, *in innocentes*, on wrong heads.
Cite we an illustrative case in point:
Mulier Smirnea quaedam, good my lords,
A gentlewoman lived in Smyrna once,
Virum et filium ex eo conceptum, who
Both husband and her son begot by him,
Killed, *interfecerat, ex quo*, because,
Vir filium suum perdiderat, her spouse
Had been beforehand with her, killed her son,
Matrimonii primi, of a previous bed.
920 *Deinde accusata*, then accused,
Apud Dolabellam, before him that sat

Proconsul, *nec duabus caedibus*
Contaminatam liberare, nor
To liberate a woman doubly-dyed
With murder, *voluit*, made he up his mind,
Nec condemnare, nor to doom to death,
Justo dolore impulsam, one impelled
By just grief, *sed remisit*, but sent her up
Ad Areopagum, to the Hill of Mars,
930 *Sapientissimorum judicum*
Coetum, to that assembly of the sage
Paralleled only by my judges here;
Ubi, cognito de causa, where, the cause
Well weighed, *responsum est*, they gave reply,
Ut ipsa et accusator, that both sides
O' the suit, *redirent*, should come back again,
Post centum annos, after a hundred years,
For judgment; *et sic*, by which sage decree,
Duplici parricidio rea, one
940 Convicted of a double parricide,
Quamvis etiam innocentem, though in truth
Out of the pair, one innocent at least
She, *occidisset*, plainly had put to death,
Undequaque, yet she altogether 'scaped,
Evasit impunis. See the case at length
In Valerius, fittingly styled *Maximus*,
That eighth book of his Memorable Facts.
Nor Cyriacus cites beside the mark:
Similiter uxor quae mandaverat,
950 Just so, a lady who had taken care,
Homicidium viri, that her lord be killed,
Ex denegatione debiti,
For denegation of a certain debt,
Matrimonialis, he was loth to pay,
Fuit pecuniaria mulcta, was
Amerced in a pecuniary mulct,
Punita, et ad poenam, and to pains,
Temporalem, for a certain space of time,
In monasterio, in a convent.

960   Ay,
In monasterio! How he manages
In with the ablative, the accusative!
I had hoped to have hitched the villain into verse
For a gift, this very day, a complete list
O' the prepositions each with proper case,
Telling a story, long was in my head.
What prepositions take the accusative?
Ad to or at – *who saw the cat?* – down to
Ob, for, because of, *keep her claws off!* Ah,
970   Law in a man takes the whole liberty!
The muse is fettered, – just as Ovid found!

And now, sea widens and the coast is clear.
What of the dubious act you bade excuse?
Surely things brighten, brighten, till at length
Remains – so far from act that needs defence –
Apology to make for act delayed
One minute, let alone eight mortal months
Of hesitation! 'Why procrastinate?'
(Out with it my Bottinius, ease thyself!)
980   'Right, promptly done, is twice right: right delayed
Turns wrong. We grant you should have killed your wife,
But on the moment, at the meeting her
In company with the priest: then did the tongue
O' the Brazen Head give licence, "Time is now!"
You make your mind up: "Time is past" it peals.
Friend, you are competent to mastery
O' the passions that confessedly explain
An outbreak, – yet allow an interval,
And then break out as if time's clock still clanged.
990   You have forfeited your chance, and flat you fall
Into the commonplace category
Of men bound to go softly all their days,
Obeying law.'

                  Now, which way make response?
What was the answer Guido gave, himself?

    – That so to argue came of ignorance
How honour bears a wound: 'For, wound,' said he,
'My body, and the smart is worst at first:
While, wound my soul where honour sits and rules,
1000 Longer the sufferance, stronger grows the pain,
'T is *ex incontinenti*, fresh as first.'
But try another tack, calm common sense
By way of contrast: as – Too true, my lords!
We did demur, awhile did hesitate:
Yet husband sure should let a scruple speak
Ere he slay wife, – for his own safety, lords!
Carpers abound in this misjudging world.
Moreover, there's a nicety in law
That seems to justify them should they carp:
1010 Suppose the source of injury a son, –
Father may slay such son yet run no risk:
Why graced with such a privilege? Because
A father so incensed with his own child,
Or must have reason, or believe he has:
Quia semper, seeing that in such event,
Presumitur, the law is bound suppose,
Quod capiat pater, that the sire must take,
Bonum consilium pro filio,
The best course as to what befits his boy,
1020 Through instinct, *ex instinctu*, of mere love,
Amoris, and, *paterni*, fatherhood;
Quam confidentiam, which confidence,
Non habet, law declines to entertain,
De viro, of the husband: where has he
An instinct that compels him love his wife?
Rather is he presumably her foe:
So, let him ponder long in this bad world
Ere do the simplest act of justice.

                    But
1030 Again – and here we brush Bottini's breast –
Object you, 'See the danger of delay!
Suppose a man murdered my friend last month:

Had I come up and killed him for his pains
In rage, I had done right, allows the law:
I meet him now and kill him in cold blood,
I do wrong, equally allows the law:
Wherein do actions differ, yours and mine?'
In plenitudine intellectus es?
Hast thy wits, Fisc? To take such slayer's life,
1040 Returns it life to thy slain friend at all?
Had he stolen ring instead of stabbing friend, –
To-day, to-morrow or next century,
Meeting the thief, thy ring upon his thumb,
Thou justifiably hadst wrung it thence:
So, couldst thou wrench thy friend's life back again,
Though prisoned in the bosom of his foe,
Why, law would look complacent on thy rush.
Our case is, that the thing we lost, we found:
The honour, we were robbed of eight months since,
1050 Being recoverable at any day
By death of the delinquent. Go thy ways!
Ere thou hast learned law, will be much to do,
As said the rustic while he shod the goose.

Nay, if you urge me, interval was none!
From the inn to the villa – blank or else a bar
Of adverse and contrarious incident
Solid between us and our just revenge!
What with the priest who flourishes his blade,
The wife who like a fury flings at us,
1060 The crowd – and then the capture, the appeal
To Rome, the journey there, the journey thence,
The shelter at the House of Convertites,
The visits to the Villa, and so forth,
Where was one minute left us all this while
To put in execution that revenge
We planned o' the instant? – as it were, plumped down
A round sound egg, o' the spot, some eight months since,
Rome, more propitious than our nest, should hatch!
Object not, 'You reached Rome on Christmas-eve,

1070 And, despite liberty to act at once,
Waited a week – indecorous delay!'
Hath so the Molinism-canker, lords,
Eaten to the bone? Is no religion left?
No care for aught held holy by the Church?
What, would you have us skip and miss those Feasts
O' the Natal Time, must we go prosecute
Secular business on a sacred day?
Should not the merest charity expect,
Setting our poor concerns aside for once,
1080 We hurried to the song matutinal
I' the Sistine, and pressed forward for the Mass
The Cardinal that's Camerlengo chaunts,
Then rushed on to the blessing of the Hat
And Rapier, which the Pope sends to what prince
Has done most detriment to the Infidel –
And thereby whet our courage if 't were blunt?
Meantime, allow we kept the house a week,
Suppose not we were idle in our mew:
Picture Count Guido raging here and there –
1090 '"Money?" I need none – "Friends?" The word is null.
Match me the white was on that shield of mine
Borne at' . . . wherever might be shield to bear;
'I see my grandsire, he who fought so well
At' . . . here find out and put in time and place
Of what might be a fight his grandsire fought:
'I see this – I see that –'

See to it all,
Or I shall scarce see lamb's fry in an hour!
– Nod to the uncle, as I bid advance
1100 The smoking dish, 'This, for your tender teeth!
Behoves us care a little for our kin –
You, Sir, – who care so much for cousinship
As come to your poor loving nephew's feast!'
He has the reversion of a long lease yet –
Land to bequeath! He loves lamb's fry, I know!

Here fall to be considered those same six
Qualities; what Bottini needs must call
So many aggravations of our crime,
Parasite-growth upon mere murder's back.
1110 We summarily might dispose of such
By some off-hand and jaunty fling, some skit –
'So, since there's proved no crime to aggravate,
A fico for your aggravations, Fisc!'
No, – handle mischief rather, – play with spells
Were meant to raise a spirit, and laugh the while
We show that did he rise we are his match!
Therefore, first aggravation: we made up –
Over and above our simple murdering selves –
A regular assemblage of armed men,
1120 *Coadunatio armatorum*, – ay,
Unluckily it was the very judge
Who sits in judgment on our cause to-day
That passed the law as Governor of Rome:
'Four men armed,' – though for lawful purpose, mark!
Much more for an acknowledged crime, – 'shall die.'
We five were armed to the teeth, meant murder too?
Why, that's the very point that saves us, Fisc!
Let me instruct you. Crime nor done nor meant, –
You punish still who arm and congregate:
1130 For why have used bad means to a good end?
Crime being meant not done, – you punish still
The means to crime, you haply pounce upon,
Though circumstance have baulked you of their end:
But crime not only compassed but complete,
Meant and done too? Why, since you have the end,
Be that your sole concern, nor mind those means
No longer to the purpose! Murdered we?
(– Which, that our luck was in the present case,
Quod contigisse in praesenti casu,
1140 Is palpable, *manibus palpatum est* –)
Make murder out against us, nothing less!
Of many crimes committed with a view
To one main crime, you overlook the less,

Intent upon the large. Suppose a man
Having in view commission of a theft,
Climb the town-wall: 't is for the theft he hangs,
Suppose you can convict him of such theft,
Remitted whipping due to who climbs wall
For bravery or wantonness alone,
1150 Just to dislodge a daw's nest and no more.
So I interpret you the manly mind
Of him the Judge shall judge both you and me, –
O' the Governor, who, being no babe, my Fisc,
Cannot have blundered on ineptitude!

Next aggravation, – that the arms themselves
Were specially of such forbidden sort
Through shape or length or breadth, as, prompt, law plucks
From single hand of solitary man,
And makes him pay the carriage with his life:
1160 *Delatio armorum*, arms against the rule,
Contra formam constitutionis, of
Pope Alexander's blessed memory.
Such are the poignard with the double prong,
Horn-like, when tines made bold the antlered buck,
And all of brittle glass – for man to stab
And break off short and so let fragment stick
Fast in the flesh to baffle surgery:
And such the Genoese blade with hooks at edge
That did us service at the Villa here.
1170 *Sed parcat mihi tam eximius vir*,
But, let so rare a personage forgive,
Fisc, thy objection is a foppery!
Thy charge runs, that we killed three innocents:
Killed, dost see? Then, if killed, what matter how? –
By stick or stone, by sword or dagger, tool
Long or tool short, round or triangular –
Poor folks, they find small comfort in a choice!
Means to an end, means to an end, my Fisc!
Nature cries out 'Take the first arms you find!'

1180 *Furor ministrat arma*: where's a stone?
　　Unde mî lapidem, where darts for me?
　　Unde sagittas? But subdue the bard
　　And rationalize a little: eight months since,
　　Had we, or had we not, incurred your blame
　　For letting 'scape unpunished this bad pair?
　　I think I proved that in last paragraph!
　　Why did we so? Because our courage failed.
　　Wherefore? Through lack of arms to fight the foe:
　　We had no arms or merely lawful ones,
1190 An unimportant sword and blunderbuss,
　　Against a foe, pollent in potency,
　　The *amasius*, and our vixen of a wife.
　　Well then, how culpably do we gird loin
　　And once more undertake the high emprise,
　　Unless we load ourselves this second time
　　With handsome superfluity of arms,
　　Since better say 'too much' than 'not enough,'
　　And '*plus non vitiat*,' too much does no harm,
　　Except in mathematics, sages say.
1200 Gather instruction from the parable!
　　At first we are advised – 'A lad hath here
　　Seven barley loaves and two small fishes: what
　　Is that among so many?' Aptly asked:
　　But put that question twice and, quite as apt
　　The answer is 'Fragments, twelve baskets full!'

　　And, while we speak of superabundance, fling
　　A word by the way to fools that cast their flout
　　On Guido – 'Punishment exceeds offence:
　　You might be just but you were cruel too!'
1210 If so you stigmatise the stern and strict,
　　Still, he is not without excuse – may plead
　　Transgression of his mandate, over-zeal
　　O' the part of his companions: all he craved
　　Was, they should fray the faces of the three:
　　Solummodo fassus est, he owns no more,

Dedisse mandatum, than that he desired,
Ad sfrisiandum, dicam, that they hack
And hew, i' the customary phrase, his wife,
Uxorem tantum, and no harm beside.
1220 If his instructions then be misconceived,
Nay, disobeyed, impute you blame to him?
Cite me no Panicollus to the point,
As adverse! Oh, I quite expect his case –
How certain noble youths of Sicily
Having good reason to mistrust their wives,
Killed them and were absolved in consequence:
While others who had gone beyond the need
By mutilation of the paramour
(So Galba in the Horatian satire grieved)
1230 – These were condemned to the galleys, as for guilt
Exceeding simple murder of a wife.
But why? Because of ugliness, and not
Cruelty, in the said revenge, I trow!
Ex causa abscissionis partium;
Quia nempe id facientes reputantur
Naturae inimici, man revolts
Against such as the natural enemy.
Pray, grant to one who meant to slit the nose
And slash the cheek and slur the mouth, at most,
1240 A somewhat more humane award than these!
Objectum funditus corruit, flat you fall,
My Fisc! I waste no kick on you but pass.

Third aggravation: that our act was done –
Not in the public street, where safety lies,
Not in the bye-place, caution may avoid,
Wood, cavern, desert, spots contrived for crime, –
But in the very house, home, nook and nest,
O' the victims, murdered in their dwelling-place,
In domo ac habitatione propria,
1250 Where all presumably is peace and joy.
The spider, crime, pronounce we twice a pest
When, creeping from congenial cottage, she

Taketh hold with her hands, to horrify
His household more, i' the palace of the king.
All three were housed and safe and confident.
Moreover, the permission that our wife
Should have at length *domum pro carcere*,
Her own abode in place of prison – why,
We ourselves granted, by our other self
1260 And proxy Paolo: did we make such grant,
Meaning a lure? – elude the vigilance
O' the jailor, lead her to commodious death,
While we ostensibly relented?

                       Ay,
Just so did we, nor otherwise, my Fisc!
Is vengeance lawful? We demand our right,
But find it will be questioned or refused
By jailor, turnkey, hangdog, – what know we?
Pray, how is it we should conduct ourselves?
1270 To gain our private right – break public peace,
Do you bid us? – trouble order with our broils?
Endanger . . . shall I shrink to own . . . ourselves? –
Who want no broken head nor bloody nose
(While busied slitting noses, breaking heads)
From the first tipstaff shall please interfere!
Nam quicquid sit, for howsoever it be,
An de consensu nostro, if with leave
Or not, *a monasterio*, from the nuns,
Educta esset, she had been led forth,
1280 *Potuimus id dissimulare*, we
May well have granted leave in pure pretence,
Ut aditum habere, that thereby
An entry we might compass, a free move
Potuissemus, to her easy death,
Ad eam occidendam. Privacy
O' the hearth, and sanctitude of home, say you?
Would you give man's abode more privilege
Than God's? – for in the churches where He dwells,
In quibus assistit Regum Rex, by means
1290 Of His essence, *per essentiam*, all the same,

Et nihilominus, therein, *in eis,*
Ex justa via delinquens, whoso dares
To take a liberty on ground enough,
Is pardoned, *excusatur:* that's our case –
Delinquent through befitting cause. You hold,
To punish a false wife in her own house
Is graver than, what happens every day,
To hale a debtor from his hiding-place
In church protected by the Sacrament?
1300 To this conclusion have I brought my Fisc?
Foxes have holes, and fowls o' the air their nests;
Praise you the impiety that follows, Fisc?
Shall false wife yet have where to lay her head?
'*Contra Fiscum definitum est!*' He's done,
'*Surge et scribe,*' make a note of it!
– If I may dally with Aquinas' word.

Or in the death-throe does he mutter still?
Fourth aggravation, that we changed our garb,
And rusticized ourselves with uncouth hat,
1310 Rough vest and goatskin wrappage; murdered thus
Mutatione vestium, in disguise,
Whereby mere murder got complexed with wile,
Turned *homicidium ex insidiis.* Fisc,
How often must I round thee in the ears –
All means are lawful to a lawful end?
Concede he had the right to kill his wife:
The Count indulged in a travesty; why?
De illa ut vindictam sumeret,
That on her he might lawful vengeance take,
1320 *Commodius,* with more ease, *et tutius,*
And safelier: wants he warrant for the step?
Read to thy profit how the Apostle once
For ease and safety, when Damascus raged,
Was let down in a basket by the wall,
To 'scape the malice of the governor
(Another sort of Governor boasts Rome!)
– Many are of opinion, – covered close,

Concealed with – what except that very cloak
He left behind at Troas afterward?
1330 I shall not add a syllable: Molinists may!

Well, have we more to manage? Ay, indeed!
Fifth aggravation, that our wife reposed
Sub potestate judicis, beneath
Protection of the judge, – her house was styled
A prison, and his power became its guard
In lieu of wall and gate and bolt and bar.
This a tough point, shrewd, redoubtable:
Because we have to supplicate the judge
Shall overlook wrong done the judgment-seat.
1340 Now, I might suffer my own nose be pulled,
As man – but then as father . . . if the Fisc
Touched one hair of my boy who held my hand
In confidence he could not come to harm
Crossing the Corso, at my own desire,
Going to see those bodies in the church –
What would you say to that, Don Hyacinth?
This is the sole and single knotty point:
For, bid Tommati blink his interest,
You laud his magnanimity the while:
1350 But baulk Tommati's office, – he talks big!
'My predecessors in the place, – those sons
O' the prophets that may hope succeed me here, –
Shall I diminish their prerogative?
Count Guido Franceschini's honour! – well,
Has the Governor of Rome none?'

                                    You perceive,
The cards are all against us. Make a push,
Kick over table, as our gamesters do!
We, do you say, encroach upon the rights,
1360 Deny the omnipotence o' the Judge forsooth?
We, who have only been from first to last
Intent on that his purpose should prevail,
Nay, more, at times, anticipating both

At risk of a rebuke?

But wait awhile!
Cannot we lump this with the sixth and last
Of the aggravations – that the Majesty
O' the Sovereign here received a wound, to-wit,
Laesa Majestas, since our violence
1370 Was out of envy to the course of law,
In odium litis? We cut short thereby
Three pending suits, promoted by ourselves
I' the main, – which worsens crime, *accedit ad
Exasperationem criminis!*

Yes, here the eruptive wrath with full effect!
How – did not indignation chain my tongue –
Could I repel this last, worst charge of all!
(There is a porcupine to barbacue;
Gigia can jug a rabbit well enough,
1380 With sour-sweet sauce and pine-pips; but, good Lord,
Suppose the devil instigate the wench
To stew, not roast him? Stew my porcupine?
If she does, I know where his quills shall stick!
Come, I must go myself and see to things:
I cannot stay much longer stewing here)
Our stomach . . . I mean, our soul – is stirred within,
And we want words. We wounded Majesty?
Fall under such a censure, we, – who yearned
So much that Majesty dispel the cloud
1390 And shine on us with healing on its wings,
We prayed the Pope, *Majestas'* very self,
To anticipate a little the tardy pack,
Bell us forth deep the authoritative bay
Should start the beagles into sudden yelp
Unisonous, – and, Gospel leading Law,
Grant there assemble in our own behoof
A Congregation, a particular Court,
A few picked friends of quality and place,
To hear the several matters in dispute,

1400 Causes big, little and indifferent,
     Bred of our marriage like a mushroom-growth,
     All at once (can one brush off such too soon?)
     And so with laudable dispatch decide
     Whether we, in the main (to sink detail)
     Were one the Church should hold fast or let go.
     'What, take the credit from the Law?' you ask?
     Indeed, we did! Law ducks to Gospel here:
     Why should Law gain the glory and pronounce
     A judgment shall immortalize the Pope?
1410 Yes: our self-abnegating policy
     Was Joab's – we would rouse our David's sloth,
     Bid him encamp against a city, sack
     A place whereto ourselves had long laid siege,
     Lest, taking it at last, it take our name
     And be not *Innocentinopolis*.
     But no! The modesty was in alarm,
     The temperance refused to interfere,
     Returned us our petition with the word
     '*Ad judices suos*,' 'Leave him to his Judge!'
1420 As who should say – 'Why trouble my repose?
     Why consult Peter in a simple case,
     Peter's wife's sister in her fever-fit
     Might solve as readily as the Apostle's self?
     Are my Tribunals posed by aught so plain?
     Hath not my Court a conscience? It is of age,
     Ask it!'

          We do ask, – but, inspire reply
     To the Court thou bidst me ask, as I have asked –
     Oh thou, who vigilantly dost attend
1430 To even the few, the ineffectual words
     Which rise from this our low and mundane sphere
     Up to thy region out of smoke and noise,
     Seeking corroboration from thy nod
     Who art all justice – which means mercy too,
     In a low noisy smoky world like ours
     Where Adam's sin made peccable his seed!

We venerate the father of the flock,
Whose last faint sands of life, the frittered gold,
Fall noiselessly, yet all too fast, o' the cone
1440 And tapering heap of those collected years, –
Never have these been hurried in their flow,
Though justice fain would jog reluctant arm,
In eagerness to take the forfeiture
Of guilty life: much less shall mercy sue
In vain that thou let innocence survive,
Precipitate no minim of the mass
O' the all-so precious moments of thy life,
By pushing Guido into death and doom!

(Our Cardinal engages read my speech:
1450 They say, the Pope has one half-hour, in twelve,
Of something like a moderate return
Of the intellectuals, – never much to lose! –
If I adroitly plant this passage there,
The Fisc will find himself forestalled, I think,
Though he stand, beat till the old ear-drum break!
– Ah, boy of my own bowels, Hyacinth,
Wilt ever catch the knack, – requite the pains
Of poor papa, become proficient too
I' the how and why and when – the time to laugh,
1460 The time to weep, the time, again, to pray,
And all the times prescribed by Holy Writ?
Well, well, we fathers can but care, but cast
Our bread upon the waters!)
                                          In a word,
These secondary charges go to ground,
Since secondary, so superfluous, – motes
Quite from the main point: we did all and some,
Little and much, adjunct and principal,
Causa honoris. Is there such a cause
1470 As the sake of honour? By that sole test try
Our action, nor demand if more or less,
Because of the action's mode, we merit blame
Or may-be deserve praise. The Court decides.

Is the end lawful? It allows the means:
What we may do we may with safety do,
And what means 'safety' we ourselves must judge.
Put case a person wrongs me past dispute:
If my legitimate vengeance be a blow,
Mistrusting my bare arm can deal the same,
1480 I claim co-operation of a stick;
Doubtful if stick be tough, I crave a sword;
Diffident of ability in fence,
I fee a friend, a swordsman to assist:
Take one – who may be coward, fool or knave –
Why not take fifty? – and if these exceed
I' the due degree of drubbing, whom accuse
But the first author of the aforesaid wrong
Who put poor me to such a world of pains?
Surgery would have just excised a wart;
1490 The patient made such pother, struggled so
That the sharp instrument sliced nose and all.
Taunt us not that our friends performed for pay!
For us, enough were simple honour's sake:
Give country clowns the dirt they comprehend,
The piece of gold! Our reasons, which suffice
Ourselves, be ours alone; our piece of gold
Be, to the rustic, reason and to spare!
We must translate our motives like our speech
Into the lower phrase that suits the sense
1500 O' the limitedly apprehensive. Let
Each level have its language! Heaven speaks first
To the angel, then the angel tames the word
Down to the ear of Tobit: he, in turn,
Diminishes the message to his dog,
And finally that dog finds how the flea
(Which else, importunate, might check his speed)
Shall learn its hunger must have holiday, –
How many varied sorts of language here,
Each following each with pace to match the step,
1510 *Haud passibus aequis!*

     Talking of which flea
Reminds me I must put in special word
For the poor humble following, – the four friends,
Sicarii, our assassins in your charge.
Ourselves are safe in your approval now:
Yet must we care for our companions, plead
The cause o’ the poor, the friends (of old-world faith)
Who are in tribulation for our sake.
Pauperum Procurator is my style:
1520 I stand forth as the poor man’s advocate:
And when we treat of what concerns the poor,
Et cum agatur de pauperibus,
In bondage, *carceratis*, for their sake,
In eorum causis, natural piety,
Pietas, ever ought to win the day,
Triumphare debet, quia ipsi sunt,
Because those very very paupers constitute,
Thesaurus Christi, all the wealth of Christ.
Nevertheless I shall not hold you long
1530 With multiplicity of proofs, nor burn
Candle at noon-tide, clarify the clear.
There beams a case refulgent from our books –
Castrensis, Butringarius, everywhere
I find it burn to dissipate the dark.
’T is this: a husband had a friend, which friend
Seemed to him over-friendly with his wife
In thought and purpose, – I pretend no more.
To justify suspicion or dispel,
He bids his wife make show of giving heed,
1540 Semblance of sympathy – propose, in fine,
A secret meeting in a private place.
The friend, enticed thus, finds an ambuscade,
To-wit, the husband posted with a pack
Of other friends, who fall upon the first
And beat his love and life out both at once.
These friends were brought to question for their help.
Law ruled ‘The husband being in the right,
Who helped him in the right can scarce be wrong ’ –

Opinio, an opinion every way,
1550 *Multum tenenda cordi,* heart should hold!
When the inferiors follow as befits
The lead o' the principal, they change their name,
And, *non dicuntur,* are no longer called
His mandatories, *mandatorii,*
But helpmates, *sed auxiliatores;* since
To that degree does honour' sake lend aid,
Adeo honoris causa est efficax,
That not alone, *non solum,* does it pour
Itself out, *se diffundat,* on mere friends, ·
1560 We bring to do our bidding of this sort,
In mandatorios simplices, but sucks
Along with it in wide and generous whirl,
Sed etiam assassinii qualitate
Qualificatos, people qualified
By the quality of assassination's self,
Dare I make use of such neologism,
Ut utar verbo.

Haste we to conclude:
Of the other points that favour, leave some few
1570 For Spreti; such as the delinquents' youth:
One of them falls short, by some months, of age
Fit to be managed by the gallows; two
May plead exemption from our law's award,
Being foreigners, subjects of the Granduke –
I spare that bone to Spreti and reserve
Myself the juicier breast of argument –
Flinging the breast-blade i' the face o' the Fisc,
Who furnished me the tid-bit: he must needs
Play off his armoury and rack the clowns, –
1580 And they, at instance of the rack, confessed
All four unanimously did resolve, –
That night o' the murder, in brief minutes snatched
Behind the back of Guido as he fled, –
That, since he had not kept his promise, paid
The money for the murder on the spot,

And, reaching home again, might even ignore
The pact or pay it in improper coin,
They one and all resolved, these hopeful friends,
They would inaugurate the morrow's light,
1590 Having recruited strength with needful rest,
By killing Guido as he lay asleep
Pillowed by wallet which contained their fee.

I thank the Fisc for knowledge of this fact:
What fact could hope to make more manifest
Their rectitude, Guido's integrity?
For who fails recognise apparent here,
That these poor rustics bore no envy, hate,
Malice nor yet uncharitableness
Against the people they had put to death?
1600 In them, did such an act reward itself?
All done was to deserve their simple pay,
Obtain the bread they earned by sweat of brow:
Missing this pay, they missed of everything –
Hence claimed it, even at expense of life
To their own lord, so little warped were they
By prepossession, such the absolute
Instinct of equity in rustic souls!
While he the Count, the cultivated mind,
He, wholly rapt in his serene regard
1610 Of honour, as who contemplates the sun
And hardly minds what tapers blink below,
He, dreaming of no argument for death
Except the vengeance worthy noble hearts,
Would he so desecrate the deed forsooth,
Vulgarise vengeance, as defray its cost
By money dug out of the dirty earth,
Mere irritant, in Maro's phrase, to ill?
What though he lured base hinds by lucre's hope, –
The only motive they could masticate,
1620 Milk for babes, not strong meat which men require?
The deed done, those coarse hands were soiled enough,
He spared them the pollution of the pay.

So much for the allegement, thine, my Fisc,
Quo nil absurdius, than which nought more mad,
Excogitari potest, may be squeezed
From out the cogitative brain of thee!

And now, thou excellent the Governor!
(Push to the peroration) *caeterum*
Enixe supplico, I strive in prayer,
1630 *Ut dominis meis*, that unto the Court,
Benigna fronte, with a gracious brow,
Et oculis serenis, and mild eyes,
Perpendere placeat, it may please them weigh,
Quod dominus Guido, that our noble Count,
Occidit, did the killing in dispute,
Ut ejus honor tumulatus, that
The honour of him buried fathom-deep
In infamy, *in infamia*, might arise,
Resurgeret, as ghosts break sepulchre!
1640 *Occidit*, for he killed, *uxorem*, wife,
Quia illi fuit, since she was to him,
Opprobrio, a disgrace and nothing more!
Et genitores, killed her parents too,
Qui, who, *postposita verecundia*,
Having thrown off all sort of decency
Filiam repudiarunt, had renounced
Their daughter, *atque declarare non*
Erubuerunt, nor felt blush tinge cheek,
Declaring, *meretricis genitam*
1650 *Esse*, she was the offspring of a drab,
Ut ipse dehonestaretur, just
That so himself might lose his social rank!
Cujus mentem, and which daughter's heart and soul,
They, *perverterunt*, turned from the right course,
Et ad illicitos amores non
Dumtaxat pellexerunt, and to love
Not simply did alluringly incite,
Sed vi obedientiae, but by force
O' the duty, *filialis*, daughters owe,

1660 *Coegerunt*, forced and drove her to the deed:
    Occidit, I repeat he killed the clan,
    Ne scilicet amplius in dedecore,
    Lest peradventure longer life might trail,
    Viveret, link by link his turpitude,
    Invisus consanguineis, hateful so
    To kith and kindred, *a nobilibus*
    Notatus, shunned by men of quality,
    Relictus ab amicis, left i' the lurch
    By friends, *ab omnibus derisus*, turned
1670 A common hack-block to try edge of jokes.
    Occidit, and he killed them here in Rome,
    In Urbe, the Eternal City, Sirs,
    Nempe quae alias spectata est,
    The appropriate theatre which witnessed once,
    Matronam nobilem, Lucretia's self,
    Abluere pudicitiae maculas,
    Wash off the spots of her pudicity,
    Sanguine proprio, with her own pure blood;
    Quae vidit, and which city also saw,
1680 *Patrem*, Virginius, *undequaque*, quite,
    Impunem, with no sort of punishment,
    Nor, *et non illaudatum*, lacking praise,
    Sed polluentem parricidio,
    Imbrue his hands with butchery, *filiae*,
    Of chaste Virginia, to avoid a rape,
    Ne raperetur ad stupra; so to heart,
    Tanti illi cordi fuit, did he take,
    Suspicio, the mere fancy men might have,
    Honoris amittendi, of fame's loss
1690 *Ut potius voluerit filia*
    Orbari, that he chose to lose his child,
    Quam illa incederet, rather than she walk
    The ways an, *inhonesta*, child disgraced,
    Licet non sponte, though against her will.
    Occidit – killed them, I reiterate –
    In propria domo, in their own abode,
    Ut adultera et parentes, that each wretch,

Conscii agnoscerent, might both see and say,
Nullum locum, there's no place, *nullumque esse*
1700 *Asylum*, nor yet refuge of escape,
Impenetrabilem, shall serve as bar,
Honori laeso, to the wounded one
In honour; *neve ibi opprobria*
Continuarentur, killed them on the spot
Moreover, dreading lest within those walls
The opprobrium peradventure be prolonged,
Et domus quae testis fuit turpium,
And that the domicile which witnessed crime,
Esset et poenae, might watch punishment:
1710 *Occidit*, killed, I round you in the ears,
Quia alio modo, since by other mode,
Non poterat ejus existimatio,
There was no possibility his fame,
Laesa, gashed griesly, *tam enormiter*,
Ducere cicatrices, might be healed:
Occidit ut exemplum praeberet
Uxoribus, killed her so to lesson wives
Jura conjugii, that the marriage-oath,
Esse servanda, must be kept henceforth:
1720 *Occidit denique*, killed her, in a word,
Ut pro posse honestus viveret,
That he, please God, might creditably live,
Sin minus, but if fate willed otherwise,
Proprii honoris, of his outraged fame,
Offensi, by Mannaja, if you please,
Commiseranda victima caderet,
The pitiable victim he should fall!

Done! I' the rough, i' the rough! But done! And, lo,
Landed and stranded lies my very own,
1730 My miracle, my monster of defence –
Leviathan into the nose whereof
I have put fish-hook, pierced his jaw with thorn,
And given him to my maidens for a play!
I' the rough, – to-morrow I review my piece,

Tame here and there undue floridity, –
It's hard: you have to plead before these priests
And poke at them with Scripture, or you pass
For heathen and, what's worse, for ignorant
O' the quality o' the Court and what it likes
1740 By way of illustration of the law:
To-morrow stick in this, and throw out that,
And, having first ecclesiasticized,
Regularize the whole, next emphasize,
Then latinize and lastly Cicero-ize,
Giving my Fisc his finish. There's my speech –
And where's my fry, and family and friends?
Where's that old Hyacinth I mean to hug
Till he cries out, 'Jam satis! Let me breathe!'
Oh, what an evening have I earned to-day!
1750 Hail, ye true pleasures, all the rest are false!
Oh, the old mother, oh, the fattish wife!
Rogue Hyacinth shall put on paper toque,
And wrap himself around with mamma's veil
Done up to imitate papa's black robe,
(I'm in the secret of the comedy, –
Part of the program leaked out long ago!)
And call himself the Advocate o' the Poor,
Mimic Don father that defends the Count,
And for reward shall have a small full glass
1760 Of manly red rosolio to himself,
– Always provided that he conjugate
Bibo, I drink, correctly – nor be found
Make the perfectum, bipsi, as last year!
How the ambitious do so harden heart
As lightly hold by these home-sanctitudes,
To me is matter of bewilderment –
Bewilderment! Because ambition's range
Is nowise tethered by domestic tie:
Am I refused an outlet from my home
1770 To the world's stage? – whereon a man should play
The man in public, vigilant for law,
Zealous for truth, a credit to his kind,

Nay, – through the talent so employed as yield
The Lord his own again with usury, –
A satisfaction, yea, to God Himself!
Well, I have modelled me by Agur's wish,
'Remove far from me vanity and lies,
Feed me with food convenient for me!' What
I' the world should a wise man require beyond?
1780 Can I but coax the good fat little wife
To tell her fool of a father of the prank
His scapegrace nephew played this time last year
At Carnival, – he could not choose, I think,
But modify that inconsiderate gift
O' the cup and cover (somewhere in the will
Under the pillow, someone seems to guess)
– Correct that clause in favour of a boy
The trifle ought to grace with name engraved
(Would look so well produced in years to come
1790 To pledge a memory when poor papa
Latin and law are long since laid at rest)
Hyacintho dono dedit avus, – why,
The wife should get a necklace for her pains,
The very pearls that made Violante proud,
And Pietro pawned for half their value once, –
Redeemable by somebody – *ne sit*
Marita quae rotundioribus
Onusta mammis . . . baccis ambulet,
Her bosom shall display the big round balls,
1800 No braver should be borne by wedded wife!
With which Horatian promise I conclude.
Into the pigeon-hole with thee, my speech!
Off and away, first work then play, play, play!
Bottini, burn your books, you blazing ass!
Sing 'Tra-la-la, for, lambkins, we must live!'

BOOK IX

Juris Doctor Johannes-Baptista Bottinius

Juris Doctor Johannes–Baptista Bottinius,
Fisci et Rev. Cam. Apostol. Advocatus

Had I God's leave, how I would alter things!
If I might read instead of print my speech, –
Ay, and enliven speech with many a flower
Refuses obstinately blow in print
As wildings planted in a prim parterre, –
This scurvy room were turned an immense hall;
Opposite, fifty judges in a row;
This side and that of me, for audience – Rome:
And, where yon window is, the Pope should be –
10 Watch, curtained, but yet visibly enough.
A buzz of expectation! Through the crowd,
Jingling his chain and stumping with his staff,
Up comes an usher, louts him low, 'The Court
Requires the allocution of the Fisc!'
I rise, I bend, I look about me, pause
O'er the hushed multitude: I count – One, two –

Have ye seen, Judges, have ye, lights of law, –
When it may hap some painter, much in vogue
Throughout our city nutritive of arts,
20 Ye summon to a task shall test his worth,
And manufacture, as he knows and can,
A work may decorate a palace-wall,
Afford my lords their Holy Family, –
Hath it escaped the acumen of the Court
How such a painter sets himself to paint?
Suppose that Joseph, Mary and her Babe
A-journeying to Egypt prove the piece:
Why, first he sedulously practiseth,
This painter, – girding loin and lighting lamp, –

30   On what may nourish eye, make facile hand;
      Getteth him studies (styled by draughtsmen so)
      From some assistant corpse of Jew or Turk
      Or, haply, Molinist, he cuts and carves, –
      This Luca or this Carlo or the like:
      To him the bones their inmost secret yield,
      Each notch and nodule signify their use,
      On him the muscles turn, in triple tier,
      And pleasantly entreat the entrusted man, –
      'Familiarize thee with our play that lifts
40   Thus, and thus lowers again, leg, arm and foot!'
      – Ensuring due correctness in the nude.
      Which done, is all done? Not a whit, ye know!
      He, – to art's surface rising from her depth, –
      If some flax-polled soft-bearded sire be found,
      May simulate a Joseph, (happy chance!)
      Limneth exact each wrinkle of the brow,
      Loseth no involution, cheek or chap,
      Till lo, in black and white, the senior lives!
      Is it a young and comely peasant-nurse
50   That poseth? (be the phrase accorded me!)
      Each feminine delight of florid lip,
      Eyes brimming o'er and brow bowed down with love,
      Marmoreal neck and bosom uberous, –
      Glad on the paper in a trice they go
      To help his notion of the Mother-Maid:
      Methinks I see it, chalk a little stumped!
      Yea and her babe – that flexure of soft limbs,
      That budding face imbued with dewy sleep,
      Contribute each an excellence to Christ.
60   Nay, since he humbly lent companionship,
      Even the poor ass, unpanniered and elate
      Stands, perks an ear up, he a model too;
      While clouted shoon, staff, scrip and water-gourd, –
      Aught may betoken travel, heat and haste, –
      No jot nor tittle of these but in its turn
      Ministers to perfection of the piece:
      Till now, such piece before him, part by part, –

Such prelude ended, – pause our painter may,
Submit his fifty studies one by one,
70 And in some sort boast 'I have served my lords.'

But what? And hath he painted once this while?
Or when ye cry 'Produce the thing required,
Show us our picture shall rejoice its niche,
Thy Journey through the Desert done in oils!' –
What, doth he fall to shuffling 'mid his sheets,
Fumbling for first this, then the other fact
Consigned to paper, – 'studies,' bear the term! –
And stretch a canvas, mix a pot of paste,
And fasten here a head and there a tail,
80 (The ass hath one, my Judges!) so dove-tail
Or, rather, ass-tail in, piece sorrily out –
By bits of reproduction of the life –
The picture, the expected Family?
I trow not! do I miss with my conceit
The mark, my lords? – not so my lords were served!
Rather your artist turns abrupt from these,
And preferably buries him and broods
(Quite away from aught vulgar and extern)
On the inner spectrum, filtered through the eye,
90 His brain-deposit, bred of many a drop,
E pluribus unum: and the wiser he!
For in that brain, – their fancy sees at work,
Could my lords peep indulged, – results alone,
Not processes which nourish the result,
Would they discover and appreciate, – life
Fed by digestion, not raw food itself,
No gobbets but smooth comfortable chyme
Secreted from each snapped-up crudity, –
Less distinct, part by part, but in the whole
100 Truer to the subject, – the main central truth
And soul o' the picture, would my Judges spy, –
Not those mere fragmentary studied facts
Which answer to the outward frame and flesh –
Not this nose, not that eyebrow, the other fact

Of man's staff, woman's stole or infant's clout,
But lo, a spirit-birth conceived of flesh,
Truth rare and real, not transcripts, fact and false.
The studies – for his pupils and himself!
The picture be for our eximious Rome
110 And – who knows? – satisfy its Governor,
Whose new wing to the villa he hath bought
(God give him joy of it) by Capena, soon
('T is bruited) shall be glowing with the brush
Of who hath long surpassed the Florentine,
The Urbinate and ... what if I dared add,
Even his master, yea the Cortonese, –
I mean the accomplished Ciro Ferri, Sirs!
(– Did not he die? I'll see before I print.)

End we exordium, Phoebus plucks my ear!
120 Thus then, just so and no whit otherwise,
Have I, – engaged as I were Ciro's self,
To paint a parallel, a Family,
The patriarch Pietro with his wise old wife
To boot (as if one introduced Saint Anne
By bold conjecture to complete the group)
And juvenile Pompilia with her babe,
Who, seeking safety in the wilderness,
Were all surprised by Herod, while outstretched
In sleep beneath a palm-tree by a spring,
130 And killed – the very circumstance I paint,
Moving the pity and terror of my lords –
Exactly so have I, a month at least,
Your Fiscal, made me cognizant of facts,
Searched out, pried into, pressed the meaning forth
Of every piece of evidence in point,
How bloody Herod slew these innocents, –
Until the glad result is gained, the group
Demonstrably presented in detail,
Their slumber and his onslaught, – like as life.
140 Yea and, availing me of help allowed
By law, discreet provision lest my lords

Be too much troubled by effrontery, –
The rack, law plies suspected crime withal –
(Law that hath listened while the lyrist sang
'*Lene tormentum ingenio admoves,*'
Gently thou joggest by a twinge the wit,
'*Plerumque duro,*' else were slow to blab!)
Through this concession my full cup runs o'er:
The guilty owns his guilt without reserve.
150   Therefore by part and part I clutch my case
Which, in entirety now, – momentous task, –
My lords demand, so render them I must,
Since, one poor pleading more and I have done.
But shall I ply my papers, play my proofs,
Parade my studies, fifty in a row,
As though the Court were yet in pupilage
And not the artist's ultimate appeal?
Much rather let me soar the height prescribed
And, bowing low, proffer my picture's self!
160   No more of proof, disproof, – such virtue was,
Such vice was never in Pompilia, now!
Far better say 'Behold Pompilia!' – (for
I leave the family as unmanageable,
And stick to just one portrait, but life-size)
Hath calumny imputed to the fair
A blemish, mole on cheek or wart on chin,
Much more, blind hidden horrors best unnamed?
Shall I descend to prove you, point by point,
Never was knock-knee known nor splay-foot found
170   In Phryne? (I must let the portrait go,
Content me with the model, I believe) –
– I prove this? An indignant sweep of hand,
Dash at and doing away with drapery,
And, – use your eyes, Athenians, smooth she smiles!
Or, – since my client can no longer smile,
And more appropriate instances abound, –
What is this Tale of Tarquin, how the slave
Was caught by him, preferred to Collatine?
Thou, even from thy corpse-clothes virginal,

180 Look'st the lie dead, Lucretia!
                         Thus at least
I, by the guidance of antiquity,
(Our one infallible guide) now operate,
Sure that the innocency shown is safe;
Sure, too, that, while I plead, the echoes cry
(Lend my weak voice thy trump, sonorous Fame!)
'Monstrosity the Phrynean shape shall mar,
Lucretia's soul comport with Tarquin's lie,
When thistles grow on vines or thorns yield figs,
190 Or oblique sentence leave this judgment-seat!'

A great theme: may my strength be adequate!
For – paint Pompilia, dares my feebleness?
How did I unaware engage so much
– Find myself undertaking to produce
A faultless nature in a flawless form?
What's here? Oh, turn aside nor dare the blaze
Of such a crown, such constellation, say,
As jewels here thy front, Humanity!
First, infancy, pellucid as a pearl;
200 Then, childhood – stone which, dew-drop at the first,
(An old conjecture) sucks, by dint of gaze,
Blue from the sky and turns to sapphire so:
Yet both these gems eclipsed by, last and best,
Womanliness and wifehood opaline,
Its milk-white pallor, – chastity, – suffused
With here and there a tint and hint of flame, –
Desire, – the lapidary loves to find.
Such jewels bind conspicuously thy brow,
Pompilia, infant, child, maid, woman, wife –
210 Crown the ideal in our earth at last!
What should a faculty like mine do here?
Close eyes, or else, the rashlier hurry hand!

Which is to say, – lose no time but begin!
Sermocinando ne declamem, Sirs,
Ultra clepsydram, as our preachers say,

Lest I exceed my hour-glass. Whereupon,
As Flaccus prompts, I dare the epic plunge –
Begin at once with marriage, up till when
Little or nothing would arrest your love,
220 In the easeful life o' the lady; lamb and lamb,
How do they differ? Know one, you know all
Manners of maidenhood: mere maiden she.
And since all lambs are like in more than fleece,
Prepare to find that, lamb-like, she too frisks –
O' the weaker sex, my lords, the weaker sex!
To whom, the Teian teaches us, for gift,
Not strength, – man's dower, – but beauty, nature gave,
'Beauty in lieu of spears, in lieu of shields!'
And what is beauty's sure concomitant,
230 Nay, intimate essential character,
But melting wiles, deliciousest deceits,
The whole redoubted armoury of love?
Therefore of vernal pranks, dishevellings
O' the hair of youth that dances April in,
And easily-imagined Hebe-slips
O'er sward which May makes over-smooth for foot –
These shall we pry into? – or wiselier wink,
Though numerous and dear they may have been?

For lo, advancing Hymen and his pomp!
240 *Discedunt nunc amores*, loves, farewell!
Maneat amor, let love, the sole, remain!
Farewell to dewiness and prime of life!
Remains the rough determined day: dance done,
To work, with plough and harrow! What comes next?
'Tis Guido henceforth guides Pompilia's step,
Cries 'No more friskings o'er the foodful glebe,
Else, 'ware the whip!' Accordingly, – first crack
O' the thong, – we hear that his young wife was barred,
Cohibita fuit, from the old free life,
250 *Vitam liberiorem ducere*.
Demur we? Nowise: heifer brave the hind?
We seek not there should lapse the natural law,

The proper piety to lord and king
And husband: let the heifer bear the yoke!
Only, I crave he cast not patience off,
This hind; for deem you she endures the whip,
Nor winces at the goad, nay, restive, kicks?
What if the adversary's charge be just,
And all untowardly she pursue her way
260 With groan and grunt, though hind strike ne'er so hard?
If petulant remonstrance made appeal,
Unseasonable, o'erprotracted, – if
Importunate challenge taxed the public ear
When silence more decorously had served
For protestation, – if Pompilian plaint
Wrought but to aggravate Guidonian ire, –
Why, such mishaps, ungainly though they be,
Ever companion change, are incident
To altered modes and novelty of life:
270 The philosophic mind expects no less,
Smilingly knows and names the crisis, sits
Waiting till old things go and new arrive.
Therefore, I hold a husband but inept
Who turns impatient at such transit-time,
As if this running from the rod would last!

Since, even while I speak, the end is reached
Success awaits the soon-disheartened man,
The parents turn their backs and leave the house,
The wife may wail but none shall intervene,
280 He hath attained his object, groom and bride
Partake the nuptial bower no soul to see,
Old things are passed and all again is new,
Over and gone the obstacles to peace,
Novorum – tenderly the Mantuan turns
The expression, some such purpose in his eye –
Nascitur ordo! Every storm is laid,
And forth from plain each pleasant herb may peep,
Each bloom of wifehood in abeyance late:
(Confer a passage in the Canticles.)

290   But what if, as 't is wont with plant and wife,
      Flowers, – after a suppression to good end,
      Still, when they do spring forth, – sprout here, spread there,
      Anywhere likelier than beneath the foot
      O' the lawful good-man gardener of the ground?
      He dug and dibbled, sowed and watered, – still
      'T is a chance wayfarer shall pluck the increase.
      Just so, respecting persons not too much,
      The lady, foes allege, put forth each charm
      And proper floweret of feminity
300   To whosoever had a nose to smell
      Or breast to deck: what if the charge be true?
      The fault were graver had she looked with choice,
      Fastidiously appointed who should grasp,
      Who, in the whole town, go without the prize!
      To nobody she destined donative,
      But, first come was first served, the accuser saith
      Put case her sort of . . . in this kind . . . escapes
      Were many and oft and indiscriminate –
      Impute ye as the action were prepense,
310   The gift particular, arguing malice so?
      Which butterfly of the wide air shall brag
      'I was preferred to Guido' – when 't is clear
      The cup, he quaffs at, lay with olent breast
      Open to gnat, midge, bee and moth as well?
      One chalice entertained the company;
      And if its peevish lord object the more,
      Mistake, misname such bounty in a wife,
      Haste we to advertise him – charm of cheek,
      Lustre of eye, allowance of the lip,
320   All womanly components in a spouse,
      These are no houschold-bread each stranger's bite
      Leaves by so much diminished for the mouth
      O' the master of the house at supper-time:
      But rather like a lump of spice they lie,
      Morsel of myrrh, which scents the neighbourhood
      Yet greets its lord no lighter by a grain.

Nay, even so, he shall be satisfied!
Concede we there was reason in his wrong, –
Grant we his grievance and content the man!
330 For lo, Pompilia, she submits herself;
Ere three revolving years have crowned their course,
Off and away she puts this same reproach
Of lavish bounty, inconsiderate gift
O' the sweets of wifehood stored to other ends:
No longer shall he blame 'She none excludes,'
But substitute 'She laudably sees all,
Searches the best out and selects the same.'
For who is here, long sought and latest found,
Waiting his turn unmoved amid the whirl,
340 'Constans in levitate,' – Ha, my lords?
Calm in his levity, – indulge the quip! –
Since 'tis a levite bears the bell away,
Parades him henceforth as Pompilia's choice.
'Tis no ignoble object, husband! Doubt'st?
When here comes tripping Flaccus with his phrase
'Trust me, no miscreant singled from the mob,
Crede non illum tibi de scelesta
Plebe delectum,' but a man of mark,
A priest, dost hear? Why then, submit thyself!
350 Priest, ay and very phoenix of such fowl,
Well-born, of culture, young and vigorous,
Comely too, since precise the precept points –
On the selected levite be there found
Nor mole nor scar nor blemish, lest the mind
Come all uncandid through the thwarting flesh!
Was not the son of Jesse ruddy, sleek,
Pleasant to look on, pleasant every way?
Since well he smote the harp and sweetly sang,
And danced till Abigail came out to see,
360 And seeing smiled and smiling ministered
The raisin-cluster and the cake of figs,
With ready meal refreshed the gifted youth,
Till Nabal, who was absent shearing sheep,
Felt heart sink, took to bed (discreetly done –

They might have been beforehand with him else)
And died – would Guido had behaved as well!
But ah, the faith of early days is gone,
Heu prisca fides! Nothing died in him
Save courtesy, good sense and proper trust,
370　Which, when they ebb from souls they should o'erflow,
Discover stub, weed, sludge and ugliness.
(The Pope, you know, is Neapolitan
And relishes a sea-side simile.)
Deserted by each charitable wave,
Guido, left high and dry, shows jealous now!
Jealous avouched, paraded: tax the fool
With any peccadillo, he responds
'Truly I beat my wife through jealousy,
Imprisoned her and punished otherwise,
380　Being jealous: now would threaten, sword in hand,
Now manage to mix poison in her sight,
And so forth: jealously I dealt, in fine.'
Concede the fact and what remains to prove?
Have I to teach my masters what effect
Hath jealousy and how, befooling men,
It makes false true, abuses eye and ear,
Turns the mist adamantine, loads with sound
Silence, and into void and vacancy
Crowds a whole phalanx of conspiring foes?
390　Therefore who owns 'I watched with jealousy
My wife' adds 'for no reason in the world!'
What need that who says 'madman' should remark
'The thing he thought a serpent proved an eel?' –
Perchance the right Comacchian, six foot length,
And not an inch too long for that same pie
(Master Arcangeli has heard of such)
Whose succulence makes fasting bearable;
Meant to regale some moody splenetic
Who pleases to mistake the donor's gift,
400　And spies – I know not what Lernaean snake
I' the luscious Lenten creature, stamps forsooth
The dainty in the dust.

Enough! Prepare,
His lunes announced, for downright lunacy!
Insanit homo, threat succeeds to threat,
And blow redoubles blow, – his wife, the block.
But, if a block, shall not she jar the hand
That buffets her? The injurious idle stone
Rebounds and fits the head of him who flung.
410 Causeless rage breeds, i' the wife now, rageful cause,
Tyranny wakes rebellion from its sleep.
Rebellion, say I? – rather, self-defence,
Laudable wish to live and see good days,
Pricks our Pompilia on to fly the foe
By any means, at any price, – nay, more,
Nay, most of all, i' the very interest
Of the foe that, baffled of his blind desire
At any price, is truliest victor so.
Shall he effect his crime and lose his soul?
420 No, dictates duty to a loving wife.
Far better that the unconsummate blow,
Adroitly baulked by her, should back again,
Correctively admonish his own pate!

Crime then, – the Court is with me? – she must crush;
How crush it? By all efficacious means;
And these, – why, what in woman should they be?
'With horns the bull, with teeth the lion fights,
To woman,' quoth the lyrist quoted late,
'Nor teeth, nor horns, but beauty, Nature gave!'
430 Pretty i' the Pagan! Who dares blame the use
Of the armoury thus allowed for natural, –
Exclaim against a seeming-dubious play
O' the sole permitted weapon, spear and shield
Alike, resorted to i' the circumstance
By poor Pompilia? Grant she somewhat plied
Arts that allure, the magic nod and wink,
The witchery of gesture, spell of word,
Whereby the likelier to enlist this friend,
Yet stranger, as a champion on her side?

440   Such, being but mere man, ('t was all she knew),
Must be made sure by beauty's silken bond,
The weakness that subdues the strong, and bows
Wisdom alike and folly. Grant the tale
O' the husband, which is false, for proved and true
To the letter, – or the letters, I should say,
The abominations he professed to find
And fix upon Pompilia and the priest, –
Allow them hers – for though she could not write,
In early days of Eve-like innocence
450   That plucked no apple from the knowledge-tree,
Yet, at the Serpent's word, Eve plucks and eats
And knows – especially how to read and write:
And so Pompilia, – as the move o' the maw,
Quoth Persius, makes a parrot bid 'Good-day!'
A crow salute the concave, and a pie
Endeavour at proficiency in speech, –
So she, through hunger after fellowship,
May well have learned, though late, to play the scribe:
As indeed, there's one letter on the list
460   Explicitly declares did happen here.
'You thought my letters could be none of mine,'
She tells her parents – 'mine, who wanted skill;
But now I have the skill, and write, you see!'
She needed write love-letters, so she learned,
'Negatas artifex sequi voces' – though
This letter nowise 'scapes the common lot,
But lies i' the condemnation of the rest,
Found by the husband's self who forged them all.
Yet, for the sacredness of argument,
470   For this once an exemption shall it plead –
Anything, anything to let the wheels
Of argument run glibly to their goal!
Concede she wrote (which were preposterous)
This and the other epistle, – what of it?
Where does the figment touch her candid fame?
Being in peril of her life – 'my life,
Not an hour's purchase,' as the letter runs, –

And having but one stay in this extreme,
And out of the wide world a single friend –
480 What could she other than resort to him,
And how with any hope resort but thus?
Shall modesty dare bid a stranger brave
Danger, disgrace, nay death in her behalf –
Think to entice the sternness of the steel
Save by the magnet moves the manly mind?
– Most of all when such mind is hampered so
By growth of circumstance athwart the life
O' the natural man, that decency forbids
He stoop and take the common privilege,
490 Say frank 'I love,' as all the vulgar do.
A man is wedded to philosophy,
Married to statesmanship; a man is old;
A man is fettered by the foolishness
He took for wisdom and talked ten years since;
A man is, like our friend the Canon here,
A priest, and wicked if he break his vow:
He dare to love, who may be Pope one day?
Suppose this man could love, though, all the same –
From what embarrassment she sets him free
500 Should one, a woman he could love, speak first –
' 'T is I who break reserve, begin appeal,
Confess that, whether you love me or no,
I love you!' What an ease to dignity,
What help of pride from the hard high-backed chair
Down to the carpet where the kittens bask,
All under the pretence of gratitude!

From all which, I deduce – the lady here
Was bound to proffer nothing short of love
To the priest whose service was to save her. What?
510 Shall she propose him lucre, dust o' the mine,
Rubbish o' the rock, some diamond, muckworms prize,
Or pearl secreted by a sickly fish?
Scarcely! She caters for a generous taste.
'T is love shall beckon, beauty bid to breast,

Till all the Samson sink into the snare!
Because, permit the end – permit therewith
Means to the end!

How say you, good my lords?
I hope you heard my adversary ring
520   The changes on this precept: now, let me
Reverse the peal! *Quia dato licito fine,*
Ad illum assequendum ordinata
Non sunt damnanda media, – licit end
Enough was the escape from death, I hope,
To legalize the means illicit else
Of feigned love, false allurement, fancied fact.
Thus Venus losing Cupid on a day,
(See that *Idyllium Moschi*) seeking help,
In the anxiety of motherhood,
530   Allowably promised 'Who shall bring report
Where he is wandered to, my winged babe,
I give him for reward a nectared kiss;
But who brings safely back the truant's self,
His be a super-sweet makes kiss seem cold!'
Are not these things writ for example-sake?

To such permitted motive, then, refer
All those professions, else were hard explain,
Of hope, fear, jealousy, and the rest of love!
He is Myrtillus, Amaryllis she,
540   She burns, he freezes, – all a mere device
To catch and keep the man may save her life,
Whom otherwise nor catches she nor keeps!
Worst, once, is best now: in all faith, she feigns:
Feigning, – the liker innocence to guilt,
The truer to the life is what she feigns!
How if Ulysses, – when, for public good
He sunk particular qualms and played the spy,
Entered Troy's hostile gate in beggar's garb –
How if he first had boggled at this clout,
550   Grown dainty o'er that clack-dish? Grime is grace
To whoso gropes amid the dung for gold.

Hence, beyond promises, we praise each proof
That promise was not simply made to break, –
No moonshine-structure meant to fade at dawn:
So call – (proofs consequent and requisite) –
What enemies allege of – more than words,
Deeds – meeting at the window, twilight-tryst,
Nocturnal entertainment in the dim
Old labyrinthine palace; lies, we know –
560 Inventions we, long since, turned inside out.
Would such external semblance of intrigue
Demonstrate that intrigue must lurk perdue?
Does every hazel-sheath disclose a nut?
He were a Molinist who dared maintain
That midnight meetings in a screened alcove
Must argue folly in a matron – since
So would he bring a slur on Judith's self,
Commended beyond women that she lured
The lustful to destruction through his lust.
570 Pompilia took not Judith's liberty,
No faulchion find you in her hand to smite, –
No damsel to convey the head in dish,
Of Holophernes, – style the Canon so –
Or is it the Count? If I entangle me
With my similitudes, – if wax wings melt,
And earthward down I drop, not mine the fault:
Blame your beneficence, O Court, O sun,
Whereof the beamy smile affects my flight!
What matter, so Pompilia's fame revive
580 I' the warmth that proves the bane of Icarus?

Yea, we have shown it lawful, necessary
Pompilia leave her husband, seek the house
O' the parents: and because 'twixt home and home
Lies a long road with many a danger rife,
Lions by the way and serpents in the path,
To rob and ravish, – much behoves she keep
Each shadow of suspicion from fair fame,
For her own sake much, but for his sake more,

The ingrate husband! Evidence shall be,
590 Some witness to the world how white she walks
I' the mire she wanders through ere Rome she reach.
And who so proper witness as a priest?
Gainsay ye? Let me hear who dares gainsay!
I hope we still can punish heretics!
'Give me the man' I say with him of Gath,
'That we may fight together!' None, I think:
The priest is granted me.

Then, if a priest,
One juvenile and potent: else, mayhap,
600 That dragon, our Saint George would slay, slays him.
And should fair face accompany strong hand,
The more complete equipment: nothing mars
Work, else praiseworthy, like a bodily flaw
I' the worker: as 't is said Saint Paul himself
Deplored the check o' the puny presence, still
Cheating his fulmination of its flash,
Albeit the bolt therein went true to oak.
Therefore the agent, as prescribed, she takes, –
A priest, juvenile, potent, handsome too, –
610 In all obedience: 'good,' you grant again.
Do you? I would ye were the husband, lords!
How prompt and facile might departure be!
How boldly would Pompilia and the priest
March out of door, spread flag at beat of drum,
But that inapprehensive Guido grants
Neither premiss nor yet conclusion here,
And, purblind, dreads a bear in every bush!
For his own quietude and comfort, then,
Means must be found for flight in masquerade
620 At hour when all things sleep. – 'Save jealousy!'
Right, judges! Therefore shall the lady's wit
Supply the boon thwart nature baulks him of,
And do him service with the potent drug
(Helen's nepenthe, as my lords opine)
Shall respite blessedly each frittered nerve

O' the much-enduring man: accordingly,
There lies he, duly dosed and sound asleep,
Relieved of woes, or real or raved about.
While soft she leaves his side, he shall not wake;
630 Nor stop who steals away to join her friend,
Nor do him mischief should he catch that friend
Intent on more than friendly office, – nay,
Nor get himself raw head and bones laid bare
In payment of his apparition!

                    Thus
Would I defend the step, – were the thing true
Which is a fable, – see my former speech, –
That Guido slept (who never slept a wink)
Through treachery, an opiate from his wife,
640 Who not so much as knew what opiates mean.

Now she may start: but hist, – a stoppage still!
A journey is an enterprise which costs!
As in campaigns, we fight and others pay,
Suis expensis, nemo militat.
'T is Guido's self we guard from accident,
Ensuring safety to Pompilia, versed
Nowise in misadventures by the way,
Hard riding and rough quarters, the rude fare,
The unready host. What magic mitigates
650 Each plague of travel to the unpractised wife?
Money, sweet Sirs! And were the fiction fact,
She helped herself thereto with liberal hand
From out the husband's store, – what fitter use
Was ever husband's money destined to?
With bag and baggage thus did Dido once
Decamp, – for more authority, a queen!

So is she fairly on her route at last,
Prepared for either fortune: nay and if
The priest, now all a-glow with enterprise,
660 Cool somewhat presently when fades the flush

O' the first adventure, clouded o'er belike
By doubts, misgivings how the day may die,
Though born with such auroral brilliance, – if
The brow seem over-pensive and the lip
'Gin lag and lose the prattle lightsome late, –
Vanquished by tedium of a prolonged jaunt
In a close carriage o'er a jolting road,
With only one young female substitute
For seventeen other Canons of ripe age
670 Wcrc wont to keep him company in church, –
Shall not Pompilia haste to dissipate
The silent cloud that, gathering, bodes her bale? –
Prop the irresoluteness may portend
Suspension of the project, check the flight,
Bring ruin on them both? – use every means,
Since means to the end are lawful? What i' the way
Of wile should have allowance like a kiss
Sagely and sisterly administered,
Sororia saltem oscula? We find
680 Such was the remedy her wit applied
To each incipient scruple of the priest,
If we believe, – as, while my wit is mine
I cannot, – what the driver testifies,
Borsi, called Venerino, the mere tool
Of Guido and his friend the Governor, –
The avowal I proved wrung from out the wretch,
After long rotting in imprisonment,
As price of liberty and favour: long
They tempted, he at last succumbed, and lo
690 Counted them out full tale each kiss required, –
'The journey was one long embrace,' quoth he.
Still, though we should believe the driver's lie,
Nor even admit as probable excuse,
Right reading of the riddle, – as I urged
In my first argument, with fruit perhaps –
That what the owl-like eyes (at back of head!)
O' the driver, drowsed by driving night and day,
Supposed a vulgar interchange of love,

This was but innocent jog of head 'gainst head,
700   Cheek meeting jowl as apple may touch pear
From branch and branch contiguous in the wind,
When Autumn blusters and the orchard rocks.
The rapid run and the rough road were cause
O' the casual ambiguity, no harm
I' the world to eyes awake and penetrative.
Yet, – not to grasp a truth I can forego
And safely fight without and conquer still, –
Say, she kissed him, and he kissed her again!
Such osculation was a potent means,
710   A very efficacious help, no doubt:
This with a third part of her nectar did
Venus imbue: why should Pompilia fling
The poet's declaration in his teeth? –
Pause to employ what, – since it had success,
And kept the priest her servant to the end, –
We must presume of energy enough,
No whit superfluous, so permissible?

The goal is gained: day, night and yet a day
Have run their round: a long and devious road
720   Is traversed, – many manners, various men
Passed in review, what cities did they see,
What hamlets mark, what profitable food
For after-meditation cull and store!
Till Rome, that Rome whereof – this voice,
Would it might make our Molinists observe,
That she is built upon a rock nor shall
Their powers prevail against her! – Rome, I say,
Is all but reached; one stage more and they stop
Saved: pluck up heart, ye pair, and forward, then!

730   Ah, Nature – baffled she recurs, alas!
Nature imperiously exacts her due,
Spirit is willing but the flesh is weak,
Pompilia needs must acquiesce and swoon,
Give hopes alike and fears a breathing-while.

The innocent sleep soundly: sound she sleeps.
So let her slumber, then, unguarded save
By her own chastity, a triple mail,
And his good hand whose stalwart arms have borne
The sweet and senseless burthen like a babe
740 From coach to couch, – the serviceable man!
Nay, what and if he gazed rewardedly
On the pale beauty prisoned in embrace,
Stooped over, stole a balmy breath perhaps
For more assurance sleep was not decease –
'*Ut vidi,*' 'how I saw!' succeeded by
'*Ut perii,*' 'how I sudden lost my brains!'
– What harm ensued to her unconscious quite?
For, curiosity – how natural!
Importunateness – what a privilege
750 In the ardent sex! And why curb ardour here?
How can the priest but pity whom he saved?
And pity is how near to love, and love
How neighbourly to unreasonableness!
And for love's object, whether love were sage
Or foolish, could Pompilia know or care,
Being still sound asleep, as I premised?
Thus the philosopher absorbed by thought,
Even Archimedes, busy o'er a book
The while besiegers sacked his Syracuse,
760 Was ignorant of the imminence o' the point
O' the sword till it surprised him: let it stab,
And never knew himself was dead at all.
So sleep thou on, secure whate'er betide!
For thou, too, hast thy problem hard to solve –
How so much beauty is compatible
With so much innocence!

      Fit place, methinks,
While in this task she rosily is lost,
To treat of and repel objection here
770 Which, – frivolous, I grant, – but, still misgives
My mind, it may have flitted, gadfly-like,

And teazed the Court at times – as if, all said
And done, there still seemed, one might nearly say,
In a certain acceptation, somewhat more
Of what may pass for insincerity,
Falsehood, throughout the course Pompilia took,
Than befits Christian. Pagans held, we know,
We always ought to aim at good and truth,
Not always put one thing in the same words:
780 *Non idem semper dicere sed spectare*
Debemus. But the Pagan yoke was light;
'Lie not at all,' the exacter precept bids:
Each least lie breaks the law, – is sin, ye hold.
I humble me, but venture to submit –
What prevents sin, itself is sinless, sure:
And sin, which hinders sin of deeper dye,
Softens itself away by contrast so.
Conceive me! Little sin, by none at all,
Were properly condemned for great: but great,
790 By greater, dwindles into small again.
Now, what is greatest sin of womanhood?
That which unwomans it, abolishes
The nature of the woman, – impudence.
Who contradicts me here? Concede me, then,
Whatever friendly fault may interpose
To save the sex from self-abolishment
Is three-parts on the way to virtue's rank!
Now, what is taxed here as duplicity,
Feint, wile and trick, – admitted for the nonce, –
800 What worse do one and all than interpose,
Hold, as it were, a deprecating hand,
Statuesquely, in the Medicean mode,
Before some shame which modesty would veil?
Who blames the gesture prettily perverse?
Thus, – lest ye miss a point illustrative, –
Admit the husband's calumny – allow
That the wife, having penned the epistle fraught
With horrors, charge on charge of crime, she heaped
O' the head of Pietro and Violante – (still

810   Presumed her parents) – and despatched the thing
      To their arch-enemy Paolo, through free choice
      And no sort of compulsion in the world –
      Put case that she discards simplicity
      For craft, denies the voluntary act,
      Declares herself a passive instrument
      I' the hands of Guido; duped by knavery,
      She traced the characters, she could not write,
      And took on trust the unread sense which, read,
      Were recognized but to be spurned at once.
820   Allow this calumny, I reiterate!
      Who is so dull as wonder at the pose
      Of our Pompilia in the circumstance?
      Who sees not that the too-ingenuous soul,
      Repugnant even at a duty done
      Which brought beneath too scrutinizing glare
      The misdemeanours, – buried in the dark, –
      Of the authors of her being, she believed, –
      Stung to the quick at her impulsive deed,
      And willing to repair what harm it worked,
830   She – wise in this beyond what Nero proved,
      Who, when needs were the candid juvenile
      Should sign the warrant, doom the guilty dead,
      'Would I had never learned to write,' quoth he!
      – Pompilia rose above the Roman, cried
      'To read or write I never learned at all!'
      O splendidly mendacious!

                        But time fleets:
      Let us not linger: hurry to the end,
      Since end does flight and all disastrously.
840   Beware ye blame desert for unsuccess,
      Disparage each expedient else to praise,
      Call failure folly! Man's best effort fails.
      After ten years' resistance Troy fell flat:
      Could valour save a town, Troy still had stood.
      Pompilia came off halting in no point
      Of courage, conduct, the long journey through:

But nature sank exhausted at the close,
And, as I said, she swooned and slept all night.
Morn breaks and brings the husband: we assist
850 At the spectacle. Discovery succeeds.
Ha, how is this? What moonstruck rage is here?
Though we confess to partial frailty now,
To error in a woman and a wife,
Is 't by the rough way she shall be reclaimed?
Who bursts upon her chambered privacy?
What crowd profanes the chaste *cubiculum*?
What outcries and lewd laughter, scurril gibe
And ribald jest to scare the ministrant
Good angels that commerce with souls in sleep?
860 Why, had the worst crowned Guido to his wish,
Confirmed his most irrational surmise,
Yet there be bounds to man's emotion, checks
To an immoderate astonishment.
'T is decent horror, regulated wrath,
Befit our dispensation: have we back
The old Pagan licence? Shall a Vulcan clap
His net o' the sudden and expose the pair
To the unquenchable universal mirth?
A feat, antiquity saw scandal in
870 So clearly, that the nauseous tale thereof —
Demodocus his nugatory song —
Hath ever been concluded modern stuff
Impossible to the mouth of the grave Muse,
So, foisted into that Eighth Odyssey
By some impertinent pickthank. O thou fool,
Count Guido Franceschini, what were gained
By publishing thy shame thus to the world?
Were all the precepts of the wise a waste —
Bred in thee not one touch of reverence?
880 Why, say thy wife — admonish we the fool, —
Were false, and thou bid chronicle thy shame,
Much rather should thy teeth bite out thy tongue,
Dumb lip consort with desecrated brow,
Silence become historiographer,

And thou – thine own Cornelius Tacitus!
But virtue, barred, still leaps the barrier, lords!
– Still, moon-like, penetrates the encroaching mist
And bursts, all broad and bare, on night, ye know!
Surprised, then, in the garb of truth, perhaps,
890 Pompilia, thus opposed, breaks obstacle,
Springs to her feet, and stands Thalassian-pure,
Confronts the foe, – nay, catches at his sword
And tries to kill the intruder, he complains.
Why, so she gave her lord his lesson back,
Crowned him, this time, the virtuous woman's way,
With an exact obedience; he brought sword,
She drew the same, since swords are meant to draw.
Tell not me 'tis sharp play with tools on edge!
It was the husband chose the weapon here.
900 Why did not he inaugurate the game
With some gentility of apophthegm
Still pregnant on the philosophic page,
Some captivating cadence still a-lisp
O' the poet's lyre? Such spells subdue the surge,
Make tame the tempest, much more mitigate
The passions of the mind, and probably
Had moved Pompilia to a smiling blush.
No, he must needs prefer the argument
O' the blow: and she obeyed, in duty bound,
910 Returned him buffet ratiocinative –
Ay, in the reasoner's own interest,
For wife must follow whither husband leads,
Vindicate honour as himself prescribes,
Save him the very way himself bids save!
No question but who jumps into a quag
Should stretch forth hand and pray one 'Pull me out
By the hand!' such were the customary cry:
But Guido pleased to bid 'Leave hand alone!
Join both feet, rather, jump upon my head,
920 I extricate myself by the rebound!'
And dutifully as enjoined she jumped –
Drew his own sword and menaced his own life,

Anything to content a wilful spouse.

And so he was contented – one must do
Justice to the expedient which succeeds,
Strange as it seem: at flourish of the blade,
The crowd drew back, stood breathless and abashed,
Then murmured 'This should be no wanton wife,
No conscience-stricken creature, caught i' the act,
And patiently awaiting our first stone:
But a poor hard-pressed all-bewildered thing,
Has rushed so far, misguidedly perhaps,
Meaning no more harm than a frightened sheep.
She sought for aid; and if she made mistake
I' the man could aid most, why – so mortals do:
Even the blessed Magdalen mistook
Far less forgiveably: consult the place –
Supposing him to be the gardener,
"Sir," said she, and so following.' Why more words?
Forthwith the wife is pronounced innocent:
What would the husband more than gain his cause,
And find that honour flash in the world's eye,
His apprehension was lest soil had smirched?

So, happily the adventure comes to close
Whereon my fat opponent grounds his charge
Preposterous: at mid-day he groans 'How dark!'
Listen to me, thou Archangelic swine!
Where is the ambiguity to blame,
The flaw to find in our Pompilia? Safe
She stands, see! Does thy comment follow quick
'Safe, inasmuch as at the end proposed;
But thither she picked way by devious path –
Stands dirtied, no dubiety at all!
I recognize success, yet, all the same,
Importunately will suggestion prick –
What, had Pompilia gained the right to boast
"No devious path, no doubtful patch was mine,
I saved my head nor sacrificed my foot?"

　　　Why, being in a peril, show mistrust
960　Of the angels set to guard the innocent?
　　　Why rather hold by obvious vulgar help
　　　Of stratagem and subterfuge, excused
　　　Somewhat, but still no less a foil, a fault,
　　　Since low with high, and good with bad is linked?
　　　Methinks I view some ancient bas-relief.
　　　There stands Hesione thrust out by Troy,
　　　Her father's hand has chained her to a crag,
　　　Her mother's from the virgin plucked the vest,
　　　At a safe distance both distressful watch,
970　While near and nearer comes the snorting orc.
　　　I look that, white and perfect to the end,
　　　She wait till Jove despatch some demigod;
　　　Not that, – impatient of celestial club
　　　Alcmena's son should brandish at the beast, –
　　　She daub, disguise her dainty limbs with pitch,
　　　And so elude the purblind monster! Ay,
　　　The trick succeeds, but 't is an ugly trick,
　　　Where needs have been no trick!'

　　　　　　　　　　　　　　My answer? Faugh!
980　*Nimis incongrue!* Too absurdly put!
　　　Sententiam ego teneo contrariam,
　　　Trick, I maintain, had no alternative.
　　　The heavens were bound with brass, – Jove far at feast
　　　(No feast like that thou didst not ask me to,
　　　Arcangeli, – I heard of thy regale!)
　　　With the unblamed Ethiop, – Hercules spun wool
　　　I' the lap of Omphale, while Virtue shrieked –
　　　The brute came paddling all the faster. You
　　　Of Troy, who stood at distance, where's the aid
990　You offered in the extremity? Most and least,
　　　Gentle and simple, here the Governor,
　　　There the Archbishop, everywhere the friends,
　　　Shook heads and waited for a miracle,
　　　Or went their way, left Virtue to her fate.
　　　Just this one rough and ready man leapt forth!

     – Was found, sole anti-Fabius (dare I say)
     To restore things, with no delay at all,
     Qui, haud cunctando, rem restituit! He,
     He only, Caponsacchi 'mid a crowd,
1000 Caught Virtue up, carried Pompilia off
     Thro' the gaping impotence of sympathy
     In ranged Arezzo: what you take for pitch,
     Is nothing worse, belike, than black and blue,
     Mere evanescent proof that hardy hands
     Did yeoman's service, cared not where the gripe
     Was more than duly energetic: bruised,
     She smarts a little, but her bones are saved
     A fracture, and her skin will soon show sleek.
     How it disgusts when weakness, false-refined,
1010 Censures the honest rude effective strength, –
     When sickly dreamers of the impossible
     Decry plain sturdiness which does the feat
     With eyes wide open!
                      Did occasion serve,
     I could illustrate, if my lords allow;
     Quid vetat, what forbids, I aptly ask
     With Horace, that I give my anger vent,
     While I let breathe, no less, and recreate
     The gravity of my Judges, by a tale –
1020 A case in point – what though an apologue
     Graced by tradition, – possibly a fact?
     Tradition must precede all scripture, words
     Serve as our warrant ere our books can be:
     So, to tradition back we needs must go
     For any fact's authority: and this
     Hath lived so far (like jewel hid in muck)
     O' the page of that old lying vanity
     Called 'Sepher Toldoth Yeschu:' God be praised,
     I read no Hebrew, – take the thing on trust:
1030 But I believe the writer meant no good
     (Blind as he was to truth in some respects)
     To our pestiferous and schismatic . . . well,
     My lords' conjecture be the touchstone, show

The thing for what it is! The author lacks
Discretion, and his zeal exceeds: but zeal, –
How rare in our degenerate day! Enough!
Here is the story, – fear not, I shall chop
And change a little, else my Jew would press
All too unmannerly before the Court.

1040 It happened once, – begins this foolish Jew,
Pretending to write Christian history, –
That three, held greatest, best and worst of men,
Peter and John and Judas, spent a day
In toil and travel through the country-side
On some sufficient business – I suspect,
Suppression of some Molinism i' the bud.
Foot-sore and hungry, dropping with fatigue,
They reached by nightfall a poor lonely grange,
Hostel or inn: so, knocked and entered there.
1050 'Your pleasure, great ones?' – 'Shelter, rest and food!'
For shelter, there was one bare room above;
For rest therein, three beds of bundled straw:
For food, one wretched starveling fowl, no more –
Meat for one mouth, but mockery for three.
'You have my utmost.' How should supper serve?
Peter broke silence. 'To the spit with fowl!
And while 't is cooking, sleep! – since beds there be,
And, so far, satisfaction of a want.
Sleep we an hour, awake at supper-time,
1060 Then each of us narrate the dream he had,
And he whose dream shall prove the happiest, point
The clearliest out the dreamer as ordained
Beyond his fellows to receive the fowl,
Him let our shares be cheerful tribute to,
His the entire meal, may it do him good!'
Who could dispute so plain a consequence?
So said, so done: each hurried to his straw,
Slept his hour's-sleep and dreamed his dream, and woke.
'I,' commenced John, 'dreamed that I gained the prize
1070 We all aspire to: the proud place was mine,

Throughout the earth and to the end of time
I was the Loved Disciple: mine the meal!'
'But I,' proceeded Peter, 'dreamed, a word
Gave me the headship of our company,
Made me the Vicar and Vice-regent, gave
The keys of Heaven and Hell into my hand,
And o'er the earth, dominion: mine the meal!'
'While I,' submitted in soft under-tone
The Iscariot – sense of his unworthiness
1080 Turning each eye up to the inmost white –
With long-drawn sigh, yet letting both lips smack,
'I have had just the pitifullest dream
That ever proved man meanest of his mates,
And born foot-washer and foot-wiper, nay
Foot-kisser to each comrade of you all!
I dreamed I dreamed; and in that mimic dream
(Impalpable to dream as dream to fact)
Methought I meanly chose to sleep no wink
But wait until I heard my brethren breathe;
1090 Then stole from couch, slipped noiseless to the door,
Slid downstairs, furtively approached the hearth,
Found the fowl duly brown, both back and breast,
Hissing in harmony with the cricket's chirp,
Grilled to a point; said no grace but fell to,
Nor finished till the skeleton lay bare.
In penitence for which ignoble dream,
Lo, I renounce my portion cheerfully!
Fie on the flesh – be mine the etherial gust,
And yours the sublunary sustenance!
1100 See, that whate'er be left, ye give the poor!'
Down the two scuttled, one on other's heel,
Stung by a fell surmise; and found, alack,
A goodly savour, both the drumstick-bones,
And that which henceforth took the appropriate name
O' the merry-thought, in memory of the fact
That to keep wide awake is our best dream.

So, – as was said once of Thucydides

And his sole joke, 'The lion, lo, hath laughed!' –
Just so, the Governor and all that's great
I' the city, never meant that Innocence
Should starve thus while Authority sat at meat.
They meant to fling a bone at banquet's end,
Wished well to our Pompilia – in their dreams,
Nor bore the secular sword in vain – asleep:
Just so the Archbishop and all good like him
Went to bed meaning to pour oil and wine
I' the wounds of her, next day, – but long ere day,
They had burned the one and drunk the other: while
Just so, again, contrariwise, the priest
Sustained poor Nature in extremity
By stuffing barley-bread into her mouth,
Saving Pompilia (grant the parallel)
By the plain homely and straightforward way
Taught him by common-sense. Let others shriek
'Oh what refined expedients did we dream
Proved us the only fit to help the fair!'
He cried 'A carriage waits, jump in with me!'

And now, this application pardoned, lords, –
This recreative pause and breathing-while, –
Back to beseemingness and gravity!
For Law steps in: Guido appeals to Law,
Demands she arbitrate, – does well for once.
O Law, of thee how neatly was it said
By that old Sophocles, thou hast thy seat
I' the very breast of Jove, no meanlier throned!
Here is a piece of work now, hitherto
Begun and carried on, concluded near,
Without an eye-glance cast thy sceptre's way;
And, lo the stumbling and discomfiture!
Well may you call them 'lawless,' means men take
To extricate themselves through mother-wit
When tangled haply in the toils of life!
Guido would try conclusions with his foe,
Whoe'er the foe was and whate'er the offence;

He would recover certain dowry-dues:
Instead of asking Law to lend a hand,
What pother of sword drawn and pistol cocked,
What peddling with forged letters and paid spies,
Politic circumvention! – all to end
1150 As it began – by loss of the fool's head,
First in a figure, presently in a fact.
It is a lesson to mankind at large.
How other were the end, would men be sage
And bear confidingly each quarrel straight,
O Law, to thy recipient mother-knees!
How would the children light come and prompt go,
This, with a red-cheeked apple for reward,
The other, peradventure red-cheeked too
I' the rear, by taste of birch for punishment.
1160 No foolish brawling murders any more!
Peace for the household, practice for the Fisc,
And plenty for the exchequer of my lords!
Too much to hope, in this world: in the next,
Who knows? Since, why should sit the Twelve enthroned
To judge the tribes, unless the tribes be judged?
And 't is impossible but offences come:
So, all's one lawsuit, all one long leet-day!

Forgive me this digression – that I stand
Entranced awhile at Law's first beam, outbreak
1170 O' the business, when the Count's good angel bade
'Put up thy sword, born enemy to the ear,
And let Law listen to thy difference!'
And Law does listen and compose the strife,
Settle the suit, how wisely and how well!
On our Pompilia, faultless to a fault,
Law bends a brow maternally severe,
Implies the worth of perfect chastity,
By fancying the flaw she cannot find.
Superfluous sifting snow, nor helps nor harms:
1180 'T is safe to censure levity in youth,
Tax womanhood with indiscretion, sure!

Since toys, permissible to-day, become
Follies to-morrow: prattle shocks in church:
And that curt skirt which lets a maiden skip,
The matron changes for a trailing robe.
Mothers may risk thus much with half-shut eyes
Nodding above their spindles by the fire,
On the chance to hit some hidden fault, else safe.
Just so, Law hazarded a punishment –
1190 If applicable to the circumstance,
Why, well – if not so apposite, well too.
'Quit the gay range o' the world,' I hear her cry.
'Enter, in lieu, the penitential pound:
Exchange the gauds of pomp for ashes, dust: –
Leave each mollitious haunt of luxury,
The golden-garnished silken-couched alcove,
The many-columned terrace that so tempts
Feminine soul put foot forth, nor stop ear
To fluttering joy of lover's serenade,
1200 Leave these for cellular seclusion; mask
And dance no more, but fast and pray; avaunt –
Be burned, thy wicked townsman's sonnet-book!
Welcome, mild hymnal by . . . some better scribe!
For the warm arms, were wont enfold thy flesh,
Let wire-shirt plough and whip-cord discipline!'
If such an exhortation proved, perchance,
Inapplicable, words bestowed in waste,
What harm, since law has store, can spend nor miss?

And so, our paragon submits herself,
1210 Goes at command into the holy house
And, also at command, comes out again:
For, could the effect of such obedience prove
Too certain, too immediate? Being healed,
Go blaze abroad the matter, blessed one!
Art thou sound forthwith? Speedily vacate
The step by pool-side, leave Bethesda free
To patients plentifully posted round,
Since the whole need not the physician! Brief,

She may betake her to her parents' place.
1220 Welcome her, father, with wide arms once more,
Motion her, mother, to thy breast again!
For why? The law relinquishes its charge,
Grants to your dwelling-place a prison's style,
But gives you back Pompilia; golden days,
Redeunt Saturnia regna! Six weeks slip,
And she is domiciled in house and home
As though she thence had never budged at all.
And thither let the husband, joyous – ay,
But contrite also – quick betake himself,
1230 Proud that his dove which lay among the pots
Hath mued those dingy feathers, – moulted now,
Shows silver bosom clothed with yellow gold.
Quick, he shall tempt her to the perch she fled,
Bid to domestic bliss the truant back!

O let him not delay! Time fleets how fast,
And opportunity, the irrevocable,
Once flown will flout him! Is the furrow traced?
If field with corn ye fail preoccupy,
Darnel for wheat and thistle-beards for grain,
1240 *Infelix lolium, carduus horridus,*
Will grow apace in combination prompt,
Defraud the husbandman of his desire.
Already – hist – what murmurs 'monish now
The laggard? – doubtful, nay, fantastic bruit
Of such an apparition, such return
Interdum, to anticipate the spouse,
Of Caponsacchi's very self! 'T is said
When nights are lone and company is rare,
His visitations brighten winter up.
1250 If so they did – which nowise I believe –
How can I? – proof abounding that the priest,
Once fairly at his relegation-place
Never once left it – still, admit he stole
A midnight march, would fain see friend again,
Find matter for instruction in the past,

Renew the old adventure in such chat
As cheers a fireside! He was lonely too,
He, too, must need his recreative hour.
Should it amaze the philosophic mind
1260 If one, was wont the empurpled cup to quaff,
Have feminine society at will,
Being debarred abruptly from all drink
Save at the spring which Adam used for wine,
Dread harm to just the health he hoped to guard,
And, meaning abstinence, gain malady?
Ask Tozzi, now physician to the Pope!
'Little by little break' – (I hear he bids
Master Arcangeli my antagonist,
Who loves good cheer – and may indulge too much –
1270 So I explain the logic of the plea
Wherewith he opened our proceedings late) –
'Little by little break a habit, Don!
Become necessity to feeble flesh!'
And thus, nocturnal taste of intercourse
(Which never happened, – but, suppose it did)
May have been used to dishabituate
By sip and sip this drainer to the dregs
O' the draught of conversation, – heady stuff,
Brewage which broached, it took two days and nights
1280 To properly discuss o' the journey, Sirs!
Such is the second-nature, men call use,
That undelightful objects get to charm
Instead of chafe: the daily colocynth
Tickles the palate by repeated dose,
Old sores scratch kindly, the ass makes a push,
Although the mill-yoke-wound be smarting yet,
For mill-door bolted on a holiday –
And must we marvel if the impulse urge
To talk the old story over now and then,
1290 The hopes and fears, the stoppage and the haste, –
Subjects of colloquy to surfeit once?
'Here did you bid me twine a rosy wreath!'
'And there you paid my lips a compliment!'

'There you admired the tower could be so tall!'
'And there you likened that of Lebanon
To the nose o' the beloved!' – Trifles – still,
'*Forsan et haec olim*,' – such trifles serve
To make the minutes pass in winter-time.

Husband, return then, I re-counsel thee!
1300 For, finally, of all glad circumstance
Should make a prompt return imperative,
What i' the world awaits thee, dost suppose?
O' the sudden, as good gifts are wont befall,
What is the hap of the unconscious Count?
That which lights bonfire and sets cask a-tilt,
Dissolves the stubborn'st heart in jollity.
O admirable, there is born a babe,
A son, an heir, a Franceschini last
And best o' the stock! Pompilia, thine the palm!
1310 Repaying incredulity with faith,
Ungenerous thrift of each marital debt
With bounty in profuse expenditure,
Pompilia will not have the old year end
Without a present shall ring in the new –
Bestows upon her parsimonious lord
An infant for the apple of his eye,
Core of his heart, and crown completing life,
The *summum bonum* of the earthly lot!
'We,' saith ingeniously the sage, 'are born
1320 Solely that others may be born of us.'
So, father, take thy child, for thine that child,
Oh nothing doubt! In wedlock born, law holds
Baseness impossible, since '*filius est
Quem nuptiae demonstrant*,' twits the text
Whoever dares to doubt.

                    Yet doubt he dares!
O faith where art thou flown from out the world?
Already on what an age of doubt we fall!
Instead of each disputing for the prize,

1330 The babe is bandied here from that to this.
Whose the babe? '*Cujum pecus?*' Guido's lamb?
'*An Meliboei?*' Nay, but of the priest!
'*Non sed Aegonis!*' Someone must be sire:
And who shall say, in such a puzzling strait,
If there were not vouchsafed some miracle
To the wife who had been harassed and abused
More than enough by Guido's family
For non-production of the promised fruit
Of marriage? What if Nature, I demand,
1340 Touched to the quick by taunts upon her sloth,
Had roused herself, put forth recondite power,
Bestowed this birth to vindicate her sway?
Like to the favour, Maro memorized,
Was granted Aristaeus when his hive
Lay empty of the swarm, not one more bee –
Not one more babe to Franceschini's house –
And lo, a new birth filled the air with joy,
Sprung from the bowels of the generous steed!
Just so a son and heir rejoiced the Count!
1350 Spontaneous generation, need I prove
Were facile feat to Nature at a pinch?
Let whoso doubts, steep horsehair certain weeks,
In water, there will be produced a snake;
A second product of the horse, which horse
Happens to be the representative –
Now that I think on 't – of Arezzo's self
The very city our conception blessed!
Is not a prancing horse the City-arms?
What sane eye sees not such coincidence?
1360 *Cur ego*, boast thou, my Pompilia, then,
Desperem fieri sine conjuge
Mater – how well the Ovidian distich suits! –
Et parere intacto dummodo
Casta viro? but language baffles here.
Note, further, as to mark the prodigy,
The babe in question neither took the name
Of Guido, from the sire presumptive, nor

Giuseppe, from the sire potential, but
Gaetano – last saint of the hierarchy,
1370 And newest namer for a thing so new:
What other motive could have prompted choice?

Therefore be peace again: exult, ye hills!
Ye vales rejoicingly break forth in song!
Incipe, parve puer, begin, small boy,
Risu cognoscere patrem, with a smile
To recognize thy parent! Nor do thou
Boggle, oh parent, to return the grace –
Nec anceps haere, pater, puero
Cognoscendo – one might well eke out the prayer!
1380 In vain! The perverse Guido doubts his eyes,
Distrusts assurance, lets the devil drive;
Because his house is swept and garnished now,
He, having summoned seven like himself,
Must hurry thither, knock and enter in,
And make the last worse than the first, indeed!
Is he content? We are. No further blame
O' the man and murder! They were stigmatized
Befittingly: the Court heard long ago
My mind o' the matter, which, outpouring full,
1390 Has long since swept, like surge i' the simile
Of Homer, overborne both dyke and dam,
And whelmed alike client and advocate:
His fate is sealed, his life as good as gone,
On him I am not tempted to waste word.
Yet though my purpose holds, – which was and is
And solely shall be to the very end,
To draw the true *effigiem* of a saint,
Do justice to perfection in the sex, –
Yet, let not some gross pamperer o' the flesh
1400 And niggard in the spirit's nourishment,
Whose feeding hath offuscated his wit
Rather than law, – he never had, to lose –
Let not such advocate object to me
I leave my proper function of attack!

'What's this to Bacchus?' – (in the classic phrase,
Well used, for once) he hiccups probably.
O Advocate o' the Poor, thou born to make
Their blessing void – *beati pauperes!*
By painting saintship I depicture sin,
1410 Beside the pearl, I prove how black the jet,
And through Pompilia's virtue, Guido's crime.

Back to her, then, – with but one beauty more,
End we our argument, – one crowning grace
Pre-eminent 'mid agony and death.
For to the last Pompilia played her part,
Used the right means to the permissible end,
And, wily as an eel that stirs the mud
Thick overhead, so baffling spearman's thrust,
She, while he stabbed her, simulated death,
1420 Delayed, for his sake, the catastrophe,
Obtained herself a respite, four days' grace,
Whereby she told her story to the world,
Enabled me to make the present speech,
And, by a full confession, saved her soul.

Yet hold, even here would malice leer its last,
Gurgle its choaked remonstrance: snake, hiss free!
Oh, that's the objection? And to whom? – not her
But me, forsooth – as, in the very act
Of both confession and, what followed close,
1430 Subsequent talk, chatter and gossipry,
Babble to sympathizing he and she
Whoever chose besiege her dying bed, –
As this were found at variance with my tale,
Falsified all I have adduced for truth,
Admitted not one peccadillo here,
Pretended to perfection, first and last,
O' the whole procedure – perfect in the end,
Perfect i' the means, perfect in everything,
Leaving a lawyer nothing to excuse,
1440 Reason away and show his skill about!

– A flight, impossible to Adamic flesh,
Just to be fancied, scarcely to be wished,
And, anyhow, unpleadable in court!
'How reconcile' gasps Malice 'that with this?'

Your 'this,' friend, is extraneous to the law,
Comes of men's outside meddling, the unskilled
Interposition of such fools as press
Out of their province. Must normal I speak my mind?
Far better had Pompilia died o' the spot
1450 Than found a tongue to wag and shame the law,
Shame most of all herself, – did friendship fail,
And advocacy lie less on the alert.
Listen how these protect her to the end!
Do I credit the alleged narration? No!
Lied our Pompilia then, to laud herself?
Still, no; – clear up what seems discrepancy?
The means abound, – art's long, though time is short,
So, keeping me in compass, all I urge
Is – since, confession at the point of death,
1460 *Nam in articulo mortis*, with the Church
Passes for statement honest and sincere,
Nemo presumitur reus esse, – then,
If sure that all affirmed would be believed,
'T was charity, in one so circumstanced,
To spend her last breath in one effort more
For universal good of friend and foe,
And, – by pretending utter innocence,
Nay, freedom from each foible we forgive, –
Re-integrate – not solely her own fame,
1470 But do the like kind office for the priest
Whom the crude truth might treat less courteously,
Indeed, expose to peril, abbreviate
The life and long career of usefulness
Presumably before him: while her lord,
Whose fleeting life is forfeit to the law, –
What mercy to the culprit if, by just
The gift of such a full certificate

Of his immitigable guiltiness,
She stifled in him the absurd conceit
1480 Of murder as it were a mere revenge!
– Stopped confirmation of that jealousy
Which, had she but acknowledged the first flaw,
The faintest foible, might embolden him
To battle with his judge, baulk penitence,
Bar preparation for impending fate.
Whereas, persuade him he has slain a saint
Who sinned not in the little she did sin,
You urge him all the brisklier to repent
Of most and least and aught and everything!
1490 Next, – if this view of mine, content ye not,
Lords, nor excuse the genial falsehood here,
'T is come to our *Triarii*, last resource,
We fall back on the inexpugnable,
Submit you, – she confessed before she talked!
The sacrament obliterates the sin:
What is not, – was not, in a certain sense.
Let Molinists distinguish, 'Souls washed white
Were red once, still show pinkish to the eye!'
We say, abolishment is nothingness
1500 And nothingness has neither head nor tail
End nor beginning; – better estimate
Exorbitantly, than disparage aught
Of the efficacity of the act, I hope!

Solvuntur tabulae? May we laugh and go?
Well, – not before (in filial gratitude
To Law, who, mighty mother, waves adieu)
We take on us to vindicate Law's self –
For, – yea, Sirs, – curb the start, curtail the stare! –
Remains that we apologize for haste
1510 I' the Law, our lady who here bristles up
'And my procedure? Did the Court mistake?
(Which were indeed a misery to think)
Did not my sentence in the former stage
O' the business bear a title plain enough?

Decretum' – I translate it word for word –
' "Decreed: the priest, for his complicity
I' the flight and deviation of the dame,
As well as for unlawful intercourse,
Is banished three years:" crime and penalty,
1520 Declared alike. If he be taxed with guilt
How can you call Pompilia innocent?
If they be innocent, have I been just?'

Gently, O mother, judge men! – whose mistake
Is in the poor misapprehensiveness.
The *Titulus* a-top of your decree
Was but to ticket there the kind of charge
You in good time would arbitrate upon.
Title is one thing, – arbitration's self,
Probatio, quite another possibly.
1530 *Subsistit*, there holds good the old response,
Responsio tradita, we must not stick,
Quod non sit attendendus Titulus,
To the Title, *sed Probatio*, but to Proof,
Resultans ex processu, and result
O' the Trial, and the style of punishment,
Et poena per sententiam imposita;
All is tentative, till the sentence come,
Mere indication of what men expect,
And nowise an assurance they shall find.
1540 Lords, what if we permissibly relax
The tense bow, as the law-god Phoebus bids,
Relieve our gravity at close of speech?
I traverse Rome, feel thirsty, need a draught,
Look for a wine-shop, find it by the bough
Projecting as to say 'Here wine is sold!'
So much I know, – 'sold:' but what sort of wine?
Strong, weak, sweet, sour, home-made or foreign drink?
That much must I discover by myself.
'Wine is sold,' quoth the bough, 'but good or bad,
1550 Find, and inform us when you smack your lips!'
Exactly so, Law hangs her title forth,

To show she entertains you with such case
About such crime: come in! she pours, you quaff.
You find the Priest good liquor in the main,
But heady and provocative of brawls.
Remand the residue to flask once more,
Lay it low where it may deposit lees,
I' the cellar: thence produce it presently,
Three years the brighter and the better!

1560   Thus,
Law's son, have I bestowed my filial help,
And thus I end, *tenax proposito*;
Point to point as I purposed have I drawn
Pompilia, and implied as terribly
Guido: so, gazing, let the world crown Law –
Able once more, despite my impotence,
And helped by the acumen of the Court,
To eliminate, display, make triumph truth!
What other prize than truth were worth the pains?

1570 There's my oration – much exceeds in length
That famed Panegyric of Isocrates,
They say it took him fifteen years to pen.
But all those ancients could say anything!
He put in just what rushed into his head,
While I shall have to prune and pare and print.
This comes of being born in modern times
With priests for auditory. Still, it pays.

BOOK X

The Pope

Like to Ahasuerus, that shrewd prince,
I will begin, – as is, these seven years now,
My daily wont, – and read a History
(Written by one whose deft right hand was dust
To the last digit, ages ere my birth)
Of all my predecessors, Popes of Rome:
For though mine ancient early dropped the pen,
Yet others picked it up and wrote it dry,
Since of the making books there is no end.
10 And so I have the Papacy complete
From Peter first to Alexander last;
Can question each and take instruction so.
Have I to dare, – I ask, how dared this Pope?
To suffer? Suchanone, how suffered he?
Being about to judge, as now, I seek
How judged once, well or ill, some other Pope;
Study some signal judgment that subsists
To blaze on, or else blot, the page which seals
The sum up of what gain or loss to God
20 Came of His one more Vicar in the world.
So, do I find example, rule of life;
So, square and set in order the next page,
Shall be stretched smooth o'er my own funeral cyst.

Eight hundred years exact before the year
I was made Pope, men made Formosus Pope,
Say Sigebert and other chroniclers.
Ere I confirm or quash the Trial here
Of Guido Franceschini and his friends,
Read, – how there was a ghastly Trial once

30 Of a dead man by a live man, and both, Popes:
    Thus – in the antique penman's very phrase.

    'Then Stephen, Pope and seventh of the name,
    Cried out, in synod as he sat in state,
    While choler quivered on his brow and beard,
    "Come into court, Formosus, thou lost wretch,
    That claimedst to be late the Pope as I!"

    And at the word, the great door of the church
    Flew wide, and in they brought Formosus' self,
    The body of him, dead, even as embalmed
40 And buried duly in the Vatican
    Eight months before, exhumed thus for the nonce.
    They set it, that dead body of a Pope,
    Clothed in pontific vesture now again,
    Upright on Peter's chair as if alive.
    And Stephen, springing up, cried furiously
    "Bishop of Porto, wherefore didst presume
    To leave that see and take this Roman see,
    Exchange the lesser for the greater see,
    – A thing against the canons of the Church?"

50 Then one, (a Deacon who, observing forms,
    Was placed by Stephen to repel the charge,
    Be advocate and mouthpiece of the corpse)
    Spoke as he dared, set stammeringly forth
    With white lips and dry tongue, – as but a youth,
    For frightful was the corpse-face to behold, –
    How nowise lacked there precedent for this.
    But when, for his last precedent of all,
    Emboldened by the Spirit, out he blurts
    "And, Holy Father, didst not thou thyself
60 Vacate the lesser for the greater see,
    Half a year since change Arago for Rome?"
    " – Ye have the sin's defence now, synod mine!"
    Shrieks Stephen in a beastly froth of rage:
    "Judge now betwixt him dead and me alive!

Hath he intruded or do I pretend?
Judge, judge!" – breaks wavelike one whole foam of wrath.

Whereupon they, being friends and followers,
Said "Ay, thou art Christ's Vicar, and not he!
Away with what is frightful to behold!
70   This act was uncanonic and a fault."

Then, swallowed up in rage, Stephen exclaimed
"So, guilty! So, remains I punish guilt!
He is unpoped, and all he did I damn:
The Bishop, that ordained him, I degrade:
Depose to laics those he raised to priests:
What they have wrought is mischief nor shall stand,
It is confusion, let it vex no more!
Since I revoke, annul and abrogate
All his decrees in all kinds: they are void!
80   In token whereof and warning to the world,
Strip me yon miscreant of those robes usurped,
And clothe him with vile serge befitting such!
Then hale the carrion to the market-place;
Let the town-hangman chop from his right hand
Those same three fingers which he blessed withal;
Next cut the head off, once was crowned forsooth:
And last go fling all, fingers, head and trunk,
In Tiber that my Christian fish may sup!"
– Either because of ΙΧΘΥΣ which means Fish
90   And very aptly symbolizes Christ,
Or else because the Pope is Fisherman
And seals with Fisher's-signet. Anyway,
So said, so done: himself, to see it done,
Following the corpse, they trailed from street to street
Till into Tiber wave they threw the thing.
The people, crowded on the banks to see,
Were loud or mute, wept or laughed, cursed or jeered,
According as the deed addressed their sense;
A scandal verily: and out spake a Jew
100   "Wot ye your Christ had vexed our Herod thus?"

Now when, Formosus being dead a year,
His judge Pope Stephen tasted death in turn,
Made captive by the mob and strangled straight,
Romanus, his successor for a month,
Did make protest Formosus was with God,
Holy, just, true in thought and word and deed.
Next Theodore, who reigned but twenty days,
Therein convoked a synod, whose decree
Did reinstate, repope the late unpoped,
110 And do away with Stephen as accursed.
So that when presently certain fisher-folk
(As if the queasy river could not hold
Its swallowed Jonas, but discharged the meal)
Produced the timely product of their nets,
The mutilated man, Formosus, — saved
From putrefaction by the embalmer's spice,
Or, as some said, by sanctity of flesh, —
"Why, lay the body again" bade Theodore
"Among his predecessors, in the church
120 And burial-place of Peter!" which was done.
"And" addeth Luitprand "many of repute,
Pious and still alive, avouch to me
That as they bore the body up the aisle
The saints in imaged row bowed each his head
For welcome to a brother-saint come back."
As for Romanus and this Theodore,
These two Popes, through the brief reign granted each,
Could but initiate what John came to close
And give the final stamp to: he it was,
130 Ninth of the name, (I follow the best guides)
Who, — in full synod at Ravenna held
With Bishops seventy-four, and present too
Eude King of France with his Archbishopry, —
Did condemn Stephen, anathematize
The disinterment, and make all blots blank.
"For," argueth here Auxilius in a place
De Ordinationibus, "precedents
Had been, no lack, before Formosus long,

Of Bishops so transferred from see to see, –
140　Marinus, for example": read the tract.

But, after John, came Sergius, reaffirmed
The right of Stephen, cursed Formosus, nay
Cast out, some say, his corpse a second time.
And here, – because the matter went to ground,
Fretted by new griefs, other cares of the age, –
Here is the last pronouncing of the Church,
Her sentence that subsists unto this day.
Yet constantly opinion hath prevailed
I' the Church, Formosus was a holy man.'

150　Which of the judgments was infallible?
Which of my predecessors spoke for God?
And what availed Formosus that this cursed,
That blessed, and then this other cursed again?
'Fear ye not those whose power can kill the body
And not the soul,' saith Christ 'but rather those
Can cast both soul and body into hell!'

John judged thus in Eight Hundred Ninety Eight,
Exact eight hundred years ago to-day
When, sitting in his stead, Vice-gerent here,
160　I must give judgment on my own behoof.
So worked the predecessor: now, my turn!

In God's name! Once more on this earth of God's,
While twilight lasts and time wherein to work,
I take His staff with my uncertain hand,
And stay my six and fourscore years, my due
Labour and sorrow, on His judgment-seat,
And forthwith think, speak, act, in place of Him –
The Pope for Christ. Once more appeal is made
From man's assize to mine: I sit and see
170　Another poor weak trembling human wretch
Pushed by his fellows, who pretend the right,
Up to the gulf which, where I gaze, begins

From this world to the next, – gives way and way,
Just on the edge over the awful dark:
With nothing to arrest him but my feet.
He catches at me with convulsive face,
Cries 'Leave to live the natural minute more!'
While hollowly the avengers echo 'Leave?
None! So has he exceeded man's due share
180 In man's fit licence, wrung by Adam's fall,
To sin and yet not surely die, – that we,
All of us sinful, all with need of grace,
All chary of our life, – the minute more
Or minute less of grace which saves a soul, –
Bound to make common cause with who craves time,
– We yet protest against the exorbitance
Of sin in this one sinner, and demand
That his poor sole remaining piece of time
Be plucked from out his clutch: put him to death!
190 Punish him now! As for the weal or woe
Hereafter, God grant mercy! Man be just,
Nor let the felon boast he went scot-free!'
And I am bound, the solitary judge,
To weigh the worth, decide upon the plea,
And either hold a hand out, or withdraw
A foot and let the wretch drift to the fall.
Ay, and while thus I dally, dare perchance
Put fancies for a comfort 'twixt this calm
And yonder passion that I have to bear, –
200 As if reprieve were possible for both
Prisoner and Pope, – how easy were reprieve!
A touch o' the hand-bell here, a hasty word
To those who wait, and wonder they wait long,
I' the passage there, and I should gain the life! –
Yea, though I flatter me with fancy thus,
I know it is but nature's craven-trick.
The case is over, judgment at an end,
And all things done now and irrevocable:
A mere dead man is Franceschini here,
210 Even as Formosus centuries ago.

I have worn through this sombre wintry day,
With winter in my soul beyond the world's,
Over these dismalest of documents
Which drew night down on me ere eve befell, –
Pleadings and counter-pleadings, figure of fact
Beside fact's self, these summaries to-wit, –
How certain three were slain by certain five:
I read here why it was, and how it went,
And how the chief o' the five preferred excuse,
220 And how law rather chose defence should lie, –
What argument he urged by wary word
When free to play off wile, start subterfuge,
And what the unguarded groan told, torture's feat
When law grew brutal, outbroke, overbore
And glutted hunger on the truth, at last, –
No matter for the flesh and blood between.
All's a clear rede and no more riddle now.
Truth, nowhere, lies yet everywhere in these –
Not absolutely in a portion, yet
230 Evolvable from the whole: evolved at last
Painfully, held tenaciously by me.
Therefore there is not any doubt to clear
When I shall write the brief word presently
And chink the hand-bell, which I pause to do.
Irresolute? Not I more than the mound
With the pine-trees on it yonder! Some surmise,
Perchance, that since man's wit is fallible,
Mine may fail here? Suppose it so, – what then?
Say, – Guido, I count guilty, there's no babe
240 So guiltless, for I misconceive the man!
What's in the chance should move me from my mind?
If, as I walk in a rough country-side,
Peasants of mine cry 'Thou art he can help,
Lord of the land and counted wise to boot:
Look at our brother, strangling in his foam,
He fell so where we find him, – prove thy worth!'
I may presume, pronounce, 'A frenzy-fit,
A falling-sickness or a fever-stroke!

Breathe a vein, copiously let blood at once!'
250 So perishes the patient, and anon
I hear my peasants – 'All was error, lord!
Our story, thy prescription: for there crawled
In due time from our hapless brother's breast
The serpent which had stung him: bleeding slew
Whom a prompt cordial had restored to health.'
What other should I say than 'God so willed:
Mankind is ignorant, a man am I:
Call ignorance my sorrow not my sin!'
So and not otherwise, in after-time,
260 If some acuter wit, fresh probing, sound
This multifarious mass of words and deeds
Deeper, and reach through guilt to innocence,
I shall face Guido's ghost nor blench a jot.
'God who set me to judge thee, meted out
So much of judging faculty, no more:
Ask Him if I was slack in use thereof!'
I hold a heavier fault imputable
Inasmuch as I changed a chaplain once,
For no cause, – no, if I must bare my heart, –
270 Save that he snuffled somewhat saying mass.
For I am ware it is the seed of act,
God holds appraising in His hollow palm,
Not act grown great thence on the world below,
Leafage and branchage, vulgar eyes admire.
Therefore I stand on my integrity,
Nor fear at all: and if I hesitate,
It is because I need to breathe awhile,
Rest, as the human right allows, review
Intent the little seeds of act, the tree, –
280 The thought, to clothe in deed, and give the world
At chink of bell and push of arrased door.

O pale departure, dim disgrace of day!
Winter's in wane, his vengeful worst art thou,
To dash the boldness of advancing March!
Thy chill persistent rain has purged our streets

Of gossipry; pert tongue and idle ear
By this, consort 'neath archway, portico.
But wheresoe'er Rome gathers in the grey,
Two names now snap and flash from mouth to mouth –
290 (Sparks, flint and steel strike) Guido and the Pope.
By this same hour to-morrow eve – aha,
How do they call him? – the sagacious Swede
Who finds by figures how the chances prove,
Why one comes rather than another thing,
As, say, such dots turn up by throw of dice,
Or, if we dip in Virgil here and there
And prick for such a verse, when such shall point.
Take this Swede, tell him, hiding name and rank,
Two men are in our city this dull eve;
300 One doomed to death, – but hundreds in such plight
Slip aside, clean escape by leave of law
Which leans to mercy in this latter time;
Moreover in the plenitude of life
Is he, with strength of limb and brain adroit,
Presumably of service here: beside,
The man is noble, backed by nobler friends:
Nay, for who wish him well, the city's self
Makes common cause with the house-magistrate,
The lord of hearth and home, domestic judge
310 Who ruled his own and let men cavil. Die?
He'll bribe a gaoler or break prison first!
Nay, a sedition may be helpful, give
Hint to the mob to batter wall, burn gate,
And bid the favourite malefactor march.
Calculate now these chances of escape!
'It is not probable, but well may be.'
Again, there is another man, weighed now
By twice eight years beyond the seven-times-ten,
Appointed overweight to break our branch.
320 And this man's loaded branch lifts, more than snow,
All the world's cark and care, though a bird's nest
Were a superfluous burthen: notably
Hath he been pressed, as if his age were youth,

From to-day's dawn till now that day departs,
Trying one question with true sweat of soul
'Shall the said doomed man fitlier die or live?'
When a straw swallowed in his posset, stool
Stumbled on where his path lies, any puff
That's incident to such a smoking flax,
330   Hurries the natural end and quenches him!
Now calculate, thou sage, the chances here,
Say, which shall die the sooner, this or that?
'That, possibly, this in all likelihood.'
I thought so: yet thou tripp'st, my foreign friend!
No, it will be quite otherwise, – to-day
Is Guido's last: my term is yet to run.

But say the Swede were right, and I forthwith
Acknowledge a prompt summons and lie dead:
Why, then I stand already in God's face
340   And hear 'Since by its fruit a tree is judged,
Show me thy fruit, the latest act of thine!
For in the last is summed the first and all, –
What thy life last put heart and soul into,
There shall I taste thy product.' I must plead
This condemnation of a man to-day.

Not so! Expect nor question nor reply
At what we figure as God's judgment-bar!
None of this vile way by the barren words
Which, more than any deed, characterize
350   Man as made subject to a curse: no speech –
That still bursts o'er some lie which lurks inside,
As the split skin across the coppery snake,
And most denotes man! since, in all beside,
In hate or lust or guile or unbelief,
Out of some core of truth the excrescence comes,
And, in the last resort, the man may urge
'So was I made, a weak thing that gave way
To truth, to impulse only strong since true,
And hated, lusted, used guile, forwent faith.'

360　But when man walks the garden of this world
　　　For his own solace, and, unchecked by law,
　　　Speaks or keeps silence as himself sees fit,
　　　Without the least incumbency to lie,
　　　– Why, can he tell you what a rose is like,
　　　Or how the birds fly, and not slip to false
　　　Though truth serve better? Man must tell his mate
　　　Of you, me and himself, knowing he lies,
　　　Knowing his fellow knows the same, – will think
　　　'He lies, it is the method of a man!'
370　And yet will speak for answer 'It is truth'
　　　To him who shall rejoin 'Again a lie!'
　　　Therefore this filthy rags of speech, this coil
　　　Of statement, comment, query and response,
　　　Tatters all too contaminate for use,
　　　Have no renewing: He, the Truth, is, too,
　　　The Word. We men, in our degree, may know
　　　There, simply, instantaneously, as here
　　　After long time and amid many lies,
　　　Whatever we dare think we know indeed
380　– That I am I, as He is He, – what else?
　　　But be man's method for man's life at least!
　　　Wherefore, Antonio Pignatelli, thou
　　　My ancient self, who wast no Pope so long
　　　But studied God and man, the many years
　　　I' the school, i' the cloister, in the diocese
　　　Domestic, legate-rule in foreign lands, –
　　　Thou other force in those old busy days
　　　Than this grey ultimate decrepitude, –
　　　Yet sensible of fires that more and more
390　Visit a soul, in passage to the sky,
　　　Left nakeder than when flesh-robe was new –
　　　Thou, not Pope but the mere old man o' the world,
　　　Supposed inquisitive and dispassionate,
　　　Wilt thou, the one whose speech I somewhat trust,
　　　Question the after-me, this self now Pope,
　　　Hear his procedure, criticize his work?
　　　Wise in its generation is the world.

This is why Guido is found reprobate.
I see him furnished forth for his career,
On starting for the life-chance in our world,
With nearly all we count sufficient help:
Body and mind in balance, a sound frame,
A solid intellect: the wit to seek,
Wisdom to choose, and courage wherewithal
To deal with whatsoever circumstance
Should minister to man, make life succeed.
Oh, and much drawback! what were earth without?
Is this our ultimate stage, or starting-place
To try man's foot, if it will creep or climb,
'Mid obstacles in seeming, points that prove
Advantage for who vaults from low to high
And makes the stumbling-block a stepping-stone?
So, Guido, born with appetite, lacks food,
Is poor, who yet could deftly play-off wealth,
Straitened, whose limbs are restless till at large:
And, as he eyes each outlet of the cirque,
The narrow penfold for probation, pines
After the good things just outside the grate,
With less monition, fainter conscience-twitch,
Rarer instinctive qualm at the first feel
Of the unseemly greed and grasp undue,
Than nature furnishes the main mankind, –
Making it harder to do wrong than right
The first time, careful lest the common ear
Break measure, miss the outstep of life's march.
Wherein I see a trial fair and fit
For one else too unfairly fenced about,
Set above sin, beyond his fellows here,
Guarded from the arch-tempter, all must fight,
By a great birth, traditionary name,
Diligent culture, choice companionship,
Above all, conversancy with the faith
Which puts forth for its base of doctrine just
'Man is born nowise to content himself
But please God.' He accepted such a rule,

Recognized man's obedience; and the Church,
Which simply is such rule's embodiment,
He clave to, he held on by, – nay, indeed,
Near pushed inside of, deep as layman durst,
440 Professed so much of priesthood as might sue
For priest's-exemption where the layman sinned, –
Got his arm frocked which, bare, the law would bruise.
Hence, at this moment, what's his last resource,
His extreme stay and utmost stretch of hope
But that, – convicted of such crime as law
Wipes not away save with a worldling's blood, –
Guido, the three-parts consecrate, may 'scape?
Nay, the portentous brothers of the man
Are veritably priests, protected each
450 May do his murder in the Church's pale,
Abate Paul, Canon Girolamo!
This is the man proves irreligiousest
Of all mankind, religion's parasite!
This may forsooth plead dinned ear, jaded sense,
The vice o' the watcher who bides near the bell,
Sleeps sound because the clock is vigilant,
And cares not whether it be shade or shine,
Doling out day and night to all men else!
Why was the choice o' the man to niche himself
460 Perversely 'neath the tower where Time's own tongue
Thus undertakes to sermonize the world?
Why, but because the solemn is safe too,
The belfry proves a fortress of a sort,
Has other uses than to teach the hour,
Turns sunscreen, paravent and ombrifuge
To whoso seeks a shelter in its pale,
– Ay, and attractive to unwary folk
Who gaze at storied portal, statued spire,
And go home with full head but empty purse
470 Nor dare suspect the sacristan the thief!
Shall Judas, – hard upon the donor's heel,
To filch the fragments of the basket, – plead
He was too near the preacher's mouth, nor sat

Attent with fifties in a company?
No, – closer to promulgated decree,
Clearer the censure of default. Proceed!

I find him bound, then, to begin life well;
Fortified by propitious circumstance,
Great birth, good breeding, with the Church for guide.
480 How lives he? Cased thus in a coat of proof,
Mailed like a man-at-arms, though all the while
A puny starveling, – does the breast pant big,
The limb swell to the limit, emptiness
Strive to become solidity indeed?
Rather, he shrinks up like the ambiguous fish,
Detaches flesh from shell and outside show,
And steals by moonlight (I have seen the thing)
In and out, now to prey and now to skulk.
Armour he boasts when a wave breaks on beach,
490 Or bird stoops for the prize: with peril nigh, –
The man of rank, the much-befriended man,
The man almost affiliate to the Church,
Such is to deal with, let the world beware!
Does the world recognize, pass prudently?
Do tides abate and sea-fowl hunt i' the deep?
Already is the slug from out its mew,
Ignobly faring with all loose and free,
Sand-fly and slush-worm at their garbage-feast,
A naked blotch no better than they all:
500 Guido has dropped nobility, slipped the Church,
Plays trickster if not cut-purse, body and soul
Prostrate among the filthy feeders – faugh!
And when Law takes him by surprise at last,
Catches the foul thing on its carrion-prey,
Behold, he points to shell left high and dry,
Pleads 'But the case out yonder is myself!'
Nay, it is thou, Law prongs amid thy peers,
Congenial vermin; that was none of thee,
Thine outside, – give it to the soldier-crab!

510   For I find this black mark impinge the man,
     That he believes in just the vile of life.
     Low instinct, base pretension, are these truth?
     Then, that aforesaid armour, probity
     He figures in, is falsehood scale on scale;
     Honor and faith, – a lie and a disguise,
     Probably for all livers in this world,
     Certainly for himself! All say good words
     To who will hear, all do thereby bad deeds
     To who must undergo; so thrive mankind!
520   See this habitual creed exemplified
     Most in the last deliberate act; as last,
     So, very sum and substance of the soul
     Of him that planned and leaves one perfect piece,
     The sin brought under jurisdiction now,
     Even the marriage of the man: this act
     I sever from his life as sample, show
     For Guido's self, intend to test him by,
     As, from a cup filled fairly at the fount,
     By the components we decide enough
530   Or to let flow as late, or staunch the source.

     He purposes this marriage, I remark,
     On no one motive that should prompt thereto –
     Farthest, by consequence, from ends alleged
     Appropriate to the action; so they were:
     The best, he knew and feigned, the worst he took.
     Not one permissible impulse moves the man,
     From the mere liking of the eye and ear,
     To the true longing of the heart that loves,
     No trace of these: but all to instigate,
540   Is what sinks man past level of the brute,
     Whose appetite if brutish is a truth.
     All is the lust for money: to get gold, –
     Why, lie, rob, if it must be, murder! Make
     Body and soul wring gold out, lured within
     The clutch of hate by love, the trap's pretence!
     What good else get from bodies and from souls?

This got, there were some life to lead thereby,
– What, where or how, appreciate those who tell
How the toad lives: it lives, – enough for me!
550 To get this good, – with but a groan or so,
Then, silence of the victims, – were the feat.
He foresaw, made a picture in his mind, –
Of father and mother stunned and echoless
To the blow, as they lie staring at fate's jaws
Their folly danced into, till the woe fell;
Edged in a month by strenuous cruelty
From even the poor nook whence they watched the wolf
Feast on their heart, the lamb-like child his prey;
Plundered to the last remnant of their wealth,
560 (What daily pittance pleased the plunderer dole)
Hunted forth to go hide head, starve and die,
So leave the pale awe-stricken wife, past hope
Of help i' the world now, mute and motionless,
His slave, his chattel, to use and then destroy:
All this, he bent mind how to bring about,
Put this in act and life, as painted plain,
And have success, the crown of earthly good,
In this particular enterprise of man,
A marriage – undertaken in God's face
570 With all those lies so opposite God's truth,
For ends so other than man's end.

               Thus schemes
Guido, and thus would carry out his scheme:
But when an obstacle first blocks the path,
When he finds there is no monopoly
Of lies and trick i' the tricking lying world, –
That sorry timid natures, even this sort
O' the Comparini, want nor trick nor lie
Proper to the kind, – that as the gor-crow treats
580 The bramble-finch so treats the finch the moth,
And the great Guido is minutely matched
By this same couple, – whether true or false
The revelation of Pompilia's birth,

Which in a moment brings his scheme to nought, –
Then, he is piqued, advances yet a stage,
Leaves the low region to the finch and fly,
Soars to the zenith whence the fiercer fowl
May dare the inimitable swoop. I see.
He draws now on the curious crime, the fine
590 Felicity and flower of wickedness;
Determines, by the utmost exercise
Of violence, made safe and sure by craft,
To satiate malice, pluck one last arch-pang
From the parents, else would triumph out of reach,
By punishing their child, within reach yet,
Who nowise could have wronged, thought, word or deed,
I' the matter that now moves him. So plans he,
Always subordinating (note the point!)
Revenge, the manlier sin, to interest
600 The meaner, – would pluck pang forth, but unclench
No gripe in the act, let fall no money-piece.
Hence a plan for so plaguing, body and soul,
His wife, so putting, day by day and hour by hour,
The untried torture to the untouched place,
As much precipitate an end foreseen,
Goad her into some plain revolt, most like
Plunge upon patent suicidal shame,
Death to herself, damnation by rebound
To those whose hearts he, holding hers, holds still:
610 Such a plan as, in its completeness, shall
Ruin the three together and alike,
Yet leave himself in luck and liberty,
No claim renounced, no right a forfeiture,
His person unendangered, his good fame
Without a flaw, his pristine worth intact, –
While they, with all their claims and rights that cling,
Shall forthwith crumble off him every side,
Scorched into dust, a plaything for the winds.
As when, in our Campagna, there is fired
620 The nest-like work that lets a peasant house;
And, as the thatch burns here, there, everywhere,

Even to the ivy and wild vine, that bound
And blessed the hut where men were happy once,
There rises gradual, black amid the blaze,
Some grim and unscathed nucleus of the nest, –
Some old malicious tower, some obscene tomb
They thought a temple in their ignorance,
And clung about and thought to lean upon –
There laughs it o'er their ravage, – where are they?
630 So did his cruelty burn life about,
And lay the ruin bare in dreadfulness,
Try the persistency of torment so
O' the wife, that, at some fierce extremity,
Some crisis brought about by fire and flame,
The patient stung to frenzy should break loose,
Fly anyhow, find refuge anywhere,
Even in the arms of who might front her first,
No monster but a man – while nature shrieked
'Or thus escape, or die!' The spasm arrived,
640 Not the escape by way of sin, – O God,
Who shall pluck sheep Thou holdest, from Thy hand?
Therefore she lay resigned to die, – so far
The simple cruelty was foiled. Why then,
Craft to the rescue, craft should supplement
Cruelty and show hell a masterpiece!
Hence this consummate lie, this love-intrigue,
Unmanly simulation of a sin,
With place and time and circumstance to suit –
These letters false beyond all forgery –
650 Not just handwriting and mere authorship,
But false to body and soul they figure forth –
As though the man had cut out shape and shape
From fancies of that other Aretine,
To paste below – incorporate the filth
With cherub faces on a missal-page!

Whereby the man so far attains his end
That strange temptation is permitted, – see!
Pompilia, wife, and Caponsacchi, priest,

Are brought together as nor priest nor wife
660   Should stand, and there is passion in the place,
Power in the air for evil as for good,
Promptings from heaven and hell, as if the stars
Fought in their courses for a fate to be.
Thus stand the wife and priest, a spectacle,
I doubt not, to unseen assemblage there.
No lamp will mark that window for a shrine,
No tablet signalize the terrace, teach
New generations which succeed the old,
The pavement of the street is holy ground;
670   No bard describe in verse how Christ prevailed
And Satan fell like lightning! Why repine?
What does the world, told truth, but lie the more?

A second time the plot is foiled; nor, now,
By corresponding sin for countercheck,
No wile and trick to baffle trick and wile, –
The play of the parents! Here the blot is blanched
By God's gift of a purity of soul
That will not take pollution, ermine-like
Armed from dishonour by its own soft snow.
680   Such was this gift of God who showed for once
How He would have the world go white: it seems
As a new attribute were born of each
Champion of truth, the priest and wife I praise, –
As a new safeguard sprang up in defence
Of their new noble nature: so a thorn
Comes to the aid of and completes the rose –
Courage to-wit, no woman's gift nor priest's,
I' the crisis; might leaps vindicating right.
See how the strong aggressor, bad and bold,
690   With every vantage, preconcerts surprise,
Flies of a sudden at his victim's throat
In a byeway, – how fares he when face to face
With Caponsacchi? Who fights, who fears now?
There quails Count Guido, armed to the chattering teeth,
Cowers at the steadfast eye and quiet word

O' the Canon at the Pieve! There skulks crime
Behind law called in to back cowardice!
While out of the poor trampled worm the wife,
Springs up a serpent!

700   But anon of these!
Him I judge now, – of him proceed to note,
Failing the first, a second chance befriends
Guido, gives pause ere punishment arrive.
The law he called, comes, hears, adjudicates,
Nor does amiss i' the main, – secludes the wife
From the husband, respites the oppressed one, grants
Probation to the oppressor, could he know
The mercy of a minute's fiery purge!
The furnace-coals alike of public scorn,
710 Private remorse, heaped glowing on his head,
What if, – the force and guile, the ore's alloy,
Eliminate, his baser soul refined –
The lost be saved even yet, so as by fire?
Let him, rebuked, go softly all his days
And, when no graver musings claim their due,
Meditate on a man's immense mistake
Who, fashioned to use feet and walk, deigns crawl –
Takes the unmanly means – ay, though to end
Man scarce should make for, would but reach thro' wrong, –
720 May sin, but must not needs shame manhood so:
Since fowlers hawk, shoot, nay and snare the game,
And yet eschew vile practice, nor find sport
In torch-light treachery or the luring owl.

But how hunts Guido? Why, the fraudful trap –
Late spurned to ruin by the indignant feet
Of fellows in the chase who loved fair play –
Here he picks up the fragments to the least,
Lades him and hies to the old lurking-place
Where haply he may patch again, refit
730 The mischief, file its blunted teeth anew,
Make sure, next time, a snap shall break the bone.

Craft, greed and violence complot revenge:
Craft, for its quota, schemes to bring about
And seize occasion and be safe withal:
Greed craves its act may work both far and near,
Crush the tree, branch and trunk and root beside,
Whichever twig or leaf arrests a streak
Of possible sunshine else would coin itself,
And drop down one more gold piece in the path.
740　Violence stipulates 'Advantage proved,
And safety sure, be pain the overplus!
Murder with jagged knife! Cut but tear too!
Foiled oft, starved long, glut malice for amends!'
And, last, craft schemes, – scheme sorrowful and strange
As though the elements, whom mercy checked,
Had mustered hate for one eruption more,
One final deluge to surprise the Ark
Cradled and sleeping on its mountain-top:
The outbreak-signal – what but the dove's coos
750　Back with the olive in her bill for news
Sorrow was over? 'T is an infant's birth,
Guido's first born, his son and heir, that gives
The occasion: other men cut free their souls
From care in such a case, fly up in thanks
To God, reach, recognise His love for once:
Guido cries 'Soul, at last the mire is thine!
Lie there in likeness of a money-bag,
This babe's birth so pins down past moving now,
That I dare cut adrift the lives I late
760　Scrupled to touch lest thou escape with them!
These parents and their child my wife, – touch one
Lose all! Their rights determined on a head
I could but hate, not harm, since from each hair
Dangled a hope for me: now – chance and change!
No right was in their child but passes now
To that child's child and through such child to me.
I am the father now, – come what, come will,
I represent my child; he comes between –
Cuts sudden off the sunshine of this life

770   From those three: why, the gold is in his curls!
Not with old Pietro's, Violante's head,
Not his grey horror, her more hideous black –
Go these, devoted to the knife!'
                      'T is done:
Wherefore should mind misgive, heart hesitate?
He calls to counsel, fashions certain four
Colourless natures counted clean till now,
– Rustic simplicity, uncorrupted youth,
Ignorant virtue! Here's the gold o' the prime
780   When Saturn ruled, shall shock our leaden day –
The clown abash the courtier! Mark it, bards!
The courtier tries his hand on clownship here,
Speaks a word, names a crime, appoints a price, –
Just breathes on what, suffused with all himself,
Is red-hot henceforth past distinction now
I' the common glow of hell. And thus they break
And blaze on us at Rome, Christ's Birthnight-eve!
Oh angels that sang erst 'On the earth, peace!
To man, good will!' – such peace finds earth to-day!
790   After the seventeen hundred years, so man
Wills good to man, so Guido makes complete
His murder! what is it I said? – cuts loose
Three lives that hitherto he suffered cling,
Simply because each served to nail secure,
By a corner of the money-bag, his soul, –
Therefore, lives sacred till the babe's first breath
O'erweights them in the balance, – off they fly!

So is the murder managed, sin conceived
To the full: and why not crowned with triumph too?
800   Why must the sin, conceived thus, bring forth death?
I note how, within hair's-breadth of escape,
Impunity and the thing supposed success,
Guido is found when the check comes, the change,
The monitory touch o' the tether – felt
By few, not marked by many, named by none
At the moment, only recognised aright

I' the fulness of the days, for God's, lest sin
Exceed the service, leap the line: such check –
A secret which this life finds hard to keep,
810 And, often guessed, is never quite revealed.
Guido must needs trip on a stumbling-block
Too vulgar, too absurdly plain i' the path!
Study this single oversight of care,
This hebetude that mars sagacity,
Forgetfulness of what the man best knew!
Here is a stranger who, with need to fly,
Needs but to ask and have the means of flight.
Why, the first urchin tells you, to leave Rome,
Get horses, you must show the warrant, just
820 The banal scrap, clerk's scribble, a fair word buys,
Or foul one, if a ducat sweeten word, –
And straight authority will back demand,
Give you the pick o' the post-house! – in such wise,
The resident at Rome for thirty years,
Guido, instructs a stranger! And himself
Forgets just this poor paper scrap, wherewith
Armed, every door he knocks at opens wide
To save him: horsed and manned, with such advance
O' the hunt behind, why 't were the easy task
830 Of hours told on the fingers of one hand,
To reach the Tuscan Frontier, laugh at home,
Light-hearted with his fellows of the place, –
Prepared by that strange shameful judgment, that
Satire upon a sentence just pronounced
By the Rota and confirmed by the Granduke, –
Ready in a circle to receive their peer,
Appreciate his good story how, when Rome,
The Pope-King and the populace of priests
Made common cause with their confederate
840 The other priestling who seduced his wife,
He, all unaided, wiped out the affront
With decent bloodshed and could face his friends,
Frolic it in the world's eye. Ay, such tale
Missed such applause, all by such oversight!

So, tired and footsore, those blood-flustered five
Went reeling on the road through dark and cold,
The few permissible miles, to sink at length,
Wallow and sleep in the first wayside straw,
As the other herd quenched, i' the wash o' the wave,
850 – Each swine, the devil inside him: so slept they,
And so were caught and caged – all through one trip,
Touch of the fool in Guido the astute!
He curses the omission, I surmise,
More than the murder. Why, thou fool and blind,
It is the mercy-stroke that stops thy fate,
Hamstrings and holds thee to thy hurt, – but how?
On the edge o' the precipice! One minute more,
Thou hadst gone farther and fared worse, my son,
Fathoms down on the flint and fire beneath!
860 Thy comrades each and all were of one mind
Straightway, thy murder done, to murder thee
In turn, because of promised pay withheld.
So, to the last, greed found itself at odds
With craft in thee, and, proving conqueror,
Had sent thee, the same night that crowned thy hope,
Thither where, this same day, I see thee not,
Nor, through God's mercy, need, to-morrow, see.

Such I find Guido, midmost blotch of black
Discernible in this group of clustered crimes
870 Huddling together in the cave they call
Their palace, outraged day thus penetrates.
Around him ranged, now close and now remote,
Prominent or obscure to meet the needs
O' the mage and master, I detect each shape
Subsidiary i' the scene nor loathed the less,
All alike coloured, all descried akin
By one and the same pitchy furnace stirred
At the centre: see, they lick the master's hand, –
This fox-faced horrible priest, this brother-brute
880 The Abate, – why, mere wolfishness looks well,
Guido stands honest in the red o' the flame,

Beside this yellow that would pass for white,
This Guido, all craft but no violence,
This copier of the mien and gait and garb
Of Peter and Paul, that he may go disguised,
Rob halt and lame, sick folk i' the temple-porch!
Armed with religion, fortified by law,
A man of peace, who trims the midnight lamp
And turns the classic page – and all for craft,
890 All to work harm with, yet incur no scratch!
While Guido brings the struggle to a close,
Paul steps back the due distance, clear o' the trap
He builds and baits. Guido I catch and judge;
Paul is past reach in this world and my time:
That is a case reserved. Pass to the next,
The boy of the brood, the young Girolamo
Priest, Canon, and what more? nor wolf nor fox,
But hybrid, neither craft nor violence
Wholly, part violence part craft: such cross
900 Tempts speculation – will both blend one day,
And prove hell's better product? Or subside
And let the simple quality emerge,
Go on with Satan's service the old way?
Meanwhile, what promise, – what performance too!
For there's a new distinctive touch, I see,
Lust – lacking in the two – hell's own blue tint
That gives a character and marks the man
More than a match for yellow and red. Once more,
A case reserved: why should I doubt? Then comes
910 The gaunt grey nightmare in the furthest smoke,
The hag that gave these three abortions birth,
Unmotherly mother and unwomanly
Woman, that near turns motherhood to shame,
Womanliness to loathing: no one word,
No gesture to curb cruelty a whit
More than the she-pard thwarts her playsome whelps
Trying their milk-teeth on the soft o' the throat
O' the first fawn, flung, with those beseeching eyes,
Flat in the covert! How should she but couch,

920   Lick the dry lips, unsheathe the blunted claw,
      Catch 'twixt her placid eyewinks at what chance
      Old bloody half-forgotten dream may flit,
      Born when herself was novice to the taste,
      The while she lets youth take its pleasure. Last,
      These God-abandoned wretched lumps of life,
      These four companions, – country-folk this time,
      Not tainted by the unwholesome civic breath,
      Much less the curse o' the court! Mere striplings too,
      Fit to do human nature justice still!

930   Surely when impudence in Guido's shape
      Shall propose crime and proffer money's-worth
      To these stout tall bright-eyed and black-haired boys,
      The blood shall bound in answer to each cheek
      Before the indignant outcry break from lip!
      Are these i' the mood to murder, hardly loosed
      From healthy autumn-finish, the ploughed glebe,
      Grapes in the barrel, work at happy end,
      And winter come with rest and Christmas play?
      How greet they Guido with his final task –

940   (As if he but proposed 'One vineyard more
      To dig, ere frost come, then relax indeed!')
      'Anywhere, anyhow and anywhy,
      Murder me some three people, old and young,
      Ye never heard the names of, – and be paid
      So much!' And the whole four accede at once.
      Demur? As cattle would, bid march or halt!
      Is it some lingering habit, old fond faith
      I' the lord of the land, instructs them, – birthright-badge
      Of feudal tenure claims its slaves again?

950   Not so at all, thou noble human heart!
      All is done purely for the pay, – which, earned,
      And not forthcoming at the instant, makes
      Religion heresy, and the lord o' the land
      Fit subject for a murder in his turn.
      The patron with cut throat and rifled purse,
      Deposited i' the roadside-ditch, his due,
      Nought hinders each good fellow trudging home,

The heavier by a piece or two in poke,
And so with new zest to the common life,
960 Mattock and spade, plough-tail and waggon-shaft,
Till some such other piece of luck betide,
Who knows? Since this is a mere start in life,
And none of them exceeds the twentieth year.

Nay, more i' the background, yet? Unnoticed forms
Claim to be classed, subordinately vile?
Complacent lookers-on that laugh, – perchance
Shake head as their friend's horse-play grows too rough
With the mere child he manages amiss –
But would not interfere and make bad worse
970 For twice the fractious tears and prayers: thou know'st
Civility better, Marzi-Medici,
Governor for thy kinsman the Granduke!
Fit representative of law, man's lamp
I' the magistrate's grasp full-flare, no rushlight-end
Sputtering 'twixt thumb and finger of the priest!
Whose answer to these Comparini's cry
Is a threat, – whose remedy of Pompilia's wrong
A shrug o' the shoulder, a facetious word
Or wink, traditional with Tuscan wits,
980 To Guido in the doorway. Laud to law!
The wife is pushed back to the husband, he
Who knows how these home-squabblings persecute
People who have the public good to mind,
And work best with a silence in the court!

Ah, but I save my word at least for thee,
Archbishop, who art under me in the Church,
As I am under God, – thou, chosen by both
To do the shepherd's office, feed the sheep –
How of this lamb that panted at thy foot
990 While the wolf pressed on her within crook's reach?
Wast thou the hireling that did turn and flee?
With thee at least anon the little word!

Such denizens o' the cave now cluster round
And heat the furnace sevenfold: time indeed
A bolt from heaven should cleave roof and clear place,
Transfix and show the world, suspiring flame,
The main offender, scar and brand the rest
Hurrying, each miscreant to his hole: then flood
And purify the scene with outside day –
1000 Which yet, in the absolutest drench of dark,
Ne'er wants a witness, some stray beauty-beam
To the despair of hell.

        First of the first,
Such I pronounce Pompilia, then as now
Perfect in whiteness – stoop thou down, my child,
Give one good moment to the poor old Pope
Heart-sick at having all his world to blame –
Let me look at thee in the flesh as erst,
Let me enjoy the old clean linen garb,
1010 Not the new splendid vesture! Armed and crowned,
Would Michael, yonder, be, nor crowned nor armed,
The less pre-eminent angel? Everywhere
I see in the world the intellect of man,
That sword, the energy his subtle spear,
The knowledge which defends him like a shield –
Everywhere; but they make not up, I think,
The marvel of a soul like thine, earth's flower
She holds up to the softened gaze of God!
It was not given Pompilia to know much,
1020 Speak much, to write a book, to move mankind,
Be memorized by who records my time.
Yet if in purity and patience, if
In faith held fast despite the plucking fiend,
Safe like the signet-stone with the new name
That saints are known by, – if in right returned
For wrong, most pardon for worst injury,
If there be any virtue, any praise, –
Then will this woman-child have proved – who knows? –
Just the one prize vouchsafed unworthy me,

1030 Ten years a gardener of the untoward ground,
    I till, – this earth, my sweat and blood manure
    All the long day that barrenly grows dusk:
    At least one blossom makes me proud at eve
    Born 'mid the briers of my enclosure! Still
    (Oh, here as elsewhere, nothingness of man!)
    Those be the plants, imbedded yonder South
    To mellow in the morning, those made fat
    By the master's eye, that yield such timid leaf,
    Uncertain bud, as product of his pains!
1040 While – see how this mere chance-sown, cleft-nursed seed,
    That sprang up by the wayside 'neath the foot
    Of the enemy, this breaks all into blaze,
    Spreads itself, one wide glory of desire
    To incorporate the whole great sun it loves
    From the inch-height whence it looks and longs! My flower,
    My rose, I gather for the breast of God,
    This I praise most in thee, where all I praise,
    That having been obedient to the end
    According to the light allotted, law
1050 Prescribed thy life, still tried, still standing test, –
    Dutiful to the foolish parents first,
    Submissive next to the bad husband, – nay,
    Tolerant of those meaner miserable
    That did his hests, eked out the dole of pain, –
    Thou, patient thus, couldst rise from law to law,
    The old to the new, promoted at one cry
    O' the trump of God to the new service, not
    To longer bear, but henceforth fight, be found
    Sublime in new impatience with the foe!
1060 Endure man and obey God: plant firm foot
    On neck of man, tread man into the hell
    Meet for him, and obey God all the more!
    Oh child that didst despise thy life so much
    When it seemed only thine to keep or lose,
    How the fine ear felt fall the first low word
    'Value life, and preserve life for My sake!'
    Thou didst . . . how shall I say? . . . receive so long

The standing ordinance of God on earth,
What wonder if the novel claim had clashed
1070 With old requirement, seemed to supersede
Too much the customary law? But, brave,
Thou at first prompting of what I call God,
And fools call Nature, didst hear, comprehend,
Accept the obligation laid on thee,
Mother elect, to save the unborn child,
As brute and bird do, reptile and the fly,
Ay and, I nothing doubt, even tree, shrub, plant
And flower o' the field, all in a common pact
To worthily defend that trust of trusts,
1080 Life from the Ever Living: – didst resist –
Anticipate the office that is mine –
And with his own sword stay the upraised arm,
The endeavour of the wicked, and defend
Him who, – again in my default, – was there
For visible providence: one less true than thou
To touch, i' the past, less practised in the right,
Approved so far in all docility
To all instruction, – how had such an one
Made scruple 'Is this motion a decree?'
1090 It was authentic to the experienced ear
O' the good and faithful servant. Go past me
And get thy praise, – and be not far to seek
Presently when I follow if I may!

And surely not so very much apart
Need I place thee, my warrior-priest, – in whom
What if I gain the other rose, the gold,
We grave to imitate God's miracle,
Greet monarchs with, good rose in its degree?
Irregular noble scapegrace – son the same!
1100 Faulty – and peradventure ours the fault
Who still misteach, mislead, throw hook and line
Thinking to land leviathan forsooth,
Tame the scaled neck, play with him as a bird,
And bind him for our maidens! Better bear

The King of Pride go wantoning awhile,
Unplagued by cord in nose and thorn in jaw,
Through deep to deep, followed by all that shine,
Churning the blackness hoary: He who made
The comely terror, He shall make the sword
To match that piece of netherstone his heart,
Ay, nor miss praise thereby; who else shut fire
I' the stone, to leap from mouth at sword's first stroke,
In lamps of love and faith, the chivalry
That dares the right and disregards alike
The yea and nay o' the world? Self-sacrifice, –
What if an idol took it? Ask the Church
Why she was wont to turn each Venus here, –
Poor Rome perversely lingered round, despite
Instruction, for the sake of purblind love, –
Into Madonna's shape, and waste no whit
Of aught so rare on earth as gratitude!
All this sweet savour was not ours but thine,
Nard of the rock, a natural wealth we name
Incense, and treasure up as food for saints,
When flung to us – whose function was to give
Not find the costly perfume. Do I smile?
Nay, Caponsacchi, much I find amiss,
Blameworthy, punishable in this freak
Of thine, this youth prolonged though age was ripe,
This masquerade in sober day, with change
Of motley too, – now hypocrite's-disguise,
Now fool's-costume: which lie was least like truth,
Which the ungainlier, more discordant garb
With that symmetric soul inside my son,
The churchman's or the worldling's, – let him judge,
Our Adversary who enjoys the task!
I rather chronicle the healthy rage, –
When the first moan broke from the martyr-maid
At that uncaging of the beasts, – made bare
My athlete on the instant, gave such good
Great undisguised leap over post and pale
Right into the mid-cirque, free fighting-place.

There may have been rash stripping – every rag
Went to the winds, – infringement manifold
Of laws prescribed pudicity, I fear,
In this impulsive and prompt self-display!
Ever such tax comes of the foolish youth;
Men mulct the wiser manhood, and suspect
No veritable star swims out of cloud:
1150 Bear thou such imputation, undergo
The penalty I nowise dare relax, –
Conventional chastisement and rebuke.
But for the outcome, the brave starry birth
Conciliating earth with all that cloud,
Thank heaven as I do! Ay, such championship
Of God at first blush, such prompt cheery thud
Of glove on ground that answers ringingly
The challenge of the false knight, – watch we long,
And wait we vainly for its gallant like
1160 From those appointed to the service, sworn
His body-guard with pay and privilege –
White-cinct, because in white walks sanctity,
Red-socked, how else proclaim fine scorn of flesh,
Unchariness of blood when blood faith begs?
Where are the men-at-arms with cross on coat?
Aloof, bewraying their attire: whilst thou
In mask and motley, pledged to dance not fight,
Sprang'st forth the hero! In thought, word and deed,
How throughout all thy warfare thou wast pure,
1170 I find it easy to believe: and if
At any fateful moment of the strange
Adventure, the strong passion of that strait,
Fear and surprise, may have revealed too much, –
As when a thundrous midnight, with black air
That burns, rain-drops that blister, breaks a spell,
Draws out the excessive virtue of some sheathed
Shut unsuspected flower that hoards and hides
Immensity of sweetness, – so, perchance,
Might the surprise and fear release too much
1180 The perfect beauty of the body and soul

Thou savedst in thy passion for God's sake,
He who is Pity: was the trial sore?
Temptation sharp? Thank God a second time!
Why comes temptation but for man to meet
And master and make crouch beneath his foot,
And so be pedestalled in triumph? Pray
'Lead us into no such temptations, Lord!'
Yea, but, O Thou whose servants are the bold,
Lead such temptations by the head and hair,
1190 Reluctant dragons, up to who dares fight,
That so he may do battle and have praise!
Do I not see the praise? — that while thy mates
Bound to deserve i' the matter, prove at need
Unprofitable through the very pains
We gave to train them well and start them fair, —
Are found too stiff, with standing ranked and ranged,
For onset in good earnest, too obtuse
Of ear, through iteration of command,
For catching quick the sense of the real cry, —
1200 Thou, whose sword-hand was used to strike the lute,
Whose sentry-station graced some wanton's gate,
Thou didst push forward and show mettle, shame
The laggards, and retrieve the day. Well done!
Be glad thou hast let light into the world,
Through that irregular breach o' the boundary, — see
The same upon thy path and march assured,
Learning anew the use of soldiership,
Self-abnegation, freedom from all fear,
Loyalty to the life's end! Ruminate,
1210 Deserve the initiatory spasm, — once more
Work, be unhappy but bear life, my son!

And troop you, somewhere 'twixt the best and worst,
Where crowd the indifferent product, all too poor
Makeshift, starved samples of humanity!
Father and mother, huddle there and hide!
A gracious eye may find you! Foul and fair,
Sadly mixed natures: self-indulgent, — yet

Self-sacrificing too: how the love soars,
How the craft, avarice, vanity and spite
1220 Sink again! So they keep the middle course,
Slide into silly crime at unaware,
Slip back upon the stupid virtue, stay
Nowhere enough for being classed, I hope
And fear. Accept the swift and rueful death,
Taught, somewhat sternlier than is wont, what waits
The ambiguous creature, – how the one black tuft
Steadies the aim of the arrow just as well
As the wide faultless white on the bird's breast.
Nay, you were punished in the very part
1230 That looked most pure of speck, – the honest love
Betrayed you, – did love seem most worthy pains,
Challenge such purging, as ordained survive
When all the rest of you was done with? Go!
Never again elude the choice of tints!
White shall not neutralise the black, nor good
Compensate bad in man, absolve him so:
Life's business being just the terrible choice.

So do I see, pronounce on all and some
Grouped for my judgment now, – profess no doubt
1240 While I pronounce: dark, difficult enough
The human sphere, yet eyes grow sharp by use,
I find the truth, dispart the shine from shade,
As a mere man may, with no special touch
O' the lynx-gift in each ordinary orb:
Nay, if the popular notion class me right,
One of well nigh decayed intelligence, –
What of that? Through hard labour and good will,
And habitude that gives a blind man sight
At the practised finger-ends of him, I do
1250 Discern, and dare decree in consequence,
Whatever prove the peril of mistake.
Whence, then, this quite new quick cold thrill, – cloud-like,
This keen dread creeping from a quarter scarce
Suspected in the skies I nightly scan?

What slacks the tense nerve, saps the wound-up spring
Of the act that should and shall be, sends the mount
And mass o' the whole man's-strength, – conglobed so late –
Shudderingly into dust, a moment's work?
While I stand firm, go fearless, in this world,
1260 For this life recognise and arbitrate,
Touch and let stay, or else remove a thing,
Judge "This is right, this object out of place,"
Candle in hand that helps me and to spare, –
What if a voice deride me, 'Perk and pry!
Brighten each nook with thine intelligence!
Play the good householder, ply man and maid
With tasks prolonged into the midnight, test
Their work and nowise stint of the due wage
Each worthy worker: but with gyves and whip
1270 Pay thou misprision of a single point
Plain to thy happy self who lift'st the light,
Lament'st the darkling, – bold to all beneath!
What if thyself adventure, now the place
Is purged so well? Leave pavement and mount roof,
Look round thee for the light of the upper sky,
The fire which lit thy fire which finds default
In Guido Franceschini to his cost!
What if, above in the domain of light,
Thou miss the accustomed signs, remark eclipse?
1280 Shalt thou still gaze on ground nor lift a lid, –
Steady in thy superb prerogative,
Thy inch of inkling, – nor once face the doubt
I' the sphere above thee, darkness to be felt?'

Yet my poor spark had for its source, the sun;
Thither I sent the great looks which compel
Light from its fount: all that I do and am
Comes from the truth, or seen or else surmised,
Remembered or divined, as mere man may:
I know just so, nor otherwise. As I know,
1290 I speak, – what should I know, then, and how speak
Were there a wild mistake of eye or brain

In the recorded governance above?
If my own breath, only, blew coal alight
I called celestial and the morning-star?
I, who in this world act resolvedly,
Dispose of men, the body and the soul,
As they acknowledge or gainsay this light
I show them, – shall I too lack courage? – leave
I, too, the post of me, like those I blame?
1300 Refuse, with kindred inconsistency,
Grapple with danger whereby souls grow strong?
I am near the end; but still not at the end;
All till the very end is trial in life:
At this stage is the trial of my soul
Danger to face, or danger to refuse?
Shall I dare try the doubt now, or not dare?

O Thou, – as represented here to me
In such conception as my soul allows, –
Under Thy measureless my atom width! –
1310 Man's mind – what is it but a convex glass
Wherein are gathered all the scattered points
Picked out of the immensity of sky,
To reunite there, be our heaven on earth,
Our known unknown, our God revealed to man?
Existent somewhere, somehow, as a whole;
Here, as a whole proportioned to our sense, –
There, (which is nowhere, speech must babble thus!)
In the absolute immensity, the whole
Appreciable solely by Thyself, –
1320 Here, by the little mind of man, reduced
To littleness that suits his faculty,
Appreciable too in the degree;
Between Thee and ourselves – nay even, again,
Below us, to the extreme of the minute,
Appreciable by how many and what diverse
Modes of the life Thou makest be! (why live
Except for love, – how love unless they know?)
Each of them, only filling to the edge,

Insect or angel, his just length and breadth,
1330 Due facet of reflection, – full, no less,
Angel or insect, as Thou framedst things, –
I it is who have been appointed here
To represent Thee, in my turn, on earth,
Just as, if new philosophy know aught,
This one earth, out of all the multitude
Of peopled worlds, as stars are now supposed, –
Was chosen, and no sun-star of the swarm,
For stage and scene of Thy transcendent act
Beside which even the creation fades
1340 Into a puny exercise of power.
Choice of the world, choice of the thing I am,
Both emanate alike from the dread play
Of operation outside this our sphere
Where things are classed and counted small or great, –
Incomprehensibly the choice is Thine!
I therefore bow my head and take Thy place.
There is, beside the works, a tale of Thee
In the world's mouth which I find credible:
I love it with my heart: unsatisfied,
1350 I try it with my reason, nor discept
From any point I probe and pronounce sound.
Mind is not matter nor from matter, but
Above, – leave matter then, proceed with mind:
Man's be the mind recognized at the height, –
Leave the inferior minds and look at man.
Is he the strong, intelligent and good
Up to his own conceivable height? Nowise.
Enough o' the low, – soar the conceivable height,
Find cause to match the effect in evidence,
1360 Works in the world, not man's, then God's; leave man:
Conjecture of the worker by the work:
Is there strength there? – enough: intelligence?
Ample: but goodness in a like degree?
Not to the human eye in the present state,
This isoscele deficient in the base.
What lacks, then, of perfection fit for God

But just the instance which this tale supplies
Of love without a limit? So is strength,
So is intelligence; then love is so,
1370 Unlimited in its self-sacrifice:
Then is the tale true and God shows complete.
Beyond the tale, I reach into the dark,
Feel what I cannot see, and still faith stands:
I can believe this dread machinery
Of sin and sorrow, would confound me else,
Devised, – all pain, at most expenditure
Of pain by Who devised pain, – to evolve,
By new machinery in counterpart,
The moral qualities of man – how else? –
1380 To make him love in turn and be beloved,
Creative and self-sacrificing too,
And thus eventually God-like, (ay,
'I have said ye are Gods,' – shall it be said for nought?)
Enable man to wring, from out all pain,
All pleasure for a common heritage
To all eternity: this may be surmised,
The other is revealed, – whether a fact,
Absolute, abstract, independent truth,
Historic, not reduced to suit man's mind, –
1390 Or only truth reverberate, changed, made pass
A spectrum into mind, the narrow eye, –
The same and not the same, else unconceived –
Though quite conceivable to the next grade
Above it in intelligence, – as truth
Easy to man were blindness to the beast
By parity of procedure, – the same truth
In a new form, but changed in either case:
What matter so the intelligence be filled?
To the child, the sea is angry, for it roars;
1400 Frost bites, else why the tooth-like fret on face?
Man makes acoustics deal with the sea's wrath,
Explains the choppy cheek by chymic law, –
To both, remains one and the same effect
On drum of ear and root of nose, change cause

Never so thoroughly: so our heart be struck,
What care I, – by God's gloved hand or the bare?
Nor do I much perplex me with aught hard,
Dubious in the transmitting of the tale, –
No, nor with certain riddles set to solve.
1410 This life is training and a passage; pass, –
Still, we march over some flat obstacle
We made give way before us; solid truth
In front of it, were motion for the world?
The moral sense grows but by exercise.
'T is even as man grew probatively
Initiated in Godship, set to make
A fairer moral world than this he finds,
Guess now what shall be known hereafter. Thus,
O' the present problem: as we see and speak,
1420 A faultless creature is destroyed, and sin
Has had its way i' the world where God should rule.
Ay, but for this irrelevant circumstance
Of inquisition after blood, we see
Pompilia lost and Guido saved: how long?
For his whole life: how much is that whole life?
We are not babes, but know the minute's worth,
And feel that life is large and the world small,
So, wait till life have passed from out the world.

Neither does this astonish at the end,
1430 That, whereas I can so receive and trust,
Men, made with hearts and souls the same as mine,
Reject and disbelieve, – subordinate
The future to the present, – sin, nor fear.
This I refer still to the foremost fact,
Life is probation and this earth no goal
But starting-point of man: compel him strive,
Which means, in man, as good as reach the goal, –
Why institute that race, his life, at all?
But this does overwhelm me with surprise,
1440 Touch me to terror, – not that faith, the pearl,
Should be let lie by fishers wanting food, –

Nor, seen and handled by a certain few
Critical and contemptuous, straight consigned
To shore and shingle for the pebble it proves, –
But that, when haply found and known and named
By the residue made rich for evermore,
These, – ay, these favoured ones, should in a trice
Turn, and with double zest go dredge for whelks,
Mud-worms that make the savoury soup. Enough
1450 O' the disbelievers, see the faithful few!
How do the Christians here deport them, keep
Their robes of white unspotted by the world?
What is this Aretine Archbishop, this
Man under me as I am under God,
This champion of the faith, I armed and decked,
Pushed forward, put upon a pinnacle,
To show the enemy his victor, – see!
What's the best fighting when the couple close?
Pompilia cries, 'Protect me from the fiend!'
1460 'No, for thy Guido is one heady, strong,
Dangerous to disquiet: let him bide!
He needs some bone to mumble, help amuse
The darkness of his den with: so, the fawn
Which limps up bleeding to my foot and lies,
– Come to me, daughter, – thus I throw him back!'
Have we misjudged here, over-armed the knight,
Given gold and silk where the plain steel serves best,
Enfeebled whom we sought to fortify,
Made an archbishop and undone a saint?
1470 Well then, descend these heights, this pride of life,
Sit in the ashes with the barefoot monk
Who long ago stamped out the worldly sparks.
Fasting and watching, stone cell and wire scourge,
– No such indulgence as unknits the strength –
These breed the tight nerve and tough cuticle,
Let the world's praise or blame run rillet-wise
Off the broad back and brawny breast, we know!
He meets the first cold sprinkle of the world
And shudders to the marrow, 'Save this child?

1480 Oh, my superiors, oh, the Archbishop here!
Who was it dared lay hand upon the ark
His betters saw fall nor put finger forth?
Great ones could help yet help not: why should small?
I break my promise: let her break her heart!'
These are the Christians not the worldlings, not
The sceptics, who thus battle for the faith!
If foolish virgins disobey and sleep,
What wonder? But the wise that watch, this time
Sell lamps and buy lutes, exchange oil for wine,
1490 The mystic Spouse betrays the Bridegroom here.
To our last resource, then! Since all flesh is weak,
Bind weaknesses together, we get strength:
The individual weighed, found wanting, try
Some institution, honest artifice
Whereby the units grow compact and firm:
Each props the other, and so stand is made
By our embodied cowards that grow brave.
The Monastery called of Convertites,
Meant to help women because these helped Christ, –
1500 A thing existent only while it acts,
Does as designed, else a nonentity,
For what is an idea unrealized? –
Pompilia is consigned to these for help.
They do help[, –] they are prompt to testify
To her pure life and saintly dying days.
She dies, and lo, who seemed so poor, proves rich[.]
What does the body that lives through helpfulness
To women for Christ's sake? The kiss turns bite,
The dove's note changes to the crow's cry: judge!
1510 'Seeing that this our Convent claims of right
What goods belong to those we succour, be
The same proved women of dishonest life, –
And seeing that this Trial made appear
Pompilia was in such predicament, –
The Convent hereupon pretends to said
Succession of Pompilia, issues writ,
And takes possession by the Fisc's advice.'

Such is their attestation to the cause
Of Christ, who had one saint at least, they hoped:
1520 But, is a title-deed to filch, a corpse
To slander, and an infant-heir to cheat?
Christ must give up his gains then! They unsay
All the fine speeches, – who was saint is whore.
Why, scripture yields no parallel for this!
The soldiers only threw dice for Christ's coat;
We want another legend of the Twelve
Disputing if it was Christ's coat at all,
Claiming as prize the woof of price – for why?
The Master was a thief, purloined the same,
1530 Or paid for it out of the common bag!
Can it be this is end and outcome, all
I take with me to show as stewardship's fruit,
The best yield of the latest time, this year
The seventeen-hundredth since God died for man?
Is such effect proportionate to cause?
And still the terror keeps on the increase
When I perceive . . . how can I blink the fact?
That the fault, the obduracy to good,
Lies not with the impracticable stuff
1540 Whence man is made, his very nature's fault,
As if it were of ice, the moon may gild
Not melt, or stone, 't was meant the sun should warm
Not make bear flowers, – nor ice nor stone to blame:
But it can melt, that ice, and bloom, that stone,
Impassible to rule of day and night!
This terrifies me, thus compelled perceive,
Whatever love and faith we looked should spring
At advent of the authoritative star,
Which yet lie sluggish, curdled at the source, –
1550 These have leapt forth profusely in old time,
These still respond with promptitude to-day,
At challenge of – what unacknowledged powers
O' the air, what uncommissioned meteors, warmth
By law, and light by rule should supersede?
For see this priest, this Caponsacchi, stung

At the first summons, – 'Help for honour's sake,
Play the man, pity the oppressed!' – no pause,
How does he lay about him in the midst,
Strike any foe, right wrong at any risk,
1560 All blindness, bravery and obedience! – blind?
Ay, as a man would be inside the sun,
Delirious with the plenitude of light
Should interfuse him to the finger-ends –
Let him rush straight, and how shall he go wrong?
Where are the Christians in their panoply?
The loins we girt about with truth, the breasts
Righteousness plated round, the shield of faith,
The helmet of salvation, and that sword
O' the Spirit, even the word of God, – where these?
1570 Slunk into corners! Oh, I hear at once
Hubbub of protestation! 'What, we monks
We friars, of such an order, such a rule,
Have not we fought, bled, left our martyr-mark
At every point along the boundary-line
'Twixt true and false, religion and the world,
Where this or the other dogma of our Church
Called for defence?' And I, despite myself,
How can I but speak loud what truth speaks low,
'Or better than the best, or nothing serves!
1580 What boots deed, I can cap and cover straight
With such another doughtiness to match,
Done at an instinct of the natural man?'
Immolate body, sacrifice soul too, –
Do not these publicans the same? Outstrip!
Or else stop race, you boast runs neck and neck,
You with the wings, they with the feet, – for shame!
Oh, I remark your diligence and zeal!
Five years long, now, rounds faith into my ears,
'Help thou, or Christendom is done to death!'
1590 Five years since, in the Province of To-kien,
Which is in China as some people know,
Maigrot, my Vicar Apostolic there,
Having a great qualm, issues a decree.

Alack, the converts use as God's name, not
Tien-chu but plain *Tien* or else mere *Shang-ti*,
As Jesuits please to fancy politic,
While, say Dominicans, it calls down fire, –
For *Tien* means heaven, and *Shang-ti*, supreme prince,
While *Tien-chu* means the lord of heaven: all cry,
1600 'There is no business urgent for despatch
As that thou send a legate, specially
Cardinal Tournon, straight to Pekin, there
To settle and compose the difference!'
So have I seen a potentate all fume
For some infringement of his realm's just right,
Some menace to a mud-built straw-thatched farm
O' the frontier, while inside the mainland lie,
Quite undisputed-for in solitude,
Whole cities plague may waste or famine sap:
1610 What if the sun crumble, the sands encroach,
While he looks on sublimely at his ease?
How does their ruin touch the empire's bound?

And is this little all that was to be?
Where is the gloriously-decisive change,
The immeasurable metamorphosis
Of human clay to divine gold, we looked
Should, in some poor sort, justify the price?
Had a mere adept of the Rosy Cross
Spent his life to consummate the Great Work,
1620 Would not we start to see the stuff it touched
Yield not a grain more than the vulgar got
By the old smelting-process years ago?
If this were sad to see in just the sage
Who should profess so much, perform no more,
What is it then suspected in that Power
Who undertook to make and made the world,
Devised and did effect man, body and soul,
Ordained salvation for them both, and yet . . .
Well, is the thing we see, salvation?

1630
I

Put no such dreadful question to myself,
Within whose circle of experience burns
The central truth, Power, Wisdom, Goodness, – God:
I must outlive a thing ere know it dead:
When I outlive the faith there is a sun,
When I lie, ashes to the very soul, –
Someone, not I, must wail above the heap,
'He died in dark whence never morn arose.'
While I see day succeed the deepest night –
1640 How can I speak but as I know? – my speech
Must be, throughout the darkness, 'It will end:'
'The light that did burn, will burn!' Clouds obscure –
But for which obscuration all were bright?
Too hastily concluded! Sun-suffused,
A cloud may soothe the eye made blind by blaze, –
Better the very clarity of heaven:
The soft streaks are the beautiful and dear.
What but the weakness in a faith supplies
The incentive to humanity, no strength
1650 Absolute, irresistible, comports?
How can man love but what he yearns to help?
And that which men think weakness within strength,
But angels know for strength and stronger yet –
What were it else but the first things made new,
But repetition of the miracle,
The divine instance of self-sacrifice
That never ends and aye begins for man?
So, never I miss footing in the maze,
No, – I have light nor fear the dark at all.

1660 But are mankind not real, who pace outside
My petty circle, the world measured me?
And when they stumble even as I stand,
Have I a right to stop ears when they cry,
As they were phantoms, took the clouds for crags,
Tripped and fell, where the march of man might move?
Beside, the cry is other than a ghost's,

When out of the old time there pleads some bard,
Philosopher, or both and – whispers not,
But words it boldly. 'The inward work and worth
1670 Of any mind, what other mind may judge
Save God who only knows the thing He made,
The veritable service He exacts?
It is the outward product men appraise.
Behold, an engine hoists a tower aloft:
"I looked that it should move the mountain too!"
Or else "Had just a turret toppled down,
Success enough!" – may say the Machinist
Who knows what less or more result might be:
But we, who see that done we cannot do,
1680 "A feat beyond man's force," we men must say.
Regard me and that shake I gave the world!
I was born, not so long before Christ's birth,
As Christ's birth haply did precede thy day, –
But many a watch, before the star of dawn:
Therefore I lived, – it is thy creed affirms,
Pope Innocent, who art to answer me! –
Under conditions, nowise to escape,
Whereby salvation was impossible.
Each impulse to achieve the good and fair,
1690 Each aspiration to the pure and true,
Being without a warrant or an aim,
Was just as sterile a felicity
As if the insect, born to spend his life
Soaring his circles, stopped them to describe
(Painfully motionless in the mid-air)
Some word of weighty counsel for man's sake,
Some "Know thyself" or "Take the golden mean!"
– Forwent his happy dance and the glad ray,
Died half an hour the sooner and was dust.
1700 I, born to perish like the brutes, or worse,
Why not live brutishly, obey my law?
But I, of body as of soul complete,
A gymnast at the games, philosopher
I' the schools, who painted, and made music, – all

Glories that met upon the tragic stage
When the Third Poet's tread surprised the Two, —
Whose lot fell in a land where life was great
And sense went free and beauty lay profuse,
I, untouched by one adverse circumstance,
1710 Adopted virtue as my rule of life,
Waived all reward, and loved for loving's sake,
And, what my heart taught me, I taught the world,
And have been teaching now two thousand years.
Witness my work, — plays that should please, forsooth!
"They might please, they may displease, they shall teach,
For truth's sake," so I said, and did, and do.
Five hundred years ere Paul spoke, Felix heard, —
How much of temperance and righteousness,
Judgment to come, did I find reason for,
1720 Corroborate with my strong style that spared
No sin, nor swerved the more from branding brow
Because the sinner was called Zeus and God?
How nearly did I guess at that Paul knew?
How closely come, in what I represent
As duty, to his doctrine yet a blank?
And as that limner not untruly limns
Who draws an object round or square, which square
Or round seems to the unassisted eye,
Though Galileo's tube display the same
1730 Oval or oblong, — so, who controverts
I rendered rightly what proves wrongly wrought
Beside Paul's picture? Mine was true for me.
I saw that there are, first and above all,
The hidden forces, blind necessities,
Named Nature, but the thing's self unconceived:
Then follow, — how dependent upon these,
We know not, how imposed above ourselves,
We well know, — what I name the gods, a power
Various or one; for great and strong and good
1740 Is there, and little, weak and bad there too,
Wisdom and folly: say, these make no God, —
What is it else that rules outside man's self?

A fact then, – always, to the naked eye, –
And, so, the one revealment possible
Of what were unimagined else by man.
Therefore, what gods do, man may criticise,
Applaud, condemn, – how should he fear the truth?
But likewise have in awe because of power,
Venerate for the main munificence,
1750 And give the doubtful deed its due excuse
From the acknowledged creature of a day
To the Eternal and Divine. Thus, bold
Yet self-mistrusting, should man bear himself,
Most assured on what now concerns him most –
The law of his own life, the path he prints, –
Which law is virtue and not vice, I say, –
And least inquisitive where least search skills,
I' the nature we best give the clouds to keep.
What could I paint beyond a scheme like this
1760 Out of the fragmentary truths where light
Lay fitful in a tenebrific time?
You have the sunrise now, joins truth to truth,
Shoots life and substance into death and void;
Themselves compose the whole we made before:
The forces and necessity grow God, –
The beings so contrarious that seemed gods,
Prove just His operation manifold
And multiform, translated, as must be,
Into intelligible shape so far
1770 As suits our sense and sets us free to feel:
What if I let a child think, childhood-long,
That lightning, I would have him spare his eye,
Is a real arrow shot at naked orb?
The man knows more, but shuts his lids the same:
Lightning's cause comprehends nor man nor child.
Why then, my scheme, your better knowledge broke,
Presently readjusts itself, the small
Proportioned largelier, parts and whole named new:
So much, no more two thousand years have done!
1780 Pope, dost thou dare pretend to punish me,

For not descrying sunshine at midnight,
Me who crept all-fours, found my way so far –
While thou rewardest teachers of the truth,
Who miss the plain way in the blaze of noon, –
Though just a word from that strong style of mine,
Grasped honestly in hand as guiding-staff,
Had pricked them a sure path across the bog,
That mire of cowardice and slush of lies
Wherein I find them wallow in wide day?'

1790 How should I answer this Euripides?
Paul, – 't is a legend, – answered Seneca,
But that was in the day-spring; noon is now
We have got too familiar with the light.
Shall I wish back once more that thrill of dawn?
When the whole truth-touched man burned up, one fire?
– Assured the trial, fiery, fierce, but fleet,
Would, from his little heap of ashes, lend
Wings to the conflagration of the world
Which Christ awaits ere He make all things new –
1800 So should the frail become the perfect, rapt
From glory of pain to glory of joy; and so,
Even in the end, – the act renouncing earth,
Lands, houses, husbands, wives and children here, –
Begin that other act which finds all, lost,
Regained, in this time even, a hundredfold,
And, in the next time, feels the finite love
Blent and embalmed with its eternal life.
So does the sun ghastlily seem to sink
In those north parts, lean all but out of life,
1810 Desist a dread mere breathing-stop, then slow
Reassert day, begin the endless rise.
Was this too easy for our after-stage?
Was such a lighting-up of faith, in life,
Only allowed initiate, set man's step
In the true way by help of the great glow?
A way wherein it is ordained he walk,
Bearing to see the light from heaven still more

And more encroached on by the light of earth,
Tentatives earth puts forth to rival heaven,
1820 Earthly incitements that mankind serve God
For man's sole sake, not God's and therefore man's,
Till at last, who distinguishes the sun
From a mere Druid fire on a far mount?
More praise to him who with his subtle prism
Shall decompose both beams and name the true.
In such sense, who is last proves first indeed;
For how could saints and martyrs fail see truth
Streak the night's blackness? Who is faithful now,
Untwists heaven's pure white from the yellow flare
1830 O' the world's gross torch, without a foil to help
Produce the Christian act, so possible
When in the way stood Nero's cross and stake, –
So hard now that the world smiles 'Rightly done!
It is the politic, the thrifty way,
Will clearly make you in the end returns
Beyond our fool's-sport and improvidence:
We fools go thro' the cornfield of this life,
Pluck ears to left and right and swallow raw,
– Nay, tread, at pleasure, a sheaf underfoot,
1840 To get the better at some poppy-flower, –
Well aware we shall have so much wheat less
In the eventual harvest: you meantime
Waste not a spike, – the richlier will you reap!
What then? There will be always garnered meal
Sufficient for our comfortable loaf,
While you enjoy the undiminished prize!'
Is it not this ignoble confidence,
Cowardly hardihood, that dulls and damps,
Makes the old heroism impossible?

1850 Unless . . . what whispers me of times to come?
What if it be the mission of that age,
My death will usher into life, to shake
This torpor of assurance from our creed,
Re-introduce the doubt discarded, bring

The formidable danger back, we drove
Long ago to the distance and the dark?
No wild beast now prowls round the infant camp;
We have built wall and sleep in city safe:
But if the earthquake try the towers, that laugh
1860 To think they once saw lions rule outside,
Till man stand out again, pale, resolute,
Prepared to die, – that is, alive at last?
As we broke up that old faith of the world,
Have we, next age, to break up this the new –
Faith, in the thing, grown faith in the report –
Whence need to bravely disbelieve report
Through increased faith in thing reports belie?
Must we deny, – do they, these Molinists,
At peril of their body and their soul, –
1870 Recognized truths, obedient to some truth
Unrecognized yet, but perceptible? –
Correct the portrait by the living face,
Man's God, by God's God in the mind of man?
Then, for the few that rise to the new height,
The many that must sink to the old depth,
The multitude found fall away! A few,
E'en ere the new law speak clear, keep the old,
Preserve the Christian level, call good good
And evil evil, (even though razed and blank
1880 The old titles stand,) thro' custom, habitude,
And all they may mistake for finer sense
O' the fact than reason warrants, – as before,
They hope perhaps, fear not impossibly.
Surely some one Pompilia in the world
Will say 'I know the right place by foot's feel,
I took it and tread firm there; wherefore change?'
But what a multitude will fall, perchance,
Quite through the crumbling truth subjacent late,
Sink to the next discoverable base,
1890 Rest upon human nature, take their stand
On what is fact, the lust and pride of life!
The mass of men, whose very souls even now

Seem to need re-creating, – so they slink
Worm-like into the mud light now lays bare, –
Whose future we dispose of with shut eyes
'They are baptized, – grafted, the barren twigs,
Into the living stock of Christ: may bear
One day, till when they lie death-like, not dead,' –
Those who with all the aid of Christ lie thus,
1900 How, without Christ, whither, unaided, sink?
What but to this rehearsed before my eyes?
Do not we end, the century and I?
The impatient antimasque treads close on kibe
O' the very masque's self it will mock, – on me,
Last lingering personage, the impatient mime
Pushes already, – will I block the way?
Will my slow trail of garments ne'er leave space
For pantaloon, sock, plume and castanet?
Here comes the first experimentalist
1910 In the new order of things, – he plays a priest;
Does he take inspiration from the Church,
Directly make her rule his law of life?
Not he: his own mere impulse guides the man –
Happily sometimes, since ourselves admit
He has danced, in gaiety of heart, i' the main
The right step in the maze we bade him foot.
What if his heart had prompted to break loose
And mar the measure? Why, we must submit
And thank the chance that brought him safely through.
1920 Will he repeat the prodigy? Perhaps.
Can he teach others how to quit themselves,
Prove why this step was right, while that were wrong?
How should he? 'Ask your hearts as I asked mine,
And get discreetly through the morrice so;
If your hearts misdirect you, – quit the stage,
And make amends, – be there amends to make.'
Such is, for the Augustine that was once,
This Canon Caponsacchi we see now.
'And my heart answers to another tune,'
1930 Puts in the Abate, second in the suite,

'I have my taste too, and tread no such step!
You choose the glorious life, and may, for me,
Who like the lowest of life's appetites, –
What you judge, – but the very truth of joy
To my own apprehension which must judge.
Call me knave and you get yourself called fool!
I live for greed, ambition, lust, revenge;
Attain these ends by force, guile: hypocrite,
To-day, perchance to-morrow recognized
1940 The rational man, the type of common sense.'
There's Loyola adapted to our time!
Under such guidance Guido plays his part,
He also influencing in due turn
These last clods where I track intelligence
By any glimmer, those four at his beck
Ready to murder any, and, at their own,
As ready to murder him, – these are the world!
And, first effect of the new cause of things,
There they lie also duly, – the old pair
1950 Of the weak head and not so wicked heart,
And the one Christian mother, wife and girl,
– Which three gifts seem to make an angel up, –
The first foot of the dance is on their heads!

Still, I stand here, not off the stage though close
On the exit: and my last act, as my first,
I owe the scene, and Him who armed me thus
With Paul's sword as with Peter's key. I smite
With my whole strength once more, then end my part,
Ending, so far as man may, this offence.
1960 And when I raise my arm, what plucks my sleeve?
Who stops me in the righteous function, – foe
Or friend? O, still as ever, friends are they
Who, in the interest of outraged truth
Deprecate such rough handling of a lie!
The facts being proved and incontestable,
What is the last word I must listen to?
Is it 'Spare yet a term this barren stock,

We pray thee dig about and dung and dress
Till he repent and bring fórth fruit even yet?'
1970 Is it 'So poor and swift a punishment
Shall throw him out of life with all that sin?
Let mercy rather pile up pain on pain
Till the flesh expiate what the soul pays else?'
Nowise! Remonstrance on all sides begins
Instruct me, there 's a new tribunal now
Higher than God's, – the educated man's!
Nice sense of honour in the human breast
Supersedes here the old coarse oracle –
Confirming handsomely a point or so
1980 Wherein the predecessor worked aright
By rule of thumb: as when Christ said, – when, where?
Enough, I find it in a pleading here, –
'All other wrongs done, patiently I take:
But touch my honour and the case is changed!
I feel the due resentment, – *nemini*
Honorem trado, is my quick retort.'
Right of Him, just as if pronounced to-day!
Still, should the old authority be mute,
Or doubtful, or in speaking clash with new,
1990 The younger takes permission to decide.
At last we have the instinct of the world
Ruling its household without tutelage,
And while the two laws, human and divine,
Have busied finger with this tangled case,
In the brisk junior pushes, cuts the knot,
Pronounces for acquittal. How it trips
Silverly o'er the tongue! 'Remit the death!
Forgive, . . . well, in the old way, if thou please,
Decency and the relics of routine
2000 Respected, – let the Count go free as air!
Since he may plead a priest's immunity, –
The minor orders help enough for that,
With Farinacci's licence, – who decides
That the mere implication of such man,
So privileged, in any cause, before

Whatever court except the Spiritual,
Straight quashes the procedure, – quash it, then!
It proves a pretty loophole of escape
Moreover, that, beside the patent fact
2010 O' the law's allowance, there's involved the weal
O' the Popedom: a son's privilege at stake,
Thou wilt pretend the Church's interest,
Ignore all finer reasons to forgive!
But herein lies the proper cogency –
(Let thy friends teach thee while thou tellest beads)
That in this case the spirit of culture speaks,
Civilization is imperative.
To her shall we remand all delicate points
Henceforth, nor take irregular advice
2020 O' the sly, as heretofore: she used to hint
Apologies when law was out of sorts
Because a saucy tongue was put to rest,
An eye that roved was cured of arrogance:
But why be forced to mumble under breath
What soon shall be acknowledged the plain fact,
Outspoken, say, in thy successor's time?
Methinks we see the golden age return!
Civilization and the Emperor
Succeed thy Christianity and Pope.
2030 One Emperor then, as one Pope now: meanwhile,
She anticipates a little to tell thee "Take
Count Guido's life, and sap society,
Whereof the main prop was, is, and shall prove
– Supremacy of husband over wife!"
Shall the man rule i' the house, or may his mate
Because of any plea dispute the same?
Oh, pleas of all sorts shall abound, be sure,
If once allowed validity, – for, harsh
And savage, for, inept and silly-sooth,
2040 For, this and that, will the ingenious sex
Demonstrate the best master e'er graced slave:
And there 's but one short way to end the coil, –
By giving right and reason steadily

To the man and master: then the wife submits.
There it is broadly stated, – nor the time
Admits we shift – a pillar? nay, a stake
Out of its place i' the tenement, one touch
Whereto may send a shudder through the heap
And bring it toppling on our heads perchance.
2050 Moreover, if this breed a qualm in thee,
Give thine own feelings play for once, – deal death?
Thou, whose own life winks o'er the socket-edge,
Would'st thou it went out in such ugly snuff
As dooming sons to death, though justice bade?
Why, on a certain feast, Barabbas' self
Was set free not to cloud the general cheer.
Neither shalt thou pollute thy Sabbath close!
Mercy is safe and graceful. How one hears
The howl begin, scarce the three little taps
2060 O' the silver mallet ended on thy brow, –
"His last act was to sacrifice a Count
And thereby screen a scandal of the Church!
Guido condemned, the Canon justified
Of course, – delinquents of his cloth go free!"
And so the Luthers and the Calvins come,
So thy hand helps Molinos to the chair
Whence he may hold forth till doom's day on just
These *petit-maître* priestlings, – in the choir,
Sanctus et Benedictus, with a brush
2070 Of soft guitar-strings that obey the thumb,
Touched by the bedside, for accompaniment!
Does this give umbrage to a husband? Death
To the fool, and to the priest impunity!
But no impunity to any friend
So simply over-loyal as these four
Who made religion of their patron's cause,
Believed in him and did his bidding straight,
Asked not one question but laid down the lives
This Pope took, – all four lives together made
2080 Just his own length of days, – so, dead they lie,
As these were times when loyalty's a drug,

And zeal in a subordinate too cheap
And common to be saved when we spend life!
Come, 't is too much good breath we waste in words:
The pardon, Holy Father! Spare grimace,
Shrugs and reluctance! Are not we the world,
Bid thee, our Priam, let soft culture plead
Hecuba-like, "*non tali*" (Virgil serves)
"*Auxilio*," and the rest! Enough, it works!
2090 The Pope relaxes, and the Prince is loth,
The father's bowels yearn, the man's will bends,
Reply is apt. Our tears on tremble, hearts
Big with a benediction, wait the word
Shall circulate thro' the city in a trice,
Set every window flaring, give each man
O' the mob his torch to wave for gratitude.
Pronounce it, for our breath and patience fail!'

I will, Sirs: for a voice other than yours
Quickens my spirit. ' *Quis pro Domino?*
2100 Who is upon the Lord's side?' asked the Count.
I, who write —
              'On receipt of this command,
Acquaint Count Guido and his fellows four
They die to-morrow: could it be to-night,
The better, but the work to do, takes time.
Set with all diligence a scaffold up,
Not in the customary place, by Bridge
Saint Angelo, where die the common sort;
But since the man is noble, and his peers
2110 By predilection haunt the People's Square,
There let him be beheaded in the midst,
And his companions hanged on either side:
So shall the quality see, fear and learn.
All which work takes time: till to-morrow, then,
Let there be prayer incessant for the five!'

For the main criminal I have no hope
Except in such a suddenness of fate.

I stood at Naples once, a night so dark
I could have scarce conjectured there was earth
2120 Anywhere, sky or sea or world at all:
But the night's black was burst through by a blaze –
Thunder struck blow on blow, earth groaned and bore,
Through her whole length of mountain visible:
There lay the city thick and plain with spires,
And, like a ghost disshrouded, white the sea.
So may the truth be flashed out by one blow,
And Guido see, one instant, and be saved.
Else I avert my face, nor follow him
Into that sad obscure sequestered state
2130 Where God unmakes but to remake the soul
He else made first in vain; which must not be.
Enough, for I may die this very night
And how should I dare die, this man let live?

Carry this forthwith to the Governor!

BOOK XI

Guido

You are the Cardinal Acciaiuoli, and you,
Abate Panciatichi – two good Tuscan names;
Acciaiuoli – ah, your ancestor it was,
Built the huge battlemented convent-block
Over the little forky flashing Greve
That takes the quick turn at the foot o' the hill
Just as one first sees Florence: oh those days!
'T is Ema, though, the other rivulet,
The one-arched, brown brick bridge yawns over, – yes,
Gallop and go five minutes, and you gain
The Roman Gate from where the Ema's bridged:
Kingfishers fly there: how I see the bend
O'erturreted by Certosa which he built,
That Senescal (we styled him) of your House!
I do adjure you, help me, Sirs! My blood
Comes from as far a source: ought it to end
This way, by leakage through their scaffold-planks
Into Rome's sink where her red refuse runs?
Sirs, I beseech you by blood-sympathy,
If there be any vile experiment
In the air, – if this your visit simply prove,
When all's done, just a well-intentioned trick,
That tries for truth truer than truth itself,
By startling up a man, ere break of day,
To tell him he must die at sunset, – pshaw!
That man's a Franceschini; feel his pulse,
Laugh at your folly, and let's all go sleep!
You have my last word, – innocent am I
As Innocent my Pope and murderer,
Innocent as a babe, as Mary's own,

As Mary's self, – I said, say and repeat, –
And why, then, should I die twelve hours hence? I –
Whom, not twelve hours ago, the gaoler bade
Turn to my straw-truss, settle and sleep sound
That I might wake the sooner, promptlier pay
His dues of meat-and-drink-indulgence, cross
His palm with fee of the good-hand, beside,
As gallants use who go at large again!
For why? All honest Rome approved my part;
40 Whoever owned wife, sister, daughter, – nay,
Mistress, – had any shadow of any right
That looks like right, and, all the more resolved,
Held it with tooth and nail, – these manly men
Approved! I being for Rome, Rome was for me!
Then, there's the point reserved, the subterfuge
My lawyers held by, kept for last resource,
Firm should all else, – the impossible fancy! – fail, –
And sneaking burgess-spirit win the day:
The knaves! One plea at least would hold, they laughed,
50 One grappling-iron scratch the bottom-rock
Even should the middle mud let anchor go –
And hook my cause on to the Clergy's, – plea
Which, even if law tipped off my hat and plume,
Would show my priestly tonsure, save me so, –
The Pope moreover, this old Innocent,
Being so meek and mild and merciful,
So fond o' the poor and so fatigued of earth,
So . . . fifty thousand devils in deepest hell!
Why must he cure us of our strange conceit
60 Of the angel in man's likeness, that we loved
And looked should help us at a pinch? He help?
He pardon? Here's his mind and message – death,
Thank the good Pope! Now, is he good in this,
Never mind, Christian, – no such stuff's extant, –
But will my death do credit to his reign,
Show he both lived and let live, so was good?
Cannot I live if he but like? 'The law!'
Why, just the law gives him the very chance,

The precise leave to let my life alone,
70 Which the angelic soul of him (he says)
Yearns after! Here they drop it in his palm,
My lawyers, capital o' the cursed kind, –
A life to take and hold and keep: but no!
He sighs, shakes head, refuses to shut hand,
Motions away the gift they bid him grasp,
And of the coyness comes that off I run
And down I go, he best knows whither, – mind,
He knows, and sets me rolling all the same!
Disinterested Vicar of our Lord,
80 This way he abrogates and disallows,
Nullifies and ignores, – reverts in fine
To the good and right, in detriment of me!
Talk away! Will you have the naked truth?
He's sick of his life's supper, – swallowed lies:
So, hobbling bedward, needs must ease his maw
Just where I sit o' the door-sill. Sir Abate,
Can you do nothing? Friends, we used to frisk:
What of this sudden slash in a friend's face,
This cut across our good companionship
90 That showed its front so gay when both were young?
Were not we put into a beaten path,
Bid pace the world, we nobles born and bred,
The body of friends with each his scutcheon full
Of old achievement and impunity, –
Taking the laugh of morn and Sol's salute
As forth we fared, pricked on to breathe our steeds
And take equestrian sport over the green
Under the blue, across the crop, – what care?
So we went prancing up hill and down dale,
100 In and out of the level and the straight,
By the bit of pleasant byeway, where was harm?
Still Sol salutes me and the morning laughs:
I see my grandsire's hoof-prints, – point the spot
Where he drew rein, slipped saddle, and stabbed knave
For daring throw gibe – much less, stone – from pale,
Then back, and on, and up with the cavalcade;

Just so wend we, now canter, now converse,
Till, 'mid the jaunNcing pride and jaunty port,
Something of a sudden jerks at somebody –
110 A dagger is out, a flashing cut and thrust,
Because I play some prank my grandsire played,
And here I sprawl: where is the company? Gone!
A trot and a trample! only I lie trapped,
Writhe in a certain novel springe just set
By the good old Pope: I'm first prize. Warn me? Why?
Apprize me that the law o' the game is changed?
Enough that I'm a warning, as I writhe,
To all and each my fellows of the file,
And make law plain henceforward past mistake,
120 'For such a prank, death is the penalty!'
Pope the Five Hundredth . . . what do I know or care?
Deputes your Eminence and Abateship
To announce that, twelve hours from this time, he needs
I just essay upon my body and soul
The virtue of his bran-new engine, prove
Represser of the pranksome! I'm the first!
Thanks. Do you know what teeth you mean to try
The sharpness of, on this soft neck and throat?
I know it, – I have seen and hate it, – ay,
130 As you shall, while I tell you: let me talk,
Or leave me, at your pleasure! talk I must:
What is your visit but my lure to talk?
You have a something to disclose? – a smile,
At end of the forced sternness, means to mock
The heart-beats here? I call your two hearts stone!
Is your charge to stay with me till I die?
Be tacit as your bench, then! Use your ears,
I use my tongue: how glibly yours will run
At pleasant supper-time . . . God's curse! . . . to-night
140 When all the guests jump up, begin so brisk
'Welcome, his Eminence who shrived the wretch!
Now we shall have the Abate's story!'

                                        Life!
How I could spill this overplus of mine

Among those hoar-haired, shrunk-shanked, odds and ends
Of body and soul, old age is chewing dry!
Those windle-straws that stare while purblind death
Mows here, mows there, makes hay of juicy me,
And misses, just the bunch of withered weed,
150 Would brighten hell and streak its smoke with flame!
How the life I could shed yet never shrink,
Would drench their stalks with sap like grass in May!
Is it not terrible, I entreat you, Sirs?
Such manifold and plenitudinous life,
Prompt at death's menace to give blow for threat,
Answer his 'Be thou not!' by 'Thus I am!' –
Terrible so to be alive yet die?

How I live, how I see! so, – how I speak!
Lucidity of soul unlocks the lips:
160 I never had the words at will before.
How I see all my folly at a glance!
'A man requires a woman and a wife:'
There was my folly; I believed the saw:
I knew that just myself concerned myself,
Yet needs must look for what I seemed to lack,
In a woman, – why, the woman's in the man!
Fools we are, how we learn things when too late!
Overmuch life turns round my woman-side;
The male and female in me, mixed before,
170 Settle of a sudden: I'm my wife outright
In this unmanly appetite for truth,
This careless courage as to consequence,
This instantaneous sight through things and through,
This voluble rhetoric, if you please, – 't is she!
Here you have that Pompilia whom I slew,
Also the folly for which I slew her!

                               Fool!
And, fool-like, what is it I wander from?
What, of the sharpness of your iron tooth?
180 Ah, – that I know the hateful thing: this way.
I chanced to stroll forth, many a good year gone,
One warm Spring eve in Rome, and unaware

Looking, mayhap, to count what stars were out,
Came on your huge axe in a frame, that falls
And so cuts off a man's head underneath,
Mannaia, – thus we made acquaintance first,
Out of the way, in a bye-part o' the town,
At the Mouth-of-Truth o' the river-side, you know:
One goes by the Capitol: and wherefore coy,
190 Retiring out of crowded noisy Rome?
Because a very little time ago
It had done service, chopped off head from trunk,
Belonging to a fellow whose poor house
The thing had made a point to stand before.
Felice Whatsoever-was-the-name
Who stabled buffaloes and so gained bread,
(Our clowns unyoke them in the ground hard by)
And, after use of much improper speech,
Had struck at Duke Some-title-or-other's face,
200 Because he kidnapped, carried away and kept
Felice's sister that would sit and sing
I' the filthy doorway while she plaited fringe
To deck the brutes with, – on their gear it goes, –
The good girl with the velvet in her voice.
So did the Duke, so did Felice, so
Did Justice, intervening with her axe.
There the man-mutilating engine stood
At ease, both gay and grim, like a Swiss guard
Off duty, – purified itself as well,
210 Getting dry, sweet and proper for next week, –
And doing incidental good, 't was hoped
To the rough lesson-lacking populace
Who now and then, forsooth, must right their wrongs!
There stood the twelve-foot-square of scaffold, railed
Considerately round to elbow-height:
(Suppose an officer should tumble thence
And sprain his ankle and be lame a month,
Through starting when the axe fell and head too?)
Railed likewise were the steps whereby 't was reached.
220 All of it painted red: red, in the midst,

Ran up two narrow tall beams barred across,
Since from the summit, some twelve feet to reach,
The iron plate with the sharp shearing edge
Had . . . slammed, jerked, shot or slid, – I shall find which!
There it lay quiet, fast in its fit place,
The wooden half-moon collar, now eclipsed
By the blade which blocked its curvature: apart,
The other half, – the under half-moon board
Which, helped by this, completes a neck's embrace, –
230 Joined to a sort of desk that wheels aside
Out of the way when done with, – down you kneel,
In you're wheeled, over you the other drops,
Tight you are clipped, whiz, there's the blade on you,
Out trundles body, down flops head on floor,
And where's your soul gone? That, too, I shall find!
This kneeling-place was red, red, never fear!
But only slimy-like with paint, not blood,
For why? a decent pitcher stood at hand,
A broad dish to hold sawdust, and a broom
240 By some unnamed utensil, – scraper-rake, –
Each with a conscious air of duty done.
Underneath, loungers, – boys and some few men, –
Discoursed this platter and the other tool,
Just as, when grooms tie up and dress a steed,
Boys lounge and look on, and elucubrate
What the round brush is used for, what the square, –
So was explained – to me the skill-less man –
The manner of the grooming for next world
Undergone by Felice What's-his-name.
250 There's no such lovely month in Rome as May –
May's crescent is no half-moon of red plank,
And came now tilting o'er the wave i' the west,
One greenish-golden sea, right 'twixt those bars
Of the engine – I began acquaintance with,
Understood, hated, hurried from before,
To have it out of sight and cleanse my soul!
Here it is all again, conserved for use:
Twelve hours hence I may know more, not hate worse.

That young May-moon-month! Devils of the deep!
260   Was not a Pope then Pope as much as now?
Used not he chirrup o'er the Merry Tales,
Chuckle, – his nephew so exact the wag
To play a jealous cullion such a trick
As wins the wife i' the pleasant story! Well?
Why do things change? Wherefore is Rome un-Romed?
I tell you, ere Felice's corpse was cold,
The Duke, that night, threw wide his palace-doors,
Received the compliments o' the quality,
For justice done him, – bowed and smirked his best,
270   And in return passed round a pretty thing,
A portrait of Felice's sister's self,
Florid old rogue Albano's masterpiece,
As – better than virginity in rags –
Bouncing Europa on the back o' the bull:
They laughed and took their road the safelier home.
Ah, but times change, there's quite another Pope,
I do the Duke's deed, take Felice's place,
And, being no Felice, lout and clout,
Stomach but ill the phrase 'I lose my head!'
280   How euphemistic! Lose what? Lose your ring,
Your snuff-box, tablets, kerchief! – but, your head?
I learnt the process at an early age;
'T was useful knowledge in those same old days,
To know the way a head is set on neck.
My fencing master urged 'Would you excel?
Rest not content with mere bold give-and-guard,
Nor pink the antagonist somehow-anyhow, –
See me dissect a little, and know your game!
Only anatomy makes a thrust the thing.'
290   Oh Cardinal, those lithe live necks of ours!
Here go the vertebrae, here's *Atlas*, here
Axis, and here the symphyses stop short,
So wisely and well, – as, o'er a corpse, we cant, –
And here's the silver cord which . . . what's our word?
Depends from the gold bowl, which loosed (not 'lost')
Lets us from heaven to hell, – one chop, we're loose!

'And not much pain i' the process,' quoth the sage:
Who told him? Not Felice's ghost, I think!
Such 'losing' is scarce Mother Nature's mode.
300 She fain would have cord ease itself away,
Worn to a thread by threescore years and ten,
Snap while we slumber: that seems bearable:
I'm told one clot of blood extravasate
Ends one as certainly as Roland's sword, –
One drop of lymph suffused proves Oliver's mace, –
Intruding, either of the pleasant pair,
On the arachnoid tunic of my brain.
That's Nature's way of loosing cord! – but Art,
How of Art's process with the engine here?
310 When bowl and cord alike are crushed across,
Bored between, bruised through? Why, if Fagon's self,
The French Court's pride, that famed practitioner,
Would pass his cold pale lightning of a knife,
Pistoja-ware, adroit 'twixt joint and joint,
With just a 'See how facile, gentlefolks!' –
The thing were not so bad to bear! Brute force
Cuts as he comes, breaks in, breaks on, breaks out
O' the hard and soft of you: is that the same?
A lithe snake thrids the hedge, makes throb no leaf:
320 A heavy ox sets chest to brier and branch,
Bursts somehow through, and leaves one hideous hole
Behind him!

             And why, why must this needs be?
Oh, if men were but good! They are not good,
Nowise like Peter: people called him rough,
But if, as I left Rome, I spoke the Saint,
– '*Petrus, quo vadis?*' – doubtless, I should hear,
'To free the prisoner and forgive his fault!
I plucked the absolute dead from God's own bar,
330 And raised up Dorcas, – why not rescue thee?'
What would cost one such nullifying word?
If Innocent succeeds to Peter's place,
Let him think Peter's thought, speak Peter's speech!

I say, he is bound to it: friends, how say you?
Concede I be all one bloodguiltiness
And mystery of murder in the flesh,
Why should that fact keep the Pope's mouth shut fast?
He execrates my crime, – good! – sees hell yawn
One inch from the red plank's end which I press, –
340   Nothing is better! What's the consequence?
How does a Pope proceed that knows his cue?
Why, leaves me linger out my minute here,
Since close on death come judgment and the doom,
Nor cribs at dawn its pittance from a sheep
Destined ere dewfall to be butcher's-meat!
Think, Sirs, if I had done you any harm,
And you require the natural revenge,
Suppose, and so intend to poison me,
– Just as you take and slip into my draught
350   The paperful of powder that clears scores,
You notice on my brow a certain blue:
How you both overset the wine at once!
How you both smile! 'Our enemy has the plague!
Twelve hours hence he'll be scraping his bones bare
Of that intolerable flesh, and die,
Frenzied with pain: no need for poison here!
Step aside and enjoy the spectacle!'
Tender for souls are you, Pope Innocent!
Christ's maxim is – one soul outweighs the world:
360   Respite me, save a soul, then, curse the world!
'No,' venerable sire, I hear you smirk,
'No: for Christ's gospel changes names, not things,
Renews the obsolete, does nothing more!
Our fire-new gospel is retinkered law,
Our mercy, justice, – Jove's rechristened God, –
Nay, whereas, in the popular conceit,
'T is pity that old harsh Law somehow limps,
Lingers on earth, although Law's day be done, –
Else would benignant Gospel interpose,
370   Not furtively as now, but bold and frank
O'erflutter us with healing in her wings, –

Law is all harshness, Gospel were all love! –
We like to put it, on the contrary, –
Gospel takes up the rod which Law lets fall;
Mercy is vigilant when justice sleeps;
Does Law let Guido taste the Gospel-grace?
The secular arm allow the spiritual power
To act for once? – what compliment so fine
As that the Gospel handsomely be harsh,
380 Thrust back Law's victim on the nice and coy?'
Yes, you do say so, – else you would forgive
Me, whom Law dares not touch but tosses you!
Do n't think to put on the professional face!
You know what I know, – casuists as you are,
Each nerve must creep, each hair start, sting and stand,
At such illogical inconsequence!
Dear my friends, do but see! A murder's tried,
There are two parties to the cause: I'm one,
– Defend myself, as somebody must do:
390 I have the best o' the battle: that's a fact,
Simple fact, – fancies find no place beside:
What though half Rome condemned me? Half approved:
And, none disputes, the luck is mine at last,
All Rome, i' the main, acquits me: whereupon
What has the Pope to ask but 'How finds Law?'
'I find,' replies Law, 'I have erred this while:
Guilty or guiltless, Guido proves a priest,
No layman: he is therefore yours, not mine:
I bound him: loose him, you whose will is Christ's!'
400 And now what does this Vicar of the Lord,
Shepherd o' the flock, – one of whose charge bleats sore
For crook's help from the quag wherein it drowns?
Law suffers him put forth the crumpled end, –
His pleasure is to turn staff, use the point,
And thrust the shuddering sheep he calls a wolf,
Back and back, down and down to where hell gapes!
'Guiltless,' cries Law – 'Guilty' corrects the Pope!
'Guilty,' for the whim's sake! 'Guilty,' he somehow thinks,
And anyhow says: 't is truth; he dares not lie!

410   Others should do the lying. That's the cause
    Brings you both here: I ought in decency
    Confess to you that I deserve my fate,
    Am guilty, as the Pope thinks, – ay, to the end,
    Keep up the jest, lie on, lie ever, lie
    I' the latest gasp of me! What reason, Sirs?
    Because to-morrow will succeed to-day
    For you, though not for me: and if I stick
    Still to the truth, declare with my last breath,
    I die an innocent and murdered man, –

420   Why, there's the tongue of Rome will wag a-pace
    This time to-morrow, – do n't I hear the talk!
    'So, to the last he proved impenitent?
    Pagans have said as much of martyred saints!
    Law demurred, washed her hands of the whole case.
    Prince. Somebody said this, Duke Something, that.
    Doubtless the man's dead, dead enough, do n't fear!
    But, hang it, what if there have been a spice,
    A touch of . . . eh? You see, the Pope's so old,
    Some of us add, obtuse, – age never slips

430   The chance of shoving youth to face death first!'
    And so on. Therefore to suppress such talk
    You two come here, entreat I tell you lies,
    And end, the edifying way. I end,
    Telling the truth! Your self-styled shepherd thieves!
    A thief – and how thieves hate the wolves we know:
    Damage to theft, damage to thrift, all's one!
    The red hand is sworn foe of the black jaw!
    That's only natural, that's right enough:
    But why the wolf should compliment the thief

440   With the shepherd's title, bark out life in thanks,
    And, spiteless, lick the prong that spits him, – eh,
    Cardinal? My Abate, scarcely thus!
    There, let my sheepskin-garb, a curse on't, go –
    Leave my teeth free if I must show my shag!
    Repent? What good shall follow? If I pass
    Twelve hours repenting, will that fact hook fast
    The thirteenth at the horrid dozen's end?

If I fall forthwith at your feet, gnash, tear,
Foam, rave, to give your story the due grace,
450 Will that assist the engine half-way back
Into its hiding-house? – boards, shaking now,
Bone against bone, like some old skeleton bat
That wants, now winter 's dead, to wake and prey!
Will howling put the spectre back to sleep?
Ah, but I misconceive your object, Sirs!
Since I want new life like the creature, – life
Being done with here, begins i' the world away:
I shall next have 'Come, mortals, and be judged!'
There's but a minute betwixt this and then:
460 So, quick, be sorry since it saves my soul!
Sirs, truth shall save it, since no lies assist!
Hear the truth, you, whatever you style yourselves,
Civilization and society!
Come, one good grapple, I with all the world!
Dying in cold blood is the desperate thing;
The angry heart explodes, bears off in blaze
The indignant soul, and I'm combustion-ripe.
Why, you intend to do your worst with me!
That's in your eyes! You dare no more than death,
470 And mean no less. I must make up my mind!
So Pietro, – when I chased him here and there,
Morsel by morsel cut away the life
I loathed, – cried for just respite to confess
And save his soul: much respite did I grant!
Why grant me respite who deserve my doom?
Me – who engaged to play a prize, fight you,
Knowing your arms, and foil you, trick for trick,
At rapier-fence, your match and, may be, more.
I knew that if I chose sin certain sins,
480 Solace my lusts out of the regular way
Prescribed me, I should find you in the path,
Have to try skill with a redoubted foe;
You would lunge, I would parry, and make end.
At last, occasion of a murder comes:
We cross blades, I, for all my brag, break guard,

And in goes the cold iron at my breast,
Out at my back, and end is made of me.
You stand confessed the adroiter swordsman, – ay,
But on your triumph you increase, it seems,
490 Want more of me than lying flat on face:
I ought to raise my ruined head, allege
Not simply I pushed worse blade o' the pair,
But my antagonist dispensed with steel!
There was no passage of arms, you looked me low,–
With brow and eye abolished cut-and-thrust
Nor used the vulgar weapon! This chance scratch,
This incidental hurt, this sort of hole
I' the heart of me? I stumbled, got it so!
Fell on my own sword as a bungler may!
500 Yourself proscribe such heathen tools, and trust
To the naked virtue: it was virtue stood
Unarmed and awed me, – on my brow there burned
Crime out so plainly, intolerably, red,
That I was fain to cry – 'Down to the dust
With me, and bury there brow, brand and all!'
Law had essayed the adventure, – but what's Law?
Morality exposed the Gorgon-shield!
Morality and Religion conquer me.
If Law sufficed would you come here, entreat
510 I supplement law, and confess forsooth?
Did not the Trial show things plain enough?
'Ah, but a word of the man's very self
Would somehow put the keystone in its place
And crown the arch!' Then take the word you want!

I say that, long ago, when things began,
All the world made agreement, such and such
Were pleasure-giving profit-bearing acts,
But henceforth extra-legal, nor to be:
You must not kill the man whose death would please
520 And profit you, unless his life stop yours
Plainly, and need so be put aside:
Get the thing by a public course, by law,

Only no private bloodshed as of old!
All of us, for the good of every one,
Renounced such licence and conformed to law:
Who breaks law, breaks pact, therefore, helps himself
To pleasure and profit over and above the due,
And must pay forfeit, – pain beyond his share:
For pleasure is the sole good in the world,
530 Anyone's pleasure turns to someone's pain,
So, let law watch for everyone, – say we,
Who call things wicked that give too much joy,
And nickname the reprisal, envy makes,
Punishment: quite right! thus the world goes round.
I, being well aware such pact there was,
Who in my time have found advantage too
In law's observance and crime's penalty, –
Who, but for wholesome fear law bred in friends,
Had doubtless given example long ago,
540 Furnished forth some friend's pleasure with my pain,
And, by my death, pieced out his scanty life, –
I could not, for that foolish life of me,
Help risking law's infringement, – I broke bond,
And needs must pay price, – wherefore, here's my head,
Flung with a flourish! But, repentance too?
But pure and simple sorrow for law's breach
Rather than blunderer's-ineptitude?
Cardinal, no! Abate, scarcely thus!
'T is the fault, not that I dared try a fall
550 With Law and straightway am found undermost,
But that I fail to see, above man's law,
God's precept you, the Christians recognize?
Colly my cow! Do n't fidget, Cardinal!
Abate, cross your breast and count your beads
And exorcize the devil, for here he stands
And stiffens in the bristly nape of neck,
Daring you drive him hence! You, Christians both?
I say, if ever was such faith at all
Born in the world, by your community
560 Suffered to live its little tick of time,

'T is dead of age now, ludicrously dead;
Honour its ashes, if you be discreet,
In epitaph only! For, concede its death,
Allow extinction, you may boast unchecked
What feats the thing did in a crazy land
At a fabulous epoch, – treat your faith, that way,
Just as you treat your relics: 'Here's a shred
Of saintly flesh, a scrap of blessed bone,
Raised King Cophetua, who was dead, to life
570   In Mesopotamy twelve centuries since,
Such was its virtue!' – twangs the Sacristan,
Holding the shrine-box up, with hands like feet
Because of gout in every finger-joint:
Does he bethink him to reduce one knob,
Allay one twinge by touching what he vaunts?
I think he half uncrooks fist to catch fee,
But, for the grace, the quality of cure, –
Cophetua was the man put that to proof!
Not otherwise, your faith is shrined and shown
580   And shamed at once: you banter while you bow!
Do you dispute this? Come, a monster-laugh,
A madman's laugh, allowed his Carnival
Later ten days than when all Rome, but he,
Laughed at the candle-contest: mine's alight,
'T is just it sputter till the puff o' the Pope
End it to-morrow and the world turn Ash.
Come, thus I wave a wand and bring to pass
In a moment, in the twinkle of an eye,
What but that – feigning everywhere grows fact,
590   Professors turn possessors, realize
The faith they play with as a fancy now,
And bid it operate, have full effect
On every circumstance of life, to-day,
In Rome, – faith's flow set free at fountain-head!
Now, you'll own, at this present when I speak,
Before I work the wonder, there's no man
Woman or child in Rome, faith's fountain-head,
But might, if each were minded, realize

Conversely unbelief, faith's opposite —
600　Set it to work on life unflinchingly,
　　Yet give no symptom of an outward change:
　　Why should things change because men disbelieve?
　　What's incompatible, in the whited tomb,
　　With bones and rottenness one inch below?
　　What saintly act is done in Rome to-day
　　But might be prompted by the devil, 'is'
　　I say not, — 'has been, and again may be,' —
　　I do say, full i' the face o' the crucifix
　　You try to stop my mouth with! Off with it!
610　Look in your own heart, if your soul have eyes!
　　You shall see reason why, though faith were fled,
　　Unbelief still might work the wires and move
　　Man, the machine, to play a faithful part.
　　Preside your college, Cardinal, in your cape,
　　Or, — having got above his head, grown Pope, —
　　Abate, gird your loins and wash my feet!
　　Do you suppose I am at loss at all
　　Why you crook, why you cringe, why fast or feast?
　　Praise, blame, sit, stand, lie or go! — all of it,
620　In each of you, purest unbelief may prompt,
　　And wit explain to who has eyes to see.
　　But, lo, I wave wand, make the false the true!
　　Here's Rome believes in Christianity!
　　What an explosion, how the fragments fly
　　Of what was surface, mask and make-believe!
　　Begin now, — look at this Pope's-halberdier
　　In wasp-like black and yellow foolery!
　　He, doing duty at the corridor,
　　Wakes from a muse and stands convinced of sin!
630　Down he flings halbert, leaps the passage-length,
　　Pushes into the presence, pantingly
　　Submits the extreme peril of the case
　　To the Pope's self, — whom in the world beside? —
　　And the Pope breaks talk with ambassador,
　　Bids aside bishop, wills the whole world wait
　　Till he secure that prize, outweighs the world,

A soul, relieve the sentry of his qualm!
His Altitude the Referendary, –
Robed right, and ready for the usher's word
640 To pay devoir, – is, of all times, just then
'Ware of a master-stroke of argument
Will cut the spinal cord . . . ugh, ugh! . . . I mean,
Paralyse Molinism for evermore!
Straight he leaves lobby, trundles, two and two,
Down steps, to reach home, write if but a word
Shall end the impudence: he leaves who likes
Go pacify the Pope: there's Christ to serve!
How otherwise would men display their zeal?
If the same sentry had the least surmise
650 A powder-barrel 'neath the pavement lay
In neighbourhood with what might prove a match,
Meant to blow sky-high Pope and presence both –
Would he not break through courtiers, rank and file,
Bundle up, bear off and save body so,
O' the Pope, no matter for his priceless soul?
There's no fool's-freak here, nought to soundly swinge,
Only a man in earnest, you'll so praise
And pay and prate about, that earth shall ring!
Had thought possessed the Referendary
660 His jewel-case at home was left ajar,
What would be wrong in running, robes awry,
To be beforehand with the pilferer?
What talk then of indecent haste? Which means,
That both these, each in his degree, would do
Just that, – for a comparative nothing's sake,
And thereby gain approval and reward, –
Which, done for what Christ says is worth the world,
Procures the doer curses, cuffs and kicks.
I call such difference 'twixt act and act,
670 Sheer lunacy unless your truth on lip
Be recognized a lie in heart of you!
How do you all act, promptly or in doubt,
When there's a guest poisoned at supper-time
And he sits chatting on with spot on cheek?

'Pluck him by the skirt, and round him in the ears,
Have at him by the beard, warn anyhow!'
Good, and this other friend that's cheat and thief
And dissolute, – go stop the devil's feast,
Withdraw him from the imminent hell-fire!
680   Why, for your life, you dare not tell your friend
'You lie, and I admonish you for Christ!'
Who yet dare seek that same man at the Mass
To warn him – on his knees, and tinkle near, –
He left a cask a-tilt, a tap unturned,
The Trebbian running: what a grateful jump
Out of the Church rewards your vigilance!
Perform that self-same service just a thought
More maladroitly, – since a bishop sits
At function! – and he budges not, bites lip, –
690   'You see my case: how can I quit my post?
He has an eye to any such default.
See to it, neighbour, I beseech your love!'
He and you know the relative worth of things,
What is permissible or inopportune.
Contort your brows! You know I speak the truth:
Gold is called gold, and dross called dross, i' the Book:
Gold you let lie and dross pick up and prize!
– Despite your muster of some fifty monks
And nuns a-maundering here and mumping there,
700   Who could, and on occasion would, spurn dross,
Clutch gold, and prove their faith a fact so far, –
I grant you! Fifty times the number squeak
And gibber in the madhouse – firm of faith,
This fellow, that his nose supports the moon,
The other, that his straw hat crowns him Pope:
Does that prove all the world outside insane?
Do fifty miracle-mongers match the mob
That acts on the frank faithless principle,
Born-baptized-and-bred Christian-atheists, each
710   With just as much a right to judge as you, –
As many senses in his soul, or nerves
I' neck of him as I, – whom, soul and sense,

Neck and nerve, you abolish presently, –
I being the unit in creation now
Who pay the Maker, in this speech of mine,
A creature's duty, spend my last of breath
In bearing witness, even by my worst fault
To the creature's obligation, absolute,
Perpetual: my worst fault protests, 'The faith
720   Claims all of me: I would give all she claims,
But for a spice of doubt: the risk's too rash:
Double or quits, I play, but, all or nought,
Exceeds my courage: therefore, I descend
To the next faith with no dubiety –
Faith in the present life, made last as long
And prove as full of pleasure as may hap,
Whatever pain it cause the world.' I'm wrong?
I've had my life, whate'er I lose: I'm right?
I've got the single good there was to gain.
730   Entire faith, or else complete unbelief, –
Aught between has my loathing and contempt,
Mine and God's also, doubtless: ask yourself,
Cardinal, where and how you like a man!
Why, either with your feet upon his head,
Confessed your caudatory, or at large
The stranger in the crowd who caps to you
But keeps his distance, – why should he presume?
You want no hanger-on and dropper-off,
Now yours, and now not yours but quite his own,
740   According as the sky looks black or bright.
Just so I capped to and kept off from faith –
You promised trudge behind through fair and foul,
Yet leave i' the lurch at the first spit of rain.
Who holds to faith whenever rain begins?
What does the father when his son lies dead,
The merchant when his money-bags take wing,
The politician whom a rival ousts?
No case but has its conduct, faith prescribes:
Where's the obedience that shall edify?
750   Why, they laugh frankly in the face of faith

And take the natural course, – this rends his hair
Because his child is taken to God's breast,
That gnashes teeth and raves at loss of trash
Which rust corrupts and thieves break through and steal,
And this, enabled to inherit earth
Through meekness, curses till your blood runs cold!
Down they all drop to my low level, ease
Heart upon dungy earth that's warm and soft,
And let who will, attempt the altitudes.
760 We have the prodigal son of heavenly sire,
Turning his nose up at the fatted calf,
Fain to fill belly with the husks we swine
Did eat by born depravity of taste!

Enough of the hypocrites. But you, Sirs, you –
Who never budged from litter where I lay,
And buried snout i' the draff-box while I fed,
Cried amen to my creed's one article –
'Get pleasure, 'scape pain, – give your preference
To the immediate good, for time is brief,
770 And death ends good and ill and everything:
What's got is gained, what's gained soon is gained twice,
And, – inasmuch as faith gains most, – feign faith!'
So did we brother-like pass word about:
– You, now, – like bloody drunkards but half-drunk,
Who fool men yet perceive men find them fools,
And that a titter gains the gravest mouth, –
O' the sudden you must needs re-introduce
Solemnity, must sober undue mirth
By a blow dealt your boon companion here
780 Who, using the old licence, dreamed of harm
No more than snow in harvest: yet it falls!
You check the merriment effectually
By pushing your abrupt machine i' the midst,
Making me Rome's example: blood for wine!
The general good needs that you chop and change!
I may dislike the hocus-pocus, – Rome,
The laughter-loving people, won't they stare

Chap-fallen! – while serious natures sermonize
'The magistrate, he beareth not the sword
790 In vain; who sins may taste its edge, we see!'
Why my sin, drunkards? Where have I abused
Liberty, scandalized you all so much?
Who called me, who crooked finger till I came,
Fool that I was, to join companionship?
I knew my own mind, meant to live my life,
Elude your envy, or else make a stand,
Take my own part and sell you my life dear:
But it was 'Fie! No prejudice in the world
To the proper manly instinct! Cast your lot
800 Into our lap, one genius ruled our births,
We'll compass joy by concert; take with us
The regular irregular way i' the wood;
You'll miss no game through riding breast by breast,
In this preserve, the Church's park and pale,
Rather than outside where the world is waste!'
Come, if you said not that, did you say this?
Give plain and terrible warning, 'Live, enjoy?
Such life begins in death and ends in hell!
Dare you bid us assist you to your sins
810 Who hurry sin and sinners from the earth?
No such delight for us, why then for you?
Leave earth, seek heaven or find its opposite!'
Had you so warned me, not in lying words
But veritable deeds with tongues of flame,
That had been fair, that might have struck a man,
Silenced the squabble between soul and sense,
Compelled him make his mind up, take one course
Or the other, peradventure! – wrong or right,
Foolish or wise, you would have been at least
820 Sincere, no question, – forced me choose, indulge
Or else renounce my instincts, still play wolf
Or find my way submissive to the fold,
Be red-crossed on the fleece, one sheep the more.
But you as good as bade me wear sheep's wool
Over wolf's skin, suck blood and hide the noise

By mimicry of something like a bleat, –
Whence it comes that because, despite my care,
Because I smack my tongue too loud for once,
Drop baaing, here's the village up in arms!
830   Have at the wolf's throat, you who hate the breed!
Oh, were it only open yet to choose –
One little time more – whether I'd be free
Your foe, or subsidized your friend forsooth!
Should not you get a growl through the white fangs
In answer to your beckoning! Cardinal,
Abate, managers o' the multitude,
I'd turn your gloved hands to account, be sure!
You should manipulate the coarse rough mob:
'T is you I'd deal directly with, not them, –
840   Using your fears: why touch the thing myself
When I could see you hunt and then cry 'Shares!
Quarter the carcass or we quarrel; come,
Here's the world ready to see justice done!'
Oh, it had been a desperate game, but game
Wherein the winner's chance were worth the pains
To try conclusions! – at the worst, what's worse
Than this Mannaia-machine, each minute's talk,
Helps push an inch the nearer me? Fool, fool!

You understand me and forgive, sweet Sirs?
850   I blame you, tear my hair and tell my woe –
All's but a flourish, figure of rhetoric!
One must try each expedient to save life.
One makes fools look foolisher fifty-fold
By putting in their place the wise like you
To take the full force of an argument
Would buffet their stolidity in vain.
If you should feel aggrieved by the mere wind
O' the blow that means to miss you and maul them,
That's my success! Is it not folly, now,
860   To say with folks, 'A plausible defence –
We see through notwithstanding, and reject?'
Reject the plausible they do, these fools,

Who never even make pretence to show
One point beyond its plausibility
In favour of the best belief they hold!
'Saint Somebody-or-other raised the dead:'
Did he? How do you come to know as much?
'Know it, what need? The story's plausible,
Avouched for by a martyrologist,
870   And why should good men sup on cheese and leeks
On such a saint's day, if there were no saint?'
I praise the wisdom of these fools, and straight
Tell them my story – 'plausible, but false!'
False, to be sure! What else can story be
That runs – a young wife tired of an old spouse,
Found a priest whom she fled away with, – both
Took their full pleasure in the two-days' flight,
Which a grey-headed greyer-hearted pair,
(Whose best boast was, their life had been a lie)
880   Helped for the love they bore all liars. Oh,
Here incredulity begins! Indeed?
Allow then, were no one point strictly true,
There's that i' the tale might seem like truth at least
To the unlucky husband, – jaundiced patch, –
Jealousy maddens people, why not him?
Say, he was maddened, so, forgivable!
Humanity pleads that though the wife were true,
The priest true, and the pair of liars true,
They might seem false to one man in the world!
890   A thousand gnats make up a serpent's sting,
And many sly soft stimulants to wrath
Compose a formidable wrong at last,
That gets called easily by some one name
Not applicable to the single parts,
And so draws down a general revenge,
Excessive if you take crime, fault by fault.
Jealousy! I have known a score of plays,
Were listened to and laughed at in my time
As like the everyday-life on all sides,
900   Wherein the husband, mad as a March hare,

Suspected all the world contrived his shame;
What did the wife? The wife kissed both eyes blind,
Explained away ambiguous circumstance,
And while she held him captive by the hand,
Crowned his head, – you know what's the mockery, –
By half her body behind the curtain. That's
Nature now! That's the subject of a piece
I saw in Vallombrosa Convent, made
Expressly to teach men what marriage was!
910   But say 'Just so did I misapprehend!'
Or 'Just so she deceived me to my face!'
And that's pretence too easily seen through!
All those eyes of all husbands in all plays,
At stare like one expanded peacock-tail,
Are laughed at for pretending to be keen
While horn-blind: but the moment I step forth –
Oh, I must needs o' the sudden prove a lynx
And look the heart, that stone-wall, through and through!
Such an eye, God's may be, – not yours nor mine.

920   Yes, presently ... what hour is fleeting now?
When you cut earth away from under me,
I shall be left alone with, pushed beneath
Some such an apparitional dread orb;
I fancy it go filling up the void
Above my mote-self it devours, or what
Immensity please wreak on nothingness.
Just so I felt once, couching through the dark,
Hard by Vittiano; young I was, and gay,
And wanting to trap fieldfares: first a spark
930   Tipped a bent, as a mere dew-globule might
Any stiff grass-stalk on the meadow, – this
Grew fiercer, flamed out full, and proved the sun.
What do I want with proverbs, precepts here?
Away with man! What shall I say to God?
This, if I find the tongue and keep the mind –
'Do Thou wipe out the being of me, and smear
This soul from off Thy white of things, I blot!

I am one huge and sheer mistake, – whose fault?
Not mine at least, who did not make myself!'
940 Someone declares my wife excused me so!
Perhaps she knew what argument to use.
Grind your teeth, Cardinal, Abate, writhe!
What else am I to cry out in my rage,
Unable to repent one particle
O' the past? Oh, how I wish some cold wise man
Would dig beneath the surface which you scrape,
Deal with the depths, pronounce on my desert
Groundedly! I want simple sober sense,
That asks, before it finishes with a dog,
950 Who taught the dog that trick you hang him for?
You both persist to call that act a crime,
Sense would call . . . yes, I do assure you, Sirs, . . .
A blunder! At the worst, I stood in doubt
On cross-road, took one path of many paths:
It leads to the red thing, we all see now,
But nobody at first saw one primrose
In bank, one singing-bird in bush, the less,
To warn from wayfare: let me prove you that!
Put me back to the cross-road, start afresh!
960 Advise me when I take the first false step!
Give me my wife: how should I use my wife,
Love her or hate her? Prompt my action now!
There she stands, there she is alive and pale,
The thirteen-years'-old child, with milk for blood,
Pompilia Comparini, as at first,
Which first is only four brief years ago!
I stand too in the little ground-floor room
O' the father's house at Via Vittoria: see!
Her so-called mother, – one arm round the waist
970 O' the child to keep her from the toys – let fall,
At wonder I can live yet look so grim, –
Ushers her in, with deprecating wave
Of the other, – there she fronts me loose, at large,
Held only by the mother's finger-tip –
Struck dumb, for she was white enough before!

She eyes me with those frightened balls of black,
As heifer – the old simile comes pat –
Eyes tremblingly the altar and the priest:
The amazed look, all one insuppressive prayer, –
980 Might she but be set free as heretofore,
Have this cup leave her lips unblistered, bear
Any cross anywhither anyhow,
So but alone, so but apart from me!
You are touched? So am I, quite otherwise,
If 't is with pity. I resent my wrong,
Being a man: we only show man's soul
Through man's flesh, she sees mine, it strikes her thus!
Is that attractive? To a youth perhaps –
Calf-creature, one-part boy to three-parts girl,
990 To whom it is a flattering novelty
That he, men use to motion from their path,
Can thus impose, thus terrify in turn
A chit whose terror shall be changed apace
To bliss unbearable when, grace and glow,
Prowess and pride descend the throne and touch
Esther in all that pretty tremble, cured
By the dove o' the sceptre! But myself am old,
O' the wane at least, in all things: what do you say
To her who frankly thus confirms my doubt?
1000 I am past the prime, I scare the woman-world,
Done-with that way: you like this piece of news?
A little saucy rose-bud minx can strike
Death-damp into the breast of doughty king
Though 't were French Louis, – soul I understand, –
Saying, by gesture of repugnance, just
'Sire, you are regal, puissant and so forth,
But – young you have been, are not, nor will be!'
In vain the mother nods, winks, bustles up
'Count, girls incline to mature worth like you!
1010 As for Pompilia, what's flesh, fish or fowl
To one who apprehends no difference,
And would accept you even were you old
As you are ... youngish by her father's side?

Trim but your beard a little, thin your bush
Of eyebrow; and for presence, portliness
And decent gravity, you beat a boy!'
Deceive you for a second, if you may,
In presence of the child that so loves age,
Whose neck writhes, cords itself against your kiss,
1020 Whose hand you wring stark, rigid with despair!
Well, I resent this; I am young in soul,
Nor old in body, – thews and sinews here, –
Though the vile surface be not smooth as once, –
Far beyond the first wheelwork that went wrong
Through the untempered iron ere 't was proof:
I am the steel man worth ten times the crude, –
Would woman see what this declines to see,
Declines to say 'I see,' – the officious word
That makes the thing, pricks on the soul to shoot
1030 New fire into the half-used cinder, flesh!
Therefore 't is she begins with wronging me,
Who cannot but begin with hating her.
Our marriage follows: there we stand again!
Why do I laugh? Why, in the very gripe
O' the jaws of death's gigantic skull do I
Grin back his grin, make sport of my own pangs?
Why from each clashing of his molars, ground
To make the devil bread from out my grist,
Leaps out a spark of mirth, a hellish toy?
1040 Take notice we are lovers in a church,
Waiting the sacrament to make us one
And happy! Just as bid, she bears herself,
Comes and kneels, rises, speaks, is silent, – goes:
So have I brought my horse, by word and blow,
To stand stock-still and front the fire he dreads.
How can I other than remember this,
Resent the very obedience? Gain thereby?
Yes, I do gain my end and have my will, –
Thanks to whom? When the mother speaks the word,
1050 She obeys it – even to enduring me!
There had been compensation in revolt –

Revolt's to quell: but martyrdom rehearsed,
But predetermined saintship for the sake
O' the mother? – 'Go!' thought I, 'we meet again!'
Pass the next weeks of dumb contented death,
She lives, – wakes up, installed in house and home,
Is mine, mine all day-long, all night-long mine.
Good folks begin at me with open mouth
'Now, at least, reconcile the child to life!
1060 Study and make her love . . . that is, endure
The . . . hem! the . . . all of you though somewhat old,
Till it amount to something, in her eye,
As good as love, better a thousand times, –
Since nature helps the woman in such strait,
Makes passiveness her pleasure: failing which,
What if you give up boys' and girls' fools'-play
And go on to wise friendship all at once?
Those boys and girls kiss themselves cold, you know,
Toy themselves tired and slink aside full soon
1070 To friendship, as they name satiety:
Thither go you and wait their coming!' Thanks,
Considerate advisers, – but, fair play!
Had you and I but started fair at first,
We, keeping fair, might reach it, neck by neck,
This blessed goal, whenever fate so please:
But why am I to miss the daisied mile
The course begins with, why obtain the dust
Of the end precisely at the starting-point?
Why quaff life's cup blown free of all the beads,
1080 The bright red froth wherein our beard should steep
Before our mouth essay the black o' the wine?
Foolish, the love-fit? Let me prove it such
Like you, before like you I puff things clear!
'The best's to come, no rapture but content!
Not the first glory but a sober glow,
Nor a spontaneous outburst in pure boon,
So much as, gained by patience, care and toil!'
Go preach that to your nephews, not to me
Who, tired i' the midway of my life, would stop

1090 And take my first refreshment in a rose:
What's this coarse woolly hip, worn smooth of leaf,
You counsel I go plant in garden-pot,
Water with tears, manure with sweat and blood,
In confidence the seed shall germinate
And for its very best, some far-off day,
Grow big, and blow me out a dog-rose bell?
Why must your nephews begin breathing spice
O' the hundred-petalled Provence prodigy?
Nay, more and worse, – would such my root bear rose –
1100 Prove really flower and favourite, not the kind
That's queen, but those three leaves that make one cup
And hold the hedge-bird's breakfast, – then indeed
The prize though poor would pay the care and toil!
Respect we Nature that makes least as most,
Marvellous in the minim! But this bud,
Bit through and burned black by the tempter's tooth,
This bloom whose best grace was the slug outside
And the wasp inside its bosom, – call you 'rose?'
Claim no immunity from a weed's fate
1110 For the horrible present! What you call my wife
I call a nullity in female shape,
Vapid disgust, soon to be pungent plague,
When mixed with, made confusion and a curse
By two abominable nondescripts,
That father and that mother: think you see
The dreadful bronze our boast, we Aretines,
The Etruscan monster, the three-headed thing,
Bellerophon's foe! How name you the whole beast?
You choose to name the body from one head,
1120 That of the simple kid which droops the eye,
Hangs the neck and dies tenderly enough:
I rather see the griesly lion belch
Flame out i' the midst, the serpent writhe her rings,
Grafted into the common stock for tail,
And name the brute, Chimaera, which I slew!
How was there ever more to be – (concede
My wife's insipid harmless nullity) –

Dissociation from that pair of plagues –
That mother with her cunning and her cant –
1130 The eyes with first their twinkle of conceit,
Then, dropped to earth in mock-demureness, – now,
The smile self-satisfied from ear to ear,
Now, the prim pursed-up mouth's protruded lips,
With deferential duck, slow swing of head,
Tempting the sudden fist of man too much, –
That owl-like screw of lid and rock of ruff!
As for the father, – Cardinal, you know,
The kind of idiot! – rife are such in Rome,
But they wear velvet commonly, such fools,
1140 At the end of life, can furnish forth young folk
Who grin and bear with imbecility,
Since the stalled ass, the joker, sheds from jaw
Corn, in the joke, for those who laugh or starve:
But what say we to the same solemn beast
Wagging his ears and wishful of our pat,
When turned, with hide in holes and bones laid bare,
To forage for himself i' the waste o' the world,
Sir Dignity i' the dumps? Pat him? We drub
Self-knowledge, rather, into frowzy pate,
1150 Teach Pietro to get trappings or go hang!
Fancy this quondam oracle in vogue
At Via Vittoria, this personified
Authority when time was, – Pantaloon
Flaunting his tom-fool tawdry just the same
As if Ash-Wednesday were mid-Carnival!
That's the extreme and unforgiveable
Of sins, as I account such. Have you stooped
For your own ends to bestialize yourself
By flattery of a fellow of this stamp?
1160 The ends obtained, or else shown out of reach,
He goes on, takes the flattery for pure truth, –
'You love and honour me, of course: what next?'
What, but the trifle of the stabbing, friend? –
Which taught you how one worships when the shrine
Has lost the relic that we bent before.

Angry? And how could I be otherwise?
'T is plain: this pair of old pretentious fools
Meant to fool me: it happens, I fooled them.
Why could not these who sought to buy and sell
1170 Me, — when they found themselves were bought and sold,
Make up their mind to the proved rule of right,
Be chattel and not chapman any more?
Miscalculation has its consequence;
But when the shepherd crooks a sheep-like thing
And meaning to get wool, dislodges fleece
And finds the veritable wolf beneath,
(How that staunch image serves at every turn!)
Does he, by way of being politic,
Pluck the first whisker grimly visible? —
1180 Or rather grow in a trice all gratitude,
Protest this sort-of-what-one-might-name sheep
Beats the old other curly-coated kind,
And shall share board and bed, if so it deign,
With its discoverer, like a royal ram?
Ay, thus, with chattering teeth and knocking knees,
Would wisdom treat the adventure: these, forsooth,
Tried whisker-plucking, and so found what trap
The whisker kept perdue, two rows of teeth —
Sharp, as too late the prying fingers felt.
1190 What would you have? The fools transgress, the fools
Forthwith receive appropriate punishment:
They first insult me, I return the blow,
There follows noise enough: four hubbub months,
Now hue and cry, now whimpering and wail —
A perfect goose-yard cackle of complaint
Because I do not gild the geese their oats, —
I have enough of noise, ope wicket wide,
Sweep out the couple to go whine elsewhere,
Frightened a little, hurt in no respect,
1200 And am just taking thought to breathe again,
Taste the sweet sudden silence all about,
When, there they are at it, the old noise I know,
At Rome i' the distance! 'What, begun once more?

Whine on, wail ever, 't is the loser's right!'
But eh, what sort of voice grows on the wind?
Triumph it sounds and no complaint at all!
And triumph it is! My boast was premature:
The creatures, I turned forth, clapped wing and crew
Fighting-cock-fashion, – they had filched a pearl
1210 From dung-heap, and might boast with cause enough!
I was defrauded of all bargained for, –
You know, the Pope knows, not a soul but knows
My dowry was derision, my gain – muck,
My wife, (the Church declared my flesh and blood)
The nameless bastard of a common whore:
My old name turned henceforth to . . . shall I say
'He that received the ordure in his face?'
And they who planned this wrong, performed this wrong,
And then revealed this wrong to the wide world,
1220 Rounded myself in the ears with my own wrong, –
Why, these were . . . note hell's lucky malice, now! . . .
These were just they, and they alone, could act
And publish in this wise their infamy,
Secure that men would in a breath believe
Compassionate and pardon them, – for why?
They plainly were too stupid to invent,
Too simple to distinguish wrong from right, –
Inconscious agents they, the silly-sooth,
Of heaven's retributive justice on the strong
1230 Proud cunning violent oppressor – me!
Follow them to their fate and help your best,
You Rome, Arezzo, foes called friends of mine,
They gave the good long laugh to at my cost!
Defray your share o' the cost since you partook
The entertainment! Do! – assured the while,
That not one stab, I dealt to right and left,
But went the deeper for a fancy – this –
That each might do me two-fold service, find
A friend's face at the bottom of each wound,
1240 And scratch its smirk a little!
                              Panciatichi!

There's a report at Florence, – is it true? –
That when your relative the Cardinal
Built, only the other day, that barrack-bulk,
The palace in Via Larga, someone picked
From out the street a saucy quip enough
That fell there from its day's flight through the town,
About the flat front and the windows wide
And ugly heap of cornice, – hitched the joke
1250 Into a sonnet, signed his name thereto,
And forthwith pinned on post the pleasantry.
For which he's at the galleys, rowing now
Up to his waist in water, – just because
Panciatic and *lymphatic* rhymed so pat:
I hope, Sir, those who passed this joke on me
Were not unduly punished? What say you,
Prince of the Church, my patron? Nay, indeed!
I shall not dare insult your wits so much
As think this problem difficult to solve!
1260 This Pietro and Violante, then, I say,
These two ambiguous insects, changing name
And nature with the season's warmth or chill, –
Now, grovelled, grubbing toiling moiling ants,
A very synonym of thrift and peace, –
Anon, with lusty June to prick their heart,
Soared i' the air, winged flies for more offence,
Circled me, buzzed me deaf and stung me blind,
And stunk me dead with fetor in the face
Until I stopped the nuisance: there's my crime!
1270 Pity I did not suffer them subside
Into some further shape and final form
Of execrable life? My masters, no!
I, by one blow, wisely cut short at once
Them and their transformations of disgust
In the snug little Villa out of hand.
'Grant me confession, give bare time for that!' –
Shouted the sinner till his mouth was stopped.
His life confessed! – that was enough for me,
Who came to see that he did penance. 'S death!

1280 Here's a coil raised, a pother and for what?
Because strength, being provoked by weakness, fought
And conquered, – the world never heard the like!
Pah, how I spend my breath on them, as if
'T was their fate troubled me, too hard to range
Among the right and fit and proper things!

Ay, but Pompilia, – I await your word, –
She, unimpeached of crime, unimplicate
In folly, one of alien blood to these
I punish, why extend my claim, exact
1290 Her portion of the penalty? Yes, friends,
I go too fast: the orator's at fault:
Yes, ere I lay her, with your leave, by them
As she was laid at San Lorenzo late,
I ought to step back, lead her by degrees,
Recounting at each step some fresh offence,
Up to the red bed, – never fear, I will!
Gaze at her, where you place her, to begin,
Confound me with her gentleness and worth!
The horrible pair have fled and left her now,
1300 She has her husband for her sole concern,
His wife, the woman fashioned for his help,
Flesh of his flesh, bone of his bone, the bride
To groom as is the Church and Spouse, to Christ:
There she stands in his presence, – 'Thy desire
Shall be to the husband, o'er thee shall he rule!'
– 'Pompilia, who declare that you love God,
You know who said that: then, desire my love,
Yield me contentment and be ruled aright!'
She sits up, she lies down, she comes and goes,
1310 Kneels at the couch-side, overleans the sill
O' the window, cold and pale and mute as stone,
Strong as stone also. 'Well, are they not fled?
Am I not left, am I not one for all?
Speak a word, drop a tear, detach a glance,
Bless me or curse me of your own accord!
Is it the ceiling only wants your soul,

Is worth your eyes?' And then the eyes descend
And do look at me. Is it at the meal?
'Speak!' she obeys, 'Be silent!' she obeys,
1320 Counting the minutes till I cry 'Depart,'
As brood-bird when you saunter past her eggs.
Departed, just the same through door and wall
I see the same stone strength of white despair.
And all this will be never otherwise!
Before, the parents' presence lent her life:
She could play off her sex's armoury,
Intreat, reproach, be female to my male,
Try all the shrieking doubles of the hare,
Go clamour to the Commissary, bid
1330 The Archbishop hold my hands and stop my tongue,
And yield fair sport so: but the tactics change,
The hare stands stock-still to enrage the hound!
Since that day when she learned she was no child
Of those she thought her parents, – that their trick
Had tricked me whom she thought sole trickster late, –
Why, I suppose she said within herself
'Then, no more struggle for my parents' sake,
And, for my own sake, why needs struggle be?'
But is there no third party to the pact?
1340 What of her husband's relish or dislike
For this new game of giving up the game,
This worst offence of not offending more?
I'll not believe but instinct wrought in this,
Set her on to conceive and execute
The preferable plague . . . how sure they probe, –
These jades, the sensitivest soft of man!
The long black hair was wound now in a wisp, –
Crowned sorrow better than the wild web late:
No more soiled dress, 'tis trimness triumphs now,
1350 For how should malice go with negligence?
The frayed silk looked the fresher for her spite!
There was an end to springing out of bed,
Praying me, with face buried on my feet,
Be hindered of my pastime, – so an end

To my rejoinder, 'What, on the ground at last?
Vanquished in fight, a supplicant for life?
What if I raise you? 'Ware the casting down
When next you fight me!' Then, she lay there, mine:
Now, mine she is if I please wring her neck, –
1360 A moment of disquiet, working eyes,
Protruding tongue, a long sigh, then no more –
As if one killed the horse one could not ride!
Had I enjoined 'Cut off the hair!' – why, snap
The scissors, and at once a yard or so
Had fluttered in black serpents to the floor:
But till I did enjoin it, how she combs,
Uncurls and draws out to the complete length,
Plaits, places the insulting rope on head
To be an eyesore past dishevelment!
1370 Is all done? Then sit still again and stare!
I advise – no one think to bear that look
Of steady wrong, endured as steadily,
– Through what sustainment of deluding hope?
Who is the friend i' the background that notes all?
Who may come presently and close accounts?
This self-possession to the uttermost,
How does it differ in aught, save degree,
From the terrible patience of God?
                                   'All which just means,
1380 She did not love you!' Again the word is launched
And the fact fronts me! What, you try the wards
With the true key and the dead lock flies ope?
No, it sticks fast and leaves you fumbling still!
You have some fifty servants, Cardinal, –
Which of them loves you? Which subordinate
But makes parade of such officiousness
That, – if there's no love prompts it, – love, the sham,
Does twice the service done by love, the true.
God bless us liars, where's one touch of truth
1390 In what we tell the world, or world tells us,
Of how we like each other? All the same,
We calculate on word and deed, nor err, –

Bid such a man do such a loving act,
Sure of effect and negligent of cause,
Just as we bid a horse, with cluck of tongue,
Stretch his legs arch-wise, crouch his saddled back
To foot-reach of the stirrup – all for love,
And some for memory of the smart of switch
On the inside of the foreleg – what care we?
1400 Yet where's the bond obliges horse to man
Like that which binds fast wife to husband? God
Laid down the law: gave man the brawny arm
And ball of fist – woman the beardless cheek
And proper place to suffer in the side:
Since it is he can strike, let her obey!
Can she feel no love? Let her show the more,
Sham the worse, damn herself praiseworthily!
Who's that soprano Rome went mad about
Last week while I lay rotting in my straw?
1410 The very jailor gossiped in his praise –
How, – dressed up like Armida, though a man;
And painted to look pretty, though a fright, –
He still made love so that the ladies swooned,
Being an eunuch. 'Ah, Rinaldo mine!
But to breathe by thee while Jove slays us both!'
All the poor bloodless creature never felt,
Si, do, re, mi, fa, squeak and squall – for what?
Two gold zecchines the evening! Here's my slave,
Whose body and soul depend upon my nod,
1420 Can't falter out the first note in the scale
For her life! Why blame me if I take the life?
All women cannot give men love, forsooth!
No, nor all pullets lay the henwife eggs –
Whereat she bids them remedy the fault,
Brood on a chalk-ball: soon the nest is stocked –
Otherwise, to the plucking and the spit!
This wife of mine was of another mood –
Would not begin the lie that ends with truth,
Nor feign the love that brings real love about:
1430 Wherefore I judged, sentenced and punished her.

But why particularize, defend the deed?
Say that I hated her for no one cause
Beyond my pleasure so to do, – what then?
Just on as much incitement acts the world,
All of you! Look and like! You favour one,
Brow-beat another, leave alone a third, –
Why should you master natural caprice?
Pure nature! Try – plant elm by ash in file;
Both unexceptionable trees enough,
1440 They ought to overlean each other, pair
At top and arch across the avenue
The whole path to the pleasaunce: do they so –
Or loathe, lie off abhorrent each from each?
Lay the fault elsewhere, since we must have faults:
Mine shall have been, – seeing there's ill in the end
Come of my course, – that I fare somehow worse
For the way I took, – my fault ... as God's my judge
I see not where the fault lies, that's the truth!
I ought ... oh, ought in my own interest
1450 Have let the whole adventure go untried,
This chance by marriage, – or else, trying it,
Ought to have turned it to account some one
O' the hundred otherwises? Ay, my friend,
Easy to say, easy to do, – step right
Now you've stepped left and stumbled on the thing,
– The red thing! Doubt I any more than you
That practice makes man perfect? Give again
The chance, – same marriage and no other wife,
Be sure I'll edify you! That's because
1460 I'm practised, grown fit guide for Guido's self.
You proffered guidance, – I know, none so well, –
You laid down law and rolled decorum out,
From pulpit-corner on the gospel-side, –
Wanted to make your great experience mine,
Save me the personal search and pains so: thanks!
Take your word on life's use? When I take his –
The muzzled ox that treadeth out the corn,
Gone blind in padding round and round one path, –

As to the taste of green grass in the field!
1470 What do you know o' the world that 's trodden flat
And salted sterile with your daily dung,
Leavened into a lump of loathsomeness?
Take your opinion of the modes of life,
The aims of life, life's triumph or defeat,
How to feel, how to scheme and how to do
Or else leave undone? You preached long and loud
On high-days, 'Take our doctrine upon trust!
Into the mill-house with you! Grind our corn,
Relish our chaff, and let the green grass grow!'
1480 I tried chaff, found I famished on such fare,
So made this mad rush at the mill-house-door,
Buried my head up to the ears in dew,
Browzed on the best, for which you brain me, Sirs!
Be it so! I conceived of life that way,
And still declare – life, without absolute use
Of the actual sweet therein, is death, not life.
Give me, – pay down, – not promise, which is air, –
Something that's out of life and better still,
Make sure reward, make certain punishment,
1490 Entice me, scare me, – I'll forego this life;
Otherwise, no! – the less that words, mere wind,
Would cheat me of some minutes while they plague.
The fulness of revenge here, – blame yourselves
For this eruption of the pent-up soul
You prisoned first and played with afterward!
'Deny myself' meant simply pleasure you,
The sacred and superior, save the mark!
You – whose stupidity and insolence
I must defer to, soothe at every turn, –
1500 Whose swine-like snuffling greed and grunting lust
I had to wink at or help gratify, –
While the same passions, – dared they perk in me,
Me, the immeasurably marked, by God,
Master of the whole world of such as you, –
I, boast such passions? 'T was 'Suppress them straight!
Or stay, we'll pick and choose before destroy:

Here's wrath in you, – a serviceable sword, –
Beat it into a ploughshare! What's this long
Lance-like ambition? Forge a pruning-hook,
1510 May be of service when our vines grow tall!
But – sword used swordwise, spear thrust out as spear?
Anathema! Suppression is the word!'
My nature, when the outrage was too gross,
Widened itself an outlet over-wide
By way of answer? – sought its own relief
With more of fire and brimstone than you wished?
All your own doing: preachers, blame yourselves!

'Tis I preach while the hourglass runs and runs!
God keep me patient! All I say just means –
1520 My wife proved, whether by her fault or mine, –
That's immaterial, – a true stumbling-block
I' the way of me her husband: I but plied
The hatchet yourselves use to clear a path,
Was politic, played the game you warrant wins,
Plucked at law's robe a-rustle through the courts,
Bowed down to kiss divinity's buckled shoe
Cushioned i' the church: efforts all wide the aim!
Procedures to no purpose! Then flashed truth!
The letter kills, the spirit keeps alive
1530 In law and gospel: there be nods and winks
Instruct a wise man to assist himself
In certain matters nor seek aid at all.
'Ask money of me,' – quoth the clownish saw, –
'And take my purse! But, – speaking with respect, –
Need you a solace for the troubled nose?
Let everybody wipe his own himself!'
Sirs, tell me free and fair! Had things gone well
At the wayside inn: had I surprised asleep
The runaways, as was so probable,
1540 And pinned them each to other partridge-wise,
Through back and breast to breast and back, then bade
Bystanders witness if the spit, my sword,
Were loaded with unlawful game for once –

Would you have interposed to damp the glow
Applauding me on every husband's cheek?
Would you have checked the cry 'A judgment, see!
A warning, note! Be henceforth chaste, ye wives,
Nor stray beyond your proper precinct, priests!'
If you had, then your house against itself
1550 Divides, nor stands your kingdom any more.
Oh, why, why was it not ordained just so?
Why fell not things out so nor otherwise?
Ask that particular devil whose task it is
To trip the all-but-at perfection, – slur
The line o' the painter just where paint leaves off
And life begins, – puts ice into the ode
O' the poet while he cries 'Next stanza – fire!'
Inscribes all human effort with one word,
Artistry's haunting curse, the Incomplete!
1560 Being incomplete, the act escaped success.
Easy to blame now! Every fool can swear
To hole in net that held and slipped the fish.
But, treat my act with fair unjaundiced eye,
What was there wanting to a masterpiece
Except the luck that lies beyond a man?
My way with the woman, now proved grossly wrong,
Just missed of being gravely grandly right
And making critics laugh o' the other side.
Do, for the poor obstructed artist's sake,
1570 Go with him over that spoiled work once more!
Take only its first flower, the ended act
Now in the dusty pod, dry-and defunct!
I march to the Villa, and my men with me,
That evening, and we reach the door and stand.
I say ... no, it shoots through me lightning-like
While I pause, breathe, my hand upon the latch,
'Let me forebode! Thus far, too much success:
I want the natural failure – find it where?
Which thread will have to break and leave a loop
1580 I' the meshy combination, my brain's loom
Wove this long while and now next minute tests?

Of three that are to catch, two should go free,
One must: all three surprised, – impossible!
Beside, I seek three and may chance on six, –
This neighbour, t' other gossip, – the babe's birth
Brings such to fireside and folks give them wine, –
'T is late: but when I break in presently
One will be found outlingering the rest
For promise of a posset, – one whose shout
1590 Would raise the dead down in the catacombs,
Much more the city-watch that goes its round.
When did I ever turn adroitly up
To sun some brick embedded in the soil,
And with one blow crush all three scorpions there?
Or Pietro or Violante shambles off –
It cannot be but I surprise my wife –
If only she is stopped and stamped on, good!
That shall suffice: more is improbable.
Now I may knock!' And this once for my sake
1600 The impossible was effected: I called king,
Queen and knave in a sequence, and cards came,
All three, three only! So, I had my way,
Did my deed: so, unbrokenly lay bare
Each taenia that had sucked me dry of juice,
At last outside me, not an inch of ring
Left now to writhe about and root itself
I' the heart all powerless for revenge! Henceforth
I might thrive: these were drawn and dead and damned.
Oh Cardinal, the deep long sigh you heave
1610 When the load's off you, ringing as it runs
All the way down the serpent-stair to hell!
No doubt the fine delirium flustered me,
Turned my brain with the influx of success
As if the sole need now were to wave wand
And find doors fly wide, – wish and have my will, –
The rest o' the scheme would care for itself: escape?
Easy enough were that, and poor beside!
It all but proved so, – ought to quite have proved,
Since, half the chances had sufficed, set free

1620 Anyone, with his senses at command,
From thrice the danger of my flight. But, drunk,
Redundantly triumphant, – some reverse
Was sure to follow! There 's no other way
Accounts for such prompt perfect failure then
And there on the instant. Any day o' the week,
A ducat slid discreetly into palm
O' the mute post-master, while you whisper him –
How you the Count and certain four your knaves,
Have just been mauling who was malapert,
1630 Suspect the kindred may prove troublesome,
Therefore, want horses in a hurry, – that
And nothing more secures you any day
The pick o' the stable! Yet I try the trick,
Double the bribe, call myself Duke for Count,
And say the dead man only was a Jew,
And for my pains find I am dealing just
With the one scrupulous fellow in all Rome –
Just this immaculate official stares,
Sees I want hat on head and sword in sheath,
1640 Am splashed with other sort of wet than wine,
Shrugs shoulder, puts my hand by, gold and all,
Stands on the strictness of the rule o' the road!
'Where's the Permission?' Where's the wretched rag
With the due seal and sign of Rome's Police,
To be had for asking, half-an-hour ago?
'Gone? Get another, or no horses hence!'
He dares not stop me, we five glare too grim,
But hinders, – hacks and hamstrings sure enough,
Gives me some twenty miles of miry road
1650 More to march in the middle of that night
Whereof the rough beginning taxed the strength
O' the youngsters, much more mine, such as you see,
Who had to think as well as act: dead-beat,
We gave in ere we reached the boundary
And safe spot out of this irrational Rome, –
Where, on dismounting from our steeds next day,
We had snapped our fingers at you, safe and sound,

Tuscans once more in blessed Tuscany,
Where the laws make allowance, understand
1660 Civilized life and do its champions right!
Witness the sentence of the Rota there,
Arezzo uttered, the Granduke confirmed,
One week before I acted on its hint, –
Giving friend Guillichini, for his love,
The galleys, and my wife your saint, Rome's saint, –
Rome manufactures saints enough to know, –
Seclusion at the Stinche for her life.
All this, that all but was, might all have been,
Yet was not! baulked by just a scrupulous knave
1670 Whose palm was horn through handling horses' hoofs
And could not close upon my proffered gold!
What say you to the spite of fortune? Well,
The worst's in store: thus hindered, haled this way
To Rome again by hangdogs, whom find I
Here, still to fight with, but my pale frail wife?
– Riddled with wounds by one not like to waste
The blows he dealt, – knowing anatomy, –
(I think I told you) one to pick and choose
The vital parts! 'T was learning all in vain!
1680 She too must shimmer through the gloom o' the grave,
Come and confront me – not at judgment-seat
Where I could twist her soul, as erst her flesh,
And turn her truth into a lie, – but there,
O' the death-bed, with God's hand between us both,
Striking me dumb, and helping her to speak,
Tell her own story her own way, and turn
My plausibility to nothingness!
Four whole days did Pompilia keep alive,
With the best surgery of Rome agape
1690 At the miracle, – this cut, the other slash,
And yet the life refusing to dislodge,
Four whole extravagant impossible days,
Till she had time to finish and persuade
Every man, every woman, every child
In Rome of what she would: the selfsame she

Who, but a year ago, had wrung her hands,
Reddened her eyes and beat her breasts, rehearsed
The whole game at Arezzo, nor availed
Thereby to move one heart or raise one hand!
1700 When destiny intends you cards like these,
What good of skill and preconcerted play?
Had she been found dead, as I left her dead,
I should have told a tale brooked no reply:
You scarcely will suppose me found at fault
With that advantage! 'What brings me to Rome?
Necessity to claim and take my wife:
Better, to claim and take my new-born babe, –
Strong in paternity a fortnight old,
When 't is at strongest: warily I work,
1710 Knowing the machinations of my foe;
I have companionship and use the night:
I seek my wife and child, – I find – no child
But wife, in the embraces of that priest
Who caused her to elope from me. These two,
Backed by the pander-pair who watch the while,
Spring on me like so many tiger-cats,
Glad of the chance to end the intruder. I –
What should I do but stand on my defence,
Strike right, strike left, strike thick and threefold, slay,
1720 Not all – because the coward priest escapes.
Last, I escape, in fear of evil tongues,
And having had my taste of Roman law.'
What's disputable, refutable here? –
Save by just this one ghost-thing half on earth,
Half out of it, – as if she held God's hand
While she leant back and looked her last at me,
Forgiving me (here monks begin to weep)
Oh, from her very soul, commending mine
To heavenly mercies which are infinite, –
1730 While fixing fast my head beneath your knife!
'T is fate not fortune! All is of a piece!
What was it you informed me of my youths?
My rustic four o' the family, soft swains,

What sweet surprise had they in store for me,
Those of my very household, – what did Law
Twist with her rack-and-cord-contrivance late
From out their bones and marrow? What but this –
Had no one of these several stumbling-blocks
Stopped me, they yet were cherishing a scheme,
1740 All of their honest country homespun wit,
To quietly next day at crow of cock,
Cut my own throat too, for their own behoof,
Seeing I had forgot to clear accounts
O' the instant, nowise slackened speed for that, –
And somehow never might find memory,
Once safe back in Arezzo, where things change,
And a court-lord needs mind no country lout.
Well, being the arch-offender, I die last, –
May, ere my head falls, have my eyesight free,
1750 Nor miss them dangling high on either hand,
Like scarecrows in a hemp-field; for their pains!

And then my Trial, – 't is my Trial that bites
Like a corrosive, so the cards are packed,
Dice loaded, and my life-stake tricked away!
Look at my lawyers, lacked they grace of law,
Latin or logic? Were not they fools to the height,
Fools to the depth, fools to the level between,
O' the foolishness set to decide the case?
They feign, they flatter; nowise does it skill,
1760 Everything goes against me: deal each judge
His dole of flattery and feigning, – why,
He turns and tries and snuffs and savours it,
As an old fly the sugar-grain, your gift;
Then eyes your thumb and finger, brushes clean
The absurd old head of him, and whisks away,
Leaving your thumb and finger dirty. Faugh!

And finally, after this long-drawn range
Of affront, failure, failure and affront, –
This path, twixt crosses leading to a skull,

1770 Paced by me barefoot, bloodied by my palms
From the entry to the end, – there's light at length,
A cranny of escape, – appeal may be
To the old man, to the father, to the Pope,
For a little life – from one whose life is spent,
A little pity – from pity's source and seat,
A little indulgence to rank, privilege,
From one who is the thing personified,
Rank, privilege, indulgence, grown beyond
Earth's bearing, even, ask Jansenius else!

1780 Still the same answer, still no other tune
From the cicala perched at the tree-top
Than crickets noisy round the root, – 't is 'Die!'
Bids Law – 'Be damned!' adds Gospel, – nay,
No word so frank, – 't is rather, 'Save yourself!'
The Pope subjoins – 'Confess and be absolved!
So shall my credit countervail your shame,
And the world see I have not lost the knack
Of trying all the spirits, – yours, my son,
Wants but a fiery washing to emerge

1790 In clarity! Come, cleanse you, ease the ache
Of these old bones, refresh our bowels, boy!'
Do I mistake your mission from the Pope?
Then, bear his Holiness the mind of me!
I do get strength from being thrust to wall,
Successively wrenched from pillar and from post
By this tenacious hate of fortune, hate
Of all things in, under, and above earth.
Warfare, begun this mean unmanly mode,
Does best to end so, – gives earth spectacle

1800 Of a brave fighter who succumbs to odds
That turn defeat to victory. Stab, I fold
My mantle round me! Rome approves my act:
Applauds the blow which costs me life but keeps
My honour spotless: Rome would praise no more
Had I fallen, say, some fifteen years ago,
Helping Vienna when our Aretines
Flocked to Duke Charles and fought Turk Mustafa;

Nor would you two be trembling o'er my corpse
With all this exquisite solicitude.
1810 Why is it that I make such suit to live?
The popular sympathy that's round me now
Would break like bubble that o'er-domes a fly –
Pretty enough while he lies quiet there,
But let him want the air and ply the wing,
Why, it breaks and bespatters him, what else?
Cardinal, if the Pope had pardoned me,
And I walked out of prison through the crowd,
It would not be your arm I should dare press!
Then, if I got safe to my place again,
1820 How sad and sapless were the years to come!
I go my old ways and find things grown grey;
You priests leer at me, old friends look askance;
The mob's in love, I'll wager, to a man,
With my poor young good beauteous murdered wife:
For hearts require instruction how to beat,
And eyes, on warrant of the story, wax
Wanton at portraiture in white and black
Of dead Pompilia gracing ballad-sheet,
Which, had she died unmurdered and unsung,
1830 Would never turn though she paced street as bare
As the mad penitent ladies do in France.
My brothers quietly would edge me out
Of use and management of things called mine;
Do I command? 'You stretched command before!'
Show anger? 'Anger little helped you once!'
Advise? 'How managed you affairs of old?'
My very mother, all the while they gird,
Turns eye up, gives confirmatory groan, –
For unsuccess, explain it how you will,
1840 Disqualifies you, makes you doubt yourself,
– Much more, is found decisive by your friends.
Beside, am I not fifty years of age?
What new leap would a life take, checked like mine
I' the spring at outset? Where's my second chance?
Ay, but the babe . . . I had forgot my son,

My heir! Now for a burst of gratitude!
There's some appropriate service to intone,
Some *gaudeamus* and thanksgiving-psalm!
Old, I renew my youth in him, and poor
1850 Possess a treasure, – is not that the phrase?
Only I must wait patient twenty years –
Nourishing all the while, as father ought,
The excrescence with my daily blood of life.
Does it respond to hope, such sacrifice, –
Grows the wen plump while I myself grow lean?
Why, here's my son and heir in evidence,
Who stronger, wiser, handsomer than I
By fifty years, relieves me of each load, –
Tames my hot horse, carries my heavy gun,
1860 Courts my coy mistress, – has his apt advice
On house-economy, expenditure,
And what not? All which good gifts and great growth
Because of my decline, he brings to bear
On Guido, but half apprehensive how
He cumbers earth, crosses the brisk young Count,
Who civilly would thrust him from the scene.
Contrariwise, does the blood-offering fail?
There's an ineptitude, one blank the more
Added to earth in semblance of my child?
1870 Then, this has been a costly piece of work,
My life exchanged for his! – why he, not I,
Enjoy the world, if no more grace accrue?
Dwarf me, what giant have you made of him?
I do not dread the disobedient son –
I know how to suppress rebellion there,
Being not quite the fool my father was.
But grant the medium measure of a man,
The usual compromise 'twixt fool and sage,
– You know – the tolerably-obstinate,
1880 The not-so-much-perverse but you may train,
The true son-servant that, when parent bids
'Go work, son, in my vineyard!' makes reply
'I go, Sir!' – Why, what profit in your son

Beyond the drudges you might subsidize,
Have the same work from at a paul the head?
Look at those four young precious olive-plants
Reared at Vittiano, – not on flesh and blood,
These twenty years, but black bread and sour wine!
I bade them put forth tender branch, and hook
1890 And hurt three enemies I had in Rome:
They did my hest as unreluctantly,
At promise of a dollar, as a son
Adjured by mumping memories of the past!
No, nothing repays youth expended so –
Youth, I say, who am young still, – give but leave
To live my life out, to the last I'd live
And die conceding age no right of youth!
It is the will runs the renewing nerve
Through flaccid flesh, would faint before the time.
1900 Therefore no sort of use for son have I –
Sick, not of life's feast but of steps to climb
To the house where life prepares her feast, – of means
To the end: for make the end attainable
Without the means, – my relish were like yours.
A man may have an appetite enough
For a whole dish of robins ready cooked,
And yet lack courage to face sleet, pad snow,
And snare sufficiency for supper.

                                        Thus
1910 The time's arrived when, ancient Roman-like,
I am bound to fall on my own sword, – why not
Say – Tuscan-like, more ancient, better still?
Will you hear truth can do no harm nor good?
I think I never was at any time
A Christian, as you nickname all the world,
Me among others: truce to nonsense now!
Name me, a primitive religionist –
As should the aboriginary be
I boast myself, Etruscan, Aretine,
1920 One sprung, – your frigid Virgil's fieriest word, –

From fauns and nymphs, trunks and the heart of oak,
With, – for a visible divinity, –
The portent of a Jove Aegiochus
Descried 'mid clouds, lightning and thunder, couched
On topmost crag of your Capitoline –
'Tis in the Seventh Aeneid, – what, the Eighth?
Right, – thanks, Abate, – though the Christian's dumb,
The Latinist's vivacious in you yet!
I know my grandsire had our tapestry
1930 Marked with the motto, 'neath a certain shield
His grandson presently will give some gules
To vary azure. First we fight for faiths,
But get to shake hands at the last of all:
Mine's your faith too, – in Jove Aegiochus!
Nor do Greek gods, that serve as supplement,
Jar with the simpler scheme, if understood.
We want such intermediary race
To make communication possible;
The real thing were too lofty, we too low,
1940 Midway hang these: we feel their use so plain
In linking height to depth, that we doff hat
And put no question nor pry narrowly
Into the nature hid behind the names.
We grudge no rite the fancy may demand;
But never, more than needs, invent, refine,
Improve upon requirement, idly wise
Beyond the letter, teaching gods their trade,
Which is to teach us: we'll obey when taught.
Why should we do our duty past the due?
1950 When the sky darkens, Jove is wroth, – say prayer!
When the sun shines and Jove is glad, – sing psalm!
But wherefore pass prescription and devise
Blood-offering for sweat-service, lend the rod
A pungency through pickle of our own?
Learned Abate, – no one teaches you
What Venus means and who's Apollo here!
I spare you, Cardinal, – but, though you wince,
You know me, I know you, and both know that!

So, if Apollo bids us fast, we fast:
1960 But where does Venus order we stop sense
When Master Pietro rhymes a pleasantry?
Give alms prescribed on Friday, – but, hold hand
Because your foe lies prostrate, – where's the word
Explicit in the book debars revenge?
The rationale of your scheme is just
'Pay toll here, there pursue your pleasure free!'
So do you turn to use the medium-powers,
Mars and Minerva, Bacchus and the rest,
And so are saved propitiating – what?
1970 What all good, all wise and all potent Jove
Vexed by the very sins in man, himself
Made life's necessity when man he made?
Irrational bunglers! So, the living truth
Revealed to strike Pan dead, ducks low at last,
Prays leave to hold its own and live good days
Provided it go masque grotesquely, called
Christian not Pagan? Oh, you purged the sky
Of all gods save the One, the great and good,
Clapped hands and triumphed! But the change came fast:
1980 The inexorable need in man for life –
Life, – you may mulct and minish to a grain
Out of the lump, so the grain left but live, –
Laughed at your substituting death for life,
And bade you do your worst, – which worst was done
– Pass that age styled the primitive and pure
When Saint this, Saint that, dutifully starved,
Froze, fought with beasts, was beaten and abused
And finally ridded of his flesh by fire,
Keeping the while unspotted from the world! –
1990 Good: but next age, how goes the game, who gives
His life and emulates Saint that and this?
They mutiny, mutter who knows what excuse?
In fine make up their minds to leave the new,
Stick to the old, – enjoy old liberty,
No prejudice, all the same, if so it please,
To the new profession: sin o' the sly, henceforth!

Let the law stand: the letter kills, what then?
The spirit saves as unmistakeably.
Omniscience sees, Omnipotence could stop,
2000 All-mercifulness pardons, – it must be,
Frown law its fiercest, there's a wink somewhere.

Such was the logic in this head of mine:
I, like the rest, wrote 'poison' on my bread;
But broke and ate: – said 'those that use the sword
Shall perish by the same;' then stabbed my foe.
I stand on solid earth, not empty air:
Dislodge me, let your Pope's crook hale me hence!
Not he, nor you! And I so pity both,
I'll make the speech you want the wit to make:
2010 'Count Guido, who reveal our mystery,
You trace all issues to the love of life:
We have a life to love and guard, like you.
Why did you put us upon self-defence?
You well knew what prompt pass-word would appease
The sentry's ire when folk infringe his bounds,
And yet kept mouth shut: do you wonder then
If, in mere decency, he shot you dead?
He can't have people play such pranks as you
Beneath his nose at noonday, who disdain
2020 To give him an excuse before the world,
By crying "I break rule to save our camp!"
Under the old rule, such offence were death;
And so had you heard Pontifex pronounce
"Since you slay foe and violate the form,
That turns to murder, which were sacrifice
Had you, while, say, law-suiting him to death,
But raised an altar to the Unknown God,
Or else the Genius of the Vatican."
Why then this pother? – all because the Pope
2030 Doing his duty, cries "A foreigner,
You scandalize the natives: here at Rome
Romano vivitur more: wise men, here,
Put the Church forward and efface themselves.

The fit defence had been, – you stamped on wheat,
Intending all the time to trample tares, –
Were fain extirpate, then, the heretic,
And now find, in your haste you slew a fool:
Nor Pietro, nor Violante, nor your wife
Meant to breed up your babe a Molinist!
2040 Whence you are duly contrite. Not one word
Of all this wisdom did you urge! – which slip
Death must atone for!"'
                So, let death atone!
So ends mistake, so end mistakers! – end
Perhaps to recommence, – how should I know?
Only, be sure, no punishment, no pain
Childish, preposterous, impossible,
But some such fate as Ovid could foresee, –
Byblis in fluvium, let the weak soul end
2050 In water, *sed Lycaon in lupum*, but
The strong become a wolf for evermore!
Change that Pompilia to a puny stream
Fit to reflect the daisies on its bank!
Let me turn wolf, be whole, and sate, for once, –
Wallow in what is now a wolfishness
Coerced too much by the humanity
That's half of me as well! Grow out of man,
Glut the wolf-nature, – what remains but grow
Into the man again, be man indeed
2060 And all man? Do I ring the changes right?
Deformed, transformed, reformed, informed, conformed!
The honest instinct, pent and crossed through life,
Let surge by death into a visible flow
Of rapture: as the strangled thread of flame
Painfully winds, annoying and annoyed,
Malignant and maligned, thro' stone and ore,
Till earth exclude the stranger: vented once,
It finds full play, is recognized a-top
Some mountain as no such abnormal birth.
2070 Fire for the mount, the streamlet for the vale!

Ay, of the water was that wife of mine –
Be it for good, be it for ill, no run
O' the red thread through that insignificance!
Again, how she is at me with those eyes!
Away with the empty stare! Be holy still,
And stupid ever! Occupy your patch
Of private snow that's somewhere in what world
May now be growing icy round your head,
And aguish at your foot-print, – freeze not me,
2080 Dare follow not another step I take,
Not with so much as those detested eyes,
No, though they follow but to pray me pause
On the incline, earth's edge that's next to hell!
None of your abnegation of revenge!
Fly at me frank, tug while I tear again!
There's God, go tell Him, testify your worst!
Not she! There was no touch in her of hate:
And it would prove her hell, if I reached mine!
To know I suffered, would still sadden her,
2090 Do what the angels might to make amends!
Therefore there's either no such place as hell,
Or thence shall I be thrust forth, for her sake,
And thereby undergo three hells, not one –
I who, with outlet for escape to heaven,
Would tarry if such flight allowed my foe
To raise his head, relieved of that firm foot
Had pinned him to the fiery pavement else!
So am I made, 'who did not make myself:'
(How dared she rob my own lip of the word?)
2100 Beware me in what other world may be! –
Pompilia, who have brought me to this pass!
All I know here, will I say there, and go
Beyond the saying with the deed. Some use
There cannot but be for a mood like mine,
Implacable, persistent in revenge.
She maundered 'All is over and at end:
I go my own road, go you where God will!
Forgive you? I forget you!' There's the saint

That takes your taste, you other kind of men!
2110 How you had loved her! Guido wanted skill
To value such a woman at her worth!
Properly the instructed criticize
'What's here, you simpleton have tossed to take
Its chance i' the gutter? This a daub, indeed?
Why, 't is a Rafael that you kicked to rags!'
Perhaps so: some prefer the pure design:
Give me my gorge of colour, glut of gold
In a glory round the Virgin made for me!
Titian's the man, not Monk Angelico
2120 Who traces you some timid chalky ghost
That turns the church into a charnel: ay,
Just such a pencil might depict my wife!
She, – since she, also, would not change herself, –
Why could not she come in some heart-shaped cloud,
Rainbowed about with riches, royalty
Rimming her round, as round the tintless lawn
Guardingly runs the selvage cloth of gold?
I would have left the faint fine gauze untouched,
Needle-worked over with its lily and rose,
2130 Let her bleach unmolested in the midst,
Chill that selected solitary spot
Of quietude she pleased to think was life:
Purity, pallor grace the lawn no doubt
When there's the costly bordure to unthread
And make again an ingot: but what's grace
When you want meat and drink and clothes and fire?
A tale comes to my mind that's apposite –
Possibly true, probably false, a truth
Such as all truths we live by, Cardinal!
2140 'T is said, a certain ancestor of mine
Followed – whoever was the potentate,
To Paynimrie, and in some battle, broke
Through more than due allowance of the foe
And, risking much his own life, saved the lord's.
Battered and bruised, the Emperor scrambles up,
Rubs his eyes and looks round and sees my sire,

Picks a furze-sprig from out his hauberk-joint,
(Token how near the ground went majesty)
And says 'Take this, and, if thou get safe home,
2150 Plant the same in thy garden-ground to grow:
Run thence an hour in a straight line, and stop:
Describe a circle round (for central point)
The furze aforesaid, reaching every way
The length of that hour's run: I give it thee, –
The central point, to build a castle there,
The circumjacent space, for fit demesne,
The whole to be thy children's heritage, –
Whom, for my sake, bid thou wear furze on cap!'
Those are my arms: we turned the furze a tree
2160 To show more, and the greyhound tied thereto,
Straining to start, means swift and greedy both;
He stands upon a triple mount of gold –
By Jove, then, he's escaping from true gold
And trying to arrive at empty air!
Aha! the fancy never crossed my mind!
My father used to tell me, and subjoin
'As for the castle, that took wings and flew:
The broad lands, – why, to traverse them to-day
Would task my gouty feet, though in my prime
2170 I doubt not I could stand and spit so far:
But for the furze, boy, fear no lack of that,
So long as fortune leaves one field to grub!
Wherefore hurra for furze and loyalty!'
What may I mean, where may the lesson lurk?
'Do not bestow on man by way of gift
Furze without some substantial framework, – grace
Of purity, a furze-sprig of a wife,
To me, i' the thick of battle for my bread,
Without some better dowry, – house and land!'
2180 No other gift than sordid muck? Yes, Sir!
Many more and much better. Give them me!
O those Olimpias bold, those Biancas brave,
That brought a husband will worth Ormuz' wealth!
Cried 'Thou being mine, why, what but thine am I?

Be thou to me law, right, wrong, heaven and hell!
Let us blend souls, be thou in me to bid
Two bodies work one pleasure! What are these
Called king, priest, father, mother, stranger, friend?
They fret thee or they frustrate? Give the word –
2190 Be certain they shall frustrate nothing more!
And who is this young florid foolishness
That holds thy fortune in his pigmy clutch,
– Being a prince and potency, forsooth! –
And hesitates to let the trifle go?
Let me but seal up eye, sing ear to sleep
Sounder than Samson, – pounce thou on the prize
Shall slip from off my breast, and down couch-side
And on to floor, and far as my lord's feet –
Where he stands in the shadow with the sword
2200 Waiting to see what Delilah dares do!
Is the youth fair? What is a man to me
Who am thy call-bird? Twist his neck – my dupe's, –
Then take the breast shall turn a breast indeed!'
Such women are there; and they marry whom?
Why, when a man has gone and hanged himself
Because of what he calls a wicked wife, –
See, if the turpitude, he makes his moan,
Be not mere excellence the fool ignores!
His monster is perfection, Circe, sent
2210 Straight from the sun, with rod the idiot blames
As not an honest distaff to spin wool!
O thou Lucrezia, is it long to wait
Yonder where all the gloom is in a glow
With thy suspected presence? – virgin yet,
Virtuous again in face of what's to teach –
Sin unimagined, unimaginable, –
I come to claim my bride, – thy Borgia's self
Not half the burning bridegroom I shall be!
Cardinal, take away your crucifix!
2220 Abate, leave my lips alone, they bite!
'T is vain you try to change, what should not change,
And cannot. I have bared, you bathe my heart –

It grows the stonier for your saving dew!
You steep the substance, you would lubricate,
In waters that but touch to petrify!

You too are petrifactions of a kind:
Move not a muscle that shows mercy; rave
Another twelve hours, every word were waste!
I thought you would not slay impenitence, –
2230 Teazed first contrition from the man you slew, –
I thought you had a conscience. Cardinal,
You know I am wronged! – wronged, say, and wronged
    maintain.
Was this strict inquisition made for blood
When first you showed us scarlet on your back,
Called to the College? That straightforward way
To that legitimate end, – I think it passed
Over a scantling of heads brained, hearts broke,
Lives trodden into dust, – how otherwise?
Such is the way o' the world, and so you walk:
2240 Does memory haunt your pillow? Not a whit.
God wills you never pace your garden-path
One appetizing hour ere dinner-time
But your intrusion there treads out of life
An universe of happy innocent things:
Feel you remorse about that damsel-fly
Which buzzed so near your mouth and flapped your face,
You blotted it from being at a blow?
It was a fly, you were a man, and more,
Lord of created things, so took your course.
2250 Manliness, mind, – these are things fit to save,
Fit to brush fly from: why, because I take
My course, must needs the Pope kill me? – kill you!
Because this instrument he throws away
Is strong to serve a master: it were yours
To have and hold and get such good from out!
The Pope who dooms me, needs must die next year;
I'll tell you how the chances are supposed
For his successor: first the Chamberlain,

Old San Cesario, – Colloredo, next, –
2260 Then, one, two, three, four, I refuse to name,
After these, comes Altieri; then come you –
Seventh on the list you are, unless . . . ha, ha,
How can a dead hand give a friend a lift?
Are you the person to despise the help
O' the head shall drop in pannier presently?
So a child seesaws on or kicks away
The fulcrum-stone that's all the sage requires
To fit his lever to and move the world.
Cardinal, I adjure you in God's name,
2270 Save my life, fall at the Pope's feet, set forth
Things your own fashion, not in words like these
Made for a sense like yours who apprehend!
Translate into the court-conventional
'Count Guido must not die, is innocent!
Fair, be assured! But what an he were foul,
Blood-drenched and murder-crusted head to foot?
Spare one whose death insults the Emperor,
And outrages the Louis you so love!
He has friends who will avenge him; enemies
2280 Who hate the church now with impunity
Missing the old coercive: would you send
A soul straight to perdition, dying frank
An atheist?' Go and say this, for God's sake!
– Why, you don't think I hope you'll say one word?
Neither shall I persuade you from your stand
Nor you persuade me from my station: take
Your crucifix away, I tell you twice!

Come, I am tired of silence! Pause enough!
You have prayed: I have gone inside my soul
2290 And shut its door behind me: 't is your torch
Makes the place dark, – the darkness let alone
Grows tolerable twilight, – one may grope
And get to guess at length and breadth and depth.
What is this fact I feel persuaded of –
This something like a foothold in the sea,

Although Saint Peter's bark scuds, billow-borne,
Leaves me to founder where it flung me first?
Spite of your splashing, I am high and dry!
God takes his own part in each thing he made;
2300 Made for a reason, he conserves his work,
Gives each its proper instinct of defence.
My lamblike wife could neither bark nor bite,
She bleated, bleated, till for pity pure,
The village roused it, ran with pole and prong
To the rescue, and behold the wolf's at bay!
Shall he try bleating? – or take turn or two,
Since the wolf owns to kinship with the fox,
And failing to escape the foe by these,
Give up attempt, die fighting quietly?
2310 The last bad blow that strikes fire in at eye
And on to brain, and so out, life and all,
How can it but be cheated of a pang
While, fighting quietly, the jaws enjoy
Their re-embrace in mid back-bone they break,
After their weary work thro' the foes' flesh?
That's the wolf-nature. Do n't mistake my trope!
The Cardinal is qualmish! Eminence,
My fight is figurative, blows i' the air,
Brain-war with powers and principalities,
2320 Spirit-bravado, no real fisticuffs!
I shall not presently, when the knock comes,
Cling to this bench nor flee the hangman's face,
No, trust me! I conceive worse lots than mine.
Whether it be the old contagious fit
And plague o' the prison have surprised me too,
The appropriate drunkenness of the death-hour
Creep on my sense, the work o' the wine and myrrh, –
I know not, – I begin to taste my strength,
Careless, gay even: what's the worth of life?
2330 The Pope is dead, my murderous old man,
For Tozzi told me so: and you, forsooth –
Why, you do n't think, Abate, do your best,
You'll live a year more with that hacking cough

And blotch of crimson where the cheek's a pit?
Tozzi has got you also down in book.
Cardinal, only seventh of seventy near,
Is not one called Albano in the lot?
Go eat your heart, you'll never be a Pope!
Inform me, is it true you left your love,
2340 A Pucci, for promotion in the church?
She's more than in the church, – in the churchyard!
Plautilla Pucci, your affianced bride,
Has dust now in the eyes that held the love, –
And Martinez, suppose they make you Pope,
Stops that with *veto*, – so, enjoy yourself!
I see you all reel to the rock, you waves –
Some forthright, some describe a sinuous track,
Some crested, brilliantly with heads above,
Some in a strangled swirl sunk who knows how,
2350 But all bound whither the main-current sets,
Rockward, an end in foam for all of you!
What if I am o'ertaken, pushed to the front
By all you crowding smoother souls behind,
And reach, a minute sooner than was meant,
The boundary, whereon I break to mist?
Go to! the smoothest safest of you all,
Most perfect and compact wave in my train,
Spite of the blue tranquillity above,
Spite of the breadth before of lapsing peace
2360 Where broods the halcyon and the fish leaps free,
Will presently begin to feel the prick
At lazy heart, the push at torpid brain,
Will rock vertiginously in turn, and reel,
And, emulative, rush to death like me:
Later or sooner by a minute then,
So much for the untimeliness of death, –
And, as regards the manner that offends,
The rude and rough, I count the same for gain –
Be the act harsh and quick! Undoubtedly
2370 The soul's condensed and, twice itself, expands
To burst thro' life, in alternation due,

Into the other state whate'er it prove.
You never know what life means till you die:
Even throughout life, 't is death that makes life live,
Gives it whatever the significance.
For see, on your own ground and argument,
Suppose life had no death to fear, how find
A possibility of nobleness
In man, prevented daring any more?
2380 What's love, what's faith without a worst to dread?
Lack-lustre jewelry; but faith and love
With death behind them bidding do or die –
Put such a foil at back, the sparkle's born!
From out myself how the strange colours come!
Is there a new rule in another world?
Be sure I shall resign myself: as here
I recognized no law I could not see,
There, what I see, I shall acknowledge too:
On earth I never took the Pope for God,
2390 In heaven I shall scarce take God for the Pope.
Unmanned, remade: I hold it probable –
With something changeless at the heart of me
To know me by, some nucleus that's myself:
Accretions did it wrong? Away with them –
You soon shall see the use of fire!

                         Till when,
All that was, is; and must for ever be.
Nor is it in me to unhate my hates, –
I use up my last strength to strike once more
2400 Old Pietro in the wine-house-gossip-face,
To trample underfoot the whine and wile
Of that Violante, – and I grow one gorge
To loathingly reject Pompilia's pale
Poison my hasty hunger took for food.
A strong tree wants no wreaths about its trunk,
No cloying cups, no sickly sweet of scent,
But sustenance at root, a bucketful.
How else lived that Athenian who died so,

Drinking hot bull's-blood, fit for men like me?
2410 I lived and died a man, and take man's chance,
Honest and bold: right will be done to such.
Who are these you have let descend my stair?
Ha, their accursed psalm! Lights at the sill!
Is it 'Open' they dare bid you? Treachery!
Sirs, have I spoken one word all this while
Out of the world of words I had to say?
Not one word! All was folly; I laughed and mocked!
Sirs, my first true word, all truth and no lie,
Is – save me notwithstanding! Life is all!
2420 I was just stark mad, – let the madman live
Pressed by as many chains as you please pile!
Do n't open! Hold me from them! I am yours,
I am the Granduke's – no, I am the Pope's!
Abate, – Cardinal, – Christ, – Maria, – God, . . .
Pompilia, will you let them murder me?

Here were the end, had anything an end:
Thus, lit and launched, up and up roared and soared
A rocket, till the key o' the vault was reached,
And wide heaven held, a breathless minute-space,
In brilliant usurpature: thus caught spark,
Rushed to the height, and hung at full of fame
Over men's upturned faces, ghastly thence,
Our glaring Guido: now decline must be.
In its explosion, you have seen his act,
10 By my power – may-be, judged it by your own, –
Or composite as good orbs prove, or crammed
With worse ingredients than the Wormwood Star.
The act, over and ended, falls and fades:
What was once seen, grows what is now described,
Then talked of, told about, a tinge the less
In every fresh transmission; till it melts,
Trickles in silent orange or wan grey
Across our memory, dies and leaves all dark,
And presently we find the stars again.
20 Follow the main streaks, meditate the mode
Of brightness, how it hastes to blend with black!

After that February Twenty-Two,
Since our salvation, Sixteen-Ninety-Eight,
Of all reports that were, or may have been,
Concerning those the day killed or let live,
Four I count only. Take the first that comes.
A letter from a stranger, man of rank,
Venetian visitor at Rome, – who knows,
On what pretence of busy idleness?

30   Thus he begins on evening of that day.

'Here are we at our end of Carnival;
Prodigious gaiety and monstrous mirth,
And constant shift of entertaining show:
With influx, from each quarter of the globe,
Of strangers nowise wishful to be last
I' the struggle for a good place presently
When that befalls, fate cannot long defer.
The old Pope totters on the verge o' the grave:
You see, Malpichi understood far more
40   Than Tozzi how to treat the ailments: age,
No question, renders these inveterate.
Cardinal Spada, actual Minister,
Is possible Pope; I wager on his head,
Since those four entertainments of his niece
Which set all Rome a-stare: Pope probably –
Though Colloredo has his backers too,
And San Cesario makes one doubt at times:
Altieri will be Chamberlain at most.

A week ago the sun was warm like May,
50   And the old man took daily exercise
Along the river-side; he loves to see
That Custom-house he built upon the bank,
For, Naples-born, his tastes are maritime:
But yesterday he had to keep in-doors
Because of the outrageous rain that fell.
On such days the good soul has fainting-fits,
Or lies in stupor, scarcely makes believe
Of minding business, fumbles at his beads.
They say, the trust that keeps his heart alive
60   Is that, by lasting till December next,
He may hold Jubilee a second time,
And, twice in one reign, ope the Holy Doors.
By the way, somebody responsible
Assures me that the King of France has writ
Fresh orders: Fénelon will be condemned:

The Cardinal makes a wry face enough,
Having a love for the delinquent: still,
He's the ambassador, must press the point.
Have you a wager too dependent here?

70   Now, from such matters to divert awhile,
Hear of to-day's event which crowns the week,
Casts all the other wagers into shade.
Tell Dandolo I owe him fifty drops
Of heart's blood in the shape of gold zecchines!
The Pope has done his worst: I have to pay
For the execution of the Count, by Jove!
Two days since, I reported him as safe,
Re-echoing the conviction of all Rome:
Who could suspect the one deaf ear – the Pope's?
80   But prejudices grow insuperable,
And that old enmity to Austria, that
Passion for France and France's pageant-king
(Of which, why pause to multiply the proofs
Now scandalously rife in Europe's mouth?)
These fairly got the better in the man
Of justice, prudence, and *esprit de corps*,
And he persisted in the butchery.
Also, 't is said that in his latest walk
To that Dogana-by-the-Bank, he built,
90   The crowd, – he suffers question, unrebuked, –
Asked, "Whether murder was a privilege
Only reserved for nobles like the Count?"
And he was ever mindful of the mob.
Martinez, the Caesarian Minister,
– Who used his best endeavours to spare blood,
And strongly pleaded for the life "of one,"
Urged he, "I may have dined at table with!" –
He will not soon forget the Pope's rebuff,
– Feels the slight sensibly, I promise you!
100   And but for the dissuasion of two eyes
That make with him foul weather or fine day,
He had abstained, nor graced the spectacle:

As it was, barely would he condescend
Look forth from the *palchetto* where he sat
Under the Pincian: we shall hear of this!
The substituting, too, the People's Square
For the out-o'-the-way old quarter by the Bridge,
Was meant as a conciliatory sop
To the mob; it gave one holiday the more.
110 But the French Embassy might unfurl flag, –
Still the good luck of France to fling a foe!
Cardinal Bouillon triumphs properly!
Palchetti were erected in the Place,
And houses, at the edge of the Three Streets,
Let their front windows at six dollars each:
Anguisciola, that patron of the arts,
Hired one; our Envoy Contarini too.

Now for the thing; no sooner the decree
Gone forth, – 't is four-and-twenty hours ago, –
120 Than Acciaioli and Panciatichi,
Old friends, indeed compatriots of the man,
Being pitched on as the couple properest
To intimate the sentence yesternight,
Were closeted ere cock-crow with the Count.
They both report their efforts to dispose
The unhappy nobleman for ending well,
Despite the natural sense of injury,
Were crowned at last with a complete success:
And when the Company of Death arrived
130 At twenty-hours, – the way they reckon here, –
We say, at sunset, after dinner-time, –
The Count was led down, hoisted up on car,
Last of the five, as heinousest, you know:
Yet they allowed one whole car to each man.
His intrepidity, nay, nonchalance,
As up he stood and down he sat himself,
Struck admiration into those who saw.
Then the procession started, took the way
From the New Prisons by the Pilgrim's Street,

140   The street of the Governo, Pasquin's Street,
    (Where was stuck up, 'mid other epigrams,
    A quatrain . . . but of all that, presently!)
    The Place Navona, the Pantheon's Place,
    Place of the Column, last the Corso's length,
    And so debouched thence at Mannaia's foot
    I' the Place o' the People. As is evident,
    (Despite the malice, – plainly meant, I fear,
    By this abrupt change of locality, –
    The Square's no such bad place to head and hang)
150   We had the titillation as we sat
    Assembled, (quality in conclave, ha?)
    Of, minute after minute, some report
    How the slow show was winding on its way.
    Now did a car run over, kill a man,
    Just opposite a pork-shop numbered Twelve:
    And bitter were the outcries of the mob
    Against the Pope: for, but that he forbids
    The Lottery, why, twelve were Tern Quatern!
    Now did a beggar by Saint Agnes, lame
160   From his youth up, recover use of leg,
    Through prayer of Guido as he glanced that way:
    So that the crowd near crammed his hat with coin.
    Thus was kept up excitement to the last,
    – Not an abrupt out-bolting, as of yore,
    From Castle, over Bridge and on to block,
    And so all ended ere you well could wink!

    Guido was last to mount the scaffold-steps
    Here also, as atrociousest in crime.
    We hardly noticed how the peasants died,
170   They dangled somehow soon to right and left,
    And we remained all ears and eyes, could give
    Ourselves to Guido undividedly,
    As he harangued the multitude beneath.
    He begged forgiveness on the part of God,
    And fair construction of his act from men,
    Whose suffrage he entreated for his soul,

Suggesting that we should forthwith repeat
A *Pater* and an *Ave*, with the hymn
Salve Regina Coeli, for his sake.
180   Which said, he turned to the confessor, crossed
And reconciled himself, with decency,
Oft glancing at Saint Mary's opposite
Where they possess, and showed in shrine to-day,
The Blessed *Umbilicus* of our Lord,
(A relic 't is believed no other church
In Rome can boast of) – then rose up, as brisk
Knelt down again, bent head, adapted neck,
And, with the name of Jesus on his lips,
Received the fatal blow.

190   The headsman showed
The head to the populace. Must I avouch
We strangers own to disappointment here?
Report pronounced him fully six feet high,
Youngish, considering his fifty years,
And, if not handsome, dignified at least.
Indeed, it was no face to please a wife!
His friends say, this was caused by the costume:
He wore the dress he did the murder in,
That is, a *just-a-corps* of russet serge,
200   Black camisole, coarse cloak of baracan
(So they style here the garb of goat's-hair cloth)
White hat and cotton cap beneath, poor Count,
Preservative against the evening dews
During the journey from Arezzo. Well,
So died the man, and so his end was peace;
Whence many a moral were to meditate.
Spada, – you may bet Dandolo, – is Pope!
Now for the quatrain!'

                        No, friend, this will do!
210   You've sputtered into sparks. What streak comes next?
A letter: Don Giacinto Arcangeli,
Doctor and Proctor, him I made you mark

Buckle to business in his study late,
The virtuous sire, the valiant for the truth,
Acquaints his correspondent, – Florentine,
By name Cencini, advocate as well,
Socius and brother-in-the-devil to match, –
A friend of Franceschini, anyhow,
And knit up with the bowels of the case, –
220 Acquaints him, (in this paper that I touch)
How their joint effort to obtain reprieve
For Guido had so nearly nicked the nine
And ninety and one over, – he would say,
At Tarocs, – or succeeded, – in our phrase.
To this Cencini's care I owe the Book,
The yellow thing I take and toss once more
– How will it be, my four-years'-intimate,
When thou and I part company anon? –
'T was he, the 'whole position of the case,'
230 Pleading and summary, were put before;
Discreetly in my Book he bound them all,
Adding some three epistles to the point.
Here is the first of these, part fresh as penned,
The sand, that dried the ink, not rubbed away,
Though penned the day whereof it tells the deed:
Part – extant just as plainly, you know where,
Whence came the other stuff, went, you know how,
To make the ring that's all but round and done.

'Late they arrived, too late, egregious Sir,
240 Those same justificative points you urge
Might benefit His Blessed Memory
Count Guido Franceschini now with God:
Since the Court, – to state things succinctly, – styled
The Congregation of the Governor,
Having resolved on Tuesday last our cause
I' the guilty sense, with death for punishment,
Spite of all pleas by me deducible
In favour of said Blessed Memory, –
I, with expenditure of pains enough,

250 Obtained a respite, leave to claim and prove
Exemption from the law's award, – alleged
The power and privilege o' the Clericate:
To which effect a courier was despatched.
But ere an answer from Arezzo came,
The Holiness of our Lord the Pope (prepare!)
Judging it inexpedient to postpone
The execution of such sentence passed,
Saw fit, by his particular chirograph,
To derogate, dispense with privilege,
260 And wink at any hurt accruing thence
To Mother Church through damage of her son;
Also, to overpass and set aside
That other plea on score of tender age,
Put forth by me to do Pasquini good,
One of the four in trouble with our friend.
So that all five, to-day, have suffered death
With no distinction save in dying, – he,
Decollated by way of privilege,
The rest hanged decently and in order. Thus
270 Came the Count to his end of gallant man,
Defunct in faith and exemplarity:
Nor shall the shield of his great House lose shine,
Nor its blue banner blush to red thereby.
This, too, should yield sustainment to our hearts –
He had commiseration and respect
In his decease from universal Rome,
Quantum est hominum venustiorum,
The nice and cultivated everywhere:
Though, in respect of me his advocate,
280 Needs must I groan o'er my debility,
Attribute the untoward event o' the strife
To nothing but my own crass ignorance
Which failed to set the valid reasons forth,
Find fit excuse: such is the fate of war!
May God compensate us the direful blow
By future blessings on his family
Whereof I lowly beg the next commands;

– Whereto, as humbly, I confirm myself . . . '

And so forth – follow name and place and date:
290   On the next leaf –
               ' *Hactenus senioribus!*
There, old fox, show the clients t' other side
And keep this corner sacred, I beseech!
You and your pleas and proofs were what folks call
Pisan assistance, aid that comes too late,
Saves a man dead as nail in post of door.
Had I but time and space for narrative!
What was the good of twenty Clericates
When Somebody's thick headpiece once was bent
300   On seeing Guido's drop into the bag?
How these old men like giving youth a push!
So much the better: next push goes to him,
And a new Pope begins the century.
Much good I get by my superb defence!
But argument is solid and subsists,
While obstinacy and ineptitude
Accompany the owner to his tomb;
What do I care how soon? Beside, folks see!
Rome will have relished heartily the show,
310   Yet understood the motives, never fear,
Which caused the indecent change o' the People's Place
To the People's Playground, – stigmatize the spite
Which in a trice precipitated things!
As oft the moribund will give a kick
To show they are not absolutely dead,
So feebleness i' the socket shoots its last,
A spirt of violence for energy!

But thou, Cencini, brother of my breast,
O fox, whose home is 'mid the tender grape,
320   Whose couch in Tuscany by Themis' throne,
Subject to no such . . . but I shut my mouth
Or only open it again to say,
This pother and confusion fairly laid,

My hands are empty and my satchel lank.
Now then for both the Matrimonial Cause
And the case of Gomez! Serve them hot and hot!

Reliqua differamus in crastinum!
The impatient estafette cracks whip outside:
Still, though the earth should swallow him who swears
30   And me who make the mischief, in must slip
– My boy, your godson, fat-chaps Hyacinth,
Enjoyed the sight while Papa plodded here.
I promised him, the rogue, a month ago,
The day his birthday was, of all the days,
That if I failed to save Count Guido's head,
Cinuccio should at least go see it chopped
From trunk – "So, latinize your thanks!" quoth I:
"That I prefer, *hoc malim*," raps me out
The rogue: you notice the subjunctive? Ah!
40   Accordingly he sat there, bold in box,
Proud as the Pope behind the peacock-fans:
Whereon a certain lady-patroness
For whom I manage things (my boy in front,
Her Marquis sat the third in evidence;
Boys have no eyes nor ears save for the show)
"This time, Cintino," was her sportive word,
When whiz and thump went axe and mowed lay man,
And folks could fall to the suspended chat,
"This time, you see, Bottini rules the roast,
350   Nor can Papa with all his eloquence
Be reckoned on to help as heretofore!"
Whereat Cinone pouts; then, sparkishly –
"Papa knew better than aggrieve his Pope,
And baulk him of his grudge against our Count,
Else he'd have argued-off Bottini's" . . . what?
"His nose," – the rogue! well parried of the boy!
He's long since out of Caesar (eight years old)
And as for tripping in Eutropius . . . well,
Reason the more that we strain every nerve
360   To do him justice, mould a model-mouth,

A Bartolus-cum-Baldo for next age:
For that I purse the pieces, work the brain,
And want both Gomez and the marriage-case,
Success with which shall plaster aught of pate
That's broken in me by Bottini's flail,
And bruise his own, belike, that wags and brags.
Adverti supplico humiliter
Quod, do n't the fungus see, the fop divine
That one hand drives two horses, left and right?
370 With this rein did I rescue from the ditch
The fortune of our Franceschini, keep
Unsplashed the credit of a noble House,
And set the fashionable cause of Rome
A-prancing till bystanders shouted "'ware!"
The other rein's judicious management
Suffered old Somebody to keep the pace,
Hobblingly play the roadster: who but he
Had his opinion, was not led by the nose
In leash of quibbles strung to look like law!
380 You'll soon see, – when I go to pay devoir
And compliment him on confuting me, –
If, by a back-swing of the pendulum,
Grace be not, thick and threefold, consequent!
"I must decide as I see proper, Don!
The Pope, I have my inward lights for guide.
Had learning been the matter in dispute,
Could eloquence avail to gainsay fact,
Yours were the victory, be comforted!"
Cinuzzo will be gainer by it all.
390 Quick then with Gomez, hot and hot next case!'

Follows, a letter, takes the other side.
Tall blue-eyed Fisc whose head is capped with cloud,
Doctor Bottini, – to no matter who,
Writes on the Monday two days afterward.
Now shall the honest championship of right,
Crowned with success, enjoy at last, unblamed,
Moderate triumph! Now shall eloquence

Poured forth in fancied floods for virtue's sake,
(The print is sorrowfully dyked and dammed,
400 But shows where fain the unbridled force would flow,
Finding a channel) – now shall this refresh
The thirsty donor with a drop or two!
Here has been truth at issue with a lie;
Let who gained truth the day have handsome pride
In his own prowess! Eh? What ails the man?

'Well, it is over, ends as I foresaw:
Easily proved, Pompilia's innocence!
Catch them entrusting Guido's guilt to me!
I had, as usual, the plain truth to plead.
410 I always knew the clearness of the stream
Would show the fish so thoroughly, child might prong
The clumsy monster: with no mud to splash,
Small credit to lynx-eye and lightning-spear!
This Guido, – (much sport he contrived to make,
Who at first twist, preamble of the cord,
Turned white, told all, like the poltroon he was!) –
Finished, as you expect, a penitent,
Fully confessed his crime, and made amends,
And, edifying Rome last Saturday,
420 Died like a saint, poor devil! That's the man
The gods still give to my antagonist:
Imagine how Arcangeli claps wing,
And crows! "Such formidable facts to face,
So naked to attack, my client here,
And yet I kept a month the Fisc at bay,
And in the end had foiled him of the prize
By this arch-stroke, this plea of privilege,
But that the Pope must gratify his whim,
Put in his word, poor old man, – let it pass!"
430 – Such is the cue to which all Rome responds.
What with the plain truth given me to uphold,
And, should I let truth slip, the Pope at hand
To pick up, steady her on legs again,
My office turns a pleasantry indeed!

Not that the burly boaster did one jot
O' the little was to do – young Spreti's work!
But for him, – mannikin and dandiprat,
Mere candle-end and inch of cleverness
Stuck on Arcangeli's save-all, – but for him
440   The spruce young Spreti, what is bad were worse!

I looked that Rome should have the natural gird
At advocate with case that proves itself;
I knew Arcangeli would grin and brag:
But what say you to one impertinence
Might move a man? That monk, you are to know,
That barefoot Augustinian whose report
O' the dying woman's words did detriment
To my best points it took the freshness from,
– That meddler preached to purpose yesterday
450   At San Lorenzo as a winding-up
O' the shows, have proved a treasure to the church.
Out comes his sermon smoking from the press:
Its text – "Let God be true, and every man
A liar" – and its application, this,
The longest-winded of the paragraphs,
I straight unstitch, tear out and treat you with:
'T is piping hot and posts through Rome to-day.
Remember it, as I engage to do!'

———————

'But if you rather be disposed to see
460   In the result of the long trial here, –
This dealing doom to guilt and doling praise
To innocency, – any proof that truth
May look for vindication from the world,
Much will you have misread the signs, I say.
God, who seems acquiescent in the main
With those who add "So will He ever sleep" –
Flutters their foolishness from time to time,
Puts forth His right-hand recognizably;
Even as, to fools who deem He needs must right
470   Wrong on the instant, as if earth were heaven,

He wakes remonstrance – "Passive, Lord, how long?"
Because Pompilia's purity prevails,
Conclude you, all truth triumphs in the end?
So might those old inhabitants of the ark,
Witnessing haply their dove's safe return,
Pronounce there was no danger all the while
O' the deluge, to the creature's counterparts,
Aught that beat wing i' the world, was white or soft, –
And that the lark, the thrush, the culver too,
480 Might equally have traversed air, found earth,
And brought back olive-branch in unharmed bill.
Methinks I hear the Patriarch's warning voice –
"Though this one breast, by miracle, return,
No wave rolls by, in all the waste, but bears
Within it some dead dove-like thing as dear,
Beauty made blank and harmlessness destroyed!"
How many chaste and noble sister-fames
Wanted the extricating hand, and lie
Strangled, for one Pompilia proud above
490 The welter, plucked from the world's calumny,
Stupidity, simplicity, – who cares?

Romans! An elder race possessed your land
Long ago, and a false faith lingered still,
As shades do, though the morning-star be out.
Doubtless, some pagan of the twilight-day
Has often pointed to a cavern-mouth,
Obnoxious to beholders, hard by Rome,
And said, – nor he a bad man, no, nor fool, –
Only a man, so, blind like all his mates, –
500 "Here skulk in safety, lurk, defying law,
The devotees to execrable creed,
Adoring – with what culture . . . Jove, avert
Thy vengeance from us worshippers of thee ! . . .
What rites obscene – their idol-god, an Ass!"
So went the word forth, so acceptance found,
So century re-echoed century,
Cursed the accursed, – and so, from sire to son,

You Romans cried "The offscourings of our race
Corrupt within the depths there: fitly, fiends
510 Perform a temple-service o'er the dead:
Child, gather garment round thee, pass nor pry!"
So groaned your generations: till the time
Grew ripe, and lightning hath revealed, belike, –
Thro' crevice peeped into by curious fear, –
Some object even fear could recognize
I' the place of spectres; on the illumined wall,
To-wit, some nook, tradition talks about,
Narrow and short, a corpse's length, no more:
And by it, in the due receptacle,
520 The little rude brown lamp of earthenware,
The cruse, was meant for flowers, but held the blood,
The rough-scratched palm-branch, and the legend left
Pro Christo. Then the mystery lay clear:
The abhorred one was a martyr all the time,
A saint whereof earth was not worthy. What?
Do you continue in the old belief?
Where blackness bides unbroke, must devils be?
Is it so certain, not another cell
O' the myriad that make up the catacomb,
530 Contains some saint a second flash would show?
Will you ascend into the light of day
And, having recognized a martyr's shrine,
Go join the votaries that gape around
Each vulgar god that awes the market-place?
Be these the objects of your praising? See!
In the outstretched right hand of Apollo, there,
Is screened a scorpion: housed amid the folds
Of Juno's mantle, lo, a cockatrice!
Each statue of a god were fitlier styled
540 Demon and devil. Glorify no brass
That shines like burnished gold in noonday glare,
For fools! Be otherwise instructed, you!
And preferably ponder, ere ye pass,
Each incident of this strange human play
Privily acted on a theatre,

Was deemed secure from every gaze but God's, –
Till, of a sudden, earthquake lays wall low
And lets the world see the wild work inside,
And how, in petrifaction of surprise,
550 The actors stand, – raised arm and planted foot, –
Mouth as it made, eye as it evidenced,
Despairing shriek, triumphant hate, – transfixed,
Both he who takes and she who yields the life.

As ye become spectators of this scene –
Watch obscuration of a fame pearl-pure
In vapoury films, enwoven circumstance,
– A soul made weak by its pathetic want
Of just the first apprenticeship to sin,
Would thenceforth make the sinning soul secure
560 From all foes save itself, that's truliest foe, –
For egg turned snake needs fear no serpentry, –
As ye behold this web of circumstance
Deepen the more for every thrill and throe,
Convulsive effort to disperse the films
And disenmesh the fame o' the martyr, – mark
How all those means, the unfriended one pursues,
To keep the treasure trusted to her breast,
Each struggle in the flight from death to life,
How all, by procuration of the powers
570 Of darkness, are transformed, – no single ray,
Shot forth to show and save the inmost star,
But, passed as through hell's prism, proceeding black
To the world that hates white: as ye watch, I say,
Till dusk and such defacement grow eclipse
By, – marvellous perversity of man! –
The inadequacy and inaptitude
Of that self-same machine, that very law
Man vaunts, devised to dissipate the gloom,
Rescue the drowning orb from calumny,
580 – Hear law, appointed to defend the just,
Submit, for best defence, that wickedness
Was bred of flesh and innate with the bone

Borne by Pompilia's spirit for a space,
And no mere chance fault, passionate and brief:
Finally, when ye find, – after this touch
Of man's protection which intends to mar
The last pin-point of light and damn the disc, –
One wave of the hand of God amid the worlds
Bid vapour vanish, darkness flee away,
590 And leave the vexed star culminate in peace
Approachable no more by earthly mist –
What I call God's hand, – you, perhaps, – this chance
Of the true instinct of an old good man
Who happens to hate darkness and love light, –
In whom too was the eye that saw, not dim,
The natural force to do the thing he saw,
Nowise abated, – both by miracle, –
All this well pondered, – I demand assent
To the enunciation of my text
600 In face of one proof more that "God is true
And every man a liar" – that who trusts
To human testimony for a fact
Gets this sole fact – himself is proved a fool;
Man's speech being false, if but by consequence
That only strength is true; while man is weak,
And, since truth seems reserved for heaven not earth,
Should learn to love what he may speak one day.

For me, the weary and the worn, who prompt
To mirth or pity, as I move the mood, –
610 A friar who glide unnoticed to the grave,
Bare feet, coarse robe and rope-girt waist of mine, –
I have long since renounced your world, ye know:
Yet weigh the worth of worldly prize foregone,
Disinterestedly judge this and that
Good ye account good: but God tries the heart.
Still, if you question me of my content
At having put each human pleasure by,
I answer, at the urgency of truth,
As this world seems, I dare not say I know

620　– Apart from Christ's assurance which decides –
　　　Whether I have not failed to taste some joy.
　　　For many a dream would fain perturb my choice –
　　　How love, in those the varied shapes, might show
　　　As glory, or as rapture, or as grace:
　　　How conversancy with the books that teach,
　　　The arts that help, – how, to grow great, in fine,
　　　Rather than simply good, and bring thereby
　　　Goodness to breathe and live, nor, born i' the brain,
　　　Die there, – how these and many another gift
630　May well be precious though abjured by me.
　　　But, for one prize, best meed of mightiest man,
　　　Arch-object of ambition, – earthly praise,
　　　Repute o' the world, the flourish of loud trump,
　　　The softer social fluting, – Oh, for these,
　　　– No, my friends! Fame, – that bubble which, world-wide
　　　Each blows and bids his neighbour lend a breath,
　　　That so he haply may behold thereon
　　　One more enlarged distorted false fool's-face,
　　　Until some glassy nothing grown as big
640　Send by a touch the imperishable to suds, –
　　　No, in renouncing fame, the loss was light,
　　　Choosing obscurity, the chance was well !'

　　　　　　　————

　　　'Didst ever touch such ampollosity
　　　As the man's own bubble, let alone its spite?
　　　What's his speech for, but just the fame he flouts –
　　　How he dares reprehend both high and low?
　　　Else had he turned the sentence "God is true
　　　And every man a liar – save the Pope
　　　Happily reigning – my respects to him!"
650　– So, rounded off the period. Molinism
　　　Simple and pure! To what pitch get we next?
　　　I find that, for first pleasant consequence,
　　　Gomez, who had intended to appeal
　　　From the absurd decision of the Court,
　　　Declines, though plain enough his privilege,
　　　To call on help from lawyers any more –

Resolves the liars may possess the world,
Till God have had sufficiency of both:
So may I whistle for my job and fee!

660   But, for this virulent and rabid monk, –
If law be an inadequate machine,
And advocacy, so much impotence,
We shall soon see, my blatant brother! That's
Exactly what I hope to show your sort!
For, by a veritable piece of luck,
True providence, you monks round period with,
All may be gloriously retrieved. Perpend!

That Monastery of the Convertites
Whereto the Court consigned Pompilia first,
670   – Observe, if convertite, why, sinner then,
Or where the pertinency of award? –
And whither she was late returned to die,
– Still in their jurisdiction, mark again! –
That thrifty Sisterhood, for perquisite,
Claims every paul whereof may die possessed
Each sinner in the circuit of its walls.
Now, this Pompilia, seeing that by death
O' the couple, all their wealth devolved on her,
Straight utilized the respite ere decease
680   By regular conveyance of the goods
She thought her own, to will and to devise, –
Gave all to friends, Tighetti and the like,
In trust for him she held her son and heir,
Gaetano, – trust to end with infancy:
So willing and devising, since assured
The justice of the Court would presently
Confirm her in her rights and exculpate,
Re-integrate and rehabilitate –
Station as, through my pleading, now she stands.
690   But here's the capital mistake: the Court
Found Guido guilty, – but pronounced no word
About the innocency of his wife:

I grounded charge on broader base, I hope!
No matter whether wife be true or false,
The husband must not push aside the law,
And punish of a sudden: that's the point!
Gather from out my speech the contrary!
It follows that Pompilia, unrelieved
By formal sentence from imputed fault,
700   Remains unfit to have and to dispose
Of property, which law provides shall lapse:
Wherefore the Monastery claims its due.
And whose, pray, whose the office, but the Fisc's?
Who but I institute procedure next
Against the person of dishonest life,
Pompilia, whom last week I sainted so?
I, it is, teach the monk what scripture means,
And that the tongue should prove a two-edged sword,
No axe sharp one side, blunt the other way,
710   Like what amused the town at Guido's cost!
Astraea redux! I've a second chance
Before the self-same Court o' the Governor
Who soon shall see volte-face and chop, change sides!
Accordingly, I charge you on your life,
Send me with all despatch the judgment late
O' the Florence Rota Court, confirmative
O' the prior judgment at Arezzo, clenched
Again by the Granducal signature,
Wherein Pompilia is convicted, doomed,
720   And only destined to escape through flight
The proper punishment. Send me the piece, –
I'll work it! And this foul-mouthed friar shall find
His Noah's-dove that brought the olive back,
Is turned into the other sooty scout,
The raven, Noah first of all put forth the ark,
And never came back, but ate carcasses!
No adequate machinery in law?
No power of life and death i' the learned tongue?
Methinks I am already at my speech,
730   Startle the world with "Thou, Pompilia, thus?

How is the fine gold of the Temple dim!”
And so forth. But the courier bids me close,
And clip away one joke that runs through Rome,
Side by side with the sermon which I send –
How like the heartlessness of the old hunks
Arcangeli! His Count is hardly cold,
His client whom his blunders sacrificed,
When somebody must needs describe the scene –
How the procession ended at the church
740   That boasts the famous relic: quoth our brute,
“Why, that’s just Martial’s phrase for ‘make an end’ –
Ad umbilicum sic perventum est!”
The callous dog, – let who will cut off head,
He cuts a joke, and cares no more than so!
I think my speech shall modify his mirth:
“How is the fine gold dim!” – but send the piece!’

Alack, Bottini, what is my next word
But death to all that hope? The Instrument
Is plain before me, print that ends my Book
750   With the definitive verdict of the Court,
Dated September, six months afterward,
(Such trouble and so long, the old Pope gave!)
‘In restitution of the perfect fame
Of dead Pompilia, *quondam* Guido’s wife,
And warrant to her representative
Domenico Tighetti, barred hereby,
While doing duty in his guardianship,
From all molesting, all disquietude,
Each perturbation and vexation brought
760   Or threatened to be brought against the heir
By the Most Venerable Convent called
Saint Mary Magdalen o’ the Convertites
I’ the Corso.’

              Justice done a second time!
Well judged, Marc Antony, *Locum-tenens*
O’ the Governor, a Venturini too!

For which I save thy name, – last of the list!

Next year but one, completing his nine years
Of rule in Rome, died Innocent my Pope
770 – By some accounts, on his accession-day.
If he thought doubt would do the next age good,
'T is pity he died unapprised what birth
His reign may boast of, be remembered by –
Terrible Pope, too, of a kind, – Voltaire.

And so an end of all i' the story. Strain
Never so much my eyes, I miss the mark
There lived or died that Gaetano, child
Of Guido and Pompilia: only find,
Immediately upon his father's death,
780 A record in the annals of the town
That Porzia, sister of our Guido, moved
The Priors of Arezzo and their head
Its Gonfalonier to give loyally
A public attestation to the right
O' the Franceschini to men's reverence –
Apparently because of the incident
O' the murder, – there's no mention made of crime,
But what else caused such urgency to cure
The mob, just then, of chronic greediness
790 For scandal, love of lying vanity,
And appetite to swallow crude reports
That bring annoyance to their betters? – Bane
Which, here, was promptly met by antidote.
I like and shall translate the eloquence
Of nearly the worst Latin ever writ:
'Since antique time whereof the memory
Holds the beginning, to this present hour,
Our Franceschini ever shone, and shine,
Still i' the primary rank, supreme amid
800 The lustres of Arezzo, proud to own
In this great family – her flag-bearer,
Guide of her steps and guardian against foe, –

As in the first beginning, so to-day!'
There, would you disbelieve stern History,
Trust rather to the babble of a bard?
I thought, Arezzo, thou hadst fitter souls,
Petrarch, – nay, Buonarroti at a pinch,
To do thee credit as *vexillifer*!
Was it mere mirth the Patavinian meant,
810   Making thee out, in his veracious page,
Founded by Janus of the Double Face?

Well, proving of such perfect parentage,
Our Gaetano, born of love and hate,
Did the babe live or die? – one fain would find!
What were his fancies if he grew a man?
Was he proud, – a true scion of the stock, –
Of bearing blason, shall make bright my Book –
Shield, Azure, on a Triple Mountain, Or,
A Palm-tree, Proper, whereunto is tied
820   A Greyhound, Rampant, striving in the slips?
Or did he love his mother, the base-born,
And fight i' the ranks, unnoticed by the world?

Such, then, the final state o' the story. So
Did the Star Wormwood in a blazing fall
Frighten awhile the waters and lie lost:
So did this old woe fade from memory,
Till after, in the fulness of the days,
I needs must find an ember yet unquenched,
And, breathing, blow the spark to flame. It lives,
830   If precious be the soul of man to man.
So, British Public, who may like me yet,
(Marry and amen!) learn one lesson hence
Of many which whatever lives should teach:
This lesson, that our human speech is naught,
Our human testimony false, our fame
And human estimation words and wind.
Why take the artistic way to prove so much?
Because, it is the glory and good of Art,

That Art remains the one way possible
840 Of speaking truth, to mouths like mine, at least.
How look a brother in the face and say
'Thy right is wrong, eyes hast thou yet art blind,
Thine ears are stuffed and stopped, despite their length,
And, oh, the foolishness thou countest faith!'
Say this as silverly as tongue can troll –
The anger of the man may be endured,
The shrug, the disappointed eyes of him
Are not so bad to bear – but here's the plague
That all this trouble comes of telling truth,
850 Which truth, by when it reaches him, looks false,
Seems to be just the thing it would supplant,
Nor recognizable by whom it left –
While falsehood would have done the work of truth.
But Art, – wherein man nowise speaks to men,
Only to mankind, – Art may tell a truth
Obliquely, do the thing shall breed the thought,
Nor wrong the thought, missing the mediate word.
So may you paint your picture, twice show truth,
Beyond mere imagery on the wall, –
860 So, note by note, bring music from your mind,
Deeper than ever the Andante dived, –
So write a book shall mean, beyond the facts,
Suffice the eye and save the soul beside.

And save the soul! If this intent save mine, –
If the rough ore be rounded to a ring,
Render all duty which good ring should do,
And, failing grace, succeed in guardianship, –
Might mine but lie outside thine, Lyric Love,
Thy rare gold ring of verse (the poet praised)
870 Linking our England to his Italy!

I. THE SOURCES OF THE POEM

The principal source of *The Ring and the Book* is a volume composed of printed pamphlets and handwritten documents collected by a Florentine lawyer named Francesco Cencini at the time of the Franceschini murder trial in Rome, and found by Browning under the circumstances related in the poem's opening lines. It is now in the library of Balliol College, Oxford.

Fourteen of the eighteen pamphlets deal with the trial of Guido and his accomplices for the murder of Pompilia and the Comparini. Of these fourteen, eleven concern points of law, six for Guido, five against him, and the remaining three contain evidence, mainly affidavits and letters from persons involved in the events or witnesses to them. Two further pamphlets relate to the petition, subsequent to the murder trial, to clear Pompilia's reputation and thus prevent her estate from falling into the hands of the Convertite nuns. All of these are official documents printed for circulation among those connected with the case as pleaders or judges; in Roman trial procedure, they took the place of the oral testimony and arguments usual in Anglo-Saxon courts. Finally, 'the Old Yellow Book', as it is always called, contains two unofficial, so-called 'anonymous' pamphlets written for popular distribution. These are the basis of the 'Half-Rome' books of the poem (II and III).

The written material bound up in the volume consists of three letters written from Rome on the evening after Guido's execution, telling of the three-day delay in favour of Guido and the Pope's rejection of his appeal – in part the basis of Book XII – and a transcript of the sentence following Pompilia's trial at Arezzo (No. 4 in the list of law cases below).

The Old Yellow Book was reproduced in facsimile, with a translation and copious notes, in a large volume edited by Charles

W. Hodell (Washington, D.C., 1908; second edition, 1915). The translation itself, unfortunately not accompanied by the long and acute essay on 'The Making of a Great Poem' which occupied pages 227–91 of the original work, was published in Everyman's Library in 1911. The Old Yellow Book was translated afresh (Boston, Mass., 1925; new edition, Philadelphia, 1927) by Judge J. M. Gest, who found many errors in Hodell's rendering of the law Latin and, more importantly, brought a vast knowledge of obscure antiquarian law to bear on the legal issues argued in the case.

In addition to the bound collection he found in Florence, Browning used another contemporary source, a pamphlet on the trial obtained for him by a woman friend in 1862. This is known to Browning scholars as 'the secondary source'.

Such – apart from various sources he consulted to verify particular points of background detail, such as the character of Pope Innocent XII – was the sum of the information Browning possessed concerning the Franceschini case as he wrote his epic-length poetic treatment. But long after his death, a considerable body of material unknown to him came to light in several instalments. In 1900 another separate account was discovered in the Royal Casanatense Library, Rome. It was printed in an appendix to Griffin and Minchin's biography of Browning and in Hodell's edition of the Old Yellow Book. In 1938 Professor William O. Raymond found a further document, concentrating on the murder and subsequent developments, in the Armstrong Browning Collection at Baylor University, Texas. Two years later Professor Beatrice Corrigan discovered in the Biblioteca del Comune, in Cortona, a collection similar to the Old Yellow Book but twice as large. It too comprised printed pamphlets (some being copies of those already known) and a long section of manuscript relating to 'the personages and events of the Comparini-Franceschini relationship', though with comparatively little bearing on the murder trial itself. Professor Corrigan published those portions of the Cortona codex which contained hitherto unknown information in her volume, *Curious Annals* (Toronto, 1956). Still other documents connected with the Franceschini case have been located in various Italian libraries.

A study of the documents Browning did not know reinforces the strong impression received from the Old Yellow Book, and from his imaginative reconstruction of the Roman atmosphere at the moment of the trial and execution, of the intense excitement the Franceschini affair generated. This was no ordinary murder case, but a *cause célèbre* in the truest sense. Moreover, by virtue of the fact that they are to a substantial degree independent documents, those found between 1900 and the present time frequently support and add details to the narrative Browning drew from the Old Yellow Book: they provide extensive corroborative evidence. And most important of all, they supply many pieces of information totally unknown to Browning. The documents Miss Corrigan found at Cortona reveal, for instance, the true circumstances of Pompilia's birth (they include a full narrative, obtained from participants and witnesses, of how Violante's deception was managed) and add many details to our previous knowledge of how Guido spent his last hours.

Although it is very satisfactory to be able to see the tangled Franceschini case from more angles, and in greater detail, than was possible to Browning, the focus of attention must remain on the poem itself. The sheer quantity of documents surviving from the 'Roman murder story' attests to its importance as an event in legal history as well as in the popular annals of Rome. But the modern reader's concern is not so much with what really happened as with what the Victorian poet Robert Browning did, by way of artistic 'resuscitation', with the facts as he knew them.

2. CALENDAR OF EVENTS

(See also list of Law Cases)

1680   *16 July*   Pompilia born and immediately adopted by the Comparini.

1693   *6 September*   Pompilia marries Guido. Three months later (30 November) they leave for Arezzo.

1694   *March*   The Comparini return to Rome and deny Pompilia's legitimacy.

1697   *28–29 April**   Pompilia and Caponsacchi leave Arezzo.

* Changed in the poem to 23 April; see note to III 1065.

1 May   Guido overtakes them at Castelnuovo and they are arrested and conveyed to Rome.

24 September   Roman court hands down verdict in the *processus fugae*.

18 December   Pompilia bears son Gaetano.

1698   *2 January*   Guido and his accomplices kill the Comparini and mortally wound Pompilia.

6 January   Pompilia dies.

(Books II–VII are set in the period 3–6 January)

Late January   Murder trial begins (Books VIII–IX).

18 February   Court finds Guido *et al.* guilty and condemns them to death. Guido appeals to Pope.

*20 February**   Pope rejects appeal (Book X) and the news is brought to Guido (Book XI).

22 February   Guido and accomplices executed (Book XII).

3. THE LAW CASES

1. *Summer 1694*   The Comparini's suit to declare Pompilia illegitimate and thereby recover her dowry from Guido. Countersuit entered (August 1695) by Pompilia and Guido to implement the dower settlement. Decisions chiefly in favour of Guido, but Pietro appealed each one. The litigation was still in the courts at the time of the murders.

2. *Summer 1697*   The suit Guido brought in Rome against Pompilia and Caponsacchi for flight and adultery (the '*processus fugae*'), the direct result of his overtaking them at Castelnuovo. The court's decision, handed down in September, was that Caponsacchi should be 'relegated' to Civita Vecchia for three years and that Pompilia, on whom no judgement was rendered, should be placed in the care of the Scalette Convent.

3. *Autumn 1697*   Pompilia's suit against Guido for divorce (or, more accurately, legal separation). Not decided at the time of the murders.

4. *Autumn 1697*   A suit, paralleling the '*processus fugae*' (No. 2),

* See headnote to Book X, in the notes.

brought at Arezzo against Pompilia. (Caponsacchi, as a cleric, was exempt from prosecution in a civil court.)

> (At this juncture, Paolo, overburdened with his brother's suits at law, tried to have the several pending cases – Nos. 1, 3, and 4 – transferred from their respective courts to an *ad hoc* session *(Congregatio)* appointed by the Pope. This manoeuvre, based on the claim of special privilege enjoyed by a holder of orders in the church, failed, the Pope refusing to intervene.)

The decision in No. 4, handed down by the Tuscan court in December, sentenced Pompilia to life imprisonment. But she was then, of course, under Roman jurisdiction.

5. *January–February 1698* The indictment and trial of Guido and four accomplices for the murder of Pompilia and the Comparini. This was the occasion for all but two of the printed documents assembled in the Old Yellow Book as well as the subject of most of the documents brought to light after Browning's death. Browning's knowledge of the previous lawsuits and the circumstances surrounding them was derived from the repeated allusions to them in the murder trial pamphlets.

6. *January 1698* The suit brought by the Convent of Convertites to acquire the estate of Pompilia (now deceased) on the ground that she was a 'debased woman'. The Franceschini entered a countersuit (Spring) claiming the property for themselves. In May the court turned the estate over to her executor and thus, in effect, to her infant son, and in September it formally and finally confirmed Pompilia's good name.

4. MOLINISM

In the poem there are over thirty references to 'the subject of the day' in Rome, 1698: the heresy of Molinism. As is to be expected, the various speakers do not refer, except casually (and inaccurately), to the ideas involved; the name itself serves rather as an all-purpose smear word to arouse irrational and irrelevant responses on the part of the speakers' respective auditors. Only the Pope, of all people, refers sympathetically to Molinism and the Molinists.

Miguel de Molinos (1627–96) was a Spanish theologian, resident in Rome, whose *Spiritual Guide* (1675) had for its fundamental principle the concept of Quietism or 'the Inner Light' – the doctrine that man's soul, maintained always in a state of perfect inaction, can and should be receptive only to the promptings of God, without the intermediation of dogma or ritual. Molinism therefore denied the efficacy of confession and, indeed, of the entire ecclesiastical system. Initially well received by the Inquisition, Molinist belief came under heavy attack from the Jesuits, who after a bitter secret trial succeeded in having Innocent XI (predecessor once removed of the Pope in the poem) condemn it as heretical in 1687. Molinos died in prison in late December 1696, but the echoes of the controversy his doctrine engendered were still loud in the Rome of January-February 1698, when the ten monologues of *The Ring and the Book* are supposed to be spoken. (On this subject, see Cook, *Commentary*, Appendix VIII, and William Coyle, 'Molinos: "The Subject of the Day" in *The Ring and the Book*', *Publications of the Modern Language Association of America* LXVII, 1952, 308–14.)

It should be made clear, however, that the Molinism of this poem is quite distinct from the Molinism described, under that name, in the *New Catholic Encyclopedia*. The latter is the body of doctrine taught by Luis de Molina (1535–1600) which was concerned chiefly with 'the problem of free will and God's fore-knowledge, providence, predestination, probation, [and] efficacious grace'. Not that the considerable difference between the two Molinisms, in both origin and content, would have been of any moment to the characters in the poem. It was the word, not one ideology or another, to which their ignorant but vigorous prejudices responded.

5. POMPILIA'S ILLITERACY AND THE 'FORGED' LETTERS

One of the dominant issues in the Old Yellow Book, which Browning naturally has his characters make much of, was whether or not Pompilia could write, for upon this question hinged the validity of a damaging piece of evidence against her and Caponsacchi, the love letters allegedly exchanged between the two. It was these letters which Guido claimed to have found in their possession when he confronted them at Castelnuovo and which his counsel offered as exhibits at their trial.

In her deposition of May 1697, in connection with the *processus fugae*, Pompilia denied that she could read or write. Seizing upon this avowal, the earlier commentators on the poem were inclined to follow Browning's own clear prejudice in her favour and conclude that the love letters were forgeries. But the evidence in the Old Yellow Book makes it quite plain that in this respect, as in some others, she was lying. Whether or not all the letters she was asserted to have written – not only those to Caponsacchi but the earlier ones to her parents – were in fact hers, she was at least as capable of writing them as Guido was capable of forging them or of forcing her to trace them from a pencilled model he provided. In addition to the evidence in the Old Yellow Book (summarized and weighed by Cook, *Commentary*, Appendix IV) there is the fact, discovered by Professor Corrigan in one of the Cortona documents, that Pompilia had gone to school for four years.

6. THE CONVERTITES

Frequent reference is made in the poem to a community of nuns, 'those good Convertites, | Those sinners saved, those Magdalens re-made' (II 1198–9), formally called the convent of Santa Maria Maddalena della Convertite. Browning's characters uniformly assert that it was these nuns who received Pompilia, by court order, after her and Caponsacchi's trial for flight and adultery, and who cared for her until the approaching birth of her child required her to be removed to the home of the Comparini. This is a mistake. The community which actually cared for her in those months was not the Convertites but the Conservatorio di Santa Croce della Penitenza ('Le Scalette'). The only true part the Convertites played in the Franceschini affair was their initiating a lawsuit, immediately after Pompilia's death, to acquire her estate on the ground that she belonged to the class of 'loose women' whose property was automatically forfeited to them by law. In his account of this (unsuccessful) attempt to defame

Pompilia's memory, Browning is faithful to the historical record.

7. CAPONSACCHI'S CLERICAL STATUS

Everywhere in the poem, as in pro-Guido contexts in the Old Yellow Book, Caponsacchi is referred to as 'a priest'. But in other documents, including Caponsacchi's own affidavit, he is called a subdeacon, which is what he actually was: a member of the lowest of the four major orders of clergy. Even though not a priest, however, he was bound as priests are by a vow of celibacy, and so the dereliction of which he was accused was no less grave.

Notes

BOOK I

1 *this Ring* A ring worn by Browning's wife, who had died in 1861. It is now in the Balliol College Library.

3 *Castellani's* A firm of Roman jewellers.

4 *Etrurian circlets* Etruscan rings.

7 *Chiusi* A town in Tuscany, noted for its Etruscan ruins.

8 *one trick* The gold-alloy metaphor which begins here and recurs throughout Book I has been the subject of much discussion. See especially Paul A. Cundiff, 'The Clarity of Browning's Ring Metaphor', *Publications of the Modern Language Association of America* LXIII, 1948, 1276–82; the exchange by Cundiff, Robert Langbaum and Donald Smalley, *Victorian Newsletter* 15–17 (Spring 1959–Spring 1960); and George R. Wasserman, 'The Meaning of Browning's Ring-Figure', *Modern Language Notes* LXXVI, 1961, 420–26.

23 *repristination* restoration to original state.

33 *this square old yellow Book* See General Note 1 (p. 629).

45 *Baccio's marble* Baccio Bandinella's statue of Giovanni della Bande Nere ('John of the Black Bands', line 47), father of Cosimo I of Tuscany.

58 *breccia* A rock composed of angular fragments embedded in a matrix of the same or different nature.

65 *scagliola* floor of inlaid stone.

66 *crazie* 1½*d* in the money of Browning's time.

67 *conch* sea shell.

69 *the imaginative Sienese* See lines 369–72 and note.

72–3 *Lionard . . . Joconde* Leonardo da Vinci's *La Gioconda (Mona Lisa)*.

75 *compeers* companions.

77 *Spicilegium* anthology.

78 *Frail One of the Flower* *La Dame aux Camélias*.

104 *festas* festival days.

112 *At the Strozzi, at the Pillar, at the Bridge* Respectively, the Palazzo Strozzi, the column in the Piazza Santa Trinità, and the Bridge of Santa Trinità.

114 *Casa Guidi* The Brownings' home in Florence, 1847–61. It was – and at the moment of writing still stands – across the Arno from the centre of Florence, near the Pitti Palace.

119 *Print three-fifths, written supplement the rest* Actually, only about a dozen of the 262 pages in the Old Yellow Book are written; all the rest are printed.

122 *Position* exposition, explanation.

125–6 Although some commentators stress that Guido belonged to an 'inferior' order of nobility, the fact is that in 1693 the Franceschini were recorded as being of the second grade (of eight), based on the age of family and the number of offices and dignities its members had held. It had risen two grades since 1658.

136–8 *a Latin cramp enough . . . But interfilleted with Italian streaks* All the legal arguments are in the late church Latin employed in the Roman courts, while the testimony of witnesses is in vernacular Italian. ('Cramp': hard to decipher or understand.)

145 *Primary lawyer-pleadings* For a list of these, see DeVane's *Browning Handbook*, pp. 326–7.

149 *At Rome, in the Apostolic Chamber's type* The imprint of the papal press, found on the printed legal documents in the Old Yellow Book.

155 *there properly was no judgment-bar* In conformance with Roman practice, there were no 'courtroom scenes' in which the two sides confronted each other. The legal arguments were presented to the court in printed form. See lines 242–4, 1119–21.

165 *'T was the so-styled Fisc began* The Advocatus of the Fisc was the official prosecutor, but Browning, probably confusing Roman procedure with Anglo-Saxon, errs in saying he began the pleading. Actually the defence had the privilege of the first argument. Despite his mistake in this line, Browning correctly orders the sequence of Books VIII and IX, where Arcangeli, leading for the defence, is heard before Bottini, the 'Fisc'.

169 *qualities of bad* aggravating circumstances, much dwelt upon in Book VIII.

171 *cockatrice* A fabulous serpent supposedly hatched from a cock's egg and having the power to kill by a look.

177 *so-styled Patron of the Poor* court-appointed defence counsel. Since lawyers on both sides in a Roman suit were provided by the state as a matter of course, there need be no implication that Guido was too poor to afford one of his own, despite Browning's remark in the next line.

195 *her tottering ark* Because it was being shaken by the oxen on Nachon's threshing floor, Uzzah sacrilegiously 'put forth his hand to the ark of God [the chest containing the ten commandments] and took hold of it'; whereupon an angry God killed Uzzah (2 Samuel vi 6–7).

205 *portentousest* This inflected superlative form of an adjective was common in Victorian times. Browning, it will be seen as the poem progresses, was particularly addicted to it.

210 *impudence* shamelessness.

213 *the precedents, the authorities* All those cited in the following passage are found in the Old Yellow Book.

215 *a firebrand at each fox's tail* Judges xv 4–5.

222–3 *Solon and his Athenians . . , Romulus and Rome* Solon (*c.* 640– *c.* 559 BC) and Romulus, the mythical founder of Rome, included severe punishment for adultery in the legal codes of their respective societies. See Plutarch's *Lives*.

223 *Justinian* Byzantine emperor (482–565), legal reformer, whose *Pandects* (533) constituted the enduring basis of Roman law.

224 *Baldo, Bartolo* Celebrated fourteenth-century Italian jurists.

226–7 *Cornelia de Sicariis . . . Pompeia de Parricidiis* Legal decisions relating to murderers contained in the *Pandects*. See note to VIII 572.

227–8 *Julia de | Something-or-other* 'Something-or-other' is *Adulteriis*.

230 *Dolabella* Roman proconsul (*c.* 70–43 BC). For the 'nice decision' see VIII 912–47.

231 For Theodoric and the 'pregnant instance' see VIII 481–6.

232 *Aelian* Claudius Aelianus (late 2nd–early 3rd century AD), author of *Variae Historiae, On the Nature of Animals*.

236 *naughty* sinning.

260 *clerkly privilege* immunity from civil prosecution on the grounds of being an ecclesiastic. The 'minor orders' Guido is said to have taken are not specified in the records; those mentioned in lines 263–5 have no warrant in the Old Yellow Book and are, as Cook remarks, 'a strange jumble'.

269 *parlous* risky (but cunning).

271 *the zealous orator* Probably Ugolinucci, one of the correspondents of Cencini, the Florentine lawyer (next line) who was interested in the Franceschini case and collected the Old Yellow Book.

276 *Quality* 'the superior social section' (line 927).

285 *Emperor's Envoy* See XII 94 and note.

287   *Civility*   the spirit of civilization, civilized standards.

297   *Herodotus*   The Greek historian (*c.* 484–425 BC) who wrote a number of stories illustrating the fall of the proud, wealthy and mighty – the vanity of human ambitions.

307   *Jansenists, re-nicknamed Molinists*   The heretical school of theology founded by Cornelius Jansen (1585–1638), which denied free will on the ground that divine grace was irresistible. In some respects Jansenism had affinities with Molinism, for which see General Note 4 (p. 633).

308   *frowsy*   dirty, untidy, musty. Browning may be recalling Byron's 'a drowsy frowzy poem, call'd the "Excursion"' (*Don Juan* III xciv).

310   *clown-like*   like a peasant.

314   *spoil*   strip (a tree of bark), peel (a twig of coating).

319   *Nepotism*   The papal practice of handing rich plums of ecclesiastical office and privilege to relatives and other favourites. Innocent XII did in fact oppose it.

324   *carlines*   A carlino was worth about 4*d* in Victorian money.

346   *particular chirograph*   own handwriting.

351   *Castle Angelo*   the Mausoleum of Hadrian, on the right bank of the Tiber.

352   *custom somewhat staled the spectacle*   An echo of 'Age cannot wither her, nor custom stale | Her infinite variety' (*Antony and Cleopatra* II ii 240–41).

358   *Pincian gardens*   East of the Piazza del Popolo, near the Porto del Popolo, Rome's northern gate (line 357).

363   *suffrage*   sympathy, support.

369   *Ademollo*   Luigi Ademollo (1764–1849), painter and engraver.

372   *Was this truth of force?*   did it carry conviction, have power?

384   *The priest*   See General Note 7 (p. 636).

396   *Might welcome as it were an angel-guest*   'Be not forgetful to entertain strangers: for thereby some have entertained angels unawares' (Hebrews xiii 2; see also Revelation iii 20).

410   *British Public, ye who like me not*   See note to lines 1379–85.

431   *Diario*   newspaper.

432   *the French burned them*   During their occupation of Rome, 1849–70.

433   *The rap-and-rending nation*   'rap and rend', common in the sixteenth and seventeenth centuries, meant 'to take or get by snatching or stealing'.

434   *gird*   attack.

435   *the Temporality*   the papal claim to power in secular affairs.

This claim, much debated in the years when the poem was being written, was abrogated by the Vatican Council of 1870.

444–6 *Manning ... Newman ... Wiseman* Three members of the Roman Catholic hierarchy in England; of these, only Wiseman was as yet a cardinal.

459 *lingot* The French version of the English 'ingot'.

466 *Thridded and so thrown fast* Both mean 'made (twisted) into thread'.

467 *djereed* wooden javelin used in tilting at a target.

473 *agate* stone slab (line 476).

479 *terrace* balcony.

490 *that gold snow Jove rained on Rhodes* 'gold snow' is wealth (*Iliad* II 670).

495 *datura* plant of the nightshade family.

498 *north* Browning's mistake for 'south' (the Roman Road leads southwest from the Casa Guidi).

500 *felt the Apennine* sensed (imagined) the Apennine mountain range.

501 *Arezzo* A Tuscan town fifty-six miles south-east of Florence and 154 miles north of Rome.

504 *spectacle for angels* 1 Corinthians iv 9.

508 *Castelnuovo* A hamlet fifteen miles from Rome.

521 *Deep calling unto deep* Psalm xlii 7.

542 *Now let us depart in peace* Simeon's words after he has beheld Jesus according to the promise of the Holy Ghost (Luke ii 29).

544 *fog o' the fen* Phosphorescence emanating from decaying matter in a swamp, thought to be a carrier of pestilence.

554 *pest* pestilence. In later books, especially V, plague imagery will be frequent.

567 *the Prince o' the Power of the Air* Satan (Ephesians ii 2).

572 *Mopping and mowing* making faces, grimacing.

585 *Saint George* The first of many allusions to Caponsacchi as a St George figure, the valiant rescuer of beleaguered women.

604 *a solitary villa* See note to II 206–7.

623 *'Gabriel!' cried Lucifer at Eden-gate* That is, Guido's use of Caponsacchi's name was analogous to Lucifer's use of the name of the guardian angel Gabriel to gain admission to Paradise.

638 *Tophet* Old Testament site (Jeremiah vii 31–2) of child sacrifices, later developed into a symbol of hell.

643–4 *the primal curse | Which bids man love as well as make a lie* Revelation xxii 15; see also 2 Thessalonians ii 11.

647 *fell* hide, skin.

667 *friable* easily crumbled.

670 *entablature* The topmost (horizontal) portion of a classic order of architecture, consisting of cornice, frieze, and architrave.

673 *shards* debris, rubble.

676 *abacus* The square-shaped top slab of a capital in a column.

678 *style* column.

684 *favoured* ornamented.

690 *commodity of carriage* portability.

694 *a client* Cencini (line 272 above).

702 *malleolable* capable of being delicately hammered into shape.

720 *Inalienable* God's alone, not to be delegated to man.

737 *Stationed for temple-service* 1 Samuel iii 3; Exodus xxvii 20–1 (the lamp in the tabernacle of the Lord).

740 *galvanism for life* stimulation from inertia into activity. In Browning's time, galvanism meant especially the therapeutic use of electrical shock to stir muscular activity.

742 *mage* magician (and, in this context, poet).

757 *By a moonrise through a ruin of a crypt* A line suggesting an engraving by the eighteenth-century Roman artist Piranese.

760 *Faust ... Elisha* Faust was assisted to the realization of his ambitions by Mephistopheles (Satan); Elisha, in contrast, was aided by God (2 Kings iv 29–35).

774 *medicinable* healing.

784 *Fifty years old* Guido's age is not mentioned in the Old Yellow Book, but another document says he was forty. The same document vouches for the truth of the other articles of Browning's description.

800 *style* title.

838 *Here are the voices presently shall sound* From this point to line 1329, Browning provides a series of previews of Books II–XI.

843 *figure* shape.

865 *sample* Two meanings – 'illustrative case' and 'warning' (compare 'example').

868 *Aeacus* King of Aegina whose reputation for justice won him one of the three judgeships in Hades (Horace, *Odes* II xiii 22, IV viii 25).

875 *Corso* A main Roman street.

899 *Bernini's creature* See note to III 118.

902 *caritellas* small figures of the Graces.

916 *tertium quid* an undefined or indefinite thing distinct from, but somehow related to, two other entities which are known and distinct.

935 *girandole* branched candlestick.

939 *observance* politeness.

962-3 *pour the blame | Of their wrong-doing, Satan-like, on Job* Job ii 1–7.

967 *shrewdness* intelligence.

979 *the Cord* The defendant was stripped and tied up, his arms twisted behind his back; he then was hoisted by a rope attached to a pulley and subjected to various additional tortures such as repeated jerks of the rope, weights hung on his feet, and a rod inserted between his feet to stretch his legs apart.

980 *Vigil-torture* Although Browning implies that this was another name for the Cord, it actually was a separate procedure. After the defendant was prepared as for the Cord and all hair removed from his body, he was fastened in a sitting position to a three-legged bench slightly raised in the middle. His shoulders were tied to the walls and his legs elevated by a rod between his feet.

986 *course* proposed line of action.

992 *recusants* persons refusing to conform (especially in religious matters).

1017 *coil* 'the entanglement caused by combining the two roles' (Cook).

1027 *seal* insignia.

1028 *chrism* consecrated oil for anointment.

1034 *excepted at* objected to.

1081 *alien* stranger.

1085 *the good house that helps the poor to die* Saint Anna's hospital (III 37). But this is a mistake: Pompilia died at the Comparini's house.

1087 *leech* physician.

1114 *The patent truth-extracting process* See note to VIII 14.

1117 *One orator, of two on either side* On each side of a Roman lawsuit were two lawyers, of equal status: the Procurator (Arcangeli for the defence), who concentrated on facts, and the Advocatus (Spreti for the defence, Bottini for the prosecution), whose speciality was argumentation. Bottini's Procurator colleague, Gambi, is not mentioned.

1118 *puissance* power.

1133 *use* are accustomed.

1139 *efficacious* influential.

1153 *levigate* reduce to powder.

1155 *inchoates* develops.

1157 *crank* fantastic figure of speech.

1165 *exordium* introduction.

1174 *To-morrow her persecutor* Browning's invention. See XII 703 13 and note.

1190 *Well done, thou good and faithful!*   Matthew xxv 21.

1201 *scrannel*   strident, shrill (Milton, *Lycidas* 124).

1202 *studio*   study.

1204 *like the cockerel that would crow*   Such as Chanticleer in Chaucer's *Nun's Priest's Tale.*

1207 *Forum and Mars' Hill*   The Roman and Athenian assembly places where orators could have full scope for their talents.

1209 *Clavecinist*   performer on the clavecin, forerunner of the piano.

1214–15 *both | I' the flesh at Rome*   Handel actually did not arrive in Rome until the autumn of 1706.

1239 *lathen*   made of 'latten', an alloy containing brass or bronze.

1250 *a huge tome*   See the opening lines of Book X.

1252 *diurnal*   daily.

1252–5 *opes page, . . . comes upon the evening's chance*   See note to V 402.

1273 *Satan's old saw*   Job ii 4.

1279 *rivelled*   shrivelled.

1305 *standard*   crucifix.

1306 *trope*   figure of speech.

1311 *Brotherhood of Death*   See XI 2413–14.

1319 *Out of the deeps, Lord, have I cried to thee*   Psalm cxxx 1.

1328 *Mannaia*   guillotine.

1333 *the wide prospect round*   the 'lay of the land' – the Franceschini story 'of so long ago'.

1334–9   Perhaps a reference to the easier kinds of Victorian poetry, whose subject was familiar experience in a placid everyday setting, such as Tennyson's domestic idylls.

1342 *wistful eagle's horny eye*   A suggestion of Tennyson's *The Eagle,* who 'clasps the crag with crooked hands: | Close to the sun in lonely lands'.

1351 *the House of Fame*   Chaucer's *House of Fame* was possibly suggested to Browning by the preceding image of the eagle.

1352 *Landscaping*   portraying.
 saved   selected? (Cook)

1367–75   The device which is the basis of this image has recently been identified as an ' "electric egg", an instrument used to show the effect of an electric discharge in a glass vessel partially exhausted of air'. The effect of passing a charge across a gap in a partial vacuum 'consisted of a bright, reddish-purple glow, spreading out from the points of the rods, forming dark and light striations as the glass "globe" is more and more exhausted'. See J. Killham, in I. Armstrong (ed.), *The Major Victorian Poets,* Routledge & Kegan Paul, 1969, pp. 167, 174–5.

1377   *Guy Faux*   Instigator of the Gunpowder Plot against James I and Parliament in 1605.

1379–85   A passage expressing Browning's rueful awareness of his lack of fame as a poet during his career thus far, when, as he says with some exaggeration in line 1385, he had an audience of one – himself. At the very moment he was writing these lines, however (the autumn of 1864), the tide was turning in his favour. His two-volume collected works, published in mid-1863, was selling well enough to require a reprint within two years, and, more important, his volume of new poems, *Dramatis Personae*, published on 28 May, had been so well received that a second edition was called for before the end of the year. Such success, though modest enough when compared with Tennyson's concurrent popular and critical acclaim, was new in Browning's experience.

1382   *all . . . could read who ran*   'that he may run that readeth it' (Habakkuk ii 2).

1383   *more careless*   caring less.

1390   *posy*   inscription, motto.

1391   *O lyric Love*   The following 'invocation to the muse' is addressed to Elizabeth Barrett Browning, although there are also faint references to Christ (1400) and the Madonna (1402).

1396   *human at the red-ripe of the heart*   One of a number of references in Browning's poetry to the 'red-ripe heart' of the pomegranate – a rabbinical-patristic symbol of special personal meaning to him and his wife (see Exodus xxviii 33–4).

BOOK II

The time is near dusk of the day after the murders, which took place on 2 January 1698. Preview: I 839–82.

14   *pearl is cast to swine*   Matthew vii 6.

29   *Honoris causâ*   a case of [defending one's] honour.

30   *delicacy*   delicate question, point of refinement.

32   *fray*   cut into strips.

55   *a string of names beside*   For these, see VII 6–7.

70   *clandestinely*   There is no evidence for this charge, except for statements that Pietro withheld his consent. The marriage was carried out in due form.

73   *top her part*   play her part to the hilt, or to perfection.

84   *Guido Reni*   Painter (1575–1642).

115   *Barbers and blear-eyed, as the ancient sings*   'a tale well known to every blear-eyed man and barber' (Horace, *Satires* I vii 3).

127 *Antichrist* the ultimate evil – the opponent of Christ and denier of his teachings, whose coming is prophesied in Scripture.

154 *the Cardinal* Cardinal Lauria, Paolo's patron. 'Guido' (line 156) is Browning's error for 'Paolo'.

164 *she confessed her crime* This was a groundless rumour. She did indeed make a deathbed confession to Fra Celestino, but in it she declared herself innocent of any wrongdoing.

175–6 *tares | Are sown for wheat* Matthew xiii 24–30, 36–43.

178 *the philosophic sin* No one seems to have satisfactorily identified the part of Molinist teaching to which this term refers.

179 *the Cardinal* The context suggests that this was Lauria, but Cook identifies him as Cardinal d'Estrées, French ambassador at Rome, who, according to current gossip, had been responsible for Molinos' arrest in 1685.

188 *the Ruspoli* A palace (I 876).

192 *handsel* use, privilege.

203 *aspectable* attractive, pleasant.

206–7 *The villa . . . I' the Pauline district* In his numerous references to the Comparini's domesticity, Browning assumes that they had two residences in Rome, one in the Via Vittoria and another, less pretentious, in the Via Paolina. The fact is that they had but one, at the corner of the two streets. See Cook, *Commentary*, Appendix II.

211 *usufruct* property producing income, interest.

212 *determine* terminate.

222 *spite of her unpromising age* A suggestion of the stories of Sarah (Genesis xviii) and of St Elizabeth (Luke i 5–25).

230 *fiddle-pin's end!* nonsense! (Seemingly a portmanteau expletive, combining 'fiddlesticks', 'not worth a pin' and 'fig's end'. 'Fiddle-pin' literally means 'tuning peg'.)

242 *after-wit* hindsight.

253–4 *lest Eve's rule decline | Over this Adam of hers* The ordained situation in Genesis iii 16–17 is actually the opposite: Eve's 'desire shall be to thy husband, and he shall rule over thee'.

260 *cats'-cradle* A game in which two players intertwine a cord on their fingers so as to produce a symmetrical pattern.

271 *policy* practice (with a suggestion of expedient, stratagem).

285–6 *that stinted due | Service and suit* the world was stingy in paying the rights due him (in the manner of a feudal lord).

291 *a shrewd younger poorer brother* Guido really was the youngest of four brothers, one of whom, Antonio, is not mentioned in the poem.

294 *Galilean* Christian; therefore, in the present context, churchly, ecclesiastical.

295 *free o' the wave* well adapted to his element, or with the freedom of the whole pond.

296 *dab-chick* a small bird, specifically the grebe.

297 *fond* silly.

308 *concurrence* competition.

318 *trimmed his lamp and girt his loins* Luke xii 35, but the phraseology is closer to Browning's in *The Statue and the Bust*, line 247.

352 *clear scores* pay debts.

358 *blind* dark.

361 *some priest-confederate* See III 455 and note.

368 *gainsay* oppose.

388 *devoir* respects, duty.

406 *fusion* Apart from its suggestion of 'melt', used here simply for effect, as a back-formation from 'confusion'.

414 *with purple flushing him* backed by influential churchmen (such as purple-wearing cardinals), and himself with the expectation of rising to the cardinalate (see III 375).

416 *moiety* share, portion.

428 *one black eye does it all* 'thou hast ravished my heart with one of thine eyes' (Song of Solomon iv 9).

436 *citizen's* ordinary man's.

  conceit fancy, imaginary notion.

442 *as if Plutus paid a whim* indiscriminately. Plutus, the Greek personification of riches, was said to have been blinded by Zeus so that he would distribute his gifts in such a fashion.

443 *what God?* The speaker gropes, unsuccessfully, for a fresh mythological analogy.

446 *minister* manage.

447–8 *Stay ... With apples and with flagons* Song of Solomon ii 5.

454–6 Compare the image at I 557.

457–8 *walk softly all his days | In soberness of spirit* Isaiah xxxviii 15: 'I shall go softly all my years in the *bitterness* of my soul.'

469 *competence* money.

474 *verjuice* sour wine.

488 *doited* old and feeble (Scottish).

490 *novercal* stepmotherly.

493 *mumps* ill humour, sulks.

495 *formal habits* empty customs.

500 *malapert* impudent one.

513 *goody, gossip, cater-cousin and sib* Collectively, busybodies, sometimes with a tenuous claim to family relationship.

537 *pricked in conscience* An allusion to the medieval religious treatise, *The Pricke of Conscience*. (Browning often uses the verb 'prick' in this poem, usually but not uniformly with the meaning of 'stir', 'urge', 'goad'.)

541 *Short shrift* hurried confession and absolution.

544 *commuted* absolved. (The usual meaning of 'commute' is 'to reduce a punishment', such as penance, but this seems negated by the following line.)

548 *compound* settle.

552 *changeling* substitute.
 grace mitigation, a mercy.

559 *Catch from the kennel* refuse from the gutter.

563 *Communis meretrix* common prostitute, the 'wanton' of line 561. A document discovered by Professor Corrigan, however, reveals that Pompilia's mother was not a Roman prostitute but a widow named Corona Paperozzi, lately come to Rome from a village southeast of Viterbo.

564 *conditioned* circumstanced.

572–3 *that crown | To the husband* 'A virtuous woman is a crown to her husband: but she that maketh ashamed is as rottenness in his bones' (Proverbs xii 4).

604 *colourable* plausible.

612 *Peter and Paul* A casual expletive.

632 *lazar-badge* leper rag.

673 *find . . . in* supply with.

676 *with three-pauls' worth' sauce*] with stale fame for sauce *1889* (A paul, obsolete by Browning's time, would have been worth about 5*d* in Victorian money.)

684 *she wrote* See General Note 5 (p. 634).

690 *qualified* characterized, described (but in this context, 'berated', 'condemned').

693 *Quiet as Carmel where the lilies live* Proverbial – not a Biblical expression.

712 *posset-cup* cup of hot milk and wine or ale, spiced and sweetened; often taken for medicinal purposes.

726 *The cause thus carried to the courts at Rome* For this and the following lawsuits, see General Note 3 (p. 632).

754 *Counter-appeal* Guido did not, in fact, contest the appeal.

767 *rubric* red.

782 *aureole* halo, possibly with a suggestion of tonsure.

786 *portly make* handsome appearance, disposition.

792 *saint of Caesar's household* Philippians iv 22.

794 *Apollos turned Apollo* Apollos (a follower of St Paul, 1 Corinthians iii 4–6) transformed into Apollo, a god of archery.

795 *spires* coils.

802 *Carnival* period of festivity preceding Lent.

814 *day-book* ledger.

824 *Mum here and budget there* 'shhhhhh'.

832 *horn-madness* the delusive insanity of a cuckold (a man whose wife is unfaithful to him). According to ancient folk belief, the outward sign of cuckoldry was the sprouting of horns from the husband's forehead.

837 *acceptance* popularity, *entrée*.

844 *The trouble of eclipse* Eclipses of the sun or moon were thought to be portents of evil.

845 *officious* meddlesome, interloping.

846 *system* That is, solar system.

847 *pressure of this spring* touch of this wire.

886–7 *the customary compliment | Of cap and bells, the luckless husband's fit!* A ballad ('fit') sung by a jester, whose emblems were cap and bells, about a cuckold. See V 1451–5.

890 *After the cuckoo* 'The point here is that Caponsacchi is the cuckoo; he has been beforehand with Guido, cuckolded him ... and has now carried his wife off' (Cook). The allusion to the cuckoo has a double point: the bird itself is an early riser, and it has the habit of laying its eggs in another bird's nest – hence the word 'cuckold'.

893 *poppy-milk* laudanum (an opiate).

894 *scrutoire* escritoire, writing desk.

899 *candid* innocent.

908 *this waif and the other stray* various pieces of property.

909 *Spoiled the Philistine* Exodus iii 22, where it is 'spoiled the Egyptians'.

939 *poppy-heads* red birettas of the higher clergy, with a play on 'poppy', the source of opium and thus of laudanum.

953 *drench* large dose (a term usually associated with veterinary medicine).

964 *impunity* immunity from civil prosecution.

994 *benedicite* blessing.

1007 *appointment* adornment, accessory.

1018 *priests to try a priest* In Rome, the papal state, the courts were composed of ecclesiastics.

1022 *Commissary* governor.

1030 *as terrible as truth* Perhaps deriving from '*O magna vis veritatis*'

(Cicero, *Pro Caelio* XXVI 63) or '*Magna est veritas, et praevalet*' (3 Esdras iv 41, Vulgate).

1037   *pains*   difficulty.

1038   *pinked*   stabbed, pierced.

1044   *sbirri*   police.

1048   *lead a measure*   dance.

1051   *poke*   pocket.

1055   *an added palm in length*   In Italian idiom, an elongated nose was a sign of disappointed expectations (compare the modern 'nose out of joint').

1072   *the love-letters*   See General Note 5 (p. 634).

1079   *proemium*   prologue.

1082   *He might go cross himself*   A colloquial phrase meaning the business was done with.

1105   *concur i' the close*   fit into a pattern, 'add up'.

1109   *thought, word and deed*   This phrase, repeated several times in the course of the poem, is from the *Confiteor* of the ordinary of the Mass.

1114–15   *Difficult to believe, yet possible,* | *As witness Joseph, the friend's patron-saint*   Perhaps an allusion to St Joseph's difficulty in accepting the idea of the virgin birth (Matthew i 18–20).

1120   *faculty*   intellectual powers.

1127   *repugns*   resists, refuses.

1130   *both in a tale*   agreeing in their story.

1137   *pearls to swine*   Matthew vii 6.

1141   *fardel*   bundle (of).

1158   *fondest*   most naïve or foolish.

1159   *apage*   'get thee hence' (Matthew iv 10).

1168   *Gordian*   The complicated knot tied by Gordius, legendary king of Phrygia, which Alexander the Great cut with his sword.

1180   *Civita*   Civita Vecchia, a seaport thirty-five miles northwest of Rome.

1197–1202   A mistake; see General Note 6 (p. 635).

1201   *patiently possess her soul*   Luke xxi 19.

1221   *Ovid, a like sufferer in the cause*   In 8 AD Ovid was exiled from Rome to Tomis on the Black Sea, ostensibly because of the immoral tendency of his love poems.

1244   *Pontifex Maximus*   The high priest of ancient Rome, who had the privilege of flogging Vestal Virgins who were lax in their duties.

1249   *old Head-i'-the-Sack*   A word play on 'Caponsacchi'.

1250   *fought at Fiesole*   See VI 228–30.

1251   *firk*   assault, trounce.

1269   *alembic*   distilling apparatus.

1270   *Canidian*   Canidia was the evil sorceress in Horace's *Satires* and *Epodes*.

1285   *He claimed in due form a divorce at least*   Not true; the Franceschini had earlier contemplated doing so on Guido's behalf, but their lawyers discouraged them.

1294   *engine*   catapult.

1306   *till he contorts his tail*   The scorpion's poison was said to be delivered by the sting of its tail.

1342   *Domus pro carcere*   house arrest.

1377   *The hoard i' the heart o' the toad*   Toads were thought to be full of deadly poison ('the toad, ugly and venomous', *As You Like It* II i 13).

1379   *wants*   lacks.

1397–8   *clown . . . clodpole*   Both words mean 'lout', 'stupid one'.

1399–1400   *held their peace, | What wonder if the sticks and stones cried out?*   'if these should hold their peace, the stones would immediately cry out' (Luke xix 40). There is also a hint of the children's chant, 'Sticks and stones may break my bones, | But names will never hurt me.'

1445   *Viper-like, very difficult to slay*   Folk herpetology held that wounded snakes survived until after sunset and in some cases had the power to make themselves whole again. ('We have scotch'd the snake, not killed it: | She'll close and be herself', *Macbeth* III ii 13–14.) Pompilia actually lived three more days.

1476   *Astraea*   The goddess of justice.

1478   *God's word 'the faithless wife shall die'*   The exact phrase does not occur in the Bible, but the idea is that of, for example, Leviticus xx 10: 'the adulterer and the adulteress shall surely be put to death'.

1484   *natural*   idiot.

1487   *male-Grissel*   Griselda (a woman) was the model of boundless patience (Boccaccio's *Decameron*, Chaucer's *Clerk's Tale*).

1495   *Rolando-stroke*   the sword of Roland, Charlemagne's nephew.

1496   *clavicle*   collarbone.

1515   *actor*   man of action.

BOOK III

The time is either the second day (I 894–5; this book, line 36) or the third (I 904) after the murders. Preview: I 883–909.

4   *white hospital-array*   See note to I 1085.
18   *the Augustinian Brother*   Fra Celestino. See XII 441–642.
39   *wicket*   small door set inside a larger one.

41   *men of art*   doctors.

47   *gifts*   virtues.

58–9   *Carlo ... Maratta*   Roman painter of great contemporary reputation (1625–1713).

75   *parterre*   formal garden.

96   *the Philosophic Sin*   See note to II 178.

103–4   *the wind | That waits outside a certain church*   The place outside the Gesù church in Rome was notoriously windy.

114   *immunity and all*   exemption from the trials incident to sainthood.

118   *yon Triton's trump*   Bernini's statue of the Triton, referred to above, I 899.

131   *composure*   equitable composition.

137–43   A philosophical notion mixing the Aristotelian concept of the 'fatal flaw' with the idea of original sin.

146–7   *Out of the very ripeness of life's core | A worm was bred*   Compare the different application of the same figure at II 209–10.

154   *God says so*   'For this cause shall a man leave father and mother, and shall cleave to his wife: and they twain shall be one flesh' (Matthew xix 5). But nothing is said about 'a child'.

159   *usufructuary*   recipient of income.

169–70   *Adam-like, Pietro sighed ... Eve saw the apple*   A repetition of the same cast (Pietro as Adam, Violante as Eve) seen at II 253–4.

179   *her own confession*   See note to II 164.

191   *Who swallowed such a tale nor strained a whit*   'Ye blind guides, which strain at a gnat, and swallow a camel' (Matthew xxiii 24).

213   *irksome chance*   embarrassment.

215   *This fragile egg*   It will be laid in Guido's nest at V 655.

222   *conscious and inconscious*   witting and unwitting.

228   *Give ... the church its group*   complete the group of three bodies; see II 136–7.

235   *tongue-leaved eye-figured Eden tree*   Perhaps, as Cook speculates, a reference to 'some allegorical woodcut of the early seventeenth century, representing the tree of knowledge of good or evil', or a suggestion of the serpent hiding in the tree, camouflaged by its leaves and knots (see note to V 1956–7). In any case, this tree has its counterpart in the stump at II 256.

250   *one day brought a priest*   Paolo's visit to the Comparini as Guido's envoy is Browning's invention.

255–7   See note to V 285–342.

282   *the red cloth*   the garb of a cardinal.

287–8   *the topmost beacon-tip | That warrants life a harbour through the haze* Compare I 1182–95, where a similar beacon results in a shipwreck.

289 *fantastic* irrational, lacking in common sense.

292 *when it fell* In line 280 it was '*if* his brother's patron-friend kept faith'.

293–4 *Irrigate far rather than deluge near,* | *Go fertilize Arezzo, not flood Rome* Compare similar imagery above, lines 165–8, 174–6, and below, 715–17.

302 *one who puts his hand to the plough* 'And Jesus said unto him, No man, having put his hand to the plough, and looking back, is fit for the kingdom of God' (Luke ix 62).

307 *Vast as a quarry* 'antres vast and deserts idle, | Rough quarries, rocks and hills whose heads touch heaven' (*Othello* I iii 140–41).

311 *Vittiano* A village nine miles from Arezzo.

316 *cicala's* cicada's.

339 *name-pecking credit-scratching* foraging in hope of finding social dignity.

352 *pant* beat.

359 *Scintillant, rutilant* glittering, shining red.

361 *spiritualty* clergy.

363 *tenement* house.

365 *Lily of a maiden* Compare the use of the lily figure at II 303 and IV 323.

368 *fillet* hair band.

375 *A certain purple gleam* 'the air of a cardinal-to-be' (Cook), suggestive also of the iridescence of certain snakes.

384 *the Hesperian ball* One of the golden apples which Earth gave to Hera on her marriage to Zeus; Hercules, outwitting the Hesperides who stood guard along with a dragon, succeeded in gathering the apples. The legend is used again at VI 1002–9.

392 *Babbuino* A street near the Piazza di Spagna; the 'Boat-fountain' (next line) is at the foot of the steps from the Piazza to the Trinità de Monti.

401 *cross i' the poke* a coin (of any denomination) in the purse.

403 *Humours of the imposthume* temperamental quirks caused by the abscess (disease).

413 *pricked* put himself in position by piercing, boring.

417 *the shift was this* A pun – this 'shift', unlike the preceding one, means 'scheme'.

419 *snuffed* sniffed out.

422 *burgesses* See note to IV 65.

432 *snuff* charred wick or puff of smoke,

439 *playing Danae to gold dreams* Danaë, imprisoned by her father Acrisius because an oracle had warned him she would be the mother of a son who would kill him, was visited by Zeus in the form of a shower of gold. The resulting child was Perseus, who did indeed kill Acrisius by accident.

455 *perhaps* Pompilia, however, says it *was* Paolo (VII 437).

456 *clandestinely* See note to II 70.

464 *chaffer* bargain, haggle.

467 *shambles* slaughter house.

477 *surnamed 'a hinge'* The word 'cardinal' is derived from the Latin *cardo, cardinis*, 'hinge, that on which something turns or depends'.

480 *naughty world* Probably suggested by *The Merchant of Venice* V i 91: 'So shines a good deed in a naughty world.'

487–8 *till faith move | Mountains* 1 Corinthians xiii 2; Matthew xvii 20, xxi 21.

493–520 Compare the quagmire image above, II 1526–33, where Guido is the victim.

499 *doit* a negligible sum (formerly a small Dutch coin).

503–4 Compare II 393.

506 *having and holding* property.

512 *charge* burden, responsibility.

515 *orts* scraps of refuse.

520 *flounced* floundered.

526 *graduated* meted out.

532 *casting coat* Suggestive of a snake's shedding its skin; see below, lines 694–6.

556 *vulgar* petty, common.

567 *the great door new-broken for the nonce* The extreme right-hand door in the west front of St Peter's, normally walled up.

572 *The poor repugnant Penitentiary* Member of a tribunal of the Holy See (the Sacred Penitentiary) charged with hearing confessions, especially of grave sins. 'Repugnant' alludes to the feelings evoked in him by the sins confessed.

592 *alienate* renounce.

618 *gave a leap for joy* 'And it came to pass, that, when Elisabeth heard the salutation of Mary, the babe leaped in her womb' (Luke i 41).

666 *losels* worthless persons.

675 *grace* kindness.

712 *excogitate* think out.

736 *derelict* deserted.

743–50 Compare the discrepant account at II 702–18.

754] As if it had been just so much Chinese *1889*.

769 *figured* described.

779–87 Note the related image at II 820–25.

785 *popinjay* fop.

789 *tenebrific* shadowy.

790 *gorge* inner portion.

806 *silly-sooth* naïve, easily deceived.

837 *facts, charactery* 'facts in black and white' (Cook); 'charactery' means 'handwriting'.

843 *decent* appropriate.

875 *adventurous* coming by chance.

887 *reckless* uncaring.

909 *She never penned a letter in her life* See General Note 5 (p. 634).

977 *opprobrious wight* disgraced one.

998 *cure their qualms* cure what ailed them.

1015 *She, as a last resource, betook herself* The sole evidence of Pompilia's appeal to the friar is her own statement in the Old Yellow Book.

1024 *pluck from out the flame the brand* Zechariah iii 2.

1034 *And woe to the friar by whom offences come* Matthew xviii 7.

1051 *So is the legend of my patron-saint* Compare II 1115.

1054 *passenger* passer-by.

1065 *on a certain April evening* The historical record identifies this as the night of 28–29 April, but Browning changed it to the twenty-third to take advantage of the fact that the latter is the feast day of St George.

1087 *convoy* escort.

1106–7 *Lies! | The woman's life confutes her word* And, in fact, her testimony was rejected by the court on the ground that immorality precludes credibility.

1140 *In a red daybreak* In all the depositions in the Old Yellow Book except Pompilia's, the time of arrival is given as nightfall.

1186 *Confirm her story in all points but one* Untrue; in the Old Yellow Book there are many discrepancies between her story and Caponsacchi's. See Cook, *Commentary*, Appendix V.

1224] Leave no least loop-hole to let murder through *1889*.

1225 *infamy* object of public reproach (Ezekiel xxxvi 3).

1228 *two short hours off* It was 'the trifling four-hours'-running' at II 978.

1233 *Perdue* hidden. Compare Guido's conduct as reported at II 955–78.

1272 *Apprized* alerted.

1289–1317 With this version of the scene at Castelnuovo, compare Half-Rome's account, II 983–1059.

1300 *froward … restif* disobedient … unruly.

1300–306 Variation of the lamb image above, lines 462–8.

1322 *Oh mouse-birth of that mountain-like revenge!* Horace, *Ars Poetica* 139.

1346 *the one hand* Caponsacchi's, as an agent of God. Compare line 620.

1353–4 *If so my worldly reputation burst, | Being the bubble it is* '… the bubble reputation …' (*As You Like It* II vii 152). Compare the bubble imagery at I 557–62 and II 454–6. There will be others at V 449–52, XI 1811–15 and XII 635–42.

1378 *Hard to believe, but not impossible* Compare Half-Rome's attribution to the court of the same attitude, II 1114, 1125.

1380 *A middle course is happily open yet* Compare similar praise of the middle course, lines 671, 711.

1381 *the social blank* the whiteness of society.

1392 *the pattern of desert* the very epitome of injury.

1409 *unshent, unshamed* The words are virtually synonymous.

1424 *breathed* rested (as a horse), therefore reinvigorated.

1429 *Guido turned the screw too much* He was a *victim* of 'one master-squeeze from screw' at II 1376. For another use of the image, see below, lines 1542–5.

1446 *this last best of the Hundred Merry Tales* At least one commentator has identified this as the story of the Patient Griselda in Boccaccio's *Decameron* – ironically appropriate to Pompilia, of course. But Hodell and Cook are probably right in seeing an allusion to Franco Sacchetti's *Libro delle Trecentonovelle (Book of Three Hundred Tales)*. Sacchetti was a contemporary of Chaucer (*c.* 1330–1400). See V 560, 1153; XI 261.

1450–55 The story of Vulcan and Mars is told in the *Odyssey* VIII 266–366. Compare Half-Rome's version, II 1003–9, where the culprits were Paris and Helen, and the injured husband Guido by implication was Menelaus. See also IX 866–75.

1461 *Back to his kennel, tail 'twixt legs* Compare II 1062.

1467–8 *the House whose weight he bore | Pillar-like* Guido in the role of Samson (Judges xvi 25–30).

1471 *efficacious* influential.

1475 *and nephews out of date* See note to I 319.

1477 *Render Caesar what is Caesar's due* Matthew xxii 21.

1480 *Made Guido claim divorce* See note to II 1285.

1514 *Domum*] *Domus 1889*.

1533–8 Note the use of a similar metaphor for Pompilia's instinct, lines 1121–4.

1541 *wrote Paolo* There is no evidence of such a letter.

1542–5 'And the winepress was trodden without the city, and blood came out of the winepress . . .' (Revelation xiv 20).

1561 *process* lawsuit.

1563–9 A reprise of the blood-baptism motif of II 1433–6.

1592 *Good will on earth and peace to man* Luke ii 14.

1598–9 *A friend of Caponsacchi's bringing friends | A letter* Note the significant difference between this version of the password and that at II 1431.

1608 *Were Caponsacchi no rare visitant* The Old Yellow Book contains no evidence on this point. The remark is based on the lawyer Arcangeli's innuendo contained there.

1629 *ticket* pass to leave Rome and cross the Tuscan frontier.

1636 *grange* farm or granary, but elsewhere they are said to have slept on straw by the wayside. In point of fact, they were arrested at an inn.

1674 *That were too temptingly commodious, Count!* Guido is being apostrophized by the speaker. ('Commodious': convenient.)

BOOK IV

The time is the night of the third day after the murders. Preview: I 910–42. 'Tertium Quid' is defined in note to I 916.

15 *Law's a machine* In the ancient Greek theatre, the plot complications at the end of a play were often resolved by the arrival of a god, lowered from heaven on a crane.

26 *tort, retort* wrong ('tort' is a legal term), reply (with the etymological implication of a fresh wrong from the other party).

31–2 *"Trecentos . . . appelle!"* 'You're packing in hundreds!' 'Hold on, that's enough!' 'Bring to here!' (Horace, *Satires* I v 12–13).

42 *Eusebius* The 'father of ecclesiastical history' (*c*. 264–*c*. 349 AD).

46 *Spreti* Arcangeli's colleague in the defence of Guido.

47 *the Fisc and the other kind of Fisc* See notes to I 165, 1117.

53 *ultimate arbiter* That is, the Pope.

54 *basset-table* Basset was a card game.

55 *Her Eminence* a cardinal. (Browning retains the feminine gender of the Italian pronoun: '*Sua* Eminenza'.)

65 *burgess-life* life of the commoner ('bourgeois'). Throughout this book, such words – others are 'cits', 'mob', 'plebs', 'rabble and brabble', 'commonalty' – carry a strong implication of social condescension.

80 *tow* hemp.

86–8] For wind to ravage, nor dropped till lamp graze ground
 Like cresset, mudlarks now here now there,
  Going their rounds to probe the ruts i' the road *1889*
('Mudlarks': street urchins, scavengers.)

87 *cresset* iron vessel to hold burning grease or other substance.

114–15 *The Pope puts meat i' the mouth of, ravens they,|And providence he* Psalm cxlvii 9; Job xxxviii 41.

121 *dollar* Approximately 2*s* 11*d* in Victorian money.

143 *frittered* tattered.

146 *house-book* ledger of household expenses.

170 *Citorio* the Piazza di Monte Citorio.

174 *criticise* see.

179 *propitious shape* But at II 570 she is said to have been only one month pregnant at the time.

191 *earnest-money-piece* down payment.

196–7 *My reproof is taken away, | And blessed shall mankind proclaim me now* St Elizabeth's words (Luke i 25), whereas the *Magnificat* (from Luke i 46) contains those of the Virgin Mary.

202 *orisons* prayers.

203 *pair of pinners and a coif* A coif is a tight-fitting cap, such as that still worn by some orders of nuns, and the pinners are the large flaps attached to it.

206 *Orvieto* A light wine.

221 *Debarred* omitted.

271 *the havings and the holdings* See note to III 506.

272 *defect* lack.

295 *chatelaine* mistress of a palace.

296 *want . . . want* A play on words – the first 'want' means both 'lack' and 'desire' and the second only 'desire'.

307 *exact* scrupulous, rigorous (with suggestion of 'niggling', 'finicky').

328 *Solomon's porch* 1 Kings vii 7, x 18–20.

338 *dimittas*] *dimittis 1889*
 Nunc dimittas 'Now let thy servant depart' (Luke ii 29).

405 *affected* imitated.

418 *chafe* impatience.

424 *recalcitrant* resentful one ('recalcitrant' is the object of 'pats').

437 *Notum tonsoribus* it's known to barbers (and therefore is common knowledge); (Horace, *Satires* I vii 3; see note to II 115). Browning uses the Latin tag as a means of introducing the peruke maker who actually served as a go-between for Guido and the Comparini.

448 *zecchines* A zecchine was worth about 10s in Victorian money.

456 *patch* 'beauty spot' worn by fashionable women.

457 *pomander* wax perfume ball.

460 *pantoufle* slipper.

470 *Her Efficacity* powerful one. (For 'her' see note to line 55.)

472–3 *the grey mare, | The better horse, – how wise the people's word!*
'The grey mare is the better horse' – proverb meaning 'the wife rules the husband'.

484 *fairy* magic.

506 *clapnet* net which can be closed by pulling a string.

515 *truck* exchange.

531 *traffic* transaction.

583 *dignity* social rank.

585 *bye-circumstance* side issue.

586 *untowardness* annoyance.

600 *round* din. (The word actually means 'whisper', but Browning regularly uses it, by extension from 'roundly', in the sense of loud, insistent utterance.)

612 *bye-blow* bastard.

658 *superfluity of naughtiness* excessive troublemaking (James i 21).

708 *baited their own hook* Compare earlier uses of the angler image at II 268–77, 321–3, 342–3, 1355–60.

712 *Hymen* The Greek god of marriage.

730 *scullions* kitchen help of the lowest order.

731 *vitriol* sulphuric acid.
devil's-dung asafoetida, a stinking drug.

733 *slab* wet, slimy matter ('Make the gruel thick and slab', *Macbeth* IV i 32).

756–7 *the man was Aretine, had touch | O: the subtle air* Michaelangelo is said to have remarked to Giorgio Vasari, the historian of painting, 'If I have anything good in me, that comes from my birth in the pure air of your country of Arezzo.' See note to XII 807.

762 *cross-buttock* a throw over the hip, in wrestling.
quarter-staff iron-tipped staff about six-and-a-half feet long.

768 *unmitigably* ceaselessly.

794 *No outlet* Compare previous uses of the figure at III 689, 780, 1039.

796 *Hell's arms* Compare III 230–2.

833 *dispensation* divinely ordained qualities.

834 *poor Hophni that I am* 2 Samuel vi 6–7. ('Hophni' is an error for 'Uzzah', which Browning substituted in 1889. See note to I 195.)

836 *In patience all of ye possess your souls* Luke xxi 19.

840 *intention* sake.

844–9 A suggestion of the story of Orpheus' rescue of Eurydice from Hades, without the unhappy ending.

849 *the circle* Compare I 574, 581.

854–6 Beginning in 1872 these lines were printed in the order 855–856–854.

856 *The serpent tempted me* Compare the same plea at III 471.

874 *cap* remove our hat.

876 *in converse* in 'criminal conversation', adultery.

887 *Lucretia* The chaste wife of Collatinus, raped by Tarquin.

 Susanna Model of virtue in the apocryphal History of Susanna (chapter 13 of the Book of Daniel in the Vulgate).

888–9 *curtaining Correggio carefully | Lest I be taught that Leda had two legs* The scene of Zeus visiting the nude Leda in the form of a swan, preparatory to begetting Castor and Pollux, was a favourite subject of Renaissance painters, among them Correggio.

895 *earnest of despair* token of hopelessness (my inability to reform you).

904 *fabric* structure, with (in this context) the implication of 'fabrication' – a lie.

925 *primacies* high authorities.

951 *mitigable* capable of being palliated, lessened in degree of guilt.

955 *rubric* heading.

 breviary book of daily prayers for priests.

965 *turbulence* troublemaker.

1014 *confidency* intimacy.

1021 *hackney chair* a hired one-horse vehicle, chaise.

1037 *converse* See note to line 876.

1054 *Cui profuerint!* Who stood to gain by it?

1065 *embassies* messages carried by a go-between.

1069 *acquetta* poison.

 stilling distilling, issuing in drops.

1091 *i' the stock* in the trunk, by main lineage or breed.

1144 *Paphos* Cyprian site of the temple of Aphrodite, vulgarized in modern times into a symbol of sexual licence.

1145 *stews* brothels.

1147 *stock-fish* hard-dried, unsalted cod.

1187 *To try conclusions* debate, try the issue.

1209 *Well done, thou good and faithful servant!* Matthew xxv 21.

1233 *mulct* fine.

1236 *Saint Rose* Falsely accused martyr burned at the stake but unscathed; the stake itself blossomed with roses.

1237 *Donna Olimpia of the Vatican* The sister-in-law of Pope Innocent X (1644–55), who dominated and unmercifully robbed him.

1261 *stripes* flogging.

1276 *wisdom to the children of this world* Luke xvi 8.

1282 *Place Navona* Largest of the Roman squares, site of markets and popular entertainments.

1305 *the three suits* See General Note 3 (p. 632).

1311 *Rota* ecclesiastical court of final appeal, subject only to papal authority.

1322 *Vicegerent* vice governor.

1347 *impunity* immunity, exemption from punishment.

1356–7 *Paolo first | Vanished* To Venice and eventually to Spain, where, in 1708, he enlisted the aid of numerous dignitaries, including two ambassadors, an admiral, two generals, a duke, and a king in a strenuous and ultimately successful effort to obtain a pension. (See F. E. Faverty, 'The Absconded Abbot in *The Ring and the Book*', *Studies in Philology* XXXVI, 1939, 88–104.)

1369 *the Paolina* The Via Paolina, site of the Comparini's home.

1371 *one in the evening* An hour after the Ave Maria, about 7 p.m.

1372 *'Friends with a letter from the priest your friend'* Compare the passwords at II 1431, III 1598–9.

1402–3 *sleeping . . . The sleep o' the just* 'Elle s'endormit du sommeil des justes' (Racine, *Abrégé de l'histoire du Port Royal* IV 517).

1404 *just and unjust* Matthew v 45, Acts xxiv 15, etc.

1412 *in a chafe* overheated.

1453 *the old Religious* Fra Celestino.

1495 *apposed to* placed on (the document of).

1498 *anotherguess* another kind of.

1511 *baulks* deprives.

1578] *Malorum* – drops first, deluge since, – which done *1872*

1618 *truth is*] truth seems *1889*

BOOK V

The time is probably the third day after the murders, although the evidence is conflicting (compare line 1683 below with VI 37). It will be noted also that at line 936 Guido speaks of Pompilia as having already died, but at 1687 he says she is still living. She did, in fact, die four days after his attack. Preview: I 943–1015.

5 *vinegar and gall* Matthew xxvii 34, 38.

28 *in and out my heart, the play o' the probe* Note Tertium Quid's use of the same image, IV 1148–9. The latter is one of many evidences of Tertium Quid's instinctive – and politic – sympathy for Guido.

38 *Vigil-torment* See note to I 979–80.

63 *sib* See note to II 513.

71 *lamb's head and purtenance* Exodus xii 9.

78 *policy* shrewdness, calculation.

118 *omoplat* shoulderblade.

127 *crease* wrinkle, or possibly the furrow worn by the yoke.

134 *my back of docile beast* At the end of the preceding book Guido was portrayed as a maddened bull.

135 *whealed* flogged (leaving welts). See note to XI 1467.

149–56 An allusion to the rivalry between the two religious orders of Franciscans and Dominicans.

158 *Homager to the Empire* holder of an estate under the (Holy Roman) Emperor.

166 *remark* noticing.

169 *pay that fault* pay for being poor.

177 *pricking* tingling with life.

183 *muse, demand* ask oneself, and ask others, why.

186–7 *Was adding to his purchased pile a fourth | Tall tower* In Renaissance Tuscany, tall towers continued to be built as status symbols long after their military usefulness had ended.

194 *suttler* peddler trading with the army.

207 *suum cuique* to each his own (Tacitus, *Annals* IV xxxv 4).

209 *Well, let me go, do likewise* Luke x 37.

227 *porporate* a wearer of cardinal's purple.

228 *Red-stockinged* in cardinal's stockings.

230 *Be not the vine but dig and dung its root* Luke xiii 7–8.

231 *gird up priesthood's loins* Luke xii 35.

249–50 *I, having a field, | Went, sold it, laid the sum at Peter's foot* 'And Joses, who by the apostles was named Barnabas, . . . having land, sold it, and brought the money, and laid it at the apostles' feet' (Acts iv 36–7).

255 *prop . . . stanchion* The words are synonymous.

275–6 *Should miracle leave, beyond what feeds the flock, | Fragments to brim the basket of a friend* Matthew xiv 19–20.

278 *Quitted me* behaved.

282 *Dives* The rich man in Christ's parable, Luke xvi.

285 *Utrique sic paratus* prepared for either event.

285–342 This detailed account of Guido's futile attempt to gain a profitable foothold in the church is almost entirely Browning's invention. We do know from the documents, however, that Guido exaggerates the lowliness of the position he held in the entourage of his patron,

Cardinal Nerli. The records also indicate that he does not exaggerate his lack of success.

293 *denizen o' the dung* Compare II 295–8 (the direct antecedent of the present image) and IV 247, where Pompilia is a rose on the dung-heap.

303 *griffin-guarded* guarded by statues of griffins, Greek mytho-logical animals with the head and wings of an angel and the body of a lion.

304 *term* pillar surmounted by a sculptured head or bust, originally that of Terminus, god of boundaries.

307 *varletry* rabble, menials.

313 *Sylla, Marius* Lucius Sulla (138–78 BC) and Gaius Marius (157–86 BC) were rival Roman generals and dictators.

314 *hexastich* six-line epigram.

318 *Purfled* fringed.

322 *tittup* frisk, prance.

328 *florins* gold Florentine coins.

345 *seventh climacteric* the age of forty-nine.

347 *fed by the east-wind* Job xv 2.

fulsome-fine fed to satiety.

349 *gorge* stomach.

364 *limes* catches by spreading a sticky substance on twigs.

378 *cross nor pile* the two sides of a coin (compare 'heads and tails'), therefore penniless.

379 *short-casting* cautious.

389 *shagrag* shaggy, unkempt.

392 *baulked of* spared.

402 *a sors . . . a right Virgilian dip* The Roman habit of opening a copy of Virgil at random in the expectation of lighting upon a particu-larly appropriate and helpful passage.

406 *counted* accounted, known.

408 *frieze* coarse, shaggy woollen fabric.

413 *Paul's advice* See line 724 and note.

416 *stomach* appetite.

418 *truck* exchange.

458 *prizer* prizefighter.

462–524 Compare Tertium Quid's account of the same bargain, IV 508–27.

488–9 *Pietro of Cortona . . . Ciro Ferri* Pietro (1597–1669) was a celebrated baroque painter, Ferri (1634–89) his pupil.

497 *Mere grace, mere coquetry* embellishment, window-dressing.

504 *Flirted* sprinkled.
  chapmen merchants.

509 *were rights of force* were justice done.

511 *writhings* Note the reflection of earlier snake imagery, for example II 1445-6.

519 *The tone o' the new sphere that absorbed the old* Ephesians iv 22–4.

522 *Greatness to touch and taste and handle now* Colossians ii 21.

523-4 *vanity, | Vexation, and what Solomon describes* Ecclesiastes i 14 and elsewhere.

540 *salamander-like* a lizard reputed in myth to live in the midst of fire.

542 *baioc* a contemporary papal coin of small value.

546 *frizzles* That is, loses his salamander-like resistance to fire and burns, briskly and crisply.

559 *Plautus, Terence, Boccaccio's Book* All classics of comedy, with special reference to cheating and disillusionment.

560 *My townsman, frank Ser Franco's merry Tales* See note to III 1446. Sacchetti was not Guido's 'townsman' but a Florentine.

565 *purblind* stupid, uncomprehending.

578 *loyalty and obedience* 1 Corinthians xiv 34.

581-2 *Father and mother shall the woman leave, | Cleave to the husband, be it for weal or woe* 'Therefore shall a man leave his father and mother, and shall cleave unto his wife. . . .' (Genesis ii 24; the same statement in Matthew xix 5). Note Guido's inversion of the Biblical text.

592 *Epithalamium* wedding song.

605-6 *when I buy, timber and twig, a tree – | I buy the song o' the nightingale inside* Compare the image at III 235-48, and below, line 705.

625 *soldo* The Tuscan equivalent of the baioc (line 542).

627 *Caligula* A mad, bloodthirsty Roman emperor (12–41 AD).

632 *Woe worth* woe be to.

637-8 *call the stones | O' the common street to save her* Earlier (II 1400) it was the stones that cried out.

657 *cockatrice* See note to I 171.

672 *Thyrsis* Stock name for a lover in pastoral poetry.
  Neaera Name of several mistresses in classical literature – Horace's (*Carmina* III xiv 21), the shepherd Aegon's (Virgil, *Eclogues* III 3), Bacchus's, etc.

673 *provençal roses* ribbon rosettes.

675 *bravo* tough bodyguard.

700 *true-love-knot* A complicated double knot, symbolic of fidelity.

701 *Venus' pet* In Renaissance art, a dove is often an attribute of Venus.

703   *hawk*   At line 606 Pompilia was a nightingale.

705   *the Rotunda*   the Piazza della Rotonda, site of Rome's bird market.

709   *hoodwink*   blindfold.

710   *should she prove a haggard*   prove untrainable. The passage echoes *Othello* III iii 260–63.

715   *falcon-gentle*   female falcon.

724   *neither marry nor burn*   1 Corinthians vii 9.

726–7   *its own blessed special ordinance | Whereof indeed was marriage made the type*   'Wives, submit yourselves unto your own husbands, as unto the Lord. For the husband is the head of the wife, even as Christ is the head of the church: and he is the saviour of the body. Therefore, as the church is subject unto Christ, so let the wives be to their own husbands in every thing. Husbands, love your wives, even as Christ also loved the church, and gave himself for it' (Ephesians v 22–5).

730   *claustral*   cloistral, monastic.

732   *supports indifferently*   barely endures.

736   *profess*   take religious vows.

738   *Francis' manna*   'Did St Francis use the manna-metaphor when teaching his disciples to take no thought for what they should eat?' (Cook). 'Quails' is from Numbers xi 31–2.

740   *Levite-rule*   rule for deacons.

742   *peccant humours*   sinful self-indulgence.

746   *lore*   teaching.

750   *pens*   feathers.

753   *turtle*   turtledove.

760   *postulant*   candidate for admission into a religious order; see lines 735–6.

802   *A proverb and a byeword*   1 Kings ix 7.

809–14   Note the same combination of images at II 627–35.

811   *Locusta*   A female poisoner in the time of Claudius and Nero.

814   *stock*   stem on which a graft is made, lineage.

850   *Bilboa*   sword made in a Spanish town famed for its steel weapons.

862   *morose*   despondent.

879–83   At II 1267–71 the poisonous drops were *falling* on Guido. Compare also III 573–4.

897   *lodge*   box, loge.

900   *Launching her looks forth*   In the manner of a basilisk, relative of (or sometimes identified with) the cockatrice, whose mere breath or look could kill.

906   *minion*   servile follower, sycophant.

R.B. – 29

908-10 Compare other quagmire images at II 1524–9; III 493–5, 520–21, 620–21; VI 1799–1800; IX 915–23; XI 400–406. (The same gadfly was *life* at I 1275–6; it reappears below, line 1539.)

922 *Stans pede in uno* an easy thing, done standing on one foot (Horace, *Satires* I iv 10).

923 *plainsong* a simple, moving chant.

931 *mulct* punishment – used ironically (so sweet and mild a punishment).

933 *Breathed threatenings, rage and slaughter* Acts ix 1 (St Paul against the disciples of the Lord).

967-8 *Malchus . . . After the incident of the ear* John xvii 10–11; but Guido omits to recall that Christ reproached Peter for cutting off Malchus' ear.

972 *Like Judas* Matthew xxvii 5–7, John xiii 26–30.

998 *admiring* wondering, excited.

1000 *intelligence* secret communications.

1023 *Torrione* the Great Tower in Arezzo.

1026 *calash* carriage.

1031 *tesselated* mosaic.

1038 *drenched* given a large dose of purgative medicine.

1046 *As Lucifer kept falling to find hell* Isaiah xiv 12.

1051 *confessed* manifest, avowed.

1096 *poltroon* coward.

1107 *Gamaliel's nod* Acts xxii 3.

1114 *amercement* penalty.

1121 *conversancy in* familiarity with.

1136 *witches' circle* Compare I 573–4, IV 849, and V 1032–4, 1512–13.

1137 *succubus* female demon.

1153 *Sacchetti again* See note to line 560. The quoted passage which follows is a pastiche of the florid style characteristic of the novella of Sacchetti's and Boccaccio's time.

1155 *placket* Either her petticoat or a pocket in her skirt.

1159 *Thy page* The same one referred to at IV 876?

1161 *losel* futile.

1174 *Law renovates even Lazarus* Luke xvi 20–24.

1175 *Caesar thou seekest? To Caesar thou shalt go!* Acts xxv 12.

1182 *runagate* runaway.

1197 *provident shepherd* Matthew xviii 12.

1209 *Did not Catullus write less seemly once?* Yes; in his *Carmina*.

1210 *doctus* learned, wise.

1219 *deviation* departure from the path of virtue.

1228 *establish* accept as true.

1234   *connection*   sexual intercourse.

1235   *pudency*   shame, modesty.

1265   *The . . . much-commiserated husband*   Menelaus.

1282   *Ultima Thule*   A locale vaguely placed in the far north by Virgil (*Georgics* I 30) and other ancient writers.

1283   *Proxima Civitas*   nearby town – Civita Vecchia, thirty-five miles from Rome.

1290   *fillip*   tap.

1302   *harbour-boom*   barrier, often of logs roped or chained together.

1311–14   A fusion of two separate episodes, Laban's tricking Jacob into marrying Leah instead of Rachel (Genesis xxix 16–25) and Lot's incest with his two daughters (Genesis xix 30–35).

1324   *colour*   justification, legal authority.

1350   *infallible*   See note to X 150.

1353   *irruption*   sudden breaking in, incursion.

1357–8   *versed in Ovid's art* | *More than his Summa*   'Ovid's art' is his *Ars Amatoria*; the 'Summa' is the *Summa Theologiae* of St Thomas Aquinas. The passage by anticipation merges II 1222 with VI 484, 500; compare VI 344–5.

1359   *Corinna*   Ovid's mistress.

1365   *merum sal*   'very spicy' (Cook).

1370   *he has sold all off, is gone*   See note to IV 1356–7.

1372   *Britain almost divided from our orb*   Virgil, *Eclogues* I 67.

1378   *titillation*   sensation, excitement.

1389   *the toad's-head-squeeze*   A poison often referred to in literature. It was especially favoured by adulterous wives who wanted to kill their husbands.

1400–403   A resumption of the angler motif; see earlier occurrences listed in the note to IV 708.

1421   *Paynims*   pagans.

1481   *bantling*   brat (with suggestion of illegitimacy).

1492   *jakes*   privy.

1494–5   *when who cut my purse,* | *Filched my name*   An echo of *Othello* III iii 157–61.

1502   *carriage*   conduct.

1505   *leviathan*   the sea monster in Job xli.

1537–8   Compare II 629 and line 912 of this book.

1549   *Quis est pro Domino?*   'Who is on the Lord's side?' (Exodus xxxii 26).

1557–9   Suggested by *The Tempest* III ii 96–8: 'There thou mayst brain him . . . or paunch [prod, poke] him with a stake.'

1574   *anterior*   early, primitive.

1583   *Joy upon earth, peace and good will to man*   Luke ii 14.

1610   *O Lord, how long, how long be unavenged?*   Revelation vi 10.

1613   *death-watch-tick*   the sound of a death-watch beetle.

1630–33   Compare previous versions at II 1406–31, III 1597–9 and IV 1371–2.

1663   *Immeasurable everlasting wave*   Compare II 1433.

1694–5   *florid prose | As smooth as mine is rough*   '. . . though I be rude in speech' (2 Corinthians xi 6; also *Othello* I iii 81).

1723   *warrant*   the 'ticket' of III 1629.

1727   *stipendiary*   paid employee, hireling.

1733   *discards*   disposes of (by killing).

1754   *fondness of conceit*   silly idea.

1775   *determinable*   explicit.

1778   *Statute*   fixed by law.

1780   *legist*   lawyer.

1781   *Justinian's Pandects*   The collection of legal codes and decisions which still served as the basis of Roman law at this time. See note to I 223.

1907   *effraction*   burglary.

1911   *Amenable*   subject.

1949–51   Resumes the image of lines 810–14.

1956–7   *fixed eye | And vibrant tongue*   This association of the eye and tongue of the serpent with the 'tree of life' sheds light on the meaning of the Eden tree image at III 325.

1980   *pink*   the flower of, perfection.

2000   *efficient*   effective, productive of results.
  comminatory   threatening.

2010   *exenterate*   disembowelled.

2020   *Shimei*   2 Samuel xvi 5–13 (the stones were thrown at David).

2032   *paladin*   perfect knight.

2045   *men of Belial*   1 Samuel ii 12, 22 ('they knew not the Lord').

2048   *Then will I set my son at my right-hand*   Acts ii 25, 34.

BOOK VI

The time is the day following Guido's appearance before the court. Preview: I 1016–75.

52–9   John xix 23–4.

67   *the four corners of this earth*   Revelation vii 1.

87   *fribble . . . coxcomb*   Both mean 'trifler', 'playboy'.

126   *lenity*   lenience.

134   *Chop-fallen*   dejected.

148 *relume the quenched flax by this dreadful light* Isaiah xlii 3, perhaps by way of *Othello* V ii 8–13.

151-2 *pluck tares | And weed the corn* See note to II 175.

156 *the other potentate* 'civility and the mode' (IV 217) – civilized custom.

183 *colour* plausibility.

202 *disadvantage* put in an unfavourable position (but here, almost synonymous with 'trouble').

229 *Fiesole* A town overlooking Florence.

230 *Capo-in-Sacco* See note to II 1249–50.

231-4 The event is mentioned in Dante, *Paradiso* XVI 121.

234 *the Old Mercato* the old market in Florence.

238 *the Salviati* A distinguished Roman family.

242 *illustration* illustrious person.

260-61 *expect ... The proper mood o' the priest* anticipate the correct priestly conduct.

283 *ineffable sacrosanct* indescribably holy.

294 *Dioclesian* Roman emperor (245–313 AD), persecutor of Christians (more usually spelled 'Diocletian').

318 *Onesimus* A servant who, after robbing and running away from his master, became a disciple of St Paul (Philemon 10, 18–19).

320 *King Agrippa* Agrippa II (27–*c*. 93 AD), last Jewish king of Palestine, before whom St Paul pleaded his case (Acts xxv–xxvi).

323 *Fenelon* François de Salignac de la Mothe Fénelon (1651–1715), French theologian. He defended the Quietist Madame Guyon when she was accused of sharing the more extreme views of Molinos (*Explication des maximes des saints sur la vie intérieure*, 1697, a book Louis XIV prevailed upon Innocent XII to condemn). Thus the bitter controversy engendered by Fénelon's unorthodox theology was reaching its climax in Rome concurrently with that of the Franceschini case.

328 *swinged* flogged.

329 *paste* quality, make.

333 *Marinesque Adoniad Adone* by the fashionable Italian poet Giovanni Battista Marino (1569–1625), a colourful treatment of the Venus and Adonis story that is twice as long as *The Ring and the Book*.

349 *tarocs* A card game played with a 78-card pack. (Trump in tarocs is the 22-card set of 'tarots', fortune-telling cards.)

352 *Benignant* useful.

360 *the subject of the day* Molinism.

370 *Crowd sail, crack cordage* hoist an unusual number of sails and strain the rigging, for the sake of speed. ('Crack' also means 'clap on full sail'.)

384 *closet-lectures*   informal, intimate discourses.

386 *body o' Bacchus*   The profane (heathen) equivalent of the Eucharist – a most unsuitable oath to pass ecclesiastical lips.

387–8 *chasms | Permissible only to Catullus*   Catullus violated metrical rules by leaving an unelided syllable ('chasm') in the middle of the second line of an elegiac couplet.

389 *break Priscian's head*   break the rules of the sixth-century grammarian Priscian (write unclassical, and therefore uncouth, Latin).

402 *facchini*   porters.

439 *louted*   bowed in obeisance or apology.

457 *Marino*   See note to line 333.

460 *Duomo*   cathedral.

463 *ortolans*   birds which were a cherished table delicacy.

467 *canzonet*   light love song.

518 *patch*   fool.

559 *Thyrsis ... Myrtilla*   Stock names of characters in pastoral poetry. In the love letters quoted in the Old Yellow Book, the writers actually used such names for each other.

572 *Concert*   arrange, agree on.

582 *Philomel, the thorn at her breast*   According to legend, the melancholy song of the nightingale (Philomel) was caused by a thorn in its breast.

596 *cates*   delicacies.

606 *hell's worm*   Mark ix 48.

669–73 Compare the similar image at III 1165–7, and see below, lines 1484–5.

707 *Our Lady of all the Sorrows*   The Virgin.

869 *'T was a thief said the last kind word to Christ*   Luke xxiii 42.

948 *In rushed new things, the old were rapt away*   2 Corinthians v 17; Revelation xxi 4–5.

960 *Saint Thomas*   St Thomas Aquinas.

961 *sinner Plato by Cephisian reed*   'Sinner' because (in contrast to St Thomas) a pagan. The Cephissus is the river flowing past Athens.

968–71 Possibly suggested by Revelation xiv 4.

977–8 *the Bride, the mystic love | O' the Lamb*   Revelation xxi 9.

988 *corona*   rosary.

1000 *scrannel*   shrill (in Milton's use in *Lycidas*, as here, the word is associated with the voice of a decadent church).

1002–9 See note to III 384.

1005 *hips and haws*   The ripened fruit of the rose and the hawthorn, respectively.

1099–1104 According to legend, St Thomas, who was not present when the other disciples witnessed the assumption of the Virgin, remained sceptical until she threw down her girdle to him; he was then cured of doubt.

1112 *day for copes* Copes (mantles) were worn by clergy on festive occasions.

1116 *octave* the eight days after Easter.

1129 *excepted* exceptional.

1161 *God's sea, glassed in gold* Revelation xv 2.

1170 *Parian, coprolite* They are, respectively, marble and the petrified excrement of reptiles.

1182 *vest* clothing.

1199 *determined* the 'clear' of line 1152.

1202 *hitherto* thus far.

1246 *blow-ball* seed head of the dandelion.

1263 *rocheted and mitred* clad in ecclesiastical garb. (The rochet is a short surplice, the mitre the headdress of a bishop.)

1266 *angelus* bell calling to prayer.

1271 *Gabriel's song* The words of the Annunciation (Luke i 26–35).

1272–3 *the little prayer | To Raphael* Raphael was 'the Sociable spirit, that deigned | To travel with Tobias' (*Paradise Lost* V 221–2). See the apocryphal Book of Tobit.

1275 *Foligno* A town between Perugia and Assisi.

1302–3 *Let God arise and all his enemies | Be scattered* Psalm lxviii 1.

1369 *coil* disturbance.

1396 *Whom the winds carry* Psalm xviii 10.

1443 *Matutinal* early in the morning.

1459–61 See III 1450–5 and note. The Cyclops were servants of Vulcan.

1468 *leman* mistress.

1478 *miscreate* misbegotten, badly made.

1484 *purulence* pus.

1487 *Molière's self* An allusion to the French dramatist's *Dom Juan*, in which Juan claims Donna Elvire as his wife.

1535 *wanted* needed to use.

1567 *getting him a countenance* gaining support or composure.

1600 *fulgurant* flashing like lightning.

1620 *paten* plate holding the Eucharist.

1626 *bravo's* ruffian's (that is, like that of one of Guido's henchmen).

1659 *Pasquin* Originally, a fifteenth-century Roman tailor (or cobbler), said to be a skilful epigrammatist; later, a disinterred statue named for him on the site of his shop in the Piazza Navona. On this broken statue were affixed coarse satirical comments (pasquinades) on current events and public figures.

1663 *character* handwriting.

1666 *Bembo's verse* The elegant verse of the scholar Pietro Bembo (1470–1547).

1667 *the tract 'De Tribus'* A medieval tract on 'three impostors' (Moses, Christ, Mohammed) ascribed to one Ochinus.

1688 *of your charity?* pray tell?

1691–2 *Sub imputatione meretricis | Laborat* had the reputation of being a prostitute. See III 1097–1108.

1715 *cloth* Note the pun on 'cloth' as a metaphor for the clergy.

1721 *smack* sensual appetite.

1722 *Abate my crest* do away with my pride or dignity.

1732 *Potiphar* Genesis xxxix.

1747 *'De Raptu Helenae'* A Greek poem on the rape (abduction) of Helen of Troy, written in Egypt about 500 AD.

1750 *the Vulgar* Dante's name for vernacular Italian.

1751 *Scazons* A scazon is an iambic line ending in a spondee or trochee (and therefore defective if it ends instead in an iamb: see lines 1752–3).

1759 *Admiring* A double-edged word here.

1767 *Full measure, pressed down, running over now* Luke vi 38.

1771 *personate Saint George* See note to III 1065–6.

1783 *You blind guides who must needs lead eyes that see* Matthew xxiii 24.

1792 *cartulary* record.

1793 *front* face.

1796 *letch* abnormal possession, frenzy.

1804 *pustules* (running?) pimples.

1917 *cramp* give him a secure grip.

1944 *Kiss him the kiss, Iscariot* Matthew xxvi 48–9.

1945 *smatch* smack, flavour.

1947 *the letters* Primarily the love letters allegedly exchanged by Pompilia and Caponsacchi, but the word 'Aretine' supplies an overtone of reference to the three to four thousand published letters of Pietro Aretino (see IX 1202 and note), many of which reveal his vicious character.

1950 *cockatrice ... basilisk* See note to V 900.

1956 *divagation* digression, wandering.

2009 *title* setting-forth of reasons.

2013 *Probationis ob defectum* in lack of proof (of adultery).

2032 *Conti is dead* The rumour is reported in a document of the Old Yellow Book.

2035 *the Moor's skin* A possible allusion to *Othello*.

2037-8 *Guillichini; he's condemned ... To the galleys* A fact reported in the Old Yellow Book. (Guillichini appears at II 934-6.)

2051 *Vincenzo Marzi-Medici* The governor of Arezzo.

2057 *Rota's* See note to IV 1311.

2060 *the Augustinian* Fra Celestino.

2072 *distemperature* disordered state of mind.

idle heat unproductive passion.

2077 *do my duty and live long* All that is subsequently heard of him is that in 1702 he resigned as canon of the church of Santa Maria delle Pieve.

2099 *Opens his Plutarch* In Plutarch's series of *Parallel Lives* the biographies of great Romans and somehow related Greeks are set side by side for the sake of instructive comparison.

BOOK VII

The time is the fourth day after the murders, the same day Caponsacchi appeared before the court. Preview: I 1076-1104.

22 *marble lion* There were two lions in the portico of the church of San Lorenzo.

30 *for a reason* See line 103 and the next note.

103 *a new saint* St Gaetano, canonized in 1671.

107 *five saints* Those in lines 6-7.

188 *Tisbe, that is you* The figure of Diana the huntress (Ovid, *Metamorphoses* III 151-252).

193-6 An allusion to the story of Daphne, who when chased by Apollo was turned into a bay (laurel) tree (*Metamorphoses* I 452-567).

235 *the other villa* See note to II 206-7.

238 *sincere* genuine, unadulterated.

263 *San Giovanni* the church of St John Lateran.

302-3 Compare the image at III 77.

333 *wife and husband are one flesh* Genesis ii 24; Mark x 8.

351-2 Compare the use of the disinfection-blood purgation motif at II 1433-7, III 1563, V 1662-4, and below, lines 1735-8.

390 *the slim young man* Perseus, rescuer of Andromeda (*Metamorphoses* IV 663-752).

400-409 Compare the previous versions of the marriage bargain at IV 508-38 and V 474-516.

413–24 Compare Guido's use of the doctor image at V 1704–7.

423 *Master Malpichi* Marcello Malpighi (1628–94), great biologist and physician to the Pope in 1691–4.

427 *the Lion's-mouth* the Via della Bocca di Leone.

448, 450 See note to V 726.

449 *turned he water into wine* The miracle at the wedding feast at Cana (John ii 1–10).

481 *impudent* immodest.

507 *syllabub* milk or cream combined with wine or liquor and whipped into a froth.

547 *a help in time of need* Psalm xlvi 1.

608 *the Spanish House* the Spanish embassy.

675 *just* Idiomatically, the word should precede 'anger'.

762 *Be fruitful, multiply, replenish earth* Genesis i 28.

767 *qualified* regarded as.

798 *God's Bread!* An oath invoking the Eucharist; unseemly in the mouth of an archbishop, but not so much so as 'body o' Bacchus' in VI 386.

821 *Without a parable spake He not to them* Matthew xiii 34.

832 *perquisite* thing to which one has a sole right, exclusive possession.

833 *restif* perverse.

992 *Had I a dove's wings, how I fain would flee!* Psalm lv 6.

1015 *cornet* twist of paper.

1057 *thrust* hardship, 'tight spot'.

1084 *city-ladies* fashionable women.

1145 *imposthume* swelling, abscess.

1145–8 Compare Guido's account of his threat, V 1705–6.

1150 *prevent* anticipate.

1153 *Mirtillo* See note to VI 559.

1173 *I am the Pope, am Sextus, now the Sixth* There was no Pope Sixtus the Sixth; the last Sixtus was the Fifth.

1174 *proclaimed to-day* 12 July 1691.

1215–19 A reference to Spinello Aretino's picture in the church of San Francesco, Arezzo, of St Michael fighting the dragon.

1307 *flying* passing irregularly from one part of the body to another.

1323–5 A reference to Vasari's picture of St George in the church of the Pieve: see VI 1771–7.

1368 *of force* required.

1392–3 *a thunderstone, | Wrapped in a flame* According to an old belief, thunder was caused by the descent of a large stone accompanying a lightning bolt.

1485 *He hath a devil* John vii 20, viii 48, etc.

1495–6] I did pray, do pray, in the prayer shall die,
    'Oh, to have Caponsacchi for my guide!' *1872*

1507   *traditionary*   traditional, set apart by custom.

1518   *recognize the orb*   perceive the sun.

1533   *mitigates*   reduces (or slows?).

1592   *a worm must turn*   Compare III 1289.

1633   *solemnized*   made solemn, serious.

1702   *affected frippery*   laid store on cheap outward show.

1720–21   *In His face | Is light, but in His shadow healing too*   A fusion of 2 Corinthians iv 6 and Acts v 15 (where, however, the 'shadow' is that of St Peter, not Christ).

1723   *importunate*   troublesome, a nuisance.

1738–9   *I am saved through him | So as by fire*   1 Corinthians iii 15.

1780   *put his breast between the spears and me*   Possibly a reference to St Peter's intervening between Jesus and 'a great multitude with swords and staves' (Mark xiv 43–9).

1827–8   *'T is there they neither marry nor are given | In marriage but are as the angels*   Matthew xxii 30, etc.

BOOK VIII

The time is late January or early February (the season of Carnival). If 'a month' (XII 333) can be taken literally, the date is 22 January. Preview: I 1105–61.

1–2   *Giacinto . . . Cinone*   The first of the many affectionate diminutives the speaker uses for his son and namesake Hyacinth.

7   *Quies me cum subjunctivo*   Shows that he understands that in some circumstances the relative pronoun *qui* should be followed by the subjunctive.

8   *Corderius*   Maturin Cordier (*c.* 1480–1564), author of Latin textbooks and teacher of Calvin.

12   *some crusty case*   As Guido said earlier (V 566), 'the case is hard'.

13   *triturate*   reduce to a fine pulp.

14   *Papinianian*   Basically a reference to a Roman jurist named Papinianius (2nd century AD) but with a multiple pun on 'pap', 'papa', and the name of Denis Papin, French physicist (1647–*c.* 1712) who invented a primitive pressure cooker, obliquely referred to in 'the patent truth-extracting process' (I 1114).

33   *tenements*   income-producing holdings.
    hereditaments   inheritable property.

42   *thrid*   make one's way through.

43   *galligaskin*   gaiter, wet-weather legging.

45 *Condotti* A street connecting the Piazza di Spagna with the Corso.

49 *chambering and wantonness* sexual license (Romans xiii 13).

58 *Nutshell and naught* Horace (Flaccus), *Satires* II v 35.

65 *dumple* Here used merely for the sake of assonance with 'dimple' and as one of the many expressions of Arcangeli's culinary preoccupation.

72 *mother-wit* native intelligence.

74 *bite his thumb* A gesture of threat or defiance, putting the thumbnail into the mouth and clicking it against the upper teeth.

79 *illustration* example, demonstration.

89–90 *this flower o' the field, no Solomon | Was ever clothed in glorious gold to match* Matthew vi 28–9.

94 *Non nobis, Domine, sed tibi laus* not to us, O Lord, but to thee must go praise.

98 *'sbuddikins* (God)'s bodikins – God's dear body.

101 *Pro Milone* Cicero's oration in defence of the accused murderer Milo.

107 *excogitate* reason out.

115 *Hortensius Redivivus* Hortensius (Cicero's rival) reincarnated.

117 *the Est-est* a fine Roman wine.

118 *mollifies* See lines 541–7.

(*Note:* From this point onward, the interpolated Latin of Arcangeli's argument, nearly all quoted directly from his and his colleague Spreti's pleadings in the Old Yellow Book, will be translated only when its sense is not sufficiently clear from the English paraphrase which accompanies it. Latinists will recognize, however, that as he translates, Browning sometimes plays sly tricks with the strict sense of the original for the sake of irony or innuendo. This is equally true of Bottini's speech in Book IX.)

130–35 'The first way of saying "Guido married" is taken from the actual Latin of the opening speech for the prosecution, and is scoffingly characterized as "commonplace"; the second is an adaptation of Catullus, but does not quite suit Arcangeli's taste; in the third, he gets exactly what he wishes from Virgil, *Aeneid*, I 73, "clear of any modern taint"' (Hodell).

145 *version* translation, with the specific suggestion of 'a translation from English into Latin prose done as a school or university exercise' (*OED*).

148 *Farinacci* Roman jurist (1544–1613), often cited in the lawyers' arguments in the Old Yellow Book.

149 *hitched* put (with some effort) into verse.

155   *idiom*   proper legal language.

165   *have I thee on hip?*   have I got you where I want you? See note to IV 762.

166   *break Tully's pate*   write unCiceronian, and therefore inelegant and even ungrammatical, Latin; equivalent to the 'break Priscian's head' of VI 389.

224   *hectic*   cadaverous, wasted.

  fine   extremely thin.

238–9   Compare the image of Chanticleer at I 1203–4.

246   *luck o' the last word*   See note to I 165.

253   *clamp and tenon*   apply devices to tighten a wooden structure.

254   *ship a sea*   receive water over the side.

262   *Torpid*   numbed.

267   *for*   instead of.

274   *Blunderbore*   One of Jack the Giant Killer's victims.

279   *choppy*   chapped.

280   *tippet*   scarf.

290   *pleasantness*   entertainment.

293   *topping*   eminent, illustrious.

306   *Thus I defend Count Guido*   It should be stressed here that most of the arguments advanced by both lawyers are taken directly from the pleadings in the Old Yellow Book. Their extravagance and absurdity are not, as a rule, Browning's, although they did inspire him to add a few fantastic touches of his own.

317   *validity of process*   legality.

328   *Gamaliel*   See note to V 1107.

329   *immortal 'Questions'*   the *Variae Quaestiones* of Farinacci (see note to line 148).

331   *Vigiliarum*   See note to I 979–80.

344   *shrewd*   discriminating, sagacious.

354   *reclaim*   object.

358   *the poet's word reversed*   'O fortunatos nimium, sua si bona norint, | Agricolas!' (Virgil, *Georgics* II 458). 'Ah, too fortunate the husbandmen, if they but knew their happiness!' (Cook).

377   *Neither do I condemn thee, go in peace*   Jesus's words to the woman taken in adultery by the scribes and pharisees (John viii 11).

382   *Is thine eye evil because mine is good?*   Matthew xx 15, where, however, the phrase is 'because *I* am good'.

390   *spiritual*   intellectual.

396   *pipkin*   small earthenware crock.

397   *May disconcert you his presumptive truth*   may spoil the proof he intends (by a fault in his apparatus).

401ₐ2] May drive into undoing my whole speech,
    Undoing, on his birthday, – what is worse, –
    My son and heir! *1872*

427 *misprision* mistaken belief, misapprehension.

471 *To whose dominion I impose no end* Virgil, *Aeneid* I 279.

474 *Poscimur!* I am called upon (for an ode) (Horace, *Odes* I xxxii 1).

481 *Theodoric* Theodoric the Great, first Gothic king of Italy (*c.* 455–526).

482 *Cassiodorus* Theodoric's chancellor (*c.* 480–575) who in his official capacity composed and collected many royal decrees under the title *Epistolae Variae*.

488 *when Aristotle doubts* He does so in *De Generatione Animalium* III 10 ('There is much difficulty about the generation of bees').

491 *copying King Solomon* Proverbs vi 6–8 (Septuagint version), where the bee – an ant in the King James version – is an example of industry and foresight rather than an enemy of unchastity.

502 *the Idyllist* Supposedly the reference is to Theocritus, Moschus, or Bion, but no commentator, including the present one, has succeeded in locating such a passage in their works.

511 *Aelian* See note to I 232.

539 *Derogate* 'act unworthily of his rank and dignity' (Cook).

540ₐ41] *Absit,* such homage to vile flesh and blood! *1872*

552–4 'For if they do these things [such as the persecution and killing of Jesus] in a green tree, what shall be done in the dry?' (Luke xxiii 31).

557 *whom our devils served for gods* 1 Corinthians x 20.

570 *the Laws of the Twelve Tables* The earliest known body of Roman law, fifth century BC.

572 *The Julian; the Cornelian; Gracchus' Law* Catch-titles referring to sections of Justinian's *Pandects* often cited in the Old Yellow Book (see notes to I 223 and V 1781). These were decisions and statutes of the periods of, respectively, Julius Caesar (100–44 BC), Lucius Cornelius Sulla (138–78 BC) and Gaius Gracchus (153–121 BC).

581 *the early Revelation*] natural revelation *1872*

584 *Saint Jerome* In one of his letters.

596 *coerce* repress.

598 *Saint Gregory smiles in his First Dialogue* That is, in his *Dialogorum Liber*.

602 *term* extreme, end of the rope.

614 *zeal* A calculated mistranslation of *zelus* (jealousy).

622 *compound* compensate (inadequately).

624 *consentaneous* pertinent.

628   *excogitate*   have regard for.

636   *Cavalier Maratta*   See note to III 58–9.

638–55   Judges xvi 21–30.

647   *Disdain*   pride.

656   *Are these things writ for no example, Sirs?*   1 Corinthians x 11.

658   *mansuetude*   gentleness.

659   *Sealing the sum of sufferance up*   'Thus saith the Lord God, Thou sealest up the sum, full of wisdom, and perfect in beauty' (Ezekiel xxviii 12).

660   *Opprobrium, contumely, and buffeting*   Matthew xxvi 67.

664   *Honorem meum nemini dabo!*   This was uttered not by Christ but by God, defending not *honorem* but *gloriam* (his being the Godhead). The source is Isaiah xlii 8 (Vulgate): '*Ego Dominus, | Hoc est nomen meum: | Gloriam meam alteri non dabo.*'

672   *this faith delivered once*   Jude 3.

673–6   The quotation is from 1 Corinthians ix 15: 'for it were better for me to die, than that any man should make my glorying [i.e., selfless worship of Jesus] void.' The suppression of the gerund ending alters the whole meaning of the verse. Compare Galatians vi 14: 'God forbid that I should glory, save in the cross of our Lord Jesus Christ.'

681   *I can't quite recollect it*   But Spreti does in the Old Yellow Book.

692   *crepuscular*   shadowy, dim (literally, twilight).

699   *Stoning by Moses' law*   Deuteronomy xxii 23–4.

700   *legislates our Lord*   In Matthew v 31.

707   *though heaven and earth should pass*   Matthew xxiv 35, etc.

712   *lapidation*   the right to throw stones.

716   *What profits me the fulness of the days*   1 Chronicles xxix 28.

722–5   'We remember the fish, which we did eat in Egypt freely; the cucumbers, and the melons, and the leeks, and the onions and the garlick: But now our soul is dried away: there is nothing at all, beside this manna, before our eyes' (Numbers xi 5–6).

731   *thorough-bred*   pure-blooded.

734–5   James iii 3.

738   *remit*   dispense with, excuse.

750   *Wherewithal should the husband cleanse his way?*   'Wherewithal shall a young man cleanse his way? by taking heed thereto according to thy word' (Psalm cxix 9).

752   *punishment*] turpitude *1872*

755   *foh!*   Explained by the next phrase – *Presumitur leno* (he is deemed a pander).

767   *cachinnation*   guffawing.

778   *a foolish trifler with a tool*   Such as Half-Rome; see II 66–7.

815   *with commodity*   conveniently.

823   *Matthaeus*   Laurentius Matthaeu et Sanz, Spanish author of *Tractatus de Re Criminali* (1676).

843–4   *there is the law, and this beside, | The testimony*   Isaiah viii 20.

861   *votarist of the mode*   follower of the current fashion, therefore a rationalist or freethinker.

863   *sciolist*   superficial scholar.

894   *Zeal of her house hath eaten us up*   Psalm lxix 9.

896   *devour poor Priam raw*   Zeus told Hera that she might satisfy her wrath if she ate King Priam, his sons, and all the Trojan people raw (*Iliad* IV 35).

929   *Hill of Mars*   The Areopagus, site of the Athenian judicial assembly in the time of Solon.

946   *Valerius*   Roman historian, first century AD.

948   *Cyriacus*   Franciscus Niger Cyriacus, Mantuan lawyer, author of *Controversiae Forenses* (1628–38).

953   *denegation*   denial.

956   *amerced in a pecuniary mulct*   fined.

971   *just as Ovid found*   See note to II 1221.

984   *the Brazen Head*   A bronze head reputedly made by Roger Bacon (*c.* 1214–92), which uttered the words 'Time is, Time was, Time's past' and then fell into pieces.

992   *go softly all their days*   Isaiah xxxviii 15.

1001   *ex incontinenti*   at once (the '*ex*' is superfluous).

1048   *the thing we lost, we found*   Luke xv 6 (the parable of the lost sheep).

1053   *rustic*] gaby *1872* ('Gaby': simpleton).

1081   *Sistine*   principal chapel of the Vatican.

1082   *Camerlengo*   papal chamberlain, highest of the cardinals.

1088   *mew*   confinement, captivity.

1102   *cousinship*   family ties.

1111   *skit*   joke, banter.

1113   *fico*   fig. (To 'give the fico' is to 'bite the thumb': see note to line 74 above.)

1134   *compassed*   plotted.

1162   *Pope Alexander*   Innocent XII's immediate predecessor.

1180   *Furor ministrat arma*   'Madness supplies its own arms' (*Aeneid* I 150).

1181–2   *Unde mî lapidem . . . Unde sagittas?*   Horace, *Satires* II vii 116–17.

1191   *pollent*   powerful.

1192   *amasius*   lover.

1194 *emprise* enterprise.

1200–205 *Gather instruction from the parable* Matthew xv 34 (for the seven loaves; other accounts, e.g. Matthew xiv 17, have five) and Matthew xiv 20 (for the twelve baskets; other accounts, e.g. Matthew xv 37, have seven). It is, of course, a miracle, not a parable.

1207–11] We word by the way to fools that cast their flout
On Guido – 'Punishment were pardoned him,
But here the punishment exceeds offence:
He might be just, but he was cruel too!'
Why, grant there seems a kind of cruelty
In downright stabbing people he could maim,
(If so you stigmatise the stern and strict)
Still, Guido meant no cruelty – may plead *1872*

1214ˌ15] Merely disfigure, nowise make them die *1872*

1222 *Panicollus* A mistake for Caesar Panimolle (Panimollus), a jurist frequently quoted in the Old Yellow Book.

1229 *Galba in the Horatian satire* The sole dissenter when 'all' others approved of the sexual mutilation of an adulterer (*Satires* I ii 46).

1240ˌ41] Obtained, these natural enemies of man! *1872*

1262 *commodious* adequate for our needs.

1268 *hangdog* 'a despicable or degraded fellow fit only to hang a dog, or to be hanged like a dog' (*OED*); in this context the word was perhaps suggested by Sir Walter Scott's 'hangdog executioner' (*The Fair Maid of Perth*).

1275 *tipstaff* court official.

1301 *Foxes have holes, and fowls o' the air their nests* The application in the original (Matthew viii 20) is to 'the Son of man', not to false wives.

1306 *Aquinas' word* 'Arise and write' (*'Surge et scribe'*) is not found in his writings, though many legends credit him with divine inspiration.

1317 *travesty* disguise.

1322–9 Acts ix 25 ('Then the disciples took him [Paul] by night, and let him down by the wall in a basket') and 2 Timothy iv 13 ('The cloke that I left at Troas with Carpus, when thou comest, bring with thee': but this was thirty years 'afterward').

1348–50 *blink his interest, . . . But baulk Tommati's office* 'Blink' and 'baulk' both mean 'ignore' (the sense is, disregard his personal feelings in respect to the alleged contempt of court, but not the dignity of his office).

1370 *envy* hostility, malice.

1390 *shine on us with healing on its wings* Malachi iv 2.

1411–13 2 Samuel xii 26–9.

1421–3 Matthew viii 14–15.

1425–6 *It is of age,* | *Ask it* John ix 21 (the words of the parents of the boy whose sight was miraculously restored).

1434 Micah vi 8.

1436 *peccable* capable of sinning.

1446 *minim* smallest particle.

1449ₐ50] (Our Cardinal engages to go read
        The Pope my speech, and point its beauties out. *1872*
        [They say, etc.]

1452 *intellectuals* mental powers.

1459–61 Ecclesiastes iii 1–8.

1462–3 *we fathers can but care, but cast* | *Our bread upon the waters* Ecclesiastes xi 1.

1500 *apprehensive* intelligent, quick.

1503 *Tobit* In the apocryphal book of the same name. See note to VI 1272–3.

1507ₐ8] By application of his tongue or paw *1872*

1510 *Haud passibus aequis* Virgil, *Aeneid* II 724 (which has '*non*' instead of '*haud*').

1517 *of old-world faith* That is, according to the teachings of Jesus, the principles of Christianity.

1532 *refulgent* brilliant.

1533 *Castrensis, Butringarius* Jurists of the fifteenth and fourteenth centuries, respectively.

1554 *mandatories* people who take orders.

1566 *neologism* The word-play on 'qualified' and 'quality' in the preceding lines.

1617 *Maro's*] Ovid's *1872* ('Maro' was Virgil.)
  Maro's phrase '*inritamenta malorum*' (*Metamorphoses* I 140).

1618 *hinds* peasants.

1628 *peroration* concluding summary.

1664 *turpitude* shame.

1675 *Lucretia's self* After being raped by the son of Tarquinus Superbus, Lucretia stabbed herself in the presence of her father, her husband, and two of their friends.

1677 *pudicity* The word means 'chastity', but Browning, deriving it from the adjective 'pudic', uses it here in the sense of 'shame'.

1680 *Virginius* To avoid his daughter's falling into the hands of the decemvir Appius Claudius as a slave, her father Virginius stabbed her to the heart. See Chaucer's *Physician's Tale*.

1689 *fame* reputation.

1714 *griesly* horribly.

1730–33 Job xli. Compare V 1504–5 and X 1102–11.

1744 *Cicero-ize* polish to the highest standards of Ciceronian Latin.

1748 *Jam satis* Martial, *Epigrammaton* IV lxxxix 1. See also note to IV 31.

1752 *toque* tall brimless hat worn by lawyers and chefs.

1760 *rosolio* cordial.

1763 *bipsi* It should have been *bibi*.

1773–4 *the talent so employed as yield | The Lord his own again with usury* Matthew xxv 27. There is probably a pun on 'talent'.

1776 *Agur's wish* Proverbs xxx 8.

1792 *Hyacintho dono dedit avus* Uncle bequeathed it to Hyacinth.

1798 *Onusta mammis . . . baccis ambulet* In thus quoting from Horace (*Epodes* VIII 13–14) Arcangeli commits a Freudian slip, *mammis* (breasts) for the Horatian *bacis* (pearls).

BOOK IX

The time is the same as that of Book VIII or shortly thereafter. Previews: I 1162–1219 and VIII 235–42.

14 *allocution* address.

29 *girding loin and lighting lamp* Luke xii 35.

32 *assistant* useful.

44 *flax-polled* tow-headed.

47 *chap* jaw.

53 *uberous* full of milk.

56 *stumped* blurred.

61 *unpanniered* relieved of its burden (of baskets).

63 *clouted shoon* patched shoes, or shoes with studs on soles (Milton, *Comus* 635).

   scrip small bag.

84 *conceit* fanciful image, with a pun on the meaning of 'self-admiration'.

91 *E pluribus unum* one from many (Virgil, *Moretum* 104).

97 *chyme* digested semi-liquid food.

105 *stole* long outer garment worn by matrons in ancient Rome.

   clout napkin (US diaper).

109 *eximious* glorious.

112 *Capena* the Porta Capena, entry for the Appian Way.

114 *the Florentine* Michelangelo.

115 *the Urbinate* Raphael.

116–17 *the Cortonese . . . Ciro Ferri* See note to V 488–9.

119 *exordium* introduction.

    Phoebus Apollo, god of poetry.

    plucks my ear Virgil, *Eclogues* VI 3–4.

145–7 *'Lene tormentum ingenio admoves ... Plerumque duro'* 'Pleasant compulsion dost thou apply to wits whose wont is dullness' (Horace, *Odes* III xxi 13–14).

148 *my full cup runs o'er* Psalm xxiii 5.

156 *pupilage* still merely students.

169 *splay-foot* flat, outward-turned feet.

170 *Phryne* Notorious Greek courtesan who won a lawsuit by exposing her body to the judges.

177 *the Tale of Tarquin* The rape of Lucretia (see note to VIII 1675).

189 *When thistles grow on vines or thorns yield figs* Luke vi 44.

190 *oblique* erroneous, unjust.

198 *front* forehead.

207 *lapidary* worker in gems.

214–15 *Sermocinando ne declamem, Sirs, | Ultra clepsydram* Source untraced.

217 *As Flaccus prompts* Horace in *Ars Poetica* 148.

    the epic plunge in medias res.

219 *arrest your love* engage your sympathetic attention.

226 *the Teian* The Greek lyric poet, Anacreon (*c.* 570–485 BC), born in Teos.

232 *redoubted* redoubtable, formidable.

235 *Hebe-slips* Hebe was the goddess of youth and spring.

240–41 *Discedunt nunc amores ... Maneat amor* A medieval adaptation of Catullus (Hodell).

242 *prime of life* youth.

259 *untowardly* refractorily, balkily.

267 *ungainly* awkward, embarrassing.

268 *companion* accompany.

282 *Old things are passed and all again is new* 2 Corinthians v 17; Revelation xxi 4–5.

284–6 *Novorum ... Nascitur ordo* Virgil, *Eclogues* IV 5–7.

289 *passage in the Canticles* Song of Solomon ii 11–13.

295 *dibbled* made holes for seeds.

297–301 Compare III 244–5.

302 *choice* prejudice.

305 *To nobody she destined donative* she did not reserve the gift (of herself) to any one man.

307 *escapes* escapades.

309   *prepense*   premeditated.

313   *olent*   redolent, fragrant.

318   *advertise*   inform.

341   *Calm in his levity, – indulge the quip!*   The 'quip' is the play on the two senses of 'levity', the state of being a levite (deacon) and lack of seriousness, inconstancy. (The Latin phrase is from Ovid, *Tristia* V viii 18.) 'Bell' in the next line redoubles the quip.

345–8   Horace, *Odes* II iv 17–18. Bottini converts Horace's *dilectam* (referring to a 'maid') into the masculine '*delectum*'.

350   *phoenix*   paragon.

351   *of culture*   well bred.

352   *precept*   maxim, proverb.

355   *uncandid*   defiled.

356–66   A conflation of three Biblical passages. The description of David, son of Jesse, is from 1 Samuel xvi 12 ('he was ruddy, and withal of a beautiful countenance, and goodly to look to'). In 1 Samuel xxv 18–23, Abigail, desiring to conciliate David and his soldiers, goes out to meet them with figs and sweetmeats, and in 2 Samuel vi 14–16, David dances before the Ark of the Covenant – not before Abigail – and Michal, the captive daughter of Saul, secretly looking on, 'despised him in her heart'.

368   *Heu prisca fides*   Virgil, *Aeneid* VI 878.

371   *discover*   reveal.

387   *adamantine*   hard and impenetrable.

392   ]   What need that, thus proved madman, he remark *1889*

394   *Comacchian*   The vale of Comacchio, noted for its large eels.

397   *fasting*   That is, in Lent.

398   *splenetic*   melancholy person.

400   *Lernaean snake*   the hydra of Lerna, slain by Hercules.

404   *lunes*   mad whims.

405   *Insanit homo*   Horace, *Satires* II vii 117.

414, 417   *foe*] fool *1872*

421   *unconsummate*   unachieved.

428   *the lyrist quoted late*   Anacreon; see note to line 226.

433   *spear and shield*   See line 228.

454   *Persius*   Latin poet (34–62 AD) in his *Satires*, Prologue: 'Who was it made the parrot so glib with its "good-morning"? That great teacher of art and bestower of motherwit, the stomach' (Hodell).

455   *concave*   vault of heaven.

   pie   magpie.

465   *Negatas artifex sequi voces*   Persius, *Satires*, Prologue.

467   *lies i'*   shares.

475 *candid* pure.

497‸500] Shall he dare love, who may be Pope one day?
Despite the coil of such encumbrance here,
Suppose this man could love, unhappily,
And would love, dared he only let love show!
In case the woman of his love, speaks first,
From what embarrassment she sets him free! *1872*

511 *muckworms* misers.

515 *Samson* It should be recalled that at VIII 640–55 Guido was
Samson (Judges xvi).

528 *Idyllium Moschi* Moschus, *Idyl* I 3–5.

535 *Are not these things writ for example-sake?* 1 Corinthians x 11.

539 *Myrtillus, Amaryllis* Lovers in Giambattista Guarini's *Il Pastor
Fido*.

546–8 *Odyssey* IV 244–8.

549 *clout* rag.

550 *clack-dish* covered wooden alms dish.

567–73 The story of Judith's patriotic decapitation of the Assyrian
general Holofernes is in the apocryphal Book of Judith xiii, which does
not, however, allude to her use of a dish; this touch probably is borrowed
from the story of Salome and John the Baptist.

571 *faulchion* sword.

575–80 The Icarus story is in Ovid, *Metamorphoses* VIII 182–235.

595 *him of Gath* Goliath (1 Samuel xvii 10).

604–6 'his bodily presence is weak, and his speech contemptible'
(2 Corinthians x 10).

606 *fulmination* thunderous diatribe.

615 *inapprehensive* stupid, slow-witted.

617 *dreads a bear in every bush* 'Or in the night, imagining some
fear, | How easy is a bush supposed a bear!' (*A Midsummer Night's
Dream* V i 21–2).

622 *thwart* perverse, obstinate.

624 *Helen's nepenthe* The drug she gave to Odysseus (*Odyssey* IV
220–21).
opine know.

625 *frittered*] fretted *1872*

626 *the much-enduring man* Odysseus, who also had a faithful wife.

634 *In payment of his apparition* as a reward for his inopportune
appearance.

644 *Suis expensis, nemo militat* 1 Corinthians ix 7.

655–6 *thus did Dido once | Decamp* In a dream, Dido learned from
the ghost of her late husband, Sychaeus, that he had been murdered by

her brother, Pygmalion, king of Tyre, and his treasure hidden at a place he specified. After she retrieved the riches, she fled with them and subsequently founded Carthage (*Aeneid* I 348–64).

672 *bale* trouble.

711–12 *This with a third part of her nectar did | Venus imbue* 'the sweet lips that Venus has imbued with the quintessence of her own nectar' (Horace, *Odes* I xiii 15–16).

719 *devious* To be read, no doubt, in two senses.

726 *she is built upon a rock* Matthew xvi 18.

732 *Spirit is willing but the flesh is weak* Matthew xxvi 41.

745–6 *'Ut vidi' ... 'Ut perii'* Virgil, *Eclogues* VIII 41.

757–62 Livy, *Ab Urbe Condita Libri* XXV xxxi 9. Archimedes actually 'was intent upon the figures which he had traced in the dust'.

780–81 *Non idem semper dicere sed spectare | Debemus* 'We ought not always to hold the same language, but we ought always to aim at the same end' (Cicero, *Epistulae ad Familiares* I ix 21).

793 *impudence* shamelessness, loose morals.

802 *the Medicean mode* like the statue of Venus de Medici (in the Uffizi, Florence).

830 *what Nero proved* The 'candid' (innocent) seventeen-year-old Nero, called upon to sign a death warrant, exclaimed '*Quam vellem nescire litteras!*' (Suetonius, *Nero* 10).

836 *O splendidly mendacious!* Horace, *Odes* III xi 30–36 (the reference is to the one Danaid who was faithful to her husband).

843 *fell flat*] succumbed *1872*

849–50 *assist | At* attend.

856 *cubiculum* bedroom.

859 *Good angels that commerce with souls in sleep* incubi (male demons who have intercourse with sleeping women).

866–7 *Shall a Vulcan clap | His net* Compare III 1450–55.

871 *Demodocus his nugatory song* Because many critics, ancient and modern, felt that this passage in the *Odyssey*, Book VIII, was un-Homeric in authorship and spirit, they called it worthless ('nugatory').

875 *pickthank* busybody.

885 *Cornelius Tacitus* Roman historian (*c.* 55–*c.* 120 AD). There is a pun on 'silence' / 'Tacitus'.

891 *Thalassian-pure* That is, nude, or 'in the garb of truth' (two lines above), a translation of Horace's *nuda Veritas* (*Odes* I xxiv 7). At II 1004 Pompilia, in the present situation, is described as 'pink and white'. The association of nudity with the sea (Thalassa) is by way of 'foam-born' Aphrodite as she emerges from the sea, for example in Botticelli's painting.

910 *ratiocinative* reasonable, derived from logical premises.

930 *awaiting our first stone* That cast by the scribes and pharisees at the woman taken in adultery (John viii 7).

937 *consult the place* It is John xx 15.

966–76 Laomedon, king of Troy, in order to placate Apollo and Poseidon, whom he had defrauded after promising to pay them for building the walls of the city, chained his daughter Hesione to a rock at the mercy of a sea monster. Alcmena's son Hercules rescued her, claiming for reward the horses Zeus had given to Laomedon. The latter again broke his promise and was slain by Hercules. (Ovid, *Metamorphoses* XI 194–220.)

970 *orc* mythical sea monster.

983–6 *Jove far at feast . . . With the unblamed Aethiop* Thetis was unable to plead Achilles' cause with Zeus because the god was absent for two weeks on a state visit to the Ethiopians (*Iliad* I 423).

986–7 *Hercules spun wool | I' the lap of Omphale* Hercules was for three years the servant, then the lover, of the masculine queen of Lydia, Omphale, to please whom he exchanged clothing with her and spun wool (Ovid, *Fasti* II 305 f.).

996 *anti-Fabius* Opposed to the Fabian policy (second Punic war) of attaining an end by gradual means.

1002 *ranged* lined up in a row as if watching a parade.

1017 *Horace* In *Satires* I i 24–5.

1020 *apologue* moral tale.

1027–8 *that old lying vanity | Called 'Sepher Toldoth Yeschu'* A Jewish attack on Christianity, dating probably from the Middle Ages.

1032 *our pestiferous and schismatic* Probably the Molinists.

1066 *so plain a consequence* so reasonable an understanding.

1098 *gust* relish, enjoyment.

1105 *merry-thought* wishbone.

1107 *Thucydides* Greek historian (*c.* 464–*c.* 402 BC).

1114 *bore the secular sword in vain* Romans xiii 4.

1116 *pour oil and wine* Luke x 34.

1134 *Sophocles* 'Justice sits with Zeus in the might of the eternal laws' (*Oedipus at Colonnus* 1382).

1156 *light* quickly, readily.

1164–5 *the Twelve enthroned | To judge the tribes* Matthew xix 28, Luke xxii 30.

1167 *leet-day* day appointed for court session.

1171 *thy sword, born enemy to the ear* Matthew xxvi 51–2.

1182 *toys* amorous sport, dallying.

1186   *risk thus much*] aim a blow *1872*

1192   *range*   grazing area.

1193   *pound*   place of confinement for stray (or straying) cattle or dogs.

1195   *mollitious*   voluptuous.

1202   *thy wicked townsman's sonnet-book*   The lascivious sonnets of Pietro Aretino (1492–1556).

1214   *Go blaze abroad the matter, blessed one!*   Mark i 45. The 'matter' was Jesus's cure of the leper.

1216   *Bethesda*   John v 2.

1218   *The whole need not the physician*   Luke v 31.

1225   *Redeunt Saturnia regna*   'The Golden Age returns' (Virgil, *Eclogues* IV 6). See note to X 779.

1230   *pots*   sheepfolds ('pots' is a mistranslation in Psalm lxviii 13).

1231   *mued*   moulted.

1239   *darnel*   grass found in grain fields, ryegrass.

1240   *Infelix lolium, carduus horridus*   Adapted from Virgil, *Georgics* I 151–4.

1246   *Interdum*   now and then.

1266   *Tozzi*   Malpighi's successor as physician to the Pope.

1280   *discuss*   consume.

1283   *colocynth*   Powerful cathartic made from a Mediterranean vine.

1295   *that of Lebanon*   'thy nose is as the tower of Lebanon' (Song of Solomon vii 4).

1297   *Forsan et haec olim* [. . . *meminisse iuvabit*] 'some day, perhaps, remembering even this will be a pleasure' (*Aeneid* I 203).

1304   *unconscious*   unsuspecting.

1316   *the apple of his eye*   Deuteronomy xxxii 10.

1319   *the sage*   Unidentified.

1323–4   *filius est | Quem nuptiae demonstrant*   'he is the son [of his father] according to the marriage contract'.

1331–3   '*Cujum pecus?*' . . . '*Non sed Aegonis!*'   Virgil, *Eclogues* III 1–2.

1341   *recondite*   secret.

1343   *the favour, Maro memorized*   The miraculous breeding of bees in the carcasses of four bulls and four heifers sacrificed by the shepherd Aristaeus (Virgil – 'Maro' – *Georgics* IV 554–8). ('Memorized': recorded.)

1347–53   According to the theory of spontaneous generation, freshly discredited by Louis Pasteur at the time Browning was writing the poem, fresh life could spring from such origins as a horsehair steeped in water or the dung (first 'product') of a horse. The 'bowels' of line 1348 is ambiguous (derived from the '*per viscera*' of Virgil's statement cited in the preceding note).

1360–64 The Latin may be translated: 'Why should I despair of becoming a mother without a husband, and of bringing forth without contact with a man, always supposing I am chaste?' (Ovid, *Fasti* V 241–2; Loeb translation).

1362 *distich* couplet.

1368 *potential* possible.

1374–9 Virgil, *Eclogues* IV 60 (which has '*matrem*', not '*patrem*').

1381 *lets the devil drive* A proverb found in Rabelais, Cervantes, Shakespeare, etc.

1382–3 Matthew xii 44–5. The 'seven' rather than the correct 'four' is traceable to verse 45: 'Then goeth he, and taketh with himself seven other spirits more wicked than himself. . . .'

1387 *stigmatized* censured, marked with infamy.

1390–91 *the simile* | *Of Homer* Iliad V 87–92.

1397 *effigiem*] *effigies 1872*

1401 *offuscated* addled, confused.

1405 *What's this to Bacchus?* The cry of conservative critics as the Greek tragedies originally produced in honour of Dionysus (Bacchus) strayed further and further from their original spirit and aims.

1408 *beati pauperes* Luke vi 20.

1434 *adduced* alleged, cited.

1457 *art's long, though time is short* Hippocrates, *Aphorisms*, quoted by Seneca, *De Brevitate Vitae* I i.

1458 *in compass* in check.

1487 *in the little she did sin*] even where she may have sinned *1872*

1492 *Triarii* the reserves of the Roman army.

1493 *inexpugnable* impregnable, irrefutable.

1504 *Solvuntur tabulae* 'Does the court adjourn?' (Adapted from Horace, *Satires* II i 86, '*Solventur risu tabulae*', 'The case will be dismissed with a laugh'.)

1525 *Titulus* statement of reasons at the beginning of the court's sentence.

1541 *as the law-god Phoebus bids* In Horace, *Odes* II x 19–20.

1544–5 *the bough* | *Projecting* From ancient Roman times onward, a bough or bush over a door was the sign of a wine shop.

1562 *tenax proposito* 'tenacious of my purpose' (Horace, *Odes* III iii 1).

1568 *eliminate* divulge (secrets).

1571 *That famed Panegyric of Isocrates* An oration advocating the invasion of Persia (380 BC), the composition of which is said to have taken ten years or more.

BOOK X

The time in the poem is 21 February, three days after the court has adjudged Guido guilty. The actual date of the Pope's response to Guido's appeal, however, was 20 February. Preview: I 1220–71.

1   *Ahasuerus*   sleepless king of Persia (Esther vi 1).

3   *a History*   If a specific history of the Popes is meant, it has not been identified.

9   *of the making books there is no end*   Ecclesiastes xii 12.

23   *cyst*   sac or bladder; here, coffin.

25   *Formosus*   Pope from 891 to 896. The long controversy the Pope describes in lines 32–149 hinged on the actions of the 'cadaveric synod' which declared all decisions of Formosus invalid, including all ordinations solemnized during his reign. The long-sustained and bitter debate split Italy into two parties.

26   *Sigebert*   Sigebert of Gembloux (*c.* 1030–1115), historian and hagiographer.

32   *Stephen*   Stephen VII, Pope in 896–7. (The other popes mentioned between this point and line 142 are: Romanus, 897; Theodore II, 897; John IX, 898–900; and Sergius III, 904–11.)

70   *uncanonic*   in violation of church law.

89   ΙΧΘΥΣ *which means Fish*   The Greek letters comprising the word for fish are the initials of the phrase 'Jesus Christ, son of God, Saviour'.

91   *the Pope is Fisherman*   Christ said to Peter and Andrew, 'I will make you fishers of men' (Matthew iv 19).

92   *Fisher's-signet*   The seal represents St Peter fishing from his boat.

121   *Luitprand*   Italian chronicler, diplomat, and Bishop of Cremona (*c.* 922–72). The name is also spelled 'Liutprand'.

133   *Eude King of France*   Odo, Count of Paris, king of the western Franks in the late ninth century.

134   *anathematize*   condemn.

136   *Auxilius*   Auxilius of Naples, early tenth century Frankish priest and polemicist who defended Formosus' claim to the Papacy and consequently the legitimacy of his ordinations.

140   *Marinus*   Pope Marinus I (882–4) brought the future Pope Formosus back from exile and restored his see.

141   *after John, came Sergius*   But Benedict IV (900–903) and Leo V (903) intervened.

150   *Which of the judgments was infallible?*   This and the poem's several other allusions to papal infallibility reflect a major topic of discussion during the years Browning was writing the poem. The doctrine was promulgated as an article of faith by the Vatican Council of 1870. See C. T. Phipps, 'Adaptation from the Past, Creation for the Present', *Studies in Philology*, LXV, 1968, 702–22.

154–6   Matthew x 28.

163   *While twilight lasts and time wherein to work*   John ix 4.

165   *stay*   rest.

169–92   Compare Caponsacchi's prophecy of Guido's fate, VI 1921–54.

181   *To sin and yet not surely die*   'And the serpent said unto the woman, Ye shall not surely die' (Genesis iii 4).

183   *chary*   zealous to preserve.

215   *figure*   semblance, shadow.

219   *preferred*   proffered, urged.

221   *wary*   wily, calculated.

227   *rede*   story.

249   *breathe*   lance.

281   *arrased*   curtained, tapestried.

286   *gossipry*   idlers.

292   *the sagacious Swede*   Unidentified.

296   *dip in Virgil*   See note to V 402.

312   *sedition*   incitement to rebellion.

329–30   *such a smoking flax, | Hurries the natural end and quenches him*   See note to VI 148.

340   *Since by its fruit a tree is judged*   Matthew xii 33.

372   *this*] these *1872*

375–6   *He, the Truth, is, too, | The Word*   John xiv 6.

383   *ancient*   former.

386   *legate-rule*   papal embassy.

393   *inquisitive and dispassionate*   disinterestedly seeking the truth.

397   *Wise in its generation is the world*   Luke xvi 8.

398   *reprobate*   guilty.

415   *Straitened*   confined.

417   *probation*   test of moral strength.

434–5   *Man is born nowise to content himself | But please God*   1 Thessalonians iv 1.

448   *portentous*   sinister.

465   *paravent and ombrifuge*   protection against wind and rain (seemingly Browning's coinages).

472   *the fragments of the basket*   Mark vi 39–40. See note to VIII 1200–205.

474 *Attent* attentive.

fifties in a company Luke ix 14.

480 *coat of proof* armour.

485 *the ambiguous fish* Any creature which, like the 'soldier crab' (hermit crab) of line 509, can detach itself from its shell. The Pope does indeed relish a sea-side simile (IX 372–3); he will use others below.

492 *affiliate* in the relation of a son.

496 *mew* place of confinement.

508 *Congenial* kindred, like.

510 *impinge* strike, but here (as Cook suggests) probably another coinage, meaning 'paint'.

513–14 *probity | He figures in* the guise of honesty.

579 *gor-crow* carrion crow.

589 *curious* cunning, elaborate (with suggestion of 'repulsive').

590 *Felicity* happy development.

599 *interest* that is, self-interest.

619 *Campagna* The countryside surrounding Rome.

620 *lets a peasant house*] overruns a hut *1889* (The original reading seems to mean 'affords housing to a peasant'.)

641 *Who shall pluck sheep Thou holdest, from Thy hand?* John x 28.

653 *that other Aretine* See note to IX 1202.

671 *And Satan fell like lightning!* Luke x 18.

690 *preconcerts* contrives, arranges for.

707 *Probation* hearing, just trial.

713 *saved even yet, so as by fire* 1 Corinthians iii 15.

714 *go softly all his days* Isaiah xxxviii 15.

717 *deigns* chooses to.

725 *spurned* kicked.

740 *Advantage proved* gain assured.

747–51 Genesis viii 6–11.

749 *coos*] coo *1872*

762 *determined* settled.

779–80 *the gold o' the prime | When Saturn ruled* the golden age of Saturn. See note to IX 1225.

781 *abash* discountenance, confound.

788–9 Luke ii 14.

800 James i 15.

814 *hebetude* stupidity.

845 *blood-flustered* half drunk with blood.

850 *Each swine, the devil inside him* Matthew viii 30–32.

874 *mage* (evil) sorcerer.

883 *This Guido*] Twice Guido *1872* (As originally written, 'Guido' was simply an error for 'Paolo'; by ingeniously changing 'This' to 'Twice' Browning converted the mistake into gain.)

886 *Rob halt and lame, sick folk i' the temple-porch!* Acts iii 1–10.

916 *she-pard* female leopard.

971 *Marzi-Medici* The governor of Arezzo.

982 *persecute* annoy, are a nuisance to.

986 *who art under me in the Church*] who art under, i' the Church *1889*

991 *Wast thou the hireling that did turn and flee?* John x 12–13.

1011 *yonder* On the Mausoleum of Hadrian.

1014–15 *That sword, the energy his subtle spear, | The knowledge which defends him like a shield* Ephesians vi 14–17.

1021 *memorized* commemorated.

1024–5 *the new name | That saints are known by* Revelation ii 17.

1027 *If there be any virtue, any praise* Philippians iv 8.

1030 *Ten*] Seven *1872*
untoward unyielding, stubborn.

1054 *did his hests, eked out the dole of pain* followed his orders, which added to the portion of suffering.

1087 *Approved so far in all docility* The substitution of 'less' for 'so' in *1872* clarifies the meaning: 'less educable'.

1096–8 A rose of gold annually given by the Pope to an eminent person to whom the Holy See was deeply indebted.

1102–8 Compare the earlier uses of the leviathan image at V 1504–5 and VIII 1728–33.

1108–9 *made | The comely terror* That is, 'turned the beautiful *into* terror'.

1110 *netherstone* 'as hard as a piece of the nether millstone' (Job xli 24).

1116–20 'After a period of merciless destruction, some classical monuments were spared by the Popes; temples were converted into churches, and statues of pagan gods were occasionally made to do duty as Christian images) (Cook; see Alexander Pope, note to *The Dunciad* III 101).

1122 *All this sweet savour was not ours but thine* Ephesians v 2.

1123 *Nard* aromatic herb.

1148 *mulct* punish.

1149 *No veritable star swims out of cloud* Compare III 846–51.

1153–4 *the brave starry birth | Conciliating earth with all that cloud* Compare VII 1405.

1162 *White-cinct* white-belted.

1163   *Red-socked*   red-stockinged (the garb of cardinals; see V 228).

1164   *Unchariness*   readiness (to shed).

1166   *bewraying*   betraying, proving unfaithful to.

1172   *strait*   crisis.

1190   *Reluctant dragons*   Horace, *Odes* IV iv 11; but the Pope uses 'reluctant' in the modern sense, whereas Horace's *reluctantes dracones* means that the 'snakes' would struggle vigorously.

1224   *rueful*   sorrowful, pitiable.

1244   *the lynx-gift*   ability to see through solid substances (see XI 917).

1256   *mount*   amount, total.

1257   *conglobed*   formed into a rounded compact mass.

1260   *recognise*   examine.

1264   *perk and pry*   'recover liveliness' and 'inquire into or investigate closely' (*OED*).

1270   *Pay*   punish.

1283   *darkness to be felt*   Exodus x 21.

1334   *new philosophy*   modern astronomy, especially that of Copernicus. A reminiscence of John Donne's *First Anniversary*: 'And new philosophy calls all in doubt'. Browning's poetry was considerably influenced by Donne's.

1350   *discept*   disagree.

1365   *isoscele*   triangle with two equal legs.

1383   *I have said ye are Gods*   Psalm lxxxii 6; John x 34.

1400   *fret*   roughness, chaps.

1402   *choppy*   chapped.

1415   *probatively*   by trial.

1459   *fiend*] wolf *1872*.

1475   *cuticle*   skin.

1481   *lay hand upon the ark*   See note to I 195.

1487   *If foolish virgins disobey and sleep*   Matthew xxv 1–13.

1490   *The mystic Spouse betrays the Bridegroom here*   Ephesians v 23–4.

1493   *The individual weighed, found wanting*   Daniel v 27.

1498   *The Monastery called of Convertites*   See General Note 6 (p. 635).

1525   *The soldiers only threw dice for Christ's coat*   Matthew xxvii 35.

1528   *the woof of price*   valuable cloth.

1545   *Impassible*   insensible to, independent of.

1565–9   Ephesians vi 14–17.

1580   *boots*   is the good of.

1584   *publicans*   corrupt tax collectors; used here because of their association with 'sinners' in the Gospels.

1590–1603 This tempest in the China teapot of theological linguistics was an actual occurrence of the time. See Cook's summary, *Commentary*, pp. 224–5.

1593 *qualm* attack of conscience.

1618 *adept of the Rosy Cross* member of the Rosicrucian sect, dedicated to finding the 'alchemist's stone' which could turn base metal into gold.

1650 *comports* permits.

1667–8 *there pleads some bard, | Philosopher, or both* Euripides, who speaks from line 1669 to line 1789.

1677 *the Machinist* Zeus. See note to IV 15.

1697 *'Know thyself' or 'Take the golden mean!'* The two most famous moral maxims of ancient Greece.

1706 *the Third Poet's tread surprised the Two* The Third Poet was Euripides, the (older) 'Two' were Aeschylus and Sophocles.

1717 *Paul spoke, Felix heard* Acts xxiv 22–7.

1720 *style* pen, stylus (instrument for writing on wax tablets).

1761 *tenebrific* dark.

1791 *'t is a legend* Contained in certain (forged) letters alleged to have been exchanged by Seneca and St Paul.

1799 *ere He make all things new* Revelation xxi 5.

1804–5 *that other act which finds all, lost, | Regained, in this time even, a hundredfold* Luke xviii 30.

1819 *Tentatives* attempts, reachings.

1823 *Druid* The religion of the ancient Celts in Gaul and Britain.

1826 *who is last proves first indeed* Matthew xix 30.

1837 *go*] dance *1889*

1888 *subjacent* underneath.

1891 *the lust and pride of life* 1 John ii 16.

1903 *antimasque* Interlude between the acts of a masque (dramatic performance involving elaborate settings and costumes, music and dancing), which it often burlesqued.

kibe (infected, ulcerated) heel.

1908 *pantaloon, sock, plume and castanet* The costume and equipment of the performer in the antimasque.

1920 *prodigy* astonishing achievement.

1924 *morrice* morris dance.

1927 *Augustine* The saint who made the church's rule 'his law of life' (line 1912).

1930 *suite* procession.

1941 *Loyola* St Ignatius Loyola, founder of the Jesuit order, celebrated for its worldliness and casuistry.

1957 *Paul's sword* The symbol of his warfare in behalf of Christ; not Biblical, but attributed to him in medieval and Renaissance art.

1968–9 *We pray thee dig about and dung and dress | Till he repent and bring forth fruit even yet* Luke xiii 8–9.

1983–6 The Pope is taken in by a sly misuse of Scripture. See note to VIII 664.

2003 *Farinacci's licence* See note to VIII 148.

2014 *cogency* convincing argument.

2027 *the golden age* See note to lines 779–80 above.

2032 *Count Guido's life, and sap society*] Guido's life, sapped society shall crash *1872*

2041 *Demonstrate* prove to be.

2047 *tenement* structure.

2049 *on our heads perchance*] on our children's heads *1872*

2055 *Barabbas' self* Matthew xxvii 16–17.

2057 *Sabbath* Originally the last day of the week, but here, by extension, the Pope's last days.

2059–60 *the three little taps | O' the silver mallet* The ceremony conducted at the death bed of a pope to verify his passing.

2065 *the Luthers and the Calvins come*] the Luthers chuckle, Calvins scowl *1872*

2068 *petit-maître* dandyish, affected.

2087–9 As Troy was about to fall and the aged Priam sought to enter the battle, Hecuba protested, 'The hour does not call for such aid or such defenders' (*Aeneid* II 521–2).

2100 *'Who is upon the Lord's side' asked the Count* The Count did so at V 1549.

2129 *that sad obscure sequestered state* Purgatory.

BOOK XI

The time is before dawn on the day following the Pope's rejection of Guido's appeal. Preview: I 1272–1329.

13 *Certosa* Carthusian monastery near Florence.

14 *Senescal* Official in charge of feasting and ceremonies in a medieval household.

37 *fee of the good-hand* tip.

70 *angelic*] archangelic *1872*

76 *coyness* reserve.

96 *pricked* galloped.
   breathe exercise.

105   *pale* fence.
108   *jauncing* prancing.

  jaunty port elegant, well-bred manner.

125   *his bran-new engine* the guillotine.
137   *tacit* taciturn, silent.
147   *windle-straws* Literally, dried stalks of grass; here used also in the figurative sense of feeble, scrawny old men.
184   *huge*] fine *1872*
188   *Mouth-of-Truth* A marble head of an open-mouthed Triton in the church of Santa Maria in Cosmedin.
243   *Discoursed* discussed.
245   *elucubrate* learnedly explain.
261   *Used not he chirrup o'er the Merry Tales* Pope Alexander VII (1655–67) was said to have been such a merry man.
263   *cullion* dupe.
272   *Albano* Francesco Albano, Bolognese painter (1578–1660).
278   *clout* clod.
281   *tablets* memorandum books.
291–2 *Atlas . . . Axis* the top vertebrae.
292   *symphyses* the unions of bones.
293   *cant* chant (with suggestion of hypocrisy, affected piety).
294–5 *here's the silver cord which . . . what's our word?* | *Depends from the gold bowl* Ecclesiastes xii 6.
303   *extravasate* escaped from the proper vessel, such as an artery.
304   *Roland's sword* See note to II 1495.
305   *lymph* body fluid which flows into the blood stream.

  Oliver's mace fatal (Oliver was Roland's companion in arms).

307   *arachnoid tunic* membrane coating.
311   *Fagon's self* Chief physician to Louis XIV.
314   *Pistoja-ware* fine cutlery (including weapons) made at Pistoia, near Florence.
327   *Petrus, quo vadis?* Fleeing Nero's persecution, St Peter met Jesus on the Appian Way and inquired '*Domine quo vadis?*' Jesus replied '*Venio iterum crucifigi,*' whereupon St Peter returned to be martyred. So runs the legend told by St Ambrose.
330   *raised up Dorcas* Acts ix 36–41.
336   *mystery of murder in the flesh* the very embodiment of the art of murder.
359   *Christ's maxim is – one soul outweighs the world* Matthew xvi 26, Mark viii 36.
371   *O'erflutter us with healing in her wings* Malachi iv 2.
380   *nice and coy* reserved, reluctant.

427–8 *a spice, | A touch of . . . eh?* The suppressed word probably is 'doubt': see below, line 721, 'a spice of doubt'.

449 *grace* credibility.

507 *Gorgon-shield* Athene's shield with the Gorgon's head in the centre; whoever looked on it was turned to stone.

553 *Colly my cow!* Variously explained; probably a mere mild expletive.

569 *King Cophetua* Legendary Ethiopian king, probably best known to Victorian readers through Tennyson's poem *The Beggar Maid*.

584 *candle-contest* To mark the end of Carnival, everyone in the streets sought to extinguish the others' lighted tapers, which were relighted as often as they were put out until they were utterly consumed.

616 *gird your loins and wash my feet* John xiii 4–14.

626 *this Pope's-halberdier* A member of the Swiss guard (above, line 208) who carried an eight-foot-long halberd (combination of axe and spear).

638 *Referendary* Important Vatican official.

667 *done for what Christ says is worth the world* That is, the saving of a soul (Matthew xvi 26, etc.).

683 *tinkle near* The ringing of the bell at the elevation of the Host.

685 *Trebbian* A wine from north-western Italy.

696 *Gold is called gold, and dross called dross, i' the Book* Psalm cxix 119, 127; Proverbs xxv 4, 11–12.

699 *a-maundering here and mumping there* Both verbs mean 'muttering'.

735 *caudatory* train bearer (literally, 'tail'; Browning's invention).

749 *Where's the obedience that shall edify?* 1 Corinthians viii 1 (which has 'charity', not 'obedience').

753 *That gnashes teeth and raves at loss of trash* Matthew viii 12.

754 *Which rust corrupts and thieves break through and steal* Matthew vi 19.

755–6 *inherit earth | Through meekness* Matthew v 5.

760–2 Luke xv 16–23.

766 *draff-box* trough of refuse, swill.

788 *Chap-fallen* slack-jawed, crestfallen.

790 *who sins may taste its edge, we see!* Romans xiii 4.

800 *genius* presiding spirit, 'good angel'.

801 *compass joy by concert* find pleasure together.

884 *jaundiced patch* jealous fool.

902 *kissed both eyes blind* The kiss of an adulterous wife was said to blind her husband to her infidelity.

905   *Crowned his head*   That is, with the horns of a cuckold.

908   *Vallombrosa Convent*   Monastery near Florence.

917   *prove a lynx*   See note to X 1244.

923   *apparitional*   spectral, phantasmal.

923₄] As the eye of God, since such an eye there glares: *1872*

929   *fieldfares*   thrushes.

930   *bent*   stiff stalk of grass.

956   *one primrose*] one primrose-patch *1889*

977   *the old simile*   In, for example, Lucretius, *De Rerum Natura* I 97–9.

996   *Esther in all that pretty tremble*   Esther xv 5–16 (Apocrypha), where Esther is repeatedly so portrayed as she petitions Ahasuerus for her countrymen.

1004   *French Louis*   See note to lines 2277–8 below.

1015   *portliness*   dignity, stateliness.

1024   *wheelwork*   clockwork.

1025   *proof*   of tested strength, impenetrable.

1028   *officious*   efficacious, with an overtone of 'officious *lie*': one 'told as an act of kindness to further another's interests' (*OED*).

1087₈] Proper appreciation and esteem! *1872*

1093   *Water with tears, manure with sweat and blood*   A repetition of the image at X 1030–32.

1096   *dog-rose*   small flower of the wild brier in hedges and thickets.

1098   *the hundred-petalled Provence prodigy*   a large rose.

1117   *The Etruscan monster*   Chimaera (line 1125).

1129   *cant*   whining.

1136   *rock of ruff*   sway of its collar of feathers.

1148   *i' the dumps*   gloomy, with a pun suggested by 'forage . . . i' the waste o' the world'.

1150   *trappings*   harness.

1151   *quondam*   former.

1153   *Pantaloon*   Foolish old man in Italian pantomime.

1274   *transformations of disgust*   disgusting metamorphoses, changes of nature (lines 1261–2).

1294   *her*] you *1872*

1297   *you*] I *1872*

1302   *Flesh of his flesh, bone of his bone*   Genesis ii 23.

1302–3   *the bride | To groom as is the Church and Spouse, to Christ*   Ephesians v 23–5.

1304   *Thy desire | Shall be to the husband, o'er thee shall he rule!*   Genesis iii 16.

1328   *doubles*   sharp or backward turns.

1378 *the terrible patience of God* Psalm vii 12 (Prayer Book version).

1381 *wards* projections inside a lock.

1386 *officiousness* servility.

1411–14 *Armida . . . Rinaldo* Characters in an opera based on Tasso's *Gerusalemme Liberata*.

1442 *pleasaunce* secluded garden.

1462 *decorum* rules of proper behaviour.

1463 *gospel-side* The left side as one faces the altar.

1467 *The muzzled ox that treadeth out the corn* Deuteronomy xxv 4; see previous use at V 136–7.

1487 *promise, which is air* 'I eat the air, promise-crammed' (*Hamlet* III ii 99).

1508 *Beat it into a ploughshare* Isaiah ii 4.

1512 *Anathema!* a curse upon it!

1529 *The letter kills, the spirit keeps alive* 2 Corinthians iii 6.

1549–50 *your house against itself | Divides, nor stands your kingdom any more* Matthew xii 25.

1604 *taenia* tapeworm.

1629 *malapert* impudent.

1648 *hacks and hamstrings* disables (by cutting tendons).

1769 *This path, twixt crosses leading to a skull* The road to Calvary (Matthew xxvii 33).

1779 *Jansenius* See note to I 307.

1786 *countervail* offset, compensate for.

1788 *trying all the spirits* 1 John iv 1.

1806–7 *Helping Vienna when our Aretines | Flocked to Duke Charles and fought Turk Mustafa* 'In 1683 Duke Charles of Lorraine was one of the leaders assisting John Sobieski when he marched to relieve Vienna from the siege of the Turks' (Hodell).

1813 *Pretty*] Solid *1889*

1826–7 *wax | Wanton* gloat.

1837 *gird* taunt, gibe.

1845–1900 Contrast Arcangeli's view of the father-son relationship.

1848 *gaudeamus* let us rejoice.

1881–3 Matthew xxi 28–30.

1920 *your frigid Virgil's fieriest word* It is '*indigenae*' (*Aeneid* VIII 314).

1923 *Aegiochus* the bearer of a goatskin breastplate.

1923–6 *Aeneid* VIII 352–5. (Guido's mistake may be a diplomatic error of the same kind that Caponsacchi's friends recommended that he make – VI 1751–3.)

1931 *gules* red (in heraldry).

1960   *stop sense*   close our ears or eyes.

1961   *Master Pietro*   Pietro Aretino. See note to IX 1202.

   pleasantry   salacious poem.

1967   *medium-powers*   intercessory gods, the 'intermediary race' of line 1937.

1974   *Revealed to strike Pan dead*   According to legend, during the reign of Tiberius – perhaps at the very moment of the crucifixion – voyagers at sea between Greece and Italy heard a voice from shore proclaiming that Pan was dead (Plutarch, *De Oracularum Defectu* 17).

1975   *live good days*   Psalm xxxiv 12; 1 Peter iii 10.

1981   *mulct*   reduce (by deprivation, punishment).

1989   *Keeping the while unspotted from the world*   James i 27.

2004–5   *those that use the sword | Shall perish by the same*   Matthew xxvi 52.

2010   *mystery*   tricks of the trade.

2027   *raised an altar to the Unknown God*   Acts xvii 23.

2032   *Romano vivitur more*   when in Rome, do as the Romans do.

2048–51   The tearful Byblis, in love with her own brother, was transformed into a fountain (Ovid, *Metamorphoses* IX 663–5). The cruel Lycaon was turned into a wolf (I 237–9).

2056   *Coerced*   restrained, curbed.

2061   *Deformed, transformed, reformed, informed, conformed*   'And be not conformed to the world; but be ye transformed by the renewing of your mind' (Romans xii 2).

2062   *pent and crossed*   dammed up.

2067   *the stranger*   alien element.

2098   *who did not make myself*   See VII 1731.

2136   *want*   lack.

2142   *Paynimrie*   heathen land.

2156   *circumjacent*   surrounding.

   demesne   estate.

2158   *my*] thy *872*

2169   *Would task my gouty feet, though*] Scarce tasks my gouty feet, and *1872*

2176   ]   Furze without land for framework, – vaunt no grace *1872*

2177   *a furze-sprig*] no furze-sprig *1872*

2179   *house and land*] gold will do *1872*

2181   *more and*] more gifts *1872*

2182   *those Olimpias bold, those Biancas brave*   Heroines of Italian romance.

2183   *will*] power *1872*

Ormuz   Diamond market on an island at the mouth of the Persian Gulf.

2195–200   Judges xvi 6–20.

2199   *sword*] knife *1889*

2202   *call–bird*   decoy bird.

2209   *Circe*   The sorceress in the *Odyssey* X 237–396, daughter of Helios (the sun), who turned Odysseus' companions into swine with her wand.

2210   *rod*] wand *1872*

2211   *honest distaff*   (genuine) staff used by women in spinning.

2212   *Lucrezia*   Lucrezia Borgia, daughter of Pope Alexander VI, formerly credited with 'picturesque crimes' and sexual licentiousness but now rehabilitated by historians.

2237   *scantling*   beam of wood, trestle.

2245   *damsel–fly*   dragon fly.

2277–8   *whose death insults the Emperor,* | *And outrages the Louis you so love*   There is some evidence that the Holy Roman Emperor attempted to exert his influence to spare Guido's life. It is doubtful whether his death would have 'outraged' Louis XIV, with whom Innocent XII had entered a rapprochement (XII 82) after an initial period of Galliphobia and who opposed the Empire. See the Venetian's statement, XII 110–12.

2280   *hate the church*] will hate God *1872*

2281   *coercive*   compelling force.

2295–6   *a foothold in the sea,* | *Although Saint Peter's bark scuds, billow-borne*   Matthew xiv 24–31.

2319   *powers and principalities*   A frequent phrase in the Pauline epistles.

2322   *flee*] claw *1872*

2324   *fit*   sudden attack of illness, with a suggestion of madness.

2327   *the work o' the wine and myrrh*   Mark xv 23.

2331   *Tozzi*   See note to IX 1266.

2336   *seventy near*   The number of cardinals.

2337   *Albano*   In his last hours, Guido had the voice of prophecy; see note to XII 43.

2344   *Martinez*   The Emperor's ambassador to Rome.

2360   *halcyon*   kingfisher.

2363   *vertiginously*   dizzily.

2408   *that Athenian*   Themistocles, the Athenian statesman who was rumoured to have poisoned himself.

2412   *Who are these*   The 'Company of Death' (I 1311).

2413   *their accursed psalm*   See note to I 1319.

BOOK XII

3 *key* keystone in an arch, therefore the zenith of the rocket's trajectory.

5 *usurpature* illegal possession or occupation.

12 *the Wormwood Star* Revelation viii 10–11.

27 *A letter* Browning's invention; not in the Old Yellow Book.

39 *Malpichi* See note to VII 423.

40 *Tozzi* See note to IX 1266.

41 *inveterate* incurable.

43 *I wager on his head* He lost; Innocent's successor was Cardinal Albano, a dark horse (see XI 2337).

63–8 Cardinal Bouillon (named in line 112), Louis XIV's representative in Rome and dean of the College of Cardinals, incurred his royal master's displeasure by failing to press for Fénelon's condemnation (see note to VI 318).

81–2 See note to XI 2277–8.

89 *Dogana-by-the-Bank* custom house.

94 *Martinez, the Caesarian Minister* The ambassador from Austria (the Holy Roman Empire, dominated by the Habsburgs).

104 *palchetto* grandstand.

105 *Pincian* See note to I 358.

140 *Pasquin's Street* See note to VI 1659.

158 *twelve were Tern Quatern* In the lottery, bets could be staked on three out of five numbers drawn (*terno*) or on four out of the five (*quaterno*). The fact that three times four equals twelve seemed, under the circumstances, a hot tip.

176 *suffrage* intercessory prayer.

179 *Salve Regina Coeli* Hail, Queen of Heaven.

184 *Umbilicus* navel.

188 *with the name of Jesus on his lips* So died the martyred St Stephen (Acts vii 59).

199 *just-a-corps* close-fitting body coat reaching to the knees.

200 *camisole* jacket.

205 *and so his end was peace* 'Mark the perfect man, and behold the upright: for the end of that man is peace' (Psalm xxxvii 37).

211 *A letter* This one, except for the postscript, is found in the Old Yellow Book; Browning has somewhat expanded and paraphrased the original.

214 *the valiant for the truth* The name of one of Christian's companions in the second part of Bunyan's *Pilgrim's Progress*.

217 *Socius* colleague.

224 *Tarocs* See note to VI 349.

239 *egregious* distinguished.

268–9 Beheading was reserved for the nobility; 'the rest' had to make do with mere hanging.

271 *Defunct in faith and exemplarity* dead, firm in the faith and the model of Christian virtue.

280 *debility* inadequacy, with a possible overtone of the astrological meaning: 'a weakness or diminution of influence [of a planet] due to unfavourable position' (*OED*).

291 *Hactenus senioribus* down to this point, for the eyes of our clients.

295 *Pisan assistance* help that comes too late.

299–300 *headpiece ... bag* Browning ekes out one more play on 'Caponsacchi'.

319 *the tender grape* Song of Solomon ii 15.

320 *Themis' throne* Themis was the goddess of justice, and Florence, not Rome – according to the discountenanced Arcangeli – her chosen seat.

326 *the case of Gomez* Had it materialized, it would have again pitted Arcangeli against Bottini; but see lines 653–9.

327 *Reliqua differamus in crastinum* put off the rest till tomorrow (Cicero, *De Re Publica* II xliv 4).

328 *estafette* courier.

358 *Eutropius* Roman historian, fourth century AD.

361 *Bartolus-cum-Baldo* See note to I 224.

367–8 *Adverti supplico humiliter | Quod* I humbly beg it may be noted that.

377 *roadster* horse for road travel.

391 *a letter* Browning's invention.

422–3 *Imagine how Arcangeli claps wing, | And crows* Compare what Arcangeli said of Bottini, VIII 237–40.

434 *pleasantry* pleasure.

437 *dandiprat* youth.

439 *save-all* A device to allow a candle to burn to the very end.

445 *man*] stoic *1872* stone *1889*

452 *his sermon* Browning's invention.

453–4 *Let God be true, and every man | A liar* Romans iii 4.

479 *culver* dove.

504 *their idol-god, an Ass* Early Roman opponents of the Christians maintained that they worshipped the ass.

525 *A saint whereof earth was not worthy* Hebrews xi 38.

538 *lo, a cockatrice*] lurks a centipede *1889*

595–7 'his [Moses's] eye was not dim, nor his natural force abated'
(Deuteronomy xxxiv 7).

607ʌ13] Plagued here by earth's prerogative of lies,
     Now learn to love and long for what, one day,
     Approved by life's probation, he may speak.

     For me, the weary and the worn, who haply prompt
     To mirth or pity, as I move the mood, –
     A friar who glides unnoticed to the grave,
     With these bare feet, coarse robe and rope-girt waist –
     I have long since renounced your world, ye know:
     Yet what forbids I weigh the prize forgone,
     The worldly worth? I dare, as I were dead, *1872*

622ʌ3] For many a doubt would fain perturb my choice –
     Many a dream of life spent otherwise –
     How human love, in varied shapes, might work *1872*

643 Bottini's letter, which was suspended at line 406 to permit him to
quote Celestino's sermon, is resumed here and continues to line 746.
The inverted commas, omitted in the received printed texts, have been
supplied.

645 *fame* reputation. Compare earlier uses of the bubble imagery.

651 *pitch* place.

663 *blatant* noisy.

667 *Perpend* listen.

669 *Whereto the Court consigned Pompilia first* For the error here,
see General Note 6 (p. 635).

672 *whither she was late returned to die* For the error here, see note
to I 1085.

675 *paul*] piece *1889*

703–13 There is no evidence that the Convertites hired Bottini to
press their claim that Pompilia was a 'person of dishonest life', though
he was uniquely qualified to do so.

708 *the tongue should prove a two-edged sword* Hebrews iv 12 (where
it is 'the word of God').

711 *Astraea redux* The goddess of justice, returned to earth (title
of a poem by Dryden, 1660).

713 *chop* shift, change course.

723 *His Noah's-dove* Compare X 747–51.

731 *How is the fine gold* Lamentations iv 1.

735 *hunks* disagreeable man.

741–2 *Martial's phrase for 'make an end'* – | *Ad umbilicum sic perven-
tum est!* A paraphrase of Martial, *Epigrammaton* IV lxxxix 1–2, where

umbilicum means a knob at the end of the roller to which a manuscript was attached; hence 'an end'.

748 *Instrument* document.

754 *quondam* formerly.

765 *Locum-tenens* substitute.

774 *Voltaire* Born 1694.

783 *Gonfalonier* supreme head of state.

807 *Petrarch* A native of Arezzo, though he left as an infant.

Buonarroti Michaelangelo was not born in Arezzo but in a town many miles away, though in the diocese of Arezzo.

808 *vexillifer* flag bearer.

809 *Patavinian* Livy, native of Padua (Patavium).

811 *Janus of the Double Face* Nowhere does Livy allege that the god Janus founded Arezzo.

814 *Did the babe live or die?* No one knows; no subsequent record of Gaetano has been found.

817 *blason* coat of arms.

820 *Rampant* standing on left hind leg with forelegs elevated.

in the slips on the leash.

842–3 *eyes hast thou yet art blind, | Thine ears are stuffed and stopped* Psalm cxv 5–6.

857 *missing* either lacking or bypassing.

mediate intervening or serviceable.

861] Deeper than ever e'en Beethoven dived, – *1889*

867 *succeed in guardianship* 'The ring preserves the truth hidden away in "the rough ore", but it also performs another office of a ring, that of a "guard-ring" or "keeper" outside a wedding ring' (Cook).

869–70 *Thy rare gold ring of verse (the poet praised) | Linking our England to his Italy*. The poet Nicolò Tommaseï wrote an inscription for the tablet on the Casa Guidi in which he spoke of Elizabeth Barrett Browning as having 'made of her verse a golden ring linking Italy and England' (*'e fece del suo verso aureo anello fra Italia e Inghilterra'*).

Penguin Critical Anthologies

Already published

Geoffrey Chaucer Edited by J. A. Burrow
Charles Dickens Edited by Stephen Wall
Henrik Ibsen Edited by James McFarlane
Andrew Marvell Edited by John Carey
Alexander Pope Edited by F. W. Bateson and N. Joukovsky
Ezra Pound Edited by J. P. Sullivan
Edmund Spenser Edited by Paul J. Alpers
Jonathan Swift Edited by Denis Donoghue
Leo Tolstoy Edited by Henry Gifford
John Webster Edited by G. K. and S. K. Hunter
Walt Whitman Edited by Francis Murphy

Forthcoming

Wallace Stevens Edited by Irvin Ehrenpreis
William Carlos Williams Edited by Charles Tomlinson
William Wordsworth Edited by John O. Hayden

Pelican Biographies

Penguin Modern Poets

Penguin Modern European Poets